D1611053

WORLD
NAVAL
WEAPONS
SYSTEMS

The Naval Institute Guide to WORLD NAVAL WEAPONS SYSTEMS 1994 Update

Norman Friedman

Naval Institute Press
Annapolis, Maryland

© 1994
by the United States Naval Institute
Annapolis, Maryland

Library of Congress Cataloging-in-Publication Data

Friedman, Norman, 1946–
    The Naval Institute guide to world naval weapons systems, 1994
update / Norman Friedman.
        p.   cm.
    Includes index.
    ISBN 1-55750-259-5
    1. Weapons systems—Handbooks, manuals, etc. 2. Ordnance,
Naval—Handbooks, manuals, etc.   I. Title.
VF346.F753   1993
359.8′2—dc20
                                                                                    93-26201

Printed in the United States of America on acid-free paper ⊗
9 8 7 6 5 4 3 2
First printing

CONTENTS

INTRODUCTION

The impact of the end of the Cold War continues to spread. If anything, it is now much more obvious than it was two years ago that the end of enmity between the two blocs has released enormously powerful passions, leading to previously unimagined levels of international instability. However, because none of the participants in local conflicts has the ability to destroy the major powers (mainly because they lack nuclear weapons), the current situation is ultimately less threatening to those powers. Their governments feel relatively comfortable in sharply reducing their military forces. They may well have forgotten that even local conflicts can have serious consequences: war was a nasty business even before the atomic bomb was invented. For example, by the time this book is published, Serbian forces, encouraged by the West's feeble response to the horrors occurring in Bosnia-Herzegovina, may well have moved from relatively minor persecution to major repression in the largely Muslim province of Kosovo. Because these Muslims are relatives of the Albanians just across the border, other Muslim states will probably be able to send aid directly to Kosovo. It is not too difficult to imagine this local war escalating into a general southern-European war. Both Bosnia and Kosovo could quite plausibly rally Muslims throughout the world to unite against the West. The minor problem would become major.

It is most unlikely that the United States or any combination of Western states will move to maintain world peace against all, or even most, local crises. There are just too many; major powers must make choices. That is nothing new. The long peace that followed the victory over Napoleon in 1815 is sometimes called Pax Brittanica because the general perception was that the Royal Navy was enforcing the peace required for an enormous upsurge in world trade. Thanks to the reach of the Royal Navy, Britain was the only global power of that era. In that sense the United States is Britain's direct heir. It is good, however, to keep in mind that the British never sought or filled the role of world police; they could not. In many cases they acquired colonies to quell local disorders or to enforce moral positions (e.g., against the slave trade). Many British historians would argue that most of the colonies were grossly counter-productive. The idea of empire had a considerable moral dimension, and it made for high morale in Britain, but it seems also to have been debilitating. It would be easy for the United States to start down the same path. The intervention in Somalia to protect the population from the effects of anarchy, for example, is not too different from the generous impulses that established many of the British colonies.

It seems generally to be imagined that the U.S. military, which was the world's police force during the Cold War, is now being pulled back from that necessary position. The reality is that the overall tensions of the Cold War helped enormously to discourage the rulers of small countries from attacking their neighbors. Many of them depended on subsidies from one or the other superpower (or played one off against the other) and thus could not afford the bigger countries' displeasure. In some cases, such as in Yugoslavia, there was a real possibility that internal war would provide an excuse for "peace keeping" in the form of occupation (in this case, by the Soviet Union). Each superpower generally tried to keep its client states from unduly irritating the other superpower for fear of unwanted escalation toward major war. In this sense the nuclear stalemate kept the peace, not only between the two opposing blocs, but also in much of the Third World.

To be sure, peace did not always reign. Every year since 1945 the U.S. Navy has been involved in some crisis, usually in the Third World. Crisis sometimes meant war, as in Korea and Vietnam, or punitive action, as in Libya and Iran, or the much more frequent threat of force to preclude open war.

Even though outbreaks of open conflict seemed bad enough at the time, they also seemed isolated. Now there is a much stronger sense of nearly continuous instability. To an important extent, the restraints that had been operating since 1945 have been removed. Throughout the Cold War, both superpowers sought positions that would have been advantageous had the war turned hot. That made many Third World countries so strategically important that it was worth subsidizing them. The Philippines and Cuba are cases in point: each provided its superpower ally with invaluable base facilities. Bases are still important in an unstable post–Cold War world, but those owning them cannot count on payment on anything like the earlier scale. Governments that survived for years on lavish foreign subsidies must now find substitutes. That explains why the Vietnamese government is now discovering the joys of capitalism, for example, in effect admitting defeat in its own version of the Cold War following the hot war it won.

Post–Cold War economic problems may often lead to local warfare. For example, two of the claimants to the Spratly Islands, which have vast oil resources, are former beneficiaries of the Cold War: the Philippines and Vietnam. It seems likely that North Korea is investing in nuclear weapons at least partly in hopes either of extorting money from the far richer south or of seizing its riches directly. The Cuban government already publicly recognizes that the end of Russian subsidies has had a crippling effect. It has chosen to retain full power rather than to risk moving toward a more open economy, in which power would necessarily be more widely distributed. Like North Korea, Cuba must wonder whether there is any way of obtaining money from its neighbors. Accommodating the drug traffic to the United States must appear to be an attractive solution to Cuba's economic problems, particularly since this policy hurts the country that the Cuban government feels is throttling it. Will the U.S. government eventually see an assault on Cuba as the appropriate key to solving the drug-importation problem?

All this is quite aside from traditional animosities, which have bred so many wars in the past. For example, throughout Central Europe, major ethnic groups straddle borders. Where they are in the minority, they are often persecuted. The home government may well feel that only a readjustment of borders (by warfare) will solve the problem. Yugoslavia is only the most dramatic case of such ethnic tension and hatred. Such conflicts were common before World War II, and it sometimes seems that the end of the Cold War resurrected the politics of half a century ago. Sometimes there seems to have been remarkably little appreciation of the horrors to which exactly such ideas led.

Europe is not the only likely venue for ethnic politics. Areas of enormous tension are to be found in South Asia and in the Far East. Some of the problems are clearly political—for example, the tension between the two Koreas, or between Taiwan and mainland China—but in other cases ethnic or religious hatreds are extremely important. The Hindu-Muslim split between India and Pakistan is probably a case in point.

Each case of tension either has produced or is likely to produce its own local arms buildup. The major powers may well not be involved, at least directly; there literally can be no single world police force (largely because there is no world government to enforce any version of world law; nor is such a government necessarily desirable). However, a local war may not always be a pure spectator sport. Many of the countries involved provide vital raw materials, or house important investments, for other countries, and the major powers might interfere to protect their own interests. In other cases, war, unimportant in itself (to a major power), may have extremely unfortunate consequences— as in the case of a possible wave of repression or "ethnic cleansing" in the Serbian-controlled province of Kosovo. Some level of intervention may be necessary.

The collapse of Soviet power has had another important consequence. Most Third World rulers did not really want the world to be dominated by either superpower. As long as the two blocs were opposed, Third World rulers could maintain their freedom of action by playing one superpower off against the other. Now the United States is the only superpower left. What Americans see as a benign attitude toward the people of the world (promoting, for example, the idea that they should be treated as humans rather than as dumb animals), many governments see as violently subversive. Americans agree so deeply on basic political principles that, for the most part, they do not realize that those principles form an ideology that is still quite revolutionary for most of the world. Third World governments fear that the United States will inevitably seek to impose its views on them (and, worse, that their populations may consider that an excellent idea). No U.S. administration can credibly recant the principle that people in other countries should have the same basic rights that Americans enjoy, so many Third World countries believe that they must do something to neutralize American power. They may, for example, decide to build up their arms, to be able to deal with approaching U.S. warships. These countries may also support subversive movements within the United States.

Just as the United States cannot shed its ideology, it cannot change the view, widely held in the Third World, that it is the driving force behind the social and economic developments of the twentieth century. Traditional ways of life have been torn apart as people have moved from village to city and, generally, from agriculture to industry, and many people find this movement alarming and unac-

ceptable. Fundamentalism, generally inchoate, is a natural reaction to this upheaval, just as anarchism was a reaction to a similar upheaval in nineteenth-century Europe. Neither movement has a center, an attack on which would solve the problem. The current situation does differ from that of the past in that a single country, the United States, may be the main focus of outrage. In the Muslim world, generalized anger may well combine with a very specific fury: the West has once more shown its disdain for and hostility against Muslims by permitting the Bosnian holocaust. Attacks on foreigners, particularly Muslim Turks, in Germany and elsewhere in Europe add to the sense of outrage.

In a post–nuclear age, navies become far more important. They are virtually the only means by which a country can meaningfully project power overseas. In many cases, it is more important to remain on the scene, displaying the ability to project power, than it is to actually kill anyone. For example, most would now agree that a strong dose of deterrence early in the Yugoslav crisis would have headed off the problem. Now it would take very large numbers of ground troops merely to police a cease-fire; the prewar situation almost certainly cannot be restored at all. Only a ship can remain off a country's coast, suggesting the potential for intervention but not actually attacking. Long-range airplanes cannot exert presence. They can affect the issue only by actually striking. Since the potential for military effectiveness is so often less than any potential the victims might imagine, actual attacks are often counterproductive.

Perhaps most importantly, ships can be effective without intruding on any nation's territory. They can, therefore, provide their owners with considerable flexibility in armed diplomacy. No other kind of military force has anything like that characteristic. Airplanes can appear overhead, but not for very long; to make much of an impression they must violate local airspace. It is almost necessary for them to attack. Ground troops must actually be based in a country for them to have much influence. Moreover, without a major threat to align them, countries are unlikely to view crises in the same way. Base facilities will be granted on a case-by-case basis, rather than (as in the past) on an alliance basis. This consideration also favors warships as instruments of armed diplomacy.

To be effective, those ships must be able to shrug off the sorts of attacks that local governments can mount. At one time that was quite simple: the Victorians could "send a gunboat" in the clear expectation that nothing on the scene could sink it. Once Third World countries bought torpedoes, the ante rose. Now that they have reasonably effective tactical air forces and antiship missiles, the naval-police role—surely the most important for the decade or so to come—demands far more.

The modern Royal Navy is an interesting case in point. It had to cancel the combat-direction system planned for its new Type 23 ("Duke"-class) frigates; the replacement is not yet in service. A Type 23 cannot defend itself against any sort of concentrated air attack because its manual system cannot keep track of more than a few aircraft at a time. That is not a new discovery; modern computer combat-direction systems were conceived exactly because of that limitation. For the Royal Navy, the lapse in system development has been particularly unfortunate. British naval commitments in places like the Persian Gulf continue to grow as the British government cuts the number of destroyers and frigates. A ship must be discarded or laid up as each new Type 23 commissions. Yet in many cases the earlier ship, which had a computerized combat-direction system, could be sent into harm's way; a Type 23 cannot, until it is modernized with the appropriate system. The load on the remaining effective ships, the Type 42 destroyers and Type 22 frigates, becomes less and less supportable. The publicity hailing the Type 23 as the "ship of the future" does not particularly help. Indeed, there is a real fear that a British treasury desperately seeking to save money will kill off the Type 23 command system unless the Royal Navy makes it clear that the ship is very nearly useless without it.

The Type 23's story also illustrates an important theme in this volume and in the 1991/92 edition. Outwardly, a Type 23 looks perfectly capable. Its weapons and radars are up to date. What is missing is invisible from outside the ship's CIC (operations room). Inside, however, it is obvious that many of the numerous electronic consoles familiar on board modern ships have not been included. The only summary of the air situation is the sort of plastic plotting board that would have been familiar half a century ago.

The British situation is not unique. We are not yet sufficiently familiar with Russian command systems. However, it appears that units built for export, such as export Kilo-class submarines (Project

877E), lack modern computer-based systems. They look exactly like their Russian sisters on the outside; the difference is inside, invisible, but absolutely vital.

The end of the Cold War will most likely raise, not lower, the demands on ships' combat systems. In the past, neither superpower was particularly anxious to supply customers with the most advanced technology, for fear that it would quickly fall into the hands of the enemy. For example, Soviet client states could often secure large numbers of airplanes or missiles, but none of them were anything like as good as what equipped the Soviet forces. Third World navies equipped by the West faced similar limitations. Western navies benefited enormously from this policy because they spent a great deal of their post-1945 time operating against Third World states. It was possible to distinguish between the big war, to be fought against a relatively sophisticated Soviet Navy, and limited operations in the Third World, where the opposition had much-less-capable equipment. That was quite aside from the skills of the Third World navies operating that equipment. Now that central war no longer seems likely at all, there is no longer a clear rationale for denying military technology to Third World clients. Even before the Soviet Union disintegrated, it was obvious to many of its citizens that its best chance of earning hard currency was to sell its highest technology, its military products. After all, for years the country had poured its treasure into its military industries. There was no longer much point in keeping particular systems secret. The Russians could hope for particular export success if the West continued to restrict access to its own top-of-the-line systems. Whatever the Western view of this development, it would have been unacceptably hypocritical to invite Russia into the larger world of trade while denying it a market for its most saleable products.

From about 1991 on, then, the Russians began to reveal their secrets. In 1992 visitors to the Moscow Air Show would see what, in the past, they had seen only on satellite photographs. Subsequent shows have revealed more and more, as the reader of this volume will see. Moreover, with the pressures of the Cold War relaxed, the Russians have become positively forthcoming in describing their equipment. Their brochures are generally not yet very well printed, but they supply just the sort of information that Western manufacturers provide. It almost seems that the Russians are running out of spectacular revelations. They have also opened up at home. For example, a privately prepared handbook of their fleet (a *spravotchik*) was printed in Irkutsk. Reportedly, the Russian Navy expects to publish an English-language version of its standard handbook of world navies, the book carried on its ships' bridges (the same reports suggest that Western security officers will be shocked by the details to be revealed).

All of this titillates the expert, but it implies something important. The Russians are now beginning to act like Westerners in their attitude toward their own forces. Openness is a precondition for selling in the open market (past Russian successes can be laid largely to the fact that their clients had nowhere else to go, and partly to the subsidies involved). For the moment, many potential buyers fear that the Russians cannot supply spares and adequate support. There are also rumors of poor quality control, which makes for poor performance. Neither problem is insuperable. If the Russians can convince the world that they can support the weapons and platforms they are selling, they may well enjoy considerable commercial success. Western arms sellers will have to follow suit. Even if their usual clients evince no great skepticism, they will have to demonstrate their products in the face of high-performance Russian hardware. Western governments far more concerned with commercial survival than with abstract security will undoubtedly disassemble the Cold War export controls. Operating in the Third World, navies (including, quite possibly, the Russian fleet) will face much more sophisticated weapons. These same navies will probably not be modernized to match. Money will be short, and even the cut-back fleets of the next decade or so will be expensive to modernize. The situation is similar to that of the U.S. Cavalry of the 1870s, which faced Indians armed with much better rifles than the U.S. Army could supply.

The new Russian openness has delivered a considerable shock. Until a year or so ago, it seemed reasonable to imagine that the Soviets knew how to build electromechanical hardware (such as missile launchers), but that they did not know much about system integration. Now we know better. Russian technical espionage seems to have been extremely effective, and there was just enough industrial capacity to exploit what was stolen. The Russians did fol-

low a very distinctive path toward computerization, and they followed it rather further than the West had imagined. We still do not know how well the Russian computer systems worked, and it may still be that the technology did not match the sophistication of the ideas. The reader can judge the extent of the difference between the descriptions in the 1991/92 edition of this book, which was reasonably sophisticated for its time, with those in this supplement, which are based on the new information.

Very few Third World countries can possibly afford large numbers of new missiles or sophisticated airplanes or submarines. They will buy only a few. However, the rules of Third World armed presence are very different from those of the World War III for which both superpowers prepared. Because the Third World is not a single unified entity, operations against any one country do not automatically affect the others. However, if the operations are dramatically successful and cost very little (at least in terms of people killed and major units damaged or destroyed), other Third World governments will get the message: attacking the superpower will likely be unprofitable. That was probably the effect of the impressive coalition victory over Iraq. Conversely, any dramatic failure encourages other Third World governments and discourages Western governments that may be pondering intervention. In contrast, it was generally accepted that losses during World War III would be heavy but would be an entirely acceptable price for victory.

Thus, in the Third World, a few very effective antiship missiles can make a big difference; the Russians have been displaying just what might be needed. It seems unlikely, for example, that any of the current defensive missiles could easily cope with the aeroballistic Kh-15 (AS-16). Big rocket-ramjets like Kh-41 (Moskit) and 3M-80 show the speed (but not the sea-skimming ability) of the Franco-German ANS, which is still in the early project stage. Until the Russian revelations, many had imagined that supersonic weapons of this type were a 21st-century threat, so work on counters (such as improved versions of SM-2 Block IV) could be slowed to save money. That no longer seems wise. Similarly, the Third World threat makes active torpedo defense even more urgent. In effect, then, Russian weapons now on offer for export present a greater threat to Western maritime forces than they did under hostile Soviet control. The reasoning is simple. As long as both sides were armed with nuclear weapons, neither was terribly anxious to fight. If war had come, it would have been devastating. But it was unlikely. Moreover, in the context of World War III there might be many ways of dealing with weapons-carrying aircraft or ships or submarines well before they could attack. In the Third World, an attacker will very likely shoot first. Our rules of engagement will be written to avoid accidentally starting a war, not to protect our ships or airplanes or submarines.

Will Western governments realize that the Third World commitment is both difficult and unavoidable, and that it requires additional sophistication on our part? The West badly wants to save money. In retrospect, it is clear that the Cold War was quite expensive, particularly during the final economic offensive of the Reagan years. Although Western military expenditures were fairly well controlled to keep them down to a sustainable level, many would argue that the expenditure of nonmonetary assets, such as concentrating scientific and engineering talent on military problems, was anything but a minor expense. Some Americans would argue that it cost the United States its trading position in the world (since the Japanese and the Germans in particular felt no similar need to concentrate their talents). But all of that effort had a real effect: the West won. The Soviet system collapsed of its own weight, but much of that weight had been built up to deal with the West. Now there is no longer a single major enemy; but there are many who wish the West, and particularly the United States, ill. It is unlikely that the Western military establishments will be allowed to melt away. However, the rate of new construction, whether of ships or of aircraft, must fall dramatically. New ships will continue to be bought in numbers by navies faced with real and immediate threats, such as those of South Korea and Taiwan. It seems likely that Western navies will find themselves concentrating more on modernization, which can be conducted piecemeal and which, therefore, has less immediate impact on a closely scrutinized budget. Much of the effect of such improvement may be almost invisible, just like the insertion of a full combat-direction system into an otherwise nearly useless Type 23. In other cases, the vastly improved successor to a given piece of equipment may receive virtually the same designation, or may deliberately be designed to use the same antennas or radomes.

Another continuing theme will be the reduced demand for personnel. For example, steam power plants require many more operators than gas-turbine systems. The U.S. Navy will probably decommission all its steam-powered cruisers over the next two or three years for just this reason, even though otherwise they are extremely effective ships (with recently modernized New Threat Upgrade systems). This raises an important question. Damage control is people-intensive. Many modern weapons, such as missiles, will damage rather than destroy a ship, so conventional damage control can make an enormous difference. Ships with distributed combat-direction systems may be better adapted than their predecessors to recover from many kinds of damage. But if there are too few people on board to fight off the damage, how much survivability will a ship really have?

This update to the 1991/92 edition is in two parts. First is the update proper, arranged much as in the previous edition. The first, and by far the longest, entry describes the revolution in the U.S. Navy (and then the allied navies) wrought by the need for over-the-horizon targeting (OTH-T). OTH-T initially became necessary because of the emergence of the Tomahawk missile in the United States and the disappearance of airborne radar platforms in the Royal Navy (the Sea Harrier carrying Sea Eagle missiles is in some, but decidedly not all, ways like a manned Tomahawk). The development of OTH-T technologies has changed the basic shape of these navies, and such changes may well be the pattern for the future.

In a few important cases it has been possible to explain the connections between different versions of a system, or between related systems. Examples are the U.S., French, and Italian combat-direction systems. In one important case, the Gabriel missile, new information (about the missile's guidance technique) radically changes the earlier description. In virtually all cases, I have been able to provide a listing of which navies, and generally which platforms, employ a particular device or weapon. This census is necessarily incomplete in a few cases. Major omissions are navigational radars

and 40-mm guns (it is virtually impossible to distinguish between types of Bofors guns, other than the Breda-Bofors twin 40-mm; much the same problem applies to many 20-mm guns and machine guns). Noncombatant ships are generally omitted from such listings.

The major departure from the previous arrangement is that all electronic-warfare equipment, airborne and shipborne, is collected in a single section. One reason is that, with the miniaturization of computers, more and more equipment exists in both airborne and shipboard versions.

The second part may be the most startling. With the end of the Cold War, vast amounts of information about the former Soviet Navy have become available, not least from Russian attempts to sell modern hardware. It is now possible to understand Soviet combat-direction systems and tactics on a level not previously available, it would seem, even in highly classified publications. Although the picture is still far from complete, it is well worth assembling. Much of the picture may seem primarily of historical interest, so the reader should keep in mind, first, that much of the equipment is being exported (to countries that the U.S. Navy may well have to engage) and, second, that the former Soviet fleet has not by any means vanished.

Again, the information on the Soviet/Russian Navy is organized in parallel to the main body of the previous edition. I have avoided reproducing previously published data; wherever data are provided in an entry, they are new, and often they came from the Russians themselves. Obviously, it is too early to say whether particular systems were made in Russia or in other now-independent republics. Certainly all of the industrial organizations (NPOs) that exhibited in Moscow in 1992 had Moscow or other Russian addresses.

As in the previous edition, I would emphasize that the material in this book comes from UNCLASSIFIED sources. That restriction inevitably limits coverage in some ways.

ACKNOWLEDGMENTS

Many friends helped enormously with this book. Among them are A. D. Baker III, editor of the companion book to this one, the superb *Combat Fleets*; Kernan Chaisson of DMS/Forecast International; Dr. Raymond Cheung; Sue Fili; CDR James Goldrick, RAN; Eric Grove; David Isby; Fu S. Mei; Antony Preston, editor of *Naval Forces* and of the invaluable quarterly, NAVINT; Alan Raven; CDR C. B. Robbins, USN (Ret.); Dr. Robert S. Scheina; David Steigman; Stuart Slade of DMS/Forecast International; Mark Wertheimer; Armin Welterhahn; John C. Wise; and Steven J. Zaloga. I would like to thank my editor, Anthony F. Chiffolo, for his invaluable help and his enormous patience. I would particularly like to thank my wife, Rhea, for her loving encouragement and assistance, without which this book could not have been written.

ABBREVIATIONS

AAAM	Advanced Air-to-Air Missile
AAM	air-to-air missile
AAW	antiair warfare
ABCAS	*Arma de Bajo Coste Anti-Submarina*
ABF	advanced bomb family
ACDS	Advanced Combat Direction System
ACDS	Automatic C/M-Dispensing System
ACS	Afloat Correlation System
ACT	Acoustic Collection Technology
ADA	U.S. standard military computer language
ADATS	Air-Defense Antitank System
ADAWS	Action Data Automation Weapons System
ADCAP	Advanced Capability
ADIMP	ADAWS Improvement Program
ADS	Advanced Deployable System
ADT	automatic detection and tracking
AGEP	Advanced Guidance Evaluation Program
AGI	intelligence-gathering ship
AGIS	*Automatische Gefechts und Informations-system Schnellboote*
AHEAD	Advanced Hit Efficiency and Destruction
AI	artificial intelligence
AIDS	AVP Improved Display System
AIEWS	Advanced Integrated EW System
AIO	action information organization (British CIC)
AIWS	Advanced Interdiction Weapons System
ALARM	Air-Launched Antiradar Missile
ALARMS	Airborne Laser Radar Mine Sensor
ALFS	Airborne Low-Frequency Sonar
ALI	automatic line integration
ALP	acoustic localization plot
ALSS	Air-Launched Saturation System
AM	amplitude modulation
AMCG	Advanced Minor-Caliber Gun
AMCGS	Advanced Minor(Medium)-Caliber Gun System
AMD	activated metal decoy
AMDAS	Airborne Mine Detector and Survey system
AMDR	Automatic Missile Detection Radar
AMNSYS	Airborne Mine-Neutralization System
AMRAAM	Advanced Medium-Range Air-to-Air Missile
AMSCOS	Airborne Maritime Situation Control System
ANODE	Ambient Noise Omni-Directional Evaluation
ANS	*Anti-Navire Supersonique* missile
AOTA	All-Optical Towed Array
AP	armor-piercing
APAR	active phased-array radar
APC	Acoustical Passive Classification
APC	air-picture controller
APECS	Advanced Programmable Electronic Countermeasures System
APFDS	armor-piercing fin-stabilized or fragmenting discarding sabot
APK	*Akustischen Passiv-Klassifizierung*
APS	Afloat Planning System
ARE	Admiralty Research Establishment
ARF	*Anti-Radar Futur*
ARM	antiradar missile
ARPA	automatic radar plotting
ARTIST	Advanced Radar Techniques for Improved Surveillance
ASAP	Advanced Systolic Array Processor
ASCORE	Air/Surface Coastal Radar Equipment
ASM	Advanced Sea Mine, air-to-surface missile
ASMA	Air Staff Management Aid
ASMD	antiship missile defense
ASMP	*Air-Sol Moyenne Portée*

ASPECT	acoustic short-pulse echo-classification technique
ASPJ	Airborne Self-Protection Jammer (ALQ-165)
ASPRO	Associative Parallel Processor
ASRAAM	Advanced Short-Range Air-to-Air Missile
ASSM	Advanced Sea Sparrow Missile
ASSTASS	Australian Surface-Ship Towed-Array Surveillance System
ASUW	antisurface warfare
ASW	antisubmarine warfare
ASWD	ASW director
ASWM	ASW module
ASWOC	ASW Operations Center
ASWS	Advanced Standoff Weapons System
ATARS	Advanced Tactical Air Reconnaissance System
ATAS	Active Towed-Array Sonar
ATD	automatic target detection; automatically extract plots; advanced technology development
ATES	Aegis Tactical Executive System
ATT	automatic target tracker
ATTAC	Automatic TMA for Tactical Commanders
AVP	Acoustic Video Processor
BB	bottom bounce
bbl	barrel
BCH	*Bloc Calcul Hybride*
BGAAWC	Battle-Group AAW Coordination
BGPHES	Battle Group Passive Horizon Extension System
BHP	brake horsepower
BIP	battle information post
BLNS	Breached-Lane Navigational System
BPDMS	Basic Point-Defense Missile System
bps	bits per second
BT	bathythermograph
BURLAP	British-U.S. Random LF Array Program
C2	command/control
C3	command, control, and communications
C&D	command and decision
ca.	circa
CAAIS	Computer-Aided Action Information System
CAC	computer-aided classification
CACS	Computer-Assisted Command System
CAD	computer-aided detection
cal	caliber
CAMLAC	Computer-Aided Master Launcher Control
CANE	Computer-Aided Navigational System
CANTASS	Canadian Towed-Array Surveillance System
CAP	Combustion-Augmented Plasma
CARDINAL	*Centre d'Archivage et Dépouillement d'Images Numeriques Acquisés par le système Lagadmor*
CARMEN	Countermeasure against Active Radar Missile Engagement
CASOW	Conventional Air-Launched Standoff Weapon
CATF	commander of amphibious task forces
CAWCS	Center for Automation of Weapon and Command Systems
CCA	Captain's Combat Aid
CCS	course-corrected shell, combat-control system
CCSC	Cryptologic Combat-Support Console
CCSS	Cryptologic Combat-Support System
CDC	combat-direction center
CDS	Combat-Direction System

CEC	Cooperative Engagement Concept or Capability
CEP	cooperative engagement processor, contact evaluation plot
CEPLO	Command Electronic Plotting System
CFA	crossed-field amplifier
CFE	Conventional Forces in Europe (arms-control treaty)
CHBDL	Common High-Bandwidth Data Link
CILOP	conversion in lieu of procurement
CIS	Confederation of Independent States (successor to U.S.S.R.)
CIU	Cryptologic Interface Unit
CIWS	close-in weapons system
CLF	commander of landing forces
cm	centimeter
CMA	contact motion analysis
CMS	Contact Management System
CNO	chief of naval operations
CO	commanding officer
COCM	coherent countermeasures capability
COEA	cost and effectiveness evaluation analysis
COMDAC/ ICES	Command, Display, and Control and Integrated Cutter Electronics System
COMINT	communications intelligence
CORAIL	*Contre-mésures Optronique et Radar Integré par Leurrage*
CORAS	correctable ammo
CORT	coherent receive/transmit
CPA	closest point of approach
CPIC	coastal patrol and interdiction craft
CPP	Compact Power Plant
CPU	central processing unit (of a computer)
CRT	cathode-ray tube
CTM	*Conduit de Tir Multisensor*
CTTLS/ QTLHNR	Countermeasures Torpedo Tube Launching System/Quiet Launcher
CU	cooperating unit
CVR	crystal video receiver
CW	continuous wave
CWC	composite warfare commander
CWI	continuous wave illuminator/injection
CZ	convergence zone
DAC	digital autopilot
DAISY	Digital Action Information System
DARPA	Defense Advanced Research Projects Agency
dB	decibel(s)
DCC	district control center
DDS	data-distribution system
DE	destroyer escort
deg	degree(s)
DEMON	demodulated noise
DEPLO	Danish version of CEPLO
DET	Distributed Explosive Technology
DF	direction finding
DFTDS	Data Fusion Technology Demonstrator System
DICASS	directional command-activated sonobuoy
DIFAR	directional LOFAR
DLPS	Data Link Processing System British)
DLRP	data link reference point
DOP	development options paper
DORNA	*Direccion de Tiro Optronica y Raddrica Naval*
DRA	Defence Research Authority (U.K.)
DRAM	dynamic random-access memory
DSG	digital signal generator
DSMAC	digital scene matching
DSP	Digital Signal Processor

DT	directional transmission		FSD	full-scale development
ECCM	electronic counter-countermeasures		FSED	full-scale engineering development
ECM	electronic countermeasures		FSK	frequency-shift keying
ECMIU	ECM Interface Unit		ft	foot, feet
ECP	engineering change proposal		FTAAS	
EDM	engineering development model		FTAS	Fast-Time Analyzer
EEZ	exclusive economic zone		FTEWA	Force Threat Evaluation and Weapon
EHF	extremely high frequency			Assignment
ELINT	electronic intelligence		G	force of gravity
EMPAR	European Multi-Purpose Array Radar		GAs	Gallium Arsenide
EMSP	Enhanced Modular Signal Processor (UYS-2)		GATT	General Agreement on Trade and Tariffs
EO	electro-optical		Gbyte	gigabyte(s)
EORSAT	ESM Ocean-Reconnaissance Satellite(s)		GFCS	gun fire control system
EPMDS	Experimental Parametric Mine-Detection System		GFLOPS	billions of floating-point operations per second
EPROM	erasable programmable read-only memory		GHz	gigahertz
ER	extended range		GPS	Global Positioning System
ERAPS	Expendable Reliable Acoustic Path Sonobuoy (SSQ-75)		GRT	gross registered tonnage
			HAIS	Hydroacoustic Information System
ERATO	Extended-Range Targeting of Otomat		HARM	high-speed antiradar missile
ERINT	Extended-Range Interceptor		HARP	Horizontal Array Random Position
ERP	effective radiated power (in jamming)		HE	high explosive
ESM	electronic support measures		HEAT	High-Explosive Antitank (shaped charge)
ESS	Evolved Sea Sparrow		HELWEPS	Highe-Energy-Laser Weapon System
ESSM	Evolved Sea Sparrow Missile		HF	high frequency
ETG	electrothermal gun		HFDF	high-frequency direction finder; height-finding direction finding
EW	electronic warfare			
EWC	electronic-warfare controller		HPIRS	High-Performance IR Sensor
EWCM	electronic-warfare coordination module		HPM	high-power microwave
EWCP	electronic-warfare coordination processor		hr	hour(s)
EWD	EW director		HSMST	High-Speed Maneuvering Surface Target
EXPAR	Experimental Phased-Array Radar		HUD	heads-up display
FAA	Fast Acoustic Analyzer		HVAR	High-Velocity Aircraft Rocket
FAC	fast attack craft		HYCATS	Hydrofoil Collision Avoidance and Tracking System
FACT	Force AAW Coordinating Technology			
FAE	fuel-air explosive		HYFIX	hyperbolic fixing
FAMS	Family of Antiair Missiles		Hz	hertz (cycles per second)
FARS	Frigate Array Radar System		I/O	input/output
FAST	Flanking-Beam Array Switching Technique		IAI	Israel Military Industries
			IANC	Inter-American Naval Conference
FCC	Fleet Command Center		ICDC	Improved Common Display Console (in submarines)
FCS	fire-control system			
FDDS	Flag Data Display Ststem		IDAP	Integrated Defense Avionics Program
FDS	Fixed Distributed System		IFF	Identification Friend or Foe
FEWS	Follow-on Early-Warning Satellite		IFM	instantaneous frequency measurement
FFAR	Folding-Fin Aircraft Rocket		IIR	imaging infrared
FFISTS	Frigate Integrated Shipboard Tactical System		IJMS	Interim JTIDS Messaging Standard
			ILC	Improved Line Clearance Charge
FFS	Force Fusion System		IMAIS	Integrated Magnetic and Acoustic Influence Sweep
FFT	fast Fourier transform			
FHLT	Fleet High-Level Terminal		INF	Intermediate Nuclear Forces (Treaty)
FIMS	Ferranti's Integrated Mine-Countermeasures System		IPADS	Improved Processing and Display System
			IR	infrared
FISCS	Ferranti Integrated Submarine Combat System		IRCCD	IR charge-coupled device
			IRCM	IR countermeasure
FLASH	Folding Light Acoustic System		IRST	infrared search and track
FLIR	forward-looking infrared		IRSTD	IR Search Track/Target Designator
FLTSAT	Fleet Satellite		ISA	instruction set architecture
FLYRT	Flying Radar Target		ISAR	inverse synthetic-aperture radar
FM	frequency modulation		ISD	integrated self-defense
FMCW	frequency-modulated continuous wave		ISDL	Inter-Site Data Link
FML	frequency-memory loop		ISPS	Integrated Strike Planning System
FMS	foreign military sales		ISUS	Integrated Sensor Underwater System
FOLWS	Fiber-Optic Laser-Warning System		ITACS	Integrated Tactical Command System
FOSP	Fleet Ocean Surveillance Product		ITALD	Infrared Tactical Air-Launched Decoy
FoV	field of view		ITAS	Improved TAS
FPA	focal plane array		IUSS	Integrated Undersea Surveillance System
FPB	fast patrol boat		IVDS	independent VDS
FRAZ	frequency-azimuth		IXS	Information-Exchange System
FSAF	Family of Surface-to-Air Defense Systems		JADDIN	Joint Air-Defense Digital Information Network
			JCLO	Joint Counter Low Observable Office

JDAMS	Joint Direct-Attack Munitions System	MCCIS	Maritime Command/Control Information System
JMSDF	Japanese Maritime Self-Defense Force	MCDV	maritime coastal-defence vessel
JOTS	Joint Operational Tactical System	MCIRSS	Mine Countermeasures Integrated Route Survey System
JPTDS	Junior Participating Tactical Data System	MCM	mine countermeasures
JSCAMPS	Joint-Service Common-Airframe Multiple-Purpose System	MCRC	Master Control Reporting Center
JSOW	Joint Standoff Weapon	MCS	Modular Combat System
JSTARS	Joint Standoff Airborne Radar System	MDAU	Multisource Data Acquisition Unit
JTIDS	Joint Tactical Information Distribution System	MEOSS	Marine Electro-Optical Surveillance System
JVIDS	Joint Video Display System	MFCS	missile fire-control system
kbit	kilobit(s)	MFLOPS	millions of floating-point operations per second
kbps	kilobits per second	MHC	minehunter, coastal
kbyte	kilobyte(s)	MHD	magnetohydrodynamic
KE	kinetic energy	MHIDAS	Multiple High Integration Distributed Architecture data-bus System
kg	kilogram(s)	MHQ	maritime headquarters (German)
kHz	kilohertz	MHz	megahertz
kloc	thousand lines of code	microsec	microsecond(s)
km	kilometer(s)	MIDAS	Mine Detection and Avoidance Sonar
kpps	kilopulses per second	MIDS	Multifunctional Information Distribution
kt	knot(s)	min	minute(s)
kW	kilowatt(s)	MIPS	millions of instructions per second
kword	thousands of words	MJ	mega-Joule (energy)
LADAR	laser radar	Mk	Mark
LAMPS	Light Airborne Multipurpose System	MLRS	Multiple-Launcher Rocket System
LAN	local area network	MLT	multiline tracker
LANTIRN	Low-Altitude Navigation-and-Targeting IR system for Night	mm	millimeter(s)
LAPADS	Lightweight Acoustic Processing-and-Display System	MMD	Multimode Device
		MMI	man-machine interface
LARIP	Low-Altitude Readiness-Improvement Program	MMIC	monolithic microwave integrated circuit
lb	pound(s)	MNS	mission need statement
LCAW	Low-Cost Antisubmarine Weapon	MOC	Multifunction Operator Console
LCC	local control center	MOPS	millions of operations per second
LCS	Low-Cost Seeker; Low-Cost Sonobuoy	MOSC	Maritime-Operations Support Center
LDS	Laser Dazzle System	MoU	memorandum of understanding
LEAP	Lightweight Exoatmospheric Projectile	MPA	maritime-patrol aircraft
LEDS	Link 11 Display System	MPU	medium PRF upgrade (for SPS-49 radar)
LEIP	Link 11 Improvement Program	mrad	milliradian
LEWA	*Lageerarbeitungs und Waffeneinsatzanlage*	MRR	Multi-Role Radar
LFA	LF adjunct	MSDHS	Mission System Data-Handling System
LGB	laser-guided bomb	msec	millisecond(s)
LIDAR	light (i.e., laser) radar	MSO	minesweeper, ocean
LLLTV	low-light-level television	MSOW	Modular Standoff Weapon
LOFAR	low-frequency analysis and recording	MSP	mission system computer
LOP	line-of-position	MSSE	multisensor situation elaboration
LOS	line of sight	MTAS	Multimission TAS
LPI	low probability of intercept	MTBF	mean time between failure
LRCM	long-range cruise missile	MTI	moving-target indicator
LSDM	Long Ship-Defense Missile	MTTR	mean time to repair
m	meter(s)	MULTS	Multilink Terminal Station
MAD	magnetic-anomaly detector	MUSL	Marconi Underwater Systems Ltd.
MADOM	Magnetic-Acoustic Detection of Mines	MW	megawatt(s)
MAGICS	Modular Architecture for Graphic and Imaging Console System	MWCS	multi-weapon control systems
		Mword	megawords
MAIGRET	*Matériel Automatique d'Interception et de Goniométrie des Radio communications en Exploitation Tactique*	NAAWS	NATO AAW Missile System
		NADGE	NATO Air-Defense Ground Environment
		NATO	North Atlantic Treaty Organization
		NAUTIS	Naval Autonomous Information System
MAINS	Minehunting Information System	NCCS	Naval Command-and-Control System
MAPS	Maritime Asset Planning System	NDI	nondevelopmental items
MAREC	Maritime-Reconnaissance Radar	NEDPS	*Näcken* Electronic Data–Processing System
MARS	Magnetic Array Sensor	NGCR	new-generation computer resources
MARTEL	Missile Anti-Radar Television	NGFS	naval gunfire support
MATES	Multiband Antiship Cruise-Missile-Defense Tactical Electronic System	nm	nautical mile(s)
		NML	Naval Multiple Launcher
MBAT	multibeam array technology	NMR	nuclear magnetic resonance
Mbps	mega bits per second	NOSC	Naval Ocean Systems Center
Mbyte	megabyte(s)	NPO	cooperative production organization (Russian design bureau plus factory)
MCC	maintenance of close contact		

NRL	Naval Research Laboratory
NSA	National Security Agency (U.S.)
nsec	nanosecond
NSIS	New Sonar Intercept System
NSWC	Naval Surface Warfare Center (U.S.)
NTDS	Naval Tactical Data System
NTTCS	Naval Tactical Command-and-Control System
NTU	New Threat Upgrade
NTU (ER)	New Threat Upgrade (Extended Range)
NTU (MR)	New Threat Upgrade (Medium Range)
OASIS	OTH-T Airborne Sensor Interface
OBM	Obstacle Breaching Munitions
OBSCLNC	Obstacle Line Clearing System
OBU	Operational Baseline Upgrade
OCP	Operational Computer Program
ODT	omnidirectional transmission
OIT/ATT	operator-initiated tracking/automatic target tracking
OKB	design bureau (Russian)
OPV	offshore patrol vessel
OR	operational requirement
OSCAD	Ocean Surveillance Communications and Display
OSD BTI	Office of the Secretary of Defense Balanced Technology Initiative
OSIS	Ocean Surveillance Information System
OTC	officer in tactical command
OTCIXS	Officer-in-Tactical-Command Information-Exchange System
OTH	over the horizon
OTH-T	over-the-horizon targeting
P3I	preplanned production improvement
PAEL	Prototype Array Electronic Location
PAINTER	Parallel Architectures for Integrated Thresholding and (Plot) Extraction (i.e., ADT) in Radar
PAP	*Poisson Auto-Propulsé*
PARIS	Passive/Active Range-and-Intercept Sonar
PASRAN	Passive Ranger
PBC	patrol boat, coastal
PCC	polarity coincidence correlator
Pd	probability of detection
PDI	Pulse-Doppler Integration
PDR	preliminary design review
PFSS	Pilot Flag Support System
PIANIST	Program for Investigation of Adaptive Nulling and Improved Super-Resolution
PID	passive ID
PINS	Precision Integrated Navigation System
PIPRS	Ping Intercept Passive Ranging System
PMU	parameter measuring unit
POST	Prototype Ocean Surveillance Terminal
PPI	plan-position indicator
pps	pulses per second
PRF	pulse repetition frequency
PRI	pulse repetition interval
PRISM	Passive Radar Identification System
PRR	pulse-repetition rate
PRS	Passive Ranging Sonar
PSI	Precision Strike Initiative
PSM	Phalanx Surface Mode
PSW	pro–submarine warfare
PUFFS	Passive Underwater Fire Control Feasibility Study (BQG Series)
PVDF	polyvinylidene fluoride
PVDS	propelled variable-depth sonar
PVF	polyvinyl fluoride
PWO	principal warfare officer
QRCC	Quick Reaction Combat Capability
R&D	research and development
RAAF	Royal Australian Air Force

RAF	Royal Air Force
RAIDS	Rapid Antiship-Missile Integrated Defense System
RAM	random access memory; Rolling Airframe Missile; radar-absorbing material
RAMSES	Reprogrammable Advanced Multimode Shipboard Electronic-Countermeasures Systems
RAN	Royal Australian Navy
RAPIDS	Radar Passive Identification System
RASP	Rapid Acquisition Spectrum Processor; Recognized Air and Surface Picture
RAWS	Role Adaptable Weapon System
RCS	radar cross section
RDE	remote data engagement
RDIDS	Rapid Deployment Integrated Defense System
RDT	rotationally directed transmission
RECO	Remote Control of Mines
RENT	Range Extension Near Term
REW	radio-electronic warfare
RF	radio frequency
RFA	Royal Fleet auxiliary (U.K.)
RFP	request for proposals
RFQ	request for quotation
RGPO	range-gate pull-off (ECM technique)
RIS	Remote Influence Sweep
RISC	Reduced-Instruction-Set Computer
RMS	root mean square
RN	Royal Navy
rnd	round(s)
RNEE	Royal Naval Equipment Exhibition
RNLN	Royal Netherlands Navy
RNTDES	RNTDS Emulation System
RNTDS	Restructured NTDS
RNZAF	Royal New Zealand Air Force
ROE	rules of engagement
ROK	Republic of Korea
ROLE	Receive-Only Link 11
ROM	read-only memory
RORSAT	Radar Ocean-Reconnaissance Satellite(s)
ROTHR	Relocatable Over-the-Horizon Radar
ROV	remotely operated vehicle
RPG	receiver-processor group
rpm	revolutions per minute
RRASL	Reactive Resource Allocation—Single Ship Level
RTADS	Royal Thai Air-Defense System
RTC	Radar Track Combiner
RV	reentry vehicle (in a strategic missile)
RWR	radar warning receiver
SABRE	Shallow-Water Breach System
SACEIT	*Système Automatisé de Commandement et d'Exploitation des Informations Tactiques*
SACLANT	Supreme Allied Commander Atlantic
SADANG	*Système Acoustique de l'Atlantique Nouvelle Génération*
SADIE	Segregation, Association, Deinterleaving, and Identification Equipment processor
SADIS	Semi-Automatic Decoy Integration System
SADOC	*Systema Automatico Dirizione della Operazioni di Combattimento*
SAFENET	Survivable Adaptable Fiber-Optic Embedded Network
SAGAIE	*Système d'Autodéfense pour la Guerre Infra-rouge et Électromagnetique*
SAIGON	*Système Automatisé d'Interception et de Goniométrie*
SALFAS	Stand-Alone LF Active Sonar
SAM	surface-to-air missile

SAMOS	SAGEM Anti-Missile Optronic System
SAP	semi–armor piercing
SAR	search and rescue; synthetic-aperture radar; Selected Acquisition Report
SARIE	Selective Automatic Radar Identification Equipment
SATCOM	satellite communication
SATIN	*Système de Traitement Automatique de l'Information Navale*
SAUV	Semi-Autonomous Undersea Vehicle
SAWS	Submarine Acoustic Warfare System
SBC	single-board computer
SBS/AC	Shipboard Gridlock System/Automatic Correlation
SCANS	Signal Collection-and-Analysis System
SCIP	Shipboard Countermeasures Interface Package
SCL	System Configuration Language
SCSI	special compartmented security information
SDC	*Système de Defense et de Commandement*
SDIO	Strategic Defense Initiative Organization
SDT	steered directional transmission
sec	second(s)
SEM	standard electronic module
SEPADS	Sonar-Environment Prediction-and-Display System
SFCS	submarine fire-control system
SFF	self-forging fragment
SFW	sensor-fuzed weapon
SGS/AC	ship gridlock system/autocorrelation
SHF	super high frequency
SHR	superheterodyne receiver
SIASS	Submarine Integrated Attack-and-Surveillance Sonar
SIMD	single-instruction multiple-data
SINBADS	Submarine Integrated Battle and Data System
SIRST	Surveillance IRST
SISC	*Système d'Intégration du Système de Combat*
SLAM	standoff land-attack missile
SLASM	*Système de Lutte Anti–Sous-Marin*
SLAT	surface-launched air-targeted
SLBM	sea-launched ballistic missile
SLIPAR	Short-Pulse-Light Alerting Receiver
SMASH	SM Autonomous Strike Homing
SMATCALS	Signature Managed Air Traffic Control and Landing System
SMCS	Signaal Modular Combat System
SMS	Search Mast SAGEM
SMTD	submarine torpedo-defense weapon
SNAPS	Smiths Navigation and Plotting System
SOBIC	Shore Information and Classification Center
SOSUS	Sound Surveillance System
SPC	surface-picture controller
SPHINX	System for Passive Handling of Intercepted Xmissions
SPV	surveillance-patrol vessel
SRAM	static random-access memory
SRBOC	Super Rapid-Blooming Off-Board Chaff
SRF	sweep repetition frequency
SSCS	Surface-Ship Command System
SSDS	Ship Self-Defense System
SSES	ship signals-exploitation spaces
SSIPS	Shore Signal and Information Processing Segment
SSIXS	Submarine Information Exchange System
SSK	ASW submarine
SSM	surface-to-surface missile
SSTD	surface-ship torpedo defense

STACOS	Signaal Tactical Command and Control System
STAP	situation threat-assessment planning
STAR	*Supersonique Tactique Anti-Radiation*
START	Strategic Arms Reduction Treaty
STIR	Separate Track and Illumination Radar
STM	service test model
STRAP	Sonobuoy Thinned Random Array Processor
STSS	Submarine Tactical Sensor System
STT	Submarine Targeting Terminal
SUBOPCEN	Submarine Operations Control Center
SURTASS	Surveillance Towed-Array System
SVLA	Steered Vertical Line Array (sonobuoy)
SVP	Spatial Vernier Processing
SWC	scan with compensation; subordinate warfare commander; surface-warfare coordinator
SWIP	System Weapons Improvement Program
SWIPS	A-6E System Weapons Improvement Program
SWPS	Stabilized Weapons Platform System
SYCOMOR	*Système de Leurrage EM et IR*
SYTIT	*Système de Traitement des Informations Tactiques*
t	ton(s)
TACAMO	"Take charge and move out."
TACCO	tactical coordinating officer
TACNAV	tactical navigation system
TACNAVMOD	P-3A/B modification with TACNAV
TADIL	tactical digital link
TADIXS	Tactical Digital Information Exchange System
TADS	Target Acquisition and Designation System
TADSTAND B	Tactical Digital Standard B
TAICOS	Tactical Action Information and Command System
TALC	Tactical Airborne Laser Communication
TALD	Tactical Air-Launched Decoy
TAMPS	Tactical Aircraft Mission-Planning System
TAO	tactical action officer
TAP	towed-array processor
TAS	Target Acquisition System; Torpedo Alert System
TASES	Tactical Signal Exploitation System
TAVITAC	*Traitement Automatique et Visualization Tactique*
TCC	tactical coordination console
TDA	tactical decision aid
TDC	tactical display console
TDD	target-detection device
TDLT	Track Data Link Terminal
TDP	Tactical Data Processor
TDS	Target-Designation Sights
TDT	tactical data transfer
TEAMS	Tactical EA-6B Mission-Planning System
TEDR	threat-emitter-data recorder
TENCAP	Tactical Exploitation of National Capabilities
TERCOM	terrain comparison
TERNA	terrain navigation
TERPES	Tactical Electronic-Reconnaissance Processing Evaluation System
TEWA	threat evaluation and weapons assignment
TFC	torpedo fire control
TFCC	Tactical Flag Command Center
THAAD	theater antimissile air defense
TIP	tactical-information processing
TIU	torpedo interface unit
TLAM	Tomahawk Land-Attack Missile

TMA	target-motion analysis
TMD	Theater Missile Defense
TMS	Track-Management System
ToA	time of arrival
TOR	tentative operational requirement
TPI	tactical plotting indicator
TRDT	tribeam rotationally directed transmission
TRUMP	Tribal Update and Modernization Program
TSA	*Tungt Styrt Attackvapen*
TSS	Tactical Surveillance Sonobuoy
TVC	thrust vector control
TWS	track-while-scan, threat-warning system
TWT	traveling wave tube
UAV	unmanned air vehicle
UEP	underwater electric potential

SURVEILLANCE AND CONTROL

TOMAHAWK, OTH-T, AND TWO REVOLUTIONS IN THE U.S. NAVY

Only recently has the profound impact of the **Tomahawk** missile on the U.S. Navy become evident. The missile's special need for over-the-horizon targeting (OTH-T) has helped shape U.S. sea surveillance, and the shore- and sea-based correlation centers on which it is based. This system in turn led directly to the new kind of decentralized command/control, with its **Copernicus** communication backbone. Other navies, particularly the Royal Navy, have followed much the same path, to an extent that is only now becoming obvious. The U.S. sea-surveillance system made the blockade of Iraq possible.

Tomahawk was conceived as an inexpensive weapon that would demand little of its platforms. For example, it would not enjoy in-flight update because it was clearly difficult and expensive to provide a jam-resistant long-range data link. Nor could Tomahawk demand a new generation of special-purpose reconnaissance devices. The navy that bought the missile in 1973 was concerned far more with ASW and AAW than with attacking small numbers of Soviet surface combatants. The irony is that the demand for simplicity and low cost changed the character of the U.S. Navy.

Tomahawk is relatively slow; it arrives in the vicinity of its target about half an hour after launch, a time during which a fast ship may have moved anywhere within about a 15-nm radius. If its seeker had to cover the whole 30-nm swath, then the target would likely detect its emissions long before the missile got close. To use a narrower (hence stealthier) search swath, the missile would have to snake through the entire circle of uncertainty; it would probably be shot down while passing alongside the target. So the missile must know upon arrival where the target is likely to be.

Shorter-range weapons such as **Harpoon** or **Exocet** can be targeted by ownship sensors, such as ESM (exploiting ducting to penetrate well beyond the horizon) or ducted radar or even sonar (working, in effect, as an under-the-horizon sensor). Harpoon arrives at its target within about 6 min, during which time a ship cannot move very far.

A Tomahawk user needs far more: a clear and current picture of shipping activity out to a radius of perhaps 250–400 nm, i.e., well over the horizon. This picture must be more than a snapshot; each ship's position must be projected ahead over the half hour or more between the targeting and the arrival of the missile. In 1973 this was not an entirely new requirement because Soviet missile-armed ships (whose weapons had ranges similar to that of Tomahawk) were beginning to threaten carrier battle groups, particularly in the Mediterranean. Indeed, in 1970 the submarine community proposed building a new class of cruise-missile–armed ships specifically to deal with Soviet surface-action groups (the missile proposal led directly to the antiship version of Tomahawk). No submarine could detect surface ships at anything like the necessary range. Submarines would have relied on intelligence information collated ashore and transmitted by secure satellite link, tentatively called **SSIXS** (Submarine Information Exchange System).

Existing assets, such as HFDF and patrol aircraft, provided intermittent information good enough for naval intelligence to maintain a plot of Soviet surface ships. By about 1971 each deployed fleet had its own operational intelligence center. However, the center's product was generally not timely enough or precise enough for missile targeting.

About 1972 Lockheed proposed a dedicated sea-surveillance system that would use a shore-based U-2 equipped with various passive and active sensors. A tactical flagship would receive the data directly and correlate them with information from sensors organic to the battle group. A planned Mediterranean test (the U-2 flying out of Sigonella) was canceled for political reasons, but the navy program sponsors managed to place the surface terminal on board a carrier.

They also radically changed the concept, from the use of a single dedicated platform to the correlation of all available sensor data, active and passive. Some data would necessarily be gathered and correlated ashore. The navy sponsors insisted that the link between correlation centers ashore and afloat, and between the centers and the sensors, be 2-way. The system benefitted enormously. For example, a shore DF network might get only a single "cut" on a signal. Because that single line of bearing could not be used to generate target position (by triangulation), it would normally be discarded. However, a very different passive sensor (e.g., SOSUS) might well get another line of bearing; when correlated, the 2 lines of bearing could provide a target position. Each correlation made the system more effective and further refined existing tracks.

The ashore correlation center became the **FCC** (Fleet Command Center, but perhaps initially meaning fleet correlation center); the afloat center (which had been the carrier terminal) became the **TFCC** (Tactical Flag Command Center). The latter includes an **ACS** (Afloat Correlation System). The correlation process is complicated because nonorganic tracks, based on somewhat time-late information, may not match information from real-time sensors within the battle group. As conceived in 1974, the TFCC had a special terminal for the nonorganic surveillance data, **POST** (Prototype Ocean Surveillance Terminal), running the software of the ACS. By 1988 the ACS was required to handle up to 4,000 tracks simultaneously. The number was very high because the same platform might well appear as 2 or more tracks in badly matched organic and nonorganic data.

The main sources for ACS are organic tracks (from the ship's combat-direction system [CDS]), **OSIS** (Ocean Surveillance Information System) data, data from the TADIXS B link, and shipboard ELINT data (collected by the ship's **TASES** [Tactical Signal Exploitation System]). ACS and the new Electronic-Warfare Coordination Module (EWCM) together form an **FFS** (Force Fusion System) to evaluate threats and handle countermeasures.

The FCC-TFCC link is **OTCIXS** (Officer-in-Tactical-Command Information-Exchange System), a high-density secure satellite link. In theory, the TFCC provides a carrier or other surface group with a surveillance picture out to a range of perhaps 1,500 nm from a battle group's center, compared to perhaps 500 nm for organic sensors.

The FCC created just the sort of sea-surveillance picture the submariners needed to support their new Sub-Harpoon missile. Unlike the ships of a battle group, a submarine did not have access to much data requiring correlation with off-board sources. The FCC picture was fed to an ashore **STT** (Submarine Targeting Terminal) at the fleet **SUBOPCEN** (Submarine Operations Control Center), which could feed a submarine's picture-keeping computer via a special 1-way satellite link, **SSIXS** (Submarine Information Exchange System, using the OTH Gold format). The submarine system, **Outlaw Shark**, was first tested in 1974–75. Numerous submarines were fitted with it. Outlaw Shark also became the basis for the surface ships' Tomahawk weapons-control system. A 1975–76 proto-TFCC experiment in the Mediterranean, **Outlaw Hawk** (using the carrier *Kitty Hawk*), was extremely successful, not only in surface but also in subsurface surveillance. However, the service version was unsuccessful at first, partly because the correlation concept was apparently not widely understood or appreciated. It bore fruit in the 1980s.

The basic ideas were all in place as early as 1974: the FCC/TFCC/OTCIXS combination, the STT/SSIXS, and a connection between the FCCs and the patrol-plane squadrons via an **FHLT** (Fleet High-Level Terminal) communicating with the **ASWOCs** (ASW Operations Centers). Clearly, maritime-patrol aircraft could contribute to surveillance and targeting. The FHLT was also important because the FCC kept track of submarine movements. In each case, the deployed commander chose targets based on the tactical picture. Thus, despite the apparent shift of fleet command ashore (to the FCC), tactical decisions were still made where they had always been made—afloat.

To simplify the design, the same computers (**UYK-19** or **Rolm 1666**) were used to maintain the sea-surveillance picture in the STT, the TFCC, and the Tomahawk system (the workstation was designated **USQ-81**). TFCCs were quite expensive, so only a few flagships could be fitted with them. A surface-ship Tomahawk WCS (TWCS) (**SWG-2/3**) could also maintain the necessary picture in the absence of a TFCC (the submarine lacked the full-fusion capability). Within a group, one ship is designated Force OTH Coordinator (FOTC); the others match their pictures to the FOTC's.

None of these systems promised true real-time surveillance because the data were all intermittent. For example, satellites had limited footprints, and it was some considerable time before they revisited the same spot. The key decision was to combine all the intermittent surveillance data with data on ship behavior to project forward the likely path of each ship. Special statistical ship-tracker software was developed.

Passive intermittent tracking levied peculiar demands on surveillance. It was not enough to say that 3 cruisers of a particular type had departed the Kola Inlet on 3 June at 1500 hours and that 3 ships of the same type were spotted in the central Norwegian Sea on 5 June at 1700 hours. The system had to know that they were the *same* 3

ships so that the transit from Kola to the Norwegian Sea could be used to measure their average speed (for projection). Since most of the sensors available to the system were passive, it became extremely important to match particular hulls to particular emitter fingerprints. Passive identification (by identifying radar emission) could also help a Tomahawk approaching a formation to choose the right target.

Quite possibly the largest of the group would not be the most valuable target. The Tomahawk's passive-ID (PID) sensor does not home on a particular ship but decides which of several radar targets to prefer.

One intelligence-gathering system probably really was developed mainly for surface surveillance: **White Cloud (Classic Wizard)**. Its satellites were apparently conceived as a way of collecting emitter data that could more easily be matched to particular underway hulls. Because the statistical ship tracker could accept intermittent data, this intelligence-collection system could also contribute to surveillance once the signatures were known. White Cloud was apparently conceived in 1970; the first satellite was launched on 30 April 1976. The system did not become fully operational until 1981 because of delays in the development and installation of its FSQ-3 ground station (the system uses 5 such stations to achieve worldwide coverage; in contrast to some satellite systems, it does not use space-based relay satellites). Naval intelligence was already developing a new communications DF system, **Classic Outboard**, which differed from its predecessors in that its stations, on different ships, were to be netted together. They would also be fed with other intelligence information (**Classic Outrigger**) to improve their work. The entire system would communicate with shore-based HFDF sites (**Classic Bullseye**) via its secure net. Outboard was clearly adaptable to OTH missile targeting. NSA already operated strategic electronic-intelligence–gathering satellites. In 1977 Congress ordered that information from such "national" systems be adapted for tactical users, a procedure called **TENCAP** (Tactical Exploitation of National Capabilities). The need for a steady stream of surface-surveillance data made it essential to formalize the data-fusion process. Ocean surveillance was organized into OSIS, feeding the FCC; OSIS is currently being upgraded (the program is called **OBU**).

By 1974 one other Western navy was intensely interested in OTH-T: the Royal Navy. As in the U.S. Navy, carrier-borne aircraft, particularly those carrying early-warning radars, had provided good surveillance out to a considerable distance. But the carriers and their special aircraft were vanishing. The new Sea Harriers could carry antiship missiles out to long range, but they could not do much scouting, certainly not in the face of serious missile opposition. A Sea Harrier with Sea Eagle missiles could be imagined almost as a manned (and reusable) Tomahawk with 1 or 2 warheads. The British followed the U.S. development with great interest, and they ordered their own version: **OPCON** is the British equivalent of the U.S. FCC (it receives a version of the U.S. surface-surveillance product from SACLANT at Norfolk). The TFCC equivalent is **PFSS** (Pilot Flag Support System) on board each of the 3 light carriers; the high-capacity link is Link R, presumably via the Skynet satellite. The tactical picture is the **FOSP**, the Fleet Ocean Surveillance Product. Like TFCC, OPCON is primarily a surface tracker, although there is clearly interest in providing supplementary submarine data (the next-generation OPCON, **MCCIS** [Maritime Command/Control Information System], will include such data in its product, **OSCAD** [Ocean Surveillance Communications and Display]).

The Royal Netherlands Navy has its own OPCON computers at Den Helder, linked to those at Northwood: a Dutch ship can talk to a British ship via radio to Den Helder, the link to Northwood, and Link R to the British ship.

OPCON is partly a NATO program; the planned NATO replacement, MANDATE, was never funded. The British government decided to buy a national system, **FOCSLE** (Fleet Operational Command System Life Extension) instead. As of the spring of 1993, a decision on 2 or 3 parallel project-definition studies was expected; FOCSLE is to reach interim operating capability in March 1995. Competitors include GEC-Marconi, BAe-SEMA-Lockheed, DESQ-Siemens Plessey, and EDS-Scicon-Tiburon.

British carriers and AAW ships have **ASMA**, the RAF-supplied Air Staff Management Aid, a text system providing information on air fields (status, readiness) and opnotes. ASMA is provided via an SHF satellite link to a dedicated terminal. An ASMA terminal is on board the USS *Mount Whitney* (for the commander of the Atlantic Strike Fleet).

France placed its own shore-based ship-tracker, **SYCOM**, in service about 1970. Unlike FCC and OPCON, SYCOM has no computer-to-computer link. Only now, in 1992, is it being superseded by a **SYCOM NG** (*Nouvelle Génération*) similar in concept to an FCC. The French equivalent of the TFCC is **Aidcomer**, and the link is via the French military satellite **Syracuse 2**.

Denmark upgraded to a Thomson-CSF system (fed in part by Cardion coastal radars) in 1986. The Turkish **TAICOS** is a small-scale equivalent of a TFCC, so there must be a Turkish FCC (which is connected to its mobile radars by Link 11). Since the consoles of the Turkish Track II frigates can handle all the necessary graphics, including maps, they do not have separate TAICOS systems.

The first Tomahawk revolution, then, was to provide the at-sea commander with an OTH-T sea-surveillance picture assembled ashore. The FCC could be more than a fusion center, however. It was almost certainly sold to the U.S. government as a means of exercising stronger control over the forces afloat, which would be carrying the nuclear version of the Tomahawk missile. Thus the FCC was the naval node of the **WWMCCS** (Worldwide Military Command-and-Control System). It was convenient to refer to the naval system as **NCCS**, the Naval Command-and-Control System.

TFCCs were expensive (and installations slow) because they required special military computers. By the early 1980s, however, commercial-grade workstations (DTCs) were much more powerful than military computers but also far less costly. They could perform the same picture-keeping and presentation roles. Some readers may remember a similar development in the civilian world. In the 1970s machines were bought as word processors or as scientific calculators. Then general-purpose desktop computers became so powerful that it was wiser to invest in specialized software; the same machine, using different programs, could perform a wide variety of functions. Computer power itself became relatively inexpensive, so it paid to invest in capacity and update through software improvements. The software itself could be reproduced quite cheaply.

JOTS began as a "poor man's TFCC" created for Rear Admiral Jerry O. Tuttle, commanding a carrier division on board the USS *America* in 1983. A powerful desktop computer (HP 9845, a precursor of the HP 9020 bought as **DTC I**), ran **FDDS** (TFCC display) software, i.e., maintained the OTH-T picture. JOTS soon adopted the standard navy desktop computer (DTC I) as its host machine. When Admiral Tuttle became the commander of Carrier Group 2, he wanted something more: tactical decision aids, to answer "what if" planning questions, such as evaluating alternative formations or alternative ECM plans. **JOTS II (USQ-112A)** includes the decision aids. Because it runs the OTH picture and conducts TDAs, it requires a multitasking computer, **DTC II**.

JOTS was revolutionary because it provided the OTH-T picture to the entire surface fleet; even ships without their own integrated combat-direction systems were given JOTS terminals. It was natural to call the sea-based OTH-T system **NCCS-A** (NCCS Afloat) in analogy to the shore-based NCCS. The most elaborate form of NCCS-A was a distributed form of TFCC, built out of DTC computers, which replaced the earlier version. Unification meant standard DTC (now TAC) hardware ashore and afloat, including the FCCs and STTs. Overall, NCCS/NCCS-A was conceived as a unified series of command systems, extending from the numbered fleet commanders in their FCCs to the officers in tactical command (OTCs) in their TFCCs, down to the composite warfare commanders (CWCs), subordinate warfare commanders (SWCs), commanders of amphibious task forces (CATFs), commanders of landing forces (CLFs), and commanding officers/TAOs.

The Royal Navy has followed a similar path, adopting a commercial workstation as its seaward terminal. The U.S. DTC I (HP 9020 workstation) was superseded by the Hewlett-Packard 330 (**Outfit PDT**) running U.S. JOTS software. PDT has also been installed as an intelligent shipboard Link 11 terminal. The MCCIS upgrade to OPCON corresponds broadly to the U.S. FCC modernization program. As in the U.S. Navy, a network of powerful workstations is replacing the large mainframes. MCCIS is currently being competed.

The JOTS software for HP workstations was written in the Rocky Mountain Basic language. When a Sun-4 station was chosen instead of the expected HP machine, the U.S. software had to be rewritten in Unix and "C" language. Since the British stayed with HP machines, they presumably cannot benefit from much of the later U.S. software.

Wide distribution of the OTH-T product made drastic change possible. If the individual computers gained enough processing power, they might do far more than merely display the FCC's product. Instead, that product could be formed cooperatively. All the fleet's workstations could be part of the same network, linked by satellites.

The implication of the JOTS revolution, then, was to replace OTCIXS and related links by higher-capacity satellite systems that could connect all the terminals. Those connections had to be made without buying many new satellites. The solution, in the new **Copernicus** architecture, is to abandon the old practice of associating each functional channel with a particular physical (e.g., satellite) channel. Instead, channels are assigned dynamically by software that adjusts to changes in demand. In theory, then, it should be possible virtually to abandon all other long-haul radio channels. Long-haul radio requires overseas communications (repeater) sites. Cold War alliances made them available where needed, but the sites will probably be withdrawn as the alliances fade. Satellites provide global service based entirely in the United States. They also cover Third World areas not readily accessible from the overseas sites.

INRI, the company responsible for JOTS software, now has a British subsidiary (set up in October 1992). It offers a form of JOTS II software commercially as **Nauticus**, using a DRS console. As of April 1993, single-workstation Nauticus was being installed on board an Italian frigate and in a shore station for evaluation.

SURVEILLANCE/CONTROL

UNITED STATES

The FY94/95 program reflects some lessons learned in Desert Storm. A joint-task-force–capable fleet flagship is planned. Under the new concept of joint force air operations, carriers must be able to receive the joint Air Tasking Order (ATO) by radio; that was not possible during the Gulf War. A carrier may have to generate an ATO. The navy has rejected an air force proposal that its ATO-generating computer, CTAPS (a follow-on to the Gulf War CAFMS [Computer-Aided Force Management System]) be installed on board carriers because it adds unnecessary features and is too costly. Too, it is a broadcast system; the navy prefers 2-way operation. Late in 1992 navy ships off the California coast received an ATO from a CAFMS at Luke AFB, Arizona (Exercise Tandem Thrust).

In 1991 the U.S. Navy was made the lead service for a new U.S. IFF program to replace the canceled Mk XV. One problem is that the navy favors noncooperative forms of IFF, whereas the air force favors cooperative systems, requiring positive identification of friendly aircraft. During the Gulf War the air force enforced such positive rules to successfully avoid blue-on-blue attacks. The navy counters that positive identification is far too cumbersome for a rapidly changing situation, particularly when missiles are involved, and that (in effect) it is more important to avoid losing ships than to avoid blue-on-blue aircraft losses. The navy is also pursuing **AUTO-ID**, a noncooperative technique that merges available information (including classical IFF).

During the Gulf War, 26 afloat **TAMPS** workstations (6 carriers, 1 battleship, and the major amphibious ships) supported Desert Storm. TAMPS was criticized as too slow; it needed flyable-quality color copiers and more data storage. The system did not provide advice on weapon choices (weaponeering) and war-at-sea planning; both are to be added as upgrades. It also needed more robust connections to the 2 other major air-planning tools, **TERPES** and **TEAMS**.

The Gulf War popularized a new U.S. naval mission: theater missile defense (TMD). Such a capability would certainly be helpful to marines operating on foreign shores, but it would also be important to allies threatened by future Saddam Husseins. The marine-protection mission entails relatively short range area air defense; missiles will generally be intercepted within the atmosphere. Allied support, particularly from the sea, requires longer-range interception, probably often outside the atmosphere. The navy signed an MoU with the Strategic Defense Initiative Organization (SDIO, now the Ballistic Missile Defense Organization [BMDO]) in October 1991. The first SM-2(ER) missile carrying SDIO's **LEAP** vehicle was launched by the USS *R. K. Turner* on 24 September 1992. The missile flew a special trajectory to eject the exoatmospheric device, achieving a record altitude for a ship-launched tactical missile. LEAP competitors are Boeing, Hughes, and Rockwell.

Phased-array radars (**SPY-1**) and command-guided missiles (**SM-2 Block IV**) always had an antimissile potential, but they re-

Antimissile interceptor nose (with LEAP vehicle) for an SM-2 Block IV missile, as displayed by Hughes at the 1993 Navy League Show. (Author)

quire cueing. The global sensor is the **DSP**, a series of IR satellites in geostationary orbits to detect strategic-missile launchings and also nuclear explosions. DSP cued Patriot antimissile batteries during the Gulf War. The successor system, now under development, is **FEWS** (Follow-on Early-Warning Satellite). The air force argues strongly for centralized control of DSP/FEWS information (the new program is **Talon Gold**). The navy and army argue that the additional delay involved in passing information to tactical units will be unacceptable. As of the summer of 1992, the navy was arguing for an uplink allowing commanders to cue FEWS. The air force refused. This controversy centers on a proposed tactical-events system that would fuse available information (tactical and FEWS) to warn that, for example, a missile is being launched. For example, there was a wartime attempt to fuse **JSTARS** radar data with DSP IR data (e.g., to localize Iraqi launchers), but the effort enjoyed no great success. On 24 April 1992 the army and navy agreed to develop a joint ground station for IR satellite data in FY93, and to field as many as 7 units (2 naval, 5 army). It would process DSP and other satellite IR data in real time, generating launch point, impact point, and trajectory-state vector to cue fire-control sensors on missile launches and other events. The navy has now largely withdrawn from this program, possibly because it already has bought DSP terminals under the **Have Glance** program described below.

During the Gulf War, Aegis ships often tracked incoming Iraqi ballistic missiles. Software modifications can easily extend this capability. SM-2 Block IV can easily be modified to intercept tactical ballistic missiles. The Aegis/SM-2 system sacrifices nothing in fleet-

Rockwell's Kinetic Kill Vehicle (KKV) for ballistic-missile defense, displayed by Raytheon at the 1993 Navy League Show. Below it is the powered upper stage that would carry it. The KKV motor is at the left; the nozzle-shaped part houses its optical sensor. (Author)

air-defense capability to add the TMD role. It may even be argued that the same improved kinetics that deal with ballistic missiles are needed to counter new threats such as AS-16 and -17 (it was always argued that SM-2 Block IV would be needed to deal with ANS, which is not too different from AS-17). The TMD version is tentatively designated **SM-2 Block IVA**. It should enter service in FY99. Block IVA should match the land-based Patriot PAC-3 version in TMD capability.

The step beyond would be a new upper stage, possibly the LEAP already under development by the army. Alternatively, the army's Lockheed **THAAD**issile (conceived as the upper layer of a 2-layer defense) may be carried in VLS cells. An upgraded SPY-1 radar, with twice the current range, will support the new interceptor. SDIO also envisages a new space-based sensor, **Brilliant Eyes**, to cue surface interceptors such as THAAD or SM-2/LEAP. The first 4 Brilliant Eyes satellites might be in service by about 1996 (as envisaged late in 1992, before the new administration took office). As of late 1992, SDIO (now BMDO) expected Phase II of the LEAP advanced-technology development to begin in December 1993 (with the interceptor selected in June 1994); the production decision on SM-2 Block IVA was expected in January 1994.

In June 1991 Unisys received a contract for a 40-month program to develop and deploy **JADDIN**, the Joint Air-Defense Digital Information Network, for Thailand, to provide naval and ground forces with information from **RTADS**, the Royal Thai Air-Defense System. RTADS was operationally deployed in 1990.

KN-NTDS, Litton's Korean Naval Command System, uses Link 11 to connect 3 *Ulsan*-class frigates (1 console each) to a shore headquarters (FCC, with 7 consoles). The frigates lead groups of smaller craft (but as yet there is no requirement for a **ROLE**, which would allow the smaller units to accept the frigate's tactical picture). The system is designed to detect and intercept small coastal craft trying to penetrate South Korean coastal waters, particularly infiltrators and intelligence-gatherers from North Korea. Five shore radars feed the FCC over 2 links (Link 11 and the HF **ISDL**, inter-site data link). The FCC is also connected to the main air-control center. The system will be installed on board the new KDX class.

The basis of the system, the **TDC** (Tactical Display Console), is widely used by the U.S. Air Force and the National Guard in the antidrug war. It is a gateway for multiple data links (TADIL A, TADIL B, ATDL [a missile link from command to battery], Link 1), using packet-switching technology. The TDC is built around a VME bus carrying 3 single-board computers (SBCs: each comprising a 68030, a math coprocessor, and 4 Mbyte of DRAM). One is the control processor; the other 2 are used for track control, link control, track position, and related functions. Function distribution is controlled by software, to keep any SBC from being overloaded. The bus can also carry a separate global memory board, I/O boards (which can connect to modems through which the links are received), and a graphics controller whose output appears on a 19-in color monitor (1,280 × 1,024 pixels; range scales 2–2,048 nm). One of the SBCs can connect to floppy- and hard-disk drives. The console can carry up to 1,024 tracks, bearing lines, EW strobes, and pointers, and it can drive a large-screen display. Litton offers the TDC in both portable and stand-alone form. The 2-screen console used in the **SSQ-91** combat-simulation test system is very similar to the Korean system's tactical coordination console (TCC).

Lockheed's **MOSC** (Maritime-Operations Support Center) is a distributed-computer alternative to P-3 mission-support centers such as ASWOCs, for pre- and postmission support. MOSC employs the Lockheed **TMS** (Track-Management System), elements of which are used in U.S. ASWOCs, and which is part of the Dowty/Lockheed bid for the British **FOCSL** system. MOSC was announced at UDT (July 1992), and at that time both Australia and Canada were showing interest. South Korea selected the U.S. ASWOC to support its P-3s, but Lockheed also hoped to sell MOSC there.

MOSC is a distributed network of UNIX-based commercial workstations. A typical installation might consist of 5 elements connected together by an LAN: OPCON (links, flight following, and operations), coordination/mission planning, brief/debrief (with large-screen displays), sensor analysis (based on a fast-time acoustic-data processor), and data processing. Because any workstation on the LAN can address all of the modules, the brief/debrief module can automatically fill out standard aircrew briefing charts. Lockheed claims that the system is unique in offering a sophisticated tactical oceanography subsystem, integrating environmental data bases, models, and decision aids so that the user can predict and thus fully exploit local acoustic conditions. MOSC includes a multilevel security system (so that it can employ other-than-acoustic data for tracks) based on experience with the new U.S. **Radiant Mercury** system.

Command Aids

UNITED KINGDOM

CCA (Captain's Combat Aid) is a target-evaluation and weapons-assignment system, part of the **ADIMP** modernization of the carriers and Type 42 destroyers. CCA is broadly comparable in concept to the U.S. C&D processor of the Aegis and Model 5 CDS systems. MUSL won the contract in 1991. Like Model 5, CCA uses its data base to add characteristics to the objects (platforms, weapons) in the tactical picture built up by the ship's combat information system. Threats are identified and ranked on the basis of filters (preset or rule-based); the ship's performance against them is continuously evaluated. For example, CCA may identify incoming objects with nonincreasing aiming errors as threats not dealt with by ECM. Responses are partly scripted, partly rule-based. Because so much of CCA's operation must involve looking up data, it uses transputers.

The projected British LPDs are to have a command support system (CSS) integrated with their CDS. The CSS will display an integrated Recognized Maritime Picture (RMP). Competitors are EDS-Scicon/INRI/MacKenzie Tribbett and GEC-Marconi/Australian Defense Industries. INRI offers a version of Nauticus incorporating software for amphibious operations. GEC considered CSS so important that the ship's CDS (a 4-console color Nautis) should be subordinate. Originally, the CDS was to have been a version of BAe-SEMA's SSCS, but in mid-1992 MoD funded parallel Ferranti and GEC-Marconi studies of lower-cost alternatives. Ferranti demonstrated its ADAWS 2000, using a pair of F2420s (as in ADIMP) in December 1992.

Ferranti's **MAPS** (Maritime Asset Planning System) is an AI-based command advice system (tactical decision aid, TDA). It plans dispositions of ships in a group, automatically taking into account local conditions (e.g., radar propagation). It can also reconfigure a force to take account of the effect of losses or battle damage. The MAPS calculations are supported by an **Oracle Relational Database** containing the characteristics of ships, their sensors, and their weapons; performance data for missiles; performance data for radars; and the geographic positions of bases and airfields. In 1991 MAPS was sold to the JMSDF for integration in their C2 systems. Ferranti claimed that other Pacific navies were interested.

Functions: sector-screen calculation, radar/communications propagation, geographic data base, large-scale disposition calculation. Sector-screen calculation uses tactical rules to estimate the stations or sectors for the units of a main body and to deal with an estimated threat, incorporating particular unit requirements (e.g., goalkeepers, inner screen, special stations) and unit characteristics and capabilities (e.g., towed arrays). MAPS also calculates a numerical measure of effectiveness for the solution it selects. It can explain its reasoning, and it can display the effect of choosing some alternative. Large-scale disposition is on a 240 × 240–nm grid, allowing for operations well away from the main body. Coverage calculations, based on weather conditions, include force antimissile systems and radar for any selected target height and for any arrangement of serviceable radars within the force. Other functions can be included: aircraft-sortie planning, EW tasking, SAR control, UNREP planning, ROE assessment, amphibious-operations planning, sonar-propagation prediction, task-force routing, MCM command planning, and ship's safety and damage control.

The BAe-Sema (formerly Dowty-Sema) **SEPADS** uses acoustic modeling to optimize sonar (including towed array) deployment; it includes a TMA package. The computer screen shows both the tactical picture and possible alternative strategies (in windows). SEPADS runs on a ruggedized DEC MicroVax 3500 (8 Mbyte of memory, two 170-Mbyte 5.25-in hard disks, and a 295-Mbyte tape unit), with 2 monochrome monitors.

Strategic Sensors

CHINA (PRC)

Passive bottom arrays protect harbor entrances, extending out to sea about 20–30 nm.

GERMANY

Thus far Atlas's **AISYS** is the only bottom surveillance system to be marketed publicly. It is already in service in 1 navy. AISYS uses linear arrays in deep water and cylindrical submarine-type arrays in shallows. Both can be connected to shore through either fiber-optic or microwave (via buoys) links. The associated Shore Information and Classification Center is **SOBIC**.

FINLAND

Nokia Data Systems's integrated coastal-surveillance system is probably the one used by Finland. Local control centers (LCCs) collect sensor data (from radar, TV, night optics, and remote MA 8530 and MA 8560 laser range-finders). Each LCC has a computer-driven 16-in CRT (and can have additional color CRTs). District control centers (DCCs) assemble LCC data into a synthetic-video tactical picture. It is not clear whether the DCCs feed into a national command center.

Presumably, Elesco's FHS-900 shallow-water (20–300 m) passive system can feed the LCCs. Each triangular group of 3 omnidirectional, wide-band (0.5 Hz–100 kHz) hydrophones has its own amplifiers and a group microprocessor; it can be as much as 30 km from the control station, which can handle up to 32 groups. The station is built around a 32-bit Unix-language computer and an FFT (i.e., LOFAR) processor. It has a pair of side-by-side, high-resolution (1,280 × 1,024 pixel) CRTs, each above a smaller monitor for alphanumeric data. The station also carries a pair of floppy disks and a standard keyboard. Targets are shown against a digitized map background (with 90%-probability-of-position circles displayed). Fiskars was responsible for the multitarget-detection algorithms, which presumably use ALI.

FRANCE

Work continues on the **Osiris** digital-imagery, radar-reconnaissance satellite and the **Zenon** ELINT satellite, both to be launched after the year 2000. They will complement **Helios** (Helios 1 will be launched in 1994, Helios 2 about 1996). Osiris is being proposed as a Pan-European project; it will cost $1.3 billion. It uses microwave sensors but is based on the civilian optical Spot Mk 2. Zenon is for ELINT and tactical communications; it is being developed by Alcatel Espace and Thomson-CSF. Zenon satellites will occupy 3 geostationary positions at 8°W, 15°E, and 19°E. France will gain ELINT experience by launching a 50-kg **Cérise** microsatellite (made by Surrey Satellite Technology of the U.K., equipped by Alcatel) with Helios. DGA (the government's military-technology agency) is also working on early-warning and secure data-relay satellites.

INDONESIA

In 1992 Indonesia signed an agreement with Thomson Pacific to develop bottom arrays. The ultimate goal is to monitor all of the Indonesian straits, beginning with the Lombok Strait.

SWEDEN

KAFUS (fixed underwater reconnaissance system) is being completed: it uses hydrophones, magnetic and other sensors, TV and other surveillance sets, linked by fiber-optic communications.

TAIWAN

Taiwan is experimenting with a SOSUS-type surveillance array system; about 1986 the Chang Shan Institute was commissioned to emplace a small system off the eastern Taiwanese coast for a 14-month evaluation (RCA had proposed such a system in 1981). The arrays were laid at 90–300 m [300–1,000 ft], probably at Su-Au in northeastern Taiwan. As in SOSUS, data from the arrays is presumably collected at a shore station and used to cue ships and shore-based ASW aircraft. The introduction of such a system might explain the purchase of shore-based S-70C(M) ASW helicopters. An official paper released in 1990 reported the acquisition of a U.S. Navy experimental harbor-defense system, which Taiwan calls **Lung Chin** (Dragon Eyes). It included harbor nets and apparently was not entirely satisfactory.

UNITED KINGDOM

Thus far Marconi has sold its HF surface-wave radar mainly in a short-range version, **OSCR** (Ocean Surface Current Radar) capable

Marconi's concept for the receiving and transmitting antennas (which in fact would be 1 km apart) of its S124 surface-wave coastal-surveillance radar. (Marconi Radar Systems)

of detecting ocean currents and pollution (which affects surface conductivity). One monitored the spread of oil slicks after the tanker *Braer* broke up off Scotland. However, the British government bought a coastal-surveillance set, and as of spring 1993, Australia was also interested. Marconi offers an **S124** coastal radar, which detects low-flying aircraft out to 150 km and ships out to 370 km within a 120-deg sector. It can plot 400 vessels simultaneously (and can be extended to track 40 aircraft). S124 uses a 50-m-wide transmitting antenna array about 1 km from its 800-m-wide receiving array. Its solid-state amplifiers transmit 32-kW pulses at 4–7 MHz; typical azimuth resolution is 15 km at 200 km, and range resolution is selectable between 0.6 and 2.4 km (depending on bandwidth). Plot accuracy is 3/4 deg, 110 m, 1/4 kt (post-processing). **S123** is a companion air-search radar, using a 600-m receiving array 1 km from a 50-m transmitting array. It detects low-fliers at 250 km and high-fliers at 500 km. It covers a 90-deg sector; power level is 160 kW (6–12 MHz); typical azimuth resolution is 10 km at 200 km (range resolution is 7–20 km). Track accuracy is typically 1 km, 2 kt. Track 100 aircraft, refresh every 10 sec. In both cases, targets are detected by their Doppler returns, so aircraft show up clearly against sea clutter. To detect much slower ships, the radar uses coherent processing over a longer dwell time.

UNITED STATES

ROTHR was terminated in FY92 after 4 had been authorized (prototype plus 3 in FY88–89), and only the prototype was delivered (the others probably will not be built). It is emplaced at Amchitka, in the Aleutians, and became operational in 1985. A projected Japanese ROTHR seems to have been shelved.

Because of the decline of the Soviet threat, **FDS** has been reduced to technology-demonstrator status. The FY93 budget provided $154.5 million (rather than the $229.2 million requested) for FDS but required the navy to spend at least $27.5 million of that on **ADS**

Lockheed's dispenser for a string of hydrophones to form part of a rapidly deployable surveillance system (advanced deployable array), displayed at the 1992 and 1993 Navy League Shows. (Author)

(Advanced Deployable System). It also provided $14.0 million separately for ADS.

ADS is to use as much FDS technology as possible. ADS is to be covertly and overtly deployable (from submarines, surface ships, aircraft, even UUVs) and modular so as to be suitable for shallow- or deep-water environments. Upward-looking acoustics would work in both cases; in shallow areas the array may be supplemented by short-range nonacoustic sensors, such as magnetic and perhaps UEP. The system would have to last at least 30 days and might have to remain in place for 5 yr. Ideally, portions would be retrievable for refurbishment and later redeployment. Congressional language in the FY93 defense bill characterized ADS as optimized for shallow-water operation against quiet diesel submarines. An RFP was released on 8 May 1992. A Lockheed ADS proposal, displayed at the 1992 and 1993 Navy League shows, used an air-deployed, 7-part, fiber-optic bottom array, which could be read out from the air. Stowed, it was about the size of a Mk 46 and could be carried under the wing of a P-3. The array would form the receiver of a bistatic system, the pinger of which would be laid separately. A single P-3 could lay several such arrays in parallel. Lockheed has been working on this sort of device since about 1988 and is now tailoring it to shallow-water requirements.

The draft RFP for **IUSS**, the Integrated Undersea Surveillance System (January 1992), included a rapidly deployable component with an open architecture and modular design for mission-specific configurations and deployment methods, i.e., corresponding to ADS. IBM received the contract for the FDS **SSIPS** (Shore Signal and Information Processing Segment). Its processors were open-architecture VME-based units, generally using Motorola 8800 processors. Each shore site would break its area of operation into sectors, with 5 desks (on an LAN) per sector (3 CRTs with boxes alongside). The 3 CRTs offer multiple presentations of the acoustic data to correlate or examine large amounts of data so as to extract subsets for processing. The associated SDS uses much the same equipment (6 consoles per sector). The consoles may provide support to battle-group commanders or to sector ASW commanders, providing some dedicated assets.

Have Gaze is a previously black program for aircraft detection from space, revealed in the mid-1992 House of Representatives report of the Defense Authorization Bill. Almost certainly it is an IR system. Have Gaze is controlled by the previously black Joint Counter Low Observable Office (JCLO), controlled by the navy, but the satellite itself is funded by the air force; probably it is the DSP satellite originally intended to detect missile firings by their IR signatures. Using the appropriate software, it can probably track hot aircraft (JCLO involvement suggests that the aircraft need not be very hot, particularly if they are flying over water). The navy is currently proposing an IR satellite (presumably an outgrowth of Have Gaze) for wide-area air surveillance (the air force supports an alternative radar system).

Slow Walker is a space-based tactical surveillance system under development by IBM for Naval Space Warfare Command. Development of the tactical ground station began in FY91. The system is expected to become operational in FY93 and to be completed in FY96. Since the total estimated procurement cost is $10 million, ($4.5 million in FY93), Slow Walker clearly uses an existing satellite. Slow Walker is listed among sensors reporting to shore stations in accounts of the new Copernicus architecture.

The current **SOSUS** upgrade is Phase III. The number of shore evaluation sites and the number of personnel per site are being reduced because the signal-classification system is more highly automated. To defeat submarine silencing, SOSUS is being adapted to detect nontraditional signals (transients, speed-dependent signals, and active-sonar emissions, as opposed to long-duration narrowband signals). The FY93 program includes installing all-source automatic detectors in 2 prototype systems, and refining and improving automatic signal classification by combining information from traditional and nontraditional signals. The FY93 program also includes the development of specifications for a processing architecture that will support real-time automatic detection, classification, tracking, and reporting using all sources, presumably including nonacoustic (e.g., signals) intelligence. In 1992 the Senate Armed Services Committee rejected proposed upgrades at some SOSUS sites considered unlikely now to detect foreign submarines (presumably because of the Soviet breakup). It suggested that the sites be closed; ADS could replace them if the threat reemerges.

Hughes is now producing the **LFA** for the advanced version of

SURTASS, using a Lockheed Sanders source and an AT&T reduced-diameter array. It has been tested in both monostatic (as on a T-AGOS) and bistatic forms. In bistatic sea trials (the deep source was towed by the research ship *Cory*), it detected targets over the whole width of the Mediterranean, from the northern (Ionian) shore to the Libyan shore, including a submarine on a shelf in the shallow Ionian basin. The receivers were on board destroyers. Pulses are a mixture of CW for Doppler and hyperbolic FM (HFM) for range. The system sees so far that it can be overwhelmed by data (often 200 detections/min), so much of the design effort goes into helping the operator filter real targets from bathymetric ones, such as sea mounts. For example, the structure of an echo can be compared with that of the transmitted waveform, and the probability of echo (hits per opportunity) can be assessed. Bathymetric targets are non-coherent, so their echoes show numerous peaks. The 2 displays on the console are typically geosit (map) above a waterfall (signal processor output) for detection by the operator. The operator correlates acoustic data and patterns with the processor. A window below the waterfall can show details of a given echo. An A-scan above the waterfall can show reflections in 3 beams.

COMMUNICATIONS

FRANCE

The **Syracuse II** satellite link was inaugurated in December 1991 (the second satellite was launched in May 1992). France hopes to put a collaborative Syracuse III in service by 1995.

Link W (an unlicensed commercial version of Link 11) is used by Saudi Arabia (in the *Al Madinah* class) and probably also by China (PRC), as Link V, (in the Luda III and Luhu classes, which are equipped with license-built TAVITAC combat systems). Link W will probably also be exported to Taiwan, in the new *La Fayette* class.

GERMANY

The Rockwell-Collins GmbH **TDLT** (Track Data Link Terminal), a stand-alone Link 11 introduced in 1990, can carry 500 tracks within a coverage area of up to 2,048 × 2,048 nm. This capacity is pre-divided into air, surface, subsurface, EW/ESM, and points tracks. When any category fills, messages that would initiate additional tracks in that category are ignored. TDLT uses data-link track filters (accept/reject based on track type/category, identification/hostility, penetration, geographic area, speed) to avoid overload. It can accommodate information beyond that normally provided in NTDS and similar systems; e.g., it can distinguish between a fighter and a strike airplane. The 1,280 × 1,024 pixel, raster-scan, color display is driven by a 68020 processor with a math coprocessor; there is also a separate data-base-manager processor. Typically, the screen is divided into a large operational situation display on the left, overlaid with a tote display area. The upper right-hand side is a mini-map, with track-data readout (for up to 3 tracks) and setup tote below it.

Users: Denmark (frigate *Olfert Fischer*), Norway (*Andenes*), Singapore (*Victory* class), United Kingdom (Nimrod aircraft in the Persian Gulf).

Denmark and Norway bought TDLT specifically to support operations in the Persian Gulf. By the spring of 1991, 14 TDLTs had been sold and 11 delivered, all within a few weeks.

INTERNATIONAL

Link Y Users: Argentina (carrier and Type 42 destroyers, possibly also MEKOs), Brazil (YB: carrier and frigates), Chile ("County" class), Ecuador (*Leanders*), Egypt (YE: in Beechcraft 1900s, to direct OTH missile fire; receive-only in *Ramadan, Descubierta, Romeo* classes; now have Ferranti DL500 in *Descubierta*s, Romeos), Malaysia (*Kasturi* class [with 9LV system; will get Link Y in new corvettes]), South Korea (integrated with Ferranti CDS in frigates, corvettes), Thailand (F-27s to support OTH missile fire, also probably missile boats). Ships with export SEWACO systems probably have the Dutch version of Link Y, which is not entirely compatible with Ferranti's. The NATO version, Link 10, is probably extinct, though it may survive in the Royal New Zealand Navy frigate *Southland* and in Nautis-equipped *Leanders*.

Link 10/Link Y has no net controller, sends only positional information, and transmits its messages serially, 1 bit at a time. It uses 10-sec time slots and is limited to 6 participants/min. Link 11 superimposes multiple modulations on each pulse: its more complex messages (which include engagement tell backs, ESM, and IFF information) are processed, in effect, in parallel.

Link 11 is now standard within NATO. Canada, France, Germany, Italy, and the United States used Link 11 from the outset. Belgium converted from Link 10 when the *Wielingen*-class frigates were modernized. The Dutch *Kortenaer*s and *Van Speijk*s (now sold to Indonesia, presumably without their data links) all received Link 11 during their big refits, beginning in 1984 (the *Tromp*s were built as gateway ships with both data links). British Type 42s and early Type 22s had Links 10 and 11, and the 3 carriers were "gateways" between the 2 data links. The Turkish Track I MEKO frigates originally had Link 10, but they were converted, and Link 11 has now been installed on board the Turkish *Gearing*-class destroyers (with the Whittaker UYQ-61 stand-alone Link 11 terminal). Turkey also has Link 11 in a shore command center, at 13 mobile radars, and on board the modernized S-2 aircraft. The Greek and Portuguese MEKOs were all delivered with Link 11. Greece also equipped her *Kortenaer*s and probably a shore command center. Australia, Japan, Saudi Arabia (in E-3 AWACS aircraft) and South Korea also use Link 11. E-2s in Egypt, Israel, and Singapore (also the *Victory*-class FPBs) use export versions. All new NATO and associated (e.g., Australian *Collins* class) submarines have ROLE so that they can share an overall tactical picture; U.S. *Los Angeles*–class submarines may be fitted with 2-way links. The Italian navy plans to use Link 11 on EH-101 helicopters (plus Link 16, the AEW version). U.S. non-naval users include the air force (E-3 AWACS aircraft) and the Customs Service.

Denmark expects soon to install Link 11 on 2 *Nils Juel*–class frigates (*Olfert Fischer* already has the Rockwell unit described above), and later on the StanFlex corvettes.

Norway has bought the **EDO** workstation for Link 11 for the modernized *Oslo*s, integrated with their MSI-3100 CDSs. The first (leased) unit was installed on board the *Trondheim* to fit the first for NATO StanNavForLant service. Link 11 may later be fitted to fast attack craft. The U.S. Coast Guard bought a similar workstation, its first Link 11, for the cutter *Dallas*. Two EDO stand-alone Link 11s were installed on board EP-3s for forward-deployed operations (because these aircraft were converted from P-3B airframes, they had no Link 11s).

ROLE is in German Sea King helicopters and in some British naval aircraft (Nimrods had to be fitted with Link 11 for Gulf duty). Ferranti's ROLE may have been fitted to British minehunters in the Persian Gulf.

In the U.S. Navy, the projected ROLE installations on all non-NTDS ships were superseded by plans to install 2-way stand-alone systems because the latter were not much more expensive. The standard U.S. Navy 2-way stand-alone Link 11 terminal is a DTC II combined with a DTS and an EDO TDP. Now most of the combatant ships involved have been decommissioned. The Whittaker **UYQ-61** stand-alone Link 11 terminal is used ashore, by the army and the marines, as a way of receiving AEW information.

Different navies use different subsets of Link 11. All versions are subject to NATO STANAG 5511, but NATO Link 11 (STANAG 1241) now includes a neutral category (which the U.S. version lacks). The Royal Navy uses its own symbology (letter only: N for neutral, U for unknown, I for interception, H for hostile, Z for zombie). The British display target data; NTDS displays data only when the contact is "hooked" by an operator. The Dutch use a combination of the U.S. and British displays.

LEIP (Link 11 Improvement Program) includes SATCOM Link 11 as well as the expansion of Link 11 to non-CDS (non-NTDS) ships. **LEDS** (Link 11 Display System) is built around **USQ-69**, including a low-cost Link 11 terminal with versions capable of forwarding data. **MULTS** is EDO's Multilink Terminal Station, connecting Link 11 to NADGE Link 1. The Inter-American Naval Conference (IANC) **"Link America"** is receive-only Link 11 hosted on a PC-compatible computer, for the antidrug campaign. Comtek produced 15–20 sets of software, which were copied by IANC navies (Argentina, Brazil, Chile, Ecuador, Mexico, Panama, Paraguay, Peru, Uruguay, Venezuela, United States). The system is receive-only because it was not clear whether foreign users would be able to provide sufficiently good track information of their own; inaccurate tracks would confuse the tactical picture. Comtek offered the option of developing a track package (i.e., stand-alone 2-way Link 11), but it was not adopted. As of March 1992, Litton had demonstrated versions of Link 11 using telephone, satellite, and Have Quick radio.

Link 11 improvements may include changed software to give priority to critical information (which is not possible at present). New message formats may allow the system to handle more tracks at a faster rate. The current Link 11 is limited to perhaps 200 out of a total of as many as 3,000 tracks/sec that a major command might require in a major war. Track capacity would be particularly stressed in a hot air engagement, when observed air targets would include, among the many other air tracks, the defending antiair missiles, as well as their boosters and decoys.

The U.S. Navy will fit **Link 16** to carriers, cruisers, and E-2C, F/A-18, and F-14 aircraft. As of 1990, **IJMS**, an Interim JTIDS Messaging Standard, was already in service; it was not interoperable with either full JTIDS or Link 11. **MIDS** (Multifunctional Information Distribution System) is being developed as a lighter and less expensive JTIDS terminal, initially for the F/A-18. Responsibility was transferred from the air force to the navy in FY90. That year the study contract was awarded to McDonnell Douglas. Thomson-CSF is a contractor, and the French navy plans to install MIDS in its aircraft. The partners are France, Germany, Italy, Spain, and the United States.

SWEDEN

Many Swedish-made combat systems such as CCIS and CEPLO use a simple point-to-point digital radio link to pass 2 or 3 tracks and engagement orders. The operator radios to set up the contact, data being sent via a modem.

UNITED KINGDOM

The **ADIMP** data-link processor is now designated **DLPS** (Outfit RTC); it handles Links 11 and 14 and will be expanded to handle Link 16 in the future.

Three more **Skynet 4** satellites are to be launched in 1997.

Users: Germany (*Bremen* and Type 123 classes), Netherlands (*Tromp* class), United Kingdom (carriers; Types 21, 22, 23, and 42; *Fearless* class)

UNITED STATES

The navy's fleet of E-6As replaces both EC-130 and air force EC-135 strategic command/control aircraft; after FY92 the navy will carry the entire strategic communications load, maintaining 1 EC-6A continuously airborne. A projected **Articsat** system, 6 small satellites for U.S. submarines in the Arctic, was dropped in 1992 in favor of transponders hosted on planned satellites. A new Common High-Bandwidth Data Link, **CHBDL**, is being developed for **BGPHES** and **ATARS** data. The X-band CHBDL down-link operates at high (274 or 137 Mbps) or low (10.71 Mbps) rates or carries voice traffic (CVSD); the up-link operates at 200 kbps. Images are transmitted at 137 Mbps (e.g., from an F/A-18 to JSIPS-N); BGPHES transmits at the low rate. The shipboard USQ-123 system uses 2 1-m dishes to handle 1 full-duplex link. A submarine-to-submarine covert data link was demonstrated as part of the U.S. Navy laboratory fleet support program in FY90. A fighter-to-fighter data link is included in the F-14D predeployment package.

A current R&D (6.2) effort explores the use of SHF for the very high data rate (1.54 Mbit/sec) ship-to-ship communications required for such programs as cooperative engagement. SHF is usually limited to LOS, but it can refract, and in many cases it can use an evaporative duct to achieve very long ranges. SHF becomes more viable as ships in battle groups operate closer together (because they no longer face a nuclear threat). It can support very high data rates. SHF satellite communication is currently a very high priority; a new SHF Information-Exchange System (IXS) is being defined. Each carrier is now being fitted with an interim SHF terminal, and new terminals are to be bought beginning in FY94.

TACNAV is a new helicopter-to-ship link connected to the **ASN-123** system on board a LAMPS I helicopter. It is a LAMPS III-like upgrade to the earlier system, automating information transfer from the helicopter: own position, sonobuoy positions, and some other data. The associated EDO TDP (Tactical Data Processor) is the interface between the communications link and the console on the ship using this data.

TALC (Tactical Airborne Laser Communication) is a controversial program for a 2-way link using low-altitude satellites. Submariners argue that it makes them too vulnerable to detection. It may be possible to limit detectability by using a fast frequency-hopping laser. A tentative operational requirement (TOR) has been issued, and NOSC San Diego ran tests with the experimental submarine *Dolphin*, a blue-green laser, and a small lightweight satellite. The House Armed Services Committee added $12 million in FY92 and $15 million in FY93 for this program.

Hughes's **UFO** (UHF Follow-On) satellite replaces **FLTSAT** and **LEASAT**, with 10 satellites (2 each over the continental United States and the Atlantic, Indian, and Pacific oceans, plus 1 orbiting spare and 1 ground spare). The first was launched in mid-1992. Beginning with satellite 4, an EHF capability was added. Satellites should last for 14 yr. The FY93 program bought the tenth UFO satellite (and leased 3 commercial UFO satellites).

COMPUTERS

UNITED STATES

HBC, a joint venture of Hughes Data Systems and BTG Inc., won the **TAC-3** (formerly DTC III) competition in March 1992. The new machine is based on the Hewlett-Packard 9000 series (the processors, all RISC devices, are the 50-MHz HP720, with a capacity of 57.5 MIPS [17.9 MFLOPS], and the 60-MHz HP730/750, with a capacity of 76.7 MIPS [23.7 MFLOPS]). Speeds are measured on the same scale on which DTC I (HP 9020) ran at 1–3 MIPS and DTC II originally ran at 7.5 MIPS (it was later modified to incorporate Sun 4/300 rather than 4/110 computers, running at 16 MIPS). There are 3 configurations: **System A**, the maximum expandable workstation; **System B**, a small desktop computer; and **System C**, a disk and file server. System A can be either a desktop machine or 1 of 2 rack-mounted machines (1 or 2 color monitors). System C can be desktop or rack-mounted. System A uses an HP750 processor with 32 Mbyte of RAM (expandable to 192MB) and 3 full-height, 5.25-in disk-drive bays. The rack carries 1 or 2 19-in color monitors. System B uses the HP730 processor and 32–64 Mbyte of RAM. System C uses the HP750 processor and 64–192 Mbyte of RAM, plus a 7-slot VME chassis and 3 full-height, 5.25-in disk-drive bays. Any monitor is external. The standard CRT is a CRX Color 2D/3D (1,280 × 1,024 pixels, 8 + 8 double buffered-color planes, i.e., images that can be displayed simultaneously, plus 1 color lookup table). The optional extension is a CRX-24 (1,280 × 1,024 pixels, 24 color planes, 8 overlay planes, plus 5 color lookup tables). Peripherals include 420-Mbyte, 660-Mbyte, 1.3-Gbyte hard-disk drives, a 1.2-Gbyte erasable optical drive, a CD-ROM disk drive, a 1.44-Mbyte floppy disk drive, and a variety of tape drives.

EDO's **TDP** (Tactical Data Processor) provides standard U.S. Navy DTCs with an interface to tactical data, both ownship (EW and sonar) and via Link 11/14 and formatted intelligence broadcasts (e.g., OTCIXS). The DTC provides tactical decision aids and displays the real-time multisource tactical picture built up in the TDP. A single TDP can connect multiple DTCs, as in FFISTS. The TDP can also measure force Link 11 performance through information derived from link-management messages and observation of network events; observing and tracking the originators of messages can determine who is actually active on the link. Displays of operational performance are the number of tracks by each participant, the time duration of each track, the detection range from a reference point, the engagement statistics, the identity and classification, and the invalid PIFs. The interfaces are MIL-STD-188, NTDS Slow and Fast, 32-bit data, and IEEE 488 (to DTC). The TDP is built around an Intel 8635 board (comparable to an 80286) with EDO-supplied frontware. It has no AN designator. TDP is the basis for tactical applications of the DTC I and II, such as FFISTS, JOTS I and II, 2-way Link 11, MULTS, TACNAV, and JVIDS. About 120 TDPs are currently in service, mostly for the Link 11 connection to JOTS. EDO's **MDAU** (Multisource Data Acquisition Unit) consists of a TDP, a DTC I, and related software to manage and display the data acquired by the TDP. MDAU has now been overshadowed by DTC II systems such as FFISTS II.

TACTICAL DATA SYSTEMS/COMBAT-DIRECTION SYSTEMS

The Unisys CDS division has been renamed Paramax, incorporating the Canadian company that developed Shinpads.

CHILE

Sisdef (Sistemas de Defensa) is developing a CDS for the *Leander*-class frigates, using IBM-compatible IMAGEN workstations programmed in ADA.

CHINA (PRC)

Weapons systems, at least in frigates, each consist of a dedicated sensor connected to the weapon via a standard **2KJ-series** console. It displays the dedicated sensor picture and also performs ballistic calculations; it is a digital workstation (using 80286 processors and 80287 math coprocessors) carrying alternative cards for different sensors and weapons. Each console can handle 10 targets. The tight coupling between sensor, control station, and weapon mirrors Soviet practice. The console suffix gives its role, e.g., 2KJ-3 is used with the Type 352 radar (and C801 antiship missiles), 2KJ-5 is used for ASW, and the Chinese version of Newton Beta uses 2KJ-8. Each console carries a vertical green or black screen (ca. 10 × 12 in) and an IBM-style QWERTY keyboard; there is no trackball. Presumably, all are standard workstations. Systems as a whole have their own designations, e.g., SJD-5 for the Jianghu-class ASW system (searchlight sonar coupled to a 2KJ-5 console, which in turn controls a rocket launcher). There is probably no separate sonar console.

DENMARK

TDS replaced the **CEPLO**s on board *Willemoes*-class attack boats and *Hvidbjørnen*-class fishing-protection frigates. TDS is now being installed on board *Falster*-class minelayers (the first in 1990, then 1 per year). The planned modernization of the *Nils Juel* class (to begin in 1995) includes replacement of CEPLO by a 9LV Mk 3 CDS (as in the *Flyvefisken* class); the 9LV Mk 2 FCS will remain.

FRANCE

SENIT 7, for the carrier *Charles de Gaulle*, will be built around 5 or 6 ruggedized CSEE/Hewlett Packard computers using PA-VME RISC processors and an Ethernet D103 bus. The parallel TAVITAC 2000 system in the *La Fayette* class uses Thomson-CSF MLX 32 computers built around 68000-series processors. Its French Navy designation is **SACEIT** (*Système Automatisé de Commandement et d'Exploitation des Informations Tactiques*). Both are programmed in ADA. All previous French Navy CDSs used military computers: **SENIT 6** uses the 15M125 computer programmed in ADA and a BSM bus; **SENIT 4** uses the P2MS computer programmed in ADA and has no bus. SENIT 6 will incorporate a Link 16 terminal from 1995.

Efforts to develop a simplified CDS, **SESIT**, based on a commercial workstation, for the A-69 class and the *Floréal*s seem to have been abandoned. A-69s may be fitted with stand-alone Link 11. At present they are limited to what amounts to **Vega I**, without any computer-driven tactical table (i.e., without any computerized tactical picture): 2 surveillance consoles, 1 FCS console (with a BCH computer), and 1 ASW FCS console (with a second BCH). There are a manual plotting table and an ASW plot.

The commercial **Vega** systems, grown from FCS rather than conceived as CDS, form a series distinct from the SENITs. The 3 generations (Vega I, II, III) are distinguished by their computers: BCH (*Bloc Calcul Hybride*) for Vega I, CDE for Vega II, 15M for Vega III.

Standard French navy Vista consoles in the *Cassard* (SENIT 6) CDS. (DCN photo by Jean Biaugeaud)

BCH combined analog ballistics with a digital track-keeper: it could engage 2 targets while tracking 6 air or surface targets (and carrying 1 ESM strobe). CDE is an *extended* (double-precision) version of CDI (each letter of BCH advanced by 1; this is *not* an acronym) in which the analog ballistic section was replaced by a separate digital (but ROM, effectively hard-wired) section, with an integral A/D converter so that it can emulate BCH. CDE capacity is 16 tracks. Both Vega I and II were designed to work with a separate tactical table (effectively a plot extractor and tactical picture-keeper, called TAVITAC in Vega II), with a capacity of 16 (Vega I) or 16–64 (Vega II) tracks. Using the fully programmable 15M, Vega III can handle 128 tracks. The successor TAVITAC 2000 uses the MLX 32 computer and smart consoles. CTH is the Vega I FCS for a large warship.

Vega I was designated according to the search radar and weapons used. The simplest **Vega Triton** versions (later renamed **Vega Canopus**) have a **Lynx** optical director instead of a radar tracker; A and B were the 1- and 2-computer versions. Vega **Pollux C** (PC) adds a Pollux tracker to **Canopus A** (both radars share the same transmitter); PCE controls Exocet, and PCET controls torpedoes. No 2-computer Vega I was ever sold; 2-computer Vega IIs are called TAVITAC.

Users: —Vega I: Ecuador (PCE I/43 in *Quito* class), France (CTH in many warships, with CDE computers), Germany (Vega PCE in Type 148 class, first major customer), Ghana (Canopus A in FPB 57, possibly in FPB 45s), Greece (PCET in Combattante IIs and first 4 Combattante IIIs, CTH in *Jason* class), Malaysia (PCE in Combattante IIDs), Portugal (CTH in *Baptiste de Andrade* class)

—Vega II: Colombia (II/89 [with TAVITAC] in FS-1500 class), Greece (II/43 in Combattante IIIs, with Pollux), Libya (II/12 in *Ibn Ouf* class, II/43 in Combattante IIGs, with Castor IIB), Nigeria (II/73 [II/53 plus second surveillance console]), Peru (II/43 in PR-72 class), Qatar (II/53 [II/43 plus TAVITAC] in Combattante IIIMs), Tunisia (II/83 in Combattante IIIBs)

—Vega III: Saudi Arabia (IIIC in *Al Madinah* class)

—TAVITAC 2000: China (PRC) (Luda III [beginning with hulls 17 and 18] and Luhu classes; made under license, probably designated CCS-3 for export), France (*La Fayette* class and trials ship *Monge*), Saudi Arabia (*La Fayette* class), Taiwan (*La Fayette* class). The Signaal-Thomson TACTICOS superseded the projected next-generation version of Vega.

ITALY

Elsag, the developer of the next-generation CDS, **SADOC 3 (IPN-S)**, announced in mid-1992 that it would be redesigned for a more-open architecture; the MARA computers (with 80386 or 80486) processors may be discarded. The planned 32-bit family of equipment, such as the **NA-25** FCS and **EMPAR**, will be retained, as will the dual MHIDAS bus. Software is written in a new modular System Configuration Language (SCL). The 1st SADOC 3 will probably be placed on board the planned 2nd Italian carrier.

The current CDS is an upgraded (federated) **SADOC 2** (1st installed on board the *Giuseppe Garibaldi* in 1987, then on board *Mimbelli*- and *Audace*-class destroyers and *Minerva*-class corvettes; the last will be on the final *San Giorgio*). It uses a fiber-optic data bus, and each console has its own 16-bit NDC-160E (CP-7020) computer. The central computer is CDG-3032 (NC-7010); some ships have a second such computer as a hot spare (the *Minerva* uses an NDC-160 as a central computer). The large-ship version uses 2 MHCs (presumably for the surface and air pictures) and 9 (*Garibaldi*) or 10 (*Mimbelli*) SVCs. The *Garibaldi*'s capacity is 200 air tracks. The *Minerva*'s version uses 1 MHC and 2 SVCs. In the *Mimbelli*, the 4 Dardo E consoles are outside CIC (2 are 1 deck below, 2 in the after superstructure), providing the ship with some self-defense capability if CIC is hit.

The earlier **SADOC 2 (IPN-10)** was NTDS using an Italian central computer (CDG-3032) and displays, for the *Lupo* and *Maestrale* classes. **SADOC 1** (*Systema Automatico Direzione della Operazioni di Combattimento*) was NTDS, using the U.S. CP-642B computer (produced by Selenia, now Alenia). Conceived in 1968, it entered service in 1970; it survives only on board the cruiser *Vittorio Veneto*. All programming was done by the Italian Navy's MARICENPROG, established in 1970.

IPN-10 users: Ecuador (*Wadi M'ragh* class), India (*Vikrant, Godavari*), Iraq (*Wadi M'ragh* class, for sale), Libya (*Dat Assawari, Wadi M'ragh* class), Peru (*Lupo* class), Venezuela (*Lupo* class). The Indian CDS in the *Khukri* and *Delhi* classes may be an IPN-10 derivative.

ISRAEL

The *Eilat* (Sa'ar V) has a 17-console federated Elbit **AIO III** CDS (with 2 central computers, 1 a spare) on a triaxial-cable Ethernet. Each Operational Control Console (OCC) has 1 or 2 18-in (1,280 × 1,024 pixel) screens and 2 9-in raster-scan displays on a VME bus with 3 68040 display processors.

JAPAN

The *Kongo* class uses an **OYQ-6** CDS to coordinate Aegis and other systems (SQQ-89, EW, and ASUW). This architecture differs from U.S. practice, in which the Aegis system *is* the main CDS.

NETHERLANDS

Officially the **SEWACO** designation is limited to the Royal Netherlands Navy. Signaal applied other designations to systems, often unofficially called Sewaco, for other navies. **DAISY** is the standard program, produced in modular form by the RNLN Center for Automation of Weapon and Command Systems (CAWCS). The current edition, common to all SEWACO versions, is Mod 3.

SEWACO 7 for the *Karel Doorman* class was designed beginning in 1985. The initial version, without **SMART**, is SEWACO 7A; 7B is the ultimate version, to appear first in the fifth ship of the class, *Abraham Van Der Hulst* (to be delivered in February 1994). This federated system is considered an enormous advance over earlier central-computer systems. SEWACO 7 uses 2 SMR-4 computers to maintain its tactical picture, plus 1 for external and 1 for internal communications control. There are also 6 68030s (sensor management and preprocessing and bus-interface control). The system is tied together by a triple Ethernet, with separate TV/IR and fiber-optic audio (internal communications) networks. This version uses more than 10 times as much software as earlier SEWACOs. SEWACO 7 uses 16 standard GOC consoles, 15 in CIC and 1 in the communications room (as a communications-management console). There are also 13 video/data displays and 2 dedicated multi-weapon–control systems (MWCS) consoles, linked to the 2 bridge-wing target-designation sights, the 2 STIRs, the 76-mm gun, and the Sea Sparrow. SEWACO 7 incorporates an elaborate data base (e.g., of charts and intelligence data) on 14 optical disks, run by 2 DEC VAX 8250 computers (later to be replaced by the more powerful VAX 4300/4500s). The data bases will ultimately feed an AI system comparable to the U.S. C&D computer or to the British CCA.

Reportedly, South Korean *Dong Hae*- and *Po Hang*–class frigates (hulls 756–65) have SEWACO 7K CDSs. The later units of this class (766–82) have the Ferranti **WSA 423**. The *Ulsans* (951–56) have the simpler Signaal **Mini-Combat System** built around a WM-series FCS. Later *Ulsans* (957 and 958) have **WSA 423**.

SEWACO 11 is a fully distributed CDS for the next-generation Dutch command and AAW ship, to replace the *Tromp* class. The ships will probably be equipped with the new **SMART-L** radar and with **ARTIST**; **SMART-S** may be the target-indication radar. SEWACO 11 is likely to use the new, fully distributed architecture described below. SEWACO 11 uses Sun/SPARC hardware (over 100 MIPS in each console), programmed in ADA (also in C and UNIX, with X-WINDOWS graphics).

Other versions: **SEWACO I**, *Tromp* class (Netherlands); **SEWACO II**, *Kortenaer* class (Greece and Netherlands); **SEWACO IV**, *Westhinder* class (Belgium); **SEWACO V**, *Van Speijk* class (Indonesia, formerly Netherlands); **SEWACO VI**, *Van Heemskerck* class (Netherlands); **SEWACO VIII**, Dutch submarines; **SEWACO IX**, Tripartite Minehunters (except French: Belgium, Indonesia, Netherlands, Nigeria); **SEWACO X**, for the abortive Dutch-Belgian-Portuguese minehunter. **SEWACO XII** has been proposed for a possible Canadian AAW variant of the "City" class (it adds the AAW elements of SEWACO XI to the Shinpads CDS). The Canadian AAW ships would be built with money obtained by selling 3 CPFs to Saudi Arabia and saved by canceling the 6 corvettes and leasing British *Upholder*-class submarines rather than buying new ones. Other frigate installations include (order date in parentheses) Spanish *Descubierta* class (1974), Egyptian *El Suez* class (1978), Nigerian *Aradu* class (1978), Moroccan *Errhamani* class (1979), Argentine *Almirante Brown* class (1980), and Argentine *Espora* class (1980). The Spanish, Egyptian, and Moroccan ships are essentially sisters. Some of these ships have **Mini-Combat Systems**. Reportedly, 2 such systems are on board Greek *Gearing*s, though they lack the "egg" usually associated with this system.

STACOS is the Signaal Tactical Command and Control System, formerly **Foresee/DAISY**. Mod 1 is the version in the Turkish Track I and Portuguese MEKO frigates. Mod 2 is the version in the Greek MEKO frigates. Mod 3 is in the Turkish Track II frigates (the contract was signed on 15 March 1991, but the Turks probably switched to TACTICOS). All are federated systems built around a picture-keeping computer. However, Mod 3 incorporates smart displays on the LAN (Mods 1 and 2 have dumb displays driven by the central computer). Mod 4 is a fully distributed system. It became the first version of the new TACTICOS.

TACTICOS, the new, fully distributed Signaal-Thomson CDS, supersedes both **TAVITAC 2000** and the distributed form of STACOS (however, most existing contracts will be filled with the older systems). TACTICOS/STACOS was formerly called **SMCS** (Signaal Modular Combat System). System consoles are **MOCs** (Multifunction Operator Consoles), formerly called **SIGHT** for export applications. The basis of the system is a new, fully modular hardware/software architecture, **Sigma-Splice**, which acts as a buffer between various system functions and the dual Ethernet data bus. Software functions are all written as separate modules, running within a TACTICOS "Kernel" that includes Sigma software interfaces. The interfaces make it possible for TACTICOS to use commercial software, such as data-base managers. The system can also support nontraditional programming concepts (e.g., expert systems, blackboard systems, neural networks) and special processors (e.g., for acoustics).

For example, a sensor is connected to a preprocessor, which feeds the bus via Sigma-Splice (the combination of preprocessor and Sigma-Splice is a Sigma-Node). Similarly, a combat-system console (MOC) conducts some system application function, which feeds (and is fed by) the bus via Sigma-Splice (the combination of system application and Sigma-Splice is also a Sigma-Node). The weapon system connects to its own control processing and interface, which is combined with a Sigma-Splice in a third kind of Sigma-Node. Each MOC carries all software files in its own mass memory, so it can shift functions very quickly. System-management software is distributed over the nodes. The system automatically (or manually) reallocates programs to processors in case of failure or battle damage. It automatically reroutes functional and data-base information via semantics-based connections. Ultimately, TACTICOS will use a fiber-optic bus, which has greater capacity than the Ethernet bus of the M-class frigates. Software is written in ADA and C; graphics are in X-Windows and OSF/MOTIF. The MOC consoles use VME backbones with double-Eurocards and UNIX-based hardware.

Each MOC carries 1 or 2 20-in CRTs (1,024 × 1,280 pixels, refresh rate of 50–72 Hz, video bandwidth of 120 MHz), a graphics engine, 2 400-Mbyte hard disks, and a keyboard with rollerball or joystick. Its backbone is a 25-slot VME carrying multiprocessor boards, dual Ethernet-interface boards, and graphics processor(s). Other boards may be radar or TV scan converters (RACO [up to 3 raw radar videos simultaneously], TVCO [for optronic trackers and for conventional RGB television]), a video bus interface (for RACO and TVCO), a graphics accelerator, a Z-buffer memory (for 3D-oriented graphics), and support for a second CRT. The application host processor is a SigMA multiprocessor node using SPARC (RISC) architecture, 2–7 SUN-1S processor boards (each 12.5 MIPS, with 16 Mbyte of on-board RAM), 1 Nodal Resource Module, plus an S-Bus Ethernet interface, a 200-Mbyte Winchester (hard) disk, and a 60-Mbyte tape streamer (backup for the hard disk). The graphics host processor is a MIPS R3000 CPU (32 bits, 20 MHz, with a 32-kbyte data cache and 64-kbyte instruction cache), a MIPS R3010 FPU, 16 or 32 Mbyte of RAM, 4 RS 232 and 8 RS 422 interfaces, a 200-Mbyte hard disk, and a 60-Mbyte tape streamer; the operating system is IRIX. Graphics hardware provides 24 bitplanes, 4 Window/ID bitplanes, 4 Overlay/Underlay bitplanes, and a 12-bit color look-up table (4,096 out of 16.7 million colors available). A second combination (with another 200-Mbyte drive) would be added to support a second CRT. The radar scan converter (RACO) can handle PRFs of up to 16 kHz (with 20% stagger); the maximum range setting is 256 nm or 512 km; the maximum antenna scan rate is 1.1 Hz (66 rpm). The output code is 4 bits/pixel (so intensity can vary by a factor of 16). The MOC will also be used in the new Sintra submarine command system. At Bourget Naval 1992 (October 1992) Thomson-Signaal displayed a mocked-up triple command console: a 29-in Barco MX2500 screen (2,560 × 2,048 pixels) flanked by 2 standard 17-in TACTICOS displays with their standard controls. The 29-in screen is repeated in a large screen display (over 1 mFD), the first in Europe.

The contract for the last 2 Turkish *Dogan*-class FPBs was switched from STACOS Mod 4 to TACTICOS. This system uses 5 MOCs (SIGHT consoles) and a SINCOS bus. The combat system includes the **Vesta** link modified with a voice component so that helicopters can support OTH-T. Other components are **LIOD** and target-designation sights. Search radar will be supplied as GFE, integrated by Signaal. Signaal provides the GFCS for 76-mm and 35-mm guns. The STACOS contract for the Track II frigates has probably also been switched. Other users are Oman and Qatar, for their new corvettes; TACTICOS is part of the Combattante IVNG package offered to Kuwait.

SPAIN

As modernized with the **Tritan-1** CDS, the *Baleares*-class frigates have a Spanish-built **UYK-20** central processor (U 1600, with a 256k memory), 5 **OJ-194** consoles, U.S.-type target-engagement and weapons-assignment consoles, an ASW console, 4 Selenia tactical and weapons-control consoles (MHC and SVC), a radar-data integrator (apparently broadly analogous to the U.S. SYS-1), and Rockwell Link 11. The system's capacity is ownship, 64 local and 64 remote tracks, 26 local and 14 remote special points, 1 local and 1 remote DLRP, 1 local and 1 remote PIM, 4 local and 4 remote ASW vectors (strobes), 4 local torpedo vectors, 4 local and 4 remote acoustic points (presumably sonobuoys), 16 local and 8 remote ESM strobes, and 4 local and 4 remote ESM positions. The CIC crew includes an air-intercept controller, an air antisurface controller, and an air ASW controller. Besides the carrier *Principe de Asturias* (Tritan 2), versions of Tritan appear in the last 2 *Santa Maria*–class frigates and will be installed in the modernized *Descubierta*s.

SWEDEN

CCIS is typically integrated with a **9LV200** series Mk 2 FCS, with which it is connected by the system bus; CCIS has probably been supplied to all buyers of 9LV200 Mk 2 systems. Thus raw radar video (as well as communications, ESM, and the output of an RWR) is normally fed directly into the radar-plot extractor of the CCIS. The CCIS in turn assigns weapons and commands the 9LV systems. In the event the central computer fails, raw radar video can be fed instead into the 9LV plot extractor, and thus into the combat-system bus. The simplest version, in the Swedish *Hugin* class (and probably in the Yugoslav *Rade Končar* class), probably has only a single vertical console. The *Hugin* class's upgrade program, begun in 1991 (to be complete in 1997), replaces the tape program-loading units with PROMs. Sonars are installed for ASW. The MARIL 880 CDS of the earlier Spica-II class was upgraded when these boats were armed with RBS 15 missiles. At least 6 will be further upgraded to remain in service through 2010. The improved MARIL 880 in the *Stockholm* class is to be modernized beginning in 1997.

Other designations are **CEPLO** (Command Electronic Plotting System), **DEPLO** (Danish version of CEPLO), **MARIL** (Swedish), and **MARIL 880** (extended version for the Royal Swedish Navy).

9LV Mk 3 (Base System 2000) completes the integration by distributing smart FCS and CDS consoles (and the dual-tactical-picture computers) on the same Ethernet system bus. More significantly, all software is written in modular form in ADA. Because ADA is an object-oriented language, program modules need not be rewritten to fit a particular system. Both hardware and software are treated as modules that can run in any location on the system, injecting their outputs into a special communications software. Thus, individual modules are generally only 10,000–30,000 lines of code, whereas the system as a whole probably involves a million lines or more. NobelTech argues that it is possible to achieve a high degree of commonality in systems for very different purposes because, e.g., a track-keeping module need not be rewritten for reuse. Typically, 70% of the code for any new application is existing code, 25% must be modified, and only 5% is entirely new. On this basis NobelTech has sold 9LV Mk 3 systems for both surface ships (e.g., the ANZAC frigate and the *Göteborg*-class corvette) and the current Swedish submarine (A-19 *Gotland* class: the system is designated **9SCS Mk 3**). This system is being offered to Kuwait (for the replacement patrol boat), to Oman (for the new patrol boat), and to Spain (for the F-100 frigate). Base 2000 has also been adopted for the new Swedish national air-defense system (**STRIC**).

The standard VME-backbone/double-Eurocard workstation, **SPL 85**, made by the Danish company Terma exists in 2 forms, Types IIA (single monitor, as in the ANZACs) and IID (double monitor, as in the *Gotland*). Monitors have 20-in color or monochrome monitors (1,280 × 1,024 pixels, refreshed at 60 Hz, using the upper 1,024 × 1,024 for a radar or tactical picture, and the lower 256 × 1,024 for a menu readout). Type IIA has a smaller 12-in raster-scan display on its upper right, to display television, radar, graphics, and text, and a second 12-in raster-scan on its lower right for television, A-scan radar data, or text. Operators call up functions by means of 2 touch-input screens showing menus, and they also use keyboards and 1 or 2 rollerballs.

The **9LV453 Mk 3** of the ANZAC frigate uses 6 SPL 85 consoles, for the CO/PWO (equivalent to the U.S. TAO), the surface-warfare coordinator (SWC), the ASW director (ASWD), the helicopter controller, the air-picture controller (APC), and the surface-picture controller (SPC). An additional console can be provided for the EW director (EWD). Compared to the *Göteborgs*' system, the ANZAC frigates' requires 6 or 8 rather than 5 operators/controllers. There are 3 separate buses: a combat-system bus, a video bus (to supply the consoles with raw video), and a command/control bus (consoles and computers). Reportedly, this version required some software redesign because it was not fully compatible with Link 11 (it did not automatically report some actions back into the data link), because its operator–machine interface did not use standard NATO symbology, and because it could not accommodate the usual fast-action buttons. In the Finnish *Helsinki-II* class, 9LV Mk 3 employs 2 SPL 85 consoles, plus 2 navigational-radar consoles and a fire-control console. The Danish **StanFlex 300 (Stanfire)** version has 6 command consoles with daylight screens (CIC is on the bridge). The version in the *Thetis* class has 4 consoles. As an indication of the system's complexity, BEAB claims that it has produced a software library amounting to 1–2 million lines of code for the *Göteborg* (missile-corvette) installation.

Users: —CCIS: Bahrein (FPB 62 and TNC 45 classes), Denmark (CEPLO: *Nils Juels* class), Finland (*Helsinki* class), Iraq (probably *Ibn Khaldum*), Kuwait (FPB 57 and TNC 45 classes), Malaysia (Spica-M class), Oman (probably ''Province'' class), Sweden (*Carlskrona, Hugin, Spica-II, Stockholm* classes), U.A.E. (FPB 38 and TNC 45 classes), Yugoslavia (*Rade Končar* class)
—9LV Mk 3: Australia (ANZAC class), Denmark (StanFlex 300 and *Thetis* classes), Finland (*Helsinki-II*), New Zealand (ANZAC class), Sweden (*Göteborg* and A-19 *Gotland* classes)

SWITZERLAND

In July 1993, **CoSys 200** was chosen for the Korean KDX destroyer, reportedly even though the rival SSCS had been found superior in 14 of 15 categories considered and was preferred by the Korean navy (technical and operational branches), the Korean Treasury, the Korean Foreign Ministry, and the Korean Security Forces. As of August 1993, the decision was being reconsidered, and possible corruption was being investigated. CoSys 200K1 is to have 10 BM 802-52 consoles, 2 of them for TMX/KA directors. The target-indication radar is Dolphin, and the sonar is the German ASO 90. The CoSys numbering scheme parallels that of the MEKOs. CoSys 100 was announced at RNEE 1991 to equip a new MEKO 100–series corvette.

UNITED KINGDOM

ARE's **DFTDS** (Data Fusion Technology Demonstrator) uses 600 knowledge-based rules to filter and associate data, particularly tracks, to form the compiled tactical picture automatically; in effect it is a next-generation CDS without any weapons-control functions. For example, knowing that a helicopter has been assigned to patrol a given zone, DFTDS will tentatively identify a helicopter-like radar contact there. Knowledge of the position of landmasses limits the possible area from which a line of bearing (such as an ESM strobe) can originate. DFTDS evaluates sonar propagation to estimate passive ranges. The system automatically gives its reasoning and the basic data for any particular identification. The inputs are messages (mainly tracks) from ownship and force sensors (via Link 11); DFTDS handles 1,000 messages/sec, all from the ship's combat system bus.

The system uses 5 VAXserver 4500 (originally 3800) computers on a fiber-optic Ethernet LAN: front-end and user-interface processors and 3 modules: data base, data fusion, planning (including situation assessment for a force). The last associates threats with their likely targets and lists which weapons can react. Output appears on 5 screens (3 in an operator array, 1 alongside the command radar display, 1 between the missile director and the EW operator). The system uses 2 data bases, 1 for geography, the other for equipment/platforms (including performance data). Ferranti is providing a combat-system tactical decision aid, **RRASL**, in effect a next-generation CCA, under an August 1990 contract. DFTDS is to be extended to time-stale (JOTS) data. Weather data (e.g., for ducting) will probably also be added. DFTDS was installed on board HMS *Marlborough*, a new Type 23 frigate (as yet without any installed CDS) in March 1991, for 1992–93 sea trials.

As of spring 1993, it appeared most likely that the future Anglo-French AAW frigate would have a BAe-SEMA **SSCS** CDS. The main competitor is Ferranti's ADAWS 2000.

ADIMP now includes VSEL's **EMCIU** (ECM Interface Unit), which connects the ESM and jammer without passing their data and commands through the central computer, in effect federalizing the system. According to a 1991 British parliamentary paper, the 19 ADIMP systems will cost a total of £115 million.

ADAWS versions are designated in a DA series, e.g., ADAWS 1 is DAB (the earlier ADA was DAA), ADAWS 2 is DAC, ADAWS 4 is DAD, ADAWS 6 is DAF, and ADAWS 7 is DAG. **CACS is Outfit DFA.**

CAAIS 400 (FM 1600B computer, WSA 400–series WCS), and **CAAIS 450** (FM 1600E computer, WSA 420–series) are the export versions of CAAIS. CAAIS 450 uses new vertical displays (12-in CRT for the single console, 16-in for the command console, all monochromatic and incorporating keyboards and rollerballs). It performs threat evaluation and can connect directly to a data link and to on-board ECM systems.

CAAIS and WSA 420–Series Export Users: Argentina (*25 de Mayo*), Brazil (CAAIS 400 in *Niteroi* class, CAAIS 450/WSA 421 in *Inhaúma* class), Chile (*Alm. Williams* class), Egypt (*Ramadan* class, probably first WSA 422), India (*Viraat*, DBA 3 version), Kenya (*Nyayo*, CAAIS 450/WSA 422), Oman (CAAIS and all-optical WSA 422 in *Al Sharquiyah* [her sisters have 9LV300-series systems]), South Korea (CAAIS 450/WSA 423 in fourth and later *Ulsan*s and later KCX classes). The Brazilian *Inhaúma* class uses an RTN-10X tracker. The Egyptian and Kenyan ships use S802s (Oman used 2 Sea Archers); the Korean ships have ST1802s and Radamec HK 409–029 E/O directors. Samsung makes WSA 423 under license in South Korea; the first contract was awarded in 1986, and by September 1989, 12 ships had been completed, an additional batch was on order, and a third was under tender. The South Korean version is almost certainly the single-headed version (2 trackers).

The Egyptian CAAIS system was reportedly derived from an earlier, previously undescribed, Marconi mini-AIO for the Egyptian 6 October class. It uses a single AD16L surface display, with a 16-in CRT. The operator can track and allocate 4 targets. Markers show targets being tracked (with rate-aiding), and automatic track-sequencing allows the operator to update tracks quickly using a trackball. A second AD16L alongside the surface display controls the Otomat missile. The operator detects the target, plots its course, and allocates it to the fire-control computer.

Racal announced a new 600 Series (presumably **CANE 600**), at RNEE 1991; this system substitutes 68030/68040 chips for the DS500s (single-board versions of the Kongsberg KS500) of the earlier systems (consoles have VME backplanes and are connected by an Ethernet). Each console has a full-color, 20-in digital display (1,344 × 1,010 pixels, refresh rate 60 Hz), which can show a 12-in-diameter PPI. 600 Series uses some of the same consoles as SSCS. Racal claimed that this system would be significantly less expensive than NAUTIS and System 500, its main competitors. It is intended for small ships such as light frigates and corvettes. **MAINS** (Minehunting Information System) is a special-purpose version of CANE (System 880, QX3/1).

CANE Users: Cameroon (*Bakassi*: first CANE 100), Denmark, Germany (Type 443 intelligence collectors), Finland, Hong Kong (450-ton police command craft *Sea Panther* and *Sea Horse*), Indonesia, Jordan (Hawk class), South Korea, Sweden (probably intelligence collector *Orion*), United Kingdom ("Island" and "Castle" class OPVs, *Argus* [DBE(1), distributed 3-console version], *Sir Galahad*, and "River"-class minesweepers), United States (QX3 in *Avenger* class, as URN-30), and Yugoslavia

The Type 23 version of **SSCS (DNA)** employs 12 identical consoles, including separate ones for the captain and the PWO. In this version, 4 consoles are mounted in line from the PWO's chair, for the long- and short-range air, surface, and subsurface track supervisors. On the PWO's right are a pair of consoles (CO and PWO). The other 6 consoles are in a row behind the PWO, facing the other way: typically 2 for weapons, 2 for sonar, and 1 each for radar and EW operators. Because the system is modular and the consoles interchangeable, this distribution can be changed as required. Consoles are initialized by inserting a key card, and their functions can be changed by changing the card; it takes about 30 sec for a console to change displays. This is the first Royal Navy color command system. It is expected to use red for enemy, blue for friendly, yellow for unknown, green for neutral, and white for unidentified or supporting. The symbology and colors were tried out on the crew of HMS *Norfolk*. There is some problem with colors. Software is written in ADA; as of September 1991, the estimated size of the program was 200,000 lines of code (200 kloc). The fiber-optic, token-passing, ring LAN was adopted because it was considered more predictable than an Ethernet.

The first full Type 23 SSCS is to be on board HMS *Westminster*. DNA is to replace CACS 5 on board Type 22 Batch III frigates. The versions are DNA(1) for Type 23 frigates (reported 70% redundancy, presumably meaning excess capacity); and DNA(2), for the AORs. Each has 12 consoles. A 1991 British parliamentary paper estimated that 8 shipboard systems plus 4 shore systems would cost a total of £345 million.

NAUTIS/SYQ-15: The versions are the following:

NAUTIS-F for frigates. There are 4 command consoles (surface, air, ASW, and command summary).

Users: Malaysia (new corvettes), New Zealand (2 *Leander*s: 5-console version)

NAUTIS-L for amphibious-warfare and logistics landing ships.

Users: United Kingdom (7-console version in refitted *Fearless* class)

NAUTIS-M for minehunters and minesweepers; up to 3 consoles (sonar, ship control [bridge], mine-disposal vehicle).

Users: Saudi Arabia (*Sandown* class), United Kingdom (*Sandown* class), United States (*Avenger* class, as SYQ-15)

NAUTIS-P for patrol vessels, strike craft, corvettes. There are 1 or 2 consoles.

Users: Thailand (*Khamronsin* class)

NAUTIS-S, a new version, is a supplement to existing command systems. Typical enhancements include ASW, point-defense-system control, CIWS control, missile/gun-system control, ESM or ECM management, control of containerized systems, aircraft detection and control, command workstations, mine-countermeasures modernization, integrated communications, and data-link operation. Not yet sold.

Kelvin-Hughes has developed a CDS based on several of its Colour Tactical Displays (**CTD**s), each with its own processor, on a fiber-optic LAN. Each CTD can track 20 contacts (a more-powerful processor, to be introduced in 1994, will probably double that); 5 or 6 can share a common track file. Software in the CTD processors solves the relative-velocity problem, so targets can be designated to an FCS (the CDS can indicate weapon bearing and range limits inside which the weapon will be effective; an alarm sounds or shows when a target is in range). An IFF can be controlled from the CTD screen. **KRIS** (Kelvin-Hughes Radamec Integrated System) for patrol boats combines CTDs with Siemens Plessey Lookout and 1007 radars and a Radamec 2300 (for a 40-mm gun) or 2400 (for a 57-mm gun). The CTD system may cost about half as much as CANE (say £125,000).

Users: Ireland (*Peacock* class), Netherlands (new AOR: 4-console version), Singapore (*Victory* class), Spain (new AOR: 3-console version)

At Brighton in March 1993, INRI displayed a Mini-Tactical Data System based on a DRS Military Systems Tactical Console (a high-resolution color workstation using commercial hardware). This CDS is to be offered to Greece for the *Adams* class's modernization.

CTC Users: Chile, China (PRC), Netherlands, Norway, Spain (*Milano* class, with 2459 radar). The other applications, reported by Racal, are not further identified.

Ferranti Series 500 Users: Denmark (GP250 in coast defense), Finland (GP250 in coast defense), Germany (MC500 SATAM in Type 332 minecraft), Hong Kong (GP250 for the police, presumably to track small craft), South Korea, and Sweden

GP250 predictor (software embedded in a series of extended double 68000 VME Eurocards, using 68020 processors) is designated **GP250P**. It analyzes target and ownship motion and solves the ballistic problem. The customer supplies the man–machine interface (MMI) and final gun drive. **GP250M** adds a color MMI. **GP250L** is the land-based coast-defense version. **GP250T**, the total gunfire-control system, adds a gun synchro drive, gun tell backs, gun-status indication, and a control/display unit. It is the FCS predictor/processor for the full WS500.

UNITED STATES

NTDS (using a CP-642 or UYK-7 computer) has been renamed **CDS** (Combat-Direction System); its UYK-43–equipped successor is **ACDS** (Advanced Combat-Direction System). U.S. CICs are now called CDCs (Combat-Direction Centers). CDS/ACDS and Aegis system software is designated by Model: Model 4.0 is used by CDS. Model 4.1, used by ACDS Block 0 (with a UYK-43 computer and UYQ-21 displays), is rewritten Model 4.0 software. It is also called RNTDS (Restructured NTDS). ACDS Block 1 uses Model 5 software. The original Aegis system used UYK-7 computers and Model 4 software; the upgraded UYK-43 version uses Model 5 software. Model 4.1 software was produced by Paramax (a division of Unisys); Model 5 is by Hughes Ground Systems.

CDS has only a single central computer, whose main function is to maintain the tactical picture. Because it had to decide automatically to engage targets, Aegis added a second computer, the **C&D (command and decision) Processor**, which applied decision-making (doctrinal) rules to the tactical picture in the first computer. The rules can be changed on board ship. They also help control the radar, e.g., to reject targets coming from particular directions in selected speed ranges.

ACDS Block 1 has a UYK-43 C&D processor running adapted Aegis decision-support software (*ATES* [Aegis Tactical Executive System]). Because UYK-43 is so much more powerful than UYK-7, it can add technical intelligence data to the tactical picture. ACDS Block 1 is the first U.S. CDS to provide this sort of data fusion. It is also the first to be designed for full integration with ESM data, including that collected by TFCC and POST (from the TADIXS B intelligence net).

The lead ACDS Block 1 ship is the carrier *Carl Vinson*; the other active carriers will likely follow in the mid- to late-1990s. The LHDs and LHAs will probably also be fitted with Block 1, as will the 2 *California*s and the *Kidd*s. All of the other potential platforms, the oil-burning NTU cruisers and the 4 *Virginia*s, are being laid up within the next 2 or 3 yr. The first ACDS Block 1 was delivered in December 1992 for an engineering test (with the accompanying carrier ASW Module Model 5.1) on board the *Constellation* in the fall of 1993. An enhanced Block 1 Level 1 program is to be delivered in June 1994.

Link processing is being removed to Hughes's separate **C2P** (command and control processor), a UYK-43 with a USQ-69 display terminal. That frees the main computer to quadruple the system's track capacity and effective surveillance range; it also increases the target-insertion rate. Because C2P is necessary to handle Link 16, it is still planned for cruisers no longer scheduled for the full ACDS Block 1. The design of the C2P is complicated because Link 16 uses different (NATO) target categories than Link 11, yet the same processor must prepare information from both for insertion into the picture-keeping computer. C2P(V)0 supports ACDS Block 0 and Aegis Model 4; (V)1 supports ACDS Block 1 and Aegis Model 5. C2P(V)0 is to be released to the fleet in FY94 (integration tests on board carriers and CGN-36/NTU–class ships were completed in FY92).

The following NTDS (non-Aegis) computers are in service:

—**CP-642A**: *Forrestal, Ranger, Constellation*
—**CP-642B**: *Bainbridge, Truxtun; Mahan* class (all being decommissioned or stricken)
—**UYK-7**: *Spruance* class; modernized *Adams* class (including JPTDS ships); *Tarawa* class; and *Perry*-class frigates
—**UYK-43**: CV/CVN (except CV-59, -61, -64), CGN-36–41 (but CGN-38 still has UYK-7); CG-16/26 classes; DDG-993–996; and *Wasp* (LHD-1)

COMDAC/ICES is the Unisys (Paramax) Command, Display, and Control and Integrated Cutter Electronics System for WMEC-270–class (*Bear*-class) Coast Guard cutters. COMDAC is a 2-seat bridge console system, each station of which has 2 CRTs (showing alphanumerics, graphics [synthetic video], radar/graphics, and closed-circuit TV [e.g., to observe a landing helicopter]). COMDAC was derived from HYCATS.

HYCATS (SSQ-87) has a capacity of 45 targets, using a **UYK-44** computer. This system has 4 digital TV displays for its 2 operator positions. HYCATS developed into Paramax's **Integrated Shipboard System**, which was developed into the **MSO, MCM-1, MSH** (abortive), and then **MHC-51 (SYQ-13)** systems.

SYQ-12 is Unisys's (Paramax) combat system for the Egyptian route-survey vessel and coastal minehunter, with an associated shore-based mine-warfare data center. This system is also on board U.S. MSOs.

RADDS (Radar Data Distribution System) is a rudimentary CDS built out of SPA-25G consoles, probably broadly analogous to the British Kelvin-Hughes system. It is being developed on an evolutionary prototype basis by the Naval Surface Weapons Center at Dahlgren for ships without CDS. There is no data link.

SYQ-13 is Paramax's combat system for the new *Cardinal* (MHC-51) -class minehunter. The system is tied together by a triple-redundant serial data bus, fed by 3 data-acquisition units (for the sonar and SLQ-48 mine-neutralization vehicle). SYQ-13 is connected to a pair of consoles in CIC, a single console in the pilothouse (for ship control and for the **SSQ-109** integrated machinery-control system), and a pair of consoles in the central (machinery) control station. SYQ-13 software is derived from that of **SYQ-12**. SSQ-109 is derived from the machinery/ship-control system of the Canadian frigates (*Halifax* class).

CDCS, the latest Hughes distributed CDS, was announced in 1992. The old Rolm 1666-series computers have been discarded in favor of 68040s (with some embedded 68030s). The consoles are based on the new **OJ-663**, with the same graphics engine but with a new scan converter (for both radar and TV images). The architecture is fully open, with VME backplanes. The data bus is fiber-optic, for high capacity.

Elements of **MCS** are in service in Egypt and Taiwan. In Egyptian *Descubierta*s it is responsible for data links (YE and Z), for Harpoon, and for EW integration. In the Taiwanese *Perry* class, MCS is responsible for SSMs and 40-mm–gun fire control. The full **H930** is in Taiwan (Wu Chin destroyers, *Lung Chiang* class).

EDO's **ITACS** (Integrated Tactical Command System) is an outgrowth of **FFISTS**. A typical system might consist of 4 DTC IIs in an LAN (Ethernet or fiber-optic network), feeding a large-screen display and other remote displays. The DTCs would be a track supervisor (connected to the ship's radar and her communications system [for data links]); a localization (TMA) console; an environmental/sonar console (connected to the sonars); and the ship's weapons-coordinator console, connected to the weapons system. EDO clearly sees ITACS as an inexpensive way of modernizing ships either lacking computerized CDSs or with obsolete systems. EDO suggests ITACS for a variety of platforms: the U.S. *Adams, Knox*, and *Hamilton* classes, which lack any computer combat systems (and the first two of which are being transferred to foreign navies); and the *Spruance* and *Perry* classes, which have combat systems but many of which have not yet been fitted with **SQQ-89** (FFISTS is broadly equivalent to parts of SQQ-89).

RNTDS Emulation System (RNTDES in the FY93 program) is a display system to replace the current **UYA-4** on board NTDS ships; it uses the **UYQ-21** hardware of the current Restructured NTDS. UYA-4 is apparently more and more difficult to maintain because of the age of its technology.

Aircraft Tactical Data Systems

AUSTRALIA

The **RAWS (Seahawk)** sonobuoy receiver is the 99-channel **ARR-84** used in the U.S. LAMPS III Block I upgrade; the helicopter carries 32 buoys. For Gulf operations, the Australian Seahawks were fitted with **AAR-47** missile detectors, **ALE-47** flare/chaff dispensers, **AAQ-16** FLIRs (not tied into the main dual 1553B data bus), and machine guns. FLIRs probably will ultimately be tied into the system; the bus has sufficient capacity, and there are open reserved terminals.

CANADA

The Canadian **EH-101 New Shipboard Aircraft** will be equipped with a Unisys (Paramax)/CDC **MSDHS** (Mission System Data-Handling System), **AWS-503**, built around a 34-lb mission system computer (MSP) using 68030/68882 chips and a VME backplane. A 1553B bus ties the system together. The system is programmed in ADA. There is still some question as to whether this helicopter will have FLIR (PAV) and MAD, but it will have a dipper (**FLASH/UYS-503** processor) and sonobuoys (2 dispensers, 7 buoys each).

Canada plans to upgrade **CP-140** patrol aircraft with the modernized APS-116 (APS-506) radar, a new acoustic processor (possibly an upgrade of the existing OL-5004), a new 99-channel sonobuoy receiver, a new communications system to include SATCOM, GPS, a new ESM system (probably ALR-76), and enhanced computer/displays. Two contractors are to be selected by April 1995, and the contract is to be awarded in July 1997.

UNITED STATES

A-6E/SWIP adds a new Kaiser Electronics display suite (including a HUD processor and a 5 × 5–in, monochrome, multifunction bombing/nav display), a larger-capacity mission computer, modified wing fillets, and a new slat. The modified wing and the HUD increase the allowable carrier-approach speed. SWIP also enjoys better self-defense capacity because of its **IDAP** and its added chaff dispenser. The new mission computer is an IBM **TC-4** (replacing the earlier **TC-3**), chosen specifically to avoid new high-order-language programming. The first SWIP aircraft flew at the end of August 1991; IDAP-compatibility tests began in March 1992. The first full-scale-development aircraft began flight testing in September 1992.

The future of this program is now in question. Early in 1993 the navy announced that all A-6Es would be retired by 1999; money released by curtailment of the upgrade program is to be used to modernize **F-14s** and convert them to deliver bombs (as "Bombcats"). A-6s are on average 15 yr older than F-14s. OSD questioned the wisdom of leaving a 10-yr gap between the A-6 retirement and the availability of some successor.

Like all other U.S. Navy fighters, the F-14 always had a surface-attack capability. The Phase 1 upgrade provides adapters in the under-body missile rails, permitting an F-14 to carry 4 unguided (iron) bombs. Phase 2 adds a capability to carry laser-guided bombs (but no designator), cluster bombs (Rockeye, CBU-59, and Gator mines), and TALD decoys, as well as an IRST, ALR-67, and JTIDS. Evaluation begins in June 1993. Phase 3, not yet funded, adds a laser designator, precision weapons such as HARM and SLAM, and more advanced smart weapons such as JDAM and JSOW. A Loral FLIR/laser-designator pod is to be flight-tested later in 1993. At present the F-14 force consists of 385 F-14As, 69 F-14Bs (-14A with F110-GE-400 engines and ALR-67, originally called -14A Plus), and 55 F-14Ds. Beginning with 30 aircraft in FY94, the 127 newest F-14As and all the -14Bs will be upgraded with AYK-14 computers (plus a digital bus and interface processor) and a programmable tactical information display (new weapons can then be carried without rewiring the airplane); the -14As will be fitted with ALR-67s in place of their ALR-45s. All will receive BOL chaff racks in missile-launch pylons. The "smart" ALE-47 is then reserved for flares and active GEN-X decoys. Too, the BOL, which is outboard, gets better dispersion because of wingtip vortices. Some F-14As will be remanufactured to -14B standard. Separate programs would add new digital flight-control systems (beginning in FY96), install GPS (beginning in FY95 for F-14Ds, FY97 for A/B upgrade aircraft), add ARC-210 radios (in FY98), and add more-robust mission recorders (in FY99). The first operational "Bombcats" were 2 squadrons (VF-14 and -32) deployed in October 1992 to the Eastern Mediterranean on board the USS *John F. Kennedy.* **IDAP** will now probably apply to the F-14D; work on components continues. A Lockheed-Sanders ALQ-156A missile war-

ner triggers the deployment of the ALE-50 towed decoy as well as conventional decoys. ALQ-156A is called VECP because it was developed under a value-added engineering change proposal. It has a receiver and digitizer near each antenna, so simple cables (rather than low-loss microwave cables) connect the antennas to the central processor. A digital clutter filter replaces the analog filter of the earlier ALQ-156.

P-3B TACNAVMOD (ASN-124) is, in effect, a "poor man's P-3C," developed in the mid-1970s for the remaining P-3As and -3Bs. The computer is the Lear-Sigler **CP-1224**, using the **ASA-66** display console (-66A for the pilot, -66B for the TACCO). These aircraft are also fitted with **AQA-7(V)** sonobuoy processors. CP-1224 is a 16-bit computer with 103 instructions and a memory capacity of 64 kword; it has 16 1-word registers and can operate in single and double precision. It is connected to a dual 1553B bus and has a 16-MHz clock. There are 8 input and 8 output channels plus 32 input and 32 output discretes (switches or synchros). The later -1224B adds a 32-kword-memory card to accommodate later software.

TACNAVMOD applies to surviving U.S. P-3Bs in the Naval Reserve and also to Portuguese P-3Ps and Spanish P-3Bs. It probably also applies to aircraft withdrawn from U.S. storage, such as the P-3As offered to Thailand and the P-3As that Australia plans to use as crew trainers. However, Iran did *not* receive TACNAVMOD in the P-3Fs acquired in the 1970s.

The **ASN-150** tactical system of the SH-60F (S-70B-4) is the basis of two export versions of the SH-60: the Greek S-70B-6 and the Taiwanese S-70C(M)-1 (Thunderhawk). ASN-150 also equips the SAR version, the U.S. Navy's HH-60H and Coast Guard's HH-60J (S-70B-5). The Australian version (S-70B-2) uses the Collins **RAWS**, and the Spanish version is identical to the U.S. LAMPS III. The Greek version is equipped with an **AQS-18(V)3** dipping sonar, with the **Penguin** missile adopted for LAMPS III Block I helicopters, and with **ALR-606(V)2** ESM. The helicopter is equipped with a sonobuoy launcher. Taiwan's version has the AQS-18(V) dipper with provision for sonobuoy processing, but the aircraft has only provision for a sonobuoy launcher. The radar is **APS-128PC** (APS-143), and the ESM set is ALR-606(V)2. ASN-150 has also been adopted for the Taiwanese upgrade of the S-2 Tracker (S-2T) and will be installed (probably with dipping sonars) on board the 12 S-2H LAMPS I helicopters that Taiwan is now receiving. Like the Thunderhawk, the S-2Ts have **ARR-84** sonobuoy receivers. The other systems are different: **APS-504** radar, **AQS-902F** sonobuoy processor, **AAS-40** FLIR, and **ASQ-504** digital MAD. At least in the case of Taiwan, ASN-150 includes an RF data link (referred to only as ASN-150).

STRATEGIC STRIKE SYSTEMS

Deletions: The French **M20** and the U.S. **Poseidon** missiles are now extinct. **Nuclear Tomahawk**s have been withdrawn from U.S. ships and submarines (in accordance with the Bush-Yeltsin agreement), but they remain in shore storage. TLAM-N production has ended. Prior to the agreement, about 100 were at sea, with another 267 stored ashore. The U.S. **Excalibur** follow-on cruise missile was canceled in 1991.

FRANCE

The alert level of French strategic submarines is being reduced, from 3 to 2. Super-Étendard squadrons equipped with the **ASMP** nuclear missile are being reduced from 2 to 1. **M4**, first fired operationally by *Le Tonnant* in September 1987, is now standard. **M5** was canceled in mid-1992 but revived the following October. By that time it was the only element of the French deterrent force still receiving funding ($223 million in 1993).

UNITED STATES

Current plans call for a total of 18 **Trident** submarines, down from 19 as planned in 1988. In February 1991 it was announced that the first 10 *Ohio*-class submarines would not be re-equipped with **Trident II** missiles. The FY92/93 program, announced in February 1991, called for 28 missiles in FY92 and 31 in FY93 (63 were bought in FY90 and 52 in FY91), at a unit cost of $39.3 million (up from $28.4 million in FY90). Under the Bush-Yeltsin agreements, these missiles will probably be downloaded to 4 warheads each. As of June 1992, the goal was a total of 1,728 warheads in the second phase of strategic-arms reduction, half the numbers as limited by the START treaty. **Poseidon (C-3)** SLBM warheads were taken off alert on 1 October 1991. All pre–*Ohio*-class submarines will probably be discarded during the life of the START treaty, leaving 240 **Trident D-5** and 192 **Trident C-4** missiles.

STRIKE/ SURFACE WARFARE

UAVS

The Canadian **CL-227** and the U.S. **Cypher** are no longer being considered for U.S. naval use. The Israeli Helistar has been canceled.

UNITED KINGDOM

GEC Avionics announced **Frigate Bird**, a new family of naval VTOL UAVs, in March 1992. They are canard tail-sitters weighing 250–1,000 lb. A typical version has a span of 12 ft and is 11 ft long; the propeller diameter is 6 ft 7 in, and take-off weight is 562 lb (payload 100 lb). Performance: 160 kt max, 82 kt economical cruising speed, 72 kt best endurance speed, 440 nm typical endurance (4 + hr), 3,148 ft/min maximum climb rate. The power plant is a 112-BHP Williams WTS-117 turboshaft or a 100-BHP Norton NR642 rotary. The Royal Navy has shown interest but has not issued an OR.

UNITED STATES

As of May 1993, the navy planned to drop out of the MR-UAV (JSCAMPS, BQM-145) program altogether because of cost, and to abandon the VTOL maritime UAV in favor of buying Hunter (JIMPACS) SR-UAVs (18 systems, each with 8 air vehicles). Hunter is to be tested on board amphibious ships. The VTOL program survives only as a fallback in the event Hunter proves unsuitable (VTOLs will be tested because the program was mandated by Congress). Hunter tests are to begin in the fall of 1993, and to be completed in the summer or fall of 1994.

During the Gulf War, **Pioneer** UAVs flew from the battleships *Missouri* and *Wisconsin*, for a total of 151 sorties (520 flight hours). They were also in army and marine service. These small UAVs managed more than 125 flight hours/month/unit, compared to the 60 that had been expected before the war.

The MR-UAV is now **JSCAMPS** (BQM-145), and **Hunter/ JIMPACS** is the ground-based SR-UAV. As of mid-1992 no long-endurance demonstration contracts had been issued.

In mid-1992, Phase I 4-month study contracts were awarded for 2 VTOL SR-UAVs: to Bell-Textron, for its version of the earlier **Pointer**, and to SAIC, for the exotic **Daedalus**. Boeing's version of Pointer lost. Phase II is an optional contract for 40 hr of flight-testing, to demonstrate VTOL performance, hovering ability, 150-kt airspeed, 10,000-ft service ceiling, 2-hr endurance, and the ability to launch and recover in a 36 × 36–ft space. Daedalus was developed under a 1989 DARPA contract. It has a single nose propeller and takes off vertically. Four foreplanes behind the propeller spin freely, as do the wings, allowing the vehicle to fly smoothly through the transition from vertical to horizontal flight. Variants of Daedalus have flown about 100 hr.

In mid-1992 2 more VTOL UAVs were proposed for maritime roles: the General Dynamics "ring wing" and the McDonnell Douglas stopped rotor. The "ring wing" is a 30-yr-old ducted-propeller (wing/duct) concept, demonstrated in 97 tethered flights in 1978. A 1.22-m-diameter model was tested in a low-speed wind tunnel in November–December 1991. The centerbody houses the sensor package forward of the propeller (the avionics is aft of the propeller). In theory, such a vehicle can rise vertically, then tilt over into forward flight. McDonnell Douglas Helicopters proposes a stopped rotor or canard rotor/wing (**CR/W**) based on studies of X-wing fast ground-attack helicopters. As of mid-1992, the company hoped that a demonstrator could fly within 2 yr. CR/W takes off vertically like a helicopter, using a 2-blade propeller tip-driven by gas from a low-bypass-ratio turbofan. At about 135 kt, the rotor is stopped and locked to form a wing; the foreplanes and tail provide lift during conversion and control in airplane mode (engine gases are directed rearward). This configuration offers a high dash speed: a 740-kg UAV can make 375 kt with a 700-lb-thrust Williams F107 cruise-missile engine. It can do even better with more thrust and a slewed wing.

Kaman proposes **Spyglass**, a UAV version of its old meshed-rotor helicopter configuration (as in the SH-2), which, the company asserts, is much simpler and more efficient than a tilt-rotor (the 1,905-kg manned version lifts a 2,725-kg external load). As of mid-1991, Kaman offered Spyglass for production by late 1993, in 3 versions, with 6, 12, or 24 hr of endurance. A manned version, **MMIRA**, flew in December 1991.

AIRBORNE SENSORS

CANADA

APS-504 is standard in Fokker maritime-patrol aircraft, which are operated by Angola, the Netherlands, Pakistan (V3 version), Peru, the Philippines, Spain, and Thailand.

Other users: Australia (GAF Searchmaster L), Brunei (CN-235: APS-504(V)5), China (PRC) (Hanzhong Y-8), Egypt (Navy Beech 1900), Iceland (Coast Guard Twin Otter), Indonesia (GAF Searchmaster L), Malaysia (CN-235), Nigeria (Twin Otter), Taiwan (Grumman S-2T), Thailand (Grumman S-2), and the United States (Customs Service GAF Nomad, Navy Beech 1900 for range safety)

Canada designated this radar **APS-504**, but the (V)2, (V)3, etc., are not formal AN designations. (V)3 is **APS-141(V)**; (V)5 is APS-140(V).

FRANCE

Ocean Master is now a joint venture between Thomson-CSF and Telefunken (part of DASA). The 2-axis stabilized antenna can be 660 × 350 or 940 × 350 or 1,800 × 300 mm (gain 30–34 dB, weight 15 or 27 kg). The tilt is selectable between +4 and -29 deg, and the scan rate is 6–30 rpm (automatically selected by mode; sector scan can be 60–210 deg). The coherent X-band, TWT, pulse-compression transmitter has a peak power of 0.1 or 0.4 kW (for Ocean Master 100 or 400). PRF is 300 Hz–125 kHz. Pulses have a high time-bandwidth product, i.e., they can be relatively short but covering a wide bandwidth. The receiver can maintain automatic TWS on 32 targets. It reduces sea clutter by pulse–pulse and scan–scan integration. Ocean Master can operate in ISAR mode, or it can produce a range profile of the target by using very short pulses.

DRAA-2 *Users:* France (Atlantics), Pakistan (Atlantics)

AGRION 15 *Users:* Bahrein (on helicopters and FPB 62s), Iraq, Israel (Dauphin helicopters), Saudi Arabia (Dauphin helicopters)

IGUANE *Users:* France (Alizés, Atlantique NGs), Italy (modernized Atlantics)

Varan *Users:* Chile (Falcon Guardian 200s), France (Gardians)

ORB-32 *Users:* Algeria (3 on Beech 200Ts), China (PRC) (12 Super-Frélons), France (97 on Nord 262s, Super-Frélons, Lynxes, Alouettes, C-160 Transalls), Indonesia (26 on Cougar/Super Puma helicopters), Kuwait (2 on Cougar/Super Puma helicopters), Portugal (10 on Pumas), Saudi Arabia (6 on Dauphins, 17 on KV-107s), Sweden (19 on KV-107s, 10 on Cougars/Super Pumas; designated Hera [9HCI 100]), and U.A.E. (2 on Cougars/Super Pumas).

Cougar (AS 332F1) flew in 1986 and is offered with an ORB-32/ Exocet combination (also with a dipping sonar).

In March 1993 the French navy selected the Thomson-TRT **Chlio** FLIR, already in service on army helicopters, for the Alizé.

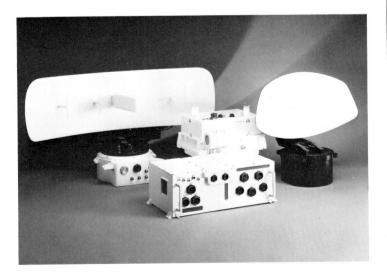

The Thomson-CSF/DASA Sea Master radar is shown with its 2 alternative antennas. (Thomson-CSF)

ISRAEL

EL/M-2022 is a new Elta maritime-surveillance radar for airplanes, helicopters, and UAVs. Features include Doppler beam sharpening, maritime (target) MTI (i.e., MTI for slow surface targets), and TWS for up to 100 targets. (V)1 is a lightweight, digital, remotely controlled radar (50 targets, small ships detected at 70 nm in sea state 3, total weight 85 kg, power 1.8 kW); (V)3 is a long-range version capable of detecting periscopes, with a 100-target track memory. Applications are not known, but EL/M-2022(V)3 may be intended to replace APS-504 on board Westwind maritime-patrol aircraft. It has been offered for installation in P-3s.

UNITED KINGDOM

The GEC-Ferranti **Seaspray/Blue Kestrel** radars are now organized in a single series, announced in August 1991: Seaspray 2000, Seaspray 3000, Seaspray 4000, Blue Kestrel 5000, and Blue Kestrel 6000. Seaspray 3000 is Seaspray Mk 3 on board Lynx helicopters; Blue Kestrel 5000 is the radar developed for the RN version of the EH-101 Merlin helicopter. Seaspray 2000 is a derated version for coastal patrol and fishery protection (EEZ enforcement). It is a 90-kW, X-band, magnetron radar with 2 pulse widths and 4 PRFs; its maximum instrumented range is 100 nm. Seaspray 3000 (formerly Mk 3) uses a high-speed, spin-tuned magnetron (PEAB type), with monopulse tracking in azimuth (to keep it turned toward the target it is illuminating for Sea Skua missiles). Seaspray 4000 is a pulse-compression version of Seaspray, using a TWT. Blue Kestrel 5000 is a pulse-compression radar for helicopters and medium maritime-patrol aircraft, using a planar-array antenna rather than the illuminated paraboloid of Seaspray. Blue Kestrel 5000 is the version adopted for the Merlin (EH-101) helicopter. Blue Kestrel 6000, now in the development stage, combines Blue Kestrel 5000 with some technology from the **Blue Vixen** of the Sea Harrier FRS 2 program. It is a pulse-Doppler radar for both air-to-air detection and surface-target classification (using ISAR). It retains the Blue Kestrel 5000 antenna.

ASV 21 The old **ASV 21** 200-kW X-band surface-search radar, not previously described, survives on board South African C-47s used for maritime surveillance (it was taken from the Shackletons, now retired). The Shackleton airframes have been retained pending the possible installation of new engines. Slow scan (8 rpm) can be selected at all ranges. A sector scan (15–360 deg) can be oriented on any bearing. At an altitude of 300 ft, ASV 21 detects a small surface craft (less than 100 tons) at 22 nm, a large one at 30 nm. At 2,000 ft, the nominal ranges are 38 and 63 nm. Pulse Width/PRF: 0.5 microsec/800 (scan 32 rpm) for 18-and 36-nm scales; 1.0/400 (scan 16 rpm) on 72-nm scale; 2.0/200 (scan 8 rpm) on 170-nm scale.

The Royal Navy is upgrading its 10 **AEW 2A Sea Kings** in 1995–98 with improved **Searchwater** radar, **JTIDS**, and more secure communications (a second Have Quick radio channel). This program was considered preferable to converting some of the new EH-101s to AEW aircraft. Searchwater is being provided with a pulse-Doppler capability to reduce clutter. New **Mk XII IFF** with Modes 1, 2, 3/A, C, and 4 integrated with Searchwater will replace the current **Jubilee Guardsman**, which lacks Mode 4.

Users: Spain (AEW Sea Kings), United Kingdom (AEW Sea Kings, Nimrods). Spain selected Searchwater for P-3 upgrades, but it was never ordered. A reported Indian order for Searchwater for 5 AEW helicopters apparently was never fulfilled.

ASR 360 (also called **ANR 360**) is a standard Racal marine radar with a new antenna.

Users: Oman (15 on Seavans [MPA versions of Skyvan]), United Kingdom (RN Jetstream navigation trainers)

MAREC II *Users:* Algeria (8 F27–400 maritime-patrol aircraft), Cameroon (3 Dornier 128s), India (14 Super-MARECs and 13 MAREC IIs on Dornier 228s for the coast guard, made under license by Hindustan Aeronautics)

The Royal Navy planned to install a new 360-deg-scan **Super Searcher Skua** (Triple S) in rebuilt Lynx helicopters, but this requirement was canceled because of cost in 1988.

Users: Australia (16 S-70B Seahawks), Brazil (10 EMB 111 patrol aircraft), Greece (14 Super Searchers on HU-16 Albatrosses), India (20 Sea King Mk 42Bs), United Kingdom (82 Sea Searchers and Super Searchers on Sea King HAS 5s and 6s)

Seaspray Mk 1 *Users:* Argentina (2 Lynxes), Brazil (23 Lynxes), Denmark (10

Lynxes), Germany (Lynxes: total 34, including Mk 3), Netherlands (22 Lynxes), United Kingdom (76 Lynxes)

Seaspray Mk 3 *Users:* Germany (Sea Kings, replacing ARI 5955), South Korea (14 Lynxes), Turkey (probably 12 for AB 212s)

UNITED STATES

Under the FY94/95 program (as proposed late in 1992), 68 P-3Cs are to be modified to **OASIS** (OTH-T Airborne Sensor Interface) configuration. Desert Storm delayed **Outlaw Viking** (S-3) to FY92; no date for **Outlaw Hawkeye** has been set. The OTH-T aircraft program also includes **Radiant Outlaw** (a feasibility study of a P-3 with LADAR, for target identification and location), **Outlaw Story Teller** (EP-3E), and **Outlaw Seahawk** (SH-60); the latter 2 were included in the FY93 program. **Outlaw Prowler** (EA-6B) is scheduled for FY94, but presumably it depends on whether the EA-6B will be provided with a new ISAR radar.

OASIS I was just too late for the Gulf War (the airplane was later assigned to VP-46). OASIS II is now on board a P-3C of VP-26. All Outlaw Hunter/OASIS aircraft were brought up to the same standard by the summer of 1992. They have stand-alone equipment in the rear of the cabin, but follow-on aircraft will integrate the system into the TACCO station. Outlaw Seahawk differs from Outlaw Hunter/ Viking in that data are down-linked to the mother ship for onward transmission via OTCIXS.

The manufacturer, Loral, claims that the **AAS-38** laser on the F/A-18 can detect and track air targets at ranges of 100+ nm; its track file can carry up to 100 targets. The pilot slaves the system scan to a selected area of the sky, and the system provides synthetic video (i.e., automatically extracted targets) of that area. It then tracks the targets automatically. All of this requires only a software change. Loral claims that the false-alarm rate approaches 4/hr.

Taiwan bought 20 Westinghouse **APG-66** X-band radars for the maritime-strike version of the AT-3 trainer. Norden may have adapted the radar to an antiship FCS. APG-66 is a TWT-driven radar using a 740 × 480–mm planar-array antenna. Air-to-ground modes include real-beam and Doppler-sharpened ground mapping and sea search (i.e., clutter reduction by integration). The APG-66 is in the F-16, in British Hawk ground-attack aircraft (APG-66H), in the RNZAF version of the A-4 (APG-66Z), in the Westinghouse Multi-Sensor Surveillance Aircraft (APG-66SR), in modernized Japanese F-4EJs (to replace APQ-120 radars), and in some U.S. naval training aircraft (including APG-66T in F-5J aggressor aircraft). A locally built version of the GE APG-67, incorporating some APG-66 components, equips the new Taiwanese fighter.

In 1991 the House Appropriations Committee ordered the navy to improve the resolution of **APQ-156** (which equips all A-6Es) for better standoff performance. Norden is proposing an ISAR modification. Funding is problematical.

If Thailand buys P-3As for surveillance, they will probably retain their **APS-80A**s. APS-80 was superseded in P-3Cs by **APS-115**, a pure ATD radar showing only synthetic video; APS-80 shows raw video. Some users feel that, in the hands of a good operator, APS-80 has a better chance of detecting a small target, such as a periscope, in sea clutter.

Users: Portugal (P-3Ps), Spain (P-3As and -3Bs), United States (Naval Reserve P-3Bs)

APS-115 *Users:* Australia (P-3Cs: APS-115B), Iran (P-3Fs), Japan (P-3Cs), Netherlands (P-3Cs), Norway (P-3Cs), United States (P-3Cs)

APS-116 *Users:* Canada (CP-140s and Arcturus aircraft as APS-506), United States (S-3As and EP-3s). AP-506 will get a "spotlight SAR" mode as part of the CP-140 upgrade.

APS-124 *Users:* Japan (SH-60Js), Spain (SH-60s), United States (SH-60B/Fs)

APS-127 *Users:* Denmark (Gulfstream IIIs), United States (coast guard HU-25As)

APS-128 *Users:* Argentina (2 C-212s), Brazil (16 EMB 111s), Chile (8 EMB 111s), Gabon (2 EMB 111s), Indonesia (2 C-130MPs), Japan (22 Beech 200Ts, 2 Falcon Jets), Malaysia (7 C-130MPs), Singapore (5 Skyvans), Spain (1 C-212, 7 C-130MPs), Uruguay (1 C-212, 1 Beech 200T), United States (ILC Aerostats and NASA Skyvans), Venezuela (4 C-212s)

APS-131/135/SLAMMR *Users:* Egypt (ordered for Beech 1900s in 1989), Indonesia (Boeing 737–200s and C-130Hs), Saudi Arabia (C-130Hs), United States (6 HU-25As, 2 HC-130Hs). It is probably on board several other C-130s in the Middle East. Probably 14 have been sold to foreign users.

The Indonesian aircraft are being refurbished; reportedly, they were used in the past only as transports and did not operate their radars. The development contract was signed in September 1989, and Boeing began work in October 1990. The first airplane returned to Seattle in July 1992. The radar will be equipped with a new digital processor and a software-controlled color display system that integrates other sensors with the radar. These aircraft may be fitted with FLIRs and ESM pods. The other 2 aircraft will be refurbished by IPTN in Bandung, Indonesia.

APS-134 *Users:* Germany (Atlantics as modernized), New Zealand (P-3Ks), Portugal (P-3Ps), Pakistan (P-3Cs). Thirty-one were made through 1990.

APS-137 *Users:* Canada (EH-101s), United States (S-3Bs, SH-60B upgrade Block 2, SH-60F, some P-3Cs, EP-3E CILOPs, coast guard HC-130Hs). Current versions: (V)1 for S-3Bs, (V)2 for P-3C Update IIIs, (V)3 planned for abortive P-3C Update IVs (but may be procured to modernize P-3Cs), (V)4 offered to Coast Guard and for similar maritime surveillance. A modified APS-137, probably (V)3, tested in 1991, had upgraded signal-processing circuits that doubled its resolution, from 6 to 3 ft. Texas Instruments calls the new helicopter version APS-137(H). There are 2 alternative antennas, a corporate-fed flatplate (gain 32.5 dB, 1.05 × 15–deg beam) and a parabolic reflector (35 dB gain, 1.3 × 4.5–deg beam, stabilized in tilt); both scan at 6, 60, 120 rpm and in sector and searchlight modes. Peak power is 50 kW (average 500 W).

APS-143 (formerly APS-128PC) *Users:* Taiwan (S-70C(M)1 Seahawks), United States (10 coast guard Aerostats, air force range safety)

RDR 1300 *Users:* Spain (500 Defender), Taiwan (500 Defender)

RDR 1500 *Users:* Portugal (Lynx Mk 95s), United States (coast guard HH-65A Dauphins)

Late in 1991 the 7th Regiment of the Polish Naval Air Force began trials with a TS-11 trainer modified to carry a Bendix **RDS-81** weather radar for surface-ship detection. This TS-11R is to replace the MiG-15UTI (SBLim-2A) reconnaissance versions now being retired. They carried cameras and navigational equipment in the rear seat.

FIRE-CONTROL SYSTEMS

FRANCE

Thomson-CSF's **AMSCOS** (Airborne Maritime Situation Control System) is, in effect, a next-generation successor to **TRES/TREW**, using the newer **Ocean Master** radar and **DR 3000**, combined with a Sextant Avionique Nadir Mk II inertial-navigation system. The simplest version, AMSCOS 100, for customs and coast guard aircraft, is limited to the radar and an altitude/heading reference system. AMSCOS 200, for medium aircraft with an antiship mission, has the full inertial reference system, as well as a FLIR (the TRT **Clio**) and **DR 3000**. AMSCOS 300 adds a sonobuoy processor (**Sadang 1000**), a MAD, a data link (Link W), and a dedicated tactical computer (in AMSCOS 100 and 200 the radar processor suffices for the tactical software). A helicopter version of AMSCOS 300 would use the Thomson Sintra **HS 312** dipping sonar.

TRES combines **VARAN** with an ESM set, probably **DR 3000A**, as an **Exocet** targeting system, either for the airplane carrying it or for surface craft (via a data link). The first buyer was Chile, for 2 Exocet-firing Falcon 200 aircraft (1990). The new Super Pumas (which carry Exocets and which fly from the "County" class) are similarly equipped. They are to be replaced by Eurocopter AS 532C Cougars, which will also carry Exocets.

Chile also ordered a simpler system, TREW, which is VARAN plus a radar warner, for 4 SA.565 Panther helicopters, but the helicopter order was canceled because of late delivery.

AIR-LAUNCHED MISSILES AND GUIDED BOMBS

Deletions: The Argentine **Martin Pescador** is probably no longer in service. The U.S. **FOG-S** program was canceled.

CHINA (PRC)

C-601 was exported to Iran and Iraq.

FRANCE

Matra's proposed **ARF** (*Anti-Radar Futur*) is a study of a family of future ARMs boosted by a "rustic" Matra-Omera ramjet. ARF would be integrated into an aircraft's detection and jamming systems, to protect low-altitude penetrators against SAM-associated surveillance and FCS radars. ARF has to be light to be accommodated in the secondary loading positions of attack aircraft, such as Rafale; the ramjet offers a combination of compactness (less than 200 kg) with excellent payload and speed. Presumably, ARF competes with Aerospatiale's **STAR**.

AS 12 *Users:* Chile (10 Alouette-IIIs), Egypt (24 SA 342 L Gazelles), France (Lynx helicopters), Greece (4 Alouette-IIIs), Libya (12 Alouette-IIIs). This missile was probably exported to Indonesia with the Wasp helicopters for the ex-British "Tribal"-class frigates (it was replaced by Sea Skua in British naval service). Other buyers, which may well use the missile from shipboard helicopters, are Argentina (Alouette-IIIs, 500 Defender aircraft), India (Alouette-IIIs [Chetaks] on *Leanders*), Iran (AB212s), the Netherlands (Lynxes), Nigeria (Lynxes on the *Aradu*), Saudi Arabia, Spain (AB212s), and the U.A.E. (Alouette-IIIs on FPB 62s). Other buyers were: Brunei, Gabon, Germany, Iraq, Italy (presumably, all Italian naval helicopters carry Marte), Ivory Coast, Kuwait, Madagascar, Norway, Qatar, Tunisia, the United Kingdom (which replaced AS 12s with Sea Skuas), and Venezuela.

The unit cost was $76,000 in 1987. AS 12 was cleared for carriage on board Atlantic and Alizé fixed-wing aircraft and also on board Gazelle, Lynx, AB212, Wessex, and Wasp helicopters.

Development of **AS 15TT** was financed as part of a Saudi program; the first deliveries were in March 1985. About 276 missiles had been delivered by the end of 1990. AS 15TT is *not* a standard French navy weapon (AS 12 is still used; only about 32 AS 15TT missiles were bought for the French navy, for trials). During the war against Iraq, the Royal Saudi Navy reported firing AS 15TTs from its Dauphin helicopters against 5 Iraqi patrol boats.

Users: Bahrein (20, for Dauphin helicopters on board the FPB 62s), Chile (Dauphins), Iraq (60 purchased in 1989), Israel (Dauphins), Saudi Arabia (254, for helicopters flying from *Al Madinah*–class frigates)

AS 30 *Users:* France (827), Germany (about 1,200), India (about 50), Iraq (70), Peru (about 50), South Africa (1,072), Switzerland (about 285), United Kingdom (probably about 550); some may also have been delivered to Israel.

AS 30L *Users:* Egypt (30), France (235), Iraq (about 240, out of 586 ordered), Jordan (10; may have canceled the order when the Mirage 2000 order was canceled). Deliveries to Iraq were suspended because of nonpayment; Iraq wanted to set up its own production line.

French air force aircraft fired a total of 60 AS 30Ls during the Gulf War, with 95% hits claimed (these weapons are also carried by Super-Étendards). The estimated unit cost is $600,000.

About 1,640 **ARMAT/MARS** have been made; ARMAT entered service in 1984 (development began in 1980). The estimated unit cost is $260,000. MARS is an ARMAT development now in the study stage. Of the earlier related **MARTEL**, 1,065 **AJ 168**s and 3,172 **AS 37**s were made.

Users: Egypt, Kuwait, Iraq, France

GERMANY

The **Kormoran 2**s currently on order are remanufactured **Kormoran 1**s.

Users: Germany (350 Kormoran 1s for Tornado strike aircraft, 262 Kormoran 2s on order), Italy (60 for Tornado strike aircraft)

UNITED KINGDOM

ALARM antiradar missiles intended for tactical trials were used successfully in the Gulf War instead. 121 were fired on 52 sorties. This missile was sold to Saudi Arabia in 1991.

Sea Eagle has been tested on board the Chilean CASA/Embraer T-36 trainer (the A-36 attack version can carry 2). The estimated unit cost was $740,000 in 1991.

Users: Chile (20 ordered for A-36Ms), India (on Sea Kings; may be bought for maritime-strike Jaguars), Saudi Arabia (for Tornadoes, ordered in 1985), United Kingdom (Sea Harrier, Tornado, and Buccaneer aircraft)

Sea Skua (CL 834) *Users:* Australia (4 on a rack on each side of the S-70 helicopter), Bahrein (FPB 62 helicopters), Brazil (about 40 for Lynxes), Germany (156 on Sea Kings), South Korea (about 126 for Lynxes), Turkey (about 120 for 10 AB212s

with Sea Spray radars), United Kingdom (about 350 for Lynxes). Portugal bought the Lynx helicopter for MEKO frigates and thus may adopt Sea Skua. A version for the Indian Dornier 228 was developed, but the requirement lapsed when the aircraft were bought for the Indian coast guard (the planned naval purchase was deferred). The German purchase comprised 140 warshot missiles, 4 telemetry missiles, and 12 missiles for training.

The unit cost of Sea Skua (FY91) is $316,600, based on the sale to Germany. By the end of 1989, more than 750 had been ordered.

UNITED STATES

In recent years, the U.S. program for advanced strike warfare R&D (6.2/6.3 program) has included work on a solid FAE warhead (completed in FY90), on an integrated fiber-optic gyro on a chip (tested in FY91; completed in FY92), on a passive IR/active RF neural-net ship classifier and aim-point selector (begun in FY91; tested in FY93), on a modular reconfigurable missile computer (demonstrated in FY92), and on a reduced-signature (i.e., low-smoke) solid rocket fuel. The navy portion of the Desert Storm weapon-replacement package included 290 **Tomahawk**s, 2,033 **HARM**s, 8 **SLAM**s, 6000 **Mk 83** bombs, and 800 **Mk 83 LGB** kits.

Texas Instruments won the **AIWS** competition in December 1991 (the contract was not formally awarded until July 1992). The required 24-nm range had already been demonstrated. AIWS was then joined with the air force's standoff weapon program under the title **JSOW** (Joint Standoff Weapon). The air force's stealthy **Tri-SSAM** (Senior Pennant: AGM/MGM-137) is to supersede the navy's companion requirement for a long-range successor to **SLAM** (ASWS). Delays in TSSAM now seem to justify further SLAM production. The baseline AIWS design was changed to incorporate a GPS receiver for better accuracy. Preplanned product improvement (P3I) is to begin in FY94, to provide improved terminal guidance (an IIR seeker), data links, a unitary warhead (the baseline carries **BLU-97** bomblets; this version could accommodate the 500- and 1,000-lb bombs planned under the **ABF** program), and to suit the weapon for attacking an expanded target set. This version will probably cost 2–3 times as much as the baseline (which was to cost $50 thousand in FY85 dollars, or $58.6 thousand in FY90 dollars). As of late 1991, the navy planned to buy 300 AIWSs in the first year of production and 1,500 in the second year. The initial contract was for a 61-month engineering and manufacturing effort.

Northrop's **TSSAM** is to have a unitary or submunition warhead and autonomous guidance. TSSAM will be air- or ground-launched (MGM-137, from the MLRS launcher). Plans call for a total of 8,650 for the three services (TSSAM would be carried by A-6Es, F/A-18s, B-2s, and B-52s). The missile is subsonic and weighs about 2,300 lb. The range of the air-launched version is 100+ nm but less than 600 km (ground-launched less than 500 km), i.e., inside INF/START limits. The estimated $15.1 billion total program cost amounts to $1.75 million per missile, but that presumably includes research and development. The program reportedly encountered severe technical problems before the first flight in June 1992. Because TSSAM has been touted as the means by which the B-2 will perform effectively in nonnuclear war (and hence the key to the airplane's future), the navy and army have expressed some skepticism as to the air force's claim of a fully successful test; both planned to test the missile themselves (it was to fly from an A-6E during the summer of 1992). Northrop received the initial contract in 1986; Boeing is the second-source producer.

The U.S. Navy is buying 1,200 **GBU-24** hard-target penetrators, as ordered by the CNO after the end of the Gulf War. In about 1987 the U.S. Navy decided to reduce its reliance on such LGBs because they expose the operator to AAW fire.

Bullpup (AGM-12) *Users:* Australia, Denmark, France (replaced by AS 12), Norway, Greece, Turkey, United Kingdom, and United States (no longer in service)

Some Block III **HARM**s were used in the Gulf War; Block III is a software change to Block II. The **LCS** program was terminated in FY91 (preproduction seekers were made). A-6s fired about 148 HARMs in the Gulf, 75% in the first 5 days. On 28 January 1991 a total of 1,328 were ordered, as a modification to the FY91 budget, including 749 for the U.S. Navy, 74 for Italy, and 40 for South Korea. As of 1990, the requirement was for 7,672 missiles for the U.S. Navy and 7,821 for the U.S. Air Force, down from 8,054 and 9,006 as stated in 1985. Procurement: FY90, 1,162; FY91, 1,320 (1,400 requested; later increased to 2,261); FY92, 749; FY93, 215 (requested, later withdrawn). As of 1987, the unit cost was about $285,000; in 1991 it was

JSOW
CONFIGURATIONS

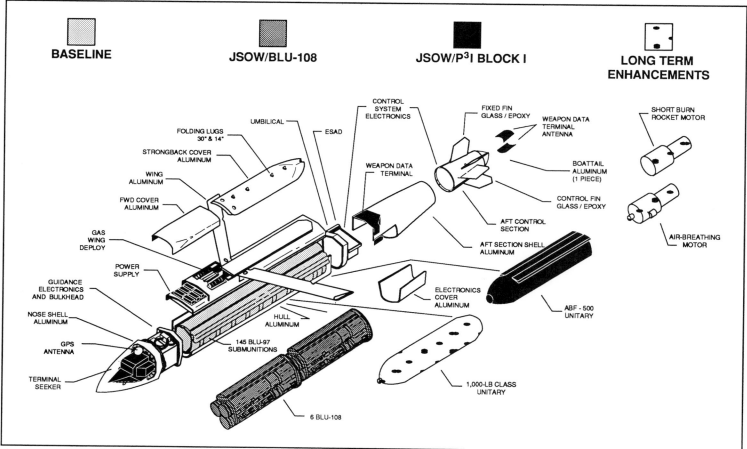

AIWS-TR0069,i B

Alternative configurations for JSOW, Texas Instruments's successful entrant in the AIWS competition. (Texas Instruments)

$281,000. The thousandth missile was delivered on 26 August 1986, and the five thousandth missile was delivered in September 1988. A 30 June 1991 Selected Acquisition Report gave a total program cost of $7,252.7 million for 22,669 missiles, i.e., a unit cost of about $320,000.

Users: Germany (announced in 1985, for Tornadoes; 1,000 ordered in 1987), Italy (September 1991), Japan (announced in January 1987), Spain (for EF-18s), South Korea, United States. Australia has expressed interest, partly inspired by the missile's performance in the Libyan raids.

No **Maverick**s were included in the FY92/93 budget submitted in February 1991. Through 1991, 60,595 had been made.

Users: Egypt, Germany, Greece, Iran, Israel, Jordan, Kuwait, Morocco, New Zealand, Pakistan, Portugal, Saudi Arabia, Singapore, South Korea, Sweden, Switzerland, Taiwan, Thailand, Turkey, United States, Yugoslavia.

In 1993 Texas Instruments obtained air force funding for preliminary work on a turbojet-powered Longhorn version of Maverick. Changes in the missile are to be minimized; existing Mavericks would be converted to Longhorn configuration. The currently planned engine, the Allison Model 150, was originally to have powered the fiber-optically guided version of Skipper. Six engines were made before that program ended. Texas Instruments estimates that, dropped from 30,000 ft and cruising at about 1,000 ft, Longhorn would have a range of about 41 nm without any attempt to extend the range by trajectory shaping. Longhorn may compete with the product-improved version of JSOW. Texas Instruments claims that development would cost only $75–80 million, compared to about $400 million for the next stage in JSOW. During the summer of 1992 a hovering Cobra attack helicopter, using its night targeting system, successfully launched the navy version of Maverick. Texas Instruments is, therefore, trying to interest the navy in buying Maverick

to arm LAMPS helicopters. The current navy position favors Hellfire because it provides more shots per helicopter, to deal with numerous, very small attacking boats. Texas Instruments's reply is that Maverick offers far greater range (10+ km from the hover, 13 km when launched at 100 kt with a lightweight warhead). Maverick has also been test-fired by a P-3, and U.S. P-3s are now being fitted to carry it.

In 1993 Hughes finally received some official support for the turbojet-powered long-endurance Longhorn version of Maverick. (Author)

SHIP- AND GROUND-LAUNCHED ANTISHIP MISSILES

CHINA (PRC)

C-801 is **HY-5**. An air-launched version of **C-802** is being developed. The H-7 interdictor/strike aircraft has been offered in the naval role carrying C-801 missiles. The NATO nickname for C-801 is CSS-NX-4 (Sardine); for C-802, CSS-NX-8 (Saccade).

Users:—C-801: China (PRC) (1 Wuhan-class submarine, Luhu, Jianghu III, Jangwei [EF-30] classes), Iran (will probably arm new Houku class), Thailand (Jianghu class)

—HY-2: Bangladesh (Jianghu, Huangfeng, Houku classes), China (PRC) (Luda, Jianghu, Huangfeng, and Houku classes), Egypt (Jianghu and Houku classes, also coast-defense version), Iran (coast-defense version), Iraq (coast-defense version), North Korea (Huangfeng class and probably coast-defense version), Pakistan (Houku, Huangfeng classes)

FRANCE

As of mid-1993, ANS is effectively dead; Aerospatiale is seeking partners for a new ASMP-C, which marries the body and engine of the strategic ASMP to the Exocet Block II seeker and ANS warhead. Development is expected to take about 5 yr at a cost of FFr 2 Billion (approximately $350 million). ANS may yet be revived if the French and German economies improve. Its manufacturers claimed that ANS enjoyed far better terminal maneuverability than its Russian and Chinese rivals. Range is 100 km [55 nm] in lo-lo-lo profile, or 200–250 km [110–137 nm] in lo-hi-lo or hi-hi-lo profile. The maneuverability limit is 15 G (compared to 6 G for Exocet).

MM 15, a surface-launched version of **AS 15TT**, was announced in February 1992. It has been tested on board a 20-m Simmoneau Marine patrol boat, equipped with a twin-arm launcher. Kuwait has ordered similar boats, but as of October 1992 no MM 15 customer had appeared. The range is 15 km [8.2 nm], with a 30-kg [66-lb] warhead. Earlier attempts to market a surface version of AS 15TT were not successful.

Exocet Users:—Shipboard versions: Argentina (MM 40: MEKO 360s and 140s, 35 MM 38s for A-69s), Bahrein (an estimated 26 MM 40s for FPB 62s and TNC 45s), Belgium (8 MM 38s for *Wielingen* class), Brazil (an estimated 26 MM 40s in *Inhaúma* and *Niteroi* classes; 10 MM 38s bought), Brunei (16 MM 38s for *Waspada* class), Cameroon (9 MM 40s for P48S class), Chile (16 MM 38s for "Counties" [except *Latorre*], *Leander*s [*Condell, Lynch*], and *Alm. Williams* class), Colombia (24 MM 38s for FS-1500 class), Ecuador (an estimated 30 MM 40s for *Wadi M'ragh* class, 12 MM 38s for *Quito* class), France (a total of 154 MM 38s and an estimated 72 MM 40s; MM 40 in *Cassard, La Fayette, Floréal* classes and *Aconit*; MM 38 in *Georges Leygues, Tourville, Suffren, Cdt. Rivière* classes and *Duperré*; 2 MM 38s or 4 MM 40s in A-69 class), Germany (350 MM 38s for *Hamburg* and S143/143A/143B/148 classes), Greece (56 MM 38s for Combattante IIs and 4 of 10 Combattante IIINs), Indonesia (26 MM 38s for *Fatahilah*, PSK Mk 6 classes and *Hajar Dewantara*), Kuwait (bought 45 MM 40s for FPB 57s and TNC 45s; had to be replaced during the war), Malaysia (an estimated 62 MM 38s for FS-1500, Spica-M, and Combattante II 4AL classes; MM 40s in new corvettes), Morocco (20 MM 38s for 4 *Lazaga* class; also bought 4 MM 40s), Nigeria (MM 38s in Combattante IIIB class), Oman (MM 40s in "Province" class and new corvettes; bought 10 MM 38s and an estimated 38 MM 40s), Peru (17 MM 38s for PR-72 class), Philippines (new *Kormoran* class, being built by Bazan), Qatar (an estimated 44 MM 40s for Combattante III class, more for new corvettes), Thailand (12 MM 38s for *Ratcharit* class), U.A.E. (32 MM 40s for FPB 38s and TNC 45s, more for new Type 62s), Tunisia (an estimated 27 MM 40s for Combattante IIIs), United Kingdom (300 MM 38s for Type 22 Batch 1/2s, Type 21s, *Leander*s). Another 172 MM 38s and 121 MM 40s are not accounted for (but may be for coast defense, below).

—Coast Defense: Qatar (2 batteries of MM 40s), Thailand (10 batteries of MM 40s ordered in 1986). The British MM 38s at Gibraltar have been withdrawn.

—Submarine version: France (79 bought through 1989 for strategic and attack submarines; operational in 1985 and still in production, probably 12/yr 1990–91). This missile may be offered to Spain to equip the new Scorpene-type submarines.

—Airborne version (AM 39): Argentina (30 for Super-Étendards and 2 L-188 patrol aircraft), Brazil (Super Pumas), Chile (Super Pumas on "County" class), France (70 for Super-Étendards, Atlantique Mk 2s), Iraq (an estimated 770 ordered, 250 delivered through 1982), Indonesia (Super Pumas), Pakistan (28 for Sea Kings, Atlantics), Peru (Super Pumas from cruisers), Qatar (an estimated 12), Saudi Arabia (Super Pumas), Venezuela (for air force Mirage V fighters, now being equipped)

China (PRC) reportedly obtained some Exocets in April 1985 via a third party, possibly using them as a basis for the C-801 missile, and there have been reports of Brazilian production under license.

MM 40 Block II is an upgrade revealed at the 1991 Paris Air Show; it had been a French "black" program. The missile can cork-screw to evade terminal defenses. It can also dogleg, changing direction by up to 90 deg. It can fly a self-adapting sea-skimming profile in sea states up to 7, and it has better ECCM. The range, about 70 km, is not affected. The missile can select targets (i.e., it has some form of target identifier on board). A new FCS, ITL/ITS 70, allows multiple targets to be engaged, fires salvos against more than 1 target and converging salvo on 1 target. Compared to earlier Exocet FCSs, it reduces operator workload. Block II was sold to 5 customers in 1992, probably Malaysia (corvettes), Oman (corvettes), Qatar (coast defense), Philippines (new 57-m patrol boats building in Spain), and Saudi Arabia (coast defense). Tests of a parallel AM 39 Block 2 were completed early in 1993.

An improved fuze (for better ECCM) is being marketed for MM 38 upgrades.

The French *Trident*-class patrol boats originally carried **SS 12Ms**, and reportedly they can be remounted.

Users: Gabon (*Gen. N. Boulinguï*), Greece (*Kelefstis Stamou* class), Libya (*Susa*-class fast attack boats), and Tunisia (P 48–class patrol boats)

ISRAEL

Radically new information is now available on **Gabriel**'s guidance and program status. Gabriel apparently adopted the beam-riding command guidance of the earlier Italian **Sea Killer**. However, it has semiactive terminal guidance, comparing returns in receiving antennas on either side of the missile's nose, each covering a 5- or 6-deg sector (Sea Killer has no terminal seeker). An operator (watching the missile's tail flares from the 2-person **OG 20** director slaved to the radar) manually steers the missile (by joystick) into the beam of the **RTN-10X** or **EL/M-2221** radar. As a backup, the missile can be command-steered all the way to the target; the command channel is also used to turn on (or off, in the event of jamming) the terminal seeker. The Israeli **TADS/RTN-10X** probably duplicates the abortive Italian **Mariner/SPQ-711**, except that it adds provision to turn on the seeker.

The original version of the system, which used a simple **OG.R7** optical sight to track the missile, survives on board the 3 Taiwanese *Sumner*-class destroyers converted under the first Taiwanese upgrade program, **Tien Hsi** (= Angel, i.e., Gabriel) in the mid-1970s; the sight is carried between the 2 Mk 51 directors and the twin 40-mm guns aft (in the later Wu Chin II destroyers, OG 20 replaces the old U.S. Mk 37 director). The simple version is probably also in the Thai *Prabrarapak* class.

OG 20 is better adapted to the command backup mode, in which 1 operator tracks the flare in the missile's tail, the other the target; it has an open sight for initial target acquisition. Presumably, the director is stabilized (the Israelis initially abandoned pure joystick guidance mainly because their boats rolled and pitched too badly). OG 20 is on board Israeli missile boats (including those for Chile and South Africa) and also on board boats converted to fire Gabriel for Ecuador and Kenya.

Gabriel II, the current production version (which appeared in 1972) accommodates a larger warhead in the same airframe by adopting a higher-thrust sustainer motor grain. The seeker may have an antijam mode and some antiradar capability.

War experience in 1973 showed a need for an active seeker. **Gabriel III** was designed and built, but the longer-range U.S. Harpoon was bought instead; tactics envisage firing a mixture of fire-and-forget Harpoons and short-range Gabriels. Work on **Gabriel IV** was abandoned, but the designation has been reserved for a future missile.

Gabriel Users: Argentina (provision for Gabriel II in 4 Israeli-supplied Daburs), Chile (Sa'ar 2/4s), Ecuador (*Manta* class), Israel, Kenya (37.5-m and 32-m boats, bought in 1979: Gabriel IIs), Singapore (FPB 45 class, provision for 2 each on 12 "Swifts"), South Africa (Sa'ar 3), Taiwan (bought in 1978), Thailand (*Prabrarapak* class). Iran reportedly received 200 Gabriels in 1987; Malaysia also reportedly received some missiles. If, as seems likely, Gabriel guidance is much like that of Sea Killer, the Iranian Gabriels may have been intended to arm the Iranian Vosper frigates.

Estimated production: 1,982 Gabriel I/IIs as of 1991; the estimated current production rate is 120/yr.

ITALY

Otomat *Users:*—Surface: Egypt (6 October and *Ramadan* classes), Iran (status unknown), Iraq (*Wadi M'ragh* class, now for sale), Italy (Mk 2s in *Garibaldi, Mimbelli, Audace, Maestrale, Lupo, Sparviero* classes), Kenya (Mk 1s in "Province" class), Libya (*Dat Assawari, Wadi M'ragh* classes), Nigeria (Mk 1s in *Aradu* and FPB 57 class), Peru (Mk 2s in *Alm. Grau* [planned but not fitted] and *Lupo* class), Saudi Arabia (Mk 2 ERATOs in *Al Madinah* class), and Venezuela (Mk 2s in *Lupos* and Mk 1s in 3 of 6 *Constitución* class). A projected Philippine Otomat-armed missile boat seems not to have materialized. This missile was reported in Argentina and Brazil, but it cannot be traced on board any ship (it may have been the coastal version, or a small number for testing).

—Coast defense: Egypt (30 missiles) and Saudi Arabia (155 missiles) use Otomat, mounted on a 6 × 6 Berliet chassis.

By September 1990, 910 Otomat missiles had been ordered for export. A French missile costs $523,900; an Italian missile costs $514,800.

A planned upgrade program (**Otomat Mk 3**) is based on work done on **MILAS**. The current analog circuitry would be replaced by digital alternatives, including a data bus connecting the seeker to a more-powerful onboard computer. The computer might be fed with target data so that the missile could attack a selected point on the target. The missile may use some form of ISAR to recognize a selected target from an array of ships. Reportedly, the computer improves ECCM and makes a (presumably programmed) terminal evasive maneuver possible. Because the missile is fully digital, and because it shares the same computer as MILAS, the same digital FCS may be able to handle both MILAS and Otomat Mk 3 interchangeably. Presumably, existing missiles can be remanufactured to Mk 3 standards.

A projected higher-speed version, **Otomach**, was dropped because Matra Defense argued that speed was no longer a guarantee of penetration.

The existing Italian **ERATO** system can launch 8 missiles (at 3-sec intervals) at 6 targets.

Marte uses the same beam-riding FCS as Gabriel, but with an Otomat active terminal seeker. Marte can now be fired by a modified MB 339; a Marte 2A was test-fired this way on 17 June 1992. The airplane was fitted with a new inertial platform, Doppler velocity sensor, and navigation/attack computers to program the missile. Target data appeared on the pilot's HUD. Since the MB 339 lacks a radar, targeting data must come from a third party. The modified aircraft is designated MB 339AM; it carries the same systems as the new MB 339C bought by the RNZAF.

Users: Italy (450 Mk 1s, 180 Mk 2s), Venezuela (100, for AB 212 helicopters). This missile may also have been exported to Peru (for AB 212 helicopters).

Sea Killer *Users:* Iran (160 sold for *Saam* class). This missile hit at least 6 ships (total 280,975 GRT) during the Iran-Iraq war, beginning in October 1986 and ending in February 1987; 2 warheads failed to explode.

NORWAY

Penguin (AGM-119) *Users:* Greece (60 Mk 2s for last 6 Combattante III class; probably others for S-70 helicopters), Norway (225 Mk 1s, 175 Mk 2s, an estimated 85 Mk 3s [with about 50 more required] for *Oslo, Hauk, Snøgg, Storm* classes and F-16 fighters), Spain (reportedly purchased in 1988 for *Lazaga* and *Barcelo* classes, but these ships do not carry missiles in peacetime), Sweden (180 Mk 2s for *Hugin* class), Turkey (40 Mk 2s for *Kartal* class), United States (for LAMPS III helicopters, as AGM-119). After the Kongsberg machine tool scandal, requests from Indonesia, Singapore, Thailand, and Venezuela were rejected. As of 1990, Japan was interested in buying Penguin for SH-60J helicopters. Missiles may be sold to Brazil (for S-2E aircraft) and to Indonesia.

As of March 1990, NFT was reportedly beginning a new program, possibly to be called **Penguin Mk 4**, with 2 external boosters, for more range, composite construction, and a new computer. The missile might also be provided with a new seeker (mm-wave, semi-active laser, dual-mode IR/laser). A future upgrade may provide submunitions for land attack, a better IIR seeker, and better ECM resistance.

SWEDEN

RBS 15 *Users:* Croatia (*King Petar Kresimir IV* class), Finland (15M: *Helsinki* classes and coast defense), Sweden (*Stockholm, Göteborg* classes, coast defense, and JAS 37 fighters [15F version]), Yugoslavia (coast defense).

As of the end of 1990, 526 missiles had been made or ordered (an estimated 139 RBS 15s plus 426 15Fs [through 1991] plus 29 15Ms in 1992) at an estimated unit cost of $525,000. In 1991 Saab received a contract for a mid-life upgrade, **TSA** (*Tungt Styrt Attackvapen*, or Precision-Guided Attack Weapon), for JAS 37 and 39 fighters attacking point targets in coastal waters. The missile will have a dogleg capability from the mid-1990s. Other likely improvements

are TERNA (terrain navigation) and automatic target recognition (using IIR, television, or imaging radar). These techniques were not yet under contract as of mid-1992, but the Swedish government was interested. The earlier **RBS 04** is still operational, awaiting replacement by RBS 15F.

TAIWAN

Where Gabriel II packs a more powerful motor into much the same space, **Hsiung Feng I** was lengthened to provide greater range with the same propellant. It encountered problems such as motor cracks and aerodynamic heating just abaft the cruciform wings. A new propellant had to be bought, and the modified missile became **Hsiung Feng IA**. Hsiung Feng I/IA probably entered service in about 1977, Taiwan having bought only 3 Gabriel systems (designated Hsi An, i.e., Angel, for *Sumner*-class destroyers). The missile's guidance system is almost certainly identical to that of Gabriel. In a *Hai Ou–* class fast attack boat, the system's sensors are the search radar (**UPS-60**), a periscope, and a tracker radar (**SPG-24**, now sometimes **SPG-21A** with a very different antenna). The consoles are side by side in that order below decks. The tracker is assigned to a target picked up by the search radar. The periscope tracks the flare in the missile's tail, to gather it into the guidance beam. It may continue to track the missile (as feedback) as the missile flies to the target. The operator in the center sees not a TV picture but an oscilloscope trace; it is probably a correlogram of the tracker and the periscope (electro-optics). As the missile approaches the target, the oscilloscope trace becomes narrower and steeper.

Hsiung Feng II is unique in using a multiple self-forging fragment (SFF) warhead (about 20 such fragments in all). All other anti-ship warheads are either blast-fragmentation or shaped-charge. This warhead is officially described as larger and heavier than that of Harpoon. The dual seeker is almost certainly a local development. A recent Hsiung Feng II shows a new IR seeker radome shape, like that of **Mistral**. Both the radar and the IR seeker are turned on simultaneously as the missile reaches the predicted target area. Each has a programmed set of predicted target returns; the guidance computer compares the inputs from both. If either deviates from the allowed range, it is assumed to be jammed, and homing shifts to the unjammed sensor. The radar uses a planar-array antenna, i.e., monopulse rather than conscan. Radar ECCM features include resistance to RGPO, a resistance reportedly due to reprogrammable software.

Hsiung Feng II is powered by a Microturbo 078 engine, the same as that in Otomat and RBS 15; the 078 burns JP-5 fuel. The maximum range is said to be "considerably farther than Harpoon." The missile's diameter is 5 cm greater than that of Harpoon, and the length is about the same, so if both have about the same length (50%) devoted to fuel, Hsiung Feng II has about 30% more fuel volume. Hsiung Feng II entered production for coast-defense service in 1991. It will also be carried on board the new *Perry*-class frigates (2 × 4-round box launchers), and an official model shows it on board a Wu Chin I destroyer. The surface-launched version entered service in 1992. An air-launched version will enter service in 1993. Development began in 1983.

UNITED KINGDOM

On 24 June 1992 the Royal Navy announced that it was seeking proposals for a long-range antiship missile, the **Surface-to-Surface Guided Weapon** (Naval Staff Target 7021) to arm the Future Frigate. Initial proposals were due on 24 August. At that time the likely contenders were **Harpoon Block ID** or its successor, **ANS**; an improved version of **Sea Eagle**; **Otomat Mk 2**; and a modified **Tomahawk**. The U.S. government specially cleared Tomahawk for sale to Britain, for air- or surface-launching (originally for an RAF requirement, SR(A) 1236, as **Air Hawk**, in 1991). The version offered to the Royal Navy has a significantly shorter range (it uses a Continental J402 engine instead of the Williams F107) and different guidance (GPS/INS/IIR plus data link). The airframe will also be different. Reportedly, Harpoon is currently favored. A Cardinal Points Specification will probably be released late in 1993. Reportedly, the required range is 150–300 km [82–164 nm], and the missile will have to attack corvettes and frigates of up to 4,000 tons, as well as fast attack craft.

The Royal Navy is also reportedly interested in a standoff missile to attack point targets ashore. McDonnell Douglas is offering **SLAM**, which can be fired from a Harpoon canister.

UNITED STATES

PSI (Precision Strike Initiative) is a project of the Office of Naval Technology begun in 1991 (to continue through 1996, with technology demonstration in 1994). The goal of PSI is to develop a Tomahawk capability for autonomous attack imaging sensors (IR, laser, and SAR) against mobile targets. Such sensors produce vast amounts of data, which require processing to compare with stored images. PSI, therefore, includes work on parallel processing, automatic target recognition, and, presumably, neural networks.

The Martin Marietta **SLAT** supersonic target was canceled in 1992. However, a new SLAT program is now beginning. In August 1992 the navy announced performance requirements: a speed of at least Mach 2.1 (with a goal of 2.36), a maximum sea-skimming altitude of 30 ft, a maneuverability of 8 G (S-turn) 12–7 nm from the end point (with a goal of 10 G at a range of 12–5 nm). Either a ship or an airplane is to launch SLAT. These characteristics presumably reflect those of current or projected foreign weapons (such as SS-N-22 and ANS), but any SLAT meeting the requirements could also be a basis for a future U.S. antiship weapon. The navy received 15 replies to an earlier request for information (pre-RFP). A draft RFP was expected by September 1992, with up to $300 million available for the new SLAT program.

As of February 1992, the unit price of **Hellfire** was $50,500.

Users: Israel (patrol boats), Sweden (RBS-17, on coast and on board patrol boats), Taiwan (on board helicopters that can be carried on shipboard, also possibly ships), United States (PBC, in SWPS mounting). Taiwan also plans to fire Hellfire from **Chaparral** launchers. Sweden has offered Taiwan the special Swedish antiship warhead. U.S. LAMPS helicopters will probably be adapted to fire Hellfire because the Penguin missiles now in service are much larger than needed to deal with small attack boats.

Harpoon Block ID's operational evaluation was completed in 1992, and production was authorized; the first retrofitted IDs (formerly ICs) will be delivered in 1993.

Block ID is 175.0 in long, compared to 151.5 in for IC and 177.0 in for **SLAM** (air-launched versions; sea-launched versions are 206.0, 182.5, and 206.2 in, respectively). Weights (air/sea): 1,400/1,750, 1,160/1,520, and 1,360/1,710 lb. Official ranges: 100+ nm for ID (unofficially reported as 240 km, or about 130 nm), 67+ nm for IC, 50+ nm for SLAM. Block ID is too long to be fired from a submarine. For submarines, Block ICs will be modified to incorporate the Block ID re-attack (cloverleaf) maneuver, but will not be given the extra range. The U.S. Navy first flew the modified IC version on 4 September 1991.

Harpoon production for the U.S. Navy was planned to end with 167 bought in FY91. SLAM: FY92, 110; FY93, 70; FY94, request for 75 (plus 6 for the Reserves). 122 Harpoons (for export) were bought in FY92. A 30 June 1991 (end of FY91) Selected Acquisition Report indicates a total planned U.S. program of 3,698 missiles, at a cost of $3,745.3 million (FY91), or $1.01 million each, which seems excessive. This figure may include ancillary equipment and R&D costs.

Combat use: Gulf of Sidra (March 1986: 3 engagements, 5 Har-

HELLFIRE MISSILE
U. S. ARMY DESIGNATION AGM-114A, B, C, AND F

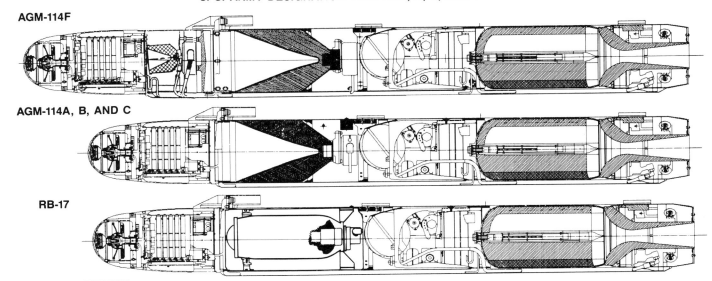

MODULAR
MAXIMUM WEIGHT KG/LBS

45.704/100.86	Laser (A, B, and C Models)
48.6/107	Laser (F Model)
47.88/105	RF/IR
47.88/105	IIRS
48.25/106	RB-17

LENGTH MM/IN.

1625.6/64.0	Laser A, B, and C Models
1803.4/71.0	Laser (F Model)
1727.2/68.0	RF/IR
1778.0/70.0	IIRS
1625/64.0	RB-17

SEEKER CONFIGURATION
Laser
Radio Frequency/Infrared (RF/IR)
Imaging Infrared System (IIRS)
Millimeter Wave (mmW)

PLATFORMS

QUALIFIED	INTEGRATED	APPLICATIONS	QUALIFIED	INTEGRATED	APPLICATIONS
U.S. AH-64	CUCV	F-16	FOREIGN SDS	A129	HARRIER
AH-1W	M-113	F/A-18		LYNX	F-5E
OH-58D	SHIPS	AV-8B		S-70	F-4
MD-530	OV-10D	A-10		BO 105	PUMA
UH-60	AH-66	AC-130			GAZELLE
HMMWV	CHAPARRAL	BRADLEY			PATROL BOAT
		UH-1			WIESEL
		LAV			

Rockwell International
Tactical Systems Division
1800 Satellite Boulevard
Duluth, Georgia 30136

HF 8/92

Hellfire versions: RB-17 is the Swedish coast-defense variant with the special unitary antiship warhead (the others have antitank shaped charges). RB-17 weighs 106 lb and is 64 in long (AGM-114F weighs 107 lb and is 71 in long). (Rockwell)

poons fired, 3 ships sunk), Persian Gulf (April 1988: 2 engagements, 4 Harpoons fired, 2 ships sunk), Desert Storm (1 engagement, 1 Harpoon fired, 1 ship sunk [by Royal Saudi Navy]).The 7 SLAMs fired during the Gulf War were controlled by the old Walleye pod (**AWW-9**) rather than the newer **AWW-13**, which was not then available. The old pod proved unreliable and probably accounts for some missile failures. In 1992 new SLAM guidance software was introduced to allow launching from twice the previously specified altitude. In April 1992 McDonnell Douglas proposed SLAM improvements that would almost double the missile's range by adding Tomahawk-style pop-out wings and a more-compact guidance system (which would leave more room for fuel or a longer penetrating warhead, while saving 5–10% in cost). A SLAM preplanned product-improvement program will begin in 1993–94. SLAM is normally an air-launched weapon, but one was fired from a Harpoon canister on board the USS *Lake Champlain* (CG-57). SLAM's current unit cost is $827 thousand.

Overseas customers account for 42% of all Harpoon production; the foreign platforms using Harpoon in early 1992 were 207 surface ships, 49 submarines, 368 aircraft, and 3 coastal batteries. Harpoon is currently being withdrawn from the U.S. *Hamilton*-class coast guard cutters fitted to fire it.

Users: Australia (P-3Cs, F-111Cs, F/A-18s, submarines, destroyers, frigates), Brazil (18 ordered in FY90), Canada (29 D-4s for CP-140s, destroyers; submarines were fitted to fire Sub-Harpoon, but none were bought), Denmark (*Nils Juels, Willemoes, Flyvefisken* classes; coast batteries, to become operational in 1994), Egypt (29 Sub-Harpoons for rebuilt submarines, also at least 20 for *Descubierta* class), Greece (16 Sub-Harpoons for modernized submarines; others in frigates and new P 100 class; Osprey 55s are fitted for it but are not armed with it), Germany (Type 122s and refitted *Adams* class), Indonesia (*Van Speijk* class), Iran (Combattante class; all 9 missiles were probably expended), Israel (Sub-Harpoon, missile boats, probably aircraft), Italy (Sub-Harpoon on at least 2 *Sauro* class), Japan (bought 301 in 1988–91, probably had others: P-3Cs, 14 submarines [2–4 Sub-Harpoons each], missile destroyers, frigates), Kuwait (40 for F/A-18s), Netherlands (destroyers and frigates; the plan to arm P-3Cs was dropped; submarines can fire Sub-Harpoon, but none were bought), Pakistan (Sub-Harpoon; also 44 bought in 1990–91 for *Brooke* class and destroyer *Shahjahan*), Portugal (MEKO 200 class), Saudi Arabia (PCG and PGG classes), Singapore (*Victory* and FPB 45 class), South Korea (52 bought in 1988, then coast defense purchase in 1989–90, 28 AGM-84s for P-3Cs, more for KDXs: *Sumner*- and *Gearing*-class destroyers [quadruple launchers], 2 *Ulsan*-class frigates [2 twin launchers each], 5 PSMM Mk 5 attack boats [2 quadruple launchers each], 3 coast batteries bought in 1987), Spain (F/A-18s; *Perry, Descubierta, Baleares* classes; AV-8S aircraft, and 4 coast-defense batteries; 55 bought before 1985, 25 ordered in 1985 for delivery in 1987–90), Thailand (PFMM Mk 16 class), Turkey (MEKO frigates [for which 40 were offered in 1990], some destroyers, FPB 57 class; Sub-Harpoon to be in new Type 209/1400 submarines; Turkey was the first export sale in 1973), United Kingdom (Nimrods, Sub-Harpoon, Type 22 Batch III and Type 23 frigates), United States (P-3Cs, F/A-18s, A-6Es, S-3Bs, Sub-Harpoon, cruisers, destroyers, frigates, PHMs; 30 air force B-52Gs, *Hamilton*-class coast guard cutters), Venezuela (*Constitución* class; 18 bought in 1989). Venezuela was the first Latin American country to buy the missile. Reportedly, the Brazilian weapons are Sub-Harpoons. Reportedly, Peru and Yugoslavia tried unsuccessfully to buy Harpoons. Bahrein and Brunei may have tried to buy Harpoons; they ended up with Exocet MM 40s. New Zealand may have bought AGM-84s for P-3K aircraft. The Danish missiles came from scrapped *Peder Skram*–class frigates. They are organized in 2 coastal batteries, each consisting of 2 trucks (4 Harpoons each) plus a control center. Their Terma C3 system is linked to the overall C3 system for the Baltic. McDonnell Douglas has a contract to upgrade all Danish Harpoon-control systems to **SWG-1A(V)** standard, to be compatible with Block 1C (-84C) missiles. The Danish batteries are scheduled to become operational at the end of 1994.

During Desert Storm, 291 **Tomahawk**s were launched; Tomahawks hit 80% of fixed Iraqi targets. For submarines, McDonnell Douglas converted 60 TLAM-Cs on very short notice to a maximum-fuel configuration so that they could reach their targets. Targeting limitations became evident. Because of a lack of TERCOM maps, no missions at all could be flown before 13 August, and the 17 January 1991 attack could not have been executed before December/January. The requirements for TERCOM maps did not begin to level off until about October 1990, and requirements for DSMAC images actually rose more steeply after mid-December. The missions required always exceeded the resources.

The first Block III live-warhead launch, from the USS *David R. Ray*, was on 20 November 1991. This version is powered by a new Williams 402 engine (19% more thrust). It has a programmable delay fuze (for penetration before explosion) and a smaller insensitive-munitions warhead (**WDU-36B**) leaving space for 50% more fuel. GPS enhances the TERCOM guidance system, making for reduced launch restrictions and seasonal effects and for faster programming.

This version also has an upgraded terminal sensor, **DSMAC-2A**. Block III's range is 1,000 nm, compared to 700 nm for a conventionally armed Block II.

The FY92 program included 236 new Block III missiles and 401 remanufactured ones, but the Desert Storm supplemental appropriation increased FY91 purchases to 678 missiles (the FY92 program was cut to 176). Procurement: FY93, 200; FY94, requested 218. Through August 1991, 2,207 Tomahawks had been delivered. Early in 1992 the planned inventory of all-up rounds was 2,250 in 1992, 2,698 in 1993, 2,981 in 1994, 3,147 in 1995, 3,449 in 1996, 3,700 in 1997. Tomahawk is the primary U.S. naval surface or submarine strike weapon for Third World conflicts, such as the war against Iraq. In November 1992 it was announced that no more missiles will be remanufactured until a Block IV program begins in FY98, saving 48% in the unit lifetime cost of each missile. The FY92/93 budget cost was $1.92 million/missile.

The Block III version of the Tomahawk WCS, the Tomahawk Mission Planning Center Upgrade, and the Afloat Planning System (APS) are to enter service in FY93. **ISPS** is to enter service in FY96.

Block IV is to have a FLIR and antijam GPS (Block III has GPS, but not the antijam version). The FLIR stores a target image, and the missile's software may be able to rotate the image to correspond to the missile's angle of approach. The combination of FLIR and GPS should drastically reduce mission-planning time (the goal is 1 hr), making missiles far more responsive to changes in the tactical situation, e.g., to cueing by JSTARS aircraft. This Tomahawk Base Line Improvement Program (TBIP) or Tomahawk Multi-Mode Missile (TMMM) version will be usable against land or sea targets because the stored image can be either a shore target or a ship. It will be the first version with a seeker; earlier land-attack Tomahawks used their scene-recognition sensors only to ensure that they were on course to the target. They were guided to a point in space, not a specific target image. GPS will now guide the missile to a point at which the target should be within the FLIR's FoV. Although the emphasis is still on autonomous operation, there is some interest in a data link. It might provide information on how well the missile was carrying out its mission (so that multiple weapons would not have to be fired at the same target), and it might also be used to switch targets en route (if the FLIR is provided with multiple images). Ultimately, the link might provide video, for aim-point adjustment. SAR or LADAR (active IIR at about 10 microns) may be substituted for the currently planned FLIR.

UNGUIDED BOMBS AND AIR-LAUNCHED ROCKETS

Durandal/CBU-15 is not used by any navy (and not by any French air arm). The standard French runway-buster is the **Brandt bomblet**. All British naval nuclear bombs and depth charges (including those for RAF Nimrods) are being scrapped. U.S. naval nuclear bombs and depth charges have been withdrawn from service, but about half are being stored for possible future use. The development of the next-generation nuclear depth bomb has been abandoned.

UNITED STATES

During the Gulf War, the typical A-6E loads were 8–12 **Mk 82s**, 8–12 **Mk 20s**, 6 **Mk 83s**, 2–4 **Mk 84s**, 2 **Mk 83 LGBs**, or 2 **Mk 84 LGBs**. LGB loads were limited mainly because one explosion throws up debris that masks the laser beam for any later bomb.

The navy's **ABF** program has been combined with the air force's Short-Range Adverse-Weather Guided Bomb (direct-attack munitions) program as **JDAMS**, the Joint Direct-Attack Munitions System. The air force will now use **AIWS** (renamed **JSOW**) to deliver its **SFW** (BLU-108) bomblet, which the navy may adopt in an insensitive-munitions version.

JDAMS will proceed in 3 phases:

—Improvements (all weather/accurate inertial-navigation system/GPS) for the weapons now in the inventory, **Mk 84** and **BLU-109**; this may also include a tactical weapons dispenser and **Mk 80**-series improvements. The air force is the lead service.
—A new sensor, the development of a penetrator with a multi-function fuze (500-lb warhead and hi/lo tail [streamlined, but capable of retarding the bomb for low-altitude delivery]). All areas need further analysis. The navy is the lead service.

—Seeker integration, a joint program. Hopefully it will use elements of the **AIWS** guidance system (inertial navigation/GPS) and seeker. That is a problem: the JDAM weapon comes in fast and steep through an overcast, hence it may have to decide and attack quickly. JSOW arrives at a shallower angle, and thus has more time to lock onto the target. The seeker demonstration/validation phase is to begin in FY94 and last 3 yr; candidates are IIR, SAR, mm-wave, and LIDAR. The air force, which will choose, currently favors mm-wave or a combination of mm-wave and LIDAR.

One problem in the joint program is that naval air weapons are currently limited to 2,200-lb (by carrier operations), whereas air force tactical aircraft can lift individual 3,500-lb weapons.

By September 1992 the air force was particularly eager to obtain bombs to arm its B-2s. It, therefore, adopted a 2-stage program, initially a **Mk 84** capable only of 1-G maneuverability (the goal is 3 G). It now plans to order 92 interim (1-G) weapons, 52 for flight tests (on B-2s and F-16s) and 40 to arm operational B-2s in the third quarter of 1996. The service would then select a contractor to build 56 bombs for operational B-2s. A formal requirement was to be issued in January 1993. The bidders are Boeing, Hughes, Martin Marietta, McDonnell Douglas, Northrop, Rockwell, and Texas Instruments.

In mid-1992 Lockheed was selected over Rockwell for a 52-month technology-demonstrator program for a **hard-target-penetrating bomb**. It is developing a 1,400-kg [2,980-lb] rocket-boosted bomb small enough to be carried by an F/A-18 (and internally by B-2s and F-117s, externally by F-16s). Rocket boost allows the weapon to be dropped from lower altitudes than the gravity-driven **GBU-28** used at the end of the Gulf War. Flight tests are planned for the final 14 months of the program. Lockheed began an initial 7-month concept-definition phase in mid-July.

Lockheed Missiles and Space/BEI won the ARS (Advanced Rocket System) competition in July 1992. The unit cost is not to exceed $452 for 271,888 rockets over 10 yr. The maximum unit cost of each of 14,496 illuminating rockets is $584. ARS employs a Lockheed launcher and the BEI 70-mm rocket.

COAST DEFENSE

By the end of 1990, ITT-Gilfillan had delivered 2 complete coast-defense systems using its **Falcon** radars, probably 1 in Latin America and 1 in Asia.

BELGIUM

At Bourget Naval 1992 (October 1992), Forges de Zeebrugge, which makes 2.75-in aircraft rockets, advertised a small-craft system, which it had tested on board a Simmoneau patrol boat. It comprises a pair of 2.75-in rocket pods (carrying multidart or unitary rounds), controlled by a GRCS firing computer, with a range of up to 6,000 m. In theory, the rockets can also be used against ships and small boats.

DENMARK

The 2 Danish postwar-built forts at the entrances to the Sound, Stevnfort and Langland Fort, each armed with 2 twin **15-cm SKC/28** guns from the battleship *Gneisenau*, are still active. They are manned mainly by reservists. Denmark also retains a few ex-U.S. **3-in/50** naval guns in coastal mountings.

NORWAY

NFT is responsible for the Norwegian fortress-modernization program, which applies to 4 obsolescent coastal torpedo batteries and 5 controlled minefields. The program also calls for 1 new torpedo battery and 2 new minefields, at a total cost of NKr 700 million [about $93 million]. The 2 new installations are at Namsen Fjord (torpedoes and mines) and in the Tromsø area (mines). The main sensors are a Terma radar and a Saab EO device; in the future there may also be a seabed sonar. The main weapons are controlled mines and wire-guided torpedoes. The mines are being fitted with new sensor and C2 packages; only their shells have not been changed. The current torpedoes are old T-1s, the last type built by the Horten Torpedo Factory (to German plans, for G-7a), modernized after World War II with wire guidance. The *Kobben*-class submarines and Norwegian motor torpedo boats carried similar weapons. Some fortresses may also be armed with old British **Mk 8s**. These weapons

Denmark retains coast-defense turrets taken from World War II German battleships. This twin 150-mm mount from the battleship *Gneisenau*, emplaced in 1952, is 1 of 2 at Stevns Fort (4 single 150-mm guns are at Langeland Fort, built in 1952 with guns taken from a German battery at Fynshoved on the island of Fyn in Denmark; 2 more guns are emplaced nearby as a practice battery). The guns are 15-cm SK C/28s in a Dreh L: C/34 mount, with 150-mm face armor, 75-mm roof armor, and 50-mm sides and back; gun range is given as 22.3 km [about 24,400 yd]. Both forts were reduced to reserve status in 1983, but a mobilization crew trains at each every year (firing live ammunition). These 2 forts are probably the only ones remaining active. Until recently there were 6 others: Middelgrundsfort (12 × 170 mm, 4 × 105 mm AA), Flakfort (6 × 210 mm, 4 × 150 mm AA), Dragørfort (4 × 150 mm, 4 × 105 mm AA), Kongelundsfort (4 × 150 mm), Bagsbofort (4 × 150 mm, 4 × 105 mm AA), and Hornbæk battery (4 × 120 mm). All the forts were originally protected against air attack by 40-mm guns, but these weapons were declared obsolete in 1983 and scrapped. (C. B. Robbins)

are likely to remain in service through about 1995. Modernization includes replacing the current above-water torpedo tubes with submerged ones. Completion of the first installation, Herdla Fort, guarding the approaches to Bergen, is planned for mid-1994; the others are to follow at 6-month intervals, to end in 1997.

Nobeltech is developing **STARKA** (Sea Front System 2000), a fixed/mobile coast artillery (KA) system, for Norway and Sweden. The 155-mm guns will be able to fire from a variety of preregistered positions, instead of from fixed sites as now. STARKA is to be procured in 1997–98.

UNITED STATES

U.S. **155-mm guns** (World War I type GPFs) supplied to Chile in 1942 are still active, controlled by a locally developed system using small commercial microcomputers. Similar guns were supplied to several other Latin American countries, including Peru and Venezuela (to protect oil fields), but the Chilean weapons are probably the only ones still in service (there is a slight chance that the Peruvian guns are still active). Brazil and Trinidad received other weapons, probably ex-naval **6-in guns**. Aruba probably had Dutch guns.

Taiwan uses ex-destroyer **5-in/38** guns (and probably also 40-mm/70 guns) for coast defense.

Chile still uses old U.S. 155-mm GPF guns, supplied during World War II, for coast defense. They were intended to protect the copper-exporting ports of Antofagasta, Barquito Island, San Antonio, and Tocopilla, but have presumably been moved since. This particular gun was an M1917A1, made in France but modified with a U.S. breech and firing mechanism. This weapon was photographed in Iquique, Chile, in June 1992. (Dr. R. S. Scheina)

ANTIAIRCRAFT WARFARE

SHIPBOARD RADARS AND FIRE-CONTROL SYSTEMS

Deletions: The U.S. Navy has abandoned the Canadian–U.S. **SAR-8** project, and the device is too heavy for Canadian ships. In 1985–87 **AWS-6** replaced the Danish CWS-1, which is now extinct. The French **DRBV 20**, the Italian **MLA-1** (replaced by a modern slotted-waveguide radar), and the British **Type 982** are all extinct (no below-decks electronics were furnished when the frigate carrying the latter was transferred to Bangladesh). The Dutch **LW-01** and **VI-01** radars on the Argentine carrier *25 de Mayo* are unlikely ever to be active again. The British Marconi **400 Series/Sea Cobra** attracted no sales.

CANADA

SPG-501 is the TWT-driven version of the Signaal **STIR**, in the TRUMP (rebuilt "Tribal") class. **SPG-502** is the Signaal **LIROD**, in the TRUMP class. **SPG-503** is the magnetron-driven version of the Signaal STIR, in the "City" class. The director associated with **SPG-515** is designated **Mk 69 Mod 2**.

CHILE

The ASMAR national shipyard and Catholic University of Chile (Valparaiso) have now produced a radar FCS for the *Alm. Williams* class. The program began about 1985 and was completed in 1990; the new system takes up about a quarter of the space of its predecessor.

CHINA (PRC)

Bean Sticks/Pea Sticks *Users:* China (PRC) (Luda class)

Eye Shield (Type 354; MX 902 [export designation]) *Users:* Bangladesh (Jianghu class), China (PRC) (Luda, Jianghu, Dajiang classes and Dakin-type training ship), Egypt (Jianghu class), Thailand (Jianghu class)

Fin Curve, a surface-search radar that was superseded by **Type 756**, is a copy of the **Decca 707**.

Users: China (PRC) (Luda [some], Jiangnan, LSM, Yanbing, Dajiang, Fuqing classes)

Type 756 *Users:* Bangladesh (Jianghu, Huchuan classes), China (PRC) (Luda [some have Fin Curve], Jianghu, Jiangdong, Riga, Huchuan, T-43, ex-U.S. LST classes, Dadie-class AGI, Dakin-class training ship), Egypt (Jianghu class), Romania (Huchuan class)

Rice Screen (Sea Eagle) is eventually to be mounted on board all Luda-class destroyers, to direct shore-based fighters in support of naval forces at sea.

Users: China (PRC) (Luda hulls 108, 110, and 132 and Jiangdong class)

◆ Fire Control

Type 331 (Square Tie) is the Chinese version of the Soviet **Square Tie** SSM missile-control radar.

Users: Bangladesh (Jianghu, Huangfeng, Houku classes), China (PRC) (Luda, Jianghu, Riga, Huangfeng [Osa], Homa, Houku classes), Egypt (Jianghu and Houku classes), Pakistan (Huangfeng, Houku classes), Thailand (Jianghu class)

The Chilean-developed gun FCS (and 2 of the 4 4-in guns it controls) on board the destroyer *Alm. Williams* in 1992. (Dr. R. S. Scheina)

Type 341 (Rice Lamp) is the X(I)-band radar for **37-mm** fire control.

Users: China (PRC) (Jianghu class), Thailand (Jianghu class)

Type 343 (Wok Wan) is the Chinese version of the old Soviet **Sun Visor** radar, for main-battery fire control. Chinese Riga-class frigates probably have Soviet-made Sun Visors.

Users: Bangladesh (Jianghu), China (PRC) (Luda, Jianghu III, Jiangdong classes), Thailand (Jianghu class)

Type 347 is the FCS radar for **twin 57-mm guns** in the Luhu-class (Type EF5) destroyers. This radar is probably the new **ESR-1.**

Fog Lamp is the **HQ-61** FCS radar, in the Jiangdong class. Other ships are to be fitted with vertically launched HQ-61 and, presumably, also with this radar (the Jiangdongs have rail-type launchers).

Round Ball, the fire-control radar for **30-mm guns,** supersedes **Bass Tilt.**

Users: China (PRC) (Haijui class, some Huangfeng [Osa-II], Dakin training ship)

Twin Eyes is the Chinese-designed optical director for **100-mm guns,** in the Jiangnan class.

DENMARK

CWS-2 (AWS-2 with a different antenna) survives on board the *Falster*-class minelayers and in the one ship of this class built for Turkey. The Royal Swedish Navy's designation for the Terma navigational radar in the *Göteborg* and *Stockholm* classes is **PN-612** (it is **Skanter 009** in older units).

The **NWS Series** are surface-search radars. **NWS-1** (in the now-defunct *Soloven* class) was a Decca slotted-waveguide radar. **NWS-3** (*Willemoes* and other classes) is Terma **20T48,** a Decca **1629** built under license. **NWS-4** and **-5** are submarine radars, presumably **Calypso** (French) antennas with Terma electronics. **NWS-6** is **Skanter-Mil X; -10** is **Skanter-Mil S.**

FRANCE

Mars is now being offered with the **MR-05** antenna under the designation **Mars 05;** it was tested on board a *Floréal*-class frigate in the fall of 1992. However, in the *Floréals* this radar is installed with a reconditioned **DRBV 22** antenna. In this form it should be able to detect aircraft at 60 nm, and the optional automatic tracker can accommodate up to 100 tracks. (Reportedly, the *Floréals* will also have a **Jupiter 08** [Jupiter electronics and the **LW-08** antenna].)

Arabel is to be carried on board the new French-built Saudi frigates (Sawari 2 program). (The corresponding *La Fayette*–class ships of the French navy will have simpler **Sea Tiger Mk 2** radars.)

Thomson, Siemens Plessey, and Inisel are developing the **Astral** 2½D monopulse (on elevation) radar. It achieves stepped-scan 3D performance and is electronically stabilized. The scan rate is 15 rpm. The **DRBV 27** designation is not definite.

The **MRR** radar was probably proposed for the Combattante IV boats offered to Kuwait.

ASCORE (Air/Surface Coastal Radar Equipment) is a simplified MRR with a 2D antenna.

Users: Qatar (new 56-m patrol boats)

The **SCORE** coastal radar uses **VARAN** (airborne radar) electronics. As of late 1992, 6 countries used SCORE as a target indicator for coastal missile batteries.

CTM (*Conduit de Tir Multisensor*) is **Castor IIJ** adapted as the **Crotale NG** FCS, but it has wider application; in effect it supersedes **Castor** (e.g., the *La Fayettes* carry it for both GFCS and MFCS).

Users: France (La Fayette class), Germany (replacement for Castor II on S148-class fast attack craft), Oman (new corvettes), Qatar (new 56-m fast attack craft), Saudi Arabia (La Fayette class), Taiwan (La Fayette class), U.A.E. (new fast attack craft). This may also be the version of Castor supplied to China (PRC) for Luda hulls 17 and 18.

DRBC 31 is the non–pulse-compressed monopulse predecessor to **DRBC 32.**

Users: Portugal (Cdt. Rivière class [31D])

DRBC 33 (Castor II) *Users:* France (*Cassard, Suffren* classes, last 3 *Georges Leygues* class)

DRBI 10 *Users:* France (*Clemenceau* class)

DRBI 23 *Users:* France (*Suffren* class)

DRBJ 11 *Users: France (****Cassard*** *class)*

DRBV 15 (Sea Tiger) *Users:* France (*Cassard* class, last 3 *Georges Leygues* class [DRBV 15A], *Duquesne* [will replace DRBV 50 in *Suffren*], *Aconit*)

DRBV 15C (Sea Tiger Mk 2) *Users:* France (*Charles de Gaulle* [first order, November 1989], *La Fayette* class, experimental ship *Monge*), Saudi Arabia (*La Fayette* class), Taiwan (*La Fayette* class)

DRBV 22 *Users:* France (22A in *Aconit, Cdt. Rivière* class, 22C in trials ship *Île d'Oléron,* 22D in *Jeanne d'Arc,* 22E in experimental ship *Rance*), Portugal (22A in *Cdt. Rivière* class), Uruguay (22A in *Cdt. Rivière* class)

DRBV 23B *Users:* France (*Clemenceau* class)

DRBV 26 *Users:* China (PRC) (26C in Luda hulls 17 and 18), France (26A in *Tourville* class, first 4 *Georges Leygues* and *Cassard,* 26C in *Jean Bart,* 26D in *Charles de Gaulle* and future AAW combatants)

Information is now available on the old but still operational **DRBV 50,** a C-band (5,350–5,750 MHz) low-flier/surface-search (and helicopter-control) radar. DRBV 50 was developed in the late 1950s specifically for the *Cdt. Rivière* class, to provide solid cover (of 1-m^2 targets) out to 10 nm, between -7 and +70 deg elevation, for cover up to 10,000 ft (the antenna is tilted up at 3 deg). The unstabilized antenna, which scans at high speed, is a pair of superimposed cheeses, with a dielectric lens across the aperture to form the csc^2 beam. Unlike contemporary British "cheeses," this one is not blocked by the feed. Instead, energy reaching the back of the bottom cheese is coupled to the upper, unblocked, cheese by a long slot parallel to the back of the antenna. The antenna radiates from its upper portion: 1.3 × 20 deg (csc^2 20 to 70 deg); the antenna gain is 28 dB. The peak power is 250 kW. Alternative pulse widths and corresponding PRFs are 1.25 microsec (750 pps) and 0.25 microsec (manually adjusted 2,000–4,000 pps).

Users: France (*Jeanne d'Arc, Suffren, Île d'Oléron*), Portugal (*Cdt. Rivière* class)

DRBV 51 (Triton) *Users:* Argentina (A-69 class [51A]), France (A-69 class [51A], *Georges Leygues* class [first 4 ships: 51C], *Tourville* class [51B], *Ouragan* class [51A])

DRUA 33 (Calypso) *Users:* Colombia (Calypso II), Denmark (with Terma electronics), Ecuador, France (standard submarine radar), Germany, Greece, Peru, Spain (*Agosta* and possibly *Daphne* class), and Venezuela, all but France and Spain in Type 209 submarines. The earlier DRUA 31 survives in Pakistani, Portuguese, South African, and possibly Spanish *Daphne*-class submarines.

Castor *Users:* —**Castor I** (TRS 3200): Greece (Combattante II and IIIN)
—**Castor II** (TRS 3203): Germany (S 148), Peru (PR-72-560)
—**Castor IIB:** Colombia (FS-1500), Libya (Combattante IIG), Nigeria (Combattante IIIG), Qatar (Combattante IIIT)
—**Castor IIC:** Saudi Arabia (*Al Madinah* class)

Pollux (THD 1280, TRS 3220) *Users:* Ecuador (*Quito* and *Manta* classes), Malaysia (Combattante II 4AL), Portugal (*Baptiste de Andrade* class), Qatar (Combattante III)

Sea Tiger (TRS 3001) *Users:* Colombia (FS-1500), Saudi Arabia (*Al Madinah*)

Triton *Users:* —**Triton** (TRS 3030, THD 1040): Ecuador (*Quito* class), Greece (Combattante II and IIIN), Libya (Combattante II), Malaysia (Combattante II 4AL), Peru (PR-72–560)
—**Triton G** (TRS 3050, DRBV 52): Germany (S 148 class)
—**Triton S** (TRS 3033): Qatar (Combattante IIIM), Tunisia (Combattante IIIT)
—**Triton IIMTI** (TRS 3035): Libya (Combattante IIG), Greece (Combattante III), Nigeria (Combattante IIIG)

At Bourget Naval 1992 (October 1992) SAGEM announced **VIGY 105** to supplement the **VIGY 50** and **VIGY 200** announced 2 yr earlier. The sight carries an IR camera, a TV camera, and a laser range-finder. SAGEM expected to complete the prototype in mid-1993 and to offer production models early in 1994. The total weight of the optronic unit is about 100 kg.

Lynx *Users* (other than with **Radop**): Bahrein (Lürssen 38-m class), France (*Cassard* class), Kuwait (TNC 45–class fast attack boats), Morocco (*LtCol. Errhamani*), and Oman (*Nasr Al Bahr*)

Panda *Users:* Bahrein (Mk 2 on FPB 62 and TNC 45 classes), Belgium (*Wielingen* class), Congo (*Pirana* class), France (*Georges Leygues*), Germany, Greece (Combattante IIIN), Libya (Combattante II), Morocco (PR-72), Nigeria (Combattante IIIB), Peru (PR-72–560), Portugal (*Baptiste de Andrade* class), and Spain (*Lazaga* class).

By 1976 more than 150 sets had been ordered. Many of those listed above were probably replaced by NAJA.

NAJA Users (other than with **Radop**): Algeria (*Kalaat Beni Hammed*–class landing ships), Cameroon (*Bakassi*), China (PRC) (Jianghu IV, to control 100-mm guns), Malaysia (*Jerong* class, *Sri Indera Sakti*–class support ships), Morocco (*Lazaga* class), Tunisia (Combattante III class), Saudi Arabia (*Al Madinah*–class frigates), Turkey (*Girne*)

NAJIR Users: France (*Cassard* and *Floréal* classes), United Kingdom (as DMAC), and 1 other foreign navy

Radop Users: —**Radop 10**: Bahrein (FPB 38 boats)
    —**Radop 20**: Argentina (A-69 corvette *Granville*), Congo (*Pirana*), Libya (*Ibn Ouf* class), and Morocco (PR-72s)
    —**Radop 30**: Algeria (Brooke-Marine–type landing ships), Argentina (A-69–class corvettes other than *Granville*), Malaysia (*Sri Indera Sakti* class), Saudi Arabia (*Durance*-class replenishment ships), Senegal (PR-72M class), Turkey (*Girne*), and Uruguay (*Vigilance* class)
    —**Radop 40**: Cameroon (P 48S–class patrol boat)

GERMANY

The C-band **TRS-3D** was ordered for the second batch of 6 StanFlex 300s, with an option for 7 more to replace the **AWS-6** radars of the first batch. The first was delivered in December 1992. The transmitter is a TWT with a solid-state driver, capable of burst-to-burst frequency agility (and pulse-to-pulse polarization agility). The stability of the transmitter permits the use of Doppler MTI and pulse compression. There are separate air and surface channels, each with its own jam detector. The radar automatically classifies helicopters and provides alerts for pop-up targets. The stabilized antenna mounting can accommodate an X-band navigational antenna below the main antenna, which is tipped back. The scan rate is 30 rpm, and the dimensions of the stabilized antenna are 1.2×0.4 m (total weight less than 370 kg). The earlier **TRS-N** has largely superseded the Kelvin-Hughes **14/9** as a standard German naval navigational radar.

Atlas 9600M is a new ARPA radar with 4 times the display resolution of **7600/8600**; it can interface with a target-indication or air-search radar. Its output can feed into a CDS. Thus far the only reported naval users are Australia and New Zealand, for the ANZAC frigates (Atlas 8600).

ISRAEL

AMDR (EL/M-2218-S) tracks 20 targets simultaneously (TWS mode). The version in the *Eilat* (Sa'ar V class) adds a 3D (multibeam array) back-to-back with the original 2D antenna; total weight is about 550 kg, compared to 220 kg for the 2D version. Both use the same high-power coherent transmitter.

Users: Israel (*Nirit*, *Eilat* class [Sa'ar V])

As of 1980, well over 50 **EL/M-2200–series** radars were reported delivered or on order, many of them for export to unspecified customers. The installations listed here add up to 42; the difference is presumably made up of shore-based radars. All the radars listed are probably the dual-frequency version because both the Sa'ars and the Taiwanese destroyers lack dedicated surface-search radars. Compared to the Neptune originally carried on board Israeli missile boats, this radar can better distinguish small seaborne targets near shore clutter.

Users: Chile (4 Sa'ar boats), Israel (22 Sa'ar boats), South Africa (12 Sa'ar IV class), Taiwan (4 Wu Chin II destroyers)

EL/M-2221 was originally a license-built version of the Italian **RTN-10X**, the first radar fitted to the Sa'ar class (1972). It is probably the unit typically described as RTN-10X in boats equipped with Gabriel.

Users: Chile (Sa'ar boats), Ecuador (*Manta* class), Israel (missile boats), Kenya (*Mamba* and 32-m class), South Africa (Sa'ar class), and Taiwan (destroyers). **EL/M-2221-GM STGR** is the version for Barak fire control.

Users: Israel (*Nirit*, *Eilat* [Sa'ar V]), Singapore (*Victory* class)

Eagle Eye is IAI's new optronic air-defense system (for 30–40-mm guns). Using a laser and an optical tracker, Eagle Eye can be cued by a radar, such as **EL/M-2106HE** (UPS-3). Eagle Eye can control up to 6 weapons simultaneously. The typical radar range is 20 km; the laser range is 7 km, and the TV identification range is 6.4 km. Track accuracy is given as 5 m.

Rafael announced the modular, stabilized, pedestal-mounted **Sea-Eye** FLIR in 1992; it has 2 FoVs: 1.7×1.25 and 4.5×3.5. It can scan at 20 deg/sec over 180 deg in bearing and 56 deg in elevation.

MSIS Users: Israel (on Dvora and Super Dvora patrol boats, ordered in 1988), possibly also Sri Lanka (Super Dvora); may also be on Dvoras in Sri Lankan service. Ultimately, MSIS is to equip all Israeli ships, including the Sa'ar Vs. One was installed on the USS *Halyburton* during the Gulf War. As of 1993, 50 were on order or delivered.

SPIRTAS (DS-35) Users: Israel (at least one Sa'ar boat) and United States (reportedly, installed on a frigate at Haifa during the Gulf War, but this may refer to MSIS)

ITALY

RAN-20S and **-25S** are new Alenia solid-state shipboard radars. RAN-20S is 2D; RAN-25S is 3D (frequency-scanned). RAN-20S has a planar-array antenna (swing diameter 4.5 m). Elevation coverage is 65+ deg, range on a fighter is 75+ nm (accuracy 20 m), and angular accuracy is 0.3 deg. It scans at 15 and 30 rpm. This radar has a solid-state transmitter.

RTN-25X is a new Alenia solid-state shipboard FCS radar, part of the new **MARA** series (see the **NA-25** FCS). The **Myriad** FCS radar uses -25X components (monopulse, coherent [TWT], pulse Doppler) but operates in X- or K-band, depending on which TWT is fitted. It will simply be called Myriad.

As of spring 1992, Alenia was beginning a family of S-band coast-defense radars based on its **ARGOS-73**.

RAN-3L (MM/SPS-768) Users: Italy (*Garibaldi*, *Vittorio Veneto*, *Mimbelli*, *Audace* classes)

RAN-10S (MM/SPS-774) Users: Ecuador (*Wadi M'ragh* class), Italy (*Mimbelli*, *Audace*, *Maestrale*, *Lupo*, *Minerva* classes), Libya (*Dat Assawari*), Peru (*Lupo*), Venezuela (*Lupo*). The *Minerva*s have new, solid **OA-7104** antennas rather than the usual mesh type.

RAN-11 L/X and **-12 L/X** Users: —**RAN-11 L/X**: Italy (*Mimbelli* and *Audace* classes and ex-Iraqi *Lupo* class), Libya (*Wadi M'ragh* class), Peru (*Lupo* class), Spain (*Príncipe de Asturias*), Venezuela (*Lupo* class)
    —**RAN-12 L/X**: Iraq (*Wadi M'ragh* class, now for sale), Libya (*Dat Assawari*), Spain (*Perry*, *Baleares* classes)

SPQ-2 Users: Italy (-2F in *Lupo* class, -2B in *Pietro De Cristofaro* class, -2 in *Albatros* class) and Venezuela (SPQ-2D in *Constitución* class)

SPQ-701 Users: Italy (*Sparviero* class)

SPS-702 Users: Italy (*Vittorio Veneto*, *Maestrale* class)

RTN-7X was the first RTN radar to use a new form of conscan, a tripod (3-slot) feed rotating instead of vibrating (as in the earlier sets, made under Raytheon license by Microlambda/Selenia, and directly descended from the U.S. wartime Mk 39). **RTN-10X**'s development began in 1970, and series production began in 1972. This radar was first installed on board Israeli Sa'ar-class missile boats (1972), then on board the Italian destroyer *Ardito*.

Users: Brazil (*Inhaúma* and *Niteroi* classes), Chile (Sa'ar II/IV), Ecuador (*Wadi M'ragh* and *Manta* classes), Iraq (*Wadi M'ragh* class and *Agnadeen* [oiler]), Israel (missile boats), Italy (*Vittorio Veneto* and *Sparviero* classes, *San Giorgio*, *Stromboli*), Kenya (32-m class), Libya (*Dat Assawari* and *Wadi M'ragh* class), Peru (*Lupo* class), Philippines (projected *Cormoran* class), South Africa (Sa'ar IV class), United Kingdom (Type 21 frigates, as Type 912), Venezuela (*Lupo*, *Alm. Clemente*, *Constitución* classes). The earlier RTN-7X (Orion 7) survives in the Italian *Pietro De Cristofaro* class.

RTN-20X (SPG-74) Users: Ecuador (*Wadi M'ragh* class), Greece (76-mm fire control on 4 FRAM I *Gearings*), Iraq (*Wadi M'ragh* class, for sale), Italy (*Garibaldi*, *Vittorio Veneto*, *Maestrale*, *Lupo*, *Minerva*, *Cassiopea* classes), Peru (*Lupo* class), Venezuela (*Lupo* class)

RTN-30X (SPG-76) is an automatic-target-acquisition and monopulse tracker that is the basis of the **NA-30** FCS; RTN-30X replaces RTN-10X in the **Albatros** missile FCS. Unlike the earlier radar, -30X incorporates CWI (no second transmitter is required). It is the most powerful tracker of the series, with twice the power of RTN-10X.

Users: Italy (*Garibaldi*, *Mimbelli*, *Audace*, *Maestrale*, *Etna* classes), Peru (*Lupo* class)

SPN-703 (3RM20-B) Users: Iraq (*Wadi M'ragh*, now for sale), Italy (*Animoso*, *Lupo*, *Lerici*, *Agile* [minehunters]), Nigeria (probably in *Lerici* class)

SPN-728 Users: Italy (*Minerva* class)

SPN-748 Users: Italy (*Audace* class, *Amerigo Vespucci* [with 2 antennas], *San Marco* class [main radar], *Cassiopea* class [main radar], *Zara* class [customs service])

SPN-749 Users: Italy (*Giuseppe Garibaldi*)

SPN-751 was apparently the last GEM navigational radar not to incorporate a digital scan converter (the company makes a scan converter for **SPN-748** and **-751**).

Users: Italy (*Zara* class [customs service])

3RM20 *Users:* Algeria (Mangusta-class patrol boats), Germany (*Bremen* class and S143/S143A/S148 classes), Italy (*Cassiopea* class, 105-ft class, *Meattini* class, *Gabriele* class), Peru (*Lupo* class), Venezuela (*Lupo* class)

3RM20 SMG (BPS-704) *Users:* Argentina (TR-1700 class), Italy (*Sauro, Toti* classes)

BX-732/764 are GEM Elettronica X-band, solid-state, navigational radars on board many Italian warships. These radars use 4- or 6-ft slotted-waveguide antennas (beam of 1.6 or 1.3 × 22 deg) scanning at 22 rpm; peak power is 10 kW, for a maximum instrumented range of 32 or 64 nm (BX-732 vs. -164). Many units have GEM's **BX-3072** or **SC-1400**.

GEM Elettronica also makes a variety of commercial navigational radars, some of which may correspond to the naval types listed above. **SC-1005-RD** is a very small X-band radar (4 kW, using a 55-cm antenna with a 4 × 24–deg beam) using a 10-in display. **SC-1510/1525** is a 10/25-kW, digital, raster-scan, X-band radar using a 4-, 6-, or 7.5-ft antenna (beams of 1.6 × 22, 1.3 × 23, 1.1 × 23 deg) and a 15-in display. Range scales are 0.25– 96 nm.

The notes that follow clarify the relationship among Italian naval FCSs. **NA-9**, the last fully analog system, survives on the cruiser *Vittorio Veneto*. **NA-10** and probably **Albatros** used a hard-wired digital computer. **Dardo** introduced a programmable 18-bit digital computer, **MAC-18**. The next step, **NA-18/21/30**, uses a 24-bit computer. The next generation, not yet in service, is the 32-bit **NA-25**, which will use **RAN-25S** and **RTN-25X** radars and **MARA 286/386** computers (1 for tracking, 1 for ballistics) and **MAGICS** consoles. The corresponding optronic FCS (NA-18's successor) is **NA-28**. In contrast to the contemporary **Vega**, the NA series could accept any search radar (they applied their plot extractors to the radar's raw video).

NA-10 versions are the following:

—Mod 0 for large ships: RTN-10X tracker radar plus 2 optical directors (periscope sights) plus optional horizon-search radar (vs. sea-skimmers). It controls 3 guns of 2 calibers. Like Vega's **BCH**, the main computer had separate ballistic (air or surface firing) and programmable sections. It was replaced by Mod 2.
—Mod 1 for smaller ships, initially the now-defunct hydrofoil *Sparviero*: RTN-10X with television camera; no periscopes; single ballistic section (1 gun caliber) and 2 outputs (2 guns). The successor version was Mod 3 (RTN-10X plus LLLTV).

Users: Italy (*Vittorio Veneto, Lupo, Cassiopea, Sparviero* [Mod 3], *Stromboli* classes), Libya (*Dat Assawari* [Mod 2], *Wadi M'ragh* class [Mod 3]), Peru (*Lupo* class), Venezuela (*Lupo* [Mod 0], *Alm. Clemente*, and *Constitución* [Mod 1] classes)

Albatros is the contemporary SAM FCS, designed to use RTN-10X as its tracker, but Albatros is adaptable to the Signaal "egg." It adds a CWI channel (**RTN-12X Sirio**) to the radar's tracker. Separate versions (Mks 1 and 2) were developed for, respectively, **Sea Sparrow** (RIM-7H) and the Italian **Aspide** missile (i.e., elements of the computer were hard-wired). Versions: Mod 3 (NA-10 FCS), Mod 5 (NA-21 FCS), Mod 7 (NA-30 FCS), and Mod 9 (Signaal WM 25 FCS). Mods 3 and 5 employ RTN-10X radar.

Users: Argentina (MEKO 360 class), Ecuador (*Wadi M'ragh* class), Egypt (*Descubierta*), Iraq (*Wadi M'ragh* class, for sale), Italy (*Garibaldi* and *Animoso, Maestrale, Minerva* classes and ex-Iraqi *Lupos*), Libya (*Dat Assawari*), Morocco (*Descubierta*), Nigeria (MEKO 360), Peru (*Lupo* class), Spain (*Descubierta*), Thailand (PFMM Mk 16 class), Venezuela (*Lupo* class). The Argentine, Egyptian, Moroccan, Nigerian, Spanish, and Thai ships have **WM 25** FCSs with Mod 9.

The **Dardo CIWS**, Selenia's first all-digital system (the name was chosen because it is digital) combines a dedicated low-flier search (target-acquisition) radar (**RAN-10S**) with a new tracker (**RTN-20X**) to control a Breda **Compact twin 40-mm/70 gun**. The associated **MAC-18** 18-bit computer adds in 2.4 microsec, multiplies in 8.7 microsec, and divides in 10.5 microsec. The capacity is 20 kword, and the programming is in the Assembly language. This computer was also used in the shore-based **Spada** AAW system.

Users: China (PRC) (Modified Luda and Jangwei classes), Ecuador (*Wadi M'ragh* class), Iraq (*Wadi M'ragh* class, for sale), Italy (*Maestrale, Lupo*), Peru (*Lupo*), Venezuela (*Lupo*). Dardo is made under license in China (PRC).

Dardo-E on the carrier *Giuseppe Garibaldi* in 1991. (Author)

NA-18/21/30 are modular systems using the 24-bit **ESA 24** computer, whose firmware includes trigonometric functions. It has a 250-nsec memory-access time (clock rate of 4 MHz). The NA-18 computer, the simplest version, can handle 2 independent sets of ballistics (for guns of 2 calibers; it has the capacity for 2 sets of ballistics for each gun) in parallel. It tracks by filtering digital 3D tracking data from the system's tracker, selecting the best of its several algorithms. All versions of the system use common console elements and a data bus.

NA-18 (Pegaso) is optronic only (it can use the ship's search radar for target acquisition). **NA-21** uses the **RTN-10X** tracker; it controls 3 guns of 2 different calibers plus the **Aspide** missile; it can also designate targets to a surface-to-surface missile. **NA-30** uses the **RTN-30X** tracker plus EO sensors (IR and television cameras and a laser range-finder). In **NA-30A** (*Maestrale*) the radar director carries the two cameras, but it is supplemented by an optronic director such as that in NA-18. NA-30A uses two consoles, one for radar and missile control and the other for the EO director. Because each console accommodates a computer, NA-30A can control 4 different weapons. **NA-30B** (*Garibaldi*) has a single director. The computer can handle 3 guns of 2 different calibers with 1 fuze-setting computation, or 1 gun plus the **Aspide** missile. **NA-30E** (Dardo E, or Extended) is a successor to Dardo based on NA-30 Mod B and a dedicated search radar (**RAN-10S**, for automatic target acquisition), first used in the carrier *Garibaldi*; it can control two weapons (e.g., twin 40-mm, 5-in/54, or Aspide).

Users: —**NA-18**: Bangladesh (-18B on *Megna* class), Italy (*Minerva, Zara* classes), Mexico (*Aguila* class), and Thailand (PSMM Mk 5 class). The version on board *Zara* may be modified; it is described as **Pegaso F**, with **CSDA-10** directors (NA-18 is probably **Pegaso L**).
—**NA-21**: Ecuador (modified *Wadi M'ragh* class), Greece (secondary control in FRAM I destroyers, Osprey 55 class), Iraq (modified *Wadi M'ragh* class, now for sale), Italy (*San Giorgio*), and Philippines (projected *Cormoran* class)
—**NA-30**: Italy (*Garibaldi* [Dardo E], *Audace* [Dardo E], *Animoso* [NA-30E], *Maestrale* [NA-30A], *Minerva* [Dardo E])

OG.R7 *Users:* Brazil (*Niteroi* class), Ecuador (*Wadi M'ragh* class), Egypt (*Descubierta* class), Germany (Type 143 missile boats, Type 331 and 351 minehunters [as modernized], Type 394 inshore sweepers, probably many others), Greece (*Kelefstis Stamou* class and ex-German *Thetis* class), Iran (*Saam* class, as adjunct to Sea Hunter 4), Italy (*Lupo* and *Maestrale* classes, probably also *Pietro de Cristofaro* and *Alpino* classes), Libya (*Dat Assawari* and *Wadi M'ragh* class), Morocco (*Descubierta* class), Peru (*Lupo* class), Spain (*Descubierta* class), Taiwan (*Sumner*-class destroyers), Thailand (*Makut Rajakuman, Prabrarapak* classes), Venezuela (*Lupo* class and modernized *Alm. Clemente* class). Germany was the main, and probably the first, customer, buying the system about 1970. The Italian navy was the other major customer (ca. 1978). Ships with Signaal FCSs bought prior to the advent of LIOD probably were fitted with OG.R7 as a backup (the French Panda series was the main alternative). The early Israeli missile boats probably had OG.R7 as

The OG.R7A lead-computing optical sight on the Spanish frigate *Descubierta* in 1991. (Raymond Cheung)

an interim director until OG 20 was ready. When integrated with an NA-series FCS, this unit is probably designated CO3. Most OG.R7s use analog computers, but late ones, probably including those ordered by Italy, have digital computers.

Galiflir is on board Italian Atlantic patrol aircraft and naval AB-212 and A109 helicopters. It has also been bought by Portugal. It is either manually aimed, slaved to a radar (as in an AB-212), or caged (fixed relative to the aircraft axis) for navigation. In the helicopter, the screen shows the radar map with the IR image in a window. Galiflir can detect a destroyer at 39 nm and identify it at 15 nm. Officine Galileo's new **PACIS** (Pilot and Close-In Surveillance) uses the same IR camera but with a less-powerful telescope (magnifications 1× and 4×, FoVs 40 × 26.7 and 10 × 6.6 deg) in a non-stabilized mounting (elevation limits +45/-70 deg).

JAPAN

OPS-1 *Platforms:* ex-DD *Akizuki*, ex-DE *Isuzu* classes

OPS-2 *Platforms: Katori*

OPS-9, an X(I/J)-band surface-search radar, with a very long slotted-waveguide antenna, is a version of the British Type 978 and was presumably bought as part of the same package that produced **ZQS-2** (Type 193).

Platforms: Utone, Hatsushima (some), *Takami, Atsumi* (LST), *Akashi, Kurihama* (9B), *Muroto, Fushimi* classes

OPS-10 *Platforms:* target-service craft ASU 81–83

OPS-11 *Platforms: Haruna* (11C), *Hatakaze* (11C), *Tachikaze* (11B), *Yamagumo, Minegumo* classes

OPS-12 *Platforms: Shirane* class

OPS-13 *Platforms:* PT 11 class

OPS-14 *Platforms: Asagiri* (14C), *Hatsuyuki* (14B), *Abukuma* (14C), *Chikugo, Souya* (MMC), *Hayase* (MMC), *Miura* (LST) classes

OPS-15 *Platforms: Katori, Azuma, Teruzuki* (ex-DD), *Akizuki* (ex-DD), *Ayanami* class (ex-DD)

OPS-16 *Platforms: Chikugo, Isuzu, Souya* (16C), *Hayase* (16C), *Miura, Sagami, Kurobe, Tsugaru* classes, *Mogami* (ex-DE), *Isuzu* (ex-DE), *Tsugaru*

OPS-17 *Platforms: Amatsukaze, Takatsuki, Yamagumo, Minegumo* classes

In the *Hatsuyuki* class, **OPS-18–1** is probably the target-acquisition set for **Sea Sparrow** and thus most likely incorporates a Japanese equivalent of **SPS-65**.

Platforms: Hatsuyuki (18–1), *Towada* (AOR: 18–1), *Awashima* (18B), *Hatsushima* (some, with 18B rather than 9), *Futami, Shirase*

OPS-19 *Platforms: Kurama, Yubari, Ishikari* classes, target-service craft ASU 85

OPS-22 *Platforms: Haruna* class, icebreaker *Shirase*

OPS-24 *Platforms:* replaces **OPS-14** on board the *Hamagiri* and later *Asagiri*-class destroyers

OPS-28 *Platforms: Shirane, Haruna, Kongo, Asagiri, Hatakaze, Hatsuyuki, Yubari* (DE—main search set)

OPS-29 *Platforms:* PB-type patrol boats, target-service craft ASU 84

No platforms for **OPS-35/36/37** have been identified.

ZPS-4 *Platforms: Uzushio* class

ZPS-6 *Platforms: Yushio* and *Harushio* classes

GFCS Model 1 (GFCS-1; Type 72) *Platforms: Shirane, Haruna, Tachikaze, Yamagumo* (DDK-120, -121 only), *Minegumo* (DDK-117, -118 only), *Chikugo, Souya, Miura* (LST) classes

GFCS Model 2 (GFCS-2) *Platforms:* —FCS 2–12/2–23: *Haruna, Asagiri* (2–12E), *Hatsuyuki, Takatsuki* (2–12B), *Minegumo* (DDK-118 only; prototype of system, for **76-mm GFCS**)
  —FCS 2–21/2–22: *Asagiri* (2–21A), *Hatakaze* (2–21C), *Hatsuyuki, Amatsukaze, Abukuma* (2–21A), *Yubari, Ishikari, Kurobe* (2–21A)
  —FCS 3 is in the new *Takao* (4,400-ton) class (2/ship, each capable of guiding 16 Sea Sparrow missiles). This ship is equipped with Mk 41 VLS forward (29 cells) and aft (61 cells). The forward cells are to be filled with quad-packed Sea Sparrows and, reportedly, a vertically launched version of the Japanese SSM-1 antiship missile. The after cells are to be filled with SM-2 Block IV missiles controlled mainly by accompanying *Kongo*-class ships using a Japanese-developed form of cooperative engagement (**CEC**). The 4,200-ton experimental ship (ASE) is reportedly intended specifically to test the FCS 3/CEC system.

NETHERLANDS

Signaal's first all-solid-state L-band transmitter, **D-SSTX**, was delivered in the spring of 1992. The power transistors consist of 7 chips in parallel, each of which has up to 216 parallel transistors; each such device produces 300 kW of peak power. The basic module (PA-Module) is a 4:1 cascade: 1 drives 4, each of which drives 4 transmitters, for a total of 4 kW. Up to 32 PA-Modules can be combined, for a total of about 100 kW from 512 final output transistors. The entire array is microprocessor-controlled. A peak power of 100 kW is quite acceptable for a pulse-compressed radar using long pulses. D-SSTX will be used in the **SMART-L** radar.

LW-09 is a solid-state transmitter offered as a replacement for that in **LW-08**; LW-09 will also be the British **Type 1022** successor.

SMART-L combines the new LW-09 transmitter with a planar passive phased-array antenna, in effect a larger equivalent to SMART (which is now **SMART-S**). SMART-L has 14 stacked beams in elevation (on receive only), reaching up to 70 deg in elevation; it applies pulse-Doppler processing to each. Like SMART-S, SMART-L is a monopulse, height-finder radar; it provides range, bearing, elevation, and target velocity on each scan. The receiver incorporates 32 parallel amplifiers. Signaal claims that it can detect a low-observable target at 50 km and a conventional target beyond 100 km. The maximum instrumented range is 400 km. The ADT track file can carry up to 1,000 aircraft and 40 surface targets simultaneously. SMART-L was conceived as part of the defunct **NAAWS** program and will probably spin off into the planned German F124 class (the Dutch-German air-defense frigate). The Royal Netherlands Navy development/delivery contract was awarded on 24 July 1991 (to combine the performance of LW-08 and SMART in a single radar).

SMART-L *Users:* Netherlands (planned: *Karel Doorman, Heemskerck*, 4 *Kortenaer* class)

Signaal feels that, compared to **Pilot**, its LPI **Scout** has gone much further in using FFTs (the key to other Signaal radars' performance) for signal processing. The price has also been reduced sharply, the limiting factor now being the Kelvin-Hughes (**Type 1007**) display. Using the display, Scout enjoys all 1007 facilities of the British radar (i.e., TWS for surface fire control). As of September 1991, Signaal was considering a D-band version. A submarine version is being developed, there have been repeated requests for a helicopter-borne ASW version, and there has been some talk (with Fokker) of a maritime-patrol version (but that will require a different processor because Doppler speeds are much higher). The current

1.8-m antenna produces a 1.4 × 22–deg beam (gain 30 dB); the scan rate is 24 rpm. The frequency sweep is 50, 25, 12.5, 6.25, 3.125, and 1.5625 MHz (corresponding to pulse width); the sweep repetition frequency (SRF, corresponding to PRF) is 1,000 Hz. The processor has 512 range cells (scales 0.75, 1.5, 3, 6, 12, 24 nm). A 1-m^2 target can be detected at about 5.5 nm, a 100-m^2 target (a large craft) at 15.6 nm. An alternative 1.2-m antenna produces a 2.1 × 22–deg beam (gain 29 dB). Signaal offers **Scout B** and **Scout D**, which incorporate conventional pulsed 25-kW transmitter/receivers. Operating with them, a ship can avoid giving away the LPI character of the radar. Scout now has a conventional-looking antenna. As of March 1992, Signaal had sold 10 to the Dutch navy (*Karel Doorman* and, presumably, *Van Heemskerck* classes) and to 2 Far Eastern navies, which required nondisclosure of these sales. In some cases the radar is cross-decked, so a navy buys fewer radars than it has platforms for. Scout was tested on board HMCS *Margary* just before she was decommissioned. As of March 1992, Signaal reported considerable interest in Canada and the United States in Scout for antidrug operations. Reportedly, Canada, the United Kingdom, and some European navies are interested in the submarine version. Scout is also offered in a mobile coast-defense version capable of detecting a fast patrol boat at 15 nm.

As marketed in the U.S. by MSSC (Magnavox-Signaal), Scout uses the Sperry Marine RASCAR (Raster-Scan Collision Avoidance Radar) 2500C display, with touch-screen controls. Average power is adjustable from 1 mW to 1 W.

Variant is a proposed 2D, dual-frequency, air-search ADT radar, operating in G- and I-bands (i.e., C- or X-band). It will be able to transmit bursts in G- or I-band or in a fixed-frequency or frequency-agile mode of both the G- and I-bands. These transmissions can cover selectable sectors of any width, using long or short pulses per sector. Additional options are (i) fully integrated, co-rotating FMCW radar system (i.e., Scout), (ii) integrated IFF antenna(s), (iii) IFF plot/track correlation.

Signaal's next-generation X(I)-band fire-control radar is an active phased-array radar, **APAR**. It will probably equip the future Dutch-German AAW ship. The current sponsors are Canada, Germany, and the Netherlands (however, as of the end of August 1992, no formal agreement had been signed). The planar arrays may be fixed (several would cover 360 deg), or a single array may rotate over a limited angle. For example, 2 planes on each of 2 directors might cover a 120-deg swath. In effect this is conceived as a **STIR** replacement for mid-life upgrades. It may be used to control the new **ESS** (Evolved Sea Sparrow) missile. A dual-plane version would weigh about 2,000 kg. Signaal has already developed quad-packed transmit-receive (Tx-Rx) modules for a prototype Experimental Phased-Array Radar, **EXPAR**. APAR may have as many as 3,200 modules (4 W of output each) in 4 fixed 4 m × 3 m faces, or a smaller number in a rotating antenna. Signaal hopes to generate about 4 separate beams/array (face). The feed controls only the waveform; the array (consisting of programmable clusters of transceivers) controls the beam pattern.

ARTIST (Advanced Radar Techniques for Improved Surveillance) is the associated software program, conceived for the defunct **NAAWS** program (the contract was signed on 1 November 1991). It uses software beam-steering, hence the name (it paints the beams across the sky). ARTIST includes **ACTOR** (Advanced Classification Techniques for Object Recognition), **MUSICIAN** (Multi-Sensor Integration Concept in an All-Supported Network), **PIANIST** (Program for Investigation of Adaptive Nulling and Improved Super-Resolution), and **Painter** (Parallel Architectures for Integrated Thresholding and [Plot] Extraction [i.e., ADT] in Radar).

The associated Dutch-German AAW missile system, using SM-2 and ESSM (Sea Sparrow successor) missiles fired from vertical launchers, is **LAMS-NL**. It is to arm both the new AAW ships for both navies and the modernized Dutch *Van Heemskerck* class (to be upgraded about the turn of the century). A subset (armed with ESSM) is to be refitted into *Karel Doorman*– and surviving *Kortenaer*-class frigates. System sensors will be SMART-L for surveillance, APAR (range 80 km) for multiple target tracking and multiple weapon guidance, and a long-range IRST (LR-IRST), probably the dual-band **Sirius** developed from the existing **IRSCAN**.

SCORADS, Signaal's C(G)-band surface and low-altitude coastal air-search radar, can track up to 100 surface and 200 air targets simultaneously; the maximum instrumented range is 67 nm. It is used by Greece.

DA-01 *Users:* Germany (*Rhein* class), Peru (*Friesland* class), Turkey (*Rhein* class)

DA-02 *Users:* Argentina (*25 de Mayo*), Peru (*Aguirre*)

DA-05 *Users:* Argentina (DA-05/2: MEKO 140 class), Belgium (*Wielingen* class), Egypt (*Descubierta* class: DA-05/2), Finland (*Pohjanmaa*), Indonesia (*Fatahilah* and *Van Speijk* classes: DA-05/2), Morocco (*Descubierta*: DA-05/2), Spain (*Descubierta* class: DA-05/2), Thailand (PFMM Mk 16 class)

DA-08 *Users:* Argentina (MEKO 360 class), Canada (TRUMP class), Germany (*Bremen* and *Hamburg* classes), Greece (MEKO frigates), Malaysia (FS-1500 frigates and new corvettes), Portugal (MEKO frigates), Netherlands (*Van Heemskerck* [to be replaced by **SMART**]), Turkey (*Köln* and MEKO-class frigates). The Canadian TRUMPs will ultimately be fitted with a 3D radar, probably SMART-S, in place of their DA-08s.

LW-02 *Users:* Australia ("River" class), Malaysia (*Rahmat*), Peru (cruiser *Aguirre* and ex-Dutch destroyers)

LW-03 *Users:* Indonesia (*Van Speijk* class)

LW-04 *Users:* Germany (*Hamburg* class)

LW-08 *Users:* Canada (TRUMP class), Greece (*Kortenaer* class), Netherlands (*Van Heemskerck* and *Kortenaer* classes), Taiwan (LW-08/2 in modernized FRAM destroyers), United Kingdom (in modified form, as **Type 1022**). As installed in the 2 *Van Heemskerck*s, LW-08 has a double transmitter with double feed, to form a high-angle beam as well as the usual fan beam (to detect high divers). The whole radar is tilted back slightly to reduce sea clutter. This radar autotracks but does *not* autodetect (SMART autodetects).

ZW-01/3 (SGR-103) *Users:* Germany (*Hamburg, Rhein* classes), Peru (ZW-03 in *Aguirre*), Turkey (*Köln* and *Rhein* classes)

ZW-06 *Users:* Brazil (*Niteroi* class), India (*Godavari, Leander,* and *Whitby* classes), Morocco (*Descubierta* class), Netherlands (*Kortenaer* and *Van Heemskerck* classes), Peru (ex-Dutch *Friesland* class), South Korea (*Ulsan* class), Spain (*Descubierta* class), Thailand (PFMM Mk 16–class corvettes)

ZW-07 *Users:* Netherlands (*Walrus, Zwaardvis, Potvis* classes)

SMART-S (formerly SMART) has been renamed to distinguish it from the larger SMART-L. It is being adapted for land use as Vanguard.

SMART-S *Users:* Germany (Type 123 frigate), Netherlands (*Van Heemskerck* [replaces DA-08] and *Karel Doorman* classes)

MW-08 can be considered **SMART-C** (in analogy with SMART-S and SMART-L).

Users: Greece (MEKO frigates), Oman (new 56-m corvettes), Portugal (MEKO frigates). In July 1991 Signaal sold 3 coastal radars, based on MW-08, to the Greek navy. All will be linked both to the existing NATO South Flank infrastructure and to the Hellenic Navy General Staff Headquarters.

STIR *Users:* Argentina (MEKO 360 class), Canada (TRUMPs and "City" class), Germany (*Bremen*, F 123 classes), Greece (*Kortenaer*s, 8 on MEKO 200s), NATO (2 for the firing range on Crete), Netherlands (*Heemskerck*s, 12 *Kortenaer*s, 16 on *Karel Doorman*s), Nigeria (*Aradu*), Peru (1 on *Alm. Grau*), Portugal (3 *Vasco da Gama*s), South Korea (36 ordered for KDX destroyers in 1991), Taiwan (14 on *Gearing*s, 7 on missile frigates [these are *not* U.S. STIRs]), Thailand (4 on Type 25T frigates being built in China [PRC], probably 4 on the 2 LPDs now on order), and Turkey (ordered for *Yavuz* class in 1982, then 4 more ordered in December 1989, probably for a project to fit *Gearing*s to fire Sea Sparrow). The Turkish *Gearing* project was dropped, and the radars are to be refurbished for use in the Turkish Track II program. As of late 1991, it was not altogether clear that the Taiwanese were buying **STIR 2.4** for their new frigates, but reportedly they wanted the larger dish to get more range to take advantage of probable later purchase of the **SM-2** missile. Some STIRs may be reordered as **STING**s.

STING is a STIR derivative, using hydraulic drive to slew and elevate more quickly. It is adaptable to future correctable ammo (CORAS). The antenna is a 1.2-m Cassegrain; the radar operates in I(X)- and K-bands (respectively, beam 1.6 deg and peak power 220 kW, and beam 0.4 deg and peak power 30 kW). In both bands it tracks by monopulse; the power tubes are TWTs, and processing is by FFT (for Doppler). Compared to STIR, STING is lighter and has a better EO package (full vs. only TV). Weights: director 750 kg, total 2,060 kg.

Users: Oman (56-m corvettes)

LIOD *Users:* Indonesia (PB 57–class ASW version), Ireland (*Eithne*), Malaysia (FS-1500–class frigates), South Korea (HDC 1150–class frigates), and Turkey (FPB 57 class)

LIROD *Users:* Argentina (MEKO 360 and 140 frigates), Australia ("River"-class frigates), Canada (TRUMP class), Greece (Osprey 55 type), Indonesia (*Fatahilah* and former Dutch *Van Speijk* classes), Kenya ("Province"-class missile boats), Mexico (*Cormoran* class), South Korea (*Ulsan* and *Dong Hae* classes), and Thailand (*Ratanakosin*-class and *Chonburi*-class fast attack craft [LIROD-8])

M4 *Users:* Germany (*Rhein*-class tenders) and Turkey (*Köln*-class frigates and *Rhein*-class tenders)

M44 *Users:* India (*Leander*-class frigates), Indonesia (former *Van Speijk*–class frigates), and Turkey (former German *Köln*-class frigates). Formerly on board Swedish destroyers.

M45 *Users:* Australia ("River"-class frigates), Germany (*Hamburg*-class destroyers and *Rhein*-class tenders), India (*Leander*-class frigates), Indonesia (former *Van Speijk*–class frigates), Peru (former Dutch *Friesland*-class destroyers), and Turkey (former *Köln*-class frigates and former *Rhein*-class tenders). Formerly on board Swedish destroyers.

WM20/M20 Series *Users:* **—M20:** Germany (Type 343 mine-countermeasures ships, formerly on *Zobel*-class torpedo boats)

—M22: Finland (*Turunmaa* class), Indonesia (PB 57–class patrol boats), Malaysia (FS-1500 frigates and the frigate *Rahmat*), Nigeria (formerly on board Vosper Mk 3 frigates), Norway (*Oslo*-class frigates, now replaced by 9LV FCS), Spain (*Lazaga*-class fast attack boats), and Sweden (*Halland*-class destroyers and *Spica*-class fast attack boats, now discarded; survives on board *Älvsborg*-class minelayers)

—WM22: Argentina (Lürssen TNC 45–class FACs), Australia ("River"-class frigates), Canada ("Tribal"-class frigates), Philippines (planned for Australian-financed patrol boats, letter of intent issued in 1992; this might be the mini-Combat System; later reported in the *Cormoran* class to be built by Bazan), and Thailand (frigate *Makut Rajakumarn*; WM22/61 in *Chonburi*-class patrol boats)

—WM24: Nigeria (*Erin'mi*-class frigates)

—WM25: Argentina (MEKO 360H2–class frigates), Belgium (*Wielingen*-class frigates), Egypt (*Descubierta* class), Germany (*Bremen*-class frigates), Greece (ex-Dutch *Kortenaer*-class and Osprey 55–class missile corvettes), Morocco (/41 version in *Descubierta*, FCS version in *Lazaga*-class attack boats), Netherlands (*Tromp*-class destroyers and *Kortenaer*-class frigates), Nigeria (MEKO 360H frigate), Peru (cruisers), South Korea (*Ulsan*-class frigates), Spain (*Descubierta*-class frigates; some may have WM22/41), Thailand (PF 103 class as modernized in 1983 and 1986–87; PFMM Mk 16 corvettes, *Ratcharit*-class missile boats), and Turkey (MEKO 200–class frigates)

—WM26: Norway (*Storm*-class fast attack boats), Singapore (110-ft Type B fast attack boats)

—WM27: Germany (S143/143A/143B-class fast attack boats)

—WM28: Argentina (MEKO 140 A16–class frigates), Bangladesh (*Megna*-class fishery-protection patrol boats), Indonesia (*Hajar Dewantara* training frigate, *Fatahilah*-class frigates, and PSK Mk 5–class patrol boats), Iran (Combattante II–class attack boats), Nigeria (WM28/41 in FPB 57–class fast attack boats), Singapore (FPB 45–class fast attack boats), South Korea (*Dong Hae*-, HDC 800–, and HDC 1150–class frigates), Thailand (*Prabrarapak*-class patrol boats), and Turkey (WM28/41 in *Dogan*-class fast attack boats)

Signaal and NobelTech (Bofors, Swedish Ordnance) offer competitive upgrades to the **WM20** series. Signaal promises overall gun-aiming accuracies better than 0.8 mrad and reaction time within 3–5 sec (detect to open fire). The modified system autodetects air targets in horizon and sector-search modes, and initiates autotracking. Increased BITE offers a drastic reduction in MTTR. Late in 1992 Signaal completed a 5-yr program to upgrade WM-27s on board German fast attack boats. The Bofors upgrade replaces 1,300 circuit boards with 13, reduces reaction time by 5–6 sec, and improves range and bearing discrimination by 15%; reliability increases enormously. Signaal is also looking at simpler upgrades of **M20**-series equipment, to bring it up to WM20 standards.

POLAND

The air-search radar of the sole Polish AGI is now offered for export (the manufacturer is RADWAR). **N-25** is a pulse-compressed radar (using a TWT/CFA transmitter) with pulse-to-pulse frequency diversity, digital MTI, and ADT. It can also discriminate between targets in different altitude zones. The ECCM features include a jammer strobe. The antenna is roll- and pitch-stabilized. The range is 100 km [55 nm], with height coverage up to 4 km [13,000 ft]; range on a low-level airplane or surface ship is 30 km [16.4 nm].

SOUTH AFRICA

A new helmet sight (**HESIS**) was announced in 1992. In the new South African coastal-patrol craft, it directly controls a 20-mm gun (carrying a gunner), and it indirectly controls a slaved **twin 107-mm rocket launcher** on the cabin roof. The sight, powered by a 9-volt battery in the helmet, presents the gunner's eye with a red dot (generated by an LED) focused at infinity. The gunner sees the dot on a half-silvered mirror and can see the target with the same eye. Hence the sight requires no calibration to adjust to different gunners' eyes. The system's angular-error detector is coupled to the gunner's helmet and to a reference point behind the gunner; it is a flexible cou-

pling between 2 flat connector plates. The plate on the helmet's back is at 90 deg to the LOS; the plate on the mount is rigid to the weapon's line of fire. The angular deviation is fed directly to the traverse and elevation servo drives. A joystick can input the lead angle and trajectory corrections. The coupling has 6 deg of freedom, allowing the gunner completely free head movement within a considerable envelope. The system has alternative search and attack modes. In search mode, it is detuned so that it follows the gunner's head with a time lag. It does not respond to quick searching movements. The firing circuit is disabled. In the attack mode, the gun follows the gunner's head. The joystick, firing button, mode selection, and power switches are on a bar suspended from the mounting. The gunner's right arm rests on this bar and thus has all the controls immediately to hand.

SPAIN

Inisel's **DORNA** (*Direccion de Tiro Optronica y Raddrica Naval*) incorporates a radar tracker, IR camera, laser RF, and high-definition TV. The director will resemble a **Meroka** turret; a *Santa Maria*–class frigate would have 2. DORNA is the first indigenous Spanish navy FCS; Inisel hopes that it will replace older U.S. equipment as frigates and corvettes are modernized. It is a joint development with Fabrica Artilleria de Bazan (FABA), to take advantage of that company's experience in systems integration, distributed architecture, and high-precision digital servos. Inisel was responsible for the software, which was written in ADA. Work began in 1986, but the Spanish navy has yet to choose a radar type, which may be single- or dual-band (Ka/X). The TV/IR tracker will be based on a TV/IR tracker Inisel used for a land-based system, **Felis.** DORNA should enter service in 1994, initially on board new ships such as the F 100–class frigates. The total estimated development cost is Pt 2,492 million.

SWEDEN

9GA218 is a dual-frequency (D-band: 1.01–1.11 and 1.25–1.35 GHz; I-band: 8.5–9.6 GHz) alternative to the usual X-band **9GA209** antenna. Physically, 9GA218 is taller than 9GA209, with dual feeds (0.7 × 2.7 m, compared to 0.3 × 2.1 m). D-band beam: 6/8 × 20/25 deg (gain is 17 and 20 dB for the 2 bands). I-band beam: 1 × 3 deg (36 dB gain). The weight, including turntable, is 260 kg, as in 9GA209. Like 9GA209, 9GA218 is stabilized in roll and pitch. It appears that unlike its predecessor, 9GA218 does not scan helically (9GA209 scans over a 40-deg vertical range).

The frequency-agility range of the standard **YJ1180** and **YJ1181** magnetrons of the **9LV200** search radar (9GA209) is 400 MHz (typically 450 MHz within 8,700–9,500 MHz). The peak power of the Mk 3 version of the **9LV200 Tracker** is 1.25 kW, compared to 65 kW for Mk 2 (pulses are compressed in Mk 3).

BEAB C/X-Band Radar's antenna produces 3 C(G)-band beams: low (gain 34 dB, 1.9 × 5 deg), high (30.5 dB, 1.9 × 9 deg), and extra high (26.5 dB, 1.9 × 3.5 deg). This portion is connected to a **Sea Giraffe** transceiver. The separate X(I)-band beam is 1.1 × 3.7 deg (37 dB). It can be fed by a **PILOT** LPI radar, although the radars sold thus far use conventional X-band systems.

Users: Australia (ANZAC class), Finland (*Helsinki II* class), New Zealand (ANZAC class), Sweden (*Göteborg* class)

Sea Giraffe *Users:* Bahrein (50HC in *Al Muharraq* class, 50 in TNC 45 class), Canada ("City"-class frigates [150HC]), Kuwait (50HC in *Istiqlal* class, 50 in TNC 45), Malaysia (150HC in new corvettes), Singapore (150HC in *Victory* class), Sweden (50HC in *Stockholm, Nörkoping, Carlskrona* classes), U.A.E. (50HC in 62-m corvettes, 50 in *Mubarraz* and TNC 45 classes). Canada and Singapore use a larger 150HC antenna, with 4 rather than 3 beams.

The Ericsson-Marconi 3D radar is now designated **Sea Giraffe 150 3D** (S1812). It can directly replace the current **150HC**, an additional processing unit being added to the signal/data cabinet below decks. According to Marconi, this radar uses C-band frequency-agile (over 500 MHz) versions of the S800/S1810 transmitter, receiver, and signal processor: 50 kW, 2-microsec pulse compressed on reception. The 130-kg antenna (an array of 24 horizontal linear feeds using phase-shifters) is stabilized mechanically or electronically. Modes: long range (scan at 15 rpm), instrumented range 66 km (detects a 2-m^2 target at 49 km); short (30 rpm), 33 km (38 km detection with Pd 0.8); anti–sea-skimmer (30 rpm), range 33 km (detect 0.1-m^2 target 5 m above sea at 13 km with Pd 0.8). There is also an I(X)-band version.

TVT-300 *Users:* Norway (*Sleipner, Hauk,* and *Storm* classes) and possibly Singapore (110-ft Type B class)

EOS-400 *Users:* Finland (*Turunmaa* class)

9LV100 Series *Users:* Bahrein, Finland (*Pohjanmaa*), Malaysia

9LV200 Series *Users:* —**Mk 1**: Denmark (*Willemoes* class), Malaysia (Spica-M class: 9LV212), Norway (9LV218 in *Norkapp* class), Sweden (*Spica-II* class), Yugoslavia (early units of the *Rade Končar* class [9LV202])
 —**Mk 2**: Bahrein (*Ahmad al Fateh* class [9LV223]), Croatia (*King Petar Kresimir IV* class [9LV249]), Finland (*Helsinki* class [9LV225]), Iraq (*Ibn Khaldum*), Kuwait (FPB 57 and TNC 45 [9LV228]), Sweden (*Hugin* class), U.A.E. (*Baniyas* class), Yugoslavia (9LV249 in later units of *Rade Končar* class)
 —**Mk 2.5** versions include **9LV230**: Malaysia (*Musytari*)
 —**Mk 3**: Denmark (StanFlex 300), Finland (*Helsinki-II* class), Sweden (*Göteborg* class)

9LV300 Series *Users:* Bahrein (FPB 62 class [9LV331]), Oman ("Province" class [9LV307, but not in *Dhofar*]), Sweden (*Stockholm* [as **ARTE 726**])

9LV400 Series *Users:* Australia (ANZAC [9LV453]), New Zealand (ANZAC [9LV453]), Sweden (*Carlskrona, Göteborg* class [9LV450, including ARTE 726E, i.e., 9LV300 for GFCS and RCI-400 for missile FCS, TORPE (torpedo fire control), 9AU300 (ASW fire control), and 9CM300 for ECM control])

SWITZERLAND

Contraves's U.S. branch displayed its new lightweight **LSEOS Mk III** (**Seahawk** successor) EO FCS at the 1993 Navy League show. Total weight is 904 lb (397 above deck) compared to 1,333 (650) for LSEOS Mk II. A single console can serve several manually directed guns, providing all with tracking and aim-point solutions. The 2-axis-stabilized pedestal carries a laser range-finder, TV, and FLIR.

Seaguard *Users:* India (trackers for **Trishul** system in *Delhi* class), Saudi Arabia (*Sandown* class, with Seahawk optronic tracker), Turkey (MEKO Track I and II frigates)

UNITED KINGDOM

Marconi's **ST1803** X(I)-band monopulse tracker, derived from **ST1802**, was announced in 1991. Presumably, ST1803 has much the same characteristics. Announced performance: beam 2.4 deg (using a 2-m twist-Cassegrain antenna, gain 37 dB); peak power 50 kW; pulse lengths 0.33, 0.67, 1.33 microsec; PRF 4.4 kHz normal, 3.0 kHz long range. Instrumented ranges: 24 km with MTI, 48 km without. Elevation limits +83/−28 deg, train and elevation rates 120 deg/sec. Weight: 550 kg above decks, 945 kg total. The set operates in fixed-frequency, pulse-burst-agility, or pulse-to-pulse-agility modes (over a 900-MHz range). ST1803 can acquire a 1-m² target at 42 km. It can accept designation from a 2D or 3D radar, or it can scan at 20 rpm to detect sea-skimmers. The pedestal carries the radar plus EO sensors.

Contraves's LSEOS Mk III lightweight director, at the 1993 Navy League Show. (Author)

Siemens Plessey announced **Lookout**, a new C-band radar, at RNEE 1991; it is intended for OPVs and small patrol vessels and auxiliaries, which in the past were limited to navigational radars. It is intended particularly to detect light aircraft used by drug runners, terrorists, and smugglers, and for self-defense. The target price was £300 thousand, compared to £40 thousand for a typical navigational radar, and about half the price of a full-up militarized radar. To hold cost down, Siemens and Kelvin-Hughes used as many existing elements as possible: the 250-kW, C-band, magnetron transmitter/logarithmic receiver came from a land-based weather radar. The antenna is new, although clearly it owes a great deal to the earlier **AWS-4**. Estimated performance is range 50+ km, altitude 10+ km [33,000 ft]; beam width is about 1.5 × 25 deg (csc² beam). At the time of announcement, PRF and pulse width were still being optimized. Lookout uses a Kelvin-Hughes color tactical display (CTD) console, which can track 40 targets, can maintain 200 maps, and has range scales of 0.25–96 nm. Target tracks are manually initiated (after which the radar autotracks). Graphics include blind axes and helicopter approach paths; Lookout is effectively a mini command system, including target indication to weapons. It has the usual navigational collision-avoidance ARPA functions. In effect, Lookout fits between the Kelvin-Hughes and Siemens Plessey radar ranges. The above-deck weight is 270 kg (500 kg below decks). A prototype was tested at Cowes in August–September 1992. A NATO navy, probably that of Norway, has expressed interest in using Lookout in its projected FPBs. There is also interest in a coast-defense version.

Type 262 *Users:* Indonesia (GWS 21 Sea Cat missile system in "Tribal" class)

Type 275 *Users:* Bangladesh (*Leopard* class and *Umar Farooq*) and India (*Leopard*-class frigate)

Type 277/278 *Users:* Bangladesh (*Umar Farooq*), Chile (Type 278, "County" class) and Pakistan ("County" class)

Type 293 *Users:* Australia (*Stalwart*), India (*Betwa*)

Type 965/966 *Users:* Argentina (Type 42s), Bangladesh (ex-British frigates, reported inoperable), Chile ("County" class and *Leander*s), Ecuador (*Leander*s), India (*Viraat*), Indonesia ("Tribal" class), Pakistan ("County" and *Leander*s).

This set is extinct in the Royal Navy.

Type 967/968 *Users:* United Kingdom (Type 22 frigates, Sea Wolf–armed *Leander*s)

The only current Royal Navy version of **Type 992** is **992R**, the solid-state version of **992Q** (at about half the size).

Users: Argentina (Type 42 class), Chile ("County" class), Pakistan ("County" class), United Kingdom (carriers *Illustrious* and *Ark Royal* prior to modernization, *Birmingham*s, Type 21 class)

Type 993 *Users:* Bangladesh (*Leopard* class and *Umar Farooq*), India (*Nilgiri*), New Zealand (*Leander* class)

Type 994 *Users:* Chile (*Gen. Banquedano*), Ecuador (*Leander*s), Pakistan (*Leander* class), United Kingdom (*Argus, Leander*-class frigates, "Castle" class OPVs, and *Fearless* class). *Argus* and the "Castles" have the **AWS-4** antenna, and current British policy is to replace the existing **AKD** antenna with the new one.

As reported in 1991, total program cost for 37 **Type 996** radars was £144 million (average £3.9 million).

Type 996/AWS-9 *Users:* Turkey (AWS-9 in Track II frigates, the first export sale), United Kingdom (996[1] replaces 992 in carriers and Type 42s, also in *Fort Victoria* class; [2] in Type 23 frigates; a twin-aerial version was associated with the abortive carrier Sea Wolf project)

Type 1006 *Versions:* 1006(1) 9,650 MHz (scan 10 rpm) for submarines; 1006(2,3) 9,445 MHz (scan 25 rpm) for major surface units and OPVs; and 1006(4) 9,425 MHz for mine-countermeasures craft ("Hunt" and "Ton" classes).

Users: Australia (*Fremantle* class, *Oberon* class, *Rushcutter* class), Brazil (*Oberon* class), Chile (*Oberon* class, *Ministro Zenteno*), Ecuador (*Leander* class), Ireland (*Peacock* class), Netherlands (*Zeeleeuw* class [designated ZW-07; these boats may have 1007]), Pakistan (*Leander* class), South Africa (*Protea, Kimberley*), United Kingdom (*Invincible* class, submarines, Type 42s, Type 22s, Type 21s, *Leander* class, *Peacock* class, "Castle" class, "Island" class, *Kingfisher* class, "Hunt" class, *Herald*)

The **Type 1007** radar can also be used for coastal surveillance; in May 1991 it was reported that a Type 1007 with a Searchwater antenna would be used for surveillance of the Clyde estuary.

Users: Australia (new helicopter ship), Canada ("City" class), Ireland (*Peacock* class), Jordan (Hawk class), Malaysia (new corvettes), Netherlands (new AOR), Norway (*Ula* class and coast defenses), Oman* (new missile boats), Qatar* (new missile boats), Portugal (MEKO frigates, *Cacine* class), Saudi Arabia* (*Sandown* class), Singapore (*Victory* class), Spain (new AOR), Turkey* (new FPBs), United Kingdom* (standard navigational radar, in Type 23, *Sandown*, *Sir Galahad*, *Fort Victoria*, *Argus* classes). This radar is also used by Bangladesh, Germany, and Indonesia; in some cases it may be used for coastal surveillance. Of the 18 navies using Type 1007 radars, 13 have the CTD tactical display either in service or on order (the exceptions are indicated by asterisks).

During the Gulf War (1991) HMS *Gloucester* reported routinely detecting stealthy F-117s using her **Type 1022** radar, typically at 40–80 nm, sometimes as far away as 120 nm. Conditions were very damp, so she may have benefited from ducting. It seems likely that some detections were the result of reflection off the sea surface.

Users: United Kingdom (*Invincible*, Type 42 classes)

Type 903/904 *Users:* Chile ("County" class and *Leander* class), India (*Nilgiri*), Indonesia ("Tribal" class), New Zealand (*Leander* class), and Pakistan ("County" and *Leander* classes)

Type 909 *Users:* Argentina (Type 42 destroyers), United Kingdom (*Invincible*-class carriers and Type 42 destroyers)

Type 910 *Users:* United Kingdom (Type 22 Batch Is and early Batch IIs [*Boxer* and *Beaver*] and Sea Wolf–armed *Leander*s [later Sea Wolf ships have Type 911])

Type 911 *Users:* United Kingdom (911(1) controls Sea Wolf GWS 25 Mod 3 in Type 22 Batch II and III frigates, HMS *Brave* and later; (2) controls VL Sea Wolf in Type 23s and *Fort Victoria* class; (3) was the canceled version for Sea Wolf in carriers and Type 42 Batch III destroyers)

The **AWS-1/AWS-2** radars sometimes appear with very different antennas. For example, the Chilean *Alm. Riveros* has AWS-2 feeding the old slotted-waveguide antenna originally installed for her Marconi **SNW-20** radar. These ships have AWS-1 (with the standard antenna) aft.

Users: Chile (*Alm. Riveros* class), Brazil (*Niteroi* class), Denmark (*Falster* class, as CWS-2, with a different antenna), Iran (*Damavand* and Vosper Mk 5 frigates), Malaysia (*Hang Tuah*), Nigeria (*Erin'mi* class), Peru (*Daring* class), Turkey (*Falster* class, as CWS-2, with a different antenna), Venezuela (*Alm. Clemente* class)

AWS-4 *Users:* Brazil (*Inhaúma* class), Kenya ("Province" class), New Zealand (as Type 994), Nigeria (*Obuma*), Norway (coast guard: *Norkapp* class), Oman ("Province" class), Thailand (*Khamronsin* class), United Kingdom (as Type 994). Reported in use by Canada, but it is not clear on board what ship. In the Royal Navy, the **Type 994** designation has been applied not only to the converted **Type 993** but also to AWS-4 as installed on board "Castle"-class OPVs and *Argus*. In the Kenyan ships, the Otomat midcourse-guidance antenna is mounted back-to-back with the main AWS-4 antenna.

The new British **Type 996 (AWS-9)** is partly based on the **AWS-5** radar. In 1991 Siemens Plessey announced 2 new versions, **AWS-5 Increased Power** (with the AWS-9 transmitter) and **AWS-5 Extended Range** (high-gain linear array and new long-range modes). The usual modes are target indication (instrumented range 60 km, scan rate 30 rpm), medium-range surveillance (120 km, 15 rpm), and long-range (240 km). Scan rate may be changed to 20/10 rpm. The Extended Range version scans at 10 rpm; its medium-range mode is instrumented for 200 km, and its long-range mode for 400 km. The Standard and Increased Power versions both use dual-beam antennas; the Extended Range version has only a main beam. Masthead weight is about the same for all: 1,300–1,430 kg for a dual-beam antenna, 1,000–1,300 kg for the high-gain antenna.

Users: Denmark (*Nils Juel* class) and Nigeria (*Aradu*)

The Danish *Thetis*-class fishery-protection frigates use an extended-range single-beam version of **AWS-6 (Dolphin)** (60/120/240 km ranges, 30/15 rpm; there is also a 20/10 rpm alternative). Shorter-range 2-beam versions have instrumented ranges of 20/30/35 km (60 rpm: **Seaguard** version in Turkish MEKO frigates) or 30/70/200 km (60/30 rpm: probably StanFlex 300 version) or 35/70/200 km (30/15 rpm, probably in the Omani "Province" class). In 1991 Siemens Plessey announced a 3D (stacked beam on receive only, as in SMART) version, **AWS-6D**. In a long-range mode, it concentrated all energy in its lower beam (at shorter ranges, it reaches 70-deg elevation). In 1993 Siemens Plessey announced a simpler 2-beam version, **AWS-6E**. Between 4 and 25–30 deg, it measures elevation to within 1 deg by comparing returns in the 2 beams. Above 30-deg elevation it is limited to the high beam and functions as a 2D radar. Similarly, below a certain angle, it is limited to the low beam. Siemens Plessey argues that such performance suffices, and that AWS-6E is far less complex and expensive, hence should be more attractive (work on the more complex -6D is proceeding at low priority).

Users: Denmark (*Thetis*, StanFlex 300, *Hvidbjørnen* classes), Greece (planned for Osprey 55 class, probably will not be fitted), Oman ("Province" class, except *Dhofar*, which has AWS-4), Turkey (MEKO Track I)

Guardsman "C" is a new, medium-range, air-search and coast-defense radar; it appears to be a version of AWS-6 (Guardsman has been redesignated **Guardsman "S"**). Guardsman "C" can be carried on an elevating mast (height 12 or 18 m). Beamwidth is 1.5 deg (2.5 × 1.1 m); peak power is 60 kW (pulse lengths 20/10 microsec compressed to 0.4 microsec, PRFs 2,200/1,100, respectively). Scan rate is 6/12 or 12/24 rpm. Blind speed is 2,000 kt. The radar is agile among 32 frequencies. Instrumented range is 100 km (200 km optional); minimum range is 1.5 km. Resolution (accuracy) is 120 (75) m, 1.5 (0.3) deg.

Marconi ST802 *Users:* Egypt (*Ramadan* and 6 October classes), Kenya (*Nyayo* class)

Marconi S810/S811 *Users:* Algeria (*Kalaat Beni Hammed*–class LSTs [version not given, probably S811]), Egypt (S810 in 6 October–class fast attack craft)

Marconi S1810 *Users:* Egypt (*Ramadan* class), South Korea (2 Korean *Ulsan*-class frigates and some of the *Dong Hae* class)

Marconi **ST1802SW** will probably form the basis for a future British lightweight **Sea Wolf** director, superseding **Type 911**. No Type number has been assigned. Characteristics: peak power is 50 kW (X-band) generated by a TWT; 4,400 pps for normal operation/surface gunnery (0.67-microsec pulses normal operation, 0.33-microsec pulses surface gunnery) and 3,000 pps at long range (1.00 microsec). The main antenna is a 1-m twist Cassegrain (36 dB, beam 2.4 deg). Instrumented range in surface mode is 24 km (e.g., can acquire a patrol vessel with masthead height of 10.7 m). The magnetron-generated J-band command link operates at 30 kW (mean 18 W). The antenna can rotate continuously at 20 rpm; it can train at 120 deg/sec (elevation 120 deg/sec). It elevates at 30 deg/sec in search mode; it tracks for Seawolf control at 11 deg/sec.

Users: Malaysia (new corvettes, controlling Sea Wolf), South Korea (Samsung-built version in *Ulsan* and *Dong Hae* classes)

Marconi's new **S1830** (a navalized S711) is being offered to Norway for the projected *Oslo*-class modernization, and to Pakistan for the Type 21s that will probably be transferred. This coherent S-band (2.8–3.1 GHz, frequency-agile over 300 MHz) radar uses an S1810 signal processor with digital MTI; the 18-microsec output pulse is compressed to 0.4 microsec on reception. Instrumented range is 200 km (108 nm); low-fliers and sea-skimmers are detected out to 20 km (11 nm). S1830 can use either a 4.7-m high-gain antenna scanning at 10 or 20 rpm (or faster for target indication or TWS) or a 2.4-m antenna scanning at 20 or 60 rpm (both produce csc^2 beams). The transmitter uses 38 solid-state modulators in parallel.

Racal 2459 is a true surface-search and often air-search radar, not a navigational set. Not all users have the dual-antenna (F/I) version.

Users: Indonesia (PB 57 class), Netherlands (*Poolster*), Portugal (this is probably the radar that replaced the old **MLA-1B** in the *João Coutinho* class), Spain (*Milano* class)

At RNEE 1991 Racal displayed a new Kevlar antenna for its standard 3-cm (X-band) navigational radars. Compared to the usual slotted waveguide, it has no squint angle, and it offers a reduced magnetic signature. It is currently selling to Scandinavian navies. The gain is 30+ dB; beam dimensions are 1.2 × 20 deg, and the scan rate is either 28 rpm or 0–60 rpm.

Standard Royal Navy **Radar Plot Extractors** are **LFA** for Type 965, **LFB** for 1022, **LFC** for 1007, and **LFD** for 996. Thorn-EMI makes LFB, LFC, and LFD. Typical capacity is 500 tracks. Thorn-EMI also makes the standard Royal Navy **Radar Track Combiner** (RTC) in *Invincible*-class carriers and Type 42 destroyers, which creates a Recognized Air and Surface Picture (RASP) for the CDS. In a ship so equipped, each radar's ATD feeds track data into the ship's combat-system bus. The RTC maintains 1,000+ tracks, with a maximum update rate of 150+ tracks/sec. RTC differs from the U.S. SYS series, operating on tracks rather than individual radar plots. RTC weights the individual radars' track data according to their measured statistics, correlating and merging them. It also projects tracks ahead during fades lasting up to a minute.

Radamec's modular EO FCS and surveillance systems are now grouped as **Series 2000** (parts of the series have been in service "from Scandinavia to North East Asia" for more than a decade, according

The new fiberglass high-gain antenna of a Decca 1226 radar on board the Norwegian frigate *Stavanger* in 1992. Other ships of the class still have the conventional slotted-waveguide antennas. (Author)

Canvas-covered DEC dazzler-laser on board HMS *Edinburgh* in 1992. (Raymond Cheung)

to the manufacturer. All are built around the **HK 409** dual-axis pedestal, well over 100 of which are in service (they were designated in an HK 409 series, e.g., 409–029). **System 2100** is the simplest, a pure surveillance system. **System 2200/2300** is a GFCS (2200 with manned, 2300 with unmanned director). **System 2400** is the most elaborate version. It incorporates a Radamec video autotracker (which automatically switches between centroid and correlation tracking); the tracker is optional in the other versions. The System 2100 pedestal carries a thermal imager (normally in the 8–12-micron band) and a daylight or LLLTV camera; it is LOS-stabilized and is normally joystick-controlled (it can also autoscan). It can be slewed to a target detected by a radar. In System 2200, the operator stands at the director, viewing the outputs of the EO sensors through a hood; the director is controlled via 2 thumb joysticks. System 2300 substitutes a below-decks console for the hooded monitor. Both versions add laser range-finders to the passive optics of System 2100. The operator fires the laser when a decision to engage is made. When the system receives the laser range datum, it calculates a gun lead angle and drives the gun; the monitor shows the sequence and the target's predicted future range. The director operator opens fire, applying spotting corrections in the case of surface fire. System 2400 uses an unmanned director with a weapons-control console below decks; it can also be connected to target-designation sights. Unlike the simpler versions, it has special shore-bombardment modes: direct fire (target height input into predictor), indirect fire (at map grid references or lat/long references), and beacon track.

Users: Denmark (*Soloven* class), Finland (two 2400 on *Hameenmaa*), Hong Kong (2100 in police launches), Jordan (2200 in "Hawk" class), South Korea (2400 in *Ulsan*, HDC 800, and *Dong Hae* classes and in "Sea Wolf"–class Maritime Police Patrol boats), Spain, United Kingdom (2100 in Type 42 destroyers). Units may have been installed on board Australian frigates for Gulf operations in 1991. Possibly also Belgium, Chile, Egypt, India, Italy, New Zealand, Norway, Pakistan, Singapore (but may be for radars only), and Sweden (but these may be pedestals, not systems). The reported sale to Australia seems not to have been consummated.

The earlier **Series 1000** designations seem to have been abandoned. Radamec refers to its **400-series** stabilized platforms as directors, although some of them carry quite different payloads. Thus **Type 409** also carries the **Guardian** (Type 675) jammer; **429** carries the antennas of the **Cygnus** jammer (**HK 440** carries the new Racal jammer for German fast attack boats). **Type 449** can carry **Blowpipe** missiles (or daylight and LLLTV cameras). **Type 459** carries an EO sensor for the land-based **Rapier** missile. Types 409, 429, and 449 are all pedestals on which sensors or other equipment are carried. 429 is a heavy-duty version of 409. As of the fall of 1991, over 200 Type 409s had been delivered (since 1980). **HK 503** is a new 3-axis radar platform, first used for **Sea Giraffe** in the Singapore navy's *Victory* class.

There are 3 **Laser Dazzle System** (LDS, Outfit DEC) modes:

(i) vs. aircraft, (ii) vs. EO missiles, (iii) vs. boats (direct burn mode). In mode (i), the laser is pointed into the water, putting up a "wall" of laser light that the airplane's HUD concentrates into the pilot's eyes. The plastic canopy fluoresces and turns opaque. Effective range may be 5 km (reported as 1,600 m in March 1990). DEC reportedly shifts between 2 very different frequencies (IR and visible) to frustrate attempts at eye protection (it burns the coating off protective goggles). DEC-1 had 2 separate lasers; DEC-3 uses a wideband laser that can shift between the 2 frequencies. DEC is reportedly controlled by the **Type 1007** radar.

Thorn-EMI's lightweight **MEOSS** (Marine Electro-Optical Surveillance System) was announced in 1991. This stabilized thermal imaging system for patrol craft down to 10 m in length uses a remotely controlled thermal imager and LLLTV on a stabilized tracking head. The imager (8–12 micron) can detect a 20-m boat at about 7.5 km and a person in the water at about 1.5 km. The wider-angle LLLTV is used for observation and navigation. The console can show either an image from one sensor or a split screen of images from both. The console carries a joystick controlling the sensor head in elevation (±30 deg) and azimuth (±170 deg); the helmsman has an override control that can slew the head 20 deg to either side of the current heading. As of September 1991, MEOSS had already been evaluated on board various patrol craft.

GDS 2* *Users:* Bangladesh (*Leopard* class and *Umar Farooq*) and India (*Leopard* class)

GDS 5 *Users:* Indonesia ("Tribal" class, with 293Q radar), Pakistan ("County" class, with 992 radar)

GSA 7 (Sea Archer 1) *Users:* Brunei (*Waspada* class), Ireland (*Peacock* class), Oman (*Dhofar* [Mk 2 version], 37.5-m–class patrol boats, and *Al Munassir*), Thailand (*Khamronsin* class [Mod 2], T 93 class [Mod 1], and PS 700 class LSTs), United Kingdom (*Peacock* class)

GSA 8 (Sea Archer 30) *Users:* United Kingdom (Type 23 and Type 22 Batch 3 classes)

GWS 1 (Sea Slug) *Users:* Chile ("County" class)

GWS 20 (Sea Cat) *Users:* United Kingdom (*Fearless* class)

GWS 21 (Sea Cat) *Users:* Indonesia ("Tribal" class)

GWS 22 (Sea Cat) *Users:* Chile ("County" and *Leander* classes), Ecuador (*Leanders*), India (*Leander*-class frigate *Nilgiri*), Pakistan ("County" and *Leander* classes)

GWS 24 (Sea Cat: WSA-4 FCS with Type-912 radar) *Users:* Brazil (*Niteroi* class) and United Kingdom (Type 21s)

GWS 25 (Sea Wolf) *Users:* United Kingdom (*Leanders* and Type 22s)

GWS 26 (Sea Wolf VLS) *Users:* United Kingdom (Type 23 and *Fort* classes)

GWS 30 (Sea Dart) *Users:* Argentina (Type 42 destroyers) and United Kingdom (carriers and Type 42 destroyers)

MRS 3 *Users:* Chile ("County" and *Leander* classes), India (*Leander* class), Indonesia ("Tribal" class), New Zealand (*Waikato*), and Pakistan ("County" and *Leander* classes)

Sapphire *Users:* Egypt (6 October and *Ramadan* classes) and Kenya (*Nyayo* class)

UNITED STATES

The current advanced R&D program includes work on multisensor technology, including a new wide-area airborne early-warning radar, an airborne IRST, and a shared-aperture airborne IR/EO system. Some of these systems may be spaceborne. The goal is to fight the AAW battle with minimum electromagnetic emissions, or at the least with minimum recognizable emissions. One approach is **HFDF** (height-finding, not high-frequency, direction finding); see the section on EW. Another is increased emphasis on IR and EO sensors. Thus the FY92 program included investigation of a multiband, multimode IR sensor with an agile FoV combined with an ISAR, for better situational awareness, i.e., for air search (the ISAR would identify targets and measure their ranges). A very few discrete range measurements might suffice for tracking, given the accurate angular information from the optics. The FY92 program also included early feasibility work on an EO multitarget tracker for fire control for all-the-way or most-of-the-way command guidance. Such a system might greatly reduce a ship's electromagnetic emissions. Work is also proceeding on superresolution sensors (which greatly exceed the usual 1/wavelength resolution limit). The FY92 program included the first over-water test of such a sensor, to measure the extent to which it might be confused by multipath effects.

Another important objective is to make the overall ship weapons system more efficient. That requires prompt kill assessment. Work on the appropriate processor began in FY92.

Martin Marietta has bought the GE Aerospace division, including its radar and Aegis interests.

Preparation for full-scale development of the **SMATCALS** (Signature Managed Air Traffic Control and Landing System) began in FY93. SMATCALS is to replace **SPN-43** and **SPN-46**. It is to provide both air traffic control *and* approach control.

SPS-48E is the **NTU** (New Threat Upgrade) version of **SPS-48**: by August 1992, 39 SPS-48Es had been delivered, with 6 more on order (3 ordered in January 1992, presumably for new LHDs). The current tracking accuracy is 0.2 deg, compared with a requirement for 0.6 deg. The low-elevation (**Low-E**) modification proved extremely effective in the Gulf War, hence NTU ships were stationed at the northern end of the Gulf. The Low-E version gives highest priority to the lowest 5 beam groups, which cover 0–28 deg (the radar's 9 pencil beams form a beam group, covering a total of 6 deg in elevation; the radar can place the beam groups at various elevation angles). The lowest 3 beams of the bottom group transmit a Doppler waveform (2,778 pps). That increases average power; a 1-m² target can be detected against sea clutter at 17 nm. Low-E was first demonstrated on board the USS *Kidd* in 1990, and it was installed on board 12 NTU ships (November 1990–November 1991: Phase IA of NTU). As of mid-1992, at least 18 ships were expected to receive this modification in the near term; ultimately it will be extended to all NTU ships. The current MTBF is 500+ hr in most ships, compared to a specified 190.

SPS-48F is a lightweight version originally intended for foreign sales. None has materialized. However, ITT-Gilfillan hopes -48F, which it can supply by 1995, will replace surviving U.S. Navy **SPS-52**s, e.g., in the LHAs. The company describes -48F as 40% less expensive than SPS-48E, and also 40% more reliable. It would use a 71-element planar array (compared to 95 for -48E: 3.96 × 3.65 rather than 5.48 × 5.18 m, 1,125 kg rather than 2,970 kg). Below-decks weight is 6,750 rather than 9,900 kg. This reduction is achieved partly by eliminating the final amplifier stage in the transmitter, cutting peak power from 2.4 MW to 660 kW (average reduced from 35 to 15 kW), thus reducing the range on a 1-m² target from 125 to 90 nm (150 nm, rather than 220 nm, on a 5-m² target). Embedded microprocessors replace the **UYK-20** and **SYS-2** associated with -48E. ITT-Gilfillan expects MTBF to increase from 650 to 950 hr (the -48E specification originally asked for only 150 hr). Accelerated retirement of NTU cruisers will probably release sufficient SPS-48s to equip the major amphibious ships without new production.

SeaAirSearch RADAR SUITE

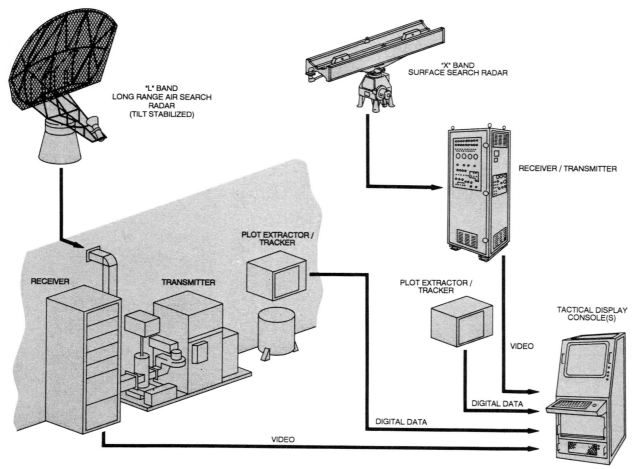

Cardion's 5544 SeaAirSearch radar, a version of which equips the new Israeli *Eilat* (Sa'ar V). (Cardion)

ITT, which makes SPS-48, is now under contract with APL for a cylindrical active aperture radar, to be demonstrated in 1993 under the **Cooperative Engagement Concept** (CEC).

TPS-44 is a land-based L-band (1.25–1.35 GHz) Cardion radar that has been navalized as the air-search radar of the new Israeli *Eilat* (Sa'ar V) class. The marinized TPS-44 is designated CLR-155. Beam is 4.9×9.6 deg (csc^2 to 20 deg), using a 4.4×2.5-m antenna (gain 26 dB, scan rate 8/16 rpm; the antenna is stabilized so that the 3-dB point of the beam is always within 2 deg of the horizon [maximum pitch and roll 7.5 and 15 deg, period at least 5 sec]). Peak power is 1 MW (pulse width 1.4 microsec/800 pps; 2.4 microsec/400 pps; 4-pulse stagger). Resolution of the associated system is 6 deg/6.5 deg at 8 rpm (narrow/wide pulses) and 6.5/7 deg at 16 rpm. Range resolution is 700 m in narrow- and 1,400 m in wide-pulse mode. Track accuracy is 1.5 nm against surface targets and 1.6 nm against non-maneuvering air targets. Track capacity is 200 tracks/scan (decreasing to 100 at maximum pitch and roll). Maximum tracking velocity is Mach 2. Antenna weight is 700 kg (swing radius 2.2 m); below-decks equipment weighs 930 kg.

The naval version replaces the MTI and video integrator of the land-based radar with digital plot extractor (ADT) functions and adds ship's motion compensation. The radar can detect fighters at 10,000 ft at 50+ nm, and larger aircraft at 10,000 ft at 75+ nm. Unambiguous range is 80/160 nm (depending on pulse rate). In the Israeli ships, TPS-44 has a plot extractor/tracker (ADT) feeding a Cardion CDS. The processor is 68000-based; the track-keeper is provided by Elta. The associated surface-search radar is **SPS-55**. Cardion is now marketing the TPS-44/SPS-55 combination as the **Type 5544 Sea-AirSearch** radar suite, with 1 or more Cardion CRD5544 color displays, and a capacity of up to 200 tracks/radar. Each radar feeds a plot extractor, and the outputs of both are sent to a single tactical display console or consoles.

Taiwan has selected Martin Marietta's (formerly GE's) S-band **ADAR-2N** over Raytheon's CMAR for its Flight 2 frigates. Aperture is about 3 m (set by deck height), beamwidth something over 2.4 deg. CMAR beamwidth would have been about 1.6 or 1.7 deg (aperture 3.1 or 2.8 m). The Martin Marietta system employs slaved illuminators.

SSDS (Ship Self-Defense System) is a series of new integrated systems, the development of which was begun under a Quick-Reaction Combat Capability (**QRCC**) program. Mk 0 is **RAIDS**, which integrates sensors and an artificial-intelligence processor (analogous to the Aegis C&D processor) to provide tactical advice on using weapons and countermeasures (it is not connected directly to any of them). The near-term **SSDS Mk 1** connects SPS-49, an IRST, SLQ-32, RAM, and Phalanx. The medium-term **SSDS Mk 2** adds the NATO Sea Sparrow Missile System and its TAS Mk 23, and is integrated with a ship's CDS. The far-term **SSDS Mk 3** will use a new multifunction radar (**MFR**), the next-generation ECM system (**AIEWS**), and a new missile (either **ESSM** or an SDIO-derived weapon), and will be compatible with the cooperative engagement concept (**CEC**).

SSDS Mk 0 is to be installed in *Spruance*-class destroyers (as interim for Mk 2) and also in *Perry*-class frigates without CORT. It should enter service with the destroyers in the second quarter of FY95 and on board frigates in the first quarter of FY96. As of spring 1993, it had completed development testing in the *John Hancock* (DD-981) and *John Rodgers* (DD-983), and it began operational testing on 21 January 1993.

SSDS Mk 1, for *Perry*-class frigates with CORT, for the LHD-1, LSD-41, LSD-49, and LX classes, is to enter service in FY96. The prototype, using an SAR-8 IRST, was installed in the USS *Whidbey Island* (LSD-41) in March–April 1993 for summer 1993 tests. The LAN is SAFENET; the weapons are 2 Phalanxes and RAM. SSDS Mk 2, for the *Nimitz, Spruance, Wasp* (LHD-1), and AOE-6 classes, is to enter service in FY98. It will be tested on board the rebuilt remotely controlled destroyer *Decatur* in late 1993 or in 1994.

About a third of the SSDS budget goes to a black program, **Link Iron**. It probably seeks counters to stealthy (low-observable) attackers.

SWY-1 is the combination of **TAS Mk 23** and NATO Sea Sparrow, in service since 1980. Currently, ESM and IR are being integrated in the TAS Mk 23 Operational Computer Program (OCP) to reduce acquisition and reaction times, using improved correlation/association and TEWA algorithms. The FY90 program began developing a single common **UYK-44** program supporting a Mk 23 interface with CDS and non-CDS equipped ships. **SWY-2** is the combi-

nation of TAS Mk 23 and RAM, for LHAs. SWY-2 was to enter service in 1993. **SWY-3** is the likely designation for the combination of TAS Mk 23, Sea Sparrow, and RAM on LHD-5 and later units.

Westinghouse proposes a shipboard version of its **TPS-63** L-band, 2D, air-defense radar, to be called **WSR-63**. It will have a new antenna and repackaged electronics.

SS-2 *Users:* Brazil (Guppy III class), Greece (Guppy IIA and III), Peru (*Dos de Mayo* class), Taiwan (Guppy II class), Turkey (Guppy II, Guppy IIA classes), Venezuela (Guppy II class)

BPS-12 *Users:* Turkey (*Tang* class), United States (*Barbel* class, stricken but probably for sale)

BPS-15 *Users:* United States (*Ohio, Los Angeles, James Madison, Permit/Sturgeon* classes, *Narwhal*)

BPS-16 is being bought for the *Seawolf* class, for the last 3 *Ohios*, and for backfit into other *Ohios*, but it is not yet planned for new *Los Angeles*–class submarines. Unlike BPS-15, -16 has a new 50-kW, X-band (8–12 GHz), frequency-agile transmitter. Pulses: 0.1 microsec/1,500 pps, 0.5 microsec/750 pps, resolution 30/100 yd, minimum range 25 yd, maximum 20 nm.

SPS-5 *Users:* Chile (ex-tug *Sergente Aldea*), Colombia (*Courtney* class), Greece (*Cabildo, Patapsco* classes), Mexico (some *Auk*-class ex-minesweepers), Philippines (*Auk*-class ex-minesweepers), Taiwan (ex–high-speed transports, *Cabildo*-class LSD), Turkey (*Portunus*-class patrol-boat tender). The Brazilian carrier *Minas Gerais* and the Chilean corvette (ex-APD) *Virgilio Uribe* may retain the very similar **SPS-4**.

SPS-6 *Users:* Brazil (*Thomaston* class), Chile (APD *Virgilio Uribe*), Colombia (*Dealey* class), Greece (*Cabildo* class), Indonesia (*Claud Jones* class), Iran (PF 103 class), Italy (*Pietro Cavezzale*), Peru (training ship *Independencia*), Portugal (AOR *São Gabriel*), South Korea (*Fletcher*-class destroyer), Taiwan (*Sumner* class not subject to major reconstruction, *Rudderow* class), Thailand (PF 103 class), Uruguay (*Cohoes* class)

SPS-10/SPS-67 *Users:* Argentina (*Cabo San Antonio*), Australia (*Adams* class [67]), Brazil (FRAM destroyers, *Garcia* class), Canada (*Annapolis, Mackenzie, Restigouche, St. Laurent* classes), Germany (*Adams* class), Greece (*Adams*, FRAM destroyers, *Terrebonne Parish* classes), Indonesia (*Claud Jones* class), Iran (FRAM destroyers), Mexico (FRAM destroyers), Pakistan (FRAM destroyers, *Brooke, Garcia* classes, *Moawin*), South Korea (FRAM destroyers), Spain (*Baleares, Paul Revere* classes), Taiwan (some destroyers [many with SPS-58], *Kao Hsiung* command ship), Turkey (destroyers, *Derya*), United States (carriers [67], *Iowa* class [67 except BB-62, SPS-10F], *California* class [67], *Long Beach* [67], *Belknap* [10F or 67], *Leahy* [10F or 67], *Arleigh Burke* [67], *Adams* [10F], *Mahan* [10B], *Knox* [10 or 67], *Blue Ridge* [10/65], *Wasp* [67], *Tarawa* [10F], *Iwo Jima, Austin, Raleigh, Harpers Ferry* [67], *Whidbey Island* [67], *Anchorage, Thomaston, Newport, Charleston, Puget Sound, Dixie, Kilauea, Nitro, Suribachi, Mars, Coronado, La Salle, Cimarron* [only AO-180, -186; others are SPS-55], *Supply* [67], *Sacramento, Wichita, Vulcan, Spear, Simon Lake, Hunley, Fulton* classes)

SPS-12 *Users:* Canada (*Mackenzie, St. Laurent* classes), Taiwan (command ship *Kao Hsiung*)

SPS-29 *Users:* Brazil (*Espirito Santo*), Greece (*Gearing*-class destroyers), Iran (*Sumner* class), Japan (*Amatsukaze*), Mexico (*Gearing*-class destroyer *Netzahualcoyotl*), Philippines (*Andres Bonifacio*), South Korea (*Gearing* and *Sumner* classes), Taiwan (*Gearing, Sumner,* and *Fletcher* classes), Turkey (*Gearing* class), Vietnam (*Barnegat* and *Savage* classes)

SPS-37 *Users:* Taiwan (*Fu Yang*)

SPS-39 *Users:* Greece (*Adams* class), Pakistan (*Brooke* class), United States (unmodernized *Adams* class; SPS-42 in JPTDS ships)

SPS-40 *Users:* Australia (*Adams* class [40C]), Brazil (*Garcia* class), Germany (*Adams* class), Greece (*Adams* class), Japan (*Azuma*), Pakistan (*Garcia, Brooke* classes), Turkey (*Berk* class), United States (*California, Truxtun* [40B], *Belknap* [CG-31 and -32 only], *Adams, Spruance* class [except DD-997], *Tarawa* [40B], *Iwo Jima, Austin, Raleigh, Anchorage, Sacramento* [AOE-1 and -2 only], *Hamilton* classes)

SPS-48 *Users:* United States (carriers, *California, Virginia, Long Beach, Leahy, Belknap, Mahan* classes, *Wasp* class except *Wasp, Blue Ridge* class)

SPS-49 *Users:* Australia (*Perry* and ANZAC classes), Canada ("City" class), New Zealand (ANZAC class), South Korea (chosen for KDX class), Spain (*Perry* class), Taiwan (*Perry* class), Thailand (new Type 25T class), United States (carriers, *Iowa* class, *Virginia* class [except CGN-38 and -39], *Ticonderoga* class, *Belknap* class [except CG-31 and -32], *Leahy, Mahan, Kidd, Perry, Wasp* classes)

SPS-49 MPU is a medium-PRF upgrade; it has doubled range and improved performance against small targets in sea clutter (i.e., against small missiles).

SPS-52 (all -52C except as noted) *Users:* Australia (*Adams* class), Germany (*Adams* class), Italy (*Vittorio Veneto* [-52B], *Animoso, Audace* classes), Japan (*Hatakaze* class; -52B in *Tachikaze, Amatsukaze* classes), Spain (*Principe de Asturias*, last 2 *Perry* class

[*Galicia, Navarra*], *Baleares* class [-52B]), United States (-52C in modernized *Adams* class, *Tarawa* class, *Wasp*)

SPS-55 *Users:* Australia (*Perry* class), Israel (*Eilat* class), Saudi Arabia (PCG, PGG, and MSC 322 classes), Spain (*Principe de Asturias, Perry* class), Taiwan (*Perry* class), United States (*Ticonderoga, Arleigh Burke, Spruance, Kidd, Perry* classes)

SPS-58 survives only in a stand-alone version developed for Taiwan. **SPS-65** survives on board *Iwo Jima*– class amphibious carriers; elsewhere it has been superseded by **TAS** Mk 23.

The **SPS-68** designation was reserved in 1983 for a planned **SPS-49** successor, for non-AAW combatants, including major amphibious ships and auxiliaries.

SPY-1/FARS *Users:* Japan (-1D in *Kongo* class), United States (*Ticonderoga* [-1A in CG-47–58, -1B in CG-59– 73]; -1D in *Arleigh Burke* class)

Mk 13 radar/GFCS Mk 38 *Users:* United States (*Iowa* class)

Mk 26 radar/GFCS Mk 52 *Users:* Chile (APD), Peru (*Bellatrix* class), Philippines (*Cannon* class), Taiwan (*Rudderow* class), Vietnam (*Savage* class)

Mk 25 radar/GFCS Mk 37 *Users:* Brazil (*Gearing, Sumner* classes), Chile (*Sumner* class), Ecuador (*Gearing* class), Greece (*Gearing, Sumner* classes), Iran (*Sumner* class), Mexico (*Gearing, Fletcher* classes), Pakistan (*Gearing* class), South Korea (*Sumner, Gearing, Fletcher* classes), Taiwan (unconverted ships and Tien Shi and Wu Chin III conversions, total of 11), Turkey (*Gearing, Sumner, Smith* classes), United States (*Iowa* class). Some Taiwanese ships retain Mk 37 without the Mk 25 radar (**H930** electro-optics has been substituted). The Mexican *Fletcher* reportedly retains her WWII **Mk 12/22** radar combination, almost certainly no longer operable.

SPG-34/Mk 34/SPG-50 and **FCS Mk 63** *Users:* Canada (*Mackenzie* class), Colombia (*Courtney, Asheville* classes), Greece (*Asheville, Terrebonne Parish* classes), Iran (PF 103 class), Japan (DDK-116/117, *Isuzu, Katori, Akizuki* classes), South Korea (PSMM Mk 5 [PGM 352–355, with **Standard ARM** missiles], *Asheville* class), Spain (*Paul Revere, Terrebonne Parish* classes), Turkey (*Berk, Asheville, Terrebonne Parish* classes)

SPG-35/FCS Mk 56 *Users:* Brazil (*Garcia* class), Japan (*Minegumo*), Pakistan (*Brooke, Garcia* classes), Turkey (*Carpenter* class), United States (*Long Beach*)

Ships without NTU are being discarded, leaving only **SPG-51D Mk 74** Mod 15 (*Kidd, California, Virginia* classes) active in the U.S. Navy. All are digital **Tartar**. *Adams*-class versions are Mod 6 (digital update with **SPG-51C**), Mod 8 (**JPTDS**; DDG-9, -12, -15, and -21; SPG-51C radar), and Mod 13 (DDG-19, -20, -22, with SPG-51C). The ships transferred to Greece have Mod 6 systems. The *Brooke* class transferred to Pakistan have the digital update (Mod 6) with SPG-51C radar. Plans to upgrade these ships further with SPG-51D radars did not come to fruition. Mk 74 versions in foreign SM-1 ships are not known.

Users: —**SPG-51B**: Japan (*Amatsukaze*)
—**SPG-51C**: Australia (*Adams* class), Germany (*Adams* class), Greece (*Adams* class), Italy (*Audace* class), Japan (*Hatakaze, Tachikaze* classes), Netherlands (*Tromp* class), Pakistan (*Brooke* class), Spain (*Baleares* class), United States (*Adams* class, for sale)
—**SPG-51D**: Italy (*Animoso* class), United States (*Virginia, California*, and *Kidd* classes)

SPG-52/FCS Mk 70 *Users:* Indonesia (*Claud Jones* class)

SPG-53/FCS Mk 68 Mod 4 is the analog version, on board 8 *Adams* class. Mod 6 is the *Mahan* class's analog version (planned replacement with the digital Mod 18 with -53F radar was not carried out). Mods 11 (FF-1052–77) and 13 (FF-1078–97) were for the *Knox* class. A planned digital modernization was not carried out, and ships with Mod 14 (to support **Standard ARM**) were converted back to Mods 11/13.

Users: —**SPG-53A**: Australia (*Adams* class), Egypt (*Knox* class), Greece (*Adams* and *Knox* classes), Taiwan (*Knox* class), Turkey (*Knox* class), United States (*Adams, Knox* classes)
—**SPG-53C**: Spain (*Baleares* class: Mk 68 Mod 11)
—**SPG-53F**: United States (*Belknap* and some *Adams* class). The *Belknap* class has Mk 68 Mod 17; all *Adams* class that did not get Mk 86 (DDG-2–16, -18, -21) were scheduled for Mod 19, but only 10 were so modified.

SPG-55C/Mk 76 *Users:* Italy (*Vittorio Veneto*), United States (*Bainbridge*).

Missiles may be controlled directly through the combat system on board the Italian *Vittorio Veneto*. Her version presumably equates to Mod 4.

SPG-55D/Mk 76 is the NTU version. Ships without NTU are being discarded, leaving only the Mod 10 version (*Leahy* and *Belknap* classes) and the NTU prototype on *Mahan*.

Users: United States (*Mahan, Long Beach, Leahy, Belknap* classes)

SPQ-9 performance improvements against targets with low radar cross sections are being tested. Current improvement efforts include a High-Speed Maneuvering Surface Target (**HSMST**) modification (completed in FY91), better detection of small low-flying missiles and aircraft, improvements to **SPG-60** (DDG-993 and CGN-38 classes) for better SM missile control, and more efficient use of available computer memory. The FY92 program included provision of a second tracking/illumination channel for **Sea Sparrow**, presumably by modifying Mk 86.

SPG-60/SPQ-9/FCS Mk 86 *Users:* Germany (*Adams* class), United States (*Spruance, Kidd*, modernized *Adams, Tarawa, Wasp* classes)

Mk 91 (NATO Sea Sparrow) *Users:* Belgium (*Wielingen* class*), Canada ("City" class [STIR tracker]), Denmark (*Nils Juel* class [Mod 1]), Germany (F 123 class [STIR tracker] and *Bremen* class*), Greece (*Kortenaer* class* and MEKO 200 class [STIR tracker]), Italy (*Lupo* class [Mod 1]), Japan (*Shirane, Haruna, Asagiri, Hatsuyuki* classes*), Netherlands (*Tromp*, Karel Doorman* [STIR tracker], *Kortenaer* [STIR tracker], Norway (*Oslo* class [Mod 1]), Portugal (MEKO 200), Thailand (new Type 25T frigate [STIR tracker]), Turkey (MEKO 200 [STIR tracker]), United States (carriers, LHAs/LHDs, *Spruance* class, AOEs, AORs [all Mods 0 and 1])

Asterisks indicate the "Netherlands" version (Signaal **WM 25** with Raytheon illuminator). Only Mods 0 and 1 (double channel) use the **Mk 95** radar. More recent Japanese ships substitute **FCS 2–21** for WM 25. The Italian version (in the original *Lupo* class) is unique in that it can control the **Aspide** missile (but these ships may be armed with **RIM-7H** and are being adapted to **RIM-7M**). U.S. ships use **TAS Mk 23** for target acquisition (the earlier **SPS-65** is limited to **BPDMS** ships).

Mk 92 *Users:* Australia (*Perry* class), Saudi Arabia (PCC and PCG classes), Spain (*Perry* class; CORT applied to last 2 ships), Taiwan (*Perry* class, with CORT), Thailand (Type 25T frigates), United States (*Perry* and PHM classes; Mk 94 in PHM-1; CORT in FFG-50, -51, -53, -55, -56, -61).

Work on a midlife upgrade to Mk 92s on board *Perry*-class frigates began in FY92. These ships may fire **SM-2 Block IIIB** missiles. Tactical improvements include Guard Gate, Priority Engage, and Sector Scan. Technical improvements include heavy-duty rate transmission for the combined antenna (the "egg") and reduction of high-failure-rate items.

Mk 51 *Users:* Argentina (modified *DeSoto County*–class LST), Brazil (*DeSoto County*–class LST), Greece (minelayers: all Mod 2), Iran (PF 103 class: Mod 2), Japan (*Chikugo, Miura, Atsumi* classes), Mexico (APDs), Peru (*Bellatrix* class), Philippines (*Cannon* class), Portugal (*João Coutinho* class), Taiwan (unconverted *Gearing*, Tien Shi *Sumners*, LSTs), Thailand (LSTs, LSMs), Turkey (*Kocatepe, Muavenet, Gearing* FRAM Is, *Mordogan*-class minelayers). Some other ships, particularly LSTs, may retain Mk 51 directors.

Mk 115 (BPDMS) *Users:* United States (*Blue Ridge*–class command ships, *Iwo Jima*–class amphibious carriers [LPH-2, -7, -9–12], and some *Knox*-class frigates [FF-1052–54, -1061, -1065, and -1071, of which only -1061 is active]. An inactive BPDMS system is on board the laid-up carrier *Midway*.)

TAS Mk 23/ITAS *Users:* United States (carriers, *Spruance* class, AOEs, AORs)

In 1992 Hughes received the first navy funds for **ITAS** (formerly **MTAS**), the 3D version. It has a new stacked-beam antenna (3 elevating beams, 1 fixed on the horizon).

R76/HR76 *Users:* New Zealand (R76C5 in *Leander*-class frigates, installation beginning in February 1985), Taiwan (HR76 in Wu Chin I–class destroyers, *Lung Chiang* class, and probably coastal defenses using H930 CDS)

W-120 *Users:* South Korea (*Paek Ku* class)

W-160 *Users:* Taiwan (Wu Chin III destroyers, in MCS CDS)

Cardion Coastal Radar *Users:* Denmark, Norway (bought in 1991)

BGAAWC-developed prototypes now in production include **SGS/AC** (Shipboard Gridlock System/Automatic Correlation), Aegis display system with color graphics, and Dial-a-Track Link 11 Quality Selection. The FY90 program included the design and fabrication of automatic ID (i.e., noncooperative ID) equipment for Aegis ships; a similar system was designed for NTU ships. The Aegis version was tested at sea during FY92, and noncooperative target recognition and IFF tracking are to be added in FY94. This program also develops **FTEWA**, a force-wide version of Threat Evaluation and Weapon Assignment (TEWA). Land-based demonstration was scheduled for FY93.

FACT (Force AAW Coordinating Technology) is a related program developing auto-identification techniques, silent gridlock, and

FTEWA. One goal is to make remote data engagement (RDE) practical. In RDE, a ship passes all engagement data to a silent unit, which actually fires the missile. This program also supports data-link improvements to help bind joint (e.g., air force) and allied forces together. The FY93 program included a demonstration of advanced multisensor tracking, FTEWA, and gridlock in fleet AAW exercises. FTEWA is to be integrated into major fleet AAW units in FY94. The next step is tighter use of nonorganic data. In FY95 FACT will conduct experiments to determine the feasibility of integrating nonorganic data to identify organic battle-group air tracks in real time.

CEC is cooperative engagement capability, to be achieved through a data-distribution system (DDS) linking cooperative engagement processors (CEPs). In effect, the jam-resistant DDS is the next step beyond Link 11/16, and CEP is the step beyond CDS. CEC needs a very high computing capacity to provide precise gridlock (to allow full use of all sensors within a battle group) and actual fire control (including the decision as to which weapon is to engage a particular threat). The CEP distributed processor will cue on-board sensors or engage targets without any onboard sensor tracks. This is a new start scheduled for FY94, building on **BGAAWC** and **FACT**. That year it should be possible to demonstrate cued self-defense missile firing and also to complete compiling a data base for composite identification/cooperative engagement. Fleet CEC tactics will be developed and tested. The navy hopes to evaluate CEC operationally and technically in FY96, and to add early-warning aircraft as cooperating units (CUs).

Cooperative engagement was tested on board the Aegis cruisers *San Jacinto* (CG-56) and *Leyte Gulf* (CG-55) in August 1990, including integration of Marine Corps ground assets. The *Dwight D. Eisenhower* battle group (including 2 Aegis cruisers, the NTU destroyer *Kidd*, and the *Wasp*) is to test CEC early in 1994 in the Mediterranean. A P-3 will be used as a demonstration air relay, and E-2s may be involved.

The *Bainbridge, Long Beach, Truxtun,* and *Mahan* class were dropped from the **NTU** program because they are to be decommissioned in the early 1990s. That leaves a total of 29 NTU ships: 6 nuclear cruisers (*California* and *Virginia* classes), 18 cruisers (*Belknap* and *Leahy* classes), and 5 *Kidd*-class destroyers. The first **Terrier NTU (ER)** ship was the USS *Biddle* (1987). The first **Tartar (or MR) NTU** ship was the *Scott* (DDG-995). Terrier (**SM-2[ER]**) NTU entered service first. The design and development of a Low-Altitude Readiness-Improvement Program (**LARIP**) for Terrier ships was completed in FY90 and tested on board an NTU/Terrier ship in FY91. The design of the follow-on Pulse-Doppler Integration (**PDI**) change, to exploit the performance of **SM-2(ER) Block III** missiles, was completed in FY92 (pulse-Doppler integration into the **SPG-55** FCS radar). The FY92 program included the first shipboard **Block III MR** developmental testing, on board the *California* (CGN-36).

Norden is currently working to reduce the size and weight of **SYS** by about two-thirds. Norden is also working to incorporate ESM data. A modernized version would be more user-friendly, with better graphics (e.g., X-Windows, MOTIF). **SYS-1** was built around 2 UYK-20s; **SYS-2** was built around 2 UYK-44s. Each has 2 standard radar consoles (1 for the radar controller, 1 for the detector-tracker-monitor). During the summer of 1992 Norden tested an **i860**. It has already fielded U.S. systems using INMOS Transputers. The next generation will use a **TAC-3** or similar workstation. Norden is also considering airborne and FAA applications of its basic sensor-fusion concept. *Perry*-class frigates without SYS-1, including the Australian ships, have **RVP/UYK-20** (which is also incorporated in **TAS Mk 23**).

Norden's systems create contact tracks from all available sensor data, partly by centroiding their detection data (and filtering out clearly erroneous points). These data are used to develop range and angle rates. Tracks are constantly examined to reject ones showing nonphysical behavior (i.e., clutter). Other radar-data-fusion systems typically choose among tracks, selecting the sensor considered most reliable. Norden claims that SYS enjoys better reaction time and greater accuracy (partly because tracks are more likely to be continuous, since they will not break at the point that one sensor overtakes another in accuracy or efficacy).

SYS *variants:* SYS-1(V)1 *Adams* class (U.S., German: 7 in all); (V)2 Italy (*Audace* class, 5 ships); (V)3 Australia (*Brisbane* class, 3 ships). SYS-2(V)1: XN-1 in *Mahan*, others in NTU/*Biddle* class (30 ships); (V)2 in U.S., Taiwan FFGs (total 21); (V)3 in *Wasp* (1 ship); (V)4 in *Kitty Hawk* (1 ship); (V)5 in *Essex* class (3 ships). SYS-3 in Israeli *Eilat* class (using 68020 processors).

The RAN currently plans to install SYS-2(V)2 in its *Perry*-class frigates as part of a 1998–2000 modernization (the other elements

are improvements to the Mk 92 FCS, new 76-mm ammunition [presumably course-corrected], and improvements to the SM-1 missile).

To form its **Coastal Protection System,** Kollmorgen combined its **Model 985** periscopic director with a **20-mm Gatling gun** (whose mount could also carry dual **Stinger** missiles). The elevation limits of the director are + 70/− 25 deg, the slew rate is 80 deg/sec, and the tracking accuracy is 1.0 mrad. FoVs (magnifications) are 30 (2×) and 7.5 (8×) deg. The GE gun could elevate to + 50/− 10 deg (train limits were + 110 deg). It could slew at 80 deg/sec with a tracking accuracy of 2.0 mrad. The system could also be combined with Kollmorgen's **Model 445** optronic director or with the **GCS-362** gun-control system. The director could be provided with an LLLTV or FLIR. The sight itself is, presumably, a version of Mk 35 (reportedly, **Mk 35 Mod L3**). The system has been called **HSV-20NCS,** but Kollmorgen does not use that designation.

Users: Honduras (*Guardian,* 105-ft and 85-ft classes), Saudi Arabia (Jetfoil tender to royal yacht), Thailand (HYUSCAT 18). Some version of this system may have been installed on board South Korean "Sea Dolphin"–class patrol boats. The same Model 985 director was used to control Hsiung Feng I missiles on board Taiwanese *Hai Ou*–class missile boats. In all, 70 Model 985 Mod Ts and Mod Hs were made between 1976 and 1988 for the Taiwanese program, for Honduras, for a Lockheed hydrofoil (HYUSCAT) and for a French CSEE contract (probably the Boeing-built Saudi yacht tender).

Model 985 is a slightly lighter and less-expensive version of Kollmorgen's Mk 35 director, of which 22 Mod 0s and Mod 1Hs were made in 1970–74 for the abortive U.S. CPIC, for Taiwanese and South Korean warships (part of **H930**), and for the South Korean PSMM class (part of H930).

As of mid-1992, 3 **Director EX-46 Mod 0s** were on order: 1 for the Naval Surface Warfare Center (delivered in May 1992), the second for DDG-52, and the third for DDG-51. Unlike earlier Kollmorgen directors, EX-46 is a stabilized pedestal flanked by 2 sensors (daylight imaging TI/CCD television and a MICROFLIR). Elevation limits are + 80/− 20 deg, and slew and elevation rates are 90 deg/sec (accuracy 1 mrad). The rotating head weighs 260 lb. Daylight FoVs are 2.0 × 1.5 deg (16×) and 5.0 × 3.75 deg (6.4×). The sensor is a 1,134 × 486 element CCD; it should detect small surface craft at 20 km and air targets at 8 km. The MICROFLIR has FoVs of 3.0 × 2.25 and 1.0 × 0.75 deg; it should detect surface targets at 16 km and air targets at 10 km. Its detector is a 9-element **SPRITE** array. The display is a 1,000-line, 14-in CRT; it tracks by correlation, centroid, or selectable edge, or it can coast (rate-aided track) if a target disappears behind some obstruction.

The projected **SIRST** (Surveillance IRST) has not yet materialized, although several prototypes have been tested at sea.

Hughes is marketing a version of the Saab **IR-700.** It carries 4 apertures along its length, stepped up in elevation, from − 5 to + 45 deg. It rotates at 180 rpm and weighs 200 lb. This device uses 2nd generation focal-plane arrays operating in both IR bands. Hughes claims that its greatest advantage is a very low false-alarm rate, about 1/hr. The company is no longer marketing **Medusa** because **EX-46** (above) won the EO FCS contest.

Loral's proposed **IRSTD** (IR Search Track/Target Designator) is derived from the defunct **SAR-8,** but the IRSTD's scanner is only

Mast-mounted sight (MMS) on board HMAS *Sydney* as modified for the Gulf War in mid-1991. (Author)

1/5th the weight, using dual-band focal plane arrays (FPAs) and real-time signal/image processing.

Kollmorgen's MICROFLIR surveillance system (**Sea Star**) is intended for small boats. The FLIR operates in the 8–12-micron band, using an 8-bar **SPRITE** detector. It can be mounted in either a 14-in sphere (single sensor) or a 24-in sphere (2 sensors, e.g., TV and FLIR or laser and FLIR). Weights are 50 and 150 lb. The sphere is controlled by a joystick; elevation limits are +90/−20 deg.

NWC Dahlgren is developing a Horizon IR Surveillance Sensor (**HISS**), using a signal processor based on the Loral ASPRO-VME.

AIRBORNE RADARS AND FIRE-CONTROL SYSTEMS

UNITED STATES

In January 1992 the Naval Air Development Center at Warminster issued a broad agency announcement for a classified airborne IR surveillance program, a demonstration program to last 12–18 months. Warminster hoped for a 12–15-in aperture within the weight and space currently required for an 8-in aperture.

The **Harrier II Plus** MoU between the United States, Italy, and Spain was signed in 1992, and the prototype AV-8B Plus flew that fall. Production deliveries will begin in the spring of 1993.

The first **APG-73** development radar was completed in mid-1991 and first flew on 15 April 1992. The first production radars should be delivered in 1994. Hughes claims an order of magnitude improvement in processor throughput and memory (the existing radar's memory and time line were full). Hardware is about 60% common with that of the F-14D upgrade radar (**APG-71**). Hughes is currently working to integrate an all-weather reconnaissance capability into this radar in lieu of a side-looking radar pod.

The current **APS-125** system (picture-keeping) computer is a dual **L-304, OL-77/ASQ** (now with a capacity of 128 kword), supported by an **ASPRO**. A current project to replace L-304 has not yet been funded. Group 2 aircraft (with APS-145 radars) have improved ASPRO processors, which more than double the number of track files in Group 1 (which more than doubled the number in Group 0). New 7-color Loral display units can show more than 2,000 tracks on 11 × 11–in screens, rather than the 250-track limit of the current 10-in Hazeltine units. They can also overlay a map and can carry 3 windows. Group 2 aircraft also have GPS. JTIDS will be introduced late in 1993 or early in 1994. Deliveries began in December 1991, and all U.S. E-2Cs are to be brought to Group 2 standard by 1998 (upgrades of earlier aircraft will begin in FY95). The United States currently has a cooperative program with Egypt (MoU signed 15 May 1991) to develop a new E-2C Software Enhanced Display System, which should increase the system's capacity from 250 to 1,600 tracks.

APS-125 Series Users: Egypt, Israel, Japan, Taiwan (APS-138 in E-2Ts), United States (E-2s, 4 EP-3s for the Customs Service, and EC-130Vs for the coast guard). France hopes to buy E-2s for the new carrier *Charles de Gaulle*.

SURFACE-TO-AIR MISSILES

CANADA

In mid-1992 Canadian Oerlikon and the French small-craft builder, CMN (the builder of La Combattante–class attack boats), began to market a new naval version of **ADATS**. The weapon had been considered too complex for small-combatant use largely because it had been assumed that the full mount would have to be stabilized. The new version stabilizes only the guidance system. Oerlikon claims that it can engage and kill 8 aircraft in close succession, the first at a range of 8 km, the last at 1.5 km (assuming that the airplanes approach in 2 flights of 2 pairs each, 5 sec between pairs, 20 sec between flights, at a speed of 250 m/sec [about 500 kt]). The response time against the first target would be less than 5 sec, with less than 2 sec between shots. ADATS missiles are credited with a maximum speed of Mach 3 + and with 60-G maneuverability.

CHINA (PRC)

According to a recent official Chinese statement, **HQ-61**, fired from a vertical launcher, is to be the standard shipboard SAM. Conventional launchers are on board 2 Jiangdong-class frigates. The PRC bought 2 **Crotale** systems and about 86 missiles from France in 1989,

to equip 2 Luda-class destroyers (which are also equipped with the **TAVITAC CDS**).

CPMIEC announced a new low-altitude missile, **FM-80**, at Farnborough in 1990. It is probably in the **Roland** or **Crotale** class. Although the brochure did not mention any naval application, one is likely, given the dual role of **HQ-61/RF-61/SD-1**. **KS-1**, which is probably the same missile, was shown at FIDAE (in Chile) in 1992. A naval version may be intended to supersede HQ-61. The land version is carried on a twin launcher; a battery consists of 24 missiles with 4 such launchers. The missile may use the same command-guidance system as the Chinese version of the old Soviet **SA-2 (HQ-1/2)**. Dimensions are 40 cm × 5.6 m (900 kg). Maximum speed is 1,200 m/sec [2,360 kt, about Mach 3.6]. Altitude limits are 500–25,000 m [1,600–80,000 ft]. Range is 7–42 km [3–23 nm]. Maximum target speed is 750 m/sec [1,480 kt]. Maximum target maneuverability is 4–5 G.

The gun-missile **Naval Combat System Type 88C/PL-9**, for destroyers and smaller craft, was announced at the 1991 Paris Air Show. The weapons are the **H/PJ 76A gun** (a twin Soviet-type 37-mm in a turret externally similar to that of the **Breda Fast Forty** or the **Oerlikon 35-mm**), the **Type 69 twin 30-mm gun**, and a quadruple ground-launched version of the **PL-9** (Python derivative) air-to-air missile. The system has probably been adapted from the Italian **Dardo**, which is made under license in China (PRC). It incorporates an IR designator (tracker and laser), a lead-computing sight, and a digital FCS computer. The system is said to be compatible with the Oerlikon 35-mm gun.

PL-9 is an all-aspect air-to-air missile made by CATIC. Dimensions are 157 × 2,900 mm (wing span 641 mm, fin span 856 mm including air-driven gyros). Launch weight is 115 kg. Maximum altitude is 21 km. Maximum range is 15 km (minimum 500 m). Maneuverability is 35 + G.

The cooled IR seeker has a 3-deg FoV; the dead zone around the sun is 15 deg wide. The missile can be fired well off boresight.

Another combined gun-missile system, by CSSC, was shown at Defense Asia (Singapore, March 1991). A mount combined a twin 37-mm power mount (**Type 715I**) with two **PL-8H** missiles, plus FCS and tracking radar. The missile was described as all-aspect IR, probably 120 kg with an 11-kg warhead, with a range of 4.5 km. This was the first appearance of PL-8 (**PL-7** and **-9** had previously been seen); this designation had earlier been associated with a medium-range AAM version of HQ-61.

The 37-mm gun has a max. range of 9,400 m (effective range less). Max. altitude is 7,200 m. Firing rate is 360–380 rounds/bbl/min. Elevating rate is 50 deg/sec. Training rate is 40 deg/sec.

The mount is unmanned (centrally controlled); missiles are launched only when the target is within their envelope.

FINLAND

Sako has developed a gun/missile launching system for the Finnish navy, to carry 2 23-mm or 6 Mistral missiles, in each case with an on-mount operator. It is locally controlled by joystick, or through a ship FCS (the local [reflex] sight is only a backup in the gun version).

The Finnish SAKO 23-mm gun mount. (SAKO)

Weight: 1,700 kg (gun version) or 2,200 kg (missile version); swing radius of the gun version is 1.570 m. Elevation limits: +80/−10 deg. Train rate: 80 deg/sec (elevation 50 deg/sec). The dispersion of the gun version is less than 3 mrad. The missile-carrying structure also carries TV and IR cameras (with monitors in the operator's cab) and argon bottles for seeker cooling; the missile version has an additional computer to control the launch-unit system.

FRANCE

Crotale *Users:* China (PRC) (Luda hulls 17 and 18), France (*Clemenceau, Georges Leygues, Tourville* classes), Saudi Arabia (*Al Madinah* class), U.A.E. (FPB 62 class).

A recent estimate of deliveries shows 280 for France and 106 for Saudi Arabia. Thomson-CSF developed a land-based version, **Chun Ma**, for South Korea (completed in 1992), and it has tried to excite South Korean naval interest.

The **VT1** missile used in **Crotale NG** maneuvers at 35 G at a range of up to 8 km (the airframe can sustain 50 G). Operating range is about 11 km [6 nm] and a ceiling of 6,000+ m [20,000 ft]. The missile reaches peak velocity (1,250 m/sec) in 3 sec, after which it loses velocity as it coasts (it is flying at 600 m/sec [1,180 kt] after 10 sec, by which time it has reached a range of 8 km [4.4 nm]). The 13-kg [28.7-lb], focused, blast-fragmentation warhead has a lethal radius of 8 m [26.2 ft]. In a typical engagement, the system locks on after 2 sec and fires after 8 sec. Thomson-CSF claims that the very high speed of the VT1 missile (which it claims is the fastest short-range air-defense missile in service) enables the system to engage and destroy targets approaching from different directions. For example, to engage 4 sea-skimming missiles approaching in pairs (5 sec apart) at Mach 0.9 [300 m/sec], 135 deg apart, the system would designate the first target at 15 km, intercepting it at 9.5 km (12.5 sec after missile firing). The second would be intercepted at 7.1 km (8 sec after firing), the third at 2.5 km (3.5 sec after firing), and the fourth at 1.9 km (3 sec after firing).

Users: France (*La Fayette* class), Oman (new corvettes). Probably also in *La Fayette* derivatives for Saudi Arabia and Taiwan.

Mistral (Sadral and Simbad Systems) *Users:* Brunei, Finland (12 Sadral bought in 1989 for *Helsinki* classes and minelayers), France (*Charles de Gaulle, Cassard, Floréal* classes), Norway (*Storm, Snøgg* classes, ordered in September 1990; options for *Hauk* class, MCM craft: 6-tube Sadral for FACs, 2-tube Simbad for MCMVs), Qatar (new light frigates), U.A.E. (FPB 62, FPB 38 classes). Mistral is included in the new Combattante IV offered to Kuwait. Buyers of the land-based version include Belgium, Cyprus, Finland, France, Kenya, Norway, Philippines, Saudi Arabia, and South Korea.

Estimated unit price (FY92) was $46,950 ($33,000 for the launcher). In November 1992 it was announced that Mistral would eventually arm *all* French surface combatants.

Sylver is DCN's vertical launcher, designed for the **Aster 15** and **30** missiles, but the French navy required that it also be able to fire the U.S.-supplied **Standard Missile**. It can also accommodate **Sea Sparrow**. As of October 1992, it had made more than 26 full-scale launches. Each module is fitted with 2 rows of 22-in missile cells surrounding the uptake for exhaust gas. A lightweight version has unarmored doors and lacks the automatic pumping device for the plenum chamber, the launcher power supply, and the electronic-launcher management bay.

INTERNATIONAL

FAMS is now called **FSAF** (Family of Surface-to-Air Defense Systems). **Aster** is the missile, developed by Aerospatiale. The only difference between versions is the booster. Britain very nearly dropped out of the consortium because **Aster 30**, with its maximum range of 30 km, could not adequately fulfill Britain's local-area air-defense requirement. Then the booster was changed, and Aster 30 is now credited with a realistic intercept range of 30 km (presumably against antiship missiles). Reportedly, each ship will be armed with 64 missiles. The missile combining the French SAMP/N and the British LAMS requirements will be called **PAAMS** (Principal Anti-Air Missile System). Late in the summer of 1992 Spain dropped out of the consortium, reportedly because of deep dissatisfaction with the extent of the industrial participation offered; Spain will probably use **Evolved Sea Sparrow** on board the new F 100–class frigates.

ISRAEL

Barak I was accepted for Israeli service in mid-1992 after a series of successful tests between August 1991 and May 1992, culminating

The Polish Wrobel 2MR combination gun-missile turret. (Author)

in a low-altitude shot on 1 May 1992. A foreign partner has always been mentioned in connection with this program. It is probably South Africa, which planned to use Barak on board a new class of corvettes (now canceled), but it may be Chile or Singapore. Reportedly, 2 foreign navies have bought Barak: they are almost certainly Chile and Singapore. Thailand may be a prospective customer. Estimated unit price (FY92) was $341,000.

Users: Israel (*Nirit* and *Eilat* class), Singapore (*Victory* class). It is not clear whether the reported sale to Chile is firm.

ITALY

Aspide (SAM version) *Users:* Argentina (MEKO 360 class), Ecuador (*Wadi M'ragh* class*), Italy (*Garibaldi* and *Animoso, Maestrale, Lupo*, and *Minerva* classes), Libya (*Dat Assawari**), Nigeria (MEKO 360), Peru (*Lupo* class), Thailand (PFMM Mk 16 class), Venezuela (*Lupo* class). The asterisk indicates a quadruple launcher. The *Garibaldi, Animosos, Maestrales*, and MEKO 360s have the autoloader version. The Iraqi *Lupos* (now bought by Italy) had no reloads, and that probably applies to the Italian, Peruvian, and Venezuelan *Lupos* as well because the launcher is atop their hangars. The Italian *Minervas* have space and weight reserved for a reload facility, but it is not currently installed.

On 17 April 1991 Alenia and Matra signed an agreement to develop an active missile to supersede Aspide Mk 2 and **Mica**.

POLAND

Wrobel 2MR, a combined gun-missile system (equivalent to the land-based **ZUR-23–2S**), consists of a twin **23-mm gun** with a single **72-mm Strela 2M** (SA-7 series) missile launcher on top. It was first mounted on board the new minelayer/transport *Gniezno*.

SWEDEN

A new stabilized mounting for **RBS 70** (Rayrider) is being developed.

Users: Finland (Helsinki-II class) and Sweden (*Landsort* class). Australian support ships used RBS 70 in the Gulf War.

UNITED KINGDOM

Sea Cat *Users:* Brazil (*Niteroi* class), Chile (*Alm. Williams* class*, "County" class, *Leander* class), Ecuador (*Leanders*), India (*Leander* class, some*), Indonesia ("Tribal" class, *Van Speijk* class*), New Zealand (*Leander* class), Nigeria (*Erin'mi* class), Pakistan (*Babur, Leander* class), and the United Kingdom (Type 21, surviving non–Sea Wolf *Leanders*, and *Fearless* class). Asterisks indicate the **M45** version. Although their Sea Cat launchers remain, the Royal Australian and New Zealand navies have retired this weapon. It has been removed from the Thai *Makut Rajakumarn*. Soviet-type twin 23-mm cannon have replaced all Iranian Sea Cat launchers (in the Battle-class destroyer and the Vosper corvettes).

The **ADIMP** upgrade of **Sea Dart** (GWS 30; CF 299) is equivalent to the U.S. **NTU**; the missile is provided with a commandable autopilot. Command antennas are located in radomes on either side of the base of the air-search radar (**Type 1022**) pedestal. The effective missile range against high-altitude targets is doubled, probably to 80 nm (the pre-ADIMP range is now given as 40 nm). Space for the command system was provided by replacing 6 circuit boards with 1 board. Since the Falkland Islands War there have been two major guidance updates, one in 1983–86, one (ADIMP and a motor im-

The radomes (similar to those of the Type 670 jammer) under the Type 1022 air-search radar on this Type 42 destroyer often contain the up-links for the Sea Dart missile system as modified under the ADIMP program, analogous to the U.S. NTU. (A. L. Raven, 1992)

provement) in 1989–91. A new IR fuze (to attack low-flying targets) is about to enter production. Upgrades run in blocks of 10; as of February 1992 the current version was **Block 610**. The missile is likely to remain in British service through 2020. Reportedly, HMS *Gloucester*'s spectacular success against a **Silkworm** (with a shot fired "over the shoulder" and redirected in flight) greatly increased the Royal Navy's interest in the weapon and clearly demonstrated how much it had changed since the Falklands.

Users: Argentina (Type 42s; 60 delivered), United Kingdom (carriers, Type 42 destroyers; total of 330 magazine slots, total production of 2,000, including missiles made to replace those fired in the Falklands)

The projected lightweight Mod 2 version of **Sea Wolf** for the carriers and Type 42 destroyers was canceled in July 1991. As of 1991, the estimated unit price was $319,000; an entire GWS 25 Mod 0 (including 24 missiles and 967/968 and 910 radars) cost $12 million in FY87. Type 22s have 6-missile launchers each backed by 12 ready-use rounds hoisted up from a magazine (in Batch I) or from fore and aft magazines (in Batches II and III). Because each magazine presumably carries another full ready-use load, the total missile loadout in a Type 22 Batch II or III is probably 60. The 32 VLS missiles are carried in individual tubes with frangible covers. Equipment for replenishment at sea is carried, although it probably can be used only in calm weather.

Users: Malaysia (VL in new corvettes; first export sale), United Kingdom (GWS 25 in Type 22s, GWS 26 [VLS] in Type 23s and *Fort Victoria* class)

VSRAD is now once again a British national program. A 14-month NATO feasibility study by the U.K., Germany, Italy, Spain, and the Netherlands was completed in September 1991, but by December only the U.K. and Italy were still very interested. Italy withdrew before signing an MoU for a joint project-definition contract. **Seastreak** may well be chosen; British studies have rejected guns because of their limited range. The British believe that directed energy is unlikely to be suitable for service before 2010. Presumably, VSRAD will arm the British version of the new Anglo-French frigate.

Starburst, in effect a cross between Seastreak and Javelin, was shown at RNEE 1991 in the form of a laser-guided Naval Multiple Launcher (**NML**). At the same show, MSI-Defence Systems exhibited its **DS30B** gun with Starburst, claiming that the combination was better than a 57-mm gun. In the fall of 1991 Shorts and Thomson-CSF signed an MoU to develop a new generation of Close Air Defence/Very Short Range Air Defence missile systems, including Starburst.

SDMS at the 1992 Navy League Show. Developed by LTV, this weapon is now marketed by Loral, which bought LTV's missile business. (Author)

UNITED STATES

The February 1991 budget (for FY92/93) included continued work on directional ordnance (i.e., shaped charges) for area-defense weapons. The budget also included initial work on an **MHD** (magnetohydrodynamic) warhead. Such a weapon would presumably generate an intense electromagnetic pulse to burn out the circuits on board an attacking weapon. Work is also proceeding on a high-PRR, high-power, microwave (HPM) weapon and on a future charged-particle-beam weapon (as well as a laser air-defense weapon).

Hughes has bought the General Dynamics missile division. Loral has bought the LTV missile division.

SDMS, Loral's (formerly LTV's) proposed short-range ship-defensive missile, is based on the **ERINT** (Extended-Range Interceptor) vehicle developed for ballistic-missile defense. As of March 1992, the naval version was only a feasibility study. SDMS uses a Ka-band terminal seeker and hits to kill. Midterm guidance is by updates (not necessarily periodic), using 180 thrusters distributed around the forebody of the missile. They are also used to steer the missile as it emerges from the vertical launchers, and for terminal steering; there are no jettisonable vanes in the jetstream. The missile uses a graphite-epoxy motor case. Dimensions are 10 × 182 in, and weight is 670 lb; 4 missiles can be accommodated in each VLS cell. ERINT made its first ballistic flight in June 1992.

The projected replacement of 2 **Sea Sparrow** cells with **RAM** (RIM-116A) has been abandoned, as it would have required replacement of the drive motors. The plan to adapt Mk 13 launchers to fire RAM has also been abandoned (there is some hope of placing Mk 49 launchers on board FFGs). The first U.S. RAM system was installed on board the LHA *Peleliu*. The first German platforms are the *Molders*, *Niedersachsen*, and *Puma*. The recent procurement authorization was as follows: FY90, 580; FY91, 540; FY92, 500; plans called for 800/yr in FY92 and FY93. However, the FY92 request was canceled. The first 30 were made under the FY85 program, and plans call for a total of 4,600 U.S. missiles and 30 **Mk 49** launchers. Low-rate production began in March 1989, with 500 ordered in June 1989 for 1992 delivery. The April 1993 budget requested 240 RAMs in FY94 (none in FY93).

Users: Germany, United States. Denmark has withdrawn to observer status. Drawings of the new Japanese 1,900-ton frigate show RAM; presumably, the Japanese plan to manufacture the missile under license.

Standard Missile-1 (Medium Range) *Users:* Australia (*Perry* class, *Adams* class), France (*Cassard* class), Germany (*Adams* class), Greece (*Adams* class), Italy (ER in *Vittorio Veneto*, MR in *Mimbelli*, *Audace*, and *Impavido* classes), Japan (*Hatakaze*, *Tachikaze*, *Amatsukaze* classes), Netherlands (*Tromp* and *Jacob Van Heemskerck* classes), Pakistan (*Brooke* class), Spain (*Perry* class), Taiwan (*Perry* class), and United States (*Perry* class [after NTU program is complete]).

Block IV is designated **RIM-66A**; Block V is **RIM-66B**; Block VI is **RIM-66E**. Hughes has placed SM-1 back into production, for export users: 171 in FY90, 242 in FY91, 153 in FY92/93. U.S. SM-1s are being modified to Block VIB standard.

Standard ARM *Users:* South Korea (PGM-352–56 [*PSMM 5* class] and PGM-351 [*Asheville* class]); possibly also Iran (*Damavand*-class destroyer)

Standard Missile-2 *Users:* Canada (TRUMP class), Japan (*Kongo* class), United States (SM-2[MR]: *Ticonderoga, California, Virginia, Arleigh Burke, Kidd* classes; SM-2[ER]: *Leahy, Belknap* classes). **SM-2 Block IV** is to be carried by *Ticonderoga* VLS ships and by the *Arleigh Burke* class; it can also be carried by the Japanese *Kongo*s.

SM-2 Block I is **RIM-66C** for MR, **RIM-67A** for ER. **RIM-66D** is **SM-2(MR) Block I** for Tartar ships (i.e., for ships lacking uplink capability). **RIM-67B** is the corresponding version for Terrier ships. Procurement of Block I ended in FY83. **SM-2 Block II** is **RIM-66G** and **RIM-67C**. **RIM-66H** is the vertically launched version of **SM-2(MR) Block II**; **-66J** is the version for **Tartar** ships. Missiles procured in FY88–90 are **Block III** (**RIM-66L, -66M** for vertical launchers, and **-67D**; there may also be a **-66K** version for vertical launchers), with an improved low-altitude fuze. Procurement ended in FY90 with 710 missiles/$390.214 million (for a unit cost of $549,000). Block III incorporates low-altitude improvements developed under a 1984 Standard Missile Improvement Program. **Block IIIA**'s production began in FY91; the plan released in 1990 called for 490/$250.126 million (at $510,000 each) that year, then 30 in each of FY92 and FY93 (for a unit cost of about $630,000). The prototype **SM-2 Block IIIA** missile flew at White Sands on 2 March 1991. **Block IIIB**'s production began with 100 modification kits in FY91 (at $195,000 each), followed by a planned 66 kits and 300 missiles in FY92 and 79 kits and 300 missiles in FY93. Block IIIB incorporates **MHIP** (approved on 17 July 1989). SM-2(MR)'s procurement was 940 in FY90, 405 in FY91, 330 in FY92, 330 in FY93, 220 planned for FY94. Presumably, the FY90 program included final purchases of one version. SM-2(ER)'s procurement ended in FY87. A Selected Acquisition Report (30 June 1991) showed a total cost of $10,725.2 million for 14,677 missiles, for an average cost of $731,000. In recent years General Dynamics and Raytheon have shared production (1991 orders were for 142 and 263 missiles, respectively).

According to an official program description, the expansion of the missile envelope of **SM-2 Aegis (ER)** (SM-2 Block IV; RIM-67E) (to a range of 200 nm, an altitude of 95,000 ft) makes the **HPIRS** (High-Performance IR Sensor) program useful. Funded for 3 yr by the OSD BTI program, HPIRS is presumably intended to deal with low-radar-cross-section targets. HPIRS was added to the navy's FY90 budget. It is *not* **MHIP**. This version will be modified to deal with tactical ballistic missiles (e.g., those fired at an amphibious assault area) as the initial phase of the naval TMD effort (as **Block IVA**). The FY91 budget request included the first 300 production SM-2 Block IV missiles. The missile first flew in July 1991 at White Sands. As of mid-1992, Block IV was expected to enter service late in 1993.

SM-2 Block IV as displayed by Raytheon at the 1992 Navy League Show. The missile above it is Raytheon's wingless version of the Evolved Sea Sparrow Missile, with an IR seeker in its extreme nose (the nose cone is cut away to show the radar dish behind it). The missile in the background is "Boxcars," Raytheon's version of the next-generation Sidewinder. (Author)

A Stinger missile position on board a *Knox*-class frigate in 1992. Similar positions are on board many other U.S. warships. (Raymond Cheung)

Hughes is developing the IR sensor for the Raytheon Block IVA missile (first guided firing was in April 1993). The 128 × 128 focal-plane array imaging sensor (which can be grown to 256 × 256) is in a bump on the side of the missile, covered by a plate that protects it from the heat of high-speed flight at low altitude. When it is needed, the protective cover blows off to reveal a sapphire dome.

Stinger *Users:* Denmark (to arm modernized *Falster* and *Willemoes* classes), Germany (Type 332– and 343–class mine-countermeasures ships), United States (issued as required, particularly for ships deploying to the Middle East). Denmark is developing a twin mounting with electronic receivers for target designation. The Danish mounting directly replaces a 20-mm gun.

AIR-TO-AIR MISSILES

British Sea Harriers will not be armed with **ASRAAM**. The U.S. **AAAM** program was terminated in 1992.

UNITED STATES

The FY92/93 R&D program (as planned in February 1991) included a breadboard, wideband, active-array, cued/supercued FCS and an integrated active array for guidance and fuzing for 8-in-diameter (Sparrow-size) missiles. A 200-element, 5–18-GHz, solid-state, active-array antenna had already been made under the FY90 program, and the integrated guidance-fuze concept tested. The FY91 program included new efforts at lock-on-after-launch guidance and also initial work on a diamond IR dome for future fast IR missiles (for FY93 survival tests).

With the cancellation of **AAAM**, the navy became interested in a longer-range version of **AMRAAM** using a new ducted-rocket engine. Recent purchases: FY91, 300; FY92, 191; FY93, 140; FY94, 44 planned. Unit cost in February 1992 was $982,000. As of August 1992, plans called for about 6,600 of the 15,450 to have warhead improvements for greater lethality.

The FY92/93 budget did not include any **Phoenix** missiles. As of May 1991, 4,213 missiles were on hand (9 per F-14), but only 2,000 were considered "warfighting capable"; the others were obsolescent **AIM-54A**s, of a hard-wired analog design whose production ended in 1981. Some **C**s were found to have defective safing/arming circuits, and AIM-54As were cannibalized for their rocket motors. As of 1991, congressional and navy sources suggested that the inventory objective should have been 7,000. A 30 June 1991 Selected Acquisition Report (SAR) showed that 2,528 **AIM-54C**s had been or were being manufactured at a total cost of $3,074 million ($1.2 million each). The navy was considering upgrading existing Phoenixes to the

AIM-54C+ (high-powered radar transmitter) configuration, and there was some possibility of new production.

The new **AIM-9R** version of **Sidewinder** was originally a joint navy/air force program. However, in about August 1991 the air force balked at the $100,000 unit price, based on a production run of 8,500–10,000 missiles, including 3,500– 5,000 for the air force. It preferred an interim modification to the existing **AIM-9M**, pending development of a new **AIM-9X**. The air force feared that unless AIM-9R was killed, the much superior AIM-9X might never materialize. The counterargument is that the Russian-made, thrust-vectored **AA-11**, which was available to Iraq during the Gulf War, was so superior to AIM-9M that something very different was needed quite urgently. Moreover, existing Russian-made decoys were considered effective against AIM-9M (3 were successfully decoyed during the Gulf War, out of 16 fired). Given the air force's withdrawal, the navy's comptroller deleted AIM-9R from the FY93 budget, despite the aviation community's objections.

AIM-9R uses a staring visual-spectrum seeker, selected under the **Pave Prism** program in 1987. The first missiles were delivered in 1991. China Lake conceived the near-visual seeker, which improves clutter and decoy rejection but lacks night capability. The air force particularly criticized this limitation, presumably because its F-16s might have to rely entirely on **Sidewinder**s (they cannot guide radar missiles such as **Sparrow**). AIM-9R also encountered severe cost overruns. The new head is completely compatible with the -9L/9M after end; the navy hoped to convert 5,000 older missiles. The weight is 193 lb, and the range is reportedly 21,125 yd.

Under the new acquisition rules, any quick decision was held up pending a trade-off study (a COEA). The alternatives were AIM-9R, **AIM-9M Plus**, and the Israeli **Python**. As of July 1992, the navy's position was that the missile should outrange **AA-11** but should not have nearly the range of the companion **AMRAAM**; the air force wanted longer range (though still shorter than AMRAAM). The navy was willing to settle for Python's maneuverability and a helmet sight; the air force wanted more maneuverability but rejected the helmet sight. The navy wanted its pilots to be able to exploit greater angles of attack.

The 2 main longer-term alternatives were China Lake's **Boa** and **Boxcars**, proposed by Raytheon and Loral. Boa has clipped canards so that it can fit inside an F-117 or F-22 weapons bay. Boxcars is faster and has tail control for better kinematics. It does not use thrust control but it does require an autopilot, which allows aircraft-style bank-to-turn tail control instead of missile-style skid-to-turn. Either version will most likely have an IIR seeker using a focal-plane array. As of mid-1992, industry was 6 months into an 18-month **AIM-9X** concept definition, which would be followed by a 2-yr seeker-demonstration/validation phase and then 5 yr of full-scale engineering development. AIM-9X, then, might appear about the year 2000. Some wags suggested that AA-11s might be bought as a near-term alternative.

Meanwhile AIM-9R, which was first fired in April 1990, made successful test shots, and the program was kept alive to provide a near-term alternative to the modified **AIM-9M-8/9** preferred by the air force. In January 1992 Raytheon proposed an **improved Sidewinder** to meet the British **ASRAAM** requirement. It was 9 in longer than AIM-9M, 120 mm in diameter, and it weighed 84.1 kg, including a 10.15-kg warhead with a laser fuze. It had a greater maximum range, and 40% shorter minimum range, with a new reduced-smoke motor and an advanced low-cost seeker. **AIM-9S** is a stripped version of -9M for Turkey (the sale of 310 missiles was announced in January 1990). This missile has been offered to Saudi Arabia and Taiwan.

As of March 1992, Martin Marietta had been working for 4 yr on its own next-generation short-range air-to-air seeker, which it hoped would be adopted for AIM-9X. It uses three 256×256 staring-imaging platinum-silicilide arrays for low cost, each operating in 1 of 3 bands within the 3–5-micron window. Each image would be processed separately, in parallel. Raytheon felt that this was the only approach that could pull targets out of clutter, including sea-surface glint. It could also deal with subsonic low-observable targets, which show no aerodynamic heating. Processing would have to be fast enough to deal with flashing countermeasures. Martin Marietta would place the seeker in a pointed nose to be able to achieve a speed of Mach 6, to deal with low-flying Mach-3.5 targets. Targets would be acquired when they filled only 1 or 2 pixels of the array.

Sidewinder *Users:* Argentina, Australia, Bahrein (-9P), Belgium (-9M), Brazil, Canada, Chile, Denmark (-9L), Egypt (-9L/-9P3), Germany (-9L/M), France,

Greece (-9P4), Indonesia (-9P), Iran, Israel (-9L), Italy (-9L), Japan (-9L), Jordan, Kenya, Kuwait, Malaysia (-9P4), Morocco, Netherlands (-9M), New Zealand, Norway (-9L), Oman (-9P/9P4), Pakistan (-9L), Philippines, Portugal, Saudi Arabia (-9L/P/P3), Singapore, South Africa, South Korea (-9P4), Spain, Sweden (-9L), Switzerland (-9P3/P4), Taiwan (-9P), Thailand (-9P), Tunisia, Turkey (-9L/S), U.A.E., United Kingdom (-9G/L), United States, Venezuela, Yemen

Sea Chaparral *Users:* Taiwan (destroyers, the LSD *Cheng Hai*, the new large transports, and the new replenishment ship *Wu-Yi*; MIM-72C, -72C/R, and -72F versions). These weapons will ultimately be supplanted by the indigenously developed **Tien Chien** (Sky Sword I) air-to-air missile, broadly comparable to AIM-9L/M.

The U.S. Army is now retiring Chaparral itself. A combined Chaparral/Hellfire system, **"Chapfire,"** was demonstrated at White Sands in August 1992, as the weapon of a proposed logistics-ship self-defense system, **RDIDS** (Rapid Deployment Integrated Defense System). Although the U.S. Navy ultimately rejected it, several foreign navies showed considerable interest. Representatives of Denmark, Italy, Japan, Norway, Saudi Arabia, South Korea, Spain, Taiwan, and the United Kingdom attended the firings. It appeared that the South Korean and Taiwanese representatives were seriously considering buying the system; the Swedes were more interested in selling the antiship version of **Hellfire** (the Norwegians were selling system components).

Sea Sparrow *Users:* Australia (ANZAC frigates), Belgium (RIM-7M in *Wielingen* class), Canada (RIM-7M in "City" class), Denmark (*Nils Juel* class), Egypt (probably RIM-7H in *Descubierta* class), Germany (RIM-7M in Type 123s), Greece (*Kortenaer* class), Italy (*Lupo* class may be armed with RIM-7H and is being adapted to take RIM-7M), Japan (RIM-7H, being replaced by RIM-7M), Morocco (probably RIM-7H in *Errhamani*), Netherlands (RIM-7M in *Kortenaer* and *Karel Doorman* classes), New Zealand (ANZAC frigates), Norway, Portugal (RIM-7M in MEKO 200s), South Korea (chosen for KDX), Spain (RIM-7H in *Descubierta* class), Thailand (Type 25T frigates), Turkey (RIM-7M in MEKO 200s), United States (RIM-7H in BPDMS, RIM-7M in others).

Work is currently proceeding on the wingless tail-controlled **RIM-7R**, which Raytheon proposed in 1988 as **ESSM** (Evolved Sea Sparrow Missile). As of mid-1992, 8 countries were participating in the program. Eliminating the wings makes it possible to neck out the rocket motor to a 9-in diameter, with much greater thrust, for 2–4 times the energy of the existing Sparrow (e.g., to get a second shot at a fast target). The new motor is all boost. The forepart of the missile (seeker and warhead) matches that of **RIM-7P**, but there is a new autopilot. The missile's existing reprogrammable computer is adaptable to multimode guidance (semiactive midcourse, IR terminal, and antiradar homing). The total weight is 540 lb [245.1 kg], and the length is 145.7 in [3.7 m]. Raytheon claims that ESSM can easily be backfitted on board ships now equipped with NATO Sea Sparrow. Hughes is developing the alternative ESSM (sometimes called **ASSM**, Advanced Sea Sparrow Missile) begun by General Dynamics; it has midlength wings (like those of SM-1/2). Like Raytheon's, this missile has an enlarged motor and is suitable for quad-packing.

In U.S. Aegis ships, ESSM will be fired from quad-packs inserted in **Mk 41** vertical launchers, complementing longer-range **Standard Missiles**. ESSM and the Standard Missiles will both share Aegis FCS.

Hughes's version of the Evolved Sea Sparrow, as displayed at the 1993 Navy League Show. This missile was begun by General Dynamics, and its configuration is reminiscent of that company's Standard Missile. RAM is in the foreground. (Author)

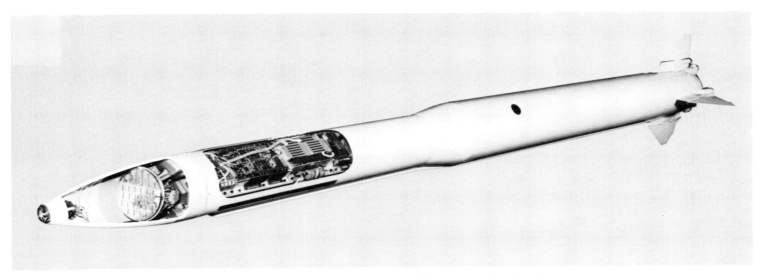

Raytheon's Evolved Sea Sparrow Missile (ESSM), showing the half-size Sidewinder IR seeker in its nose. (Raytheon)

The advent of ESSM will justify the elimination of **Phalanx CIWS** in follow-on ships of the *Arleigh Burke* class. ESSM's development may be somewhat protracted because Congress has objected that it should be considered a new start (hence subject to a COEA) rather than a simple development of an existing weapon. Some later DDG-51s may, therefore, have to retain Phalanx guns.

A further stretched version, **LSDM** (Long Ship-Defense Missile), which Raytheon claims could be in service by 1998, would offer Mach-3 speed and twice the current range. ESSM and LSDM would have common control and tail-fin (jet-vane) systems. The missile would receive midcourse guidance by modulation of the illuminator signal. Raytheon proposes a 4-missile canister launcher for these weapons, each cell of which would be about 11 in across (total width 25 in). The ESSM/LSDM combination was Raytheon's candidate for NAAWS.

TRW displayed the latest version of its shipboard laser air-defense system (**HELWEPS**) at the 1992 U.S. Navy League show. This version, including its fuel tanks and its beam director, fits in approximately the space and weight currently occupied by a 5-in/54 Mk 45 gun. Unlike the earlier version, this one would not displace the forward vertical launchers in, for example, an Aegis cruiser. In addition to its lethal effect on missiles, the new laser could attack shore targets, and it could also provide low- powered pulses for the laser-dazzler effect now used by the Royal Navy.

SHIPBOARD GUNS AND GUN SYSTEMS

The only remaining U.S. **8-in–gun** cruisers have now been stricken, as has the Chilean *O'Higgins*, with the last U.S.-supplied **6-in/47**. The Peruvian submarines that mounted the only remaining deck guns (U.S.-supplied **5-in/25s**) are also gone, as are the Paraguayan river monitors that mounted the prewar Italian **4.7s**. The only other heavy-gun ships left, the U.S. battleships and the Peruvian cruisers (with **6-in** guns), have been laid up. The French **SAMOS and Satan 30-mm guns** have been abandoned. Reportedly, **Tround** encountered severe technical problems. U.S. Navy funding was dropped, but the system is not altogether dead.

CHINA (PRC)

The **NG15–2** gun in the locally produced version of Dardo is a twin 37-mm (not 40-mm) using the design of the Breda Fast Forty (the Russian 37-mm from which the original Chinese 37-mm was copied is derived from an earlier Bofors 25-mm gun, so the Fast Forty design concept is applicable to it).

FRANCE

DGA/DCN displayed a 25-mm mount carrying a new **GIAT M811** gun at Bourget Naval 1992 (October 1992). The entire mount weighs less than 500 kg [1,100 lb]. The muzzle velocity is 1,100 m/sec [3,600 ft/sec], with an effective range of 2,500 m [2,730 yd]. The elevation limits are +55/−15 deg. The rate of fire can be set at 125/400 or 125/650 rnd/min. The gun can fire single rounds, short (3-rnd) or long (8-rnd) bursts, or automatically. The weapon's lifetime is 16,000 rnd plus 20% unloaded cycles. The GIAT gun, which weighs 105 kg [231 lb] fires all standard NATO 25-mm ammunition.

100-mm *Users:* Argentina (A-69 class [M 1968]), China (PRC) (Jianghu IV class*), France (carriers [M 1953], *Jeanne d'Arc* [M 1953], *Cassard* [M 1968], *Georges Leygues* [M 1968], *Tourville* [M 1968], *Suffren* [M 1953], *Aconit* [M 1968], A-69 [M 1968], *Cdt. Rivière* [M 1953] classes), Malaysia (FS-1500* and *Musytari** classes), Portugal (MEKO*, *Bapt. de Andrade* [M 1968], *Cdt. Rivière* [M 1953] classes), Saudi Arabia (*Al Madinah* class*), Uruguay (*Cdt. Rivière* [M 1953] class).

Asterisks indicate the **Compact** export version.

GIAT 20-mm (20F2 gun) *Users:* Belgium (Tripartite minehunters), France (*Floréal*, Tripartite minehunters, P400, CDIC, EDIC classes; most 20-mm in service are Oerlikons of U.S. or U.K. manufacture), Indonesia (Tripartite minehunters), Malawi (*Kasunga*), Netherlands (Tripartite minehunters), Pakistan (Tripartite minehunters), Saudi Arabia (NAJA 12 class).

This weapon is based on the **HS 820** gun.

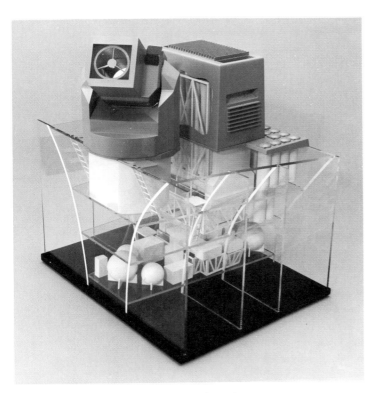

TRW's proposed shipboard laser in 1992. (TRW)

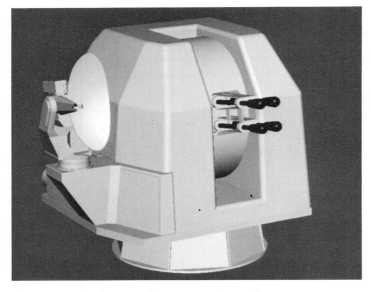

The Mauser-Signaal MIDAS close-in weapon. (Signaal)

OTO-Melara's new non–deck-penetrating version of its 76-mm gun, displayed in model form at the 1993 Navy League Show. (Author)

Mortars *Users:* Chile (81-mm in BATRAL class), France (120-mm on *Ouragan*, 81-mm in *Champlain* class), Gabon (81-mm in *Champlain* class), Ivory Coast (81-mm in *Champlain* class), Lebanon (81-mm in EDIC III class), Libya (81-mm in *Ibn Ouf* class), Madagascar (81-mm in landing ships *Toky* and *Aina Vao Vao*), Morocco (81-mm in *Champlain* class, 120-mm in EDIC class), Romania (81-mm in VB 76 class), Senegal (81-mm in EDIC type).

The 81-mm weapons are probably of U.S. type (and, often, manufacture).

GERMANY

The production version of the Mauser **Vierling** (quad 27-mm gun, formerly Taifun) is **MIDAS** (AMS 27–4), a joint Mauser-Signaal development (contract signed spring 1992). It carries a K-band monopulse tracking radar based on STING (1.5 × 0.6–deg beam, peak power 1 kW, average 100 W; capable of passively tracking a jammer). The guns diverge slightly, to cover the target (their cones of fire overlap slightly). The 360 rnd/gun is considered sufficient for 12 engagements, each lasting about 1 sec. These guns would not be effective against aircraft, so the mounting can carry a pair of **Stingers** (not included in the weights given below). The missiles would not be needed by ships, such as fast attack craft, that have other AAW weapons. MIDAS is planned for the new *Brandenburg-* (Type 123) class frigates (in place of RAM), and will probably go on board the Type 124 AAW ships (it may be retrofitted to the *Bremen*s). The prototype is to be delivered in the second half of 1994, with series production to begin in 1995. Earlier plans to fit a radarless version to Type 148 fast attack craft, on a modified 40-mm mount, have been abandoned. Total weight, including 850 kg of ammunition, is 4,000 kg. Train/elevation rates are 80 deg/sec (acceleration 210 deg/sec^2). Elevation limits are +80/−10 deg. Vierling (controlled by the boat's Vega FCS) was tested on board the fast attack boat *Dommel* in September 1991, replacing her 40-mm mount.

The Rhinemetall **20-mm Mk 20 Rh202** is essentially the World War II **MG 151**, which is used by South Africa and Yugoslavia.

ITALY

The OTO-Melara-BAe course-corrected shell (CCS) system is still under development, having flown in tests. This system uses an antenna atop the 76-mm–gun mount.

OTO-Melara 5-in/54 *Users:* Argentina (MEKO 360 class), Italy (*Animoso, Audace, Maestrale,* and *Lupo* classes), Japan (*Kongo* class), Nigeria (MEKO 360), Peru (*Lupo* class), and Venezuela (*Lupo* class).

The Italian navy has awarded a contract for a new-generation mount (for year 2000 and beyond) using the electronics of the intermediate model (on *Kongo*) but weighing 30% less, with a low-RCS shield, redesigned mechanism, and modular magazine and hoist in place of the current 3-drum type. Two loading arms will feature progressive ramming.

OTO-Melara 76-mm/62 Compact Mounting/Mk 75 *Users:* Algeria (Bulgarian C-58–class patrol boats and Brooke Marine 37.5-m patrol boats), Argentina (*Intrepida*-class FACs), Bahrein (FPB 62– and TNC 45–class missile boats), Brazil (Vosper-design patrol boats), Canada (TRUMP frigates [Super Rapido]), Chile (Sa'ar III class), Colombia (FS-1500–class frigates), Denmark (*Nils Juel, Thetis, Willemoes,* and StanFlex 300 [Super Rapido] classes), Ecuador (*Wadi M'ragh* class and *Quito* class), Egypt (*Descubierta* class, *Ramadan* class), Germany (*Bremen*-class frigates and S143/143A/143B/S148–class fast attack boats), Ghana (FPB 57 class), Greece (*Kortenaer* class, *Rhein* class, P 100 class, Osprey 55 class, Combattante IIIN class, and Jason-class LSTs), India (see below), Indonesia (*Van Speijk* class), Iran (Combattante II class), Ireland (Peacock class), Israel (*Romat* class; Sa'ar III, IV, and 4.5 classes), Italy (*Animoso* [Super Rapido], *Audace* [Super Rapido], *Minerva, Sparviero* classes), Kenya (''Province'' class), Kuwait (FPB 57 and TNC 45 classes), Libya (*Wadi M'ragh* class and Combattante II class), Mexico (*Cormoran* class, as planned), Morocco (*Descubierta* class, *Lazaga* class), Netherlands (*Karel Doorman* [Super Rapido] and *Kortenaer*-class frigates), Nigeria (*Erin'mi*, Combattante IIIB, and FPB 57 classes), Oman (new corvettes, ''Province'' and 37.5-m classes, and *Al Munassir*), Peru (PR-72–560 class), Philippines (*Cormoran* and Australian patrol-boat classes, both projected), Qatar (Combattante III class), Senegal (PR-72 MS class), Singapore (*Victory* class [Super Rapido]), South Africa (''Minister'' class), South Korea (Ulsan HDF-2000 and HDC-800 classes, *Dong Hae* class, PSMM 5 class, HDC-1150 patrol ships), Spain (*Lazaga* class), Taiwan (rebuilt destroyers, *Lung Chiang* class), Thailand (PFMM Mk 16, *Khamronsin*, and MV 400 classes), Tunisia (Combattante III class), Turkey (FPB 57 class), U.A.E. (Type 62, FPB 38, and TNC 45 classes), United Kingdom (Peacock class), Venezuela (*Constitución* class).

About October 1991 Bharat Heavy Electricals Ltd. and OTO-Melara signed an MoU for the production of at least 100 76-mm, all but the first batch to be made in India. Of the initial 18, 16 would be for the Indian coast guard and 2 for the navy. The Indian navy opposed the deal, thinking that other projects should enjoy higher priorities, and that the requirement for a modern gun mount could be met by modernizing the existing Soviet-supplied **76.2-mm** weapon. OTO-Melara is now marketing a non–deck-penetrating version of this gun.

U.S. Mk 75 (76/62 built under license) *Users:* Japan (*Asagiri, Hatsuyuki, Minegumo, Abukuma, Yubari, Ishikari* classes), Saudi Arabia (PCGs, PGGs), and United States (*Perry, Pegasus, Hamilton, Bear* classes)

Breda's most noticeable addition to standard Bofors guns was a much greater magazine capacity, achieved either by extending the magazine above the gun (in open-topped mounts) or by moving most of the ammunition below the gun (within the barbette). The **Compact** and successor **Fast Twin Forty** and **Fast Single Forty** exemplify the latter approach. Compared to standard Bofors guns, they require less manning and can react more quickly and, Breda claims, more accurately. Externally, the Compact and the new Fast Forty twin mounts are nearly indistinguishable, but the Fast Forty adds an upper magazine carrying 200 rnd of APFSDS (armor-piercing fin-stabilized discarding sabots). In the antimissile role, the gun fires proximity-fuzed HE rnd until the target gets to within 1,000 m, switching over automatically to APFSDS to penetrate and fuze the missile's warhead. No sales of the single-barrel Fast Forty, which uses the same new recoiling mass, have been announced.

Breda-Bofors 40-mm *Users:* Algeria (Brooke Marine LSTs), Argentina (MEKO frigates and corvettes), Bahrein (FPB 62s, TNC 45s, FPB 38s), China (PRC) (for Dardo in Luda III and Jiangwei classes, made under license in 37-mm caliber), Colombia (FS-1500 class), Ecuador (*Wadi M'ragh* class), Egypt (*Ramadan* class), Greece (P 100, Osprey 55 and *Jason* classes), Iraq (*Wadi M'ragh* class, for sale), Italy (*Garibaldi, Vittorio Veneto, Maestrale, Lupo* classes), Kuwait (FPB 57 and TNC 45), Libya (Combattante IIs, *Ibn Ouf* class), Nigeria (*Aradu*, Combattante IIIs, FPB 57s), Oman ("Province" class, *Nasr al Bahr*), Peru (*Daring, Lupo,* PR 72 classes), Philippines (*Cormoran* and Australian patrol boat classes, both projected), Qatar (Combattante III class), Saudi Arabia (*Al Madinah, Boraida* classes), South Korea (*Ulsan* class 955–58, *Bukhansan* class), Thailand (PFMM Mk 16s, MV 400s), Tunisia (Combattante III class), U.A.E. (TNC 45 class), and Venezuela (*Lupo, Alm. Clemente, Capaña* classes)

Breda 30-mm *Users:* Italy (*Zara* class for Customs Service) and Thailand (twin: *Khamronsin* class)

NETHERLANDS

Goalkeeper (SGE-30) *Users:* Netherlands (*Tromp, Karel Doorman, Van Heemskerck, Kortenaer* classes), Oman (new corvettes), U.A.E. (FPB 62s), United Kingdom (*Invincible*, Type 22 Batch 3 classes). Temporarily on German *Bremen* class during the Gulf War. Goalkeeper may be on board the new Kuwaiti fast attack craft. The RNLN version has a 30-deg radar vertical beamwidth, compared to 60 deg in the RN version, on the theory that because the primary target is a sea-skimmer, it is better not to spread the available energy. Programmed range is 8 nm, but the radar will detect targets at 16. The system tracks 30 targets, engaging the 4 most urgent. If there are more, it minimizes salvo length to engage as many as possible. The gun fires for about 0.2 sec/engagement, and can deal with 2 pairs of sea-skimmers about 5 sec apart.

NORWAY

NFT offers a manual mounting for the **Mauser 25-mm/73 Model E** gun, based on its mounting for the Rhinemetall **Rh202** 20-mm gun. Elevation limits are +70/−15 deg. The gun weighs 109 kg and fires 900 rnd/min from boxes on either side. The **Breda 25KBA** is comparable.

SOUTH AFRICA

Small combatants are armed with an **MG-151 20-mm** gun (probably similar to the Rhinemetall 20-mm). A new nonpenetrating power-operated deck mount carries the gun with 100 rnd; the elevation limits are +80/−15 deg, and it trains at 70 deg/sec and elevates at 80 deg/sec. The mount is joystick- and helmet-controlled (see **HESIS**).

SPAIN

Each **Meroka** burst consists of 4 groups of 3 rnd (to limit recoil effects), lasting 0.08 sec; the weapon fires 2 bursts/sec. Barrels are slightly skewed to spread out the lethal area of the weapon. Meroka is currently credited (presumably by the Spanish navy) with an 87% probability of destroying an incoming missile with a single 12-rnd

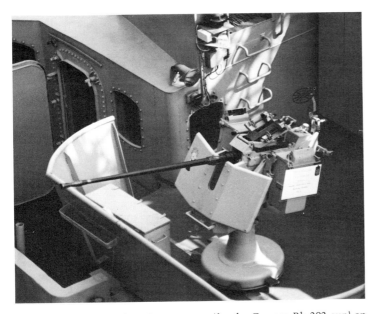

The Norwegian KV-SK/20 20-mm mount (for the German Rh 202 gun) on board the frigate *Stavanger* in 1992. (Author)

burst. Merokas now have an Israeli-designed IR tracker (in place of the original LLLTV), tested on board the *Santa Maria* in the spring of 1988. All Merokas are to be upgraded to the new Mod 2B standard, adding a new fire-control processor and a digital processor for system control. Future Merokas will be redesigned for reduced RCS. The version in the next class of frigates (F 100 type) may combine light missiles with the guns.

Sardin is a Meroka replacement now under development by Bazan. Reportedly, Sardin will be a hybrid weapon (guns and missiles); presumably, this project was the reason Spain entered the NATO **VSRAD** consortium.

SWEDEN

4.7-in/50 [120-mm] *Users:* Netherlands (*Tromp* class), Peru (*Friesland*-class destroyers)

4.7-in/46 (TAK 120) *Users:* Finland (*Turunmaa* class and *Pohjanmaa*) and Indonesia (*Fatahilah* class)

76-mm *Users:* Norway (*Storm* class), Singapore (110-ft "Type B")

57-mm/60 *Users:* Peru (ex-Dutch cruiser)

57-mm/70 Mk 1 *Users:* Croatia (*King Petar Kresimir IV* class), Finland (*Helsinki* class), Malaysia (Spica-M, *Jerong* classes), Sweden (*Carlskrona*, Spica-II, *Hugin* classes), Yugoslavia (*Rade Končar* class)

57-mm/70 Mk 2 *Users:* Canada ("City" class), Gabon ("Super PATRA" class), Malaysia (new corvettes), Mexico (*Aquila* class), and Sweden (*Göteborg*, Spica-III classes)

40-mm L70/Trinity *Users:* Sweden (*Smyge*).

As of 1992, Bofors was also advertising a **40-mm L70 Mk 3** in a powered mount carrying the operator (enclosed) and sufficient ammunition for 10 engagements. In effect, it is Trinity without the on-mount FCS.

Carl Gustav A/T Weapon (84-mm): Israel (Super Dvora class)

SWITZERLAND

Reportedly, **Sea Zenith** was less than successful in Turkish trials conducted by the British. The guns were too close together (their rounds interfered, like those of some pre-WWII triple turrets, so the shot pattern was too large). The mounting also vibrated excessively, probably because it had to be so flexible (to reach such extreme angles). Individual guns jammed during lengthy firings (such as those associated with relatively slow incoming missiles, lasting about 5 sec for a Mach 0.9 target), throwing the pattern off completely. One reported consequence of this failure was a Turkish decision to cancel **CoSys 200** in favor of **STACOS** for the TRACK II frigates.

Users: Turkey (Track I and II MEKO frigates)

AHEAD (Advanced Hit Efficiency and Destruction), a new Oerlikon antimissile ammunition, was first shown at the Paris Air Show in 1991. It is in final development for 35-mm guns, to enter service by the mid-1990s. The prefragmented heavy metal shell has a programmable base time fuze, set at the muzzle velocity gauge. The gauge consists of 3 coils: the first 2 measure muzzle velocity. The third sets the fuze as the projectile passes through it. The projectile is set to burst into a cone of pellets through which the target must fly. Oerlikon-Contraves claims that the pellets can defeat any front-end armor protecting a missile, drone, or RPV.

The unpowered **GBM-A01** mount, carrying a **25-mm KBA** gun, was an outgrowth of the **GAM** series, developed about 1975. Because the gun is fed from both sides, the mount can be reloaded while firing from the other side. This mount is used only by the Seychelles, in the FPB 42 class. Reportedly, the new Philippine patrol boats (*Cormoran* class), to be built by Bazan, will be armed with the new **Breda-Oerlikon 25-mm** mounts. They would represent the first sale of this weapon.

Oerlikon 35-mm (Type GDM-A) *Users:* Iran (1 mount aft on the single Mk 7 frigate), Greece (2 each on 4 Combattante II–class boats), and Turkey (ex-U.S. destroyers, FPB 57 class).

The Japanese Maritime Self-Defense Agency uses a single version of this gun, probably **GDM-B**, with a sidecar for the operator.

GDM-C *Users:* Libya (*Wadi M'ragh* class)

Oerlikon 20-mm (Type GAM-B01) *Users:* Argentina (Z-28 class), Austria (*Niederösterreich*), Bahrein (FPB 62–class fast attack boats and 65-ft Commercial

Cruiser class), Chile (*Reshev*), Egypt (Timsah-II class), Gabon (42-m CNE boat), Guatemala (*Broadsword* type, 85-ft type), Guyana (*Peccari*), Iran (Vosper Mk 5s and PF 103s), Ireland (P 21), Israel (Dvora and *Reshev* classes), Malaysia (*Lang Hitan*), Mauritania (PATRA class, *Barcelo* class), Mexico (*Azteca* class), Morocco (*Lazaga, Osprey*), Nigeria (*Lerici*, Type 502 landing ships), Oman (new Vosper Thornycroft corvettes, 37.5-m class, *Al Bahr* class, *Al Munassir*, CG-29, CG-27, and Haras classes), Papua New Guinea (AS 315 class), Saudi Arabia (*Al Souf* and ''Explorer'' classes), Senegal (Osprey 55 and Interceptor classes), Singapore (''Swift'' class, *Jupiter*), South Africa (*Reshev*s, *Drakensberg, Tafelberg*), Spain (*Lazaga, Barcelo*), Taiwan (*Wu Yi* class), Thailand (*Ratanakosin, Thalang, Bangrachan*, T 213, PS 700 classes), Tunisia (103-ft class), United Kingdom (*Fearless* class, *Sir Galahad, Fort Grange* class, *Diligence,* some ''Hunt'' class), Venezuela (*Capaña*).

This manual mount carries a **KAA** cannon. This 20-mm cannon, essentially equivalent to the World War II Oerlikon (but with a higher muzzle velocity), is mounted on board most British warships as a result of the Falklands emergency. The Royal Navy uses the **GAM-B01** designation. Development of the GAM series began in 1974; GAM-B01 entered production in 1976. In 1991 BMARC began development of a **Hybrid GAM** mounting, which could accommodate earlier 20-mm guns: Oerlikon Mks 1SS and 2SS and British and U.S. Mks 2 and 4. It was scheduled to enter production in 1992.

Oerlikon 20-mm (Type GAM-C01) *Users:* Libya (Thornycroft security craft), Singapore (Type As, Type Bs, ''Swifts''), Trinidad (CG-40).

This weapon is very similar to GAM-B01, but the gun is a **Hispano-Suiza 820** (which is also the basis of the French **20F2**). BMARC developed the new pedestal mount, which it called **A41/820**, in 1968–70 as a private venture, and production began in 1970.

Oerlikon 20-mm (Type A41A) *Users:* Brunei (*Perwira*), Egypt (Timsah, MV 70 classes), Gabon (Super PATRA class), Gambia (Tracker 2), Greece (*Kelefstis Stamou* class, Osprey corvettes), Guyana (*Peccari*), Ivory Coast (PATRA class), Kenya (*Nyayo*), Libya (Vosper Mk 7, 37-m Customs craft), Malaysia (*Duyong*, Brooke Marine 29-m, PX/Improved PX, Vosper 32-m), Morocco (P 32), Nigeria (*Erin'mi*, Intermarine patrol boats, *Lana*), Oman (Brooke Marine type, Vosper 25-m, *Al Mabrukah, Nasr al Bahr, Al Munassir*, CG-29, P 2000, Vosper Thornycroft 75-ft), Qatar (Combattante, *Polycat* 1450 classes), Senegal (Tracker 2), Singapore (*Endeavour*), Thailand (*Sattahip*, T 213, *Chula, Chasanyabadee, Chawengsak Songkram, Sriyanont,* Halter boats), Trinidad (Vosper patrol craft), Togo (32-m CNE type), Tunisia (Vosper Thornycroft patrol craft, P 48), U.A.E. (*Kawkab* class, Camcraft 77- and 65-ft and CG-23–class patrol craft)

TAIWAN

Small and medium combatants are being armed with the **Type 75 20-mm** gun, an adaptation of the U.S. **M39** fighter weapon.

UNITED KINGDOM

In 1992 Royal Ordnance PLC bought BMARC out of receivership. A victim of the Iraqi super-gun scandal, BMARC's parent company, Astra, had collapsed after buying PRB in Belgium.

At RNEE in 1991 VSEL announced **N114–2000**, a successor to **4.5-in Mk 8**, using newer technology to simplify the mount and reduce maintenance costs. The autoloader has been redesigned, and hydraulics are replaced by electric power. This version was described as particularly well adapted to the new High Explosive/Extended Range (HE/ER) round, which increases range from 22 to 27.5 km. The gun is unchanged (it is still a 4.5-in/55). Rate of fire is 25 rnd/min. Maximum train and elevation rates are better than 40 deg/sec. Mount's weight (excluding ammunition) is 23,250 kg. Elevation limits are +55/−10 deg. Barrel life is 3,300 rnd.

VSEL announced a new 155-mm/52 weapon, **N155–2000**, at RNEE 1991; the company probably hopes to sell it for the new-generation British AAW frigate. Muzzle velocity is 945 m/sec; range is 30 km (40 km with rocket assistance). Rate of fire is 10 rnd/min (3 rnd/min sustained). Elevation limits are +80/−15 deg. Estimated weights are 20,000 kg gun mount, 3,500 kg hoist. Crew: 1 gun captain, 1 gunbay attendant, 3 or 4 magazine operators.

4.5-in Mk 4 *Users:* Iran (*Damavand*)

4.5-in Mk 5 *Users:* Egypt (*El Fateh*), Indonesia (''Tribal''-class), Malaysia (*Rahmat*)

4.5-in Mk 6 *Users:* Australia (''River'' class), Chile (''County'' and *Leander* classes), New Zealand (*Leander* class), Pakistan (''County'' and *Leander* classes)

4.5-in Mk 8 *Users:* Argentina (Type 42), Brazil (*Niteroi, Inhaúma* classes), Iran (Vosper Mk 5 class), Libya (*Dat Assawari*), United Kingdom (Type 42, Type 22 Batch III, Type 21 classes)

4-in Mk 19 *Users:* Egypt (*Tariq*), Malaysia (*Hang Tuah*)

Vickers 4-in *Users:* Chile (*Alm. Riveros* class)

3-in Mk 6 *Users:* Canada (frigates)

30-mm (Type GCM-A01) *Users:* Brunei (*Waspada* class: B01 version), Egypt (6 October class, Timsah, MV 70 classes: A32 version), Israel (*Shimrit* class), Jordan (Hawk class: A03–2), Saudi Arabia (A32 in *Sandown* class), U.A.E. (A32 in 110-ft class), and United Kingdom (A02 bought during Falklands War, A03 currently in service; in *Fearless* class and some others). Other users of Oerlikon 30-mm gun: Qatar (Combattante III class), Tunisia (Combattante III class)

DS 30B *Users:* Malaysia (new corvettes), United Kingdom (Type 23s, Type 22 Batch 2s and 3s, ''Castle'' class, *Sandown* class, some ''Hunt'' class).

MSI is offering a version of this mount carrying a **25-mm Bushmaster** for the U.S. **AMCGS** requirement. The U.S. designation is **EX-39**. Malaysia was the first export customer.

UNITED STATES

The U.S. Navy is removing and scrapping all surviving **40-mm Bofors** guns. Similarly, **Mk 67 20-mm** guns are being scrapped as they are returned for overhaul. Both weapons will soon be replaced by standard **25-mm** guns.

A current (1992) Dahlgren naval-fire-support study considers both near-term (ca. 1997) and far-term (2010/2020) solutions to replacing the **16-in gun**. Both guns (including a 60-cal version of the 8-in Mk 71) and missiles (carrying bomblets) are possibilities. Weapons that can be fired from a Mk 41 VLS include **ATACMS, SeaSLAM, Beachcomber** (a **Patriot** derivative, formerly proposed for the Assault Breaker program, which produced the army's ATACMS), **Seabear** (**Skipper** guided by fiber optics or IR), and **SMASH** (an **SM-1** derivative; the SM Autonomous Strike Homing round, probably using GPS guidance). Beachcomber is a 16-in-diameter missile using the Patriot's body, motor, and inertial guidance (plus GPS). ATACMS is 23.96 in in diameter and thus would have to be carried in a new thin-wall (0.5-in) canister. The most likely gun concept is the electro-thermal gun (**ETG**); as of March 1992, FMC held the world record for muzzle energy (14 MJ) with its new **5-in/54 ETG**.

Advanced Gun Weapon System (renamed **WARSHIPS**) is an FY92 new start, financed initially from funds earmarked for the canceled **SLAT**, to develop a new gun system by the year 2000, to deal with fast maneuvering surface targets, small boats (cheap kill), and enemy targets near friendly ones in confined areas; and to attack beyond the horizon in support of OTH amphibious assaults. Presumably, this program will develop CAP and other exotic gun technologies, as well as new smart munitions with increased range, guidance, and payload lethality. It is also to investigate OTH-T ac-

Martin Marietta's proposal for a liquid-propellant 155-mm naval gun mount to meet the AGWS requirement, as displayed at the 1993 Navy League Show. (Martin Marietta)

quisition techniques utilizing GPS. The FY93 program is to begin the design/development of an Advanced Gun Weapon System (gun, FCS, ammunition) as well as an EO FCS. The system may go to sea on board the post–DDG-51 destroyer (DDV) or the new amphibious ship (LX).

At a presolicitation conference on 4 September 1991 at NOS Louisville, the navy representatives said that WARSHIPS was intended to develop either an improved 5-in or a new 8-in gun. Two full-scale gun weapon systems are to be developed, incorporating and demonstrating advanced technologies for AAW, ASUW, NGFS, strike, and suppress air defense. The program will include range-extension technology for existing 5-in guns.

Four notional systems or levels of performance are envisaged: (i) current technology, as baseline; (ii) a 5-in gun substantially exceeding 60 nm in range using 105-lb shells about 61 in long; (iii) a 5–8-in gun to substantially exceed 100 nm in range using rocket-assisted smart munition; (iv) a gun of at least 8-in caliber, to exceed 200 nm, with ammunition exceeding 300 lb. This last could fire special-purpose munitions. The first-year effort concentrates on smart munitions with increased range, guidance, lethality; advanced propulsion; and OTH-T acquisition using GPS. RENT is Range Extension Near Term.

AMCGS (Advanced Minor-Caliber Gun System) was inspired by U.S. experience in the Persian Gulf in 1987–88, when unstabilized light guns were unable to hit fast boats, such as Boghammers. A stabilized, pedestal-mounted gun, probably of 25–35-mm caliber, was needed. British and Italian weapons were evaluated in 1989, but they did not meet the requirements. An RFP was planned for the summer or early fall of 1991, but it fell afoul of the new requirement that new weapons projects had to undergo a trade-off process (COEA, cost and effectiveness evaluation analysis) before any RFP could be issued. In this case, the COEA (August 1992) found that the most cost-effective solution to the AMCGS problem would be a **Phalanx Surface Mode** (PSM), probably using a FLIR for target acquisition.

There was a shrewd suspicion that PSM was too convenient a solution to the AMCGS problem (there was already opposition from the fleet). The fleet had favored a 30-mm or larger round for AMCGS because a good-sized explosive shell was needed to deal with a small boat or airplane. Phalanx uses a small-diameter penetrator, which should burst a missile's warhead, but which might well pass through a boat without doing much damage. There was also some fear that arranging Phalanx to engage surface targets might detract from its primary antiair role. Ironically, Phalanx was originally designed with

an antisurface mode, which was never officially approved. Moreover, many units requiring AMCGS are not equipped with Phalanx. As of September 1992, the House Armed Services Committee had rejected the navy's COEA position. Congress still wants some AMCGS to be adopted soon; in September 1992 the Senate Appropriations Committee wrote language into the FY93 defense bill requiring live-fire tests as soon as possible. None of this affected the parallel **SWPS** project.

The original SWPS specification was written by the Crane Naval Weapons Center in June 1990; it was briefed to industry in January 1991. The weight budget for the Special Warfare PC (the *Cyclone* class) is 9,000 lb for 2 SWPS, their FCSs, and their ammunition. An RFP was scheduled for the summer of 1992, following a cost and effectiveness (trade-off) study in the spring. This is a Special Operations Command program for the new PBC. The SWPS gun is the current 25-mm or a future 30-mm weapon, not yet specified. The mount will also carry **Hellfire, Stinger,** and **Hydra/2.75-in rockets**. As of April 1992, likely competitors were AAI/Rockwell/Texas Instruments, FMC (possibly with DES), LTV (**Crossbow**, possibly with ELOP), and Boeing (**Avenger**, possibly with Kollsman). The main distinguishing feature of the FMC design is apparently protected storage for the Hellfires, to keep their seekers free of water damage. Crossbow apparently inspired the SWPS program in 1985–86. However, its future is unclear; although Loral bought the LTV defense business, it is not advertising Crossbow. About October 1992 a COEA study recommended that SWPS be built out of existing (NDI) weapons: a 25-mm gun, **Stinger**, and on-mount fire control; if affordable, an off-mount sensor and Hellfire could be added. In April 1993 an RFP was expected within 4 months.

FMC is developing a **5-in/54 ETG** in 2 phases. Phase I fires a 25-kg shell at 1,200 m/sec [3,940 ft/sec]; the maximum mass accelerated is 28 kg. The Phase II gun fires a 4–6-kg shell at 2,500 m/sec [8,200 ft/sec]; the maximum mass accelerated is 150 kg. Velocity is repeatable to within 0.25% in Phase I, and to within 0.5% in Phase II.

The FMC **60-mm Electro-Thermal Gun** and its Martin Marietta (formerly GE) guided round (Small-Caliber Smart Munition, **SCSM**) have now been tested successfully. The SCSM contract was awarded in the fall of 1991. The 2.75-kg rolling-airframe steel shell uses a K-band guidance up-link and an S-band telemetry down-link. It carries a thermal battery and a miniature propulsion control using a small solid-propellant thruster. Muzzle velocity is 1.3 km/sec (4,260 ft/sec); SCSM can maneuver at 40 G at Mach 3. Like Phalanx, this

Naval 60-mm ET Technology Demonstrator Characteristics

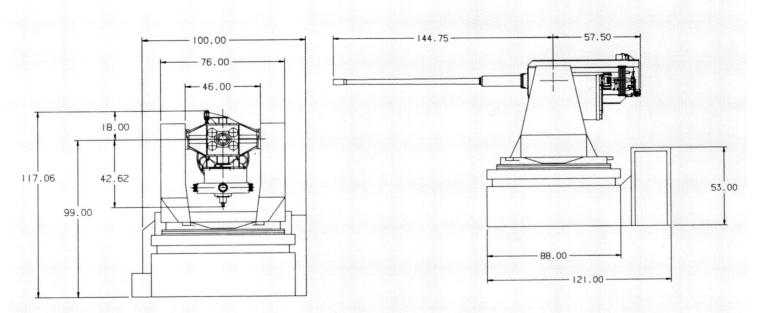

FMC's electrothermal technology-demonstrator gun. (FMC)

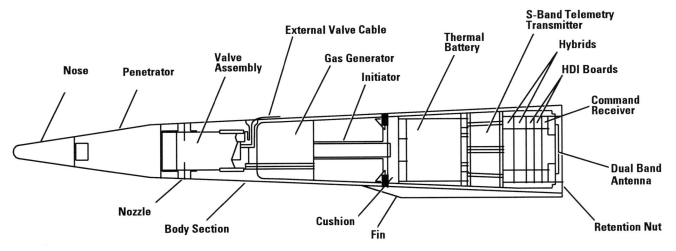

The 60-mm small-caliber saboted smart munition designed for the ET gun. (Martin Marietta)

weapon kills by impact, not by explosion. Seven saboted projectiles were successfully fired at Dahlgren in the second half of 1992, 2 carrying live gas generators and thermal batteries. The K-band command link was tested over water at Dahlgren in February 1993. Tests against airborne targets are scheduled for late 1993. The gun is an autoloader on a Phalanx mounting. Firing rate is 4 rnd/sec (10-rnd burst); elevation limits are +30/-5 deg. **TASD** is being developed specifically to acquire sea-skimmer targets for this gun.

At Navy League 1993, Martin Marietta announced a **lightweight 155-mm liquid-propellant naval gun mount** for the advanced gun program described above. It hopes to reach 35 nm with existing army ammunition, and to exceed 100 nm with new projectiles. The weapon is based on the Defender, under development for the U.S. Army Advanced Field Artillery System (AFAS), to enter service in 2005. The army's 155-mm liquid-propellant gun (XM300) is to begin tests in 1994 to demonstrate a range of over 45 km, a rate of fire of 12–16 rnd/min, and a velocity accuracy of better than 0.25%. It should then be able to fire a 4–8-rnd simultaneous impact mission at 6–40 km. Range is increased because there is a capability to precisely inject propellant throughout the combustion process, the system offers soft launch with reduced chamber pressure, and ammunition-storage volume is reduced (because there are no cartridge cases). Martin Marietta estimates that this 155-mm/52 will weigh 40,000 lb (compared to 110,000 lb for an 8-in/55), and will achieve a range of 53,000 yd; elevation limits are +65/−15 deg. Rate of fire is 16–20 rnd/min (60 ready-use rounds).

5-in/54 Mk 39 Users: Japan (Akizuki class ex-destroyers)

5-in/54 Mk 42 Users: Australia (Adams class), Germany (Adams class), Greece (Adams class), Japan, Spain (Baleares class), Taiwan (Knox class), United States (Belknap, Truxtun, Mahan, Adams, Knox classes)

5-in/54 Mk 45 Users: Australia (MEKO frigates), Greece (MEKO frigates), New Zealand (MEKO frigates), Thailand (Type 25T frigates), Turkey (MEKO frigates), United States (Virginia, California, Ticonderoga, Arleigh Burke, Kidd, Spruance, Tarawa classes).

FMC's proposed **Super Lightweight** version omits the below-decks loader drum, to reduce weight (by about 6,000 lb) and cost. It responds to foreign requests. There is also a Mk 45 technical-improvement program: a lateral-transfer cradle, an enhanced interface with the FCS, electric train and elevation drives, a new shield, and an index-drive and lower-hoist-servo controls.

5-in/38 twin mounts Users: Brazil (FRAMs), Greece (FRAMs), Mexico (FRAMs), Pakistan (FRAMs), South Korea (FRAMs), Taiwan (FRAMs and Sumners), Turkey (FRAMs), United States (Iowa class)

5-in/38 single enclosed mounts Users: Brazil (Garcia class), Chile (APD), Mexico (Fletcher class, APDs), Pakistan (Brooke and Garcia classes), Taiwan (Fletcher and Rudderow classes)

5-in/38 single open mounts Users: Peru (Independencia), Taiwan (Yu Tai, Rudderow class)

3-in/50 automatic mounts (Mks 33 and 34) Users: Brazil (Ceará, Duque de Caxias), Canada (Annapolis, Mackenzie, Restigouche, St. Laurent classes), Colombia (Boyaca, Asheville class), Denmark (Falster class), Greece (Asheville and Terrebonne County classes), Indonesia (Claud Jones class), Japan (Amatsukaze, Yamagumo, Minegumo,

Chikugo, Isuzu, Miura classes), Norway (Oslo, Sleipner classes), Portugal (João Coutinho class), South Korea (Asheville class), Spain (Paul Revere, Terrebonne Parish classes), Turkey (Carpenter, Berk, Asheville, Falster, Terrebonne Parish classes), United States (Tripoli, Blue Ridge, Austin, Raleigh, Anchorage, Newport, Charleston, Kilauea, Suribachi, Mars, Ashtabula classes)

3-in/50 semiautomatic mount (Mk 26) Users: Chile (Sgt. Aldea, Yelcho), Dominican Republic (Cohoes and Admirable classes), Ecuador (Abnaki class), Greece (Aris, Patapsco class), Iran (PF 103 class), Mexico (Auk and Admirable classes), Peru (river gunboats, Independencia), Philippines (Cannon, Auk, Admirable, PCE/PCER, LSSL classes), Spain (Anaga class), Taiwan (Auk class, LSTs, auxiliaries), Thailand (PSMM Mk 5 class, LSSL, Damrong Rachanuphat class), United States (coast guard: Reliance, Cherokee classes)

Chain Gun (25-mm Mk 38/Mk 88 mounting) Users: Saudi Arabia (77-ft class), United States.

U.S. Procurement: FY86, 29; FY87, 25; FY88, 22; FY89, 57; FY91, 55; FY92, 55 (last year procured). It seems likely that more will be bought because this gun has now been chosen to replace all existing 40-mm and 20-mm weapons. It will certainly arm U.S. special-forces boats (Mk III and Cyclone class) and the later LSD-42 class, and it is issued to ships deploying to the Middle East.

EX-74/Emerlec-30 Users: Ecuador (Manta class), Ethiopia (104-ft Commercial Cruiser type [2 with twin 23-mm instead]), Greece (Combattante IIIN class), Malaysia (FS-1500–class frigates, Hang Tuah, and corvettes), Nigeria (Combattante IIIB and FPB 57 classes, Abeking & Rasmussen and Brook Marine type patrol boats, and Lerici), Philippines (Katapangan class), South Korea (Ulsan HDF-2000 and HDC 800 classes, Dong Hae class, PSMM 5 class, "Sea Dolphin" class), Taiwan (Lung Chiang class)

Phalanx (Close-In Weapons System Mk 15) Users: Australia (Perry and Adams classes [Block 1]), Canada (Block 0 in TRUMP and "City" classes), Greece (Block 1 in MEKO 200 class), Israel (Block 0 in Sa'ar 5, Romat, Sa'ar 4.5, and Sa'ar IV classes), Japan (Block 1 in destroyers and recent DEs), Pakistan (Block 0 in Babur- and Gearing-class destroyers), Portugal (Block 0 in MEKO 200 class), Saudi Arabia (Block 0 in PCG and PGG classes), Taiwan (Block 1 in Wu Chin III destroyers and Perry-class frigates), United Kingdom (Block 1 in carriers [being replaced by Goalkeeper] and Type 42 destroyers), and United States (Block 1 in carriers and most surface combatants; replaced BPDMS on most Knox class).

Plans for a follow-on Block 2 were shelved in 1992 in favor of continued incremental improvements to Block 1. The GE contract for a Phalanx radar upgrade was canceled in December 1991. Phalanx was experimentally integrated with a FLIR at Dahlgren in the spring of 1992. CIWS Block 1 Baseline 3, to enter service in FY97, includes a major sensor upgrade (for better tracking, to better detect small targets in high clutter, and for better ECCM) and a high-order-language (HOL) computer upgrade to increase capability against maneuvering targets. Recent purchases: 18 in FY89, 15 in FY90, 16 in FY91, 14 in FY92, 12 in FY93. Unit cost including integration is $5.3 million in FY93 (the weapon itself cost about $3.3 million in FY90).

In February 1992 NSWC Dahlgren requested industry proposals for a 60–76-mm gun to be used as a future CIWS, with a total weight of about 10,000 lb (Phalanx weighs 12,000). It was to fire long (12–15-cal) rockets at a sustained rate of at least 200/min, with a total capacity of 40–50 rnd. The rocket's airframe would include a terminal seeker, a midcourse command-link receiver, a control system, a KE penetrator, and a sustainer motor; it would have to be extremely agile and be able to sustain a high rate of acceleration on a continuous basis.

Sea Vulcan 25 *Users:* Israel (*Eilat* class)

Sea Vulcan 20 (EX-84)/20P *Users:* Honduras (*Guardian*, 105-ft and 85-ft classes), Japan (new hydrofoil attack craft, also minecraft), Saudi Arabia (Jetfoil tender to royal yacht), South Korea (specially designed weatherproof mounting)

The **Mk 19 grenade launcher** is a 40-mm grenade-launching machine gun, developed during the Vietnam War and carried on board small combatants, auxiliaries, and coast guard ships; it is also exported. It fires 300 rnd/min and has a range of 2,400 yd. The current version is Mod 3. Procurement: 25/yr in the late 1980s, then FY89, 350; FY90, 123; FY91, 321; FY92, 568; FY93, none. Many of the recently bought weapons are for the marines.

Mortars *Users:* Bolivia (60-mm in PBR Mk II), Brazil (81-mm in *Piratini*-class patrol boats and in river patrol ships), Burma (60-mm in PBR Mk II), Colombia (60-mm in PBR Mk II), Costa Rica (60-mm in 105-ft, 42-ft, and 36-ft types), Malta (81-mm in "Swift" type), Paraguay (81-mm in *Itaipu*), Philippines (60-mm in 7 Mini-ATC type; provision for 81-mm in 77-ft class), Sweden (81-mm in *Stridsbåt* 90 type), Thailand (PB Mk III and "Swift" Mk II classes), Vietnam (81-mm in ex-U.S. *Savage* class DER, and 60-mm in PBR Mk II class).

Virtually all the 60-mm and 81-mm mortars are probably of U.S. design (and, mostly, manufacture).

Recoilless Rifles (probably U.S. Army types) *Users:* Guatemala (*Broadsword* and 85-ft type: 75-mm), Iran (106-mm in some of 32 Boghammer boats). Iran also uses the Soviet-supplied 107-mm recoilless rifle, in some Boston Whalers.

YUGOSLAVIA

Yugoslavia probably makes the triple Hispano-Suiza **20-mm mount**.

Users: Honduras (*Hibures*), Yugoslavia (river minesweepers, riverine command ship *Kozara*, DTK 211– and RTK 401–class landing craft)

20/4 M75 *Users:* Hungary (river minesweepers), Iraq (PB 90 class), Yugoslavia (Type 80, Silba class, and Type PO transports)

ELECTRONIC WARFARE

In what follows, a distinction is drawn between systems that are wholly analog, those that digitize pulses one by one, and those that deinterleave. A wholly analog system displays signal direction (obtained either from multiple monopulse ports or, in the U.S. **SLR/WLR-1** series, from a spinning antenna). A signal can be selected (strobed) by bearing and by band for further analysis using a CRT. In some cases a separate omni antenna is used for this purpose. The next step is to digitize the incoming pulse (measuring pulse width, time of arrival, and, using an IFM, frequency; bearing can also be measured pulse by pulse). The operator can select (strobe) a signal (by bearing and band) and measure PRF (in effect, manually). A fully automatic system associates sets of pulses detected by wide-open CVRs (for direction) with sets detected by an IFM (fed by an omni antenna). It *deinterleaves*, i.e., it separates the stream of pulses into sets corresponding, in theory, with particular emitters. Multipath reflections off the sea and off the ship's structure distort pulses and inject spurious ones, complicating deinterleaving. Many systems have 2 libraries, a small tactical one against which signals are automatically compared, plus a larger one for manual lookup. For example, the Canadian CANEWS has a 128-mode tactical library and a 2,000-mode main library.

Some recent HF/DF systems offer SSL, **single station location** (as opposed to the usual triangulation), by measuring the angle of incidence of the sky wave. For example, phase differences across an array of receiving antennas can be measured. At shorter ranges, out to about 300 km [about 160 nm], it is probably possible to compare the times of arrival of the surface and near-vertical-angle-of-incidence sky waves (NVIS). The angle of arrival depends on the structure of the ionosphere, which can be measured either by periodic sounding or by periodically measuring the angle of arrival of signals from known locations. Accuracy is not so good as from triangulation (AWA of Australia claims 5% for its new CELTIC), but SSL does offer a single ship a fully passive means of location. The new French HF/DF systems (such as Altesse) provide SSL, and the use of an extended hull array in the U.S. Classic Outboard suggests a similar capability. Current SSL producers include AWA of Australia, Rhode & Schwartz and TST of Germany, Thomson-CSF of France, and South West Research Institute and TCI in the U.S.

Canada abandoned work on the **ULQ-6** upgrade (CCP/Tecmus has gone out of business, and the DFML and programming loop planned by Canadian Astronautics Ltd. has been abandoned). The German **Schalmei** never attracted any sales. The U.S. **SLEWS** program was canceled on 6 January 1992. Up to 4 contracts had been planned for competitive ground tests, with 2 to have been chosen for sea tests. **Carol**, a version of **APECS II** for the Swedish *Göteborg* class, has been dropped in favor of **Sceptre Lens**. **DCJSS**, listed previously, does not exist (work was abandoned about 1987).

AUSTRALIA

AWA Defence Industries' **PRISM** (Passive Radar Identification System, Type 133) is an austere ESM system for fast patrol boats intended specifically to counter smugglers who have their own RWRs. The 14-kg, cylindrical, mast-antenna unit contains all RF processing elements; the antenna array itself is a set of 4 cavity-backed spirals near its bottom. The receiver is a series of channelized CVRs, and DF is by amplitude comparison. The console houses the emitter processor. The display is the usual combination of a polar plot plus the listed parameters (apparently 3 at once); the system provides both visual and audio alarms, as well as emitter PRF in audio form. The current PRISM 133 uses CVRs to cover 2–4 and 8–12 GHz (sensitivity −75 and −73 dBm, respectively; DF accuracy 10 and 8 deg, respectively; elevation coverage +35/−10 deg), measuring pulse width to within 0.05 microsec (over a range of 0.05–1,000 microsec). Throughput is 350 kpps. PRF range is 200 Hz–350 kHz (PRI accuracy is 200 nsec, resolution 100 nsec). Circular or conical scan range is 1–40 sec (resolution 0.1 sec). A new emitter is reported within 1 sec (if it is staring at the array) or within 4 scan periods. PRISM 133 can track 32 emitters simultaneously, and the operator library is 100 modes (mission library is 600 radar modes). PRISM I extends the frequency range to 2–18 GHz (sensitivity −73 dBm for 2–8 GHz, −67 dBm for 8–18 GHz); DF accuracy is 11 deg. This version adds the ability to recognize complex radars. PRISM II extends the frequency range down to 0.5 GHz (sensitivity −64 dBm for 0.5–2 GHz). A CM version can trigger an ECM system. PRISM III adds an IFM for frequency measurement (resolution 4 MHz over the entire 0.5–18-GHz range). It has a new array: bearing accuracy is 10 deg for 0.5–2 GHz, 7 deg for 2–8 GHz, and 5.5 deg for 8–18 GHz. PRISM III (PA) adds a pulse analyzer. Pulses with widths greater than 128 microsec are classed as CW, but resolution is much better (for ELINT): 0.0002 microsec for 0.05–0.127 microsec, 0.02 for 0.128–1.28 microsec, and 0.05 for 1.20 microsec up. Throughput increases to 500 kpps, and PRF range to 10 Hz–500 kHz (PRI accuracy improves to 0.1 nsec; resolution is to 4 decimal places of PRF). This version can track 500 emitters, and the mission library is 2,600 emitter modes. PRISM AD is a land-based air-defense version roughly comparable to PRISM I. PRISM C (8–12 GHz only, DF accuracy 6 deg) is intended for commercial vessels navigating by taking bearings on specific radars ashore.

First sea trials were carried out on board HMAS *Launceston* in February 1991 and HMAS *Warrnambool* in June 1991. Acceptance trials followed on board HMAS *Cessnock* in February 1993, with the remaining systems (for the Australian *Fremantle* class) to be delivered in 1993–94. Type 133 will be bid for the Pacific Patrol Boat mid-life modernization and forthcoming RAN coastal-minehunter program. PRISM is being tested on board the Canadian fishery-protection ship *Cygnus*, and is to be tested by Malaysia. It is being sold to the RAAF for early-warning aircraft detection.

AWA also produces a series of CELTIC HF/DF sets; the RAN patrol boats will be fitted with **CELTIC SAILOR**, which covers 2–30 MHz (bandwidth 3 kHz with resolution better than 25 Hz). CELTIC can detect signals down to 50 msec in duration and can take 40 DF cuts/sec. It can detect surface waves at sea out to 250–300 km.

Winnin is currently being developed for the U.S. Navy under a 1986 Memorandum of Agreement; the U.S. contractor is Sippican. However, there is no current U.S. Navy procurement plan because of weight and cost problems. In FY93 Congress authorized $2 million to consider alternative deployment concepts. Nulka completed U.S. technical and operational evaluation in 1992 (the OpTevFor report was released in March 1993). Triggered by a ship's ESM system (it is adapted to SLQ-32), it is launched and fully powered up in less than 10 sec; total endurance is 55+ sec. Nulka dimensions are about 5.9 in × 7 ft (weight 110 lb), so it needs a special launcher. AWA hopes to develop PRISM to trigger Nulka (its FCS can fit a slightly enlarged PRISM), and to cut down to 2 launchers for smaller ships. PRISM should be adequate because Nulka can work with less than 10 deg of DF accuracy.

CANADA

Lockheed Canada bought MEL Canada, which was responsible for **CANEWS** and **RAMSES**; this company is also Racal's Canadian agent for **SLR-504** (Kestrel).

For operations in the Persian Gulf in 1990–91, 8 Canadian naval Sea King helicopters (CH-124s) were converted at the Shearwater base to a surface-surveillance role, with self-protective systems: a Tracor **SLIPAR** (Short-Pulse-Light Alerting Receiver) laser warner (the Iranians have **RBS-70** laser-guided missiles), **APR-39A(V)1**, and the **AAR-47** passive missile-warner. They were fitted with **ALE-39** chaff dispensers, **M130** flare dispensers, and **ALQ-144** IR jammers. SLIPAR is a portable unit first sold in 1989 and used mainly by the U.S. Air Force. The main surface-search sensor added was a nose-mounted FLIR 2000(G). The only armament added was a door-mounted C-9 machine gun. GPS was also added at this time.

CANEWS (SLQ-501) is a close relative of **Sphinx** and **UAA-1**, using a Canadian processor. Unlike UAA-1, CANEWS is fully automatic (i.e., deinterleaves). The computer is **UYK-502**. R&D for a CANEWS upgrade for mid-life refits of "City"-class frigates has begun. **CANEWS II** will probably use the same arrays. An auxiliary receiver may extend coverage up to 40 GHz. CANEWS II will have a new distributed (multiprocessor) architecture built of ASICs and 68040s; it will operate over a wider bandwidth, in greater pulse density, and against more exotic emitters. The development team consists of Lockheed, Computer Devices Co., and Software Kinetics. Sea trials are expected in 1996.

Users: Canada ("City" and TRUMP classes)

Light Ship ESM is a new modular CANEWS export derivative (2–18 GHz, optional extension to mm-wave), to cost less than Can $1 million in its simplest form. The 45-kg antenna array (DF plus omni: 432 × 521 × 305 mm) can be mounted on its own mast or clamped to an existing mast. It is connected to the below-decks 19-in console by optical fibers. The system measures pulse width, frequency, bearing, PRI, scan time and interval, and amplitude. It is intended to operate in pulse densities greater than 500,000/sec, tracking up to 128 emitters (reporting new ones in less than 1 sec). DF accuracy is 2 deg RMS. Elevation coverage is +40/-10 deg. Sensitivity is -60dBm. An enhanced version would double the pulse density and the number of track files. Software is written in ADA.

Lockheed Canada is advertising an **Advanced MM-Wave ESM Subsystem** (presumably intended as an extension for Light Ship ESM) covering the Ka-band (higher bands are optional); sensitivity is -60 dBm, and accuracy is 5 deg. Elevation coverage is +40/-10 deg. Pulses between 50 nsec and CW can be handled, and the receiver recovers from a pulse in less than 100 nsec (so it can, in theory, handle about 10 million pps if they are short enough). The receiver reports pulse width, amplitude, bearing, and time of arrival. The receivers are packaged with the antennas (4 ports on each of 2), feeding a below-decks processor via fiber-optic cables. Up-mast weight is 23 kg.

SLQ-502 is the Shield chaff/IR decoy system. **SLQ-504** is Racal Type 242 (Kestrel) for the AORs and the new MCDVs. **SRD-501** is an HF/DF developed from the earlier (and now defunct) Model 100. It is in the TRUMP and older Canadian frigate classes. **SRD-502**, for the "City" class, is made by Southwest Research Institute of the United States, which also makes **SRD-19** (part of **Classic Outboard**); the two systems seem to share the same masthead (VHF/UHF) array, but SRD-502 uses a masthead (rather than hull) array for MFDF and HFDF. **UPD-501** is an older countermeasures radar direction finder, in the *Mackenzie* and *St. Laurent* classes; it was formerly in the "Tribal" class.

CHINA (PRC)

A frigate advertised at Abu Dhabi in 1993 showed an RWD8 RWR, NJ81–3 noise jammer, and 2 PJ46 decoy launchers. These may merely be new designations for the equipment listed below. In 1993 the Jianghu-class frigate *Siping* carried a flat-sided ESM antenna similar in appearance to that of SLQ-32, together with the usual pair of RW 23-1s.

Type 921-A (Golf Ball) is a Chinese version of the Russian **Stop Light**.

Users: China (PRC) (Han and Romeo classes), North Korea (Romeo class)

RW-23–1 (Jug Pair) is a Chinese version of the Russian **Watch Dog**.

Users: Bangladesh (Jianghu-class frigates), China (PRC) (Chengdu-, Luda- [except 3], and Jiangdong-class destroyers, Jianghu- and Jiangnan-class frigates, Yukan-class LSTs, Fuqing-class AOR, T-43 class), North Korea (Najin- and Soho-class frigates), Pakistan (Fuqing-class AOR)

BM/HZ 8610 uses 2 rows, each of 8 monopulse ports, in sections clamped around a mast, e.g., below a masthead radar.

Users: Albania (Shanghai-II, Huchuan, T-301 classes), Bangladesh (Hainan, Shanghai-II, Houku, Huangfeng, and Huchuan classes), Burma (Hainan class), China (PRC) (Haijui, Hainan, Shanghai-II, Houku, Hola, Huangfeng, Huchuan, and Type 206 OPV classes), Egypt (Hainan, Shanghai, Houku classes), Gambia (Shanghai-II class), North Korea (Hainan, Shanghai-II, Huangfeng, Soju, Taechong classes), Pakistan (Hainan, Shanghai-II, Houku, Huangfeng, Huchuan classes), Romania (Shanghai-II, Huchuan classes), Sierra Leone (Shanghai-II class), Sri Lanka (Shanghai-II class), Tanzania (Shanghai-II, Huchuan classes), Tunisia (Shanghai-II class), Zaire (Shanghai-II class)

CPMIEC's new **945PJ** shipboard decoy-launching system employs groups of IR and chaff magazines, each with 2 groups of decoys (9 launch barrels per chaff group, 3 per IR group). For example, a Jianghu III–class frigate carries 10 magazines on each side, at her stern. The controller can be on the bridge or in CIC. The computer sounds an alarm (upon radar warning), displays threat bearing (digits and lamps), fires the decoys, and recommends an evasive course. Alternatively, the decoys can be launched manually. The launcher is 500 × 250 × 370–mm (empty weight 36 kg [steel] or 26 kg [titanium alloy]). The chaff round covers the 7.5–18-GHz bands (I, J); each cluster provides a 1,500-m^2 radar cross section, which lasts 60+ sec. Average IR power is 950 W/Sr (3–5-micron band), lasting 40+ sec.

ERC-1 consists of 15 tubes and a fire-control unit and fires IR or chaff decoys singly or in salvos. Decoy modes are attraction (persists in the air for 2 min), distraction (6 min), and dump (4 min).

Users: China (PRC) (Jianghu 053H1, Jiangnan, and Luda [except for hulls 165, 17, and 18] classes), Egypt (Jianghu 053H[E] class), Pakistan (Fuqing-class AOR)

FRANCE

The French navy is apparently buying a new SSL-type HF/DF, probably to support the **ANS** and Exocet Block II missiles, both of which need an approximate target range. ANS must dive to sea-skimming altitude some distance from the target, and Exocet Block II is probably best used in an indirect approach, doglegging rather than merely following the line of bearing to the target. The competitors are apparently the Thomson-CSF **ALTESSE** (on board the destroyer *Tourville*, and planned for the *La Fayette*s and the *Charles de Gaulle* class) and the new German **MAIGRET**. The accompanying precision UHF-VHF system will be either Dassault's **SAIGON** (*Système Automatisé d'Interception et de Goniométrie*) or Thomson-CSF's **Sequoia** (on board *Aconit* and *Tourville*); the system selected will equip the *Cassard*s. DF accuracy should be about 0.5 deg.

All 3 Thomson-CSF ESM systems cover the C–J bands.

DR 2000 is an analog system. Signals (pulse trains) strobed by the operator are passed to a digitizer/recognizer, **Dalia** (which replaced the earlier hard-wired **Arial** with a 15-mode library). The Arial/DR 2000 combination, **DR 3012** (TMV 026), is used to trigger **DAGAIE** decoy launchers; it is analogous to the British **Matilda**. DR 3012 is absent from a DAGAIE ship only when the launcher is controlled by the ship's CDS, fed by an ESM system. DF accuracy is 5 or 6 deg. **DR 2000 Mk 2**, now in production for EMB 111s and Sea Kings, is smaller and has a manual SHR. The new Mk 3 is more sensitive and has a more powerful processor (pulse digitizer, capacity several hundred thousand pps). **SAGE** is an interface between DR2000/4000 and a **TAVITAC** combat system.

DR 4000, with an integrated deinterleaver, is the next generation digital version for frigates and large maritime aircraft. It has 2 (rather than 1) sets of DF antennas (6 per set in a submarine, 8 in a frigate) to handle its 2 bands. Accuracy may be as good as 2–3 deg.

DR 3000 is a new lightweight equivalent to DR 4000, with only a single set of DF antennas, originally for aircraft. The processor uses MMIC technology, and the radar identifier uses artificial intelligence (it is an expert system). DF precision is normally about 6 deg. The S2 version selected for the French *La Fayette* class uses interferometry for higher precision, for OTH missile targeting (it uses an array of 4 rectangular antennas rather than the usual 6 ports). There is also a high-precision submarine version.

DR 2000A *Users:* Atlantic MPA (in French and Pakistani service, 40 aircraft), Gardian (5 French naval aircraft), Super-Frélon helicopters (24 built for the French navy for patrol out of Brest in support of SSBNs), and Super Puma naval helicopters (8 for Abu Dhabi, 6 for Brazil, 26 for Indonesia, 6 for Kuwait, 2 for Oman, 6 for Saudi Arabia, and 6 for Singapore).

Sequoia is shown on board the frigate *Aconit* in 1992. (Author)

It is not certain how many of the helicopters were fitted with **DR 2000H**. Although DR 2000H was adapted for the EMB 111 and the Fokker Maritime Defender, aircraft of those types generally carry Elettronica's ESM equipment.

DR 2000S *Users:* Argentina (A-69–type corvettes), Belgium (*Wielingen*-class frigates and Tripartite minehunters), Cameroon (*L'Audacieuse* class), China (PRC) (Luda-class destroyer hull 165), Ecuador (3 *Quito* and 3 *Manta* class), Croatia (4 *Kobra*, 1 *Končar* class), Finland (*Turunmaa* class), Germany (10 Type 143s [to be replaced by **Octopus**], 18 Type 331 minehunters [not certain], 10 Type 343 minesweepers, 8 *Lüneberg*-class tenders, *Steigerwald*), Ghana (2 TNC 45 and 2 TNC 57 classes), Greece (10 Combattante IIIN, 4 Combattante IIs, 6 *Jaguars*, *L'Audacieuse* OPVs), Indonesia (4 PB 57s, 2 PSK-5s, 2 Tripartite minehunters, and 4 TNC 57 OPVs), Iran (12 Combattante II class, 2 now lost), Ivory Coast (4 *L'Audacieuse*-class OPVs), Libya (10 Combattante IIs, 1 now lost, and LSD *Zeltin*), Madagascar (*Malaika*), Malaysia (4 Combattante IIAL class), Mauritania (*El Nasr*), Morocco (*L'Audacieuse*-class OPVs), Peru (6 PR-72–560 class), Qatar (3 Combattante IIIs), Saudi Arabia (*Jaguar, Durance* classes), Senegal (*L'Audacieuse* class), Serbia (*Končar* class), Tunisia (*L'Audacieuse* class), Turkey (*Jaguar, Kartal* classes), Uruguay (*Cdt. Rivière* class), and Venezuela (6 *Constitución* class)

ARBR 16 (DR 2000) *Users:* 2 *Clemenceau*-class carriers, *Jeanne d'Arc*, 4 (of 7) *Georges Leygues* class, 3 *Tourville* class, *Aconit, Duperré*, 17 A-69 class, *Cdt. Rivière* class (being transferred to Uruguay), 5 *Durance* class, Tripartite minehunters, *L'Audacieuse*-class OPVs, *Ouragan*-class LSDs.

ARBR 16 works either with an **ARBB 31** or **32** jammer and **Syllex** medium-range chaff (for large ships); or with **DAGAIE** chaff launchers (and **Alligator** jammer in the case of the A-69s). The associated frequency-measurement device (SHR) is **ARBX 10**.

DR 2000U *Users:* Argentina (Type 209), Brazil (Type 209), Chile (*Oberon*s), China (PRC) (Ming class and Wuhan), Colombia (Type 209), Denmark (Type 205 *Narhvalen* class), Ecuador (Type 209), France (all submarines), Germany (Type 205s, 206s, 206As), Greece (last 4 Type 209s; first 4 have Sea Lion), Indonesia (Type 209), Pakistan (*Agosta* and *Daphne* classes), Peru (*Abtao* and Type 209 classes), Portugal (*Daphne* class), Serbia (*Sava* class), Turkey (*Atilay, Batiray, Saldiray*), Venezuela (Type 209).

ARUR 10 was the French navy's version. The associated frequency-measurement device (SHR) is **ARUX 1**.

DR 3000A *Users:* France (modernized Alizé aircraft, as ARAR 12A)

DR 3000S *Users:* China (PRC) (Luda-class hulls 17 and 18), France (*Charles de Gaulle, La Fayette* class, and experimental boat *Iris*), Oman (Muheet-class light frigates), Qatar (probably in new light frigates), Saudi Arabia (*La Fayette* class), Taiwan (*La Fayette* class)

DR 3000U *Users:* France (*Le Triomphant* class SSBNs)

DR 4000A *Users:* France (as **ARAR 13**, replaced **ALR-8** on Atlantiques)

DR 4000S *Users:* France (as **ARBR 17**: *Cassard, Suffren* classes, last 3 *Georges Leygues* class, *Floréal* class, *Bougainville, Foudre*), Saudi Arabia (*Al Madinah*–class frigates)

DR 4000U *Users:* Brazil (Type 1400 submarines), France (as **ARUR 11**: all submarines except *Le Tonnant* and the new *Le Triomphant* class), Pakistan (*Agosta* and *Daphne* classes), Portugal (*Daphne* class).

DR 4000 is **TMV 201/202**.

TRC 281/284 are communications jammers for, respectively, 2–30 and 100–500 MHz.

ARBB 32 *Users: Aconit, Georges Leygues* class (32B).

The two carriers and the *Jeanne d'Arc* have the older **ARBB 31**.

ARBB 33 *Users: Charles de Gaulle* (planned), *Cassard, Suffren, Tourville* classes

ARBR 10 *Users:* Portugal (*Cdt. João Belo* class)

Alligator *Users:* Argentina (A-69 class), China (PRC) (Luda hulls 17 and 18), France (A-69 class), Greece (Combattante II and III classes), Iran (Combattante II class), Libya (Combattante II class and *Zeltin*), Malaysia (Combattante II class), Peru (PR-72 class)

Janet *Users:* Saudi Arabia (*Al Madinah* class)

Salamandre *Users:* France (*Charles de Gaulle* and *La Fayette* class), Oman (Muheet-class light frigates), Saudi Arabia (*La Fayette* class).

It appears that DCN has selected Salamandre in preference to **Janet** or a Janet derivative. Salamandre will be integrated with **DR 3000S**, at least in the new French ships. It is the French candidate jammer for the Kuwaiti Combattante IV NG boats.

Sherloc/Shiploc *Users:* Canada (MCDV class), France (Super-Étendard and Crusader aircraft upgrades), Saudi Arabia (*Sandown* class)

The **SYCOMOR/CORAIL** decoy system, ordered into production in December 1989, has been adopted for French navy Super-Étendards and Crusaders. CORAIL is the conformal pod, which ejects flares down and chaff aft. New decoys now under development include **Spider** (active electromagnetic, in collaboration with Thomson-CSF) and **LICA** (adapted kinematic IR). A new ISIS modular-cartridge system is under development. It can be fitted internally, in conformal gondolas, or in pods, with a minimum of integration with the airplane carrying it.

DAGAIE (AMBL-1B) Users: Argentina (MEKO 360, MEKO 140, A-69 classes), Bahrein (TNC 45 and 62 classes), China (PRC) (Luda hulls 17, 18, 165), Colombia (FS-1500 class), Ecuador (TNC 36 class), Egypt (*Descubierta* class), France (*Clemenceau, Cassard, Tourville* classes, *Georges Leygues* class [replacing **Corvus**; now in 4 of 7 ships], *La Fayette, Floréal, Cdt. Rivière, Durance* classes), Ghana (TNC 57 class), Indonesia (TNC 57 FAC and OPV classes), Italy (for 12 ships, delivered in 1987; presumably, for MCM operations in the Persian Gulf), Kuwait (FPB 57 and TNC 45), Malaysia (FS-1500 class), Morocco (2 sold for the *Descubierta*-class frigate in 1979), Qatar (3 double sets for the Combattante III–class boats, sold in 1981–83), Peru (ordered for the 2 ex-Dutch cruisers, but never paid for and therefore not delivered), Saudi Arabia (8 sold in 1980 for the *Al Madinah*–class frigates), Thailand (2 sold for the PFMM Mk 16–class corvettes in 1983), Tunisia (3 sold for the Combattante III–class boats in 1981), and U.A.E. (10 for the Type 62–, FPB 38–, and TNC 45–class boats).

The other 3 users are unknown; Italy was the 16th, and the first to order DAGAIE Mk 2. It seems likely that the last 2 purchases were emergency procurements for the Gulf operations; the likely candidates include Belgium and the Netherlands, for minecraft or mine-support units. The other *Descubierta*-class corvettes (for Egypt and Spain) use the U.S. **Hycor/Mk 137** system. DAGAIE was removed from the *Cdt. Rivière* class before its transfer to Uruguay. CSEE offers **Sidewind**, which integrates and displays EW interfacing with a DAGAIE Mk 2 launcher. The ECM tactical situation is shown in synthetic video, and the response is optimized after the threat is detected. Sidewind coordinates dilution, distraction, seduction, and also the follow-up.

SAGAIE (AMBL 2A) Users: France (*Charles de Gaulle, Clemenceau, Cassard, Suffren* classes), Italy (*de la Penne* and *Maestrale* classes), Saudi Arabia (the 3 new *La Fayette*–class frigates).

The Italian sales may be DAGAIE Mk 2, which fires both DAGAIE and SAGAIE rounds. The *Maestrale* class refits began about May 1991.

GERMANY

Deutsche Aerospace (AEG) announced **MAIGRET** (*Matériel Automatique d'Interception et de Goniométrie des Radio communications en Exploitation Tactique*), incorporating **Telegon 10**, in 1992 for the French SSL HF/DF requirement; it was shown at Bourget Naval. MAIGRET uses the **A 1284/1** antenna developed for Telegon 10 (it can also use an **A 1288** antenna, or an **A 1289** adapted to submarines). An antenna switch connects the antenna either to the Telegon 10 DF or to an HF receiver (**E 1800/3**) or to a V/UHF receiver (**E 1900/3** or **E 1900/S**). All three connect to an audio-frequency switch powering a headset and loudspeaker and to a computer. The single color CRT can operate either in PPI (frequency measured from the center out, color for strength) or in histogram/A-scan modes. Like **ALTESSE**, MAIGRET can scan adaptively (detecting alerts), or over preselected channels, or operate in fixed-frequency mode. In the HF range, it can display statistics of band occupancy. Of the V/UHF receivers, E 1900/3 has a single channel detector; E 1900/S has 10, for faster scanning. Bearing accuracy is 3.5 deg RMS. The associated computer can use an emitter data base for automatic identification. MAIGRET covers 1–500 MHz (it can be extended down to 250 kHz and up to 1 GHz). In HF, it scans at approximately 50 channels/sec (E 1800/3). In V/UHF, it scans at 3,300 channels/sec in linear scan (E 1900/S) or 330 MHz/sec in adaptive scan (E 1900/3) or a maximum of 1 GHz/sec in adaptive scan for E 1900/S. The system scans in 2-MHz bands in the adaptive mode.

Telegon (type not known) Users: Brazil (*Inhaúma* class), Colombia (FS-1500 class), Denmark (*Thetis, Nils Juels, Hvidbjørnen, Willemoes, Falster, Agdlek* classes), Ecuador (*Wadi M'ragh* class), Egypt (*Descubierta* and *Ramadan* classes), France (*Durance* class and *L'Audacieuse*-class OPVs), Malaysia (FS-1500 class), Morocco (*Descubierta*), Spain (*Lazaga* class), Thailand (Jianghu 053HT, 053HT[H], and *Naresuan* classes), Turkey (*Nusret*), United Kingdom (as CXG: SSNs *Sovereign, Splendid, Superb, Torbay, Trafalgar, Turbulent*)

Telegon 4 Users: Argentina (*25 de Mayo*, MEKO 140 class), Belgium (Tripartite Minehunters), Canada (*Mackenzie, Restigouche, St. Laurent, Protecteur* classes and Bay- and Fort-class OPVs), France (*Clemenceau, Jeanne d'Arc, Cassard, Suffren, Aconit, Duperré, Georges Leygues, Tourville* [except *Tourville* herself], *Cdt. Rivière, A-69, Floréal* classes, LSDs *Bougainville* and *Foudre* and *Ouragan* class, and Tripartite Minehunters), Greece (*Kortenaer* class), India (*Sandhayak*-class AGIs, *Magar*-class LSTs, *Sukanya*- and *Vikram*-class OPVs, *Deepak*- and *Rajaba Gan Palan*–class AORs, *Tir*-class training ships), Indonesia (*Fatahilah* class, frigates *Ahmad Yani, Oswald Sihaan, Slamet Riyadi, Yos Sudarso*, T-43 class), Italy (*Garibaldi, Vittorio Veneto, Animoso, Audace, Maestrale, Lupo, Minerva, Sparviero, San Giorgio, Gaeta, Lerici, Cassiopea, Etna, Stromboli* classes), Malaysia (*Musytari, Lerici* classes), Netherlands (*Tromp, Van Heemskerck, Kortenaer, Karel Doorman, Poolster*, and Tripartite Minehunter classes), Nigeria (*Aradu, Lericis*), Norway (*Oslo, Sleipner* classes), Pakistan (Tripartite Minehunters), Peru (*Alm. Grau, Lupo*, PR-72 classes), Portugal (MEKO 200, *Cdt. João Belo, Baptiste de Andrade, João Coutinho* classes), Spain (*Principe de Asturias, Perry, Baleares, Descubierta* classes), Tunisia (Combattante IIIM), Uruguay (*Cdt. Rivière*), Venezuela (*Lupo* class)

Telegon 6 Users: Argentina (A-69 class), Belgium (*Godetia, Zinnia*), Germany (*Adams, Hamburg, Bremen*, Type 143/143A/148 attack boats, Type 332/343/394 minecraft, *Rhein, Lüneberg, Steigerwald*-class tenders), Greece (*Rhein* class), Saudi Arabia (*Al Madinah, Sandown, Durance*, PCG, PGG classes), Singapore (*Landsort* class), Sweden (*Landsort*), Thailand (*Ratcharit, Ratanakosin* classes), Turkey (*Köln, Rhein, Yildiz*, MEKO 200 classes)

Telegon 7 Users: Iceland (OPVs)

Telegon 8 Users: Bahrein (TNC 62 class), Germany (*Brandenburg*-class frigates, planned for Type 124 frigates), Ghana (TNC 57 class), Indonesia (TNC 57 class), Turkey (*Kartal, Dogan* classes), U.A.E. (TNC 62, TNC 45, TNC 38 classes)

Telegon 10 Users: Greece (MEKO 200)

FL-1800S Users: Germany (*Adams-, Brandenburg-, Bremen*-class destroyers/frigates, *Alster*-class AGIs, S143A-class attack boats, Type 332 minecraft)

FL-1800U Users: Germany (Type 212 submarines)

In 1993 Deutsche Aerospace announced a new small-ship system, **DFS 2000**, using a combination of amplitude comparison and interferometry to achieve 1.8-deg accuracy. It has 8 horns for amplitude and 8 spirals for phase comparison. The coarse amplitude comparison is used to resolve ambiguities in phase comparison. DFS 2000 operates over 2 subbands: 2–7.5, 7.5–18. The full array is 2 omnis (each biconical) atop 2 stacks, each carrying spirals with horns below, for each subrange. Coverage can be extended down to 0.5 GHz. Elevation coverage is +45/−10 deg. Sensitivity is −60 dBm. DFS 2000 handles pulse lengths from 50 nsec to CW. Approximate dimensions are 500 mm dia × 700 mm (weight 70 kg).

Hot Dog/Silver Dog are simple adaptations of standard armored-fighting-vehicle devices. The other land-combat rounds are smoke, thermal smoke, and fragmentation grenades.

Users: Germany (Type 343 minesweepers)

INDIA

The *Khukri* may have **INS-3**, but the others in the class are to have **Ajanta**, as will the *Delhi*-class destroyers. The associated jammer has not been named. In 1986 India announced that its Armament R&D Establishment at Poona had developed a multibarrel medium-range chaff launcher.

INTERNATIONAL

Sea Gnat Users: Australia (*Adams* and ANZAC classes), Denmark (*Nils Juel* class), Netherlands (*Karel Doorman* class), New Zealand (ANZAC class, *Canterbury, Wellington*), United Kingdom, United States

ISRAEL

The Peruvian *Lupo*-class frigates are to be modernized with Elisra EW equipment.

Tadiran's new COMINT, radar DF, and HFDF systems are intended for small business-type aircraft. **ACS-500** covers the 20–500-MHz band (it can be extended to 1.5–1,000 MHz). It scans in programmable frequency sectors and can display up to 100 preprogrammed frequencies (showing signal level, direction, and time of reception). The frequency band is split into 16 subbands (for search), and the system can be set to ignore up to 127 channels. **TDF-500** is the corresponding DF system, with a typical accuracy of 2 deg and a 10–300-msec response time. **RDR-500** is an interferometer radar DF system, operating over the UHF radar band (200–500 MHz) used by some LF long-range, land-based, early-warning radars. Pulse width is 3–100 microsec, PRF is 100 Hz–5 kHz, and response time is less than 3 sec. Accuracy is 3 deg. Elevation coverage is −2 to +7 deg.

Rafael's **C-Pearl** ESM system for submarines, small surface ships, and aircraft was introduced in 1991. The 40-kg radome-enclosed array comprises an IFM and 3 sets of IDF ports (2–4, 4–8, and 8–18 GHz, extendable down to 0.5–2 GHz). Typical elevation coverage is 40 deg. Sensitivity is −60 dBm, and typical elevation coverage is 40 deg. Accuracies are 1.5 MHz and 1 deg (2 deg at 2–4 GHz). The inboard console weighs 125 kg. Signal processing is by distributed microprocessors. **Kingfisher** is probably an airborne version of C-Pearl, also first shown in 1991. Kingfisher has somewhat different directional accuracy (1 deg fine DF [reduced to 2 deg for 2–6 GHz], 10 deg instantaneous DF).

Like Rafael, Elisra offers a multibeam antenna (MBAT), but the configuration is quite different. Elisra's uses a pair of semicircular (in plan) antennas projecting 90 deg apart from a box shaped like that of **SLQ-32**. Each antenna is probably a dielectric lens (Lüneberg lens) fed directly by the jamming signal.

Rafael's EW systems appear to be modular. The **RAN-1100** series is the complete system. Jammers seem to be in the -1000 series. **Shark** may be a particular variant of SEWS/RAN-1100. **RAN-1010** and **-1020** are both MBATs using flat circular RKR lenses to form their beams instantaneously, in azimuth but not in elevation. The RAN-1010 MBAT box contains a single such horizontal RKR circular lens, fed from above, forming beams for the 2 array antennas 90 deg apart. Several jamming beams can be formed simultaneously to deal with multiple threats. RAN-1020 has dual inputs and carries 4 antennas to cover 360 deg. The box, which is air-cooled, can be mounted on trunnions for stabilization. RAN-1010 follows a target by switching (in 150 nsec) among its 32 6 × 25–deg beams. Shark/SEWS is an integrated system driving both the MBAT jammer and chaff launchers. It uses monopulse DF receivers and IFMs; accuracies are 2 deg and 1.5 MHz. Signal parameters include frequency, amplitude, pulse width (or CW), scan rate, and pulse coding.

RAN-1110 probably uses a later pulse processor than RAN-1101, capable of dealing with a higher pulse density. Both systems can drive either a pair of RAN-1010s or a single RAN-1020 (for a smaller ship). Jamming is controlled by a power-management computer, which chooses jamming techniques (implemented by a "techniques" [i.e., waveform] generator) and which allocates the system's jamming power among the threats.

Rafael's standardized **RAMOC** EW operator console has a CRT, a plasma touch-screen, a keyboard, and a rollerball. **SEWS** uses a distributed processor. It provides a combination of omnidirectional pulse-on-pulse (i.e., deception) jamming and directional jamming (presumably noise) against up to 8 simultaneous threats. The combination is reminiscent of that in the Italian **Farad** and **Newton** systems. The **Rattler** (RAN-1001) designation may apply to an earlier version of SEWS, with directional rather than lens antennas, its electronics possibly derived from **ELT 521**.

Reportedly, only 3 **CR-2800**s were made, 2 of which were installed on board Westwinds for maritime surveillance (the third was a ground-system prototype). As of early 1991, 1 of the 2 Westwinds had reportedly been destroyed.

EL/L-8300 *Users:* Argentina (bought in 1985, 5 in all, 2 on Electras), Australia (20 downsized versions bought in 1989 for P-3C Upgrade), China (PRC) (on board ELINT Badgers), Indonesia (bought in 1983, probably on 1 or more 737s), Israel, Singapore (for new Maritime Enforcers), South Africa, Thailand (on board a converted DC-8F)

MN-53 *Users:* Chile (Sa'ar III and IV classes), Israel (Sa'ar II, III, IV, 4.5 classes), Malaysia (Spica-M class), Singapore (Sea Wolf class), South Africa (Sa'ar III class).

Reportedly, this system is derived from the Elettronica Newton Alpha. The integral jammer is probably based on ELT 318.

NATACS *Users:* Israel (Sa'ar II, III, IV, 4.5), Singapore (Victory- and Sea Wolf–class fast attack boats)

NS-9003 and **-9010** both use the Elbit **EA-917** lightweight circular receiving array. Typically NS-9003 or -9010 controls an **NS-9005** jamming-and-deception system.

NS-9003PR/9005PR *Users:* Flagstaff 2 class, *Chetz, Nirit, Eilat*

NS-9009 *Users:* Dabur and Improved Dvora classes; secondary ESM on Flagstaff 2, *Eilat, Chetz,* and *Nirit.*

This system was specially designed for the *Dabur* class.

NS-9010PR/9005PR *Users:* Sa'ar V (*Lahav*) class

Rafael SEWS *Users:* Israel (*Eilat* [Sa'ar V class]), Singapore (*Victory* class).

The *Eilat* uses 2 nonstabilized MBATs based on **RAN-1010**. **RAN-1110** and possibly **-1101** may be in operational Israeli service. In the *Eilat,* Elisra was system contractor (providing the NS-9003 ESM system), and Rafael was principal subcontractor. Compared to the **NS-9005** jammer, RAN-1110/1101 cover a wider frequency range, 1–18 GHz rather than 7.5–18 GHz.

Owl *Users:* Argentina (on board the modernized S-2Es), Israel (4 or 5 on Aravas), and Thailand (3 on Aravas, 1 in a ground station); South Africa is a likely user.

Rattler *Users:* Chile (Sa'ar III and IV classes), Malaysia (Spica-M class), Singapore (Sea Wolf class), South Africa (Sa'ar III class)

TIMNEX 4 CH is optimized for ELINT and OTH missile targeting rather than for threat warning. In the Mk 2 version, the system has 4-channel IFM associated with an enlarged DF array covering its frequency range (expandable to 0.5–40 GHz). There is also an optional miniature DF mast atop the periscope, for threat warning (2–18 GHz omni and 8–18 GHz IDF array, accuracy 3–5 deg, resolution 10 deg RMS). Both feed the same processing cabinet and the same operator console. The IDF on the main ESM mast is an array of 8 spirals for the low band (2–8 GHz) and 8 corrugated horns for the high band (8–18 GHz). The omnidirectional antennas are stacked biconicals. Typical IDF gains: low band +3 dBi, high band +8 dBi. Antenna weight is 200 kg. The omnis are stacked on top, then the row of high-band horns, then below them the row of spirals inside radomes (concave horns). The mast's maximum outer diameter is 290 mm. The two arrays total 270 mm in height, and the omni on top is 220 mm in diameter × 280 mm. Array or optional miniature mast: Omni 120 mm in diameter × 200 mm; IDF array 120 mm in diameter × 50 mm; RF head attached to IDF antenna 150 mm in diameter × 170 mm. Group weight is 15 kg.

Elbit claims PRF and time-of-arrival measurement accuracies of better than 0.25%; frequency accuracy and resolution (for the associated IFM) are 1.5 and 0.5 MHz. Outputs are frequency, pulse width, PRF, modulation, amplitude, direction of arrival, and time of arrival. The system is designed to deal with up to 100,000 pps. Its emitter library lists 64 radars, including 32 preset threats. The associated computer is a ROLM 1602B (16 bits, 64 kword). Control is either manual or automatic; the displays are alphanumeric, polar, and rectangular-coordinate.

Users: Australia ((V)2 in *Oberons*), Israel ((V)1 in *Gal* class since 1982, (V)2 planned for Dolphins), South Africa ((V)2 in *Daphne* class), Taiwan ((V)2 in *Hai Lung* class).

The Australian systems may have been replaced by the domestic AWA **Mavis**. The *Eilat* (Sa'ar V) has a new, rotating, stabilized, 72-rnd decoy launcher.

ACDS *Users:* Chile (22 systems), Israel (122), South Africa (28; 8 more scrapped), and Taiwan (208).

Each chaff/flare fire-control unit (FCU) is controlled either by a central computer unit or manually (as backup) via its front-panel keyboard. Launching is timed and processed by microprocessor. In automatic mode, the missile threat is defined by an external source such as the CDS or the ESM/RWR. ACDS receives radar data as well as wind and ship's course and speed data directly. The main unit incorporates a manual keyboard and displays. This unit also reports to the main tactical display and to the active ECM units (for time correlation). There is also an optional remote-control unit. The main unit incorporates 44 kbyte of EPROM and 12 kbyte of RAM. The serial interface with NTCCS is 4,800 bps; similarly with the ESM/RWR system. Payload interval is 150 msec–8 sec; resolution is 150 msec. Range display is up to 99,000 yd (resolution 1,000 yd). Bearing display is 360 deg (resolution 1 deg). There is a battery backup. The manual mode is probably via the main unit rather than the three deck units. ACDS was introduced about 1982.

ITALY

Portuguese P-3Ps carry an ESM system described as **ET-2300**. It is probably an Elettronica product but is not identified.

Elettronica's digital ESM/ECM systems are distinguished by their processors. **Farad** (SLQ-A) uses a separate ELT 123 preprocessor (including DF and programmed warners on a pulse-by-pulse basis) and an optional **ELT 261** IFM/library (presumably operating on strobed signals). **Newton** (SLQ-B, -C, -D) replaces both with a single unit, **ELT 211**, which presumably includes a deinterleaver. The NATO version (for Italy, the Netherlands, and Spain; the Italian navy's designation is **SLR-3/4**) uses the more powerful **ELT 311**, which includes a supplementary SHR. The jammers come in 3 versions: SLQ-B for C-band, SLQ-C for X-band, SLQ-D for combined C/X-bands. **SLQ-B** and **-C**, using different versions of ELT 814, are combined in large ships. **SLQ-D** is on board *Lupo*- and *Maestrale*-class frigates. The NATO version uses an **ELT 511** jammer instead of the usual **ELT 521**. The Dutch navy bought an **SLQ-01** version, pending the availability of **RAMSES** (SLQ-02). As installed on board the *Van Speijk*–class frigates (and, presumably, exported to Indonesia with those ships), it has 1 large cylindrical radome (on the centerline) and 2 shorter ones (on either side of the tower mast). SLQ-01 was also installed on board the *Tromp*s and the Dutch *Kortenaer*-class ("Standard") frigates. It was replaced by RAMSES only when ships were modernized. Thus the unmodernized units transferred to Greece retain Newton (with 2 small cylindrical antennas, one on either side just abaft the bridge). The *Kortenaer*s were completed with both Newton and **Sphinx** ESM arrays.

Farad Patrol *Users:* Italy (*Cassiopea* [probable], *Gaeta, Lerici* classes), Nigeria (*Lerici*)

Farad Attack *Users:* Italy (A1 version in *Sparviero* class)

Farad Coastal and High-Value Target Defense *Users:* Thailand (*Prabrarapak* and *Chonburi* classes)

Newton Alpha *Users:* Morocco (*Lazaga* class), Spain (*Lazaga* class), Thailand (*Ratcharit* class).

Elbit **MN-53** is a derivative.

Newton Beta *Users:* Australia (River class), China (PRC) (Jianghu IV/V), Egypt (*Descubierta* and Jianghu 053H[E] classes), Morocco (*Descubierta*), Spain (*Descubierta* [and, originally, *Baleares* class, now modernized]), Thailand (Jianghu frigates, PFMM Mk 16 class).

Newton Beta jammers on board the Spanish frigate *Descubierta* in 1991. The large radome abaft the mast is for satellite communications. The ESM antennas (hat and cylinder) are just visible on the yard above the Signaal FCS "egg." (Raymond Cheung)

China (PRC) replaces the ELT numbers with Type numbers, e.g., **Type 211** ESM, **Type 318** noise jammer, **Type 521** deception, **Type 923** omni, **Type 981** omni, **Type 929** directional antennas. In this Chinese version, resolution is 6 deg.

Newton Gamma *Users:* Ecuador (*Wadi M'ragh* class), Greece (*Kortenaer* class), Indonesia (*Van Speijk* class), Italy (*Lupo* class), Netherlands (early *Kortenaer*s).

For 1,000–3,000-ton ships the system consists of ELT 211, 1 ELT 318, 2 ELT 521s (2 or 3 ELT 828 antennas), and 2 or 3 ELT 814s. Gamma covers the 2–18-GHz range in 4 bands. The 4 outputs are displayed on 2 CRTs that can discriminate between pulse and CW signals. Two other CRTs display signal-analysis data, and a fifth gives D-band data. Several jammers are provided, including radar-angle jamming to confuse TWS radars.

Newton Lambda (SLQ-D/SLR-4) *Users:* Italy (*Maestrale* class), Peru (*Lupo* class), Venezuela (*Lupo* class).

ELT 211/311, 1 ELT 318, and 3 ELT 511/521s, or 2 ELT 318s and 2 ELT 511/521s, in each case with 4 ELT 828 antennas. Lambda (rather than Delta) indicated the commercial *Lupo* application. Despite reports, this version was not exported to Iraq. Iraq received the Selenia **INS-3**, which the Italian navy had not, as of then, adopted; later the Italian navy did adopt it for *Minerva*-class corvettes.

Newton Epsilon *Users:* 5-unit system for the *Vittorio Veneto*; consists of ELT 311, 2 ELT 318s, and 3 ELT 511s, i.e., SLR-4, SLQ-B, and SLQ-C.

Nettuno (MM/SLQ-732) *Users:* Italy (*Garibaldi, Audace, Animoso, San Giorgio*), Spain (Nettunel: *Principe de Asturias, Santa Maria* class)

Colibri (ELT 161) *Users:* Italy (AB 212, for special jamming).

Vittorio Veneto carries 6 helicopters, probably 2 ASW pairs (1 dipping, 1 carrying torpedoes) and 1 ASUW pair (1 EW, 1 Sea Killer shooter). Alternatively, there may be 1 Colibri helicopter per flight of 3.

CO-NEWS *Users:* Italy (*Garibaldi, Ardito, Audace, Maestrale, Lupo* [Italian only] classes), Spain (*Principe de Asturias, Santa Maria, Baleares* classes)

ELT 263 was originally designed for the Beech 200T light maritime-patrol aircraft but has been adapted for others, including the P68T, Casa C212, Bandeirante, F27, Gardian, GAI Searchmaster, Learjet 36A, Maritime Defender, and the Piaggio P-166. In February 1992 it was reported that the Thais were replacing their **ELT 263**s with **Argo 700**s because the former was not sufficiently precise to target **Harpoon** missiles. Fokker's name for the Argo 700 fit was reported as **Black Crow**.

Users: Algeria, Finland, Indonesia, Italy, South Africa, Spain, Thailand, and the United Arab Emirates (total at least 60)

IHS-6 *Users:* Egypt (Commando helicopters), Italy (ASH-60 Leonardo helicopter, with APS-784 radar; probably also in EH-101), formerly Iraq (ASH-61 helicopters and supersonic aircraft)

INS-1 *Users:* Libya (*Wadi M'ragh* class)

INS-3 *Users:* India (*Vikrant, Viraat, Khukri,* and *Godavari* class), Iraq (*Wadi M'ragh* class, now for sale, with PAW-1 pulse analyzer and RQN-1 jammer), Italy (ex-Iraqi *Lupo* class, with PAW-1 and RQN-1, and *Minerva* class [as SLQ-747]), Libya (*Wadi M'ragh* class)

MM/SPR-A *Users:* Italy (*Pietro de Christofaro* class)

THETIS (MM/BLD-727) *Users:* only Italian submarines

Breda 105-mm Rocket Launchers (SCLAR) *Users:* Argentina (MEKO 360H2 class, supplemented by DAGAIE), Denmark (*Nils Juel* class, possibly not installed), Ecuador (*Wadi M'ragh* class), Germany (*Hamburg* class and *Offenburg* [her sisters have Hot Dog/Silver Dog]; planned for the Type 123 frigates), Italy (*Garibaldi, Vittorio Veneto, Audace, Maestrale, Lupo, San Giorgio* classes, *Stromboli*- and *Etna*-class AORs), Nigeria (*Aradu*), Peru (*Lupo* class), Turkey (36 launchers on board 9 FRAM destroyers, 6 on board 3 *Köln*-class frigates), and Venezuela (the *Lupo* class)

The Breda **L105** light chaff system was ordered only by Iraq (*Wadi M'ragh* class, now for sale).

JAPAN

NOLQ-2 is the system in the new *Kongo*-class DDG. Like the U.S. **SLQ-32** (to which it is broadly equivalent), it uses antennas in boxes at the top of the superstructure. The **OLR** series all use CVRs (only NOLQs have scanning SHRs). **OLT-3** is a noise jammer; **OLT-5** is a deception jammer. **OPN-7B** is a broad-frequency VHF/DF. **OPN-11** is a high-precision RDF (HF and VHF).

NETHERLANDS

Signaal and the British MEL company were both members of the Philips group, and Signaal transferred its countermeasures systems to the British company in 1985. Then Philips sold its defense companies; control of Signaal went to the French company, Thomson-CSF. Thorn-EMI bought MEL (Lockheed Sanders bought MEL Canada). Signaal/MEL products are listed here under the original parent company.

RAMSES *Users:* Canada (SLQ-503: "City" class), Colombia (FS-1500–class frigates), Greece (*Kortenaer*s), Malaysia (FS-1500–class frigates), Netherlands (SLQ-02 in *Kortenaer*-class frigates, SLQ-03 in *Van Heemskerck* class; also in *Karel Doorman*–class frigates with SPHINX, *Poolster* class).

An order for units to equip the Argentine MEKO 140 frigates was canceled because of the Falklands War. There is some question as to whether the full installation planned for the Peruvian cruisers was ever completed because some equipment had to be postponed for financial reasons.

RAPIDS *Users:* Malaysia (FS-1500 class), Turkey (MEKO 200 Track I)

Scimitar *Users:* Argentina (*25 de Mayo*, MEKO 360 destroyers), Colombia (FS-1500 class), Malaysia (FS-1500 class and new Yarrow frigates), Netherlands (*Tromp* class), Peru (*Alm. Grau*)

SPHINX *Users:* Argentina (*25 de Mayo*, MEKO-360 destroyers), Greece (*Kortenaer* class), Netherlands (SPR-03/00 *Tromp, Van Heemskerck, Kortenaer* classes, also *Karel Doorman, Tjerk Hiddes, Van Amstel, Willem Van Der Zaan* of *Doorman* class)

NORWAY

SR-1A *Users:* Norway (*Sleipner, Hauk, Snøgg, Storm* classes)

VR-1B *Users:* Norway (*Svenner*) and Spain (*Daphne* class)

VR-1C *Users:* Greece (*Jaguar* class), Saudi Arabia (*Jaguar* class), Turkey (*Jaguar* class).

This fast-attack-boat set is related to the submarine RWR. The Germans bought it for *Zobel*-class torpedo boats.

SOUTH KOREA

ECM sets for corvettes (4 have **ULQ-11K**) and frigates (**ULQ-12K** on 18 *Dong Hae*s) are described as **Hughes/Gold Star**, which probably means Hughes TWTs in Gold Star systems. Their outward appearance suggests that they are modified ARGOSystems designs. These systems were developed by ADD, the South Korean Agency for Defense Development.

SPAIN

In March 1991 it was reported that a state-owned company, INISEL, would buy out ELTSA, which is jointly owned by Elettronica and CAE (Spanish majority shareholder), and which has been responsible for systems such as Nettunel. ELTSA would then become the primary Spanish EW firm, concentrating all state-owned assets. Under an agreement that lapsed in 1989, ENSA made ESM systems, Inisel ECM systems. Inisel has since worked on ESM for submarines and small surface craft; its submarine work may be part of the Manta program for the *Galerna* class.

ENSA's **Deneb** is an interface to integrate the Elsag Mk 1000 ESM system with the Tritan CDS being installed in the *Baleares* and *Descubierta* classes. ENSA is also developing a new system to replace ELT/114 and /116 (Gamma) in these classes. **Canopus**, begun in September 1989 by Inisel, is to replace ELT/311 and /511 noise and deception jammers in the *Descubierta* class. **Kochab** is Inisel's decoy-launch controller, to be refitted to older ships with Tritan CDS; it may be the chaff-launcher element in Deneb.

Aldebaran (Inisel/ENSA) is an integrated ESM/ECM suite for offshore-patrol vessels; its ECM element may only be a chaff launcher/FCS. The first unit was delivered for evaluation in 1989.

ENSA markets an unidentified COMINT system that can track up to 200 signals correlated by time, frequency, and bearing. ENSA claims that it detects any emission lasting longer than 7.5 sec. It uses artificial intelligence for post-processing. ENSA also makes a communications intercept/jamming system, **Elnath**.

ENSA's **EN/SLQ-610 (V)** is a shipboard ECM system. (V)1 operates over the E–J-bands, with a sensitivity index of -60 dBm, and determines direction to within 8 deg. Capacity is 800,000 pps, and the library contains 2,000 emitter modes. It includes an active jammer. (V)2 and (V)3 versions probably achieve better DF accuracy and add more bands, but no information is available.

SWEDEN

The new **9CM300** equips the *Göteborg* class. It employs a new ESM system (**Sceptre Lens** replacing the ARGOSystems **Carol** originally selected) using new Lüneberg lens and omnidirectional antennas and laser-warning receivers and a new 8-magazine trainable chaff launcher. The lens antennas are used for both ESM and jamming. Finland uses **9EW300** (ESM only) in Helsinki-II–class fast attack boats.

Philax *Users:* Finland (Helsinki-II class), Singapore (*Landsort* class), and Sweden (*Göteborg, Stockholm, Hugin, Nörrkoping, Landsort, Älvsborg, Carlskrona* classes)

Protean *Users:* Egypt (6 October and *Ramadan* classes), Nigeria (*Erin'mi* class, may no longer be mounted), South Korea (KDX, *Ulsan, Dong Hae*, Po Hang classes).

Protean was also reportedly sold to civilian ship owners during the Iran-Iraq War.

TAIWAN

Cheng Feng III ECM antenna on board a Taiwanese Wu Chin III destroyer, probably the *Liao Yang*, in 1992. (Fu S. Mei)

A CR-201 decoy launcher on board a Taiwanese destroyer in 1992. (Fu S. Mei)

Masthead ESM radome associated with Cheng Feng III, on board a Taiwanese Wu Chin III destroyer in 1992. The larger spherical radome houses a W-160 FCS antenna. (Fu S. Mei)

UNITED KINGDOM

For the Gulf War, Royal Navy helicopters (Lynxes and Sea King Mk 5s) were specially fitted with emergency countermeasures. Lynxes, used in combination with U.S. SH-60B (LAMPS) for antisurface operations, carried **Yellow Veil** jammers and Loral **Challenger** IR jammers and GEC **Sandpiper** FLIRs. Chaff and flare launchers, heavy machine-gun pods, and secure communications were added. U.S. LAMPS helicopters provided the ASUW commander with a surface picture via their data links. The Lynxes probed and then attacked with **Sea Skua**s modified to hit small ships. The Sea Kings, which operated from the replenishment ships *Olna* and later from the Dutch *Zuiderkruis*, were fitted with chaff and flare launchers and with the **Owl** FLIR (positive ID system).

A **Trident Self-Protection Mast**, otherwise undefined, was listed among naval *weapons* in a description of British naval programs given to the House of Commons late in 1991. The estimated cost of 4 systems plus a trainer was £128 million, with peak expenditure in 1990–92. It seems unlikely that the Self-Protection Mast carries a missile, but it may incorporate a laser dazzler.

The Royal Navy reportedly plans to standardize on the Thorn-EMI/MEL **Manta/Sceptre** series, e.g., **UAT** (the program, Novation, calls for standardization in all possible areas). The designators UAI, UAO, UAQ, and UAV have not been used, to avoid confusion. The following were abortive systems: UA-5, -6, and -7 were hand-held horns for S-, C-, and X-bands, for small combatants. UA-14, Racal's portable threat warner for helicopters and fast attack boats, was probably tested about 1975. UAM was an abortive UAA replacement, for which a specification was issued in 1987–88.

Ferranti's new missile-warning RWR (**AWARE 3** [ARI 23491]) weighs less than 13 kg and handles pulse-Doppler, pulse, and CW signals at 2–18 GHz. AWARE uses a pair of dual CVRs plus an IFM; the library's capacity is 1,000 radar modes (2,000 in AWARE 4). There are 2 side-by-side displays: tabular (for a selected signal: bearing, identification [with confidence level], frequency, PRF [with jitter or stagger], scan period, received power level, system status; also bearings and identities of current threats) and polar (up to 20 symbols, with a cursor to select one for tabular display). Bearing accuracy is better than 10 deg, using 4 planar spiral antennas. Separate processors characterize the signal, classify it, and manage tracks. Signals are processed on the basis of direction of arrival and time of arrival, but not pulse width (hence they are classified by PRF, fre-

quency, and scan rate). AWARE can feed the mission-management system via a 1553B bus, or it can be a stand-alone system. System software must be loaded for each mission, so it is relatively easy to modify.

AWARE 4 is the AWARE 3 receiver plus a new control indicator unit for airborne ESM in the front seat. **AWARE 5** is a fixed-wing RWR for aircraft such as Hawk. **AWARE 6** is a further ESM set for integration with a specialized console at an ESM station in an airplane.

Users: Netherlands (Navy Lynx helicopters [AWARE 3], combat support ships [AWARE 4]), United Kingdom (army Chinook, Lynx, Puma, and next-generation helicopters; planned for navy Lynxes in the Gulf War [**Prophet** had to be substituted])

Further details of Racal's current ESM systems (Cutlass and SADIE families) are now available. **Cutlass** was Racal's first series of digital high-performance systems, built around the **KS500** (Cutlass) computer. It was developed for a Middle Eastern customer that considered manual systems inappropriate in the sort of intense electronic environment encountered in the October War of 1973. Denmark was an important early customer. Cutlass entered production in 1979. It was the second-generation Racal system, the first being the analog **RDL**. **Cutlass E** uses the same antenna; **Cutlass B1** uses the **Anaren** antenna. **Octopus** (for German S148-class fast attack boats) is Cutlass B1 plus a **Scorpion** jammer and an AEG threat analyzer/library. Racal planned to offer Cutlass to the U.S. Navy for the abortive **SLEWS** competition. To achieve an accuracy of 1 or 2 deg, as demanded for SLEWS (V)2, Racal would have offered a rotating-dish antenna (developed for its land-based **Weasel** system).

Porpoise is Cutlass modified for submarine installation, originally for Type 209s. A modified Porpoise, **UAJ**, was developed for the *Oberon* class, but the Royal Navy bought **UAH/UAL** instead. A few UAJ(1)s may have entered service in 1984. **UAC**, for British submarines, uses a Cutlass-based processor (of different capacity, with different algorithms). Like the later **UAP**, UAC incorporates a dish antenna for high-precision direction-finding (e.g., OTH **Harpoon** targeting). UAC-1 entered service about 1985; in all, 6 were supplied. The current version is **UAC-2**.

Cutlass (with a very different antenna) won a 1982 competition to become the Type 23 frigate's ESM suite, **UAF**. Each of 8 antenna groups consists of a stack of 3 semicylindrical radomes with a prominent horn below. Each element covers 1 band. Top to bottom, the semicylinders cover 12–18 GHz, 2–6 GHz, and 6–12 GHz. The big horns (which are wrapped with wire) cover 500 MHz–2 GHz. Instantaneous bearing accuracy is 3 deg, but signals can be processed to improve that considerably for OTH-T. As in the SADIE systems, there is no separate IFM.

The next generation replaces KS500 with a new special (ASIC) chip, **SADIE**. It handles about twice the pulse density and uses more radar signal parameters to improve its chances of fitting variable signals (e.g., those with pulse-to-pulse frequency agility) into trains. SADIE is currently operational in the Royal Navy and abroad (presumably in the Royal Danish Navy). The current **SADIE V** uses 1.5-vice 3-micron technology to achieve 2–3 times the performance of its predecessor. Racal is developing an as-yet-unnamed ASIC chip to replace SADIE in the mid-1990s. Besides the new processor, systems in this family have color rather than monochrome displays (generally tabular in order of threat significance, denoted partly by color, plus B-scan [bearing vs. frequency]). Several have IFMs inserted into the DF channels, so there is no separate omni for IFM. This architecture is attractive for a system coping with a very dense pulse environment; otherwise, the IFM may measure a pulse other than the one that the system is processing for direction and pulse width.

Kestrel (**Orange Reaper**, **ARI 18242**) is for the Royal Navy's Merlin (EH-101) helicopter. In effect it adds a deinterleaving computer to the earlier analog **MIR-2/Orange Crop**, retaining the same antennas. Mk 1 has the older KS500 computer, pending availability of SADIE; Mk 2 is the full SADIE version. The Kestrel DF antennas feed a parameter measuring unit (PMU) incorporating both an IFM and an SHR (so that it can handle pulse and CW signals simultaneously). The design emphasizes accurate frequency measurement for radar identification over bearing accuracy. The PMU passes frequency, time of arrival, and direction of arrival for each pulse to the SADIE VLSI processor. There is a 2,000-emitter threat library. The output feeds the 1553B bus to the tactical display. Detection of pre-programmed high-priority threats is automatically displayed to the crew, and an audio threat warning is sounded.

Type 242 (named after **ARI 18242**) combines **Cutlass/SADIE** (0.6–18 GHz) with **Scorpion** in a single console; Racal describes 242 as one-fifth the weight of its predecessors (as well as cheaper and more reliable). The jammer is driven by the frequency-measurement unit of the ESM system, and the ESM-data processor feeds the jammer directly. Directional accuracy is about 5 deg.

Sabre and **Sea Lion** (for surface ships and submarines, respectively) are high-precision (2 deg in bearing) ESM systems derived from Cutlass via Type 242. Like it, they have IFMs in each DF channel. Sabre uses amplitude comparison to achieve a DF accuracy of 5–8 deg. To do better, for missile targeting, it uses pairs of antennas as interferometers. To minimize cost, Sea Lion uses a dish for direction finding, with an omni antenna (with IFM) for threat warning. There is no multiport antenna. The Danish Sabre system originally was to have been unmanned; it would have fed directly into the ship's command bus. However, it was feared that in a dense pulse environment it could overload the system. Therefore, it was provided with a single 14-in operator screen (rather than the usual pair), permitting the EW operator to filter the system's output.

The Royal Navy's equivalent to Sea Lion is **UAP**, selected in 1987. It uses the same high-definition **VU1400C** display as **UAF(1)** but has a **SADIE** processor. UAP underwent sea trials late in 1989. The UAP(1) version will equip most British submarines; UAP(2) is the existing UAC, updated and with new antennas added. UAP(3) is for Trident submarines. UACs are being upgraded to UAP standard. UAP does provide a 4-port antenna on the search periscope (for 5-deg accuracy at 2–18 GHz), plus an omni for IFM and warning; there is a separate dish for greater DF accuracy. It is claimed that 95% of the ESM task can be done from the search periscope.

Racal is experimentally superimposing ESM and raw radar pictures on the same screen, on the theory that the 2 should no longer be separated in a ship's CDS. A window can display the table of emitter identifications. The company is also trying the standard Decca radar antenna as a precision ESM antenna, much as the Russians have done with many of their radars.

Cutlass *Users:* Algeria (*Kalaat*-class LSTs), Argentina (E in TNC 45 fast attack boats), Bahrein (E in 2 TNC 45s and all FPB 62–class fast attack boats), Brazil (B1 in *Inhaúma* class), Canada (SLQ-504), Denmark (B1 in *Nils Juel, Falster, Hvidbjørnen,* Improved *Hvidbjørnen, Willemoes* classes), Egypt (Cutlass E in *Ramadan* class), Germany (B1 in S148 class, Octopus to replace DR 2000S in S143 class), India (B1 in frigates *Taragiri* and *Vindhyagiri,* E in Osa-IIs and in 4 Tarantuls [*Vinash, Vipul,* K-49, -50]), Kenya ("Province" class and *Madaraka* and *Mamba*), Kuwait (FPB 57 and TNC 45), Nigeria (*Erin'mi* class), Oman (E in "Province" class, B1 in Brooke Marine boats), Qatar (Combattante III class supplementing DR 2000), Thailand (E in *Khamronsin* class), Tunisia (Combattante IIIM class), Turkey (FRAM *Gearing*-class destroyers [B1 and Cygnus installed in 1988–91], *Yildiz* class, B1 in Track II MEKOs *Barbarossa* and *Orucreis,* minelayer *Nusret,* and *Tekirdag*), U.A.E. (TNC 62, TNC 45, and TNC 38 classes), and United Kingdom (UAF[1] for Type 23 Batch I [first 4, possibly first 8] frigates)

Cygnus *Users:* Algeria (*Kalaat*-class LSTs), Bahrein (FPB 62 and TNC 45 classes), Brazil (*Inhaúma* class), Denmark (StanFlex 300 class), Egypt (*Ramadan* class), India (frigates *Taragiri* and *Vindhyagiri* and Osa-II class), Kenya ("Province" class and *Madaraka* and *Mamba*), Kuwait (FPB 57 and TNC 45), Tunisia (Combattante IIIM), Turkey (FRAM destroyers, *Yildiz* class, MEKOs *Barbarossa* and *Orucreis,* and *Tekirdag*), U.A.E. (TNC 62, TNC 45, TNC 38 classes), and United Kingdom (Type 23 Batch 1, ordered in 1985).

Racal's jammer has a 2-deg (approx.) beam; it produces 300 kW of power and has a gain of about 30 dB. Pointing accuracy is about 2 deg, to keep the beam on target.

FH-4 *Users:* Bangladesh (*Umar Farooq*), Egypt (*El Fateh*), Malaysia (*Hang Tuah, Rahmat*)

FH-5 *Users:* Argentina (Type 42), Bangladesh (*Leopard* class), Brazil (*Niteroi* class), Chile ("County" class), India (*Vikrant, Viraat, Leander, Whitby, Leopard* classes), Indonesia ("Tribal" class), Iran (*Damavand* and FRAM *Sumner* destroyers and Vosper Mk 5– and PF 103–class frigates), Pakistan (*Babur*), Peru (*Aguirre, Daring* and *Friesland* classes), Thailand (*Makut Rajakumarn, Chonburi,* PF 103, TNC 45, and *Sattahip* classes), United Kingdom (Type 21s, "Ton" class)

FH-12 *Users:* Argentina (MEKO 360), Australia ("River" class), Chile (*Leander* class), Ecuador (*Leanders*), Indonesia (frigates *Abdul Halim Perdanakasuma, Karel Satsui Tubun* [others of this type all have Telegon 4]), Malaysia (planned for new Yarrow frigates), New Zealand (*Leanders*), Pakistan (*Leander* class), Spain (*Sandown* class), Thailand (*Khamronsin* class), United Kingdom (*Invincible* class, Type 42, Type 22, Type 23, *Leanders, Fearless,* "Hunt," "River," *Sandown,* "Castle," "Island" classes and OPVs *Polar Circle* and *Sentinel*)

Hermes *Users:* India (Sea King Mk 42Bs), United Kingdom (Tornado GR 1s, as ARI 18241)

Kestrel *Users:* Denmark (9 Lynxes), United Kingdom (selected for EH-101 Merlins)

Manta/Sceptre 0 *Users:* Saudi Arabia (ex-U.S. minecraft; first export sale was in 1992).

Manta 0 was **UAH**, an *Oberon*-class ESM suite. It was modified as **UAL-2** (presumably, midway between Manto 0 and Manta X) before entering service. It equips British *Oberon*s (except *Ocelot*). Manta completed sea trials on board an *Oberon* in August 1988.

Manta X was adopted for Royal Navy service as **UAL-1** (*Churchill, Valiant* classes). **Manta/Sceptre X** are roughly equivalent to Racal's **Cutlass** series.

Manta/Sceptre XL *Users:* Australia (*Oberon*s, to be fitted to *Collins* class as *Oberon*s retire, ANZAC frigate), Malaysia (new corvettes), New Zealand (ANZAC frigate), Spain (*Agosta* class), Sweden (A-19 class, *Göteborg* class [Sceptre Lens using the NobelTech lens antenna [on the fore and aft faces of the tower mast]), United Kingdom (UAT, with the antenna and probably also the display of the earlier UAF(1); UAT will probably be installed in the carriers, beginning in 1995)

Manta and Sceptre are the submarine and surface-ship versions of the Thorn-EMI (formerly MEL) ESM system; the land-based version is **Setter**. All are derived from the earlier **RAPIDS**, combined with new Signaal technology. Versions 0 and X were developed in parallel (X is more sophisticated). All versions incorporate an IFM (but versions differ in their measurement precision). The base threat library is 144 modes for automated alarms. The X and XL versions add look-up libraries containing, respectively, 2,000 and about 6,000 radar modes. These systems use the standard Royal Navy bearing-vs.-frequency B-scan display instead of the more common polar one. The alphanumeric display (tote) shows upper and lower limits on an emitter's frequency, PRF, and pulse width; this system is designed to deal with frequency- and PRF-agile radars.

MEL began work on the XL series as a response to its defeat in the Type 23 ESM competition. It developed a series of hardware modules, including a proprietary Philips digital channelized receiver, an 18-MIPS pulse-train analyzer, and transputers for parallel processing (to recognize pulse trains). The parallel software was modular, much of it written in ADA so that it could be transported to different commercial computers as CPU technology developed. Track capacity is 255. The combination of the fast analyzer and the parallel processor is Thorn-EMI's alternative to Racal's **SADIE**.

Matilda *Users:* Australia (*Durance, Tobruk,* and *Balikpapan*-class LCTs), Egypt (6 October and *Ramadan* classes), Finland (*Hameenmaa* and Helsinki-I/II classes: Matilda E), Kuwait (as backup for Cutlass), Singapore (*Landsort* class), South Korea (*Ulsan, Dong Hae,* Po Hang classes), United Kingdom (12 Matilda Es bought in 1984 as UAR, for integration with Barricade chaff launchers, for "Hunt"-class minesweepers sent to the Persian Gulf; also on board the "Castle"-class OPVs [with UAN], in RFA *Diligence* [with Shield], on the survey ship *Herald* [when operating as an MCM command ship in the Persian Gulf], and on many auxiliaries: *Fort Grange, Leaf, Olwen, Rover, Hecla* classes).

The British **UAR**s bought for the "Hunt"-class minehunters on the Armilla Patrol had been made for, but not delivered to, Iran. They had been purchased to counter **Exocet**-targeting radars (the Iranians' **DR 3012** threat warners, on their fast attack boats, did not cover high enough frequencies). At least in the "Hunts," Matilda is associated with the **Barricade** chaff launcher (it was designed to trigger **Protean/Philax**).

MIR-2 *Users:* South Korea (12 on Super Lynxes), Spain (may be on Sea King AEWs), United Kingdom (5 in the RAF as Orange Blossom, 183 on RN aircraft as Orange Crop, 2 [as UAN] on the "Castle"-class OPVs).

The British "Island"-class OPVs lack ESM of any kind.

Porpoise *Users:* Chile (Type 209), Turkey (Type 209–1400)

Prophet *Users:* Egypt (MiG-21s), United Kingdom (helicopters).

A few of the equivalent **Sea Saviours** have been sold, but the buyers have not been identified.

RCM-2 (only version in service) *Users:* Argentina (*Hercules* and MEKO-140 class), Egypt (6 October class), Malaysia (Spica-M class, probably replaced by Rattler), Nigeria (*Aradu, Obuma*), South Korea (8 *Ulsans* and 22 Po Hang–class frigates)

RDL/UAB *Users:* Argentina (Type 42 destroyers and MEKO 140 class), Bahrein (TNC 38 class and 2 of 4 TNC 45 class), Brazil (*Niteroi* class), Nigeria (MEKO 360 *Aradu*), Brunei (*Waspada* class), Egypt (6 October class), Iran (RDL-1 in *Damavand* and Mk 5 frigates), Malaysia (TNC 45 and Spica-M classes, at least in the latter probably replaced by MN-53), Nigeria (*Aradu, Obuma,* Combattante IIIBs, TNC 57s), Oman (*Nasr Al Bahr*), South Korea (8 *Ulsan* class, 22 Po Hang–class light frigates), Thailand (*Makut Rajakumarn* and *Chonburi*, TNC 45, PF 103, *Sattahip* classes), U.A.E. (TNC 45 class), and United Kingdom (UAB in *Sovereign, Splendid, Swiftsure, Torbay, Trafalgar, Turbulent*).

The basic RDL wraparound antenna is also used in the later **Cutlass**, so it is difficult to distinguish visually between the 2 systems. UAB is effectively a submarine version of RDL, bought as an interim replacement for **UA-11/12**. The first small directional warner for the Royal Navy, UAB is a 4-port system. Compared to the 4-port antenna of **UAP**, UAB lacks gain because antenna and radome design were not so advanced then (in the mid-1970s). UAB appeared about 1975 and is being replaced by UAP.

Scorpion operates over the 7.5–18-GHz range in 2 modes: area defense (40 × 40–deg beam in a horn that can be tilted ±60 deg to match the polarization of the radar, with sufficient power to dilute an attack) and point defense (using a steerable 8-deg dish antenna). Point defense is intended to jam the incoming missile until it reaches gun- or missile-engagement range, say 3 km or less. Earlier systems could not measure radar polarization and, therefore, wasted half their power (3 dB) because they had to cover both polarizations. An antenna mounted on the mast measures the radar polarization, and the jammer is steered to match. The jammer can also modulate the polarization angle up to ±15 deg about the nominal angle, to deal with copolar or cross-polarization radars. Scorpion time-shares a single TWT to deal with up to 8 threats (some Racal literature says 5) simultaneously. Peak power is 160 kW in midband. **Scorpion B** is a wide-beam jammer version, being supplied to the German navy as part of the **Octopus** system (see above); it occupies the big radome above the bridge. It provides 150-kW midband ERP (minimum 50-kW) and can jam up to 16 threats. **Scorpion B1** is the small-ship version; **B2** is a double-headed version for larger ships. Typically, Scorpion is integrated with a Racal ESM system, both sharing a common operator console and threat library.

Users: Brazil (*Inhaúma* class), Denmark (*Thetis* class), Germany (B version: S148 class), Oman ("Province" class), Turkey (MEKO 200 Track II frigates)

Sabre *Users:* Denmark (*Thetis*, StanFlex 300 classes)

Sea Lion *Users:* Denmark (Type 207 class), Greece (first 4 modernized Type 209s), Norway (Type 207s and Type 210s, except for 4 unmodernized submarines with VR-1B)

Sky Guardian 200 *Users:* Austria (J-35s), India (Sea Harriers), Indonesia (Hawks), Malaysia (20 Hawks), Oman (12 Hawks), Spain (AV-8A Matadors), United Kingdom (Sea Harriers, Jaguars, Buccaneers, VC 10 tankers, army Lynxes).

Sky Guardian is also on board some Sea King and Puma helicopters. As of 1991, reported production was 1,230. Lynx installations are interim for **AWARE 3**.

Sky Guardian 300 *Users:* Brunei (CN 235s), Malaysia (CN 235s)

Mentor is the shipboard equivalent to Sky Guardian. Mentor 1, 2, and 3 came first, then Sky Guardian 200, then Mentor A and B. **Mentor A** is Sky Guardian 200, **Mentor B** is Sky Guardian 300. **UAG** is a Royal Navy development of Mentor, for the *Fort*-class AORs. It was also bid for the *Argus* refit, for the new LPH, and for the *Fort* class's follow-on. The Royal Navy tested, but did not adopt, Sky Guardian 200 (as Mentor A) in the late 1980s, after privately funded trials. The EDM was tested successfully on board RFA *Gold Rover* in 1987, then in the assault ship *Intrepid*. Reportedly, the Royal Navy was disappointed that this RWR did not provide near-ESM performance at an RWR price. A French **ARUX** taken from a Nimrod was tried on board HMS *Fearless*, presumably in a parallel effort. At Abu Dhabi in 1993, Marconi announced **Mentor 2002**, which combines a software-controlled H/I/J-band jammer with Mentor 2 (capable of tracking 200+ emitters, with a 3,000+ emitter library). The jammer antenna and transmitter are in a combined above-decks housing.

Users: Malaysia (new corvettes), United Kingdom (*Fearless*, "Hunt" class [*Berkeley, Cattistock, Chiddingfold, Ledbury, Quorn*], *Sandown* class, *Polar Circle, Fort Grange* class)

Susie *Users:* Colombia (FS-1500 class, with ARGO Phoenix II), Indonesia (*Fatahilah* class), Sweden (*Älvsborg* class), Turkey (*Dogan* class). Susie may also be part of the original ESM suite of the Swedish *Stockholm* and *Norrköping* classes (see above under Sweden). Reportedly, Susie was bought for Malaysian Spica-M–class boats, but it appears to have been replaced by Israeli equipment. Susie-3 is more sensitive and more accurate. It is probably the system on board the Indonesian frigate *Hajar Dewantara*, built in Yugoslavia. The South Korean navy may also have bought Susie.

Type 242 *Users:* Canada (*Protecteur* class [as SLQ-504])

Type 667 (Cooky) is an S- and X-band spot noise jammer.

Users: Chile ("County" class), Ecuador (*Leander*), India (*Dunagiri, Himgiri, Nilgiri, Udaygiri, Talwar, Trishul*)

Type 668 is a variant of 667 limited to X-band, developed for frigates fitted with UA-13, whose console squeezed out 1 Type 667 operator position.

Users: Chile (*Leanders*), New Zealand (*Southland, Waikato*)

Type 669 (Bexley: X-band), previously listed, is extinct (now reported withdrawn from RN service by the end of 1983).

Type 670 (Heather) was a Racal commercial jammer derived from RCM-2, adopted after the Falklands War (the Royal Navy had emphasized ESM but not jamming). Of 37 made, 34 were installed on board ships (3 were used ashore). Type 670 entered service in 1983. Reportedly, the IFM was excellent, but the TWT proved quite unreliable in service. Type 670 modes are probably RGPO, conscan deception, and continuous/burst noise. Racal is now improving guard circuits, mechanical components, and radome heaters.

Users: United Kingdom (Type 42 Batch Is [except *Cardiff*] and IIIs, Type 21s, Type 22 Batch I/IIs, *Andromeda, Scylla*)

Type 675 (2) is typically cued by **UAA** or **UAF**, although it can also use a radar track. **Type 675** carries 2 sets of paired DF receiving antennas, each paired with 2 horns. The horns have limited gain, so this version is probably limited to point defense. Reported tactics include RGPO and amplitude pull-off. Type 675 (2) adds a dish, which would provide the sort of high gain needed for long range (i.e., for area defense). It probably generates false targets to screen formations; the reported maximum range is 500 km [275 nm]. Type 675 (2) became operational in 1987. **675 (1)** had severe reliability and maintainability problems and never reached full specified performance. 675 (2) is officially described as "significantly better." Reportedly, it suffers from waveguide losses (the jammer TWTs are below decks) and poor frequency discrimination. The Royal Navy has stated that power output is sufficient and that frequency discrimination is not a problem because the system uses parameters besides frequency to recognize threats. A projected integral Early Threat Warner (ETW) is intended to respond to quick changes in radar mode and other parameters. **Type 695** is the planned next-generation jammer, but it may really be **675 (3)**.

Type 675 (2) *Users:* United Kingdom (*Invincible* class, Type 42 Batch IIs [and Batch I *Cardiff*], Type 22 Batch IIIs, Type 23 Batch IIs, *Argus*)

UA-1 was the first modern British ESM system, using 4 ports (horns) for wide-open DF. The operator switched the single CRT to any of 3 antennas, one per band (AYA, 8–11 GHz; AYC, 2.4–4 GHz; AYD, 4–7 GHz; AYE, 7–11 GHz). The CRT showed bearing and amplitude, and earphones gave PRF (measured against an adjustable reference signal). **UA-2** was the equivalent S-band submarine system, using a cylindrical antenna housing each with 4 slots cut at 45-deg angles (to accept signals of both polarizations). **UA-3** is the solid-state equivalent of UA-1, with a single CRT. UA-3 was later fitted with EMI's **YAF** pulse analyzer, developed in parallel with the later **UAA**. This system was modified to extend coverage to the Ku(J)-band.

Users: Bangladesh (*Umar Farooq*), Egypt (*El Fateh*, last UA-1), India (*Talwar, Trishul*), Malaysia (*Rahmat*)

UA-4 (Naive) is a developed UA-3, using 3 CRTs to cover all 3 main bands (2.5–11.5 MHz) simultaneously. The AVG antenna is a series of nested slotted cylinders, separated by baffles. Bearing can almost always be measured to within 10 deg, and often to within 5 deg. Like UA-3, -4 was modified to cover the Ku(J)-band and was fitted with YAF.

Users: Bangladesh (*Leopard*-class frigates), Brazil (*Oberon* class), Canada (*Oberon* class; being replaced), United Kingdom (*Ocelot*)

UA-8/9/10 (Porker) added omnidirectional antennas (1 per band) for frequency measurement; Porker was designed to work with a YAZ pulse analyzer. Like UA-4, Porker used submarine-style cylinders with angled slots. Coverage: UA-8, 2.5–4.1 GHz; UA-9, 7–11.5 GHz (antenna AYL); UA-10, C-band. Each omni antenna feeds a broad-band (TWT-amplified) receiver with a microwave discriminator; its output (amplitude vs. frequency) is displayed on a CRT. In at least some cases a manually tuned SHR was inserted into the omni circuit. A signal displayed on either the bearing or the frequency CRT can be selected to feed the pulse analyzer, which measures pulse width, PRF, sweep rate, and modulation on an additional CRT. Because the bearing CRTs are larger than those of earlier sets, operators can track multiple signals (differing in bearing and frequency) simultaneously. Analysis (by looking at and adjusting the CRT traces) took about a minute, compared to about 1 sec in later automatic systems. Porker was later provided with an automatic signal-identification device, **YAG** (incorporating MEL's **SARIE II**, first tried on board HMS *Achilles* [with UA-8/9] in November 1972). As in the case of YAZ, YAG could analyze only one signal at a time, manually chosen by strobing (i.e., manually deinterleaved). **YAW** was a similar SARIE II–based analysis and data-transfer set, for "County"-class destroyers equipped with the **ADAWS** command system. **YAK** was a contemporary bearing and data-transfer set for ships *other* than the "Counties." Eventually, Porker was fitted with MEL's IFMs.

Users: Chile ("County" and *Leander* classes), Ecuador (*Leander*s), India (*Dunagiri, Himgiri, Nilgiri, Udaygiri*), Indonesia (*Van Speijk* class and "Tribal" class [UA-9/ YAZ only]), Malaysia (*Hang Tuah*), New Zealand (*Southland, Waikato*)

UA-15 was an add-on for towed-array *Leander*s, extending coverage to 12–18 GHz. The antennas were 4 small cylinders arranged around the mast, under the **Porker** cylinders (each of which surrounds the mast). Like Porker, UA-15 could be used with YAG and YAZ.

UA-11/12, a submarine-based ESM warner system, was probably introduced in the late 1960s. UA-11 was the omnidirectional warner. UA-12 had a directional antenna. **UAB** was the initial interim replacement.

Users: United Kingdom only (*Resolution*-class SSBNs, *Sovereign, Splendid, Swiftsure, Torbay, Trafalgar, Turbulent*)

UA-13/SPR-02, a passive system (25–1,400 MHz) on *Ariadne, Cleopatra,* and *Phoebe* (and probably 2 others) plus Dutch *Leander*s (now in Indonesian service), uses a conical omni antenna at the masthead, with projecting dipole DF arrays. It is a lower-frequency (partly communications band) equivalent of **Porker**, to achieve longer range, probably with the same sort of DF accuracy, 5–10 deg. Like Porker, it could use the YAZ pulse analyzer (and also **YAQ**, which was associated with the lower, communications, frequencies). In Dutch service UA-13 (with Signaal electronics) was designated **SPR-02**.

Users: Indonesia (frigates *Abdul Halim Perdanakasuma, Karel Satsui Tubun,* formerly Dutch *Van Speijk* class)

UAA (Abbey Hill), the first British digital (but not deinterleaving) ESM set, met a 1966 staff requirement; it entered service in 1978. Compared to its predecessors, UAA doubles the number of DF ports to 8 (so DF accuracy is probably 2.5 deg; UAA is often credited with 3 or 3.5 deg). It also increases the number of bands to 5. The antenna is designated **AYV**. The DF receivers are all CVRs, each covering a 2-GHz slice of the 1–18-GHz spectrum. The associated omni (1 per band) feeds a bank of IFMs (incorporated for the first time in a British ESM system). Reported IFM accuracy is 1.5 MHz. The frequency and DF measurements are integrated for the first time in a British system: the display is a B-scan (direction shown horizontally, frequency vertically). Pulses are tagged individually by time of arrival (ToA), to associate each IFM-measured frequency with a bearing. For example, a frequency-agile signal will appear as a vertical row of dots (because the bearing will be constant). In effect, the operator can use bearing to filter signals and thus to detect complex ones. This is not quite digital deinterleaving, but it is a step in that direction.

The system is hard-wired to sound an alarm when particular pulses (recognized by a comparator on a pulse-by-pulse basis) are received. UAA is also hard-wired to react when the operator-strobed signal matches one of a few particular pulse trains (PRFs). To analyze a signal, the operator selects it (by bearing), in effect manually deinterleaving it. The system then measures its parameters and provides them in digital form for automatic library lookup. This degree of automation makes for quick analysis, typically on the order of a few seconds per signal. Results are displayed on a second CRT alongside the frequency-bearing unit. Such analysis is still far too slow for the very dense modern environments, in which hundreds of signals may be present simultaneously. Thus, Abbey Hill is an intermediate step between fully analog systems like **Porker** and modern systems,

such as **UAF**, which automatically analyze hundreds of thousands of pulses per second.

UAA-2 has several times as many hard-wired alarms associated with particular pulses (it does not have larger numbers of programmed pulse trains because, at least in its original form, it does not incorporate a deinterleaver). It probably has a larger library; better electronics allows a search in the same time as in UAA-1. Reportedly, UAA-2 is designed to localize emissions within 2 deg, but it can sometimes do as well as 0.5 deg.

The modernized UAA-2 can be recognized by the presence of 2 half-cheese–shaped, phased-array ESM antennas under the **Type 1022** radar (in a Type 42 destroyer). It has 4 other antennas spread around a ship. As seen on board HMS *Gloucester* in June 1991, UAA-2 was further enhanced, with a new doughnut antenna and new antennas on the foremast. She was the control ship for access to and egress from Iraq during the war. MEL is currently under contract to modernize UAA-1s to -2 standard and to update UAA-2. Reportedly, the latter enlarges the emitter library and drastically reduces reaction time. That presumably means that a modern pulse-deinterleaving computer has been installed, perhaps something like the type in **Manta/Sceptre**. Staff requirements for a further modification, **UAA-3**, are expected in 1994. The major improvement would be in the currently user-unfriendly operator-machine interface. This version would go on board Type 22 frigates and Type 42 destroyers.

Users: United Kingdom (carriers, Type 42 destroyers, Type 21 and 22 frigates, Sea Wolf *Leander*s)

UAC(2) *Users:* United Kingdom (*Trenchant, Unseen, Upholder*)

UAD and **UAK** are British versions of the U.S. **Classic Outboard**. **UAD-5** is a Racal COMINT system in the British version of Outboard.

Users: United Kingdom (carriers, Type 22 frigates)

UAE (Sandman), a U.S.-supplied threat-warner, was installed for Operation Corporate (Falklands War, 1982). It is probably the U.S. **S3000**; presumably, it replaced **UA-4**.

Users: United Kingdom (3 SSNs)

UAP *Users:* United Kingdom (*Sceptre, Spartan, Superb, Talent, Triumph, Unicorn, Ursula,* Trident submarines [without the targeting mast])

UAS(1), the Falcon Electronics **RX-740** microwave surveillance system (1–18 GHz), was bought specifically for the Gulf War, to provide immediate warning of **Silkworm** attacks. It is an add-on to **UAA-1**, cross-decked to ships deploying to the Gulf.

Users: Australia (2 sets), United Kingdom (12 sets). Probably about 50 were sold.

UAX is the likely designation for the **EW Control Processor** for the carriers and possibly for the Type 42 destroyers. It is to integrate existing on-board EW assets, providing on-line management and co-ordination, reducing operator workload, and also providing off-line planning tools (in this it is analogous to the U.S. **EWCM**). EWCP is a step toward a fully integrated EW System, planned for the Future Frigate now in the concept stage. An RFP was issued in the fall of 1991. The *Ark Royal* would probably get the first upgrade, controlling the existing EW assets. Phase 1 of the EWS package is by Thorn-EMI as part of the Ferranti International Future Frigate combat-system study awarded earlier in 1991. Phase 2 (Project Definition) is to follow sometime in 1993. Phase 3 (development and production) is to begin in the mid-1990s.

France having withdrawn, the offboard active decoy is now a British national project, DLH. The Thorn-EMI/Thomson-CSF **CARMEN** (Countermeasure against Active Radar Missile Engagement) is a 2-kW smart noise jammer using a digital radio-frequency memory (DRFM); the competing Marconi/Dassault **Siren** has an analog memory loop. In addition to the launchers listed below, the Royal Navy uses **Chaff Charlie** (I- or J-band) 4.5-in rnd and **Chaff Hotel** manually released from helicopters.

The Royal Navy's current decoy outfits are the following:

—**DLA** is a 6-tube **Sea Gnat** decoy rocket launcher, interim for DLB, mounted in 2 sets on each side of a ship, 1 at 30- and 1 at 120-deg angle to the centerline. Each barrel is elevated at 30 deg. It shares the Corvus control system. Sea Gnat is used because it provides a **Mk 416** IR-seduction round; Corvus was retained because DLA was introduced before the Sea Gnat chaff round became available. Essentially the U.S. **Mk 36**, DLA is in the *Invincible* class and Type 42 Batch IIIs.

—**DLB** is a Thorn-EMI decoy-control system plus **SRBOC** launcher for **Sea Gnat**: 2 barrels for **Mk 214**, 2 for **Mk 216**, 2 for **Mk 416**. **DLB*** is an interim system with 4 SRBOC barrels and 2 **Corvus** barrels on top. Ships on Armilla Patrol (in the Persian Gulf) have carried a modified DLB in which the 2 rear 130-mm launch tubes are replaced by 102-mm Mk 1 tubes firing N4 BBC (Corvus) rockets in distraction mode pending full service introduction of Mk 216.

—**DLC** is Corvus (introduced in 1968; this may not be the official designation).

—**DLD** is a twin Mk 36 Mod 1 SRBOC bought after the Falklands War (in HMS *Birmingham* and some auxiliaries).

—**DLE Plessey (now GEC-Marconi) Shield** fires N5 BBC rounds (which are modified N4s with inductive coupling and fin assembly). In 11 ships, including the 2 "Castles," RFA *Diligence* and RFA *Sir Galahad*.

—**DLF Irvin "Rubber Duck"** is a floating corner reflector; it is also in U.S. service (as **SLQ-49**). **DLF(1)** was a copy of a Soviet decoy; **DLF(2)** is the Irvin **"Replica,"** and a request for quotation for **DLF(3)** was issued in September 1991.

—**DLJ** is a **Sea Gnat** decoy rocket launcher, a combined **DLA** and **DLB** on a single mounting, for larger ships. DLJ(1)/(2) is modified DLB with extra launchers: 4 DLBs plus 4 DLDs (SRBOC) per ship; DLJ(2) has 8 SRBOCs.

—**DLK** is a Barricade lightweight chaff/IR–launching system (Stockade for medium/long range and Palisade for close range). By early 1991, 27 (2 18-barrel launchers each) had been supplied: Barricade Mk II was bought in 1984; Mk III entered service in 1990 for "Hunts" going to the Gulf. Mk III has more reliable electronics and firing coils, is easier to load, and has better coverage. Its control unit has greater flexibility. It is also in frigates and destroyers on Armilla Patrol, as it fires the only available IR decoy.

Barricade *Users:* Algeria (*Kalaat*-class LSTs), Bahrein (2 TNC 38s), Chile (4 "County" class and 3 *Leander*s, all with Corvus), Croatia (1 *Končar*, 2 Osa-I class), Denmark (*Falster* and *Lindormen* classes, possibly also *Thetis*), Finland (*Turunmaa* class, *Helsinki* class, *Keihässalmi*, *Pohjanmaa*), Greece (Osprey and Improved Osprey OPVs), Ireland (*Eithne* [as flare launcher; no associated ESM]), Italy (*Minerva* class), Jordan (Hawk class), Kenya ("Province" class, *Madaraka, Mamba*), Malaysia (Combattante II), Oman ("Province" and Brooke Marine types, *Nasr Al Bahr*), Serbia (*Končar* and Osa-I classes), United Kingdom ("Island" class, "Castle" class, *Sandown* class, *Hecla, Herald*)

Super Barricade *Users:* Finland (*Hameenmaa*), Oman (Muheet-class light frigates), Spain (*Sandown* class)

Corvus *Users:* Argentina (Type 42 destroyers), Bangladesh (*Umar Farooq* and *Leopard* class), Chile ("County" and *Leander* classes and AOR *Alm. Montt*), France (*Jeanne d'Arc, Aconit, Duperré, Dupleix, Georges Leygues, Latouche-Tréville*), Greece (*Kortenaer* class), India (*Viraat*), Indonesia (*Fatahilah, Hajar Dewantara, Van Speijk* [note that the Netherlands navy used SRBOC on these ships], and "Tribal" classes), Iran (Saam and *Hengam* classes), Malaysia (*Rahmat*), Pakistan ("County" and *Leander* classes), and United Kingdom (Type 42 destroyers, *Bristol, Amazon* class, Type 22 frigates, and *Leander* class)

Shield *Users:* Brazil (*Inhaúma, Niteroi* classes), Canada (TRUMP, *Restigouche, Protecteur* classes), Malaysia (planned for new Yarrow frigates), Pakistan (FRAM *Gearings* modernized with APECS II ECM suit), Singapore (*Victory* class), Thailand (*Khamronsin* class), and United Kingdom ("Ton" class, "Knight" class (LSLs), *Argus, Fort Grange, Rover*-class AORs, Orangeleaf, Diligence).

Brazil, Canada, and Singapore all use the automatic **Shield 2** (Britain uses the manually fired version).

UNITED STATES

The 1993 report of the Ship Self-Defense System program revealed a previously black program, **Outlaw Bandit**, to reduce ships' radar cross section. It is being applied "aggressively" to the *Spruance* and *Perry* classes, both of which have large cross sections because of their massive flat superstructures. Since none of these ships has particularly changed in appearance, Outlaw Bandit clearly involves the application of radar-absorbing material (RAM), a technique also being used by several foreign navies (e.g., Australian, Canadian, Israeli, Royal Navy). In the U.S. Navy, one object is to reduce the cross section at least below that of standard decoys.

The heavily censored account of the advanced EW program suggests greater interest in higher-frequency microwave threats and in counters to multispectral (e.g., EO/IR) sensors. Work is also proceeding against both monopulse and LPI (stealthy) radars. New and recent projects include: closed-loop ECM for real-time effectiveness

Super Barricade at the 1991 Royal Naval Equipment Exhibition. (Author)

(1989–91); advanced threat-warning receivers (precision ECM, 1990–92); antidiscrimination decoy (**Long Duration Decoy**, 1991–93, presumably including **FLYRT**, NRL's electric prop-driven Flying Radar Target, tube-launched, with unfolding wings, to carry a jammer, due in FY93); IR Decoy (**IRCM**, 1992–94); false range/Doppler imaging (Counter-SAR, 1992–94); small-ship compatible decoy (the small **UAV**, as well as improvements to current expendable decoys); advanced missile simulations/counter targeting, and coherent-delay. An AMD (activated metal decoy) was developed specifically for Desert Storm. **FOLWS** (quadrant-resolution Fiber-Optic Laser-Warning System) was demonstrated in FY91. A new adaptive monopulse countermeasure began engineering development in FY92. The FY92 program included work on countermeasures against spaceborne SARs. A counter-targeting pod suitable for fighter/attack aircraft in the outer air battle was developed by a naval lab (probably NRL) under the FY91 budget. Negotiations with Britain for a joint program on ASMD countermeasures (algorithms, waveforms, generic tactics) began in March 1992. Early in 1991 Rockwell International received a U.S. Navy contract, under the NRL Fly's Eye program, for a prototype 2-color, staring, midwave IR sensor based on a 128×128 array.

Development of the low-cost Height-Finding/DF surface-ship interferometer system (which actually measures elevation, not height, and bearing) was included in the FY90 and later programs. HFDF is probably the passive-DF **Anaren** system that APL tested at sea in October 1991 on board the missile cruiser *Leyte Gulf*. Developed from the angle tracker in the British **Cygnus** jammer, Anaren demonstrated a tracking accuracy of 0.1 deg in azimuth and elevation. The tracker covered 2 of the 4 90-deg quadrants. Given its accuracy, the ship's unique (hence identifiable) radar need be switched on only very briefly, to inject ranges into the track file. The passive tracker could use reflected energy from other ships' radars, allowing the valuable Aegis cruiser to remain largely silent and thus immune to ARM attack.

NRL's **BTI-IRCM** is intended to provide aircraft with a counter to IR-guided missiles such as the **SA-7/14/16** family. It was to be demonstrated in 1993 on board a P-3. The BTI designation indicates that it is funded by the Balanced Technology Initiative. NRL plans to use a developed **Fly's Eye** as its threat warner (using the Rockwell array), a modified **LANTIRN** (AAQ-14) targeting pod as its control element, and a small laser to attack the missile's IR seeker. BTI-

IRCM is somewhat similar in concept to the shipboard **MATES** but is much simpler.

MATES (Multiband Antiship Cruise-Missile-Defense Tactical Electronic System) is a module to add to **SLQ-32** and **-54**. MATES jams IR-guided missiles. The sensors will be IR and optical imagers/trackers (such as FLIRs) capable of tracking multiple targets and discriminating between IR and non-IR threats. They will feed a signal processor, with an associated threat library. Based on these data, an executive controller will activate and control a pointer-tracker carrying a laser. Presumably, the laser will help distinguish IR threats because an IR dome will reflect rather differently than a radome. Low-powered pulses can also range on the target and, thus, determine just how much power is required for jamming or destruction. The laser can be turned to high power either to produce, in effect, jammming noise, or to burn out the missile sensor. MATES is to monitor its effectiveness against the targets it engages. MATES is also a potential laser radar; the RFP mentions its use in ranging against cooperative and noncooperative targets. Operating in the IR spectrum, it would be relatively covert. Hence the interest in ranging against noncooperative targets (so that a ship could operate some of the time in radar silence). Too, it seems likely that a laser radar could detect and track aircraft and missiles designed for low radar cross section. MATES might also be valuable for covert carrier air-traffic control (an application involving ranging against cooperative targets). Because a future combat system would almost certainly use an open data-bus architecture, data from MATES would automatically be available for such applications. Loral won the MATES contract in 1992.

ALSS (Air-Launched Saturation System) is an alternative to the canceled **Tacit Rainbow**: a low-cost programmable-before-launch loitering-missile system capable of searching out and attacking emitters. A Joint Services Operational Requirement was issued on 15 December 1988. The FY92 budget included plans for exploring alternative concepts via trade-off studies and/or RFQs. An armed version of **ITALD** may well be bought as an alternative to ALSS, or it may be equipped with some Tacit Rainbow electronics. FSED may begin as early as FY94. According to the January 1992 budget, the major contract award was to be $3 million in FY93, with previous funds all spent in-house (FY90 $1.69 million, FY91 zero expenditures, FY92 $7.2 million, FY93 $3.9 million).

The **BGPHES** (**SLQ-50** terminal/**ULQ-20** system) airborne system is now entering service. The XN-1 version of the surface terminal, incorporating a UYK-44 computer, was tested on board the USS *Eisenhower* in FY87. Then the navy asked that the system be downsized and integrated with other shipboard ESM. The XN-2/3 versions use DTC-2 computers. The XN-2 version, to be tested in the summer of 1993, is essentially an improved shipboard SSES (ship signals-exploitation space) using the existing SSQ-80 shipboard COMINT system. It has no up-link to an ES-3A (as yet the airborne portion of BGPHES operates independently). The production prototype XN-3 version will incorporate the ES-3A link (via **CHBDL**) for which BGPHES was conceived in the first place. BGPHES XN-3 uses 3 DTC-2s; the full version will use up to 5 (and may use TAC-3s instead). Each operator can directly control the airborne signal-intercept/collection devices via the CHBDL up-link, searching designated frequency ranges for particular signals of interest, remotely seizing and tuning a particular receiver, designating a receiver to a specific frequency of interest upon intercept, and extracting an airborne DF "cut" on that signal on command. Analysis tools include a data base of known information. Because the outputs of the airborne receivers are pooled, the system operators have a broad view of the signal environment: they can correlate a wide variety of short-term signals.

SLQ-54, formerly **AIEWS**, is the next-generation shipboard countermeasures set. It is to combine (and improve) the short-range defensive features of **SLQ-32** with long-range precision ESM. There is some fear that SLQ-32 would turn on its jammer too late when faced with a fast incoming missile. A tentative OR was issued in December 1990. The alternatives are an upgraded SLQ-32, integrated off-the-shelf components, or a completely new system. SLQ-54 is envisaged as an open-architecture system suitable for later upgrades. As of July 1991, plans called for freezing SLQ-32 development in 1995, but the SLQ-54 new-start may be delayed or aborted to save money. SLQ-54 Block 0 was to enter service about 2000, having passed its Milestone III (full-scale development) review in 1997 (with Block 1 following in 2007); up to 150 were then planned for battle-group ships (including DDG-51) and protection-of-shipping ships (such as *Perry*-class frigates). At that time concept evaluation/definition and demonstration/evaluation were expected from mid-1992 through the end of 1993.

ASTECS is the ESM suite projected for the next-generation U.S. attack submarine, Centurion. It is a new start (the OR was issued in October 1991).

The current EA-6B version is **ICAP-2** (carrying **ALQ-99F**). The next, **ADVCAP**, incorporates a new RPG (receiver-processor group), the universal exciter upgrade (**UEU**), a Band 2/3 Transmitter, a coherent countermeasures capability (COCM, i.e., against pulse-compression radars), and **ALQ-149**. UEU technology satisfied the communications/radar exciter and ALQ-149 interface requirements. RPG was needed to counter radar improvements, such as more complex (coded) pulses, to overcome spot jamming, and pulse-to-pulse frequency agility. It can analyze pulse and pulse-train patterns so that they can be mimicked. Moreover, radars can now tune over wider bands, so jammers limited to specific narrow frequency ranges may no longer be effective. Hence the interest in a "universal exciter" and in faster scanning of the spectrum. Increasing civilian use of the electromagnetic spectrum increases signal density and also makes it easier for a jammer to be seduced into action against a nontarget signal. RPG substitutes a disk recorder for the digital tape of the earlier version, for greater signal density and higher speed. ADVCAP aircraft will add a third display, for the front cockpit. The forward operator currently is underutilized, and as the electronic environment becomes more complex, this operator will become vital to the 2 NFOs in the rear. A new High-Power Band 9/10 RF Transmitter has been in development by AEL Defense Corp. since August 1991; it is a joint air force/navy program (for the EF-111 and EA-6B).

The new Lockheed Sanders **ALQ-149** jams communications signals (including the 20–70-MHz band specifically requested by the marines) for the first time. It also attacks early-warning radars operating at metric (often communications) frequencies. ALQ-149 occupies 8 wire rack assemblies within the EA-6B equipment bay. It uses cooperative jam/look-through cycles to allow simultaneous operation with **ALQ-99**, sharing the airplane's **AYK-14** central computer for library look-up of received and analyzed signals. Automated responses are monitored and can be overridden. The threat library and processing priorities can be reprogrammed in flight. Virtually all of the system's operating and threat parameters are field reprogrammable. Technical problems and legal disputes between the original joint-venture partners, ITT and Sanders (Sanders alone survived), delayed development. Although ALQ-149 was planned for ICAP-2, it had to be made part of ADVCAP (FY91 and beyond). Reportedly, part of the problem, the overambitious specification in frequency range, has now been remedied. ALQ-149 is vital because the Vietnam-era **ALQ-92**, which covers the LF bands, was removed some years ago; **ASQ-191** was purchased as an interim solution. Improvements under a P3I contract are a more-reliable, digitally tuned, set-on receiver; a new, digital, wide-band signal processor; and improved RF-distribution and power-supply units.

The U.S. Navy plans to standardize the 3 current EP-3 ELINT configurations: **EP-3B Batrack** and 2 versions of **EP-3E** (**ARIES I and II**) by 1995; VQ-2 is being upgraded to ARIES II standard. ARIES II retains the **ALR-52** and/or **ALR-60 Deepwell** COMINT suite, but there is a major sensor upgrade. The major external differences are the extensive "farms" of blade antennas beneath the wings and rear fuselage, and the introduction of the IBM **ALR-76** ESM/RWR at the wingtips. ALR-60 is GTE's computer-controlled, 5-operator, communications-intercept and -analysis system (100–150 MHz). The receiver incorporates 2 separate digitally tuned modules. The **CP-1131** 16-bit computer (with 16-kword core memory) uses an external magnetic drum memory, MU-600 (16 Mword: 64 tracks, each of 500 data blocks, each of 523 words; access time 17 msec, 2,247 bits/sec; the drum spins at 1,800 rpm). The improved **ALR-60A** uses an **AYK-14** computer but retains the drum. **EP-3J** is a new jamming version of the P-3 for fleet EW training, to replace the existing heavy jammer aircraft (the EC-24 and 2 NKC-135As); it carries USQ-113 and 8 wing pods (e.g., for ALQ-167s, -170s, AST-4s and -6s, ULQ-21 radar jammers, ALE-43 bulk chaff dispensers). A Phase II would upgrade the aircraft to the full training (FAEWS) system using ALT-40 jammers and ALR-75 ESM pods with HP 9826 control computers.

At least 200 **ALQ-157**s were either in service or under contract by 1988, and 200 had probably been exported by 1991 (the first export sale was in 1985). Export use includes both aircraft and patrol boats.

There are 2 announced versions, (V)1 (for the CH-46E; probably 147 made) and (V)2 (for the CH-53; probably 114 made). ALQ-157 is also on board Marine Corps C-130Fs. Some may also be on board SH-3s and P-3Cs, presumably in the Middle East. Exports: probably Saudi Arabia, possibly some other Middle Eastern countries, United Kingdom (probably some Lynxes).

The future of **ASPJ** (ALQ-165) is in question. Congress eliminated production funds late in 1992 after operational tests produced ambiguous results. However, no alternative is readily available. In the spring of 1993 the navy was trying to find funds to integrate the existing ASPJs (136 were bought) with F-14D fighters. There is some interest in foreign sales, but the navy opposes the transfer of the digital RF memory (DRFM) unit technology (Finland and South Korea have ordered ASPJ for F/A-18s). No formal requirement for an alternative has been issued, but at Navy League 1993 Loral announced an **Autonomous Jammer** derived from its **ALQ-178** (used by Israel and being tested by Turkey, on F-16s). It would use the existing ALR-67 with the DRFM built for the ASPJ by Anaren.

Canadian Sea Kings and probably Australian Seahawks carry **AAR-47**. It was installed on AV-8Bs beginning in 1992; this version has upgraded algorithms to handle their higher speed and maneuverability. Loral offers a laser-warning version, with 4 IR detectors mounted around the UV detector, operating in the 0.4–1.1-micron band.

Texas Instruments won the **GEN-X** active expendable competition in April 1992.

ALD-2 is the airborne DF for some P-3A/B aircraft, superseded by **ALQ-78** in P-3Cs.

ALD-2 Users: Iran (P-3Fs), Spain (P-3A/Bs), United States (about 6 P-3Bs in Reserve service)

The estimated unit cost of **ALQ-78** is $160,000.

Users: Australia, Japan (license production began in 1981, was completed in 1992), Netherlands, United States (some P-3Cs, being superseded by ALR-66)

Estimated cost of **ALQ-162** (Shadowbox) is $75,000–120,000; 688 had been made through 1991.

Users: Canada (CF-18s), Denmark (F-35s, F-16s), Spain (EF-18s), United States (AV-8Bs and army aircraft)

ALR-66(V)2 Users: P-3Bs and (as interim) P-3Cs

ALR-66B(V)3 was announced at Navy League 1993, to replace the current -66A(V)3. It can use either the aircraft radar antenna or a separate spinner; Litton claims that it embodies new signal-processing concepts.

Reportedly, the shared-antenna technique of **ALR-66(V)3** and **-66A(V)3** has not been entirely successful, hence the spinner in the (V)5 version adopted for the abortive P-3C Update IV.

Users: Japan (planned for P-3Cs), United States (P-3Cs, B-52 bombers armed with Harpoon missiles, planned for SH-2G upgrades of LAMPS I helicopters)

ALR-66(V)4 Users: United States (E-6A TACAMO aircraft)

ALR-66(V)6 Users: United States (PHM 6 only)

ALR-66(V)7 is the RWR version for C-130 aircraft, for operation in high pulse density. Sales are not known.

ALR-66(VE) Users: Greece (A-7Es; about 120 bought in 1981), Morocco (50 bought in 1980), New Zealand (A-4s), Portugal (P-3Ps), United Kingdom (C-130s, in some cases replacing Orange Blossom), United States (LAMPS Is), Venezuela. There was also an unidentified Middle Eastern customer (1984).

ALR-66(VC) is the transport aircraft version. Sales are not known.

ALR-66A(V)1 is the version for LAMPS I helicopters and foreign Sea Kings.

ALR-79 Users: United States (SH-2F LAMPS I helicopters operating in the Persian Gulf)

ALR-606(V)2 Users: Pakistan (P-3Cs), Taiwan (S-2Ts), Venezuela

ALR-45s, probably upgraded with digital processors, still equip some A-6Es and all F-14As.

In Desert Storm **ALR-67** reportedly proved less effective than the air force's **ALR-56**; that made the **ASR** upgrade more urgent. Reportedly, ALR-67 can be overloaded by high-PRF radars. Reportedly, too, there were some problems in reprogramming ALR-67 and **ALQ-126** to deal with the Persian Gulf threats. Not all aircraft had

identical equipment; some could be reprogrammed directly, others required the physical insertion of new memory modules (tripling the time needed). A new **Advanced Rapid Reprogramming Terminal**, a hand-held unit that can be plugged into an aircraft to download fresh data into an ALR-67, will help solve the problem. The ASR is designed for rapid reprogramming. ASR promises improvement factors of 50 in signal-processing throughput and 40 in memory. In 1990 Litton proposed **ECP-510**, which would be halfway between ALR-67 and -67ASR. ECP-510 has an interface with the host aircraft's INS, increases detection range by a factor of 6 (10 when in the presence of a wingman's radar signals), and can handle 5 times the signal density. Sensitivity can be selected by frequency band. It uses an IFM receiver (plus a fast-tuning superheterodyne for pulse-Doppler and CW emitters) to identify emitters unambiguously. It also provides better directional information for passive weapon targeting. Litton claims that ECP-510 is better able to detect LPI emitters. Operational evaluation was completed in April 1992.

ALR-67 Users: Australia (F/A-18s), Canada (CF-18s), Germany (modified as ALR-68), Kuwait (F/A-18s), Spain (EAV-8Bs), United States (A-6Es, AV-8Bs, F-14As, F-14Ds, F/A-18s)

ALR-76 Users: Canada (EH-101s; -76C version), United States (S-3Bs)

The U.S. Navy uses **APR-39(V)2**s on board OV-10s and AH-1, H-46, and UH-1 helicopters.

APR-39A(V)2 is the ESM system on board U.S. Patrol Boats Mk III and IV. It has now been adopted for the PBC. The manufacturer, Litton, has been asked unofficially whether APR-39 can cue the **SWPS** weapons platform through a 1553 or 422 bus. The aircraft version of APR-39A will be proposed as the radar warner of the new PB Mk V. There is a Threat-Warning System (TWS)/EW controller (EWC) version, communicating with other shipboard defenses (e.g., decoy launchers). APR-39A accepts video from an **AVR-2** laser warner, communicates with an **AAR-47** missile warner (which triggers an **ALE-39** dispenser) via an **RS-422** interface and discrete connectors, connects directly with an **ALE-47** decoy dispenser via a 1553B bus, connects via a 1553B bus with an **ALQ-136** jammer, and connects via discrete signals with an **ALQ-162** jammer. It can feed a threat-emitter-data recorder (TEDR). The system can be rapidly reprogrammed in the field, using an **ASM-687** with a memory loader/verifier. Litton is now considering integration with an IR/EO sensor. This version was specifically designed for helicopters and fixed-wing aircraft; applications include the SH-60F, MH-53, and C-130. It can be integrated with **AVR-2, AAR-47, ALQ-136, ALQ-162**, and **ALE-47** chaff launcher.

APR-39A(V)3 is the export version, for Egypt (6 October class) and Yugoslavia (patrol boats).

BLD-1 is Litton Amecon's precision submarine ESM set, used for tactical surveillance and OTH-T. BLD-1 is primarily an interferometer direction finder, but it also provides frequency and PRF on command. It works in 2 bands, with 2 receivers per band. The associated computer is **UYK-20**. BLD-1 entered service in 1985. It is on board the *Los Angeles* and *Seawolf* classes.

BLR-6 is a CVR submarine RWR.

Users: Turkey (*Tang* class)

BRD-7/8/9 are monopulse DF antennas that are capable of analyzing signals. BRD-8 is a more-sophisticated version, with a spectrum analyzer. BRD-9 is physically larger and covers a wider frequency range but uses the BRD-7 antenna.

Users: *Los Angeles* (BRD-7) and *Seawolf* (BRD-9) classes. The earlier BRD-6 is on surviving *Permit*s and *Sturgeon*s.

SLQ-32: a digital RF memory unit is being developed for the (V)3 and (V)4 versions. **SLQ-32(V)4**, for carriers, works in conjunction with the **WLR-1H** narrow-band receiver. **SLQ-51** was an abortive attempt to marry SLQ-32 electronics to the **SLQ-17** system. The current upgrade package is designed to improve performance against missiles and their targeting systems (i.e., countertargeting). Signal-processing and throughput capacity are increased, additional waveforms and techniques are provided, and SLQ-32 is integrated with the Mk 36 decoy–launcher system.

SLQ-32 Users: Australia (*Perry* class with (V)2), Greece (*Adams* class with (V)2), Pakistan (*Brooke* class with (V)2), Saudi Arabia ((V)1 in PCG and PGG classes), United States, Venezuela (reported that (V)3 will replace Elettronica's EW systems in 2 *Lupo*-class frigates under refit by Ingalls)

Shields/Sidekick *Users:* South Korea (KDX), Taiwan (*Perry* class), Thailand (*Naresuan* [Type 025T class])

SSQ-72 (Classic Outboard I) and **-108** (Classic Outboard II) is the netted HF/DF and signal-exploitation system for OTH-T, conceived in 1973. The related Cryptologic Combat-Support Console (**CCSC**, for battle group commanders) and Cryptologic Combat-Support System (**CCSS**, for all Aegis ships) were developed by Unisys (now Paramax). Paramax's Cryptologic Interface Unit (**CIU**) sanitizes the information produced by Outboard for use by the ship's CDS. Some Royal Navy ships have **SSQ-72(V)2**. The modification of **SSQ-108(V)1** to (V)2 was specified by the Royal Navy; **SSQ-108(V)2** is built under license in the U.K. Outboard is on all Type 22 and Type 23 frigates and has been backfit to the light carriers. Reportedly, within a British task group, the frigate Outboards provide information to the carrier, which alone has a data-processing system. In 1991–92 Paramax proposed **Tactical DF**, an Outboard successor, to measure HF sky-wave bearing and presumably angle of incidence with high resolution. The system needs only 3 sensors, with a baseline of only 3–4 m. The mathematical approach (finding an eigenvector to fit a matrix of data) also automatically estimates the accuracy of the measurement (covariance).

Southwest Research Institute, which makes the **SRD-19** Outboard antenna/receiver, also makes **SRS-1** (Combat DF), the **Seagle** HF/DF system for the Italian carrier *Giuseppe Garibaldi*, a system for a Hellenic Navy auxiliary (reportedly the AGI *Hermis*), and the Canadian **SRD-502** (on board the "City" class). All use characteristic SWRI multipolarization techniques that permit measurement of the direction of arrival of long-wavelength signals with small antennas.

SSQ-74 is being replaced by a new carry-on **Counter Communications System**. The existing vans take up too much deck space on board small combatants and add too much radar cross section and top weight to other ships. The new system will be installed internally. It will incorporate an open architecture, hence will be able to simulate any radar within its RF coverage through a computer-controlled modulation system. Initially, they will be able to simulate 2 radars identified by the C&D program sponsor.

ULQ-6 and **SLQ-22/23/24/30** *Users:* Australia (*C. F. Adams* class), Brazil (*Gearing* class, *Garcia* class, *Espirito Santo*), Canada (frigates), Ecuador (FRAM *Gearing*), Greece (FRAM *Gearings* and *Sumner*), Iran (*Sumner* class), Mexico (FRAM *Gearings*), South Korea (FRAM *Gearings* and *Sumners*), Spain (*Paul Revere* class), Turkey (*Zafer*, *Muavenet*)

USQ-113(V), a Rockwell VHF/UHF communications jammer, replaces **ASQ-191** (which was limited to 225–400 MHz). It is at some fixed sites, is on board EP-3s and some other aircraft, and is being installed on board some EA-6Bs. The current contract is for 70 units, half on EA-6Bs and half on larger aircraft. Modes are ESM, ECM, ECCM, and communications jamming. Communications, rather than radar, jamming requires specialist waveforms and frequency ranges. The basic version operates over 20–500 MHz, but some versions are more limited (e.g., 100–500 or 225–400 MHz). USQ-113 scans over frequencies and can indicate the activity (in dB) at various frequencies. Compared to a radar jammer, USQ-113 is not directional; it varies the timing of a signal, and it can time-share amplifier power among several signals at rates and dwell periods tailored to voice or data-link signals. It can concentrate on a particular data-link frequency. It can use noise, time, or deception jamming, or it can be linked to an external modulator, optimized against a particular network. It can also be a communications radio. Procurement began under the FY90 program. USQ-113 will also be carried by Marine Corps UAVs, to disrupt communications from the rear echelons of enemy troops, replacing the current **ULQ-19**.

WLR-1 signal analyzers are fed by omni "derby" and "sword" antennas (the corresponding DF systems [SLR series] use spinners; they pick up signals too infrequently for analysis, but they do provide early warning and precise direction). **WLR-1G** is the ultimate version of the original WLR-1, with solid-state tuners. It covers 9 bands, extending from 50 to 10,750 MHz (50–100, 90–180, 160–320, 300–600, 550–1,100, 1,010–2,600, 2,575–4,450, 4,406–7,375, and 7,300–10,750 MHz). The redesigned **WLR-1H** covers 6 bands (it eliminates everything below 550 MHz and adds a 10–20-GHz high band). All the bands are simultaneously electronically scanned in 100 microsec. Signals are digitized; up to 3 can be deinterleaved in each band. WLR-1H can therefore capture and analyze many emitters simultaneously, whereas WLR-1G and its predecessors analyze only 1 at a time. The WLR-1H signal-analysis display uses 6 sweeps

(1 per band) and can store up to 8 frequencies per band for display. Limits: pulse width, 1–50,000 microsec; PRF 20 Hz–2 MHz; bandwidth 20 MHz. The system digitizes pulse data for insertion into its memory. Its alphanumeric display (54 lines, 80 characters each) shows its emitter file, its threat-alarm file, emitter-classification parameters, and candidate matching-radar/platform data. The (V)3 version combines a new set of fixed antennas with servo-controlled spinners. The new fixed units obtain coarse DF data (by amplitude and phase, i.e., interferometer, comparison). The additional units are port and starboard antennas in 3 tiers. Each low-band antenna has 3 elements; each of the 2 higher bands uses 4 elements (3 for DF, 1 for elevation). WLR-1H works with **SLQ-32(V)4**. One version was designed for *Permit*-class submarines. **WLR-11** is a 7–18-GHz combination radar-warning system and upward frequency extension (SHF and IFM) used with earlier versions of WLR-1, sharing the same antennas (WLR-1 cannot respond quickly enough to provide effective warning).

WLR-1 *Users on surface ships:* Australia (-1F on *Adams* class), Brazil (*Garcia* class, FRAM *Gearing* class, *Espirito Santo*, probably *Minas Gerais*), Canada (-1C in *Mackenzie*, *St. Laurent* classes), Chile (*Alm. Williams* class), Colombia (*Courtenay* class), Germany (-1B in *Rhein* class), Greece (FRAM *Sumner*, Fram *Gearing*, *Rhein* classes), Indonesia (-1C in *Claud Jones* class), Iran (*Sumner* class), Mexico (FRAM *Gearings*), Pakistan (*Garcia* and *Gearing* [without APECS] classes), Philippines (*Cannon* class), Spain (*Paul Revere* class), Turkey (*Rhein* class, *Dixie*-class tender, *Sumner* [unmodified], *Berk* class [WLR-1C]), United States (with SLQ-32(V)4 in carriers; earlier version [probably -1G] on the carriers *J. F. Kennedy*, *Ranger*, and *Forrestal*, working with their SLQ-22 and -26 systems)

WLR-1 *Users on submarines:* Brazil (Guppy III), Greece (Guppies), Peru (Guppy 1A), Taiwan (Guppy II), Turkey (*Tang*, Guppy II, and Guppy IIA classes), United States (*Cheyenne*, *Columbia*, *Greeneville*, *Flasher*, *Gato*, *Greening*, *Haddock*), Venezuela (Guppy II)

WLR-3 *Users:* Brazil (*Alagaos* and *Sergipe*), Pakistan (*Garcia* class), Taiwan (Guppy II)

WLR-6 is a Sylvania ESM set, originally designed for SSNs; about 40 were made. It survives mainly on board surface ships.

Users: Australia (*Adams* class), Brazil (*Garcia* class), Germany (*Hamburg* class), Japan (a ruggedized Watkins-Johnson commercial version of WLR-6, covering the range from VLF to 40 GHz, equips 4 [ultimately 10] Japanese submarines of the *Yushio* class)

WLR-8/10 share the same telescoping mast. WLR-8 is the ELINT system ((V)2 for *Los Angeles*, (V)5 for *Ohio* class); -10 is the corresponding threat warner.

WLR-14/WJ 1140 *Users:* Denmark (2 AGIs), Germany (AGIs), South Korea (*Jeong Buk* and KDX class), United States (Coast Guard "Island" class)

WLR-18 (Classic Salmon) is a Watkins-Johnson COMINT system (5 kHz–2 GHz), standard on *Los Angeles*– class submarines. It uses an existing antenna, the communications sleeve on the standard Type 18 periscope. **WJ-32770-X** is similar. It is built around a **WJ-9195** Rapid Acquisition Spectrum Processor (RASP), which scans the 20– 512-MHz (extendable to 2–1,400 MHz) spectrum at a rate greater than 1 GHz/sec (with resolution of 25 kHz) and displays the signals intercepted on a digitally refreshed display. The system typically employs three types of operator stations: the supervisor station (including the RASP) and 2 collection operators. The supervisor uses the RASP to locate signals of interest, then hands them off to the collection operators, who actually operate the miniceptor (**WJ-8607**) receivers; they can also scan for signals. The system can support up to 8 miniceptors (20– 512 MHz, extendable to 2,000 MHz) and 2 dual receivers (for 5 kHz–32 MHz), a total of 12 channels.

WSQ-5 (Cluster Spectator) is Watkins-Johnson's companion submarine ESM (radar ELINT) system (30 MHz–40 GHz), normally coupled to **WLR-18**. WSQ-5 uses an existing antenna, the **BLA-4** omnidirectional bicone atop the **Type 18** periscope.

Mk 105 (Target Acquisition Console) *Users:* United States (*Pegasus* class except PHM-6 and possibly PHM-2 and -4); possibly Iranian destroyers armed with Standard ARM; possibly also South Korea (*Paek Ku* class armed with Standard ARM)

ARGOSystems must have been among the first to use digital deinterleavers, initially developed for an abortive U.S. Navy monopulse system, **WLR-16** (6 bands, 0.5– 18 GHz, 1976; **AR-627**). The first known export system, **AR-680/681** (for Taiwan), used trainable jammers. Later systems (**AR-700** series) were built around 2 generations of signal processors: **ASP-32** (capacity 200 signals) and then

The Phoenix AR-700 masthead ESM array on board the Norwegian frigate *Stavanger* in 1992. (Author)

ASP-2000 (capable of tracking 500 signals). ASP-2000 can handle a maximum pulse density of 1.5 million pps (it can sustain 1 million); maximum reaction time is 1 sec (excluding scan-time measurement). It can handle PRFs between 123 and 250,000; pulse widths between 0.1 and 99.9 microsec. It identifies new signals within 1 sec of interception. The earliest ARGO systems were credited with DF accuracy of 10 deg, but the current generation (as in MEKO frigates) is accurate to 5 deg. It appears that **Phoenix** was the first-generation ECM system, and **APECS** (Advanced Programmable Electronic Countermeasures System) the second (with ASP-2000). The AR-700 series is the ESM element.

Typical ESM antennas, in a Portuguese MEKO frigate, are a masthead omni antenna and a pair of monopulse (cavity-backed spiral) DF antennas. Each of the ESM antennas is a stack of three: for 0.5–2, 2–8, and 8–18 GHz, each layer consisting of 4 cavity-backed spirals. Each omni feeds a digital 12-bit IFM (accurate to within 3 MHz). Instantaneous (monopulse) DF accuracy is 5-deg RMS; fine DF (by differential phase comparison) accuracy is 1-deg RMS in the 2 high bands, 1.5 deg in the low band. Submarines use a smaller antenna.

The associated jamming antennas are a pair of big, stabilized, air-cooled cylinders, each of which covers a pair of phased-array antennas fed by a bank of mini-TWTs. The ECM section tracks up to 24 threats simultaneously, concentrating jamming power on 16

priority threats, shifting power among fixed 6-deg beams. Maximum effective radiated power is 230 kW. Among its techniques, the system provides cross-polarization (automatic polarization tuning) jamming to defeat monopulse seekers. The ECM system employs ARGO's own frequency-memory loop (FML). Each of the 2 ECM transmitters covers 180 deg with 30 overlapping time-shared beams, sufficient to noise-jam 8 or deceive 16 threats (of which 8 may be frequency and/or PRF agile). The associated ECM library contains 255 technique parameter sets.

AR-730 is a new, modular, maritime-patrol-aircraft version; its ESM/ELINT version adds an omni antenna (feeding digital IFMs) and a rotating directional antenna (for precision DF) to the usual array of monopulse DF antennas; it can also accommodate an SHR to operate over the 0.5–2-GHz band.

The new **AR-900** announced in 1993 uses a monopulse DF array (8 broad-band spirals, 2–18 GHz, accuracy 3.5 deg at 2–6 GHz, 2 deg at 6–16 GHz; 1 deg with interferometry). An omni antenna feeds a DIFM receiver. The electronic signal processor (ESP) can handle 1 million pps. It identifies an emitter within 1 sec of signal acquisition, using a 5,000-mode (500 radar) library. Displays: activity, tactical (PPI), frequency-bearing, frequency-amplitude, and frequency-PRI. Sensitivity is −65 dBm. Frequency resolution is 1 MHz (accuracy 3 MHz at 2–6 GHz, 6 MHz above 6 GHz), pulse-width range is 0.1–99.9 microsec (resolution 0.1 microsec), amplitude range is over 60 dB (resolution 0.5 dB), PRI range is 2–10,000 microsec (resolution 0.1 microsec). AR-900 can handle all polarizations and scan types; threat, steady, and CW signals. The antenna unit is 14.6 in diameter × 23.3 in (28 kg).

Phoenix II (AC-672) *Users:* Colombia (FS-1500 class [with Susie and Scimitar]), Peru (*Lupo* class)

AR-680 is the ESM system; **AR-681** is the associated jammer.

Users: Taiwan (*Sumner* and FRAM *Sumner* destroyers)

APECS II/AR-700 *Users:* Finland (Helsinki-I/II and *Turunmaa* classes and *Pohjanmaa* [the latter without the APECS jammer]), Greece (APECS II/AR-700 in MEKO 200 class), Netherlands (APECS II in *Karel Doorman*–class ships: *Abraham Van Der Hulst, Van Galen, Van Nes, Van Speijk*), New Zealand (*Canterbury, Wellington*), Norway (*Oslo* class), Pakistan (APECS II in *Babur* and FRAM destroyers *Alamgir, Taimur, Tughril*), Portugal (APECS II/AR-700 in MEKO 200 class; may replace ARBR 10 in *Cdt. Rivière* class), Sweden (*Stockholm* and *Nörrkoping* classes; no jammers). The Dutch version was selected in 1987 (at a unit cost of $3.75 million) in place of a more expensive Signaal system.

AR-700-S5 *Users of submarine version:* Australia (*Collins*), Denmark (Type 207), Egypt (4 Romeos), Greece (Type 209), India (Type 1500 and Kilos), Netherlands (all), Norway (Type 207), Pakistan (*Daphne*), Sweden (all), Taiwan (Hai Lung), Turkey (Type 209), Venezuela (Type 209)

Ferret *Users:* South Korea (Type 209s and Tolgorae-class midgets)

Guardian Star *Users:* Canada (selected in 1993 for *Oberon* class, possibly as SLR-503)

Sea Sentry *Users:* Argentina (TR1700 class), India (submarines)

SLR-600 Series *Users:* Thailand (*Ratcharit* class)

SR-200 *Users:* Peru (2 *Darings* and 6 PR-72s) and one other (11 sets)

This ARGOSystems jammer was displayed at the 1993 Navy League Show. The vertical circular plate at the right is the beam-former. Two such modules, oriented like this, and pointed 90 deg apart, fit within each big cylinder of an APECS II jammer (the smaller cylinder above it holds a cooling fan, with a heat exchanger below the big cylinder). (Author)

ARGOSystems AR-900 ESM system, showing the array in front of its radome, the shock-mounted processor, and the operator console at right. (ARGO-Systems)

The Watkins-Johnson **WJ 8957 (SCANS)** Signal Collection-and-Analysis System (for 1–2,000 MHz) was adopted for the Royal Australian Navy's *Collins* class and is currently being considered by the Royal Navy. In the Australian ships it is coupled to a **WJ 34901** antenna intercept and acquisition system. An RF data bus distributes signals to three positions: 2 for intercept/collection, 1 for early warning. A separate DF antenna feeds a tasked precision DF system. Typically, 1 intercept position deals with FSK, Morse, and AM/FM signals; the other deals with tactical voice signals. Each is equipped with 2 HF receivers (5 kHz–30 MHz) and 3 V/UHF receivers (20–1,400 MHz), all feeding the same display. The early-warning position has an HF receiver and a V/UHF receiver, both feeding a spectrum processor and a display. It deals with special signals. The spectrum processor and the DF system both feed into the system CPU. The DF antenna is a stack of 3 quadrature dipole arrays (1,100–2,000, 330–1,100, and 45–330 MHz) and a pair of crossed ferrite loop arrays, plus the appropriate preamplifiers and RF switches in a radome (total height 29.5 in). Below 45 MHz, the antenna finds signal direction by Watson-Watt (amplitude comparison) techniques, using the ferrite arrays. Above, it uses dipoles and interferometry (integration times 100, 200, 500 msec and 1, 2, and 5 sec). Bearing accuracy is 3 deg; bearing resolution is 0.1 deg. Elevation coverage is 45 deg.

WJ 8958 (DFS) shipboard DF system (1 MHz–2 GHz) uses the same DF antenna; it is planned for the South Korean KDX class and probably U.S. and foreign service (details are not known; there is no official nomenclature).

The U.S. Navy uses Comtek's **SADIS** (Semi-Automatic Decoy Integration System) special-purpose, decoy-launch processor and display as an interface between **SLQ-32** and **Mk 36** decoy launchers. The contract was let in 1988, and units entered service in 1989. SADIS incorporates its own Mil-Spec computer, based on an 80286 processor. Base memory is 64 kbyte, but it is expandable; the box has 8 slots, of which only 4 are used at present (including the I/O card). The internal bus is an 8-bit-wide Intel Multibus (specified by the user), which is described as somewhat slow for the processor. SADIS will be the **Nulka** FCS. As of July 1991, Comtek was upgrading 15 SADIS with 80386 processors to support **Nulka** decoys.

Hycor's **CAMLAC** (Computer-Aided Master Launcher Control) for Mk 36 SRBOCs uses a microprocessor with ROM, with sufficient space for 10 tactical-engagement sequences programmed by the user. Another 8 are programmed at depot level and cannot be changed on board ship. The display is a plasma panel. Wind (speed, direction) and threat (type, range, direction) are entered either manually or via interfaces with the ship's combat system; the appropriate sequence is automatically selected. CAMLAC seems to replace the standard U.S. Navy launcher control (Mk 158 Mod 1 or 2), which shows status but fires manually. There is also a standard bridge-launcher control (Mk 164 Mod 1 or 2). Cartridges listed: Mk 182 Mod 1 chaff, Mk 193 Mod 1 practice, Mk 191 Mod 0 test.

Tracor's **SCIP** (Shipboard Countermeasures Interface Package) controls Mk 33 and Mk 36 chaff launchers; it can handle any known chaff cartridge. It receives threat data (from the ship's RWR), ship's heading and speed data, and launcher status and loading data, all of which are entered into its RAM memory. The system can incorporate its own anemometer for wind data and its own inclinometer for roll. The system's ROM contains its engagement algorithm. It can operate either manually (recommending reactions to the threat) or automatically. SCIP also indicates the appropriate course to steer. The control console can be located either on the bridge or in CIC.

Users: Egypt, Singapore, and one other: as of late 1992, a sale was pending in Asia.

Early in 1993 Laguna Aerospace was marketing (and SSDS was considering) a 9-rnd **MBL-9** chaff launcher to replace the existing 6-rnd type of about the same size and weight. The FCS is ARES.

During the Gulf War, the U.S. Navy launched 137 **TALD** (ADM-141) decoys from A-6, A-7, F/A-18, and S-3 aircraft. Most were used to force Iraqi radars to remain active (and thus to succumb to anti-radar missiles), but in at least one case an Iraqi fighter locked onto a TALD and gave chase. ADM-141A is the active/passive (Lüneberg lens for RCS augmentation) version. ADM-141B is the chaff version. The first TALD was bought in December 1985; production was then split between Brunswick and Israel Military Industries (IAI). TALD entered service in 1987. As of March 1992, 4,000 TALDs had been bought in 3 lots. In September 1992 a contract for 1,480 TALDs was awarded to IAI, but it was suspended after Brunswick protested. The **ITALD** (ADM-141C) self-propelled version (CAE 312 turbojet) was expected to begin flight tests in April 1993 and to go into low-rate production in August 1993. Brunswick is seeking money for an advanced technology demonstration (ATD) of a lethal version of TALD, which could be mixed with TALDS (if the enemy failed to turn off radars, the lethal TALD would kill them). The company also proposes a miniature version, Maxi-TALD (6 × 6 × 30 in, range 60 nm, compared to 10 × 10 × 92 in and about 400 lb for ADM-141A). As of the spring of 1993, several countries were on the point of buying TALD.

ANTISUBMARINE WARFARE

SONARS AND UNDERWATER FIRE-CONTROL SYSTEMS

In passive signal processing, LOFAR/DIFAR typically detect machinery noise (including noise made by auxiliaries). DEMON generally extracts blade rate (i.e., propeller turn counts) from flow noise.

DIFAR cardioid processing is a more sophisticated directional technique. A DIFAR buoy provides 3 signals: 2 directional (north-south and east-west) and 1 omnidirectional. The ratio between the processed directional beams gives a bearing, as in radio direction finding; the omni beam resolves the 180-deg ambiguity. The directional beams are processed separately (incoherently). If each directional signal is added to or subtracted from the omni signal before processing, 4 directional cardioid (heart-shaped) beams are formed, each with a null opposite. That more than doubles the processing load, but the null excludes enough noise to add about 2 dB of processing power.

ANODE is a noise-measurement technique (Ambient Noise Omni-Directional Evaluation) that uses a DIFAR buoy. The pure omnidirectional signal is compared with an rms average of the 2 directional signals. If the noise is not directional, the 2 should match exactly, but directional noise (e.g., from nearby shipping) will unbalance the two. Typically, the comparison is matched against frequency, largely to determine which frequency ranges are best for buoy operation (i.e., which do not suffer from highly directional ambient noise). ANODE is commonly used by airborne ASW platforms, but more rarely in postmission analysis.

AUSTRALIA

Mulloka was chosen when the RAN was most concerned with southern waters, with short inherent ranges. The shift to **Spherion** was due to the strategic shift north, where the water is shallow but where the inherent range can be quite long, hence the preference for lower frequency (and a vertically steered beam).

PIPRS (which uses the Micro-PUFFS array) is in production at Sonartech (Sydney) for Australian *Oberon*s. It is a cooperative program with Canada, which also uses **Micro-PUFFS** (BQG-501), and the Royal Navy is likely to adopt it for its own version of Micro-PUFFS, **Type 2041**, on the *Upholder* class.

The 1991 force-structure review rejected the SURTASS concept for **ASSTASS** in favor of frigate-tactical arrays. The name ASSTASS was retained. **Kariwara** is now in FSED by GEC-Marconi. The first 2 will be on board the first 2 *Collins*-class submarines; another will be tried on board the frigate *Adelaide*. Thomson Pacific showed a competing array, **Narama**, at Bourget Naval in 1992. Unlike Kariwara, it is optimized for surface, not submarine, use (it is towed at higher speeds and shallower depths). Like Kariwara, it uses extruded threads, with a diameter of 45 mm (a conventional array might be 80 mm). Work began in 1991. It has now run successful sea trials.

AWA's **Krait** small-ship towed-array sonar uses the **Shearwater** fast acoustic processor (see below under airborne ASW) and a new, thin-line (25-mm, 32 or 64 hydrophones), low-noise streamer. Krait weighs less than 2 tons, and its total footprint is 3 m². The 32-hydrophone version operates at 200–400, 400–800, and 800–1,600 Hz; the 64-hydrophone version at 100–200, 200–400, and 400–800 Hz. The array is streamed at 2–20 kt, at 10–50 m. Operator aids include noise cancellation and autodetect and track. Krait is conceived primarily as an OTH *surface ship* detector; typical claimed shallow-water ranges are 40+ km for a trawler, 50+ km for a small surface warship, and 65+ km for a merchant ship. Claimed MTBF is 1,000 hr, and MTTR is 30 min.

CANADA

An RFP for an *Oberon*-class towed array was issued in August 1991; the first will be installed on board the *Ojibwa* during her 1994 MUSL **SUBTASS** refit. The prototype is in HMCS *Onandaga*. Indal Technologies developed its unusual hybrid towing system: the 2,000+ ft of cable is reeled into a wet handling and stowage system atop the pressure hull (under the casing), but the array proper is clipped to the end of the cable. The array's towing depth is controlled by varying the length of the tow (e.g., the submarine can listen both in and below the layer simultaneously). Indal is developing a handling system that would reel in a thin-line or fluid-filled array with the tow cable.

Westinghouse's **Type 5051**, announced in June 1992, is an improved commercial version of the existing **SQS-505**. Versions are

5051–5 (5 kHz), **-7** (7 kHz), and **-10** (10 kHz). In effect, Type 5051 supersedes the **HS-1000** series formerly advertised by Westinghouse Canada. Work began in 1990. The SQS-505 transducer and hull outfit are combined with a new digital (vice analog) transmitter (from the **SQQ-89[I]** program) and a new digital signal processor, which can reconfigure itself to work around failed components. The targeted reliability is 2,000 hr MTBF.

The transmitter, common to all versions, operates at 4.8–10 kHz, with variable output power and shaped-pulse control. Thus, the typical transmitting modes of -5 are 4.8, 5.4, and 6.0 kHz; of -7, 6.4, 7.2, and 8.0 kHz (-10 operates only at 10 kHz). The sonar transmits in ODT, TRDT (triple rotational), DT (single beam directional), and dual-pulse modes, at a source level of 224–233 dB; CW pulses are 2.5, 40, and 100 msec. It can also transmit in wide-band mode (linear or hyperbolic FM or CW-FM hybrid) using 40-, 100-, and 500-msec pulses. The receiver provides 24 or 36 preformed beams (depending on the version) with 1 steered beam; bandwidth is 1–15 kHz, and dynamic range is 120 dB. Software configures the parallel processor array dynamically (i.e., while it runs). Active processing techniques include FFT for CW pulses (to measure target speed, with a Doppler speed of ± 40 kt) and correlation for FM. Passive processing techniques are FFT (for spectral data, over a 2-kHz window) and short- and long-term integration for bearing-time (waterfall) display.

The display is a single 19-in, high-resolution, monochrome monitor; modes are A-scan (range vs. time) and B-scan (range vs. bearing), Doppler (2 targets: Doppler vs. range), passive, and spectrum (presumably LOFAR). Passive is a dual waterfall; the screen is divided into 2 sections, an upper one of 128 lines, each representing 85 msec of integration time, and the lower of 128 lines, each representing 32 lines of the upper display (2.7 sec). Alternative integration times are 341 msec and 10.9 sec. In each case, a bright pulse along the line indicates noise at that bearing. Spectrum mode displays 256 lines of LOFAR data (87 sec). Range scales are 500 yd–64 kyd. The screen can also be split into 2 displays: A-scan/passive, B-scan/passive, B-scan/Doppler, and A-scan/B-scan.

Types 5051–5 and -7 use 36-stave (360-element) hull transducers (1.6 m diameter $\times$ 1.6 m high and 1.2 $\times$ 1.2 m); -10 uses a 24-stave (144-element) transducer (0.6 $\times$ 0.6 m). The system can also incorporate a 6–10-kHz VDS (Fathom Oceanology **Model 15-1000**, 1.525 m diameter $\times$ 4.572 mm long, 3,600 kg), which can be launched at up to 16 kt (and towed at 30) on a 270-m faired cable. Beamwidth: 10 $\times$ 10 deg in -5/7, 17 $\times$ 17 deg in -10. Accuracy: 1% in range, 1 deg in bearing, 0.5 kt in Doppler. For passive detection, the filter is set to admit signals over any 2-kHz band within the transducer bandwidth. The two higher-frequency versions also have a mine-avoidance mode. In this case the sonar transmits at 8 (5051–7) or 10 (5051–10) kHz, using 1-msec FM pulses (bandwidth 1 kHz); the receiver's beamwidth is 8 $\times$ 10 deg, and the minimum range is 300 m.

In **SQR-501** (CANTASS) the displays are 4 or 6 high-definition (1,152 $\times$ 1,536–pixel) monochrome monitors. The display outputs include LOFAR, DEMON, and broad-band in beam and bearing-stabilized modes. Up to 240 signals can be tracked and displayed. The **UYS-501** processor, also used in **SQS-510**, is a single-instruction multiple-data (SIMD) parallel processor with 8 identical arithmetic modules in parallel; the central executive processor is a 68020. UYS-501 has up to 5 independent signal-processor I/O interfaces. It is built up of 59 cards in 2 racks. Memory comprises 4 million 32-bit words of DRAM (expandable to 64 million complex [64-bit] words); the cache memory is 32 thousand 32-bit words in fast SRAM. Output is 32 MFLOPS; UYS-501 can compute a 1,024-point complex FFT in 160 microsec. SQR-501 ran sea trials in 1987–90; 15 are to be delivered by 1995. The *Annapolis* has CANTASS in place of her VDS.

SQS-503 *Users:* Canada (*Restigouche*-class and earlier UNREP ships), France (*Foch*-class carriers)

A new (1992) contract adds a mine-avoidance capability (using a new transmitter module and WE signal processor) to Canadian **SQS-505**s.

Users: Belgium (*Wielingen* class [505A]), Canada (''Tribal''- and ''City''-class frigates, *Protecteur* class), Greece (*Kortenaer* class), Netherlands (*Kortenaer* class)

SQS-509 *Users:* Netherlands (last 4 *Kortenaer* class)

The Canadian ''City''-class frigates will be fitted with **SQS-510** in 1995, with a new **UYS-501** signal processor.

Users: Portugal (MEKO frigates; may replace SQS-17/DUBA 3 on *Cdt. Rivière* class)

CTS-36 is now on board HMCS *Restigouche*. An AN designator is being assigned. The first **CTAS-80** harbor-surveillance set for the Royal Swedish Navy began formal tests in February 1993 (Sweden has an option for production quantities). This sonar is the basis of C-Tech's **CIDS** (Coastal Intrusion Detection System), which has been sold to the U.S. Navy. CIDS normally includes an X-band radar, TV and IR cameras, and CDC's **ISIS** command/control.

At Brighton (March 1993) **OpTech** showed a programmable LIDAR, which could use different scan patterns for MCM and ASW (the company had provided the 200-Hz [PRF] laser for the Northrop ALARMS). OpTech credited the helicopter-borne ALARMS laser with a coverage rate of 48 km²/hr for ASW (3 km²/hr for MCM). A 400-Hz LIDAR (1995) should about double these rates. A future 2-kHz LIDAR might give 450 km²/hr for ASW (30 for MCM). Maximum submarine detection depth is probably about 50–70 m.

FRANCE

SLASM, which incorporates a 2-kHz towed pinger, began tests on board the trials ship *Cdt. Rivière* in 1991. The production version, with a 1-kHz pinger, will go to sea on board the *De Grasse* in 1994. The SLASM's towed body is 5.5 m $\times$ 1.8 m wide $\times$ 4.6 m high, and the composite shell weighs 2 tons. The operational version, to equip the *Georges Leygues* class in their mid-life upgrade, will probably be the Anglo-French-Italian **Type 2087** (see below). The Italian navy hopes to develop it on a cooperative basis with France, as it is a very ambitious project.

DMUX 20 is the first fully integrated French submarine sonar; it is for *Améthyste*-class SSNs with **SUBICS** combat systems. Sonars are integrated at the data level. For example, a frequency line seen by 1 sonar may coordinate with a broad-band strobe seen by another, so the combination may be meaningful to a track manager. Sonars, therefore, feed processed data (detections, lines of bearing) into the system bus. However, raw acoustic data is retained in memory at each sonar, to compensate for processing errors. The passive cylinder, the active sonar, and the sonar intercept unit all feed the same pair of processing cabinets. The towed array has its own processor, which feeds a separate console on the bus. Each processor houses massively parallel processors for beam-forming and spectral analysis (LOFAR). 68000-series CPUs are used for postprocessing, e.g., automatic detection of passive contacts by ALI.

DMUX 80 is the integrated sonar suite for the new-generation SSBNs (*Le Triomphant* class), formerly known as **SNLE NG Sonar or SNG** (*Sonar Nouvelle Génération*). It is the first French system to include a spherical bow array. The sphere is the only ceramic element. There are 4 other elements: the PVDF flank array, the first WAA-type ranger in French practice (previous passive rangers all used triplets of hydrophones; a WAA beam-forms), an acoustic intercept array, and a towed array. The prototype was being installed on board the new SSBN *Le Triomphant* at the end of 1992. DMUX 80 requires 14 electronic cabinets, accommodating 28 digital signal processors and 65 digital processors (CPUs) with a total processing power of 6 GFLOPS, plus 14 data processors (total 140 MIPS). Program software amounts to 2 million lines of code (100 Mbyte). Sonar data input rate is 256 Mbyte/sec; sonar data output (to tactical systems) is 3 kbyte/sec.

Thomson Sintra's **SUBICS** is the integrated submarine combat system of the *Améthyste*-class SSNs; it is also in the refitted *Rubis* class (the first of which was at sea as of October 1992). SUBICS was developed from the first French integrated submarine combat systems, which entered service on board the SSBNs in 1985. The sonar portion (but not the fire-control portion) will be in the 3 new Pakistani *Agosta*-class submarines (they retain **DLT 3**), and as of October 1992, it appeared that the full SUBICS would be installed in the Spanish SCORPENEs. The current version is Mk II. It employs the same consoles as in the minehunters, but a future version will probably employ the Thomson-Signaal **MOC** (and dispense with some or all of the separate computers). See the entry on the **TACTICOS** CDS for details of the MOC console.

All the sensors feed a tactical-information processing (TIP) subsystem via a TIP bus. A separate bus connects the TIP to the tactical-weapons launching system in the torpedo room. Preprocessing for each sensor includes automatic detection and tracking (ADT) and the associated contact motion analysis (CMA). CMA is an initial filter: it rejects contacts outside a preset range of interest. Contact data are fed into the system bus; the operators can also refer to raw acoustic data (waterfalls, LOFAR) for sensor fusion. An operator associates different sensor data for track management (a process Thomson calls MSSE, multisensor situation elaboration). MSSE filters the processed sensor data to form a clear tactical picture. The system's memory retains earlier track data. The ADT function is used to associate different lines representing the same track. For example, different sensors may see the same track at different times. These lines are automatically merged at the plot-extractor level. Typically, the system may pick up about 270 tracks at sensor level, filtering them to 100 at the MSSE level.

MSSE includes track classification and interactive TMA. The filtered tactical picture formed at the MSSE level is used for tactical planning. This stage, STAP, situation threat-assessment planning, provides tactical decision aids to help in planning attack or escape (using Thomson Sintra's patented method based on kinematic constructions). STAP helps optimize hit probability. Because the system is digital and software-based, it can easily be adapted to a wide variety of weapons: torpedoes, mines, and the **SM 39** standoff Sub-Exocet missile (Thomson Sintra emphasizes the value of the towed array in extending a submarine's sensor range for missile engagement).

Typically, SUBICS uses 4 multifunction duty stations (5 if fitted with a towed array) and 5 processing cabinets. In the patrol state, 3 would be manned: long-range sensor operator, short-range sensor operator, and sensor coordinator/tactical operator. When a potential threat is classified, 4 duty stations are automatically configured: 2 sensor operators, 1 tactical operator (situation evaluation), and 1 classification operator. The sensor coordinator is responsible for situation elaboration. Once tactical planning has been completed, the system is again reconfigured; the classification console becomes the weapons-control console. Attack reconfiguration time is 5 sec.

The system can accept data from 8–12 sensors, including radar and ESM. The acoustic sensors are a towed array, a PVDF flank array, a bow array (passive and intercept detection), distributed arrays for ranging, an obstacle- and mine-avoidance array, an intercept array, an active array, and a stern-arc array. Presumably, this amounts to **DMUX 20** (see above).

MSSE can handle 300 sensor tracks for 8 hr, or 100 for 24 hr, or 20 target tracks stored for the entire mission. STAP can plan for up to 20 targets, develop attack scenarios for 10, and compute hit probabilities for 10. The weapons-control system can control 4 weapons simultaneously. On the operator level, system acknowledgment time is less than 0.1 sec, and picture access time is less than 1 sec. Localization accuracy is 1 deg in bearing, 5% in range, 5% in speed, and 1 deg in course (time to achieve these figures by TMA is not given). A hostile-weapon warning is given within 10 sec, and a snapshot can be fired in reply within 45 sec.

The ADT and operator-initiated tracking/automatic target tracking (OIT/ATT) functions are in service on board French and Pakistani *Agosta*-class submarines and French *Améthyste*-class submarines, and they are part of the Australian *Collins*-class suite. MSSE and STAP are at sea on board French SSBNs. The Spanish *Agosta* class is being modernized with a new command system, presumably SUBICS. Work will begin with the *Galerna* in 1993.

Gudgeon, a third-generation adaptation of a helicopter dipper, ultimately derived from **HS 12**, was announced in 1992. The cylindrical MF transducer (diameter 0.2 m) can be either hull- or VDS-mounted (1 processor can serve both). It is unusually tall, presumably to form beams in the vertical for CZ operation. Operation can be active (with synthetic video for ADT or multi-ping display) or passive (tracking by ALI). Transmission is ODT, with directional and tribeam optional. For shallow water, Gudgeon uses FM and CW-matched filters. In October 1992, Thomson Sintra claimed that an unnamed foreign customer had ordered several units.

For **PVDF/PVF** (TSM 2253), each panel (1 m high × 0.42 m wide × 65 mm long, 45 kg) acts as a single transducer, effective between 10 Hz and 3 kHz (the frequency depends on panel size; narrower staves are effective to 5 kHz). The prototype installation is a 30-m flank array with a beam-former working at 2.5–3 kHz. Typical beamwidth is 5 deg in bearing, and the beam can be directed within 60 deg of the vertical, to avoid surface noise. To overcome self-noise, this array uses an electronic noise-canceler, driven by an accelerometer on the hull. Flow and vibration noises are reduced by averaging the noise pattern, in effect, over a wide surface. Thomson Sintra claims that this is the first array to be applied directly to the hull. It is part of the *Collins* class's suite and will probably be used on

board the new French SSBNs. First sea trials began in September 1992 on board the French nuclear submarine *Saphir*. This array was also supplied for 1 Norwegian *Ula*-class submarine. The basic PVDF technology is to be used in future semiconformal bow arrays, to replace the current cylinders and spheres.

Digilog's new **SYTIT** (*Système de Traitement des Informations Tactiques*) is a stand-alone, towed-array TMA/tactical-advisor system, for the nuclear submarines and also for surface ships now fitted with towed arrays (the prototype was on board a surface ship). Typically, SYTIT is connected to ownship data sources (navigation, time, etc.), to the hull-mounted and towed-array sonars, to the passive signal processors, to the ELINT sensor, to the search and attack periscopes, to the acoustic-performance analyzer, and to the FCS. Thus SYTIT offers the track-management and tactical functions, other than weapons control, of **SUBICS**, for ships and submarines that do not already have fully integrated systems. SYTIT is analogous to the U.S. Navy's **FFISTS**.

The surface version, **SYTIT(L)**, consists of a pair of high-resolution color displays (1,780 × 2,200 pixels) and a commercial-grade VME-based processor rack. **SYTIT(M)** is a fully militarized submarine version, consisting of 2 high-resolution consoles, typically flanking a larger PPI display console, plus a VME-based processing rack. SYTIT acquires sonar track data and ownship data, displays tracks in bearing and in frequency, manages tracks (creation, labeling, exchange, and removal), and conducts TMA. It displays the tactical situation in PPI form (including tracking selected targets, recommending course, evaluating threats, showing go/no-go areas, displaying acoustic advantage, and providing torpedo alerts), and it can provide system control. The processing console is built around a VME backbone carrying a 68030 board for graphics, another for system control, and a **SPARC** processor; special tactical boards can be added for tactical decision aids, carrying SPARC or 68030 processors. The submarine CRT is monochrome but displays colors by polarization (yellow and green only).

The digital array of **DSBV 61A/Anaconda** has about 8 modules, with an acoustic aperture about 300 m [984 ft] long, diameter about 80 mm [3.1 in].

Users: France (*Georges Leygues* class, streamed from a DUBV 43C VDS body), Netherlands (*Karel Doorman* class: Anaconda, streamed at a critical angle; uses a Mangouste Mk 2 processor)

DSUV 2 *Users: Daphne* class in Pakistan, Portugal, South Africa, and Spain

The Australian **Scylla** employs 2,000 hydrophones in 7 arrays (bow cylinder, 2 PVDF flanks, active array [in the sail], towed array, mine-avoidance sonar, and an intercept array [2 elements, fore and aft]). Total array surface is about 70 m², compared to 10 m² for typical current sonars (for diesel submarines) with 3–5 arrays. The system performs 60 acoustic functions (compared to 16 in a typical existing type), including nulling to defeat jamming, self-noise cancellation, and automatic detection (none of which is currently common).

DSUV 22 (Eledone, TSM 2272)/Scylla/Type 2040) *Users:* Australia (Scylla, in *Collins* class), France (*Rubis* and *Agosta* classes), India (6 sets bought in May 1991 for delivery 1997–99, probably for Type 1500 submarines), Netherlands (as Octopus), Spain (*Agosta* class), United Kingdom (Type 2040 in *Upholder* class)

DSUV 23 is the passive LF hull array of French SSBNs.

DSUV 61 is the towed array for French SSBNs. The current version is **DSUV 61A**; **61B** is being developed.

Thomson Sintra claims 2nd CZ performance for **DSUV 62/Lamproie (TSM 2933)**. In April 1991 the Spanish submarines *Sciroco* and *Mistral* conducted towed-array trials, probably with this sonar, in the Gulf of Cádiz and the Atlantic. The Spanish *Agosta*-class submarines, beginning with the *Galerna* in 1993, are to be modernized with a towed array (as well as a new combat system, presumably SUBICS).

Users: France (*Agosta* [62A], *Rubis* [62A], *Améthyste* [62C] classes), Pakistan (*Agosta* class)

DSUX 21 was the first French multifunction sonar serving an integrated combat system. This sonar may be redesignated **DMUX 21**, in parallel with the DMUX systems described above.

Users: French SSBNs (*L'Inflexible*, backfitted into modernized *Le Redoutable*–class French SSBNs)

DUAA-2 *Users:* Colombia (Type 209), Ecuador (Type 209), France (*Daphne*; -2B in *Agosta* and *Rubis* classes), Pakistan (*Daphne* class; -2B in *Agosta*), Peru (Type

209), South Africa (*Daphne* class), Spain (*Daphne* class; -2B in *Agosta* class), Venezuela (Type 209)

DUAV 4 (HS 71) operates in 3 modes: (i) fixed-frequency active (around 20 kHz) to measure bearing, range, and Doppler (for speed); (ii) variable-frequency (to detect motionless targets); (iii) passive, at 10–20 kHz. Transducer depth is typically 140 m [460 ft] on a 160-m cable. The maximum effective range is about 6,000 yd. French Lynx helicopters equipped with DUAV 4 have a mission computer that can handle up to 15 way points (to be upgraded to 100) with up to 6 moving or sonar targets. It can accept geographic, radar, or grid coordinates, providing the pilot with bearing and range and with the next way or hover point. The standard tactic is to dip at the last known target contact ("jumping on the contact"). With a reliable sonar range of 1,500 yd, 1 Lynx in daylight or 2 at night are expected to keep contact with any submarine. With a reliable range of 3,000 yd, the French navy estimates that a Lynx can maintain contact with a 35-kt submarine in daytime or a 22-kt submarine at night (night dipping is slower, using a complex autopilot). In 1991 the helicopter system was integrated with GPS.

Users: France (58, many replaced by HS 12), the Netherlands (12 on Lynx 27/81s), Libya (6 Super-Frélons with HS 73 and L5 torpedoes), and Sweden (14 on KV-107s, 1975, at least 8 of which are being upgraded under a June 1992 contract with Thomson Sintra). Both India and Indonesia ordered DUAV 4 for large helicopters but ultimately received **HS 12** instead. The Swedish upgrade involves improved signal processing and operator-machine interface. The acoustics, already optimized for the Baltic, will not be changed. The prototype upgrade was ordered in 1988 and delivered in April 1992. South Africa bought both the Super-Frélon and the Puma, and some of its helicopters may carry dipping sonars. Israel bought the Super-Frélon and may have bought some French dipping sonars. According to Thomson Sintra, more than 150 DUAV 1/DUAV 4 winch assemblies have been delivered, of which only 90 are listed above (**DUAV 1** was a predecessor, on board perhaps 20 French navy Super-Frélons). It seems likely that both India and Indonesia use the hoist assemblies originally ordered for DUAV 4, a total of 44–50.

DUBA 25 (Thomson Sintra TSM 2400 Tarpon)/**TSM 2080**

Users: France (C70AA and A-69 classes)

DUBV 23 *Users:* China (PRC) (Modified Luda class, Jangwei class), France (*Suffren*, first 4 *Georges Leygues* class, *Tourville* class, *Aconit*).

China (PRC) makes the **DUBV 23/43** combination under license; DUBV 23 is the sonar associated with the **CY-1** standoff missile.

DUBV 24 *Users:* France (last 3 *Georges Leygues*– class frigates)

DUBV 43 is now being modified for deeper running (700 vice 400 m) in 12 ships (1 while building); the project is due for completion in 1994.

Users: China (PRC) (Modified Luda class), France (7 *Georges Leygues*, 3 *Tourvilles*, 2 *Suffrens*, *Aconit*)

DUUA 1A/B/C *Users:* France (*Daphne, Agosta* classes), Pakistan (*Daphne, Agosta* classes), South Africa (*Daphne* class), Spain (*Daphne, Agosta* classes)

DUUA 2 *Users:* France (modernized *Daphne, Rubis, Agosta* classes)

DUUX 2A/B/C *Users:* Argentina (Type 209), Australia (*Oberon* class), Brazil (*Oberon*), Canada (*Oberon*), Chile (*Oberon*), Ecuador (Type 209), France (*Daphne* [2A], *Rubis* [2B], *Agosta* [2B], *Redoutable* classes), Germany (Type 206 [2C]; 2A was tested on board the experimental *Wilhelm Bauer*), Greece (Type 209), Pakistan (*Agosta* [2B], *Daphne* [2A] classes), Peru (Type 209 [2C]), Portugal (*Daphne* class), Peru (Type 209), South Africa (*Daphne* [2A] class), Spain (*Agosta* [2A], *Daphne* [2A] classes), Turkey (Type 209), United Kingdom (*Porpoise* and *Oberon* classes), Venezuela (Type 209).

The British designation was **Type 2005**; it was replaced in Australian and Canadian service by **Micro-PUFFS**. DUUX 2 was the standard acoustic range-finder on board most Type 209s (after 1980 Krupp-Atlas supplied its alternative, **PRS**).

A version of **DUUX 5** (Fenelon) is incorporated in the **Eledone** sonar system (see above). Compared to **DUUX 2**, DUUX 5 has integral switching and a microprocessor. The advertised export version of the Chinese Romeo includes both DUUX 5 and an enlarged chin sonar dome (presumably carrying a French cylindrical array). DUUX-5 may also be part of the sonar suite of the **E5SG** design offered for export (carrying 6 **C801** missiles).

Users: China (PRC) (1 modified Romeo [2 sets exported in 1983; this sonar may be locally produced]), France (*L'Inflexible*– and *Redoutable*-class SSBNs, *Rubis*-class SSNs), India (2 bought for the 2 Type 1500s, 2 for refit of the other pair in 1995), Norway (probably in *Ula* class)

Diodon (TSM 2630)/**Sorrel** (TSM 2630)

Users: Argentina (A-69–class corvettes), Ecuador (*Wadi M'ragh* class), India (TSM 2630 in *Nilgiri* class), Libya (Vosper Mk 7 frigate and *Wadi M'ragh* class), Portugal (*Baptiste de Andrade* class), Saudi Arabia (*Al Madinah*– class frigates: TSM 2630 version)

FLASH (TSM 8260) may replace the Bendix **HELRAS** in the Italian version of the EH-101 helicopter. Thomson Sintra and Atlas are developing a scaled-down version for the NH 90 (Lynx successor) shipboard helicopter. The Ferranti sonar processor in the British version (**Type 2095**) uses the new **T9000** Transputer (also called T9), which has 10 times the power of the earlier **T800**. The U.S. **ALFS** version reportedly operates at 1.2–5.6 kHz. The operational requirement was for 35 consecutive 4-sec pings per dip and sufficient processing power (8 FFTs) for 8 DIFAR or 4 DIFAR plus the sonar.

Users: Canada (EH-101 NSAs [New Seaborne Aircraft]), France (presumably, to replace HS 12 on Super-Frélons, using a French processor), United Kingdom (Type 2095, using a Ferranti processor), United States (ALFS, using a Hughes dry end with a UYS-2 processor)

HS 12 (TSM 8252) *Users:* Chile (HS 312: 4 Dauphins, for which 20 Murène torpedoes (later canceled) were ordered in 1989), Finland (2 on Super Pumas, others on Mi-8 and -14 helicopters), France (at least 30 on board Super-Frélons and Lynxes, with more as DUAV 4 is replaced on board Lynxes), India (24 on Mk 42B Sea Kings), Indonesia (20 or 26 on board Pumas), Iraq (8 on board Super-Frélons, possibly others planned for 6 Super Pumas and 6 Dauphins on order in 1990), Portugal (5 Super Pumas), Saudi Arabia (12 on board Dauphins), and Singapore (on at least 5 of 22 planned Super Pumas). Other Super Puma naval operators who may use HS 12 are Brazil (6, plus 7 on order) and Saudi Arabia (6). Not all of these helicopters necessarily carry sonars. Chile has 3 Super Pumas used only to carry **Exocet**s (with 4 more on order); it is unlikely that Kuwait (6) and U.A.E. (8) bought their aircraft for ASW. The Finnish installation is interesting because other operators of Soviet naval helicopters may follow suit.

More than 50 **HS 12/HS 312** winch assemblies had been delivered as of 1992. Almost certainly earlier winches were used wherever possible (otherwise the numbers here would greatly exceed the sales figure).

HS 312 (TSM 8240–43) *Users:* China (PRC) (3 for Super-Frélons, but they may actually be HS 12s; more may be made locally for further Zhi-8 Super-Frélons), France (4)

SS 12 *Users:* China (PRC) (both prototypes were sold to the PRC in 1987; one is on board Haijui-class patrol boat hull 688)

Salmon (TSM 2640) *Users:* Denmark (*Thetis* and StanFlex 300 classes), Finland (1 ship, probably *Hameenmaa*), Singapore (*Victory* class [not the EDO 786 often reported]), Sweden (*Stockholm* class, *Göteborg* class [TSM 2643 version])

Spherion (TSM 2633) *Users:* Australia (ANZAC frigate), India (*Delhi* class; 2 delivered in March 1991), New Zealand (ANZAC frigate), Norway (*Oslo* and *Sleipner* classes [replacing SQS-17 and -36, respectively] as modernized), Taiwan (*La Fayette* class).

The Mk 2 version for the ANZACs has TRDT to increase its source level by 6 dB, and also a torpedo warner.

GERMANY

Krupp Atlas Elektronik (KAE) is now Atlas Elektronik.

German submarine sonars, examples of all of which remain in service, fall into generations: (i) 2 generations of unintegrated suites, consisting of separate passive arrays (based on the wartime **GHG**) and trainable active planar-array attack sonars; (ii) integrated sonars (**CSU 3**, for 3rd-generation Compact Sonar U-boat, in which both arrays and a sonar intercept receiver feed a single console; (iii) **Standard Sonar 80** (ASO 80, CSU-83: DSQS-21 and DBQS-21D in German navy service), which added a passive ranger (PRS in its stand-alone version), a spectral (LOFAR/DEMON) processor (sonar information processor: **SIP 3**), and beam-preforming; and (iv) **Standard Sonar 90** (DSQS-23, DBQS-21DG), in which all arrays, including towed and flank arrays, feed a common bus (it provides integrated TMA). U-12 (Type 205B) is trials ship for Sonar 90.

The first-generation active searchlight sonar, **AN 407**, operates at 8–12 kHz and has a range of 1.5–9 m. It can operate independently, or its pings can be detected by the passive array. The successor trainable/tiltable planar array (in German Type 206 and later export Type 209 submarines), **AN 410** (WSU in the German navy), uses preformed overlapping beams (beamwidth about 20 deg) at 8 kHz (pulse 35 msec) over a 110-deg sector, in either ODT or RDT mode. AN 407 uses a single CRT (A-scan); AN 410 adds a PPI. The corresponding bow arrays were a 288-element bow horseshoe/

19-element stern array, **AN 526** (**GH** in the German navy), succeeded by the cylindrical **AN 5039** (diameter 3 m, 384 elements). Both used analog processors (1–10 kHz) and CRT displays; they could track a single target automatically. These systems survive in Type 209 export submarines, which generally have French sonar intercept receivers (**DUUG 1A/AUUD 1C**) and passive rangers (**DUUX 2C**) and Signaal **M 8/8** FCS.

Users of first/second generation systems: Argentina (2 Type 209s), Germany (5 Type 205s), Greece (first 4 Type 209s). The 2 Colombian Type 209s were refitted with CSU-83s in 1990–91, and the Greek boats were fitted with CSU-83s. The German Type 206s were all refitted with CSU 3–4s. The Danish Type 205s and the Norwegian Type 207s (3 bought by Denmark) were all refitted with DBQS-21Fs.

The integrated third-generation system uses a single CRT, which can switch between the 3 sensors (active and passive sonars and a German-made ISK sonar intercept receiver [which measures frequency, pulse rate, and amplitude] and can display up to 8 pulses at the center of the CRT; it also determines target-elevation angle). For example, an operator may identify a target by its sonar emission, then switch to the passive array for long-range tracking, and to the active array for short-range fire control. In this version the passive bow array was rearranged into 24 3-element staves; there are 4 analog trackers. CSU-3/2 or 3–2 uses the AN 410 active array; CSU-3/4 or 3–4 uses a 96-stave cylinder (diameter about 1 m). The prototype CSU 3–2 entered service in 1974 on board a Venezuelan Type 209.

CSU 3–2 *Users:* Ecuador (2 Type 209s), Greece (4 later Type 209s), Indonesia (2 Type 209s), Peru (6 Type 209s), Turkey (6 Type 209s), Venezuela (2 Type 209s).

CSU 3-4 *Users:* Argentina (3 TR-1700 class), Australia (CSU 3–41 in 6 *Oberon*s), Canada (CSU 3–41 in 3 *Oberon*s), Chile (2 Type 209s), Germany (18 Type 206s, 12 of which were modernized with CSU-83), India (2 SSK-1500s), Israel (3 Type 206s), Sweden (5 *Sjöormen* class), Yugoslavia (2 *Sava* class, systems bought through Italy). Colombia, Peru, and Yugoslavia (*Sava* class, possibly stand-alone in *Heroj* class) have the stand-alone **PRS 3–15** passive ranger.

Sonar 80 introduced a standard BM 802-series color console (red for new targets, green for targets already being tracked, gold for passive surveillance). The submarine version (CSU-83) initially replaced the monochrome CRT of CSU 3 with 1 such display, supplemented by a paper gram recorder for the SIP. Later the gram recorder was replaced by a second CRT, which was also used for passive ranging. SIP 3 can also be retrofitted into the earlier CSU 3–4. It can analyze data from 4 targets simultaneously, displaying them 1 by 1. Besides spectral analysis and automatic line tracking (ALT), the SIP provides automatic maneuver detection (AMD) and high-resolution target-bearing measurement. Part of the automatic tracker and its spectral analyzer may also be used in some active sonar modes. The spiderweb system bus carries raw video, not processed video, so each console can process it as required (German wire-guided torpedoes can supply their own raw video to the same bus). In German submarines the Signaal FCS is replaced by a new **LEWA** (*Lageerarbeitungs und Waffeneinsatzanlage*). This combination of sonar and FCS is called **ISUS**. The German navy version has 4 **BM 802** consoles (each with 2 screens): typically 2 for sonars, 1 for position-keeping (using a contact-evaluation plot and a waterfall)/FCS, and 1 for weapons control. The system can accommodate up to 9 consoles, which some users want. A separate **STU 5** console, provided for training, can be the CO's console during combat. The first CSU-83s were on board Brazilian Type 209/1400 submarines; the German DBQS-21DN version was tested in 1985 on board a Type 206.

KAE has developed a stand-alone LF (up to 2.5 kHz) flank array (**FAS 3–1**) to supplement CSU-83: the typical 30-m array has 96 hydrophones (on each side of the submarine) covering a 160-deg sector and achieving a typical bearing accuracy of 1 deg (the array can be up to 48 m long, with 144 hydrophones). The associated processor provides 8 BB, 8 DEMON, and 8 LOFAR channels. The array is carried within a shell mounted on the submarine, backed by a layer of plastic to keep signals from being reflected into the array by the submarine's hull. Reflectors protect the array from structure-borne noise.

PSU-83 (DBQS-21F) is a small-submarine passive version of CSU-83, using the old AN 526 array (bow and stern sector) of the German Type 205 class. It has the same 8-target dual-mode (short integration time for surveillance, long integration time for long-range detection) automatic tracker as CSU-83 and has a single BM 802–series console. KAE markets the associated FCS as FSU 83; the integrated system is **OSID 83**. The key development seems to have

been a beam-former suited to arrays of arbitrary shape, such as the horseshoe.

TAS 83 is a stand-alone clip-on towed array suited to CSU-83, typically with an 80-m acoustic aperture on a 300-m cable, operating at 150–1,200 Hz BB, 10–1,200 LOFAR, and 600–1,200 Hz DEMON with 2-deg bearing accuracy and resolution (128 beams cover 5–175 deg on each side). TAS 83–2 (TAS 83–1) provide 8 (4) 8-line trackers for multiline (MLT) LOFAR detection and tracking, 8 (4) BB detection and tracking channels, 16 (4) LOFAR classification channels, 8 (4) DEMON classification channels, and 1 target-related broad spectral analysis (not in 83–1). TAS 83–2 also provides a transient noise detector (TND).

DBQS-21 (CSU 83) *Users:* Brazil (2 Type 209s), Colombia (2 Type 209s as refitted), Denmark (-21F in 2 Type 205s and in 3 Type 207s bought from Norway), Egypt (PSU-83 in modernized Romeos), Germany* (12 Type 206As), South Korea* (Type 209s), Norway (-21N in *Ula* class, -21F in *Kobben*s), Sweden (*Näcken, Västergötland*, and *Sjöormen* [mid-life modernization of 2 units was funded under the FY87–91 plan]), Turkey* (CSU 83/1 in new Type 209/1400 submarines), Venezuela* (Type 209s refitted to 206A standard in 1990–92). The Norwegian version omits a passive ranger (Norway probably used **DUUX 5**). Starred classes all use the 4-console version of **ISUS**. Chile reportedly bought SIP 3 to enhance Type 2007 flank-array performance in its *Oberon*s.

CSU-90 has 8 automatic target trackers (ATTs) following compound tracks formed by the outputs of the active sonar, the DEMON analyzer, and the LOFAR analyzer (which is fed by the towed and flank arrays). Of the 3 consoles, 1 monitors the active sonar (with its 8 ATTs), 1 monitors the passive arrays, and 1 compiles the tactical picture using TMA; it is also responsible for passive ranging. **SIP 3** is replaced by a new Acoustical Passive Classification (APC) module. Signals are classified using expert-system techniques. In broad outline this combination is analogous to the U.S. **BSY-1/2** or **SQQ-89**, which are built around integrated TMA. CSU-90 ran its first sea trials on board a Type 205 submarine in early 1992.

CSU 90 *Users:* Chile (modernized *Oberon*), Germany (Type 212s), Greece (modernized Type 209s), Israel (*Dolphin* class), Sweden (*Gotland* [A-19] class)

The **ASO** series are surface sets corresponding to the CSUs. **ASO 90** introduces a new computer (68030 processors, VME bus, ADA software), raster-scan color displays, pull-down menus, and better passive operation (it can operate simultaneously active/passive). It can work more than 1 frequency simultaneously in active mode (2 frequencies within a single ping). Pings can be FM slides (with pulse-compression processing). Transmission is still analog. The number of transducers depends on the diameter of the array (normally each stave consists of 6, for a total of about 150–400). A towed array can be added as either an integrated element or as a stand-alone system.

ASO 94/95 operates actively at 6–9 kHz, passively at 2–11 kHz, using 32 or 64 preformed beams. Active modes: ODT/RDT/SDT, with CW and FM pulses (lengths 5, 50, 300 msec, with pulse compression, Doppler filter, and energy-level pulse detection). Capabilities include ALADIN (ASPECT in German). The ASO series uses the **MPR 2300** multiprocessor, using 68030 chips, a VME bus, and ADA software. This sonar automatically tracks up to 10 targets, transferring the data to the CDS.

Surface ships will use the same towed array as submarines; their version (TAS) can have either a single display console (**TAS 6–2**), a double display console (**TAS 6-3, 6–31,** and **5–3**), or two double-display consoles (**TAS 5-2**). These arrays operate at 15 Hz–1.2 kHz (with broad band in the 2.4-kHz range). A prototype was tested at sea in 1990, and development was to be completed early in 1993.

TAS 6–3 uses an 80-m acoustic aperture (3 frequency bands) in a 240-m towed body on a 1,000-m tow cable. TAS 6-31 uses the same tow cable and acoustic aperture, but at higher frequency (4 bands) in a shorter towed body (200 m). 6–3 uses a 165-m aperture (in a 320-m body) on a 1,000-m cable (3 bands). 5–3 uses a 330-m aperture (3 bands, lower frequency) in a 490-m body on a 1,500-m cable. Finally, 5–2 uses the long body (4 bands) on a 2,000-m cable. The array is conventional, with preamplifiers in the body and without multiplexing; it uses 2 wires per channel. The nested array has 72 channels; the HF part has at least 3 hydrophones per group, the LF part fewer. An experimental version was leased to Sweden. The frigates will probably get longer ones, for better LF performance (the Baltic has minimum attenuation at 200–600 Hz). Type 122 and 123 frigates may be modernized with either a passive or a bistatic towed-array sonar. One possibility is to use towed arrays on board Type 212 submarines as bistatic receivers for LF pingers towed by a frigate.

DSQS-21/ASO80 Series *Users:* Argentina (ASO 80 series in 10 MEKO frigates), Brazil (4 *Inhaúma* class, ASO 84–2), Colombia (4 FS-1500 class, ASO 84–2), Germany (DSQS-21 in 3 *Adams* and 8 *Bremen* classes), Iraq (DSQS-21C [ASO 84-41] in *Wadi M'ragh* series, now for sale), Italy (DSQS-21B in ex-Iraqi *Lupo* class), Malaysia (2 FS-1500 class, ASO 84-5), Nigeria (replaced PHS-32 in *Aradu*), Taiwan (10–15 DSQS-21CZ sonars in refitted non–SQS-23 destroyers and DSQS-21CZ for the modified *Perry* class), and Thailand (DSQS-21B in PFMM Mk 16s [*Ratanakosin* class]; DSQS-21CZ in the frigate *Makut Rajakumarn* [replacing PMS 26], in the U.S.-supplied PF 103 class [replacing SQS-17], in the 3 new *Khamronsin* class, and in the last 2 frigates to be built in the PRC)

DSQS-23 *Users:* Germany (F 123 *Brandenburg* class)

ELAC 1BV *Users:* Germany (*Hamburg, Thetis* classes)

PSU 1–2 *Users:* Colombia (probably on 2 SX-506–class midget submarines), Pakistan (4 SX-756s), South Korea (*Tolgorae* and SX 756–class midget submarines), and Yugoslavia (6 *Una* class). The Yugoslav boats also have a Krupp-Atlas **PP-10** active sonar. Argentina is sometimes listed as a user but has no known midget submarines.

INTERNATIONAL

There are now 3 versions of **ATAS**: (V)1 purely active, (V)2 active or passive, (V)3 simultaneously active and passive with 3.5 kHz in tandem with the Lamproie array. Taiwan (for the *La Fayettes*) is the only customer (ATAS will work with a Spherion hull sonar).

ISRAEL

Rafael's **Coris** passive linear arrays, named after a fish, were announced in 1992: they were probably 3–4 yr from service at that time. Unlike existing systems, they use the entire array for all frequency bands. **Coris-TAS** is a towed array for surface ships; **Coris-5** is a flank array for submarines; **Coris-M** is a moored surveillance version. Coris-TAS operates in 4 LF bands (10–1,600 Hz). Resolution at LF is 0.3 Hz. It employs 2 interchangeable 19-in color monitors (search and track/classification, only one of which is manned when the submarine is cruising). Processing modes are broad band, narrow band (LOFAR), and DEMON. Eight targets can be tracked automatically. Rafael claims that jammers can be rejected automatically. Coris-5 is modular to allow for different submarine lengths. Although in theory it covers the full 360 deg around the submarine, detection probability is greatest in the 120-deg sector on either side of the submarine. Detection bandwidths are 10–1,500 Hz for narrow band, and 10–1,000 Hz for broad band; dynamic range is 70 dB. Both arrays are intended primarily to track surface targets; the Coris-5 brochure appears to claim second or third CZ performance.

ITALY

SEA 90, the sensor suite for the new S90 submarine class, includes bow, flank, and towed arrays and a passive ranger. Selenia-Elsag is the manufacturer, with Thomson Sintra's cooperation.

IP-64 *Users:* *Enrico Toti* class

IPD 70/S *Users:* *Sauro* (with SEPA Mk 1 FCS), *Pelosi, Longobardo* classes.

The associated LOFAR/DEMON spectral analyzer is **SARA** (Selenia's spectral analyzer and classification system), using the bow array and LF flank transducers (probably from **MD 100/S**); lines are detected automatically or manually and are automatically compared to a signature library.

MD 100/S passive ranger *Users:* *Sauro* (retrofit), *Salvatore Pelosi* (with BSN-716(V)1 and SEPA FCS Mk 3) and *Primo Longobardo* (with BSN-716(V)2)

The reported sale of **SEPA Mk 3** and **A-184** torpedoes to Peru in 1986 probably was not consummated because of a lack of funds.

JAPAN

The new trials ship (ASE) to be built under the JFY92 budget has a flank-mounted active/passive bow array and a new towed array. The bow arrays extend back as far as the tower foremast.

OQR-1 (SQR-19) *Users:* *Kongo* class, 4,400-ton destroyer class

OQS-3 *Users:* Later *Yamagumo* class, *Chikugo* class

OQS-4 *Users:* *Asagiri, Hatakaze, Hatsuyuki, Yubari,* and *Ishikari* classes

OQS-12 *Users:* *Isuzu* class (OQA-1 VDS hoist)

OQS-101 *Users:* *Shirane* class

OQS-102 is reportedly equivalent to **SQS-53**. *Users:* *Kongo* (Aegis) class

ZQQ-2 *Users:* *Uzushio* class (training submarines)

ZQQ-3 *Users:* *Takashio* and later, with **SQS-36J** active sonars

ZQQ-4 *Users:* *Yushio* class, with **SQS-36J** active sonars. From the *Okishio* on they have U.S.-supplied **BQR-15** towed arrays (*Okishio* conducted trials in 1988–89).

ZQQ-5 suite includes a towed array (**S-TASS**) and flank arrays.

Users: *Harushio* class

ZYQ-1, a computer display system (CDS) is in the *Yushio* class only.

NETHERLANDS

CWE-10N/PAE-1 *Users:* Argentina (*25 de Mayo*), Peru (cruisers and *Friesland*-class destroyers), Turkey (*Köln* class). PAE-1 is installed only on board the destroyers and frigates.

PHS-32 *Users:* Indonesia (training frigate *Hajar Dewantara, Fatahilah*- and *Van Speijk*–class frigates, and the PB 57–class patrol craft *Andau* and *Singa*), Netherlands (*Tromp* class), Nigeria (MEKO 360–type frigate *Aradu*), and South Korea (*Ulsan* class and some *Dong Hae* class, a total of 25 sets)

PHS-36 *Users:* Netherlands (*Karel Doorman* class, with French wet ends)

SIASS *Users:* Taiwan (*Hai Lung* class). Attempts to market SIASS to other customers (particularly to the Royal Netherlands Navy) failed. **Spectrum** is the associated CDS.

M5 *Users:* Germany (*Hamburg* class), Greece (*Thetis* class), Turkey (*Köln* class)

M8 *Users:* Argentina (M8/24 in Type 209s), Denmark (M8/24 may be in *Narhvalen* class), Ecuador (M8/24 in Type 209s), Germany (M8/8 in Type 206s), Netherlands (M8/7 in *Zwaardvis* class), Turkey (first 2 Type 209s)

M9 Series *Users:* Egypt (*Descubierta* class), Indonesia (*Hajar Dewantara* and *Fatahilah* class and possibly the 2 fast ASW attack craft), Malaysia (FS-1500 class), Morocco (*Descubierta* class), Nigeria (*Aradu*), and Spain (*Descubierta* class)

M11 *Users:* Argentina (*Intrepida*-class [TNC 45–type]) and probably part of **Vega** versions controlling wire-guided torpedoes, e.g., on Greek Combattante II and III attack boats

SINBADS *Users:* Argentina (TR-1700 class), Chile (Type 1300), Greece (later Type 209s), Indonesia (Type 209s), Peru (later Type 209s), and Turkey (Type 209s after first 2). SINBADS may also have replaced **M8/24** on board the Ecuadorian Type 209s.

GIPSY (*Geintegreerd Informatie en Presentie Systeem*, used with SEWACO VIII)

Users: Netherlands (*Walrus* class)

NORWAY

Simrad abandoned searchlight sonars because they could not be stabilized against the motion of a small boat. SS and ST scanning series are numbered according to frequency (**SS 240** and beyond operate at 24 kHz, **SS 575** at 57 kHz; **SS 105** operates at 14 kHz).

ST240 produces 64 preformed beams (8 × 12 deg) at 24 kHz; it transmits in sector mode over 30, 60, or 120 deg. CW pulse lengths are 1.3–200 msec; FM pulse widths (bandwidth 1.9 kHz) are 1.3, 2.6, 5.2, and 10.4 msec. Ranges are 0.5, 1, 2, 4, 6, and 12 km.

SS 575/576 is the new HF (57-kHz) digital sonar, intended for ASW, presumably in the short-range conditions of the Norwegian coast. The 256-element spherical array was presumably inspired by Thomson Sintra's Spherion, installed on the *Oslo* class. SS 576 is mounted on a stalk. Both versions are hoistable. Signal processing: ASPECT, Doppler. The array preforms 64 beams (each 11 × 11 deg). It can transmit on 1–64 beams (ODT). The transmitting beam can be tilted between +10 and −90 deg. Transmission modes: CW short, CW normal, FM-0 (1 pulse), FM-1 (2 pulses), FM-2 (4 pulses), FM-3 (8 pulses), FM-auto. CW pulse length is 0.6–160 msec (depending on range; 60 msec in ODT mode). FM pulse width is 0.6, 2.5, 10, or 40 msec (bandwidth 1.78 kHz in each case). Range settings are 250 and 500 m and 1, 1.5, 2, 4, and 6 km. Power output is 25 W per transducer (total 6.4 kW). The display is a 20-in, high-resolution, color CRT with zoom mode. These sonars can transmit plots and tracks directly to a CDS. Presumably, SS 575/576s are planned for the next-generation Norwegian fast attack craft, now in the concept stage.

SQ3-D/SF *Users:* Finland, Sweden (*Carlskrona, Hugin* class)

SQ3-D *Users:* Norway (*Vidar* class), Sweden (coast guard ships *Gotland* and Kbv 171 class)

SU Series *Users:* Australia (SU-2 in *Flinders*), Ireland (*Eithne, Deirdre* class), United Kingdom ("Island" and *Hecla* classes)

SS105 *Users:* Finland (*Turva* class), Norway (*Norkapp* class)

ST240 *Users:* Finland (Helsinki II class; may be VDS of *Kiisla* class), Sweden (at least 13 ordered). Simrad sold a total of about 12 hull and 20 VDS versions of the SS 240 series; Taiwan may use this sonar in minehunters and in anti-frogman PCLs. Sweden is now refitting the *Hugin* class for ASW, with ST240 Toadfish (VDS search) and 95-kHz SA950 attack (normally minehunting) sonars for Elma FCS (covers a 45- or 60-deg sector with 32 1.7-deg beams). Both feed a single operator console. The Toadfish can dip or be towed at up to 16 kt.

SS242 *Users:* Finland (*Tiira*-class patrol boats)

SS 304 (Spira) *Users:* Finland (*Helsinki, Turunmaa,* and *Kiisla* classes), Sweden (*Göteborg* and *Stockholm* classes [with Salmon])

MSI-70U *Users:* Norway (*Kobben* class)

MSI-90U *Users:* Germany (Type 212 submarine), Norway (*Ula* class)

SWEDEN

The **Spider** FCS for the Tp 45 lightweight torpedo is based on the earlier **GII** tactical plotter (electronic chart table), which is also the basis for the Swedish COOP system. It uses 80386/80387 CPU and math-coprocessor and a Texas Instruments TMS 34010 graphics processor; it has a keyboard, up to 3 trackballs, and a touch-panel that has its own simulated trackball. Maps are shown on a 1024 × 1024–pixel 12-in AC plasma screen. Software is modular: Master and Tactical Plotting Indicator (TPI) in GII, with torpedo fire control (TFC) and the appropriate interface added in Spider. Master manages the internal bus and mass storage (hard and floppy disks). One TFC can handle up to 4 torpedoes simultaneously.

AI-FCS *Users:* Sweden (A 17 class, modernized *Sjöormen* class [reduced version])

NEDP (Swedish **NIBS**) *Users:* Sweden (Mk 1 in *Näcken* class; Mk 2 in *Västergötland* and *Sjöormen* classes)

9SCS Mk 3 *Users:* Sweden (*Gotland* class [version of 9LV Mk 3])

TORCI guides torpedoes less modern than **Tp 45** and **Tp 2000**.

Users: Denmark (*Willemoes* class), Norway (*Snøgg* class), and Sweden (*Spica*-II class)

UNITED KINGDOM

Submarine sonars normally operate passively. A "captain's key" (which must be kept in the captain's sight at all times) has to be inserted in order to ping.

In May 1991 Thorn-EMI announced that under a 1988 demonstration contract it had installed a new type of passive-ranging sonar, using PVF (polyvinylidene fluoride) transducer panels, on a British submarine for trials. The transducers may have been developed for the new **Type 2082** intercept sonar.

Type 2052 became extinct with the decommissioning of the older British nuclear submarines. **Type 2075**, which would have been the first integrated British sonar, was canceled in 1991 when the second batch of *Upholder*s was canceled; the prototype is not being retained (as had been reported) as a technology demonstrator. Presumably, Ferranti abandoned the corresponding **FIS 3**. **Type 2078**, the planned new SSN sonar, has been abandoned (the next SSNs will probably have an Anglo-French suite). Type 2057 and 2080 (Anglo-French LF hull sonar) have been superseded by a new **Type 2087** (integrated hull sonar and active/passive towed array) for the new AAW frigate. Type 2087 is the British-French-Italian successor to SLASM, with French processors and Italian displays. The DUBA 25 planned as the SLASM bow sonar has been dropped in favor of a new LF active/passive sonar. The 2087 designation was chosen to recall the combination of 2057 and 2080.

Type 2090 is an integrated sound-propagation-information system, replacing Type 2039 (submarines) and Types 2015 and 2060 (surface ships). It includes a VLF (5–500 Hz) loss model.

Type 2020 uses the **2001** array but new inboard electronics; it was retrofitted to the *Trafalgar, Spartan,* and *Splendid* and was the original sonar in the remaining *Trafalgar*s. The current upgrade is **2020EX**. The array is a chin strap running back about 20–22 ft from the bow on either side of the submarine; it consists of 80 staves (14 Tonpilz transducers each). Each stave is 6 ft 9 in tall, and the staves are tilted down (for BB and CZ operation) at an angle of 20 deg. Dis-

plays include 3 CRTs (2 in sonar, 1 in the control room) and 2 paper (presumably gram) printers. There is no depression/elevation display.

Type 2027 is a passive ranger using the **2001/2020** array (Swiftsure, *Trafalgar* classes), probably estimating range by measuring the depression/elevation of the same sound received over different paths, then using a sonar-propagation model to find the distant point at which those paths converge.

Some ships with **2031Z** towed arrays have a Logica tracker, which uses image processing techniques to enhance grams, seeking buried tonals (an alternative to ALI methods). The image processor can integrate *along* a line (which may vary in frequency, due to Doppler) rather than along a fixed frequency (as in ALI); it can also follow the line across different beams as the target maneuvers. The host computer uses an array of 16 68000-series chips running in parallel. The tracker automatically detects, tracks, and classifies contacts. It is to be on board all Type 23 frigates. As of June 1992, 8 had been made and 6 were at sea.

Type 2032 uses 15 detuned transducers for LOFAR passive detection; it is analogous to the U.S. linear array wrapped around submarines' bows.

Users: 3 later *Resolution*s, some SSNs

Type 2074 is a further upgrade of the basic system (Phase II Upgrade) first delivered in mid-1990. It is probably a processor upgrade to the existing systems.

Type 2050 was conceived as a wholly new CZ sonar in a bow dome. The transmitter has been badly delayed, so the program is being carried out in two phases. The first, now sometimes called **2016/50**, provides a new receiver. The number of electronic cabinets is cut from 16 to 4, and it requires 1 rather than 2 operators because it autodetects and tracks in active mode. This sonar can track up to 40 targets simultaneously, using linear FM or CW pulses; it also operates passively (in broad- and narrow-band modes) for torpedo detection. A total of 41 were bought or projected (27 ordered as of February 1990). Confusingly, the Type 22 and Type 23 versions of 2016/50 are officially designated **2016H22** and **2016HN**.

The ultimate version has a much larger (lower-frequency) transducer and, therefore, is limited to ships with bow domes. It is expected to operate at 4.5 kHz (but can operate at a still lower frequency); unlike 2016/50, it will reach CZ in the Atlantic. The test ship was HMS *Scylla*, and the first 2 will be on board the Type 23 frigates *Monmouth* and *Iron Duke*. The fully developed Type 2050 should become operational in 1994. Ultimately, it is to equip all Type 22 Batch III (circa 1996) and all Type 23 frigates. Type 22 Batch IIs will receive only 2016/50.

Type 2072 is a broad-band, linear, passive flank array (30 × 3 m [about 3.3 × 98.4 ft]), for the last 2 *Trafalgar* submarines, superseding **2007**. The display incorporates an **FMS 12** narrow-band processor, to detect VLF tonals.

The following are other new sonars. **Type 2076** is the Phase III submarine suite (parallel PD studies by MUSL and Ferranti-Thomson) for the Swiftsure, *Trafalgar,* and projected *Trafalgar* Mk 2 classes; it may also be used to modernize the *Upholder* class. **Type 2079** is probably the bow portion of 2076. **Type 2077** is an HF under-ice navigation sonar in 4 Swiftsures and 7 *Trafalgar*s. **Type 2081** is reportedly an Anglo-French VDS for 3 Type 23 frigates; it is probably an adapted Salmon. This designation was previously associated with an environmental sensor suite, so the VDS may be intended as an experimental device to explore operations in relatively shallow water. The program includes nonacoustic sensors. **Type 2095** is **FLASH** (selection announced in September 1991).

The following is new information on other current sonars: **Type 2041** is the U.S.-supplied **Micro-PUFFS** for the *Upholder* class. **Type 2044** is a reel-able towed array, a modified **2026**, for the *Vanguard* class, being tested on board HMS *Turbulent* (which also has a heavily upgraded **2020 (MODEX)**, presumably the test unit for the *Vanguard* class's bow array). **Type 2046** is the current submarine clip-on array processor, using 2 **FMS 13** narrow-band (3-octave) processors. Display formats include multibeam waterfalls (for detection) and LOFARgrams (for classification). A total of 27 has been ordered. As of May 1991, Ferranti was updating the processor. **Type 2047AC** is on 3 *Resolution* and 4 Swiftsure class. **Types 2048/2049** are minehunting-sonar processors; 2049 was BAe's unsuccessful competitor to 2048. One prototype was delivered to either the Royal Netherlands Navy or the Royal Danish Navy for trials.

Types 162 and **162M**

Users: Canada (as SQS-501), United Kingdom

Type 170B/Type 199 *Users:* Bangladesh (*Umar Farooq*), Canada (as SQS-502), Chile (ex-HMS *Achilles* has 170B; the other *Leander*s have had their Limbos removed but may retain the sonar), India (*Leander*s, *Betwa*, and *Trishul*), Indonesia ("Tribal" class), Iran (Vosper Mk 5 frigates and possibly *Damavand*), Malaysia (*Rahmat* and *Hang Tuah*), New Zealand (*Southland* [sole Type 199]), Pakistan (*Leander* class), United Kingdom (*Leander*-class frigates retaining Limbo mortars)

Type 174/Type 176 *Users:* Argentina (*25 de Mayo*: 176), Bangladesh (*Umar Farooq*, with Type 170), India (*Vikrant*: 176), and Pakistan (*Babur*: 176); in other cases, **PMS 26** replaced Type 174.

Type 177 *Users:* Chile (*Condell* and *Lynch*), Indonesia ("Tribal"-class frigates), and Pakistan (*Babur*)

Type 184P has a solid-state Doppler display. **Type 184S** has a solid-state PPI.

Type 184 and 184M/Graseby G750 Users: Chile ("County" class, *Alm. Williams* class [184M as modernized in 1971–74], *Leander* class [some 184P]), Ecuador (*Leander* class [184P]), India (*Godavari* [G750], 4 *Nilgiri* class [G750], *Trishul* [G750]), New Zealand (*Leander* class [G750]), Pakistan (*Leander* class), United Kingdom (Type 21 and 2 towed-array *Leander*s). The last 2 *Nilgiri*s were completed with French **Spherion** sonars. The Indian APSOH is a Type 184 derivative. APSOH is almost certainly the sonar in the new *Delhi*.

Type 195/2069 *Users:* Australia (Sea King Mk 50), Argentina (7 Italian-built Sea Kings and 2 Lynxes), Canada (31 CH-124s; replaced by AQS-13), Egypt (18 Sea King Mk 47s), India (Sea King Mk 42s), Pakistan (6 Sea King Mk 45s), and the United Kingdom (Sea Kings).

Only the Royal Navy operates the improved Type 2069 (44 purchased for Sea King HAS.6s).

Type 2001 *Users:* United Kingdom (*Resolution* class, all but the last 2 Swiftsure class; in eyebrow position in SSBNs and discarded older SSNs [2001(AA) version], in chin position [2001(BC) version] in modern attack submarines)

Type 2007 *Users:* Australia (Oberon class), Brazil (Oberon class), Canada (Oberon class), Chile (Oberon class), United Kingdom (*Resolution*, Swiftsure, Oberon, first 5 *Trafalgar*s)

A total of 34 **Type 2016**s has been made; it is being replaced by **Type 2016/50** except in *Leander*s.

Users: United Kingdom (*Invincible* class, Type 42, Type 22, Batch III *Leander*s)

Type 2023/2061/2062 *Users:* United Kingdom (SSBNs).

The interim processors are 2061 in the *Resolution* (by Dowty Maritime Ocean Systems) and 2062 in the *Repulse* (by MUSL); both are to be replaced by 2046.

Type 2024 *Users: Superb, Sceptre, Splendid.* Type 2024 includes **2030** and **2035**, the latter to be replaced by **2047.**

Type 2026 is being replaced by **Type 2046.**

Type 2026 Users: Netherlands (*Walrus* class), United Kingdom (*Upholder*, first 5 *Trafalgar* class)

Type 2050 *Users:* New Zealand (*Leander* class [2016/50]), United Kingdom (Type 42 Batch IIs and IIIs [both 2016/50], Type 22 Batch IIs [2016/50], Type 22 Batch IIIs [2050], Type 23s [2050])

Type 2051 is a 2-octave, narrow-band, passive sonar using some bow-array transducers, analogous to **2032.**

Users: Canada (Oberon class), United Kingdom (Oberon class)

Type 2074 *Users: Sovereign, Superb, Sceptre, Spartan, Splendid,* and all *Trafalgar*s

FMS 12 is in **Type 2051, Type 2046,** and **Type 2072.**
FMS 15 was the first Ferranti system to use transputers, to which Ferranti-Thomson is now heavily committed.

Users: New Zealand (FMS 15/2 for *Leander* class's updates, for delivery in 1991), South Korea (8 sets, presumably for Type 209 submarines)

FMS 21 is the beam-forming processor in **Type 2050** sonars.
FMS 52 has a bearing resolution of 3 deg, using steerable transmitter beams; coverage can be expanded to a full 360 deg.

Users: Germany (Type 212 submarines), South Korea (Type 209 submarines)

Plessey PMS 26/27 *Users:* Denmark (*Nils Juel*–class frigates, fishery-protection ship *Beskytterren*, *Daphne*-class ASW craft), Indonesia ("Tribal"-class frigates), Iran (destroyer *Damavand* and Vosper Mk 5 frigates), Ireland (*Eithne* [PMS 26L]), Malaysia (*Rahmat* and *Hang Tuah*), Mexico (2, applications unknown), Nigeria (*Obuma* and Vosper Mk 9 frigates), Turkey (patrol boat *Girne* and probably also AB 25 class), Venezuela (2 *Alm. Clemente*– class corvettes)

Plessey PMS 40 Series *Users:* Denmark (*Hvidbjørnen* class [PMS 46])

The Swedish **Plessey Hydra** contract was awarded in March 1988, and the first arrays were delivered late in 1989.

Users: Sweden (*Sjöormen* [as modernized under FY87–91 plan] and *Västergötland* classes).

These ships have Hydra flank and towed arrays (129-m [423-ft] array on 457-m [1,500-ft] cable). They have their own beamformers but share the **SIP 3** signal processor of the German-supplied **CSU-83** system.

The F2420 version of **DCB** (the upgrade contract let in September 1990) can track 20 targets (probably maintaining TMA solutions) and engage 2. There are 6 operator positions, each with a pair of circular CRTs. In each, the left-hand CRT shows tabular data, the right-hand shows graphics. In a typical installation, a pair of AIO consoles flanks a single CRT showing a geographic (PPI-type) plot of all sonar contacts. To one side is an automatic paper plotter (contact evaluation plot, CEP). To the other is a pair of FCS consoles (using the same hardware as the AIO consoles). Unlike a U.S. system, this one performs its TMA entirely automatically, using Kalman-filtered target-bearing data (it can also exploit **Type 2027**'s passive range data). The AIO graphics display shows target bearing (ownship at center); once an acceptable TMA solution has been found, it is sent to the FCS position. The paper CEP plot is used as a check on the machine-generated TMA solution. The FCS display is generally a PPI showing ownship and target position and weapons position, projected course, and enable point. Weapon presets are displayed on the left-hand CRT. An associated Smiths Navigation and Plotting System (**SNAPS**, a tactical plotter) can keep track of up to 128 targets, their bearings provided by DCB (the AIO-assigned number is input via a keypad at the table). SNAPS provides a line-of-position (LOP) plot. Reliance on automatic TMA (rather than the manual interaction in U.S. submarines) may be a major weakness because the automatic solution can fail if bearing-rate data are imperfect (e.g., because of multipath). Future integrated British submarine sonars may include passive rangers comparable to the U.S. **WAA.**

Users: United Kingdom (Swiftsure, *Trafalgar* classes)

The Trident version of **DCC, DCC(BN),** was superseded by the distributed **SMCS-V,** just as the centralized **CACS** (for Type 23s) was superseded by **SSCS.** Reportedly, **DCH** is disliked because it cannot track multiple targets very effectively. However, in 1991 DCH was used successfully as the towed-array tracker-processor of the Type 22 Batch 2 frigate *Coventry:* it automatically extracted and tracked contacts and performed TMA. Capacity is 30+ contacts. DCH uses 3 multifunction miniconsoles built around **M700 Argus** processors, with high-resolution CRTs, touch-sensitive controls, trackerballs, and numeric keypads. Ferranti won the contract in November 1987 (following about 2 yr of private development as **KAFS**), and the prototype was installed on board HMS *Opossum* during a 1989 refit at Devonport. Ferranti claims that its integrated **FISCS/KAFS** suite can track 60 targets and conduct simultaneous TMA on 35 of them. It can wire-guide torpedoes simultaneously at 2 targets (expandable to 8).

DCC/DCH/KAFS *Users:* Brazil (KAFS: Type 1400 class; installation in *Oberon*s abandoned because of cost in 1989), Chile (KAFS in *Oberon*s, possibly also Type 209s), United Kingdom (DCC: *Upholder* class; DCH: modernized *Oberon*s)

As of 1991, the estimated total cost of 14 **SMCS**s (Outfit DCMs) was £115 million.

Users: United Kingdom (to become the standard submarine system; variants are -V for *Vanguard* class (1993), -T for *Trafalgar* class, -U for *Upholder* class [will probably be canceled], and -S for Swiftsure [may be canceled]).

TIOS-D, with the **FM 1600D** instead of the **1600B** computer, could handle 6 tracks simultaneously.

Users: Brazil (TIOS-B, *Oberon*s), Israel (TIOS-C, Vickers 540 class)

UNITED STATES

Martin Marietta's purchase of GE defense interests included the naval division responsible for BSY-2, SQS-53, and SQQ-89; Martin Marietta is already the major towed-array producer and makes the WAA (BQG-5). **SQY-1** (formerly **SQQ-89I**) was canceled in 1991 as unaffordable within the planned FY94 budget. Existing **SQQ-89**s will be upgraded instead. However, Hughes' work on a battle-force multistatic system (MSS) is proceeding; the proof-of-concept demonstration will be complete by September 1993. **SALFAS** (Stand-Alone LF Active Sonar) is a planned follow-on, a pinger to be towed by a *Spruance*-class destroyer. The experimental ship *Glover* towed a receiving array while using a source (half an SQY-1 planar array) in her sonar dome. In other experiments, the research ship *Trojan* towed a 15-ton EDO source 1–2 CZ from the receiving array (it sank on 29 July 1992). In both cases, the receiver was the Martin Marietta **RMES**, which can accommodate up to 9 linear arrays (they typically used 9 in cruciform arrangement, but also tried a linear arrangement of 3 longer arrays [3 linear arrays end-to-end]). Tests of the SALFAS body showed that it could be located precisely enough to track targets tactically.

MSS differs from LFA (see above) in energy management. To detect relatively nearby targets, it uses 2- and 4-sec waveforms (sweep and tone) every 30 sec–1 min, with quarter- or half-scale keying for more range (LFA uses long pulses over many minutes). In quarter-scale, the sonar pings every minute, using 4 unique ping types (the cycle repeats every 4 min, so the sonar gets 4 looks in 4 min). Like LFA, MSS uses CW pulses for rate and HFM for range, as well as linear FM (LFM) and FM; it also uses short single tones (FSK) for Doppler and range (a succession of tones at different frequencies).

The French **FLASH** wet end combined with a Hughes dry end (using a **UYS-2** processor) won the **ALFS** competition in December 1991. By September 1992 a Bendix protest had been rejected. However, Congress demanded a review to see whether a simpler sonar may not be preferable. The cable was originally to have been 2,500 ft long, but in mid-1992 it was reduced to the 1,500 ft of the **AQS-13F** that ALFS replaces. Hughes is currently marketing its ALFS as AADS (Active Acoustic Detection System).

Current R&D initiatives include Full-Spectrum Signal Processing (i.e., processing over more than the frequencies typically examined by LOFAR and its derivatives) and a new **High-Gain Array**, possibly a potential **FDS** replacement (tested in the Atlantic during FY91). A Litton team, including Bendix Oceanics, successfully tested **AOTA** (All-Optical Towed Array) in March 1991. An Acoustic Collection Technology (ACT) project develops a family of A-size acoustic buoys to replace the current **SSQ-57**, to obtain signature data. Unlike LOFAR/DIFAR, signature collection demands a broad frequency range but sufficient precision to locate frequency lines (which will later be used to detect and classify submarines).

During trials in the USS *Stump*, the EDM model of **SQS-53C** regularly demonstrated second CZ capability. In many cases the ship was farther from a contact than other ASW ships but still made the first contact. She also regularly detected targets at ownship speeds that were formerly considered transit speeds. Shallow-water operations at extended ranges were demonstrated using the sonar's improved waveforms and frequency agility. The digital transmitter provides waveforms better suited than their predecessors to discriminate background from a target in shallow (high-reverberation) water. Earlier analog transmitter systems tend to suffer from alignment problems and offer only a very few waveform options.

For operations in the Persian Gulf, **SQS-56** was modified by Raytheon (in cooperation with the U.S. Navy Underwater Sound Laboratory) for obstacle (e.g., mine) avoidance (as **Kingfisher**). This modification uses a special PCC (polarity coincidence correlator, a right–left correlator) receiver (as detector) and an auxiliary display console, extracting 3 adjacent beams, which the operator can see (in A-scan form) and hear. It turned out that identification was largely by ear. The beams are still 10 × 16 deg, so they cannot easily distinguish between small objects. The Sound Lab added an electronic range recorder, showing up to 80 pings on 7 beams, to give a picture of the area ahead of the ship. It draws a horizontal line—in effect, an MTI line. The 3 special beams are then trained on the suspicious object. This was the system used by the USS *Nichols*. Similar modifications were considered (and probably tested) for **SQS-53** and **AQS-13** sonars. Kingfisher was developed in parallel with the installation of Plessey mirror sonars in bulbous bows strapped onto the forefeet of some U.S. frigates.

In May 1991 the navy abandoned its opposition to the **AVP** (Acoustic Video Processor), succumbing to congressional pressure. AVP and **UYS-2 (EMSP)** will be inserted into existing **SQQ-89** systems; the program is tentatively designated **AIDS** (AVP Improved Display System). There had been a question as to whether AVP could emulate existing **UYQ-21**–series stroker displays. Because AIDS is an engineering change proposal (ECP), it does not require major milestone reviews.

A new **CMS** (Contact Management System) is being developed for Aegis ships and *Spruance*-class destroyers, to improve **SQQ-89**'s tactical performance.

Loral Librascope is developing **SEPACS** (Submarine Engagement Automated Planning and Control System) under a 4-yr DARPA contract; it is broadly analogous to GE's **SOAS**. SEPACS uses AI techniques to recommend appropriate defensive and offensive actions. The program includes development of proof-of-concept automated torpedo attack and defense. An operational version could be available in 1996. This work is based partly on Loral's earlier ARMOR (Attack Response Mission-Oriented Reasoner) decision aid.

The heavily censored version of the FY92/93 program (released in February 1991) mentions 4 main nonacoustic projects: (i) **NA-1/16** (Clipper Shale), which seems to be a submarine wake-sensing system. At-sea tests with an improved Clipper Shale were scheduled for April–June 1993, with a preliminary design review of the advanced sensor system in September 1993. (ii) **NA-4**, a high-powered laser (technical review expected in October 1993), presumably a blue-green LIDAR similar in concept to the mine-detecting **Magic Lantern**. (iii) **NA-17** (Spotlight), whose name suggests bioluminescence. (iv) **NA-20**, which is for the SH-60B helicopter (to be developed for fixed-wing aircraft as well). The nonacoustic **STSS** (Submarine Tactical Sensor System), tested at sea in FY91–92, may be intended to counter possible foreign airborne nonacoustic systems. **TSUNAMI** is a congressionally mandated CIA program (reportedly entirely unsuccessful) to study nonacoustic detection. Congress feared that the navy would resist technologies that might nullify its sea-based deterrent; it wanted an entirely independent audit of nonacoustic technology. Total FY91 nonacoustic funding was $13.9 million, and estimated FY92 and FY93 funding was $26.2 and $58.9 million, respectively.

MARS (Magnetic Array Sensor) is a joint program with Norway to develop a fiber-optic magnetic bottom sensor, suitable for shallow-water underwater surveillance. This will be the first such sensor array to be evaluated as an ASW surveillance sensor. Funding began in FY88, and the concept exploration/demonstration and validation MoU was signed on 18 January 1991 by the United States and on 7 March 1991 by Norway. The array was installed in FY92, at which time it was estimated that 3 yr of tests would be required.

Beginning in FY88, the United States has funded work on a MAD buoy. An MoU with France (i.e., presumably with Crouzet) to develop and test a MAD buoy carrying an NMR sensor was signed on 4 December 1990.

AQS-13 *Users:* Brazil (Sea Kings), Canada (CH-124 Sea Kings), Greece (AB 212s), Iran (Sea Kings and AB 212s), Italy (Sea Kings and AB 212s), Japan (Sea Kings, as HQS-101), Peru (Sea Kings and AB 212s), Spain (Sea Kings and AB 212s; -13Bs being replaced by -13Fs in Sea Kings), Turkey (AB 212s), United States (SH-3 Sea Kings and SH-60F Carrier Inner Zone Helicopters [AQS-13F]), Venezuela (9 AB 212s, 3 delivered in 1990)

Non-NATO versions of **AQS-18** generally lack sonobuoy-processing capability.

Users: Germany (Sea Kings and Lynxes), Greece (S-70C[M]s), Italy, Japan (SH-60Js), Portugal (Lynxes), South Korea (Super Lynxes), Spain, Taiwan (S-70s). The Greek version omits all sonobuoy capacity (receiver, on-top indicator, mission tape recorder).

BQG-4 (PUFFS) *Users:* Brazil (Guppy III class), Greece (Guppy III class), Turkey (*Tang* and Guppy III classes)

BQQ-5/6 is the standard U.S. submarine sonar, superseding **BQQ-2**. In variants prior to -5E, the (V)1 version is for the *Los Angeles* class, (V)2 is for the *Sturgeon*, and (V)3 is for the *Permit* class (now retired). BQQ-5C is the current version. BQQ-5D adds the thin-line **TB-23** array. BQQ-5E is the newest version, using the **TB-29** array; E(V)3 is in *Los Angeles*–class submarines. E(V)4 is in *Ohio*-class submarines, superseding **BQQ-6** (and integrated with **CCS Mk 2**). BQQ-6 equips most *Ohio*-class submarines. Planned improvements to BQQ-5 for the 688I class include the LF adjunct (LFA), **TAP** (towed-array processor), ICDC (color display, dual towed-array processing [**TB-16** and **-29**], and full Spatial Vernier Processing [SVP] for the TB-29). TB-29 is to be tested at sea late in 1993. The wide-aperture array (WAA) is too heavy to install on board most *Los Angeles*–class submarines. A much lighter fiber-optic version began lake tests in March 1993.

BQQ-9 is Rockwell's broad-band towed-array processor for the long **BQR-15** (SPALT 9080) array, as long as TB-23 (the latter failed its tests, hence the **SPALT** applied to the earlier array). BQQ-9 uses an expanded **UYK-20** and a **UYS-1** signal processor. The next 5 *Ohio*s have the less-expensive **BQR-23** (and hence lack broad-band capability). Rockwell is negotiating to provide a **Towed Array Broadband Interim Display Unit** using the new FFT technology developed for **FAAS**.

BQR-2B *Users:* Brazil (Guppy II, Guppy III), Greece (Guppy IIA, III), Taiwan (Guppy II), Turkey (*Tang*, Guppy IIA, Guppy III)

BQR-3 *Users:* Peru (*Iquique*)

BQR-7 *Users:* United States (*James Madison* class)

BQR-15 *Users:* United States (*James Madison* class)

BQR-20A/22/22A *Users:* Greece (*Adams* class: signal processor for SQQ-23 sonar), United Kingdom (as Type 2030), United States (*Los Angeles-*, *Sturgeon-*, *Permit-*, *James Madison*-class submarines; *Adams*, *Mahan*, *Leahy*, *Los Angeles* classes [as SQQ-23 signal processor).

BQR-22A(EC15), the latest version, is used in ASWOCs serving P-3C Beartrap squadrons.

BQR-21 *Users:* United States (*James Madison* class)

BQR-23 *Users:* United Kingdom (as Type 2035) and United States (*Los Angeles*, *Sturgeon*, *Permit*, *James Madison*, *Ohio* classes)

BQS-4 *Users:* Brazil (Guppy II, Guppy III), Greece (Guppy IIA, III), Taiwan (Guppy II), Turkey (*Tang*, Guppy IIA, Guppy III), United States (*James Madison* class)

BQS-14 *Users:* United States (*Sturgeon* class's under-ice sonar)

BQS-15 *Users:* United States (*Los Angeles* class's under-ice sonar)

BQS-24 is descended from a **BQS-14** modified for short-pulse multibeam operation, with separate transmit and receive arrays.

Users: United States (MIDAS for late *Los Angeles*, *Seawolf*, *Ohio* classes)

BSY-1 *Users:* United States (*Los Angeles* class [from SSN-751]).

Compared to BQQ-5, BSY-1's major improvements are a digital transmitter (SADS, Submarine Active Detection System) providing much greater beam agility and also more flexible waveforms (much as in **SQS-53C**) and an integrated control system for the vertical launcher. BSY-1 does *not* include the submarine combat control system, so it is not being replaced by **CCS Mk 2** (which simply replaces the separate **CCS** Mk 1).

BSY-2 *Users:* United States (*Seawolf* class)

QBE-3 *Users:* Turkey (83-ft Coast Guard class)

QCU-2 was supplied to foreign navies on board ex-U.S. 95-ft coast guard cutters and their PGM derivatives. It may also survive on board other ex-U.S. warships. The Spanish P311 class had their U.S.-supplied **QCU-2** and **QHB-A** sonars removed.

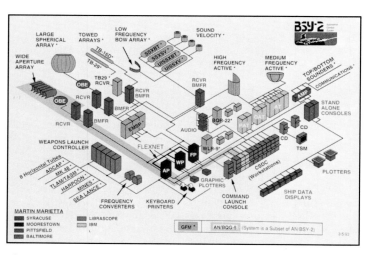

The BSY-2 system layout. Note the separate large spherical array, MF active array, and LF bow array. The large spherical array is the receiver for the MF active array; the pair correspond to the earlier BQS-6 and -13. The LF bow array, which is wrapped around the large spherical array, corresponds to the earlier BQR-7 and to the hull array of BQQ-5. BQR-22 is a separate signal processor. BMFRs are beam-formers; RCVRs are receivers. Ps denote processors: AP for active, FP for Fourier (narrow-band), WP for wide-band. ATs are active transmitters. (Martin Marietta)

Users: Italy (*Albatros*-class corvettes), Portugal (*João Coutinho* class)

SQQ-23 are all modified with **DE 1191**.

Users: Greece (*Adams* class), United States (*Adams*, *Leahy*, *Mahan*, *Long Beach* classes). Deactivated in the *Bainbridge* in 1993.

SQQ-28 *Users:* United States (*Burke*, *Ticonderoga*, *Spruance*, *Perry* classes)

SQQ-89 *Users:* United States (*Arleigh Burke*, *Ticonderoga*, *Spruance*, *Perry* classes). As of February 1991, the following *Perry*-class frigates were not expected to receive SQQ-89: FFG-10, -24, -27, -31, -34, -37, -51, -52, and -54. The following ships had already been fitted: FFG-8, -28, -29, -32, -38, -55–57.

SQR-17 *Users:* United States (*Ticonderoga* [CG-47 and -48 only], *Belknap*, *Kidd*, *Knox* classes; also used by Mobile Inshore Underwater Warfare units); presumably transferred to Egypt, Greece, Taiwan, and Turkey on board *Knox*-class frigates

SQR-18 *Users:* Greece (*Knox* class), Netherlands (2 units), Japan (6 units, but reported in 8 *Asagiri* class), Taiwan (*Knox* class), United States (*Knox* and some *Perry* class)

SQR-19 *Users:* Spain (*Perry* class), United States (*Ticonderoga*, *Arleigh Burke*, *Spruance*, *Perry* classes)

SQS-4 Series *Users:* Brazil (SQS-31 and -44 in FRAM II destroyers), Chile (SQS-40 in FRAM II destroyers), Greece (SQS-4 and -29 in FRAM II and *Fletcher*-class destroyers), Iran (SQS-29 in FRAM II destroyers), Italy (SQS-39 in *Impavido*), South Korea (SQS-29 series in FRAM II destroyers, SQS-4 in the surviving *Fletcher*), and Turkey (SQS-29 in *Berk* class, FRAM II *Sumner*-class destroyers). SQS-4 sonars in the Taiwanese navy have been replaced by Krupp-Atlas **DSQS-21**s.

SQS-10/11 *Users:* Canada (*St. Laurent* and Improved *St. Laurent* classes), Japan (*Azuma* [may have been removed])

SQS-17 was probably installed on board exported World War II–era PCs modernized in the 1960s with fixed Mk 32 tubes. It was on board Greek *Cannon*-class frigates, now discarded.

Users: Chile (PC 1638 class), France (*Cdt. Rivière* class and *Ouragan*), Iran (PF 103–class corvettes), Philippines (*Cannon*-class escorts and *Auk*-class corvettes), Portugal (*Cdt. Rivière* class), Taiwan (*Auk*-class corvettes), Thailand (PF 103–class corvettes), Turkey (PC 1638 and PGM 71 classes), Uruguay (*Cdt. Rivière* class)

SQS-23 *Users:* Australia (*Adams* class: SQS-23F [with DE 1191]), Brazil (2 FRAM Is), Colombia (*Boyaca*), Greece (SQS-23D on 6 FRAM Is [3 plus option on 3 DE 1191s]), Italy (*Vittorio Veneto* [SQS-23G]), Japan (SQS-23 in *Amatsukaze*, *Takatsuki* class, same as OQS-3], and auxiliaries *Akizuki* and *Teruzuki*; as OQS-3 in *Haruna* and *Chikugo* classes), Mexico (2 FRAM Is), Pakistan (SQS-23D in 4 FRAM Is [with DE 1191]), South Korea (5 FRAM Is and 2 FRAM IIs [8 DE 1191s bought, not clear whether all refitted]), Taiwan (12 FRAM Is, 2 *Gearing* FRAM IIs [12 DE 1191s bought]), and Turkey (2 ex–*Carpenter*-class ships, 7 FRAM Is, 1 *Gearing* FRAM II)

SQS-26 *Users:* Brazil (*Garcia* class [AXR]), Egypt (*Knox* class [CX]), Greece (*Knox* class [CX]), Pakistan (*Brooke*, *Garcia* classes [AXR in both]), Taiwan (*Knox* class [CX]), Turkey (*Knox* class [CX]), United States (*California* [CX], *Belknap* class [except name ship: CX], *Knox* class [CX])

SQS-35 was deactivated in U.S. ships in 1992 but may be reactivated in some of the export *Knox* class.

Users: Japan (*Shirane* class, *Takatsuki*-class destroyers, and *Minegumo*; 5 *Chikugo*-class escorts), Spain (*Baleares* class)

SQS-36 *Users:* Japan (submarines, as SQS-36J); removed from Italian *Pietro de Cristofaro* class (which also had SQS-35 IVDS)

SQS-38 *Users:* United States (*Hamilton* class)

An **SQS-53A/B** product-improvement program (PI) replaces the **-53B** receiver subsection with **-53C** digital components. Engineering Change 16 to SQS-53A is intended for CG-47–55 and the DDG-993 class. As of late 1992, the only -53Cs in service were on board the USS *Stump*, *Arleigh Burke*, and *Anzio*.

Users: United States (*Virginia* [-53A], *Ticonderoga* [-53B], *Arleigh Burke* [-53C], *Belknap* [-53A], *Spruance* [-53B], *Kidd* [-53A]; -53B is being retrofitted to existing *Spruance-* and *Ticonderoga*-class ships; -53C will be retrofitted to *Spruance*s and *Ticonderoga*s)

SQS-54 *Users:* United States (*Truxtun* only)

SQS-56/DE 1160 *Users:* Australia (SQS-56 in *Perry* class), Greece (4 DE 1160s in MEKOs), Italy (4 DE 1160s in *Lupo*s, 1 DE 1160LF in *Garibaldi*), Morocco (1 DE 1160 in *Descubierta*), Saudi Arabia (7 SQS-56s in 4 PCGs), Spain (6 DE 1160s in *Descubierta* class, 5 DE 1160LFs in *Baleares* class in place of SQS-23, and 6 SQS-56SPs in *Perry* class), Taiwan (6 SQS-56s in *Perry* class), Thailand (DE 1160Cs in 2 Type 25T frigates), and United States (51 SQS-56s in *Perry* class). Raytheon's

DE 1160/SQS-56 Improvement Program (IP) adds Kingfisher and improves shallow-water performance by superposing several different types of signal detectors.

DE 1164 *Users:* Greece (4 VDSs for MEKO 200s), Italy (Hull/VDS in *Maestrale* class, 2 DE 1164LFs in *Mimbelli* class, DE 1164 hull/VDS in *Alpino* class [replacing SQS-43])

DE 1167 *Users:* Egypt (LF/VDS in *Descubierta* class), Italy (8 DE 1167s in *Minerva* class; probably also in the 2 modernized *Audace* class, replacing EDO 610), Japan (4 DE 1167LFs, presumably for the MSA), and South Korea (26 DE 1167s for *Po Hang* class, some replacing PHS-32s; may also be in 2 *Ulsans*). *Minerva* sonars were the first to be made in Italy.

EDO 610 Series *Users:* Brazil (610E in all Vosper Mk 10 frigates; ships also have EDO 700E VDS), Peru (*Lupo* class), Venezuela (*Lupo* class)

EDO 700/701/PDE-700 *Users:* Brazil (EDO 701 in Vosper Thornycroft frigates), Indonesia (*Van Speijk* class, as PDE-700), Japan (presumably MSA)

EDO 780 Series (780, 786, 796, 795, 7860, 7960, 7950) *Users:* Indonesia (*Claud Jones* class [786, replacing SQS-42]), Israel (780 on 4 Sa'ar II class, 796 in *Eilat* class), South Korea (786 may be on some corvettes)

EDO 900/910 *Users:* Germany (Type 206 submarines)

EDO 1102/1105 *Users:* Peru (*Abtao* class)

EDO 1110 *Users:* probably Israel (Vickers 540 submarines)

Micro-PUFFS/PASRAN/BQG-501 *Users:* Australia (*Oberon*s), Canada (*Oberon*s), United Kingdom (*Upholder*s, as Type 2041)

For the **LAMPS III** upgrades, Block I adds provision for IR jammers, missile detectors, and door guns; helicopters have 3 stores stations. A fourth station is planned on the starboard side. The pylons are currently qualified to 1,000 lb, but Sikorsky has proposed that LAMPS and SH-60F helicopters carry **SLAM** missiles (which require 1,500-lb pylons). The GPS receiver, sonobuoy receivers, and other new equipment require 2 additional dual 1553B buses. There is an ECP to add a FLIR, which could be used to identify surface contacts at night (the planned ISAR would have much the same purpose). Three different FLIRs were installed on LAMPS IIIs during Desert Storm: the Hughes **AAQ-16** (Seahawk of HSL-48), the Texas Instruments **AAQ-17** (HSL-42), and the GEC **30X Night Owl** (HSL-46). These FLIRs were hung from the starboard weapons station, but they could be moved to the forward data-link antenna, which is little used. Texas Instruments is offering a modified AAQ-17, now carried by air force AC-130s, using a new 240 × 1– element focal-plane array, with a maximum FoV of 30 × 40 deg, plus medium and narrow fields; it operates in the 8–12-micron band.

Block II is entering FSED. It adds an APS-137 ISAR, a tactical data transfer (TDT) system, and provision for an integrated self-defense (ISD) package. It is not clear whether the planned dipping sonar (**ALFS**) has been deleted from the planned upgrade. The current **ASQ-81** MAD will presumably be replaced by **ASQ-208**. The Block II specification was released in FY91. The schedule slipped 2 quarters in FY91 because of the delay in ALFS selection. FY91 funding was increased to add upgraded ESM to Block II. Integration is to be completed in FY95, with tests and corrections of deficiencies through FY97.

The LAMPS I ships are the *Ticonderoga*s (CG-47–48 only), *Belknap*, *Kidd*, *Knox*, and some *Perry* class (reserve ships). LAMPS I will probably soon be retired to the reserves. The first 2 *Ticonderoga*s cannot easily be modified to operate the larger and heavier LAMPS III helicopter (they would be too top heavy). The *Belknap*s have never been well-adapted to operating helicopters.

LAMPS transfers: Egypt (5), Taiwan (12). Argentina has asked for 8 SH-2F helicopters.

In October 1992 Congress ordered the **P-3C Update IV** program terminated, on the ground that deep-water ASW was becoming less important with the end of the Cold War. At that time only 28 update kits (a total of 109 was planned) were included in the current 5-yr plan. The navy then decided to bring all 247 existing P-3Cs up to Update III standard. According to early FY94/95 budget statements, 68 aircraft will be fitted for better surface surveillance, with the **APS-137(V)** radars and presumably the OTH-T ESM planned for Update IV; they may also receive **OASIS** OTH-T hardware and software. Spanish plans to modernize 5 ex-Norwegian P-3Bs to Update III standard have been dropped. In February 1992 the program's budget was cut in half. It seemed likely that modernization would be limited to off-the-shelf equipment, as in the upgrade of Portuguese

P-3Ps by Lockheed and OGMA. The emphasis may be on improving the **APS-80** radar for surface surveillance.

Loral acquired Librascope Corp. in December 1991. It had already acquired another U.S. ASW manufacturer, Goodyear; to some extent the former Goodyear (Akron) and Librascope divisions compete with each other. Loral Librascope has just upgraded Canadian **SFCS Mk I**s, integrating the new **Triton** (Type 2051) sonar with the FCS and replacing the existing plotter with a plasma panel.

In **CCS Mk 2**, the submarine's **BQQ-5** sonar detects targets, passing their bearings (and ranges, in active mode) to the CCS, which manages the tracks and conducts multiple automatic TMA. Like earlier combat systems CCS Mk 2 uses a star architecture, with a central **UYK-43** interfaced to 4 **Mk 130**s. System software is carried in the UYK-43, then applications are down-loaded to individual workstations. The consoles can also connect to an Ethernet LAN, and they have VME backplanes. Each console carries its own shadow data base (the main base is carried in the UYK-43). With the appearance of the workstations, the UYK-43 is reduced largely to I/O tasks; it becomes the system bottleneck. The next step is a fully distributed system on an LAN. CCS Mk 2 performs all the functions of BSY-2 and can use some of the same software.

The **Kanaris** upgrades of the Greek Type 209/1100 submarines (*Glavkos, Nereus, Triton, Proteus*) are complete; work is about to begin on the slightly larger Type 209/1200s (*Amfrititi, Okeanos, Pontos, Poseidon*). Kanaris can engage 4 targets simultaneously. The associated **Sea Lion** ESM is used to help engage OTH targets with **Harpoon**.

Users: Egypt (modified form to modernize Romeo class), Greece (Type 209s). The Egyptian Romeo-class submarines being modernized under an FMS contract have German Atlas sonars supplied via Loral. Loral Akron bought out Tacoma Boat as system integrator of the Romeo modernization. As of mid-1992, Egypt hoped to buy new submarines with U.S. assistance. The main combat-system competitors are Loral Akron and Loral Librascope (SFCS).

ACS (for the Australian *Collins* class) incorporates **SFCS Mk III**. It is credited with automatically detecting 1,000 targets, initiating tracks on 200, and automatically localizing (conducting automatic TMA) on 25. A recent brochure compares it with systems at sea, which can track only 8–12 targets and which are limited to 2–4 octaves for analysis (the *Collins* system can handle 50). Its sonar produces 1+ Mbit/sec of sonar data, compared to about 100 kbit/sec for earlier systems; signal processing is 1,500+ MOPS (each equivalent to 1 multiplication and 1 addition), compared to fewer than 500 for earlier ones; and its data-processing power is 100+ MIPS (38 CPUs), compared to fewer than 10 MIPS (2–5 CPUs) in earlier systems. System memory exceeds 130 Mbyte (compared to fewer than 8 Mbyte in systems currently at sea). Perhaps most impressively, ACS/**Scylla** divides the area around itself into about 1 million resolution cells (beam/amplitude bin/band), compared with 64 in a typical existing system. These figures combine the capabilities of the French-supplied Scylla sonar with those of the ACS itself.

SUBICS (Loral Librascope 900 series) is a developed **SFCS Mk III**, incorporating the sensor-data converter (combat-data manager) and weapons-data manager (switcher for torpedo-tube inputs) developed for Mk II. The passive ranger and intercept sonars have a separate processor. The combat data manager forms contact (track) files for the workstations. The workstations are used for combat navigation, tactical planning, integrated surveillance (presumably monitoring the combat-data manager), and monitoring/fault location. Each incorporates a pair of 19-in CRTs (1,280 × 1,024 pixels, refresh rate 60 Hz). Singer-Librascope (now a division of Loral) proposed a 4-workstation version (Type 901) for projected Egyptian submarines. This SUBICS configuration probably uses Atlas sonars (medium-range passive cylinder, long-range flank array, passive ranger, and active cylinder). The system can maintain 68 target tracks and can engage 4 targets simultaneously (3 wire-guided torpedoes and a salvo of missiles [presumably Sub-Harpoons]).

Loral is currently marketing a surface-ship version of SUBICS, competing with EDO's integrated ASW combat system. A **Mk 114** upgrade would feed sonar and ASW helicopter data into a combat data manager (as in the submarine system), which would communicate with a standard Librascope multifunction workstation via a data bus. The station would also receive data-link information. It would embody a contact-management system, including automatic contact correlation and TMA. Tactical decision aids would include screen planning, maneuvering tools, missile strike planning, OTH-missile targeting, and navigation improvements. The workstation would determine target position, course, and speed, and transmit that data to a modified Mk 53 attack console (it would replace the display and analysis sections of the Mk 53). The system would control ASROC and torpedo launchers, presetting and launching weapons. Loral also offers a more ambitious version, in which the combat data manager would accept air- and surface-sensor data (from search and fire-control radars, EO sensors, and surface-search radars). In this case the LAN would include extra workstations (the company's drawing shows both a 1-screen and a 2-screen station) and a command plot. It would control missiles and guns. Both versions of the Surface Ship Integrated Combat Control System appear to be intended for the modernization of *Knox*-class frigates transferred abroad.

SFCS Mk I *Users:* Australia (*Oberon* class), Canada (*Oberon* class)

SFCS Mk I+ *Users:* India (Type 209 class)

SFCS Mk II *Users:* Israel (*Gal*-class submarines; canceled after production, now in arbitration; may be installed later)

SFCS Mk III *Users:* Australia (*Collins* class, element of Rockwell ACS)

Mk 101 Mod 20 is the FCS of the stricken U.S. *Barbel* class, which may eventually be transferred abroad.

Users: Turkey (*Tang* class [Mod 18])

Mk 105 *Users:* Brazil (FRAM II destroyers), Chile (FRAM II destroyers and PC 1638 class), Greece (FRAM II, *Sumner, Cannon* classes), Indonesia (*Claud Jones* class), Iran (*Sumner,* PF 103 classes), Philippines (*Cannon* class), South Korea (FRAM II destroyers), Taiwan (FRAM II–, *Sumner-, Fletcher*-class destroyers and destroyer *Lai Yang,* destroyer escorts and APDs and *Auk* class), Thailand (PF 103, *Auk* classes), Turkey (FRAM II destroyers and *Yücetepe, Berk,* PC 1638 classes)

Mk 106 *Users:* Brazil (Guppy [Mod 14]) Greece (Mod 17 on ex–SS-365, Mod 20 on ex–SS-487), Peru (probably *Dos de Mayo* class), Turkey (Mod 14 in ex–SS-344, -346; Mod 17 on ex–SS-394, -402, -410, -418, -421), Taiwan (Mod 16 on ex–SS-426, -478)

Mk 111 *Users:* Brazil (*Mariz E. Barros*), Greece (ex–DDG-15), Pakistan (*Tughril*), Taiwan (*Shao Yang, Lai Yang* [with Mk 105 Mod 10], *Kai Yang*), Turkey (*Yücetepe* [with Mk 105], *M. Fevzi Cakmak,* United States (*Long Beach, Bainbridge, Mahan, Adams* classes [but DDG-16–24 were completed with Mk 114 instead])

Mk 113 *Users:* United States (*James Madison*–class SSBNs)

Mk 114 *Users:* Brazil (FRAM I destroyers, *Garcia* class), Greece (*Adams* class and FRAM I destroyers), Italy (*Vittorio Veneto* [Mod 21]), Japan (ASROC ships), Mexico (FRAM I destroyers), Pakistan (FRAM I destroyers, *Brooke, Garcia* classes), South Korea (FRAM I destroyers), Taiwan (FRAM I destroyers, *Knox* class), Turkey (FRAM I destroyers), United States (*California* [Mod 27], *Truxtun* [Mod 12], *Belknap* [except CG-26; Mod 25 replacing Mod 9 in CG-27, Mod 26 replacing Mod 12 in CG-28–34], *Leahy* [Mod 24], *Adams* [DDG-16–24], *Knox* classes)

Mk 116 *Users:* United States (Mod 0 in *Spruance* class, being replaced; Mod 1 in *Virginia* class; Mod 2 in *Kidd* class; Mod 3 in *Belknap* (only); Mod 4 in *Ticonderoga* class; Mod 5 in *Spruance* class as modernized with SQQ-89; Mod 6 in VLS *Ticonderoga* class [CG-65 and later]; Mod 7 in *Arleigh Burke* and later *Ticonderoga* class [CG-65 and later] and also in modernized *Spruance*s with UYK-43B computers; Mod 8 in modernized VLS *Ticonderoga* class [with UYK-43B computers]; Mod 9 is the non-VLS version of Mod 8; Mod 10 is the non-VLS version of Mod 7)

When combined with Tomahawk control, **Mk 117** becomes **CCS Mk 1**; in the *Los Angeles* class, CCS Mk 1 is being replaced by **CCS Mk 2**.

Users: *Permit, Sturgeon, Los Angeles* classes

Mk 118 *Users:* *Ohio* class; being replaced by CCS Mk 2

Mk 309 Fire-Control Panel *Users:* Australia (*Perry* class [Mod 1]), Saudi Arabia (*Badr* class [Mod 0]), Spain (*Perry* class [Mod 1]), Taiwan (*Perry* class [Mod 1]), United States (*Perry* class [Mod 1], *Hamilton* class [Mod 0])

FFISTS software includes Automatic TMA for Tactical Commanders (ATTAC).

Users: all *Knox* class have either FFISTS 1 (FF-1078, -1079, -1084, -1085, -1089, -1090, -1095, -1097) or FFISTS 2. It appears that ships transferred to Taiwan (FF-1073, -1086, -1087) retained their FFISTS.

SUBMARINE PERISCOPES

FRANCE

PIVAIR (Type K') for French SSNs is the former **Type K** with a fairing. **L,** for SSBNs, omits the sextant (SSBNs have a separate **MRA-2** star-tracker periscope). The prototype of a new **M92** periscope for the *Le Triomphant* class, together with a nonpenetrating **Opto-Radar Mast,** was to be delivered by SAGEM at the end of 1992. This mast combines L and MRA-2 functions in one mast. These masts operate in both visible and IR spectra. Magnifications: $1.5\times$, $3\times$, $6\times$, $12\times$. FoV: 36, 18, 9, 4.5 deg. All are 2-axis, LOS-stabilized, using a gyro in the periscope head (hence the ability to handle $12\times$ magnification, which is quite unusual in a periscope). PIVAIR uses a micromonitor in the ocular box (displayed in the eyepieces); it can also feed a remote monitor. There are 2 automatic modes: quick-look (1 revolution in 5 sec, with the panoramic picture retained in memory), and panoramic search. Both can be in IR. The mast can also function manually, with a real picture in manual control. Typically, in IR mode the mast can detect a patrol airplane or helicopter at 10 nm. The SAT-made **CT-10** IR camera operates at 8–12 microns, using a 96-element HgCdTe linear array scanned across the FoV. However, it is being replaced by an **IRCCD** camera (288 × 4 elements). French SSNs still use the old **ST5** attack periscope; SSBNs have no attack periscope, only the search types and the star-trackers.

SMS (Search Mast SAGEM) is an export nonpenetrating mast based on PIVAIR. Sea trials began in July 1992 on board the *Daphne*-class submarine *Psyche.* The TV LOS elevates between +80 and −10 deg, and the IR LOS between +30 and −10 deg. There are 4 TV FoVs (32/16/8/4 deg) and 1 (9 deg) or 2 (13/5 deg) IR FoVs. The TV camera is a black-and-white CCD (color is optional) operating at 0.4–1.1 microns; the IR camera operates at 8–12 microns, using a closed-cycle cooler. The entire mast is covered in RAM; the sensor head is 320 mm in diameter and weighs 280 kg. Claimed MTBF is 1,250 hr (3,600 for TV only); MTTR is 30 min (inboard)/8 hr (outboard).

SAGEM is currently manufacturing a nonpenetrating IR periscope, **IMS-1,** for Danish *Narhvalen*-class submarines. This mast has a 2-axis, stabilized (LOS), cooled IR head (external diameter 208 mm, including RAM [200 mm bare]). The sensor pod weighs 180 kg. The body of the mast has a diameter of 235 mm. The cooled IR head operates at 8–12 microns, with elevation limits of +30/−9 deg. There are 2 options: (i) 1 FoV, with a **SPRITE** scanning camera (focal length 234 mm, FoV 6.4 × 4.3 deg) or an IR CCD camera (FoV 5.4 deg for search, 7 × 5.4 deg for imaging); or (ii) 2 FoVs, both using IR CCD cameras (focal length 154 mm, 3.8 × 3 deg, and focal length 58 mm, 10.2 × 8 deg).

The standard operating mode is manual scan, like that of a conventional periscope. Alternatively, the operator can program the mast for a quick scan of the horizon (in less than 5 sec at constant elevation), after which it retracts. The horizon scan's picture is recorded for replay submerged. Another alternative is panoramic surveillance at 15–20 rpm. The monitor displays a processed IR picture, threats being displayed as alarm spots (i.e., the mast acts as an IRST). The mast can be used at submerged speeds of up to 12 kt.

OMS is an optoradar mast, gyrostabilized in 1 (rather than 2) axis, carrying both TV (elevation +50/−20 deg) and IR (elevation +50/−20 deg) cameras, with 2 FoVs (32 and 4 deg) for TV and 1 FoV (9 deg) for IR. It also carries an X-band (9.2–9.5 GHz) navigational radar, with an angular accuracy of 2.5 deg. The sensor pod is 370 mm in diameter (weight 450 kg); MTBF is 1,000 hr (3,600 for TV only). The LOS-stabilized radar has 4 range scales (4–32 km), acquires targets automatically, and can track up to 5 of them. OMS is now in production for the newest French submarines, presumably the *Améthyste* class.

As of October 1992, SAGEM claimed that it had delivered more than 25 periscopes since 1980, beginning with French navy contracts for PIVAIR for SSNs and SSBNs. The Spanish *Galerna* (*Agosta*) class is being modernized with optronic periscopes, presumably SAGEM models.

GERMANY

All periscopes are made by Carl Zeiss. **ASR C 13, C 14,** and **C 15** (respectively, 6, 3, and 3 units), now out of service, were the earliest German types. **STAS C 3** (30 made) was the periscope of the German Type 205 and 207 classes. **NLSR C 8** (1 unit) was a prototype. **NLSR C 12** (5 units) was in the Italian *Toti* class; **NLSR C 13** (2 units) was in the experimental German submarine *Bauer.* **AS C 17** (24 units) was the attack periscope of the German Type 206; **NAVS** (22 units) was the navigational periscope of the same type. Both AS C 17 and NAVS were special small-boat types with fixed oculars (to limit space taken up in the boat); NAVS was in the snorkel mast. **AS C**

18 and **BS 19** were, respectively, the attack and search (*beobachtung*) periscopes of the early Type 209 export submarine (21 of each were made). Magnifications: 1.5×, 6×; FoV 32 × 24 deg (vertical) for 1.5×. These periscopes were overhauled when the Colombian Type 209 submarines were refitted in 1991 at HDW. However, the Venezuelan *Sábalo* had her AS C 18 replaced by an **AS 40** (she retained her **BS 19**).

AS 40 and **BS 40** (12 and 11 units, respectively) introduced electrical control for Type 209 boats. They are power rotated, and the prism is electrically elevated. Magnification and other functions are controlled electrically, by push buttons. Magnifications are 1.5× and 6×; FoV is 36 × 28 deg (vertical) for 1.5×. The ocular box shows true and relative bearing, elevation angle, target height, and target range. Prism elevation limits are normally +75/−15 deg (the upper limit is reduced to +60 deg when an antenna is fitted).

Later AS 40 and BS 40 periscopes (12 and 11 made, respectively) are stabilized (by dynamically tuned gyroscopes, sensors, and computers) in 2 axes in LOS; they are installed in some Type 209s and in the Taiwanese *Sea Dragon* class. These periscopes are currently advertised as the **40 Stab** series. These periscopes are modular in design; in most cases search and attack periscopes are identical.

The newest types are the optronic **SERO 14 (search) and SERO 15** (attack), prototypes of which were delivered in 1982 and 1983; 6 pairs were produced (beginning in 1986) for the Norwegian *Ula* class. They will equip the German Type 212. SERO is for *sehrohr*, periscope in German. SERO 14 incorporates an IR (8–12 micron, using a 180-element U.S. modular detector) camera with 2 FoVs. The optical element has a zoom lens (1.5–12×, with stops at 1.5×, 6×, and 12×). SERO 15 has optical (stadimeter, or double-image) and laser range-finders (the latter use a Neodymium-YAG laser). These periscopes are in the German Type 212 and the Norwegian *Ula* classes.

UNITED KINGDOM

CK043 search and **CH093** attack periscopes will equip the Australian *Collins* class. The **CH085** attack periscope equips the British *Upholder* class. **CH093** has an image intensifier and LLLTV rather than the thermal imager of the earlier CH085; both CH093's image intensification and optical channels are stabilized. Both CH085 and CH093 are 254 mm in diameter; the corresponding 190-mm attack periscope is **CH088**.

UNITED STATES

The RFP for the operational nonpenetrating (photonics) mast was issued in January 1992. At this time Kollmorgen's mast, funded by DARPA, is on board the test submarine *Memphis*. The navy maintains that it is nonoperational, but Kollmorgen is offering it for sale. As of July 1992, the photonics mast teams (for *Seawolf*, the new Centurion, and modernized *Los Angeles*–class submarines) were Kollmorgen with Riva Calzoni, Librascope, and Unisys; General Electric with Zeiss; Raytheon with Plessey Naval Systems and SAGEM; Rockwell with Barr & Stroud, McTaggert Scott, and Watkins-Johnson; and Sperry Marine with Martin Marietta (both Electronic Systems and Aero and Naval Systems Divisions) and Texas Instruments. Sperry Marine has been making U.S. periscopes in competition with Kollmorgen.

AIRBORNE SIGNAL PROCESSORS AND SONOBUOYS

AUSTRALIA

Barra operates in narrow-band (frequency-azimuth [FRAZ]) or broadband (power-bearing) modes; modes include 12-beam (8 LOFAR channels) and 4-beam (quadrant, 4 LOFAR channels).

AWA's new fast-time acoustic processor (**Shearwater/FTAAS**) for postmission analysis can replay mission tapes at up to 32 times real-time speed and can process 32 channels simultaneously. The basic 8-channel module is mounted in a 19-in rack (a 32-channel system requires 4 such modules). Capacity: 32 DIFAR or 8 Barra or 8 FRAZ or 8 power-bearing or 32 sound velocity (BT). Displays: LOFARgrams, FRAZ, power-bearing (as in Barra), histograms (ALI, for example), and Delta Y Plots. AWA's earlier FTAAS, in RAAF service since 1990, operates at 8 times real time (16 channels).

CANADA

Canadian destroyers carry sonobuoy processors for "DesJez" (Destroyer Jezebel, i.e., LOFAR) operation. This is *not* the U.S. LAMPS technique; the destroyer monitors sonobuoys directly, e.g., in a helicopter-laid barrier. Helicopters cannot transmit acoustic data directly to destroyers; they generally operate more independently. TRUMP-class destroyers carry 1 sonobuoy/attack (Bravo) and 1 dipping sonar (Alfa) Sea King (the "City" class carry only a Bravo). Standard practice is to use the dipper to direct the attacking helicopter.

The only current sonobuoys are **SSQ-525A** (out of service at the end of 1993), **-527B** (out of service at the end of 1994), **-536**, and **-53D**. **SSQ-53D(1)**, made by Hermes, is more sensitive than SSQ-53D. An improved **-53D(2)** entered production late in 1992. **Icebuoy** is an experimental, ice-penetrating, A-size, passive buoy using a thermochemical process to embed itself 8–10 in into the ice. **UYS-502** is no longer in service.

UYS-503 is the sonobuoy processor in the "City" and TRUMP classes, but it is *not* the sonar processor of the **SQS-510** and **SQR-501** sonars. It *is* the processor of the dipping sonar in the Canadian version of the new EH-101 (the wet end is the French **FLASH**). The current (**V)5** can process 32 DIFAR buoys, can simultaneously process buoys and a dipping sonar, and has acoustic fusion algorithms that combine passive tracking with other acoustic data. Besides LOFAR (narrow-band) analysis, it can detect and track on the basis of broad-band and transient signals. A new color display reduces operator workload.

UYS-503 Users: Australia (S70), Canada, Japan (probably in the SH-60J), Sweden (sonobuoy craft), and the United States (SH-2G). It may also be used by Norway.

FRANCE

The French navy expects to use the **Lynx** successor, **NH 90**, in a LAMPS-like mode, using a repackaged **SADANG 1C** processor on board the ship. It will carry up to 50 buoys, using an 8-buoy launcher (8 A- or 16 F/G-size buoys). It will receive and retransmit signals from 16 of them simultaneously. NH 90 must be able to handle **VLAD** and **Barra** buoys and **HARP** arrays (see the U.K. entry below). These are digital rather than analog buoys, and SADANG will have to be modified to handle them (a digital buoy requires more memory in the processor). It can accommodate the beam-former required by Barra (and especially by HARP). The helicopter will also carry an active sonar with 1,500 ft of cable and a reliable range of 10,000 yd, and with multiple-target automatic-tracking capability and a MAD.

The French navy currently uses A-size only for active buoys. LOFAR buoys are all F- (A/3-) size. As yet there is no interest in array buoys (**VLAD, SVLA**, etc). However, a DIFAR buoy is reported under development. The **DSTA-3** active buoy is no longer in service; the last ones were used in the Bay of Biscay in 1991. It was replaced by **TSM 8030/8050**. Production of the TSM 8030 DICASS buoy began late in 1986. TSM 8050 is a range-only buoy. **DSTV 4L**'s production ended early in 1989. **DSTV 4M** is the corresponding F-size LOFAR buoy. **DSTV 4N** is the corresponding ambient-noise buoy. These buoys operate from a few Hz up to 2,400 Hz. DSTV 4L was tested in 1968 (procurement began in 1970); DSTV 4M's procurement began in 1986. Development of the successor **DSTV 7** began in 1985; it entered service in 1989. DSTV 7 versions correspond to radio channels: **7B** uses the first 33 of 99, **7C** uses channels 34–66, **7D** uses channels 67–99, and **7E** is a true 99-channel buoy. A total of 20,000 DSTV 4s were made, plus 5,000 Italian **MSR-810s** (license-made DSTV 4Ls). About 3,000 DSTV 7s were made between 1989 and March 1992, at a reported unit price of $8,500.

SADANG is the French navy's sonobuoy processor; **Lamparo** (TSM 8220) is the export equivalent. Each is built around a data bus carrying 1–4 **TSM 8230** signal processors, each with its own VHF buoy receiver, multiple data processors, multiple video processors, and multiple RAM-ROM; also an I/O port and system-management block. There is also a UHF controller/sonobuoy localizer. The system connects to the 1553B aircraft bus. It provides both a CRT and an optional graphics recorder for hard copy. Lamparo, for medium or heavy ASW helicopters, was announced in 1986; it processes 4 or 8 buoys. SADANG (1989) introduced a new 8-buoy processor. Versions are **SADANG 1000**, for light MPA (**TSM 8221/8222**, 1 operator, 8/16/32 buoys), and **SADANG 2000**, for heavy MPA (**TSM 8200/8202/8203**, with 2 operators, 16/32/64 buoys). The version of SADANG in the Atlantique 2 is designated **DSAX 1** (TSM 8210).

The contract for 2 prototypes and 2 FSED models of **SADANG 2001C** was to be completed by July 1993. A prototype was delivered for integration into an Atlantique 2 in September 1992; it will replace the existing **SADANG 1A**. **C** indicates the new generation, with a VME bus, Texas Instruments DSP (signal processor), and 68000-family CPUs. **1C** compresses the 5 ATR-size processor boxes of 1A into 1 (50 × 30 × 25 cm, 25 kg). It can handle up to 16 LOFAR or 8 DIFAR buoys; 2 processors can be ganged together in a single console, so 1 console can handle 32 LOFAR (2 can handle 64). The Lamparo equivalent is 1001C. Thomson Sintra is bidding SADANG 1C for the RAAF P-3 upgrade.

TSM 8200 (SECBAT) *Users:* France (Atlantic Mk 1 as modernized, replacing AQA-5)

TSM 8210 (DSAX 1) *Users:* France (Atlantique Mk 2)

TSM 8220 (Lamparo) *Users:* Brazil (EMB 111s and probably modernized S-2s), Chile (EMB 111s and probably AS.365F helicopters), China (PRC) (as part of HS-312 in Zhi-8 helicopter), Netherlands (Lynxes), Saudi Arabia (AS.365F); probably other AS.365F and AS-332F Super Pumas

SOUTH KOREA

In July 1992 it was reported that South Korea wanted Motorola's sonobuoy technology as part of P-3 offsets; Gold Star Precision would make the buoys.

UNITED KINGDOM

Work on a pair of new buoys, to staff requirements ST(A)902 (passive) and ST(A)903 (active), has been suspended pending a decision on a Nimrod replacement. An experimental active sonobuoy (**EAS**), developed by the Active Sonar Group at ARE Portland, was announced at the 1991 UDT conference. Under development since about 1986, this sonobuoy incorporates 10 LF bender-transmitters. It indicates the current state of active buoy technology. EAS could almost certainly be packaged in A-size, but not in the much smaller sizes of current British passive buoys. The buoy stores a total of 64 sec of sonar waveforms at 1 kHz; modes include CW, FM, and pseudorandom noise. Its battery suffices for 200 ping-sec (which can probably be upgraded to 500), operating at 300 Hz–10 kHz at a source level of 210 dB. As of 1991, it was being used as the HARP source; given its LF, ranges of tens of km could be achieved. Radio command range is 8 km.

Recent brochures show the frequency range of **SSQ-906** extended down to 2 Hz rather than 4 Hz. That is so low that, in theory, the buoy can pick up blade rate directly, rather than via DEMON processing (2 Hz is 120 rpm).

AQS-902 (LAPADS)/**AQS-920 Series**/**ASN-920 Series** *Users:* Greece (LAPADS in 14 HU-16Bs), India (902C: Sea Kings), Italy (update of Atlantic Mk 1 with AQS-902C), Netherlands (probably 902B in 2 Fokker Maritime Enforcers), Nigeria (probably 902B in 2 Fokker Maritime Enforcers), Pakistan (projected Atlantic Mk 1 modernization with AQS-902), Peru (probably 902B in 1 Fokker Maritime Enforcer), Philippines (probably 902B in 3 Fokker Maritime Enforcers), Spain (probably 902B in 3 Fokker Maritime Enforcers), Sweden (6 AQS-924s ordered in 1984 for patrol boats, AQS-928 ordered for similar installation in 1990, plus probably 3 AQS-902s on aircraft), Taiwan (32 Turbo-Tracker conversions with AQS-902F), Turkey (projected Turbo-Tracker conversion of 18 S-2Es with AQS-902F), United Kingdom (902D: Sea King HAS.2 and HAS.5 helicopters; being replaced by 902G-DS in HAS.6 version)

The acoustic localization plot (ALP) is an unusual feature: it replaces the separate tactical plot of many airborne systems so that one piece of equipment does the job normally reserved for two. **AQS-928G/SM**, a surface-ship variant based on Swedish experience with floating sonobuoys, incorporates the ALP. In each case, the display is a 12-in CRT. The associated **ASN-920** series is presumably built around the ALP, with a separate tactical display unit showing a ground-stabilized tactical plot. It displays the sonobuoy pattern, contact track, weapon engagement zones, etc.

The follow-on **AQS-903/930** series includes an ALP. **GEMMA**, the GEC Avionics MPA Mission Avionics, is built around AQS-903/930. In April 1992 GEC Avionics and Boeing agreed to share ASW technologies for the U.S. and British patrol-airplane-replacement programs. At the time it appeared that GEC and Dassault would offer GEMMA, perhaps with some Update IV infusions, for the Nimrod replacement. **ASN-990** is probably an export designation for GEMMA. The only current user is the British EH-101 Merlin.

The **HARP** (Horizontal Array Random Position) program is analogous to the U.S. **STRAP** program, described below. Unlike the fully passive STRAP, HARP is a bistatic system, using 16 LF buoys, including 3 or 4 pingers, plus 1 DIFAR buoy (containing a compass) to orient the entire array. Intended as the next-generation patrol-airplane sonobuoy system, to staff requirement SRA(SA)-902, HARP is covered by an MoU signed in 1989, BURLAP (British-U.S. Random LF Array Program).

AQS-901 *Users:* Australia (P-3C: 60 bought), United Kingdom (Nimrod: 83 bought). Production figures suggest 2 per airplane plus spares. This is probably the processor in the RNZAF P-3Ks.

UNITED STATES

The **STRAP** (Sonobuoy Thinned Random Array Processor) concept was tested in May 1991 on board P-3Cs. This is a coherent, rather than the usual incoherent, combination of buoy signals, so the system can form beams in real time (the buoys in effect form a single sensor). The acoustic signals from the buoys are combined into beams *before* they are processed to detect the frequency lines representing submarines. Since the elements of the array move randomly, the system must not only calculate the appropriate weighting coefficient (for each element in a given beam), it must also change that weighting over time. The interferometer under the airplane does not suffice for buoy location because beam-forming requires high precision (and because the buoys of the array are far closer together than those used for incoherent signal processing). STRAP uses 2 randomly thinned sonobuoy arrays, each comprising 20 **SSQ-53D** and 4 **PAEL** (Prototype Array Electronic Location) buoys. Sonobuoy outputs combine raw acoustic data with retransmitted timing chirps from the PAEL buoys. The timing delays are used to calculate buoy position relative to the PAEL buoys. Directly transmitted PAEL chirps locate the two STRAP arrays relative to each other.

The 2 Hewlett-Packard **HP 3565** front-end processors in the P-3 digitally separate the chirps from the raw acoustic data (arriving at up to 70 kbyte/sec), and they calculate conventional or adaptive beam-forming coefficients. The buoys differ in depth, so STRAP presumably forms 3D beams. Acoustic data is processed by 3 AP Labs VME mainframes, each containing a **SPARC 1E** main processor (12.5 MIPS, 1.5 FLOPS) and a SPARC 1E graphics processor. Nine SKY Computer Warrior digital signal-processing boards and 2 Mercury Computer **MC860** boards are distributed among the 3 VME stations, for an additional 234 MFLOPS of throughput. In addition to 320 Mbyte of Sun and VME memory, the system has 3.54 Gbyte of disk capacity and 4.4 Gbytes of 8-mm video cassette. The workstations and 3 operator positions, each with a 19-in color monitor using Update IV symbology, are connected by an Ethernet LAN. Targets are automatically detected (by ALI). The paired arrays locate and track targets by cross-fixes. System output is a PPI-type display showing targets.

Rockwell's shore-based postmission-analysis processor (**FAAS**) for French navy Atlantic MPAs is part of a new family of processors, which will include a towed-array processor for later *Ohio*-class submarines (see **BQQ-9**). The family uses standard common hardware: spectrum analyzer, beam-former, acoustic display. It can be used with a variety of sensor inputs, such as towed arrays and sonobuoys, using unique Rockwell-developed software for each role. Hardware is modified commercial types (VME architecture), for low cost. Operators have single-CRT workstations, with keyboards, plasma touch-screens, and trackballs. In a 1990 brochure, Rockwell emphasized a **Torpedo Alert System** (TAS) version. Presumably, FAAS is the unit Rockwell was advertising in 1992 as the **Sonobuoy Fast-Time Analyzer**, details of which follow. The analyzer handles 16 LOFAR or 8 DIFAR buoys (32 bands) at up to 16 times real time, using 4k-point complex or 8k-point real FFTs. It stores 1 Gbyte of acoustic data (expandable to 4 Gbyte), operating at 1.6 GFLOPS. Beside standard narrow-band and DEMON analysis, it can use short integration times (down to 0.08 sec) to detect transients and intercept active sonar emissions; short-time integration is also needed for HYFIX processing (hyperbolic fixing of a signal). Thus it can accept acoustic data at up to 20-kHz bandwidth, with selectable vernier bands up to 10 kHz. Measurement functions include 20 line trackers (ALI) and a harmonic family detector. The system uses standard VME cards and a pair of 19-in CRTs, typically stacked vertically. As of 1992, Rockwell has delivered acoustic processors to the Australian, Dutch, French, U.K., and U.S. navies. These include special-purpose, multichannel, acoustic signal processors, such as the U.S. BQQ-9. Rockwell's **UQX-5** is the standard U.S. postmission analysis machine, in ASWOCs and in carrier ASWMs.

Scientific Atlanta's new **FTAS** (Fast-Time Analyzer) will replace Rockwell's UQX-5 in U.S. service; the first 2 units were shipped in December 1992. At that time no formal (AN-series) nomenclature had been assigned. FTAS uses commercial hardware to achieve a processing speed of 8.5 GFLOPS. It accepts up to 32 analog (acoustic) channels, processing in 64 channels at 1, 2, 4, 8, or 16 times real time. A typical FTAS has a pair of large acoustic monitors, flanked by tactical display workstations (using VAX 3100s with desktop monitors, QWERTY keyboards, and trackballs). Processing options are LOFAR, DIFAR, DEMON, ANODE, Cardioid, Null Steer (to null out noise), and XBT. The system can display up to 16 LOFAR grams (frequency-time), bearing-frequency, or ALI, either separately or in split-screen format. Alternatively, it can show absolute sound-power level (which is used in **Julie** systems and also to measure submarine signatures). Up to 1,024 independent vernier bands (up to 16 per channel) can be presented. The standard monitor shows up to 1,600 lines of data in waterfall (LOFAR) format. On-screen aids include Doppler, Lloyd's Mirror, CPA, and harmonic cursors (to identify the higher harmonics of a detected line, as a means of confirmation). These systems convert up to 419,000 samples/channel of acoustic data to digital (12-bit) data; the cutoff frequency can be set at any of 5 values. Signal processing is at up to 8.5 GFLOPS, with a 32-bit (1,500-dB) dynamic range. Disk storage amounts to 8 hr of 64-channel data. A typical system has 1 or 2 25-in (20 × 15–in) monitors, each with 2,000 × 2,000 pixels (refresh rate 60 Hz) and up to 32 thermographic printers (to print out LOFARgrams).

Users of earlier Scientific Atlanta fast analyzers (particularly the GD-850 series): French, German, Italian, Japanese, Portuguese, and Swedish navies, for postmission (sonobuoy) analysis and, in some cases, to process towed-array data

Sonobuoy purchases, as of February 1992:

	FY91	FY92	FY93
SSQ-53	216,736	—	—
SSQ-62	19,865	10,947	—
SSQ-77 VLAD	—	97,325	124,800

ERAPS (SSQ-75) reportedly operates at 4.1 or 4.6 kHz. Contractor demonstration tests began in FY91, and as of early 1991, low-rate production was scheduled for FY93 and full-rate production for 1995 after a 1994 technical and operational evaluation. In shallow water the same ERAPS buoy can be used as a sort of super-DICASS, exploiting direct-path and duct propagation.

The current **SSQ-77B** has 2 selectable sonar beams, for better signal-to-noise performance. **SSQ-77A** was produced from 1982 through January 1990; SSQ-77B entered production in April 1992. Sparton currently advertises **SSQ-41N**, an extended-frequency version of the **SSQ-41B** LOFAR buoy (5 Hz– 2.4 kHz rather than 10 Hz–20 kHz). The company currently offers dwarf (12-in) and G-size (16.5-in) versions of **SSQ-53B**; the latter is **SSQ-53C**. Magnavox's latest version of SSQ-53D is **-53D (Low Noise)**. **TSS** and **LCS** have both been canceled.

AQA-1 *Users:* only Iran (P-3F: to process active buoys)

AQA-3/4 *Users:* Argentina (6 S-2Es), Brazil (possibly in 8 S-2Es), Italy (8 S-2Fs), Peru (9 S-2Es), South Korea (36 S-2Es), Spain (2 P-3As), Thailand (S-2Fs, being retired due to structural problems), Turkey (18 S-2Es or more, subject to Turbo-Tracker modernization), Uruguay (S-2Gs), and Venezuela (8 S-2Es). The Argentine aircraft have been fitted with tactical computers, but apparently not with new sonobuoy processors, since 1982.

AQA-5 *Users:* Germany (Atlantics), Iran (P-3Fs), Pakistan (Atlantics)

AQA-7(V) *Users:* Brazil (plans to buy 10 P-3A/Bs), Greece (plans to lease 4 P-3Bs, buy 2 P-3As), Japan (70 P-3Cs), Morocco (plans to buy 3 P-3A/Bs), Netherlands (13 P-3C Update II.5s with AQA-7(V)8/9), Norway (P-3Cs), Pakistan (3 P-3Cs with AQA-7(V)11D, embargoed), Portugal (6 P-3Ps), Spain (7 P-3A/Bs), Turkey (plans to buy 10 P-3As), United States (AQA-7(V)11/12 in 108 P-3C Update I/II/II.5s and in 88 P-3A/Bs). All P-3A/B/Ps have **TACNAVMOD**. Japan plans to modify 40 existing AQA-7– equipped P-3Cs (30 with AQA-7(V)7/8, 10 with newer versions) to Update III standard, with **UYS-1** (see below). Thus far no AQA-7s have been sold to update other aircraft (some were on board S-2s, but they were removed when the aircraft were transferred). However, France is reported interested in AQA-7(V)18/19 (formerly **IPADS**) because of its very good broad-band performance. A lightweight, miniaturized version of AQA-7(V) will be offered to the RAAF in its P-3C modernization competition. The

only P-3s currently on offer without either AQA-7 or UYS-1 are intended for surface surveillance: P-3A TACNAVMODs for Thailand and UP-3As for Chile. The latter have no acoustic processors at all; the Chileans plan to develop new communications/radar suites of their own.

AQA-7(V)18/19 successfully completed its technical evaluation at Patuxent River in April 1991. Reportedly, its broad-band capability is much superior to that of the UYS-1, which replaced AQA-7.

UYS-1 *Users:* Japan (30 P-3C Update IIIs), Norway (6 P-3C Update IIIs, more planned), Saudi Arabia (plans 6 P-3C Update IIIs), South Korea (planned for 8 P-3C Update IIIs), United States (140 P-3C Update IIIs)

UYS-2 demonstrated its full 54-channel (full-band DIFAR) processing capability in April 1991, exceeding the threshold by 2/3 during integration testing of a P-3C Update IV program at Bell Laboratories. This was the **SEM-E** version with 7 arithmetic processors, 6 global memory SEMs, and a 64-channel input signal conditioner.

Users: United States (SURTASS, BSY-2 for submarines, SQQ-89; would have been in Update IV P-3s, but the program has died). Projected foreign sales of Update IV were 12 to Germany, 15 to Italy, and 25 to the United Kingdom.

MISSILES

Ikara has been retired by the RAN, although launchers remain in place (they would have cost more to remove than to leave). Reportedly, it has been out of service in Brazil for some years. Australia no longer supports it logistically, so almost certainly the Royal New Zealand Navy has also retired it.

CHINA (PRC)

CY-1 is the missile in 6-cell, fixed-train (but elevatable) launchers on board the 2 new "Jangwei"-class frigates, abaft their forward 100-mm guns. The individual tubes are loaded separately, by crane, with the mounting elevated. This weapon is also in the box launchers (originally for **C801** missiles) on board modified Luda-class destroyers. CY-1 is intended to engage submarines operating at 150–300-m depth at speeds of up to 33 kt. It carries a lightweight homing torpedo, probably **A244**.

UNITED STATES

Efforts to revive the **Sea Lance** (UUM-125A) program, canceled in 1989, failed. **Tomahawk/Mk 50** has not attracted navy funding.

The **VLA** (RUM-139A) launch canister is Mk 15. Revised dimensions: 14.1 × 192.6 in (maximum fin span 27.4 in); weight 1,409 lb in warshot configuration (1,371 for exercise shot). The missile is controlled by a digital autopilot (DAC), which uses a thrust vector control (TVC) to pitch it over into the appropriate elevation (initially 40 deg, then 29 deg). Trajectory height is minimized to avoid errors caused by high-altitude wind. As in conventional **ASROC**, thrust cut-off and then airframe separation control range. Compared to conventional ASROC, VLA is more maneuverable (thanks to its autopilot). Loral, the manufacturer, proposes that it be substituted for standard ASROC (in standard launchers), and the extra capability be used to cover arcs currently masked. The launcher itself would no longer have to be stabilized. Alternatively, VLA could be launched directly from its VLS canister, like **Harpoon**. Maneuverability would be such that only a small sector directly abaft the ship would be masked. Procurement: 300 authorized in FY89, 40 requested for FY94; 60 ordered for Japan. VLA was approved for production late in March 1993.

The total production of **ASROC** (RUR-5A), 1960–70, was about 12,000. The nuclear version was withdrawn under the 1991 Bush-Yeltsin agreement.

Users: Brazil (FRAM I destroyers, *Garcia*-class frigates), Germany (*Adams* class), Greece (*Adams* and *Knox* classes and FRAM I destroyers), Italy (*Vittorio Veneto*, from ASTER launcher), Japan (*Kongo* [VLA], *Asagiri, Hatakaze, Hatsuyuki, Tachikaze, Amatsukaze, Takatsuki, Yamagumo, Minegumo, Abukuma, Chikugo* classes), Mexico (FRAM I destroyers), Pakistan (FRAM I destroyers), South Korea (FRAM I destroyers), Taiwan (FRAM I destroyers, *Knox* class), Turkey (*Carpenter* class, FRAM I destroyers, *Knox* class), United States (*California, Virginia, Truxtun, Long Beach, Belknap, Leahy, Ticonderoga* [VLA], *Arleigh Burke* [VLA], *Spruance* [some VLA], *Kidd, Adams, Mahan, Knox* classes)

TORPEDOES

Murène and **A-290** have been replaced by a Franco-Italian **Impact** (EU 90) project. The U.S. **Mk 15** is probably extinct (the last platform is the Mexican *Cuitlahuac*, which is unlikely to carry any).

CHINA (PRC)

Chinese torpedoes are designated in a **Yu** (fish) series. **Yu-1** is a straight-running thermal torpedo for torpedo boats, originally planned as a license-produced version of a Soviet oxygen torpedo. The Chinese decided to substitute compressed-air propulsion for safety. Production was ordered in 1962, but a prototype assembled in 1966 failed its tests (it ran deep, its power output was unstable, and the motor tended to flame out). These problems were solved only in March 1970, the torpedo being type-classified in September 1971. Dimensions: 533 mm × 7.8 m, 3.5 km/50 kt or 9 km/39 kt; warhead 400 kg.

Yu-2 is a copy of the old Russian 45-cm **RAT-52** rocket torpedo; it is the only standoff weapon the H-5 (Il-28 copy) can carry. RAT-52s were imported in 1954, and in 1958 the Chinese had complete drawings. The first 2 were completed in July 1960, but they failed in air drops. Then all Soviet aid was withdrawn, and the project was suspended. It was revived in 1964, and type-classified in June 1971 (it remains in service). To indicate its capabilities: a 1957 Soviet manual estimated that 8 RAT-52 hits would sink a *Midway*-class carrier or an *Iowa*-class battleship; 1 to 2 would suffice for a *Gearing*-class destroyer. The weapon was quite inaccurate, however: it would take 58 shots (dropped from 7,000 m [about 23,000 ft]) to make 8 hits.

Yu-3, a submarine-launched electric torpedo, was the PRC's first ASW weapon, a tremendous step beyond the earlier straight-runners. Work began in 1965, in conjunction with the new SSN design (a water-slug torpedo-ejection system was designed specifically for the new submarine). Components were first tested in a lake in the fall of 1969, and small-scale production began in 1971. However, the homing system was far from ready. The first version used a mechanically scanned transducer, which could not overcome much flow noise, so the torpedo had to slow near its target. A beam preformed seeker solved the problem. Yu-3 was approved for production in 1984. The next year work began on the improved **Chinese Sturgeon II**, which was successfully tested in January 1991.

Yu-4 is a submarine-launched antiship homing torpedo. Work began in 1958, when a Soviet electric acoustic torpedo was bought. Manuals were translated, and work began on the electric motor, but in 1963 priority shifted to the simpler Yu-1. Work resumed in 1966, and 5 pilot models were completed in 1971. They were too slow. Two parallel programs began in 1976. The Dong Feng Institute Factory proposed an all-passive weapon, which became **Yu-4A**. The Northwest (Xi Bei) Industrial University proposed a passive/active weapon, **Yu-4B**. Both were approved for production in February 1984.

Yu-5 may be an improved passive acoustic homer. A big Otto-fueled wire-guided torpedo was tested but not adopted.

FRANCE

French submarines are currently armed with the **F17 Mod 2** for offensive action, with **L5 Mod 3** for self-defense against attacking submarines, and with the **SM 39 Exocet** missile.

As of mid-1992, DCN was experimenting with a laser-radar TDD operating in the 0.45–0.55-micron (blue-green) "window." It uses a pair of 50-cm "eyes" (emitter and backscatter receiver); it can probably also detect a wake. The range is 0.8–10 m, the FoV is 11 × 11 deg (2 × 2 m at 5 m). Transverse resolution is 50 cm, image rate is 100 Hz (13 × 13 pixels at 17 kHz).

E14/15 *Users:* Pakistan (*Daphne* class), Portugal (*Daphne* class), South Africa (*Daphne* class: E15)

E18 *Users:* Spain (*Agosta* class)

   F17 Mod 2 entered service in 1989.

F17 Users: France, Pakistan (*Agosta* class), Spain (*Agosta* and *Daphne* classes)

L3 *Users:* France (*Duperré, Cdt. Rivière* class, all from triple 550-mm tubes; can be fired by A-69 class), Portugal (*Cdt. Rivière* class), Uruguay (*Cdt. Rivière* class)

L4 *Users:* France (as Malafon payload)

L5 *Users:* Belgium (*Wielingen*-class frigates), France (submarines, also surface ships: *Cassard, Georges Leygues, Tourville, Suffren, Aconit* classes, all from catapults; can be fired by A-69 class), Libya (from Super-Frélon helicopters), Pakistan (*Daphne* class), South Africa (*Daphne* class), Spain (*Agosta* and *Daphne* classes)

GERMANY

German 2-way wire-guided torpedoes transmit raw acoustic data back to the launching platform. Others, such as later versions of **Mk 48**, transmit back processed data, i.e., acoustics as seen by the torpedo's sonar processor.

The *Hamburg, Thetis* (now Greek), and *Köln* (now Turkish) classes are all equipped with 21-in torpedo tubes, probably initially for U.S.-supplied **Mk 37**s and British **Mk 8**s. It is unlikely that they can launch modern German wire-guided weapons.

A few **DM2A3** *Seehecht* (Seahake) exist for trials; this torpedo will enter service in 1994–95. Series production began in 1989. This torpedo adds a new Selenia homing head and low-noise skewed propellers to **DM2A1**. Attitude is controlled by a new course-attitude reference gyro system, which uses pressure cells to maintain depth. It also has a new wire-guidance system. The torpedo uses distributed 16-bit processors (e.g., separate ones for guidance, fuzing, attitude control, and data communications), with a total program length of about 520 kbyte.

DM2A4 is still in the study stage. Germany, France, and Italy signed an MoU concerning heavy-torpedo propulsion; as of July 1992, the participants were STN, DCN Saint-Tropez, and Whitehead. The candidates are (i) electrical system, using an HF permanent magnet motor (based on the Murène Compact Power Plant [CPP]) or an LF motor by GEC-Alsthom (powered by aluminum silver-oxide batteries; (ii) Battelle closed-cycle system, using a Wankel engine; and (iii) lithium heat-exchanger and turbine from STN. The choice is due in 1994. The export version of DM2A4 will be Seahake Mod 1.

DM1 *Seeschlange Users:* Germany (Type 205 and 206 submarines)

DM2A1 Seal/SST-3/SST-4 *Users:* Argentina (Type 209s and TR-1700s, with the U.S. NT-37C; *Intrepida* class), Chile (Type 209s and possibly *Oberon*s), Colombia (Type 209s), Ecuador (Type 209), Germany (DM2A1 in Type 205 and 206 submarines and Type 143 fast attack boats; their tubes are to be deleted in favor of RAM missiles and mine rails), Greece (Combattante II and III classes), Peru (Type 209), Turkey (Type 209 and *Kartal*-class attack boats), Venezuela (Type 209). Brazil and possibly Chile switched to **Tigerfish** for their submarines, and Indonesia adopted the dual-purpose **SUT**. This torpedo was probably also supplied to Denmark and Norway, which ultimately adopted the Swedish **Tp 61**.

   SST-4 is impact-fuzed, but Mod 1 has a proximity fuze for under-the-keel shots.

SUT *Users:* Chile (Type 209s), Greece (Type 209s), India (Type 1500s), Indonesia (for both Type 209 submarines and *Hajar Dewantara* and PB 57–class surface ships), South Korea (for new Type 209s), Taiwan (200 ordered in 1988 from Indonesia for *Sea Dragon* class)

INTERNATIONAL

Thomson-CSF and MUSL plan a joint study of advanced torpedo-sensor technology. European torpedo makers (other than MUSL) plan a joint heavyweight-torpedo propulsion project.

Eurotorp's **Impact** (EU 90) retains the **Murène** seeker (but without the flank transducers originally planned) and **Mangouste** acoustic computer (now with 68020 CPUs). The guidance computer uses X86 series CPU chips. Software has been written jointly by Whitehead and DCN, and the after end is mainly **A-290**. The motor is supplied by the German torpedo maker, STN; Eurotorp claims that it is the first variable-speed (rather than 2- or 3-speed) electric torpedo motor (speed is software controlled). Eurotorp sees Impact as far more than a simple combination of Murène and A-290, but rather the product of a careful rethink of both (hence, e.g., the elimination of the flank arrays in the nose—the new acoustic head provided better beam definition). Performance will roughly match that planned for Murène, with a maximum speed of 50+ kt and a range of 10+ km at that speed. As of October 1992, Eurotorp hoped to run qualifying trials in 1994, delivering some to the French navy by the end of 1996, with export deliveries in 1997.

Compared to **Mk 46**, Impact must be supplied with much more information, such as protection zones for friendly ships and a bathythermal profile. That requires a special control console. It can, however, be fired in a degraded mode, with much less information. Eurotorp emphasizes Impact's ECCM capability, thanks in part to its ability to use multiple sonar frequencies (Mk 46 is more limited).

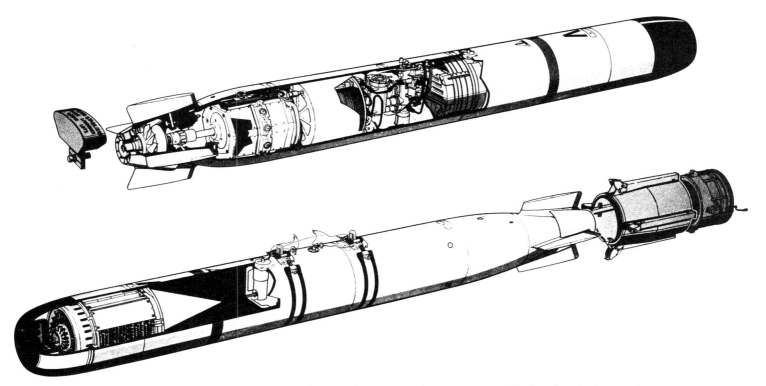

Eurotorp's Impact lightweight torpedo replaces both Murène and A-184. The pumpjet tail section is essentially that of A-184. (Eurotorp)

On the other hand, Impact is likely to be extremely expensive. It was reported in October 1991 that Murène was being built at a rate of 20/yr at a unit cost of about $1.7 million. The planned 1997 delivery date is too late for Chile, which had ordered Murène but needs torpedoes in 1993/94. Chile will presumably buy Mk 46 or Stingray instead. Eurotorp hopes to sell Impact to Germany to replace Mk 46; it claims that in a German evaluation, Murène and A-290 were first and second, with **Mk 46 Mod 5** well behind. The company considers **Mk 50** equal to Impact but argues that its propulsion is more dangerous (and, moreover, that Mk 50 will not be released for general export).

The current **LCAW** competitors are NFT-Whitehead and Lockheed. NFT-Whitehead offers a rocket-boosted, ultra-lightweight, electric torpedo, **A-200**, which is about the size of an A-size sonobuoy. It is in effect a self-propelled variation of the scare charges used by Norway and Sweden. A-200 has an active seeker (by USEA) and uses electric propulsion (3 min at 18 kt, range 2+ km). The warhead is a contact-fuzed, 4-kg, shaped charge. It has been suggested as an armed submarine decoy, to discourage trail.

Lockheed offers a new rocket-propelled torpedo, 15 × 130 cm [5.9 × 51.2 in], weighing about 35 kg [77 lb]. It would be fired with

a 30-kg [66-lb] rocket booster (15 × 90 cm [5.9 × 35.4 in]). Dimensions were set by a requirement that the weapon be manually handled, and that it use some existing launchers (6 can fit in a VLS canister). Guidance is by an active pinger driving a tail shroud. The warhead is a shaped charge, already demonstrated by Dynamit Nobel. Other members of the team are Atlas, Raufoss, and Dyno (Norway: builds the underwater rocket developed by Dynamit Nobel).

ITALY

A-184 *Users:* Italy (submarines and *Audace* and *Maestrale* classes), Peru (reported in Type 209s, but this sale may not have been consummated), Taiwan (Sea Dragon class). This torpedo may have been sold to India, which was dissatisfied with German torpedoes after the Falklands War. Argentina reportedly came close to buying A-184 after suffering torpedo failures (with German **SST** torpedoes) during the Falklands War.

A-244 and **A-244/S** *Users:* Argentina, Ecuador, Greece, India, Indonesia, Iran, Iraq, Italy, Libya, Nigeria, Pakistan, Peru, Singapore, Taiwan, Turkey, and Venezuela.

Eurotorp (the Impact consortium) is now marketing **A-244/S Mod 1**.

SOUTH KOREA

South Korea is reportedly working on a heavy torpedo, possibly based on a reverse-engineered **Mk 37**. The ROK navy may buy German torpedoes for its new Type 209 submarines, but the South Korean defense-development agency (ADD) would prefer to develop its own.

SWEDEN

Swedish lightweight torpedoes do not use seawater batteries because the salinity of the Baltic varies so much. The torpedo manufacturer is Swedish Ordnance, a product of the merger of FFV and Bofors.

The new **Type 45** was formerly designated **Type 43X2**. It is to become operational in the Royal Swedish Navy in 1993. Type 45 has both antisubmarine and anti–surface ship capability. It can be container-launched from a 21-in submarine tube or fired or dropped by a surface craft. These are not classical wire-guided torpedoes; the wire does not continuously transmit steering commands. Instead, it periodically updates (reconfigures) the torpedo's guidance system, e.g., for reacquisition and reattack. The wire is a 2-way link, carrying torpedo-sonar data back to the launch platform. Dimensions:

Lockheed low-cost torpedo as displayed at the 1992 and 1993 Navy League Shows. The torpedo steers with its tail shroud; it is rocket-propelled. The dots at the front end are the transducers. (Author)

400 × 2,800 mm (310 kg including the wire). A 3-speed DC motor (4.2 kW-hr AgZn secondary battery) drives the contraprops.

Users: Sweden (*Västergötland*-class submarines and *Göteborg*- and *Stockholm*-class corvettes)

The **Type 2000** guidance wire can carry 80 types of messages; Swedish Ordnance offers an alternative optical fiber. Control is by an onboard computer; its software controls safe/attack volume, search pattern, and torpedo behavior in the event the guidance wire breaks. The sonar seeker uses preformed beams. Target data, such as elevation and bearing and data for ECCM (not raw acoustics) are transmitted back down the wire. Fuzes are contact and acoustic proximity. The calculated shelf life is 20 yr, assuming power-up testing every 2 yr and EPROM refreshment every 3 yr; torpedoes must be reprepared every year. Propulsion is by a 7-cylinder, axial piston (swashplate) steam engine driving a pumpjet. Dimensions: 533 × 5,990 mm [21 × 236 in], weight 1,314 kg [2,896 lb]. The exercise version weighs 1,182 kg. Range may exceed 45 km [49 kyd]. **T96** is a tropicalized export version. **Type 62** is the official Swedish designation (a follow-on to the **Type 61** series). Test firings begin in 1993.

Type 42 Series *Users:* Sweden (Type 421 in *Näcken* class, Type 422 for helicopters).

An export **Type 427** is described as "in service" since 1982, but no customer can be identified.

Type 61 *Users:* Denmark (Types 613 and 617), Norway (Type 617), Sweden (Type 613), and probably Yugoslavia (*Sava* class)

UNITED KINGDOM

After fits and starts, Marconi was asked to tender (for return on 8 April 1993) for a **Spearfish** production batch. The search for a European partner was fruitless, and the MoD apparently no longer considers **Tigerfish** sufficient. About 100 torpedoes already exist; only the *Trafalgar*, *Trenchant*, and *Talent* carried full Spearfish outfits in late 1992.

The reported British war-stock requirement is 2,500 **Stingray**s. As of 1991, the estimated total cost of the Stingray program was £2,044 million (about $3.5 billion); if that amount was for 2,500, the unit cost was about $1.4 million. The Royal Navy is installing twin DMTS 90 (STWS 3) torpedo tubes on earlier Type 42s (the export DMTS retains Mk 46 capability; STWS is Stingray only). The reduction in tube numbers is reportedly accepted partly because Stingrays cannot be fired in salvo (they may tend to attack one another). The Stingray closed-cycle program was canceled in 1991. **Mk 46** is retained only as a war-reserve weapon.

Users: Egypt, Norway, Thailand, United Kingdom

A total of 2,000 **Tigerfish** (Mk 24) were on order for the Royal Navy as of 1988, and the 600 Mod 1s in service were updated by mid-1988 to improve reliability. Mod 2 entered service in 1986. There is a swim-out version for the after torpedo tubes of *Oberon*-class submarines. Tentative or active contracts for license production have been reported for Chile, Indonesia, and Turkey.

Users: Brazil (Mod 1 [dual-purpose]; first export sale in 1982 for both Type 209s and *Oberons*), Turkey (40 Mod 2s bought late in 1991), United Kingdom. Possible: Chile, Venezuela

UNITED STATES

The FY93 program included integration of a new propulsion system (internal combustion or advanced battery) with a large-diameter half-length vehicle; this may be a 30-in-diameter body suited to the new tube in the *Seawolf*. Work on more lethal warheads, inspired by the sheer size of recent Russian submarines, is now less urgent because relatively small Third World diesel submarines are far more likely targets.

An **ADCAP** upgrade program for better silencing (to preclude snap shots fired as the torpedo approached) began in 1985. Closed-cycle propulsion (for high performance at great depths) was added in 1988 but terminated in February 1992 because the expected Soviet threat was unlikely to materialize (diesel submarines generally cannot dive below about 1,000 ft). Guidance software will probably be altered for shallower water operation. A 30 June 1991 Selected Acquisition Report shows a total ADCAP program cost of $10,023.6 million in FY91 dollars. ADCAP procurement: FY91, 240; FY92, 108; FY93, 108; FY94 request, 108. Unit cost as of February 1992 was $2.1

Alliant's new Seahuntor torpedo. (Alliant)

million. A block upgrade is due in FY95 (to enter production in FY96).

In 1992 the cancellation of **Mk 50** was proposed, on the ground that it was designed to deal with deep fast targets, whereas the most likely future targets would be slow and shallow. However, it turned out that Mk 50 was much superior to **Mk 46 Mod 5AS** against just such targets. The alternative is to redesign **Mk 46** with a higher-capacity digital signal processor, with special software, and with new guidance. The **VLA** version was terminated in February 1992; VLA will use the Mk 46 torpedo instead. A 30 June 1991 Selected Acquisition Report shows a total program cost of $8,971.7 million to buy 7,851 torpedoes (average $1.14 million per torpedo). Procurement: FY91, 265; FY92, 218; FY93, 212. As of May 1993, Mk 50 procurement was suspended pending completion of a "bottom-up" defense review. Mk 50 was the only program suspended this way. Unit cost (February 1992) was $1.1 million, but Alliant expected a substantial reduction as quantity production began.

In 1993 Alliant announced Seahuntor (Sea-Hunting Torpedo), a new torpedo derived from NT-37 (in effect the generation beyond NT-37F). The torpedo has completely new electronics (new guidance, new sonar, and a proximity fuze) and a multispeed Otto engine for higher speed. Seahuntor is 190 in long compared to 177 for NT-37; there is also a 200-in option with a bigger warhead. The prototype was tested in September 1993. Range is 2.5 times that of Mk 37, speed is about 1.6 times, passive and active detection ranges are double, and warhead size is about 1.75 times.

Mk 14 and **Mk 23** Series *Users:* Brazil, Greece, Peru, Taiwan, Turkey (Mk 23), in ex-U.S. submarines

Mk 37 *Users:* Argentina, Brazil, Canada, Chile, Germany, Greece, Italy, Japan, Netherlands, Pakistan, Peru, Spain (Mod 3 in *Baleares* class), Taiwan, Turkey, United States, Venezuela. Many navies no longer use Mk 37; this torpedo may survive in service only in Argentina, Greece, and Turkey.

NT-37 *Users:* Argentina (-37C), Brazil (-37F+: larger warhead, improved exploder sensor), Canada (-37C), Egypt (-37F for Romeo class, to be delivered in 1994), Greece (may have modified Mk 37s to -37D standard), Israel (-37D; -37E design sold to Israel to upgrade -37Ds), Netherlands (-37D), Norway (-37C: bought but stored), Peru (-37C)

Mk 44 *Users:* Australia, Brazil, Canada, Chile, Colombia, Germany, Greece, Indonesia, Iran, Italy, Japan, Malaysia, Netherlands, New Zealand, Norway, Pakistan, Philippines, Portugal, South Africa, South Korea, Spain, Thailand, Tunisia, Turkey, United States, Uruguay, Venezuela. In many cases Mk 44 is retained only as a reserve weapon. South Korea and reportedly Pakistan bought the upgrade kit.

Mk 46 *Users:* Australia (468 bought prior to 1974; will probably buy Mod 5), Brazil (131 bought in 1990; Mod 2 and Mod 5), Canada (428 bought; 200 Mod 5 kits bought in 1981, 150 bought in 1992), France (100 bought; 93 Mod 5 kits bought in 1981), Germany (204 bought in 1978), Greece (100 bought prior to 1974), Indonesia (48 bought in 1984), Iran (694 bought, 280 of them prior to 1974, and 414 in 1975), Israel, Italy, Japan (made under license by Mitsubishi [coproduction agreement July 1982]), Morocco (12 bought in 1984), Netherlands (168 bought before 1974, 50 in 1979; modification kits bought in 1981), New Zealand (6 bought before 1974), Norway (not certain), Portugal (on MEKO 200 frigates), Saudi Arabia (52 bought in 1978), South Korea, Spain (231 Mod 5s bought in 1988 to supplement Mod 2 bought earlier; 118 Mod 5 kits had been bought in 1981; total of 500 Mod 5s on hand in 1991), Taiwan (5 bought pre-1972, 50 Mod 2s in 1973, 150 in 1978; now has Mod 5), Thailand, Turkey, United Kingdom (950 bought before 1974, 500 in 1979; now war reserve only), United States. Belgium plans to buy 65 Mod 5s to replace **L5** torpedoes on board the *Wielingen*-class frigates. Portugal hopes to substitute Mk 46 Mod 5s for the current French **L3** torpedoes on board the *Cdt. Rivière* class. Malaysia, which needs 50–60 replacements for Mk 44s for Wasp helicopters, will probably follow Australia in buying Mk 46 Mod 5. This torpedo has been approved for export to China (PRC) and to Yugoslavia (February 1992). China had already recovered some Mk 46s, but reportedly its attempt at reverse engineering failed because Mk 46 was designed to imperial (ft-in-lb) rather than to metric standards. The PRC's Mk 46 program fell afoul of the 1989 arms embargo. Reportedly, too, the Japanese Mk 46 program has encountered difficulties. The figures above may not be complete for some navies, probably because some torpedoes were provided as direct aid rather than as FMS purchases.

As of early 1992, the U.S. Navy was considering three levels of **Mk 46** upgrade. The most austere would involve minor improvements. The intermediate level would replace the current iron gyro, and there would be other guidance adjustments. The most elaborate would replace almost the entire guidance system and much of the warhead. The navy will probably prefer to buy Mk 50s. Mk 46 production ended in 1990, but as of 1992 the U.S. government planned to support the weapon through 2017. A SLEP program is to begin in FY94, with production in FY96 or FY97. Of the 2 latest versions, Mod 6 (for **Captor** mines) never entered production. Mod 7 is a version modified for surface ships' torpedo defense (172 converted).

Mk 48 *Users:* Australia (127 supplied in 1979, 27 ordered in 1980), Canada (48 ordered in 1985, 13 in 1988; 26 Mod 4s ordered in 1989 for 1991 delivery), Netherlands (100 supplied in 1980), Turkey (10 ordered in 1990 for 2 *Tang* class [cannot be fired by other Turkish submarines]), United States (only current ADCAP user)

UNGUIDED WEAPONS

The Italian **Menon** mortar is now extinct.

FRANCE

305-mm Mortar *Users:* Portugal (*Cdt. Rivière* class), Uruguay (*Cdt. Rivière* class). This weapon has been removed from French ships.

SPAIN

The Spanish low-cost ASW weapon (**ABCAS** (*Arma de Bajo Coste Anti-Submarina*) completed an 18-month project-definition phase in November 1991. It carries 24 rockets (6 across) in a stabilized launcher (2 m high, diameter 1.80 m). The rockets, cheap enough to be fired at an unconfirmed target, would be fired in salvos. Range is 1–8 km. The rockets have shaped-charge warheads to penetrate pressure hulls. Three prototypes were built for trials: 1 of the warheads, 1 of the stabilizer, and 1 to test the rocket motor.

SWEDEN

Saab/FFV has developed an active HF (100–200-kHz FMCW) sonar seeker and fins for a depth charge dropped by an airplane, helicopter, or ship. The movable fins steer the depth charge as it sinks. As of June 1992, the Swedish MoD was supporting this autonomous-homing-munition program. In tests, all depth charges fell within the area of uncertainty. The Swedish version is applied to a ship's standard depth charge (**Model 33**, about 50 cm in diameter, 300 kg). SAAB has considered numerous applications, including **Mk 11**, the **Bofors 375-mm** charge, and **Elma**.

Saab's **ASW-600** is a modified form of **Elma** announced in 1992. As in Elma, ASW-600 has 4 launchers, each with 9 grenades; the range is 400 m. The pattern can be varied from 80 × 10 to 80 × 100 m. The shaped-charge grenades are 100 × 465 mm (5.7 kg); they have a unique nose device intended to hold them to the target (and to prevent their tumbling in the water). Saab also offers a shore equivalent to protect coastal installations, in conjunction with local sonar systems. The new **M90** grenade has a more powerful charge, capable of penetrating a pressure hull (the original **M83** was a Carl Gustav antitank round) and flip-out fins that improve flight stability. Range is extended from 350–400 m to 600 m. Export variants may reach up to 1,000 m.

Users: Finland (Helsinki-II class), Sweden (fast patrol craft and *Landsort*-class minesweepers)

Bofors 375-mm Rocket Launcher (* indicates the 2-barrel version, ** the 4-barrel version; others are 6-barrel)

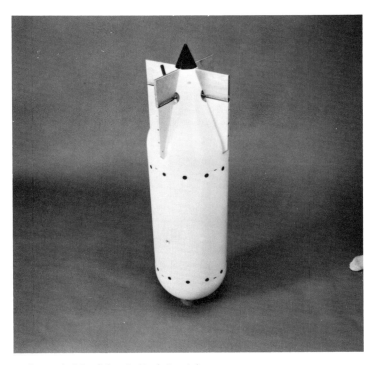

Saab's guided depth bomb. (Saab-Scania)

An ELMA (ASW-600) launcher with its new M90 grenades. Range exceeds 400 m, and the grenade is armed virtually instantly upon entering the water. (Saab-Scania)

Users: Belgium (4 *Wielingen*s), Brazil (6 *Niterois**), Egypt (2 *Descubiertas**), France (17 *D'Estienne d'Orves*, being replaced by Syracuse satellite-communications antennas), Germany (4 *Hamburgs***), Greece (5 *Thetises***), Indonesia (3 *Fatahilahs**), Japan (6 *Yamagumos***, 3 *Minegumos***, 2 *Yubaris***, 1 *Ishikari***, 4 *Isuzus***, and 2 *Akizukis***), Malaysia (2 FS-1500s*), Morocco (1 *Descubierta**), Nigeria (2 *Erin'mis**), Peru (6 *Frieslands***), Spain (6 *Descubiertas**), and Turkey (3 ex-German *Kölns***)

UNITED KINGDOM

As of March 1991, the **Mk 11 Mod 3 air-dropped depth bomb** was in service with the Royal Navy.

Likely Users: Brazil, Chile, India, and Pakistan. A new Middle East customer, probably Egypt, had just adopted this weapon. France obtained some in 1988, but the U.S.-supplied **Mk 54** is its standard depth bomb.

Limbo *Users:* Canada (*St. Laurent, Mackenzie,* and modified *Restigouche* classes), Chile (*Gen. Banquedano*), India (*Leander*s and *Trishul*), Indonesia (the ex-"Tribal" class), Iran (Mk 5 frigates), Malaysia (*Rahmat* and *Hang Tuah*), and Pakistan (*Leander* class)

Squid *Users:* Bangladesh (*Umar Farooq,* reported inoperative), Chile (*Alm. Williams* class), Iran (*Damavand*)

UNITED STATES

The U.S. Navy no longer uses air-dropped nonnuclear depth bombs, but the World War II **Mk 54 depth bomb** is standard in at least the French, German, Italian, and Norwegian navies, and probably in most others using U.S. weapons.

Hedgehog (Mk 10/11) *Users:* Brazil (5 FRAM IIs), Chile (1 *Charles Lawrence*), Greece (1 *Sumner*), Indonesia (4 *Claud Jones*es), Myanmar (1 PCER and 1 former minesweeper), Philippines (1 *Cannon* and 2 *Auk*s), South Korea (2 FRAM II *Gearing*s, 2 FRAM II *Sumner*s, and 1 *Fletcher*), Taiwan (1 Wu Chin II *Gearing*, 2 Wu Chin I *Sumner* FRAM IIs, 4 *Sumner*s, 4 *Fletcher*s, 3 *Auk*s, probably still some ex-APDs), and Turkey (1 FRAM II *Sumner*, 2 *Berk*s)

Hedgehog (Mk 15) *Users:* Chile (PC 1638 class), Turkey (*Kocatepe*, PC 1638 class)

Mousetrap (Mk 20/22) *Users:* Iran (1 Cape-class cutter), Spain (3 U.S. 83-ft types), and Turkey (*Girne*, 12 AB 25 class, 4 PGM 71 class, and 4 U.S. 83-ft types). Mousetrap may also be mounted on board U.S.-supplied or license-built PGM 39/71 series gunboats in Brazil (6), Dominican Republic (1), Philippines (5), and Vietnam (10). It was originally on board the U.S. Coast Guard 95-ft patrol boats, on which the gunboats were patterned.

COUNTERMEASURES

FRANCE

The first **Spartacus** installations (1991) are on board *Tourville*-class frigates, to be followed by the *Georges Leygues* class (beginning in 1995). The carrier *Charles de Gaulle* will be the first ship to be completed with Spartacus. **Albatros**, similar to **ATAS** but with a different array, is the active torpedo-detector sonar. The current passive detector/classifier, Safare-Crouzet's **SPDT-1A** (URDT-1A), entered service in 1990; it is an add-on to any of a range of existing sonars. The standard console contains the processor and shows 2 screens (LOFAR for classification above waterfall for initial detection, the color showing the noise level).

Reported Platforms: Jean Bart, Georges Leygues, Suffren class, and *Aconit*

DUUG-1/6 (Velox) *Users:* Argentina (Type 209s), Australia (*Oberon* class), Brazil (*Oberon* class), Canada (*Oberon* class), Colombia (Type 209s), Chile (*Oberon* class), France (*Daphne* class), Germany (Type 205s and 206s), Greece (first 4 Type 209s), Italy (*Enrico Toti* class), Pakistan (*Daphne* class), Peru (Type 209s), Portugal (*Daphne* class), South Africa (*Daphne* class), Turkey (*Tang* class), United Kingdom (*Oberon* class and early nuclear submarines, as Type 197). This set was also installed on early Type 209s, before the German equivalent became available as part of the **CSU 3** suite.

DUUG uses spot hydrophones positioned around the submarine's sail. It worked with the **AUUD-1** sonar analyzer. **DUUG-6** (Velox M5) is the replacement; **Velox M6** is a similar unit for direct integration into a submarine's combat system.

DUUG-6 Users: France (*Agosta, Rubis,* and SSBN classes), Italy (*Salvatore Pelosi* and *Nazario Sauro* classes), Pakistan (*Agosta* class), Spain (*Agosta* class), and probably the Netherlands. About 70 **DUUG-6**s were made.

DUUG-2 (PARIS) is a directional scanner. As in ESM systems, DUUG-1 was the (nearly) omnidirectional pulse analyzer, **DUUG-2** the DF set operating in several channels with analog output.

Users: France (*Agosta* and *Rubis* classes), Netherlands (all submarines; superseded LWS-30), Pakistan (*Agosta* class), Spain (*Agosta* class), United Kingdom (as 2019: all SSBNs and SSNs, to be replaced by Type 2082)

DUUG-7 (Velox M7) is the replacement for **Velox M5/M6**, entering service in 1992. **M7** provides bearing, frequency, strength (in dB), duration, and recurrence of a signal. Signals are characterized as CW, FM, or DEMON. Bearing is shown both as a number (within a degree) and graphically (by an indicator lamp lit, like that of an RWR, around a submarine sketch [within 15 deg]), for a quick response. The console shows the last 2 intercepted signals. There is an auto-track function, so it measures the recurrence period; M7 can follow up to 8 tracks. M7 operates at 2.5–100 kHz, which can be extended to 500 Hz– 250 kHz; Safare Crouzet claims this is the widest range now available.

ISRAEL

An upgrade to **ATC-1** will add a passive element to the towed fish for very short range detection and will also add a towed array (**TDTA**, now on sea trials) for long-range torpedo detection and identification: e.g., an 8-m array might detect a torpedo at 2 kyd. As of July 1992, ATC-1 was in production and in use by the Israeli navy; none had yet been exported.

Rafael's submarine-launched torpedo decoy, **Scutter**, was announced in 1991. It is not preprogrammed but generates deception signals based on the torpedo pings it receives. Dimensions: 101 × 1,020 mm (7.8 kg); Scutter operates for 5–10 min at depths of 10–300 m. The decoy has a nose propeller to maintain depth or simulate a diving or rising submarine, and it can respond to several signals simultaneously. Rafael is proposing a ship-launched version to be fired from a standard chaff launcher.

ITALY

C303 Effector, powered by a lithium battery, can be used either as a wide-band jammer or as a torpedo decoy (Doppler or range-gate deception). Typically, Effector is launched from the signal ejector in the submarine's sail (at 40 m/sec), but Whitehead is proposing a multitube external launcher, typically 21 tubes to port and 21 to starboard, each with 2 stores (jammer and decoy). The sequenced launching of the 2 types is controlled by an onboard console. Standard operating depth is 20–400 m. Dimensions: 76.2 × 1,125 mm (10 kg).

UNITED KINGDOM

Thorn-EMI has considerably modified British **Type 2019** (PARIS) sets in service, replacing the CRT with plasma panels and the numerous (about 50) analog controls with soft keys (e.g., to call up bands and change frequency and functions). Digital processors and data recorders were updated. A 1553B interface now allows the sonar intercept receiver to communicate directly with the submarine's combat system. Thorn-EMI developed improvements to algorithms for high-performance signal processing, for extended frequency coverage, and for short-pulse detection; to automatic pulse-to-pulse association and track management; to sonar-parameter extraction; and to classification. The 2019 array is in a fin about 5 ft high just in front of a submarine's sail. Bearing resolution is 3–5 deg, and the set covers frequencies from ship to torpedo sonars, i.e., about 1 kHz up to about 30 kHz or more. The original display was a pair of CRTs side by side (presumably bearing/amplitude in 2 different bands).

Type 2082, Thorn-EMI's 2019 replacement, is the last stand-alone British submarine sonar before the advent of the fully integrated **2076**. Compared to 2019, 2082 will have much-improved signal extraction (using frequency-domain processing) and will automatically detect signals and initiate tracking (Thorn has already developed track-extraction software for the 2019 upgrade). Tracks formed by 2082 are passed directly to the submarine's command system. Type 2082 retains the 2019 array but adds a new processing cabinet that communicates with the **Type 2074** multifunction console and also with a separate command display. Development is to be completed by mid-1993 for deliveries to be completed by 1995 for all SSKs/SSNs.

Type 2042 is a self-protection (presumably sonar-jamming) submarine system. **Type 2066** is the **Bandfish** decoy (*not* known as Amulet in RN service, but there have been references to a **Temula** [anagram of Amulet] soft-kill SSTD decoy; Ferranti received a contract to retrofit Temula to RN SSKs/SSNs in 1991). **Type 2070** is the **Talisman** SSTD program (joint U.S./U.K.). **Type 2071** is a programmable submarine noise-augmentation device, for exercises and for self-protection (decoy, i.e., jammer), made by Gearing & Watson, using the **UWS300S** hydrosounder. **Type 2058** (TARTT) is a towed version (in **Type 182** decoy dimensions) carrying a **UWS300F** hydrosounder. The associated digital signal generator (DSG) can produce 11 signals simultaneously (single tones, swept tones, bands of random noise, modulated noise, or pulses). The DSG can store up to 8 programs and can also repeat prerecorded signals.

Type 2071 Users: France (1 *Agosta* class), United Kingdom (3 *Resolution* class, *Upholder, Swiftsure*s, *Trafalgar*s, planned for *Vanguard*s).

A 1991 Ferranti brochure mentions air-launched torpedo countermeasures.

UNITED STATES

A **SAWS** successor is being developed. The sensor is a New Sonar Intercept System (NSIS, now designated **WLY-1**, replacing **WLR-9/12/17**); the processor/command system is **CMC2** (replacing **WLR-14**), and the decoys are **ADC Mk 4**, **MMD**, and a special-purpose decoy (**NLQ-1**). The system will also deploy a hard-kill countermeasure. Unclassified descriptions do not mention a sonar jammer to replace the current GNATS. WLY-1 was to have been installed and tested on board SSN-756 in FY90, but the program slipped, and Norden did not receive a contract for the advanced development model (ADM) of the new receiver until January 1992. WLY-1 is expected to recognize an oncoming torpedo for early acquisition, classification, and tracking. Work on the CMC2 ADM began in FY91 and was to be completed in FY93. The sonobuoy countermeasure (**ADC Mk 4**) program began in FY90. Engineering-development models of **NLQ-1** were to be completed during FY93.

Some of the exotic devices previously described under SSTD are more likely to be submarine torpedo-defense weapons (SMTDs). An ADM contract was expected in FY93. The SMTD will be launched from a new Countermeasures Torpedo Tube Launching System/Quiet Launcher (**CTTLS/QTLHNR**), which is probably the electromagnetic launcher mentioned under the SSTD program. It is to replace the noisy gas generators (Mks 72 and 77) used in **CSA Mk 2 Mods 0 and 1**. The quiet electromagnetic launcher was fabricated in FY90, subjected to laboratory test in FY91, and passed to development in FY92. DARPA developed the technology.

Many older U.S. and Allied ships credited with **Nixie** (SLQ-25) actually carry the earlier **T Mk 6** (Fanfare).

More than 3,000 ADC Mk 2s have been delivered since 1978, and more than 2,000 more were ordered for delivery in 1990–94. Mod 1 is the 6-in version. Bendix received a $13 million contract for 367 **Mk 3s** (6-in) in 1989. **ADC Mk 4** has been under development by Hazeltine since 1988. EDM design and fabrication were completed in FY91, and a service test model (STM) begun. Technical and operational evaluations were conducted in FY92; a production contract was due in FY93. As of 1991, **ADC Mk 5** was in early development by Bendix. The successor is **MMD** (Multi-Mode Device), which operates against both sonars and torpedoes. No Mk number has been assigned (Mk 6 has been reported, but that number was used long ago). As of early 1991, it was planned to issue EDM/STM contracts in FY93, leading to a delivery of 20 test units in 1994–95.

SSTD Phase I is **SLQ-25A**, an enhanced Nixie, now in production. A total of 240 were required. Prototypes appeared in December 1987, and the first operational units were installed in 1988. This phase was expanded to include all ships fitted with Nixie, beginning in FY90. SSTD Phase II is the U.S. national program, specifically to deal with wake-following torpedoes, using **Mk 46 Mod 7** as the kill vehicle. The detector/classifier is the GE **SLR-24**, which uses a short array streamed abaft the Nixie countermeasure, feeding a Martin Marietta **ASAP** (Advanced Systolic Array Processor). Phase II originally applied only to major combatants, but by 1991 plans called for it to be expanded to all combatants, combat logistics ships, and selected major amphibious ships beginning in FY95. The OR was issued in March 1985 (following a formal proposal in July 1984). The full-scale development contract was awarded in 1988, and 2 development models were delivered in 1992. Between July 1989 and early 1991, Mk 46 Mod 7 torpedoes ran 86 in-water tests against modified **Mk 48** torpedoes. SLR-24 was tested on board the carrier *John F. Kennedy*.

SSTD Phase III is the U.S.-U.K. cooperative program, to deal with all types of torpedoes. The U.S./U.K. MoU was signed on 26 October 1988. This system is to enter service 1997–98. The U.S./U.K. consortia are (1) Martin Marietta (ex-GE)/Alliant/Plessey Naval Systems; (2) Westinghouse/Librascope/Dowty/Ferranti; (3) Martin Marietta/Hughes Aircraft/BAe/Frequency Engineering Labs (Farmingdale). In April 1991 France and Germany stated their interest in entering the international SSTD program.

MINE WARFARE

MINES AND MINE COUNTERMEASURES

AUSTRALIA

The ADI Minesweeping and Surveillance System (**AMASS**), developed for the RAN COOP program, is now offered for export. Two drone precursor craft use mechanical and influence sweeps (the RAN found GRP drone boats more cost-effective than helicopters in this role). AMASS includes a degaussing system for the follow-up MCM craft. The influence and mechanical sweeps can operate in up to sea state 4; they are claimed effective to a depth of 180 m. The forward-support unit is containerized.

BRAZIL

Consub Equipamentos e Servicos Ltda of Rio de Janeiro has developed the new **MCF-100** contact mine. The body is cylindrical, with a domed top and bottom, and with 4 horns protruding from the top. It is laid with its axis horizontal, so these dimensions include the anchor: 1.4 m long × 1.02 m wide × 1.5 m high (770 kg, including 160-kg Trotyl charge); laying depth 10–100 m. The mine can be set for delayed release from its anchor. The Brazilian navy ordered 100 MCF-100 mines in August 1991. MCF-100 is envisaged as the first of a modular family of weapons, which will carry up to 3 modular charges (presumably 160 kg each) and will use influence (acoustic and magnetic) sensors. The ground-mine version will be layable from submarine torpedo tubes, hence must have a smaller diameter.

CANADA

The **MCDV** is to conduct only coastal surveillance, route survey (with a towfish), mine inspection, and mechanical sweeping. The Canadian navy has not bought **Trail Blazer** and **Manta**.

CHINA (PRC)

EM52, a rocket-propelled rising mine, was displayed at Defense Asia 1991 (March 1991). Presumably, it was inspired by the Russian rising mine. EM52 resembles a finned bomb. It is deployed in intermediate depths (maximum reported 110 m). It uses an acoustic sensor and a ship counter (1–99). Dimensions are 450 × 3,700 mm (620 kg, including 140-kg explosive). Service life is 360 days. In 1985 China began marketing its versions of the Soviet **AMD/KMD** series as **Type 500** or **Type I** (500 kg) and **Type 1000** or **Type II** (1,000 kg). Reported customers include Bangladesh.

Chinese mine production began in 1958 with Soviet contact mines. In 1962 the large **L-1** (L for *Lao*, moored) moored mine was standardized, followed in 1964 by the medium **L-2** and in 1965 by the **L-3** antenna mine. **L-4** is an acoustic mine for deep water, standardized in November 1973. Work on an improved **L-4A** with better fuzing began in 1980 (it was standardized in November 1982); a solid-state **L-4B** appeared in December 1985. The first bottom mine, **C-1** (C for *Chen*, sinking [to the bottom]), was standardized in 1966. **C-2** was the first ground mine developed entirely in China, beginning with a proposal in 1956; sea tests followed in 1966. It used transistors rather than tubes. Improved in 1969–70, it entered production in 1975 as **C-2A**. Development of **C-3** began in 1969; it entered production in 1974. This mine has antisweep features and can be laid in 6–50-m depth with a dual magnetic/acoustic pistol (or in 100-m with a single pistol). **C-4** is a small noncontact modular bottom mine with combination or single pistol. It can be disassembled for carriage by mule, and can be used for demolition. **C-5** is a similar pressure mine (probably the first to be made in China); it can be drifted into position. It entered production in July 1975. **T-1** is the PRAM mine; work began in 1981 and was completed in 1987. **T-2–1** is a remotely controlled mine, using a combination of coded commands and a pistol (it has 3 modes: safe, armed, or command-detonated). Work began in 1978, and the design was frozen in December 1986. There are also floating mines and a riverine mine with a combined HF acoustic and remote pistol.

DENMARK

The new **MTP-19** is a controlled mine. Dimensions: 878 mm high × 1,000 mm × 1,000 mm; the lower part is a trolley to ride mine-laying rails. With a buoyancy unit on top, the mine is 1,128 mm high. Total weight is 500 kg, including a 300-kg charge. Maximum laying depth is 20 m. The mine carries acoustic and magnetic sensors with microprocessor control. Minimum distance between mines is 50 m. The buoyancy unit with a marker buoy rises after the mine hits bottom so that a follow-up crew can hook the mine into the control network. The buoy also carries 40 m of cable. The cables are linked on the surface to distribution boxes and extension cables, which sink to the seabed. The boxes are microprocessor controlled, so the system can configure automatically. The cables can be connected in random order, for rapid deployment. The weapons-control unit shows the entire minefield and the state of each mine. The control unit can be up to 12 km from a mine.

At Brighton in March 1993, Eiva A/S displayed a COOP MCM system based on its Navipack navigational software system, which runs on an HP computer. An Ethernet LAN connects the Navipack data-acquisition and navigation system with an EG&G 272TD towed sidescan sonar and with a tactical and target display running on an 80486 computer. The system is packaged in a special low-magnetic-signature aluminum and plywood container with its own diesel generator. One was sold in 1991 to the Royal Swedish Navy and another in 1992 to the German Navy.

Lockheed's expendable mine-destruction torpedo, at the 1993 Navy League Show. (Author)

FRANCE

Ibis MCM systems are classed by sonar and by tactical system. **Ibis III**, for the Tripartite Minehunters, uses the **DUBM-21** sonar and the **TSM 2060/NAVIPLOT** tactical system. The Mk II version has a **DUBM-21B** sonar and **TSM 2061**. **Ibis V** is a lightweight version with **TSM 2022** sonar (and sometimes a lightweight NAVIPLOT, **TSM 2026**). In analogy to Ibis III, the Mk II version uses TSM 2061 and a Mk II version of the sonar. **Ibis V NG** (*Nouvelle Génération*) uses a **TSM 2022 NG** sonar with paired line arrays, for sequential or simultaneous detection and classification. **Ibis VII** uses a propelled VDS (PVDS) carrying the TSM 2022 NG sonar.

TSM 2023N was developed jointly by Thomson and Simrad for the new Norwegian minehunters, based on experience with a **TSM 2021N** installed on board the old Norwegian sweeper *Tana* since 1977. It combines a 256-stave electronically stabilized cylindrical array and a mechanically stabilized flat 100-stave classification array working at 3 frequencies. It also tracks the RoV. The classification sonar selects the object closest in size to a possible mine from among the objects it detects (at LF and maximum range, its resolution is close to the size of a small mine). Detection range is 400/600/900/1,200 m, classification range is 200/300 m, and minimum range is 50 m. Search sectors are 20/60/90 deg; classification sectors are 5/17.25 deg. This sonar is effective down to 100 m and at speeds of up to 6 kt (12 kt in side-looking mode, using either the detection sonar on both sides or the classification sonar on 1 side).

Ibis 42, for the abortive deep-water *Narvik* class, used the **DUBM 42** sidescan sonar. **Ibis 43**, for the Danish *Flyvefisken*, uses a **TSM 2054** sidescan sonar to search intermediate water depths (60–200 m). The 3-m fish is shorter than that of DUBM 42, the software is modified to suit Danish water conditions, and it can be towed at a higher speed (15 kt). **DUBM III/43** and **V/43** are combinations of the hull- and towed-sonar systems. **Ibis 51** uses a **TSM 5451B** with a short array, which can be oriented horizontally or vertically (5451A is the relocation and identification sonar of the **PAP 104** mine-neutralization vehicle).

Users of Ibis systems: Belgium (III in 10 Tripartite/SEWACO systems), Denmark (43 in 5 *Flyvefisken* class), Egypt (V in 6 COOP minehunters, sonar made by Thoray Thomson-Raytheon joint venture), France (III in 10 Tripartites), Indonesia (V in 2 *Alkmaar* class), Malaysia (V in 4 *Lericis*), Netherlands (III in 15 Tripartite/SEWACOs), Nigeria (V in 2 *Lericis*), Norway (V Mk II with 2023N sonar/MICOS system in 4 new minehunters), Pakistan (III in 3 Tripartites, 1 ex-French), Singapore (V Mk II in 4 *Landsorts*), Sweden (7 *Landsort*/MJ 400 CDSs), Turkey (III planned for 6 Tripartite Minehunters), Yugoslavia (V in 2 updated *Sirius*)

PAP 104 *Users:* Australia (*Rushcutter* class), Belgium (Tripartite class), France (Tripartite class), Germany (Type 331s), Indonesia, Malaysia, Netherlands (Tripartite class), Norway (*Tana*), Pakistan (Tripartite class), Saudi Arabia (*Sandown* class), Singapore (*Landsort*), South Africa (*Umkomaas*-class inshore sweepers), United Kingdom, Yugoslavia (*Sirius* class). As of early 1992, 341 (including 46 Mk 5s) had been sold.

GERMANY

STN and Lockheed have developed the **NSSV/EMDV** expendable torpedolike ROV for the future (about the turn of the century), when route surveys are really effective. Dimensions are about 25 × 150 cm, 120 kg (lightweight-torpedo size). STN/Lockheed hopes to minimize cost (the target is DM 60–70 thousand, including about 20

thousand for the neutralization charge) by using a fiber-optic link to the controlling ship; they argue that the alternative, Bendix's fully autonomous vehicle, is inherently too expensive. As of mid-1992, the main problem was assuring the quality of the sensor system without accepting excessive cost. A future minehunter will carry 30 vehicles (the navy would buy 5–10 ship loads/system). The basic idea has already been tested; this vehicle supersedes the Lockheed **LENS**.

The original version of the **DSQS-11** sonar, **-11A**, was apparently less than successful. It and the improved **-11H** both use a single software-controlled array for both detection and classification. German DSQS-11H sonars are being upgraded to **-11M**. This much more successful version adds a second (linear) array for detection, operating at a frequency different from that of the original array (which is retained for classification). The Australian version has a longer linear array (2.0 vice 1.5 m) and filtering to cope with local seabed and temperature conditions.

The German navy accepted **MWS 80–4** (with DSQS-11M sonar) in 1991 for the Type 332 class. MWS 80–4 will probably be retrofitted to Type 343s (*Pegnitz* class). **MWS 80–5** is a containerized version for the RAN (one container for the operations room, one for the sonar). It has now been accepted (trials with the original version were not satisfactory). MWS-80 includes the Ferranti **SATAM** (MC500) command system.

Users: Australia (*Rushcutter* class), Germany (DSQS-11M in Types 332 and 343, -11A in Types 331 and 351 [-11H in *Fulda*, trials ship]), Thailand (2 M48 class). Taiwan reportedly uses the German **Pinguin** mine-disposal vehicle (Pluto has also been reported) but not the German sonar.

INTERNATIONAL

In October 1991 France and Britain signed an MoU for a joint feasibility study of future MCM systems. In April 1992 France, Italy, and the Netherlands signed an MoU to begin a new mechanical sweep program (**NATO PG 22**). Three more NATO countries are interested.

The main problem is deep-sweeping, particularly for rising mines close-tethered to the bottom (within 1–3 m: existing team sweeps can come within about 15 m of the bottom). Depth control becomes very difficult; reaction time may be too slow for the sweep to avoid bottom obstacles. A 1988 NATO study called for a maximum sweep depth of at least 600 m [about 2,000 ft]; 1,000 m [about 3,000 ft] was desired. Desired maximum sweep speed was 14 kt (compared to 8–10 kt as now) with a 350-m swath width (currently 200–350 m, reduced to 50–100 m for bottom-contacting sweeps) capable of dealing with a bottom gradient of 7% (possible at present only with team sweeps). A 350-m sweep towed at 14 kt at 600-m depth imposes a load of 1,200–1,400 tons on the towing ship (2,400–3,700 tons for a sweep contacting the bottom). Too, at great depth the towing winch must heave and veer at an enormous rate, e.g., about 130 m/min for a 250-m-deep sweep at 14 kt.

The British/French/Dutch **EPMDS** buried-mine detector began trials on board the Dutch *Tydemans* in March 1991, continuing through early 1992. BAe (receiver array and processing) and Thomson Sintra (transducers and display) made the sonar. EPMDS is intended to detect mines buried at 0.5–2.0 m, and it operates at a constant height above the sea floor, at 2 frequencies, about 195 and

205 kHz, at high power (230 dB). The high frequencies make for a narrow beam. The resultant signal is a combination of the 2 base frequencies and the sum and difference signals, and a narrow, 10-kHz, high-powered beam capable of penetrating bottom sediment is produced.

IRAQ

Of about 1,300 mines laid in the Persian Gulf before war broke out, about half were **LUQM-145**s (see below). Russian-supplied **MYAM**s accounted for about 7% and **KMD-500**s for about 3%. **Manta**s were about 5%. Another 16% were classified as unknown bottom mines, probably mainly Russian-supplied **UMD**s. Another 18% were beached/floating mines. So far as can be determined, the exotic weapons displayed at Baghdad in 1989 (and described in the 1991–92 edition) did not exist. The LUQM-145 "cheeseburger mine" was encountered for the first time in the Gulf War. It is essentially a Russian-type contact mechanism (as in **M08**) married to a larger floating body, an ovoid rather than a sphere, to carry more explosives.

ITALY

Whitehead is now working on a **Captor**-type mine. Originally, it was to have been armed with an **A290** torpedo; the project is now in abeyance because of the merger with **Murène** (as **Impact**).

The current version of **MIN** is Mk 2. Maximum operational depth is 350 m; maximum speed 6 kt; umbilical length is 1,000 m; weight is 1,100 kg. MIN carries a CCD TV camera with automatic iris, and a high-resolution HF sonar (mechanical sector scan, pulsed transmission). The TV and sonar are orientable 150 deg in the vertical plane.

Users: Italy (*Lerici* class)

Pluto *Users:* Italy (*Lerici* class, used with MIN 77, and converted *Adjutant* class), Nigeria (*Lerici* class), Norway (new minehunters), South Korea (SK5000 class), Spain (chosen for modified *Sandowns*), Thailand (M 48 class)

JAPAN

The current **S-7** mine-neutralization vehicle, made by Mitsubishi, is 1.5 m wide × 1.2 m high × 2.8 m long (860 kg); it has 2 5.5-kW electric motors that can tilt up and down to steer, and also a vertical propulsor. S-7 is linked with the hunting ship by an umbilical (which provides both power and commands) and carries a transponder for tracking. The vehicle carries an imaging sonar, a searchlight, and an LLLTV. The console on the hunting ship shows the images from these sensors; a smaller console maneuvers the device. S-7 carries one PAP-size explosive charge (detonated acoustically) and explosive cable cutter.

The associated sonar, **ZQS-3**, is probably comparable to **SQQ-30**. The saucer-shaped **S-4** operates at shallower depths; it is associated with the **ZQS-2B** sonar. It is also less well equipped.

NORWAY

SA 950 *Users:* Finland (probably 4 Helsinki-II class to control Elma, also on minecraft), Norway (mine-avoidance for minesweepers), Sweden (*Hugin* class, for ASW, Taiwan (minehunters), and Turkey (6 *Mercure* class)

SOUTH AFRICA

It was reported in 1991 that Armscor had produced a number of mine designs originally sold by West Germany to Chile in the 1960s; presumably, they are distantly related to the current **SGM 80**. The principal mine can operate either by contact or by magnetic or acoustic fuzing and can change its main sensor after having been laid, for a period of up to 5 yr. The South African navy reportedly bought 2,000, of which 500 were sold back to Chile and 1,020 to Iraq; 3,000 more were sold to other users, possibly including Libya. Reportedly, too, South Africa retains very large stocks of British mines built up during 1944–45 for use in the Indian Ocean and the Pacific; few if any were returned when the British naval presence at Simonstown ended in 1962.

SWEDEN

The Royal Danish Navy bought a **Double Eagle**, probably the first of 12, in June 1992; it uses a Danish **Reson** sonar. The U.S. Navy

bought 2 **SAM** remotely controlled boats just before the Gulf War for $7 million; they performed well, and a follow-on **Remote Influence Sweep** (RIS) is being considered.

The current mines are the SA Marine **M9** and the **F80** anti-clearance mine, which can be laid by a submarine (via its mine belt) or by a fast attack boat. SA Marine's rising **P85** has a terminal active sonar seeker.

TAIWAN

The new mines are the air-dropped cylindrical **WSM 110** and the conical (Manta-like) **WSM 210**.

UNITED KINGDOM

The Royal Navy uses only **Mines Mks 5** and **12**. **Stonefish** was never bought for home use, only for export. **PAP 104 Mk 5** won the RCDMS competition. The Royal Navy buys 3 **PAP**s per minehunter in case of attrition. The **FIMS** autonomous submersible ran trials in Saudi waters (for the Royal Saudi Navy) in April 1991.

Type 193 *Users:* Argentina (2 "Ton" class), Australia (1 "Ton" class), Germany (Type 331A minehunting boats [with Mk 20(G) plotting table]), Japan (ZQS-2 is a license-made Type 193), Norway (*Tana*), South Africa (*Kimberly*), South Korea (SK5000 class, based on *Lericis*), United Kingdom, Yugoslavia (2 of 4 *Sirius* class). The South Korean boats have the Racal-Decca **MAINS** system. The Dutch "Ton"-class minesweepers converted to hunters in 1968–73 with Type 193M have been disposed of. As of July 1991, all Hunts have Type 193M Mod 1s; the only Mod 0 is in a surviving "Ton."

Mod 1 has LF elements to detect self-burying mines. Eight RN Type 193s have **Mills Cross** add-ons, produced by MUSL as a private venture. They are intended for mine avoidance; the Mills Cross was used on U.S. frigates in the Persian Gulf in 1987.

Type 2093 *Users:* Saudi Arabia (*Sandown* class), United Kingdom (*Sandown* class).

In 1993 GEC-Marconi announced Archerfish, a self-propelled semiautonomous command-controlled (by fiber-optic link) antimine torpedo (approx. 10 × 90 cm) integrated with the Type 2093 sonar. Onboard sensors are sonar and TV, and the vehicle has a 10-min lifetime. GEC-Marconi claims that it achieves a clearance rate at least 4 times that of a conventional RoV system.

UNITED STATES

Differences in the number of mines required under Cold War and post–Cold War estimates probably reflect an assumption that diesel submarines will be the primary mine targets in a post–Cold War conflict, and that the United States will have to mine only limited areas against surface targets. Even so, large numbers may be needed; about 300,000 Destructors were used in Vietnam (and 11,000 in North Vietnam in 1972).

Many existing mines may be impossible to use effectively. Mk 56, the only U.S. medium-depth ASW mine, is considered inadequate because of its very limited actuation width (less than 2% of that of Mk 60). Thus, large numbers of mines are needed to mine substantial areas (e.g., 5,000 P-3 sorties would have been required to execute the planned Cold War *defensive* mining mission around the continental United States). That makes the medium-depth rising

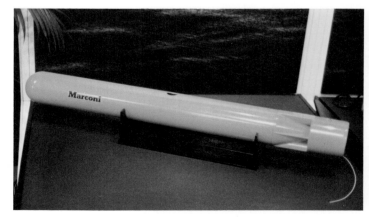

Marconi's Archerfish expendable antimine vehicle, at the 1993 Navy League Show. (Author)

	Current Inventory as a % of Requirement	
	Cold War Assessment	Post–Cold War (1999) Requirement
Mk 60 (Captor)*	35%	40%
Mk 67*	40%	60%
Mk 52**	100%	n/a
Mk 55**	100%	n/a
Mk 56**	50%	110%
Destructor	300%	2,150%
Quickstrike	10%	85%

*January 1992 figures
**1990 figures

IBM displayed this buried-mine-detector concept at the 1993 Navy League Show. The 2 tandem bodies apparently use a combination of side-looking sonar and a sensitive superconducting magnetometer. (IBM)

mine (**Substrike**) very attractive because a few such weapons can replace large numbers of Mk 56s.

The new **Mk 71** target-detection device (TDD) is microprocessor controlled and, thus, is far more flexible (also much more compact) than the older, hard-wired **Mk 57/58s** used in Quickstrike mines. Mk 71 may be able to detect the signatures of specific targets, thus limiting expenditure against others.

The FY92/93 R&D program (6.3 program) projects are **Captor Improvement/Advanced ASW Mine (Substrike), Remote Control of Mines (RECO)**, and **Advanced Sea Mine (ASM) 2000**. Funds for RECO and ASM were eliminated in FY91. Improved Captor is **Mine Mk 60 Mod 2** armed with a **Mk 46 Mod 6** torpedo (now canceled) and equipped with a new sensor. Substrike is a shallower-water rising mine for wide-area ASW coverage. During FY93 work was to begin on 2 Substrike sensors, a volumetric array and a magnetic device. The objective is to develop common Captor Mod 2/Substrike technology (the restructured Captor Improvement Program is to include Substrike). ORs were issued for Captor Improvement in March 1987 and for Substrike in March 1990. The planned FY93 program includes completion of algorithms for UEP and enhanced pressure sensors.

The helicopter carrier *Inchon* is being converted into a command ship to support MCM helicopters; her JOTS system will incorporate new MCM Decision Aids.

Experience in Kuwait shows a need for some means of very rapidly clearing a beach ahead of an amphibious assault. Possible approaches include minehunting in the surf zone (**AMDAS**) and using line charges or other explosives to neutralize or destroy very shallow anti-invasion mines. Large quantities of explosive may be needed because mines are designed not to explode when nearby mines go off (to avoid countermining). Current surf and shallow-water zone efforts include **BLNS** (Breached-Lane Navigational System), **DET** (Distributed Explosive Technology), **ILC** (Improved Line Clearance Charge), **OBM** (Obstacle Breaching Munitions), **OBSCLNC** (Obstacle Line Clearing System), **SABRE** (Shallow-Water Breach System), and **SAUV** (Semi-Autonomous Undersea Vehicle, for minehunting). As of early 1991, the projected FY93/94 program called for several new starts: rapid shallow-water clearance (development begun in FY91, FSED contract due in FY94, with operational evaluation in FY96 and Milestone III approval in FY98), buried mine detection (FSED contract in FY94–95, operational evaluation in FY96), and remote minehunting (FSED contract to be awarded in FY94, and operational evaluation to be in FY98). DOPs for all three were completed in FY90. **MADOM**, Magnetic-Acoustic Detection of Mines, is a combined cryogenic gradiometer and synthetic-aperture sonar to detect and classify buried mines. It is to be towed by surface craft. An RFP has been issued for **AMNSYS** (Airborne Mine-Neutralization System), which would be expendable mine-killing torpedoes dropped from a helicopter.

At the 1993 Navy League show, IBM advertised a **buried-mine detection system** in a pair of bodies towed in tandem, 1 with sonar plus a magnetometer, the other with sonar only. Data from different sensors will be fused for detection. The team consists of IBM, ARAP (UUV hydrodynamics), Ball Corp. (cryogenics), Dynamics Technology (underwater sensor analysis), Quantum Magnetics (SQUID: superconducting quantum interference devices), Rockwell International (UUV design), and Sonatech (Advanced Mine Detection System sensor developer; UUV sonar developer). IBM reportedly advocates electromagnetic pulse (EMP) rather than explosive charges for mine-neutralization.

Raytheon was awarded the contract for **AQS-20**, the **AQS-14** replacement, in the summer of 1992. The 10 ft, 1,000-lb towed body has a 5-ft wingspan; it carries 4 sonars: ahead-looking, belly-band (for volume search), side-scan, and gap-filler (for right below). Some data are processed in the tow body, with further processing in the helicopter. One mission control/display subsystem can handle 3 helicopters simultaneously via a UHF data link. Navigation is now so good that the AQS-20 map of a minefield can be used for follow-up attacks on individual mines by neutralization torpedoes (concept definition of which is to begin in FY94). AQS-20 uses some SQQ-32 technology, especially for volume search (belly-band), power amplification, and some SQQ-32 algorithms.

An ECP for the **Mk 105** sled (providing a new higher-powered generator and a larger-diameter sweep wire) was approved in February 1992. As of March 1992, the U.S. Navy was interested in a new shallow-water sweep to counter influence mines, *not* a replacement for the existing sled. Work on **ALQ-166** was suspended in 1990.

Although never adopted by the U.S. Navy, **AQS-17** has been sold to Indonesia as a towed sonar, to equip 8 of the 9 ex–East German Kondor II class minesweepers. The sonar was demonstrated in Indonesia in August 1992, and it was installed on board the ships before they left Germany.

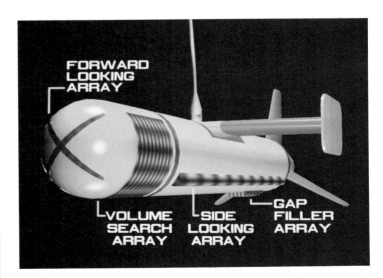

FORWARD LOOKING ARRAY

VOLUME SEARCH ARRAY   SIDE LOOKING ARRAY   GAP FILLER ARRAY

Raytheon's successful entry in the AQS-20 helicopter-minehunter competition. The 10-ft-long towed body is 18 in in diameter and contains the beamformers and signal processors for all 4 arrays. It maintains either a constant height above the bottom or a constant depth below the surface. (Raytheon)

SSDS has now been designated **SLQ-53**; it is a ship version of the helicopter **A/N37U-1**. SLQ-53 is to be operationally evaluated in FY95.

In the Persian Gulf, the EDM of the **SQQ-32**, on board the USS *Avenger*, detected a **Manta** mine at 900 yd. SQQ-32 achieves relatively long range detection because it uses a relatively LF detection sonar. The classification sonar is a development of the French Thomson Sintra series.

Users: Japan (new deep sweepers), United States (*Avenger* and *Cardinal* classes)

Kaman's **Magic Lantern** is a LIDAR (flash-pumped Nd:YAG laser [doubled]) developed in response to the Gulf crisis of 1987–88 and bought under rapid prototyping procedures; it was used in the Gulf early in 1991. Although reports of this trial varied, they were sufficiently encouraging for the program to continue. Compared to **AMDAS** and the earlier **ALARMS**, Magic Lantern uses a large spot size and low PRF, in a step-stare mode, to form an image of the underwater scene. The other systems use smaller spot sizes and a higher PRF. In March 1991 Magic Lantern was credited with a 200-ft search swath at a speed of advance of 40–50 kt (maximum depth 65 ft), and with a potential for a 500–1,000-ft search swath if automatic detection could be used. Magic Lantern may now be combined with the Marine Corps' **AMDAS** surf-zone mine-detection program, for depths down to 40–50 ft, with a projected sweep width of 1,000 ft and a 180-kt speed of advance.

Several other mine-avoidance systems were tried in the Gulf: **Kingfisher** (see **SQS-56**, above), **Midnight** (a modified DICASS active buoy; 2 prototypes made and tested: detection range 400 yd vs. -17-dB target, 1,000 yd at Pd 0.95 was predicted), and **Lightweight Minehunting Sonar** (a modified DICASS transducer sprint-and-dipped ahead of the force, with a demonstrated range of up to 800 yd and a predicted range of up to 3,000 yd). A surface version of the **BQS-15** submarine obstacle-avoidance sonar was considered, as was a modified **SQQ-32**.

SQQ-14/SQQ-30 *Users:* Belgium (6 *Dash* class), Italy (locally manufactured SQQ-14/IT in 6 new *Lerici* class [incorporate Plessey 2048 Speedscan], SQQ-14A in 4 original *Lerici*s, 6 converted *Adjutant* class [replaced original UQS-1]), Saudi Arabia (4 MSC 322 class), Spain (4 *Aggressive* class), and the United States (SQQ-14 in 2 *Acme* and 19 *Aggressive* class, SQQ-30 in early *Avenger* class; to be replaced by SQQ-32).

SQQ-14, which entered service in 1960, is essentially the 80-kHz **UQS-1** combined with a version of the 350-kHz classification array (CXRP) of the British **Type 193**. It differs from 193 in that SQQ-14 is on an articulated strut that carries the sonar to 150 ft below the hull. These sonars are being modified with electronic compasses (to indicate orientation) and conventional tow cables (tow depth 400 ft). SQQ-30 is essentially a solid-state SQQ-14 and was originally designated SQQ-14 Deep Mod. SQQ-30 has a tow cable (rather than the strut) and can operate at greater depths than SQQ-14, including the towed version. The transducer is modified for better vertical coverage.

UQS-1 *Users:* Belgium (4 *Adjutant* class), Denmark (3 *Adjutant* class), Greece (9 *Falcon* class, 5 *Adjutant* class), Iran (1 *Falcon*), Italy (9 *Adjutant*s and 4 *Agile* class), Japan (as ZQS-1, on 4 former *Kasado* class), Norway (7 *Falcon* class), South Korea (probably 5 MSC 289s, 3 MSC 268 class), Spain (8 *Adjutant* class), Taiwan (13 *Adjutant* class), Thailand (4 MSC 289 class), and Turkey (12 *Adjutant* class, probably 5 ex-Canadian Bay class and 1 ex-U.S. Cape class)

A proposed Westinghouse Integrated MCM System (**WIMS**) employs a multibeam Westinghouse Minehunting Reconnaissance Sonar-III (WMRS-III) based on AQS-14, feeding an automated target-detection and -classification system (ATD) on board the ship. The tactical subsystem is based on a QUILS II integrated navigation and data-management system. Pluto is the neutralization vehicle.

YUGOSLAVIA

M-70 is an improved version of the Soviet **KMD-II**. Reportedly, M-70 has been exported to Libya.

THE SOVIET/ RUSSIAN NAVY

COMMAND/CONTROL

The Soviets included computers with nuclear weapons and jet and rocket engines as part of the post-1945 revolution in warfare. Computers were particularly attractive to the "scientific" Soviet mindset; they promised to reach mathematically correct conclusions (e.g., for appropriate tactics) without the risk of human infirmity. By the early 1960s the Soviets foresaw a generation of ground tactical computers to help a commander choose among his options, probably on the basis of deterministic gaming calculations. The shipboard equivalent was the "Second Captain," which worked on the basis of the complete tactical picture it maintained, including ownship data (such as weapons loadout and even damage-control status). The computer's tactical advice probably amounted to modifying a series of relatively simple scripted responses. A senior officer on the *Moskva* (which had the prototype "Second Captain") complained that it would produce unthinking officers, too dependent on a machine's decisions.

Such computers dealt with a major, if unexpressed, concern. The Soviet system produced a profoundly pessimistic (not to mention paranoid) society. In theory, initiative was rewarded, but in practice, failed initiatives were often treated as sabotage. Hence the popularity of canned ("book") solutions based on masses of statistical data. Individuals could hardly be aware of all the rules, but the computer could follow them all. Like its modern Western CDS counterparts, the "Second Captain" records decisions taken on board ship (in its case, alongside the decisions it suggests). A wag suggested that it made the "Second Captain" the "second commissar" as well. Western navies are beginning to provide automated command advice (e.g., in the U.S. C&D machine and the British CCA), but with far more computer power (and with far less executive power).

Like its Western counterparts, the "Second Captain" grew directly out of World War II–type manual CICs, which the Soviets called "battle information posts" (BIPs). The BIP differed from a Western CIC in the extent to which it gathered ownship information (damage control and weapons system status). Frigates designed well into the 1970s retained manual systems. For example, a Krivak-I has a horizontal plot on which operators move magnetic counters. Eventually, Krivaks were fitted with a primitive "Second Captain," a computer fed by radar and ESM video (and providing printed output), but it was never integrated into the ship's combat system. The computer's advice is based on its own tactical picture (independent of the horizontal plot) produced by automatically detecting and tracking targets and correlating them with ESM strobes.

The tactical picture displayed to the CO or admiral generally includes target identification (based on ESM and IFF replies), probably in icon form. "Second Captain" outputs appear in the main weapons-control spaces. The CO can fight the ship via the "Second Captain" console in the BIP (or on the bridge), or can let the "Second Captain" fight the ship virtually autonomously. Ships in a group feed their sensor data to a flagship's computer center via digital data links, such as Bell Crown (equivalent to Link 11, for radar). The computer aboard the flagship (which might be called a "Second Admiral") receives operational instructions and other data from ashore, via special high-capacity links (originally Vee Cones and successor HF antennas and, later, Low Ball satellite antennas).

This recalls the U.S. system, in which data from FCCs ashore, as well as battle-group data, feed TFCCs and TWCSs afloat. However, the Russians lacked the computer capacity enjoyed by the U.S. FCCs; their shore centers could not provide enough data for missile targeting. Deployed antiship formations thus had to rely heavily on specially cued reconnaissance assets (e.g., Bear-D and satellites) to establish updated target positions. At least for antiship attacks, each strike unit obtained its own final targeting (fire-control) data, although there was apparently a means of relaying data from, e.g., a Bear-D, between attacking units.

The "Second Admiral" can direct the other ships' weapons via their own "Second Captains." Ships without a higher-order command function are not capable of correlating offboard data with that of their own sensors; unlike their Western equivalents, they do not receive such data by link. On its own ship, the "Second Admiral" is separate from one or more "Second Captains," each optimized for a particular warfare area.

The most elaborate version of this architecture was the command system planned (but not realized) for the carrier *Kuznetsov.*

Her "Second Admiral" would have generated a prioritized list of options for the group commander. When an option was chosen, the "Second Admiral" would have selected and instructed the relevant subordinate systems within the task group (not necessarily on board the carrier). In effect, "Second Captains" on board other ships of the carrier's pro-SSBN battle group, associated Bear-F aircraft, and submarines ranked equal to the combat area "Second Captains" (for AAW, ASW, and ASUW) on board the carrier. Information could be passed either directly (via data link) or relayed by a Bear or a specialized Ka-27 helicopter. This relay role is so important that 12 data-link helicopters were included in the carrier's limited air group (with 12 Su-27K fighters, 18 Ka-27 ASW helicopters, and 2 SAR helicopters).

Remote weapon firing might be exemplified by the planned use of carrier-borne fighters. The Soviets apparently believed (incorrectly) that, like themselves, Western navies would attack using long-range standoff missiles, probably air versions of Tomahawk. Like the U.S. Navy, they hoped to deal with the "archer" before it could fire its arrows. Area AAW defense was, therefore, built around the Sky Watch phased-array radar and the Su-27K fighter, the latter carrying long-range air-to-air missiles. Su-27K flight leaders were data-linked to the carrier and also to other members of the flight (MiG-31 interceptors use a similar air-to-air link). On patrol, the Su-27s would relay their radar data back to the carrier, which could steer them out along the threat axis or into a patrol formation. The carrier command system would prioritize radar-detected targets, and it would have fired Su-27 missiles once the airplanes had locked on. The Sky Watch radar in the smaller carrier *Adm. Gorshkov* was probably intended to work much the same way with land-based interceptors. The air-to-air data link has been quite successful, but a few years ago the Soviets were publicly complaining that the ship-to-air data link aboard the *Gorshkov* was not working properly. Air targets penetrating inside Su-27K range were to have been handed over automatically to shipboard missiles and point-defense guns. In Soviet/Russian practice, damage control is integral to combat control: when the targets were handed over, damage control was automatically alerted.

One of 2 "Second Captain" multifunction consoles on the bridge of the *Slava*-class cruiser *Marshal Ustinov*; the other is to the left. The curtains are to screen off ambient light; in addition, the entire area is curtained off from the front of the bridge. Another pair are in the ship's BIP. The ship has a total of about 20 such consoles. This type of console appears to be standard in recent ships, such as *Udaloys* and *Sovremennyys*. (Author)

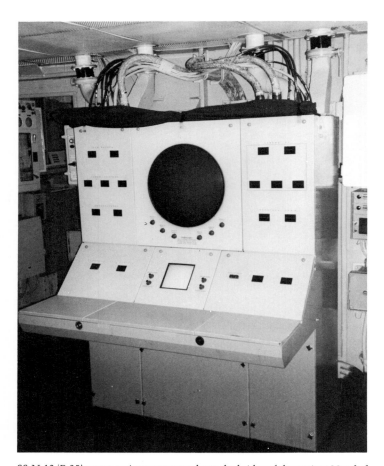

SS-N-12 (P-35) target-assignment console on the bridge of the cruiser *Marshal Ustinov*. A duplicate console is in the ship's BIP. A *Sovremennyy* has similar consoles on its bridge and in its BIP, to target its SS-N-22 missiles. (Eric Grove)

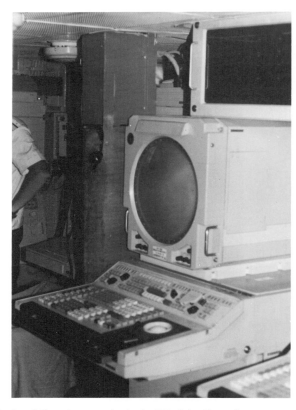

Standard multifunction consoles in the BIP of the *Slava*-class cruiser *Marshal Ustinov*. (Author)

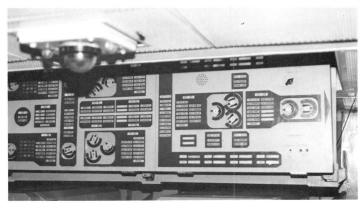

System status board (above multifunction consoles) in the SA-N-6 weapons-control space of the *Slava*-class cruiser *Marshal Ustinov*. Each panel indicates the status of a weapon or system sensor. The entire space is quite dark; it appears light only because the photograph was taken with a flash. (Author)

SA-N-6 engagement console in the weapons-control space of the *Marshal Ustinov*. There are 3 such consoles in the compartment. (Author)

There is sometimes an intermediate level between a "Second Admiral" and individual unit "Second Captains." For example, *Udaloy*-class destroyers (such as the *Adm. Kharlamov*) have what might be called a "Second Commodore" in a special space (with a pair of standard multifunction consoles and a data-link console). It is not clear whether the "Second Commodore" shares the ship's main computer with her "Second Captain." A Bear-F Mod 4 can control an ASW operation. For example, it can fire ASW missiles (SS-N-14s, -15s, -16s) carried by surface ships (it is not clear whether it can fire submarine-borne weapons).

Multifunction console in the weapons-control space of the *Marshal Ustinov*, with a status board (black-faced console) alongside. (Author)

SA-N-6 engagement-status board in the weapons-control space of the *Marshal Ustinov*. One is alongside each engagement console. The 6 rows of lights presumably indicate 6 missiles, 2 per target. (Author)

SS-N-12 control console in the BIP of the *Marshal Ustinov*. Standard practice seems to be to place such consoles only on the bridge and in BIP, never in a weapons-control space. (Author)

The single "Second Captain" console on the bridge of the *Udaloy*-class destroyer *Adm. Kharlamov*, screened against ambient light. (Author)

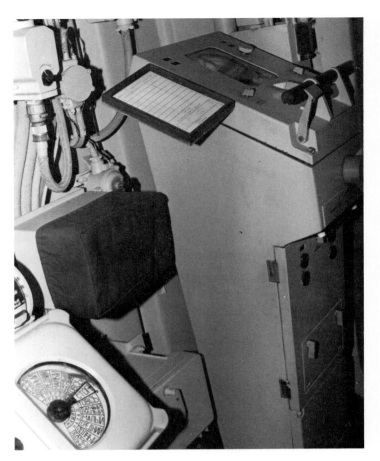

Steering stand and engine-room telegraph in the BIP of the *Adm. Kharlamov*. (Author)

The main "Second Captain" multifunction computer consoles are generally to be found in a screened-off area at the rear of the bridge and in the BIP. For example, in a *Slava*, each space holds 2 consoles (presumably, one for the air picture, one for the surface engagement) plus a weapons-assignment console for the long-range SS-N-12 (P-35) missiles. The BIP also contains the SS-N-12 operating console. In a *Udaloy*, there is only 1 multifunction console on the bridge, but there are 2 in the BIP. What is most striking is the absence of the numerous radar-tracker consoles to be found in Western CICs. The consoles in BIP show the picture the "Second Captain" forms.

"Second Captain" consoles in the BIP of the *Adm. Kharlamov*. (Author)

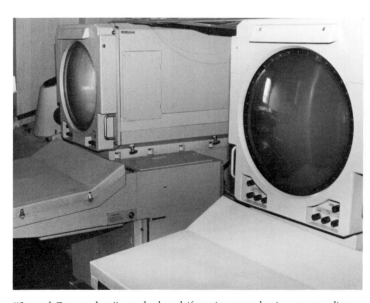

"Second Commodore" standard multifunction consoles in a space adjacent to the BIP of the *Adm. Kharlamov*; note the radar repeater in the background. (Author)

Data-link terminal in the "Second Commodore" space on board the *Adm. Kharlamov*. (Author)

The Russians apparently feel no need to resolve ambiguities between the outputs of different onboard radars, or between the outputs of ownship and consort sensors. It seems to follow that the "Second Captain" of a ship relies on the output of a single long-range radar, such as Top Sail or Top Pair in cruisers and carriers. The *Moskva* had radar consoles in her BIP; their operators entered data into the "Second Captain" via their pedals. Modern ships (at least the *Slava* and *Udaloy*) lack *any* radar consoles in their BIPs, so presumably in their cases the operators have been displaced by automatic target detectors in the radars. The BIP is in effect an alternative bridge; together with multifunction and surface-to-surface consoles it contains a steering stand and engine-order indicator. There may also be a vertical plot. As in other navies, COs differ as to whether they prefer to fight from the bridge or from the protected BIP.

The BIP is adjacent to, and opens into, a weapons-control space. Each weapon system relies on its own sensor or sensors tied to a dedicated console and computer. For example, ships generally have shorter-range air-search radars that serve their primary air-defense missiles. These radars are not, as is sometimes imagined, insurance against the failure of the main air-search set. They are more analogous to the separate target-acquisition radars (short-range air-search radars) of British and some European practice. The Soviets took this idea further; their architecture explains why point-defense missile systems (SA-N-4 and -9) have their own target-acquisition radars on their directors. Gun FCS directors, such as Bass Tilt and Kite Screech, combine the target acquisition and tracking functions in a single unit (see below under radars). The *Udaloy* is unusual in interposing a separate target-acquisition radar between the "Second Captain" and the SA-N-9 system. The *Sovremennyy* class of the 1980s seems unique among major units in depending on a single air-

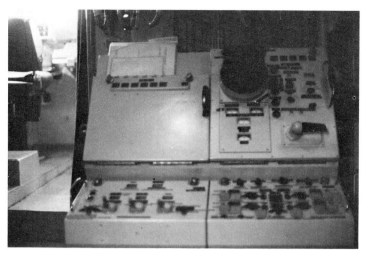

The bridge console on the *Hiddensee* (Tarantul-class missile boat). The hood at right is for the Plank Shave radar. The ship's missile system is controlled through this console (the bridge itself is to the left). (Author)

search radar (presumably, it employs a data bus, so that 1 radar can serve 2 functions). Typically, the executive officer controls weapons, fighting the ship warfare area by warfare area (different weapons are controlled from physically separate parts of the weapons-control space).

Ships too small for automation have much the same system architecture; they must be controllable by external command computers. For example, a Tarantul-class missile boat has a small CIC space abaft her bridge. It includes a plotting table and a console for the ship's main battery, her SS-N-2D missile system (Korell). There is no AAW display of any kind. The console has a "data link" setting allowing an external commander to control the ship and fire her missiles, concentrating fire by coordinating several ships. The weapons-control center below decks contains the main SS-N-2D control console and also the sole console of the gun FCS radar (Bass Tilt).

"Second Captains" form a family of versions emphasizing different warfare areas. The *Moskva*, *Volga* (submarine tender, i.e., group flagship), and Kresta-II versions share a common technology, although the latter is much less capable. Reportedly, the Kara class, construction of which began 2 yr after that of the Kresta-II class, has a next-generation version, which can handle more tracks and form a net with more ships. Karas have a ship-to-air data link (which Kresta-IIs lack) to work closely with May (Il-38) patrol aircraft.

The main surface-ship "Second Captain" types are

—Rocket Cruiser (RKR), initially on board the Kresta-Is, primarily for target selection, discrimination, and engagement. The main sensor was presumably the Big Bulge radar of a Bear-

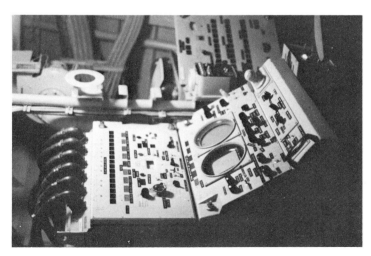

Korell control console for the SS-N-2D (P-20M) missile system on board the Tarantul-class missile boat *Hiddensee*, in the boat's below-decks weapons-control space. On the panel above the 2 CRTs (just above the B-scan) is a switch used to choose between 8 ESM frequencies. (Author)

D bomber. This computer also controlled the Side Globe jammer, which was considered a means of holding off counterattack until the SS-N-3 missiles could be fired. There was probably no intership data link.

—Rocket Cutter (MRK) on later Nanuchkas, to control their own SS-N-9 missiles and (probably later) also to coordinate the fire of accompanying missile boats with SS-N-2 missiles. The next-generation version is on board the surface-effect boat *Bora* (Project 1239, NATO "Dergach"), to work with Tarantuls. Reportedly, as of mid-1992, the transmitting section of the system did not work.

—ASW medium range, controlling SS-N-14 missiles, in Kresta-II- and Kara-class cruisers. The main sensor is the Bull Nose sonar. Presumably, the *Udaloy* class, with its longer-range sonar, has a later version of this system. Krivak-IIIs have a "Second Captain" embedded in a CDS similar in architecture to 9LV Mk 3 or to the Norwegian MSI-3100 (Krivak-I/IIs have no "Second Captain").

—ASW short range, on board a destroyer controlling groups of smaller ships firing RBU-6000s. This was probably the first approximation of a "Second Captain" to go to sea, on board the Kashin-class destroyer *Odarennyy* (ca. 1965). It is a seagoing version of a shore-based computer designed to control the RBU-6000 projectors on board small ASW craft such as Mirkas and Petyas. Given sonar data from the hunters, the computer evaluates the probability that the target is within a circle of a given size. Once the probability is high enough, the hunters are commanded to saturate the circle with projected depth bombs. Command was probably exerted via a data link (Fig Jar) to a bridge console on board each hunter. Newer corvettes fitted with RBU-6000s generally have their own fire-control computers (Burya) on board.

—AAW, controlling SA-N-3 missiles, in Kresta-II- and Kara-class cruisers. The main sensor is the Top Sail radar; the same computer probably handles the Bell Tap/Side Globes combi-

nation. SA-N-6 and -7 ships have their own versions. The associated data link is Bell Crown.

—Submarines, probably initially in the Victor-III class. As modernized (as Project 671RTMK rather than 671RTM), Victor-IIIs have "Second Captains" integrated into a CDS (Viking) via a data bus; reportedly, the system was adapted from a compromised version of the Norwegian MSI-90U (as in the new *Ula* class). A similar system is installed in some Kilos.

—ELINT ships (AGIs) probably have their own version of "Second Captain."

The "Second Admiral" was developed after the Soviets discovered that their old shore-based centralized system of multiship control could not work effectively as they pushed their fleet well out to sea. The centralized system, adapted from ground-warfare practice, seemed attractive because the single commander could easily coordinate the action of dissimilar forces (such as coastal craft and shore-based artillery and aircraft). Too, a single senior political commissar could monitor the whole operation. The central command directed its own reconnaissance (including radio direction-finding) assets; deployed units did not generally communicate much among themselves. Western observers wondered whether so rigid a system, with so little feedback from the deployed units, could possibly withstand the stress of combat. In land warfare, a senior commander manipulates large numbers of interchangeable units in close contact; top-down control works reasonably well. Ships well out to sea are spread widely. A central commander then faces complex choices, requiring large amounts of information. The greater the responsibility, the better the chance that the commander will be unable to process that information quickly enough.

In 1970 the Soviets tested their new techniques for naval warfare (including early "Second Captains") in the global Okean exercise. During the Five Year Plan ending that year, their fleet had moved well out to sea, forming pro-submarine warfare (PSW) groups to support Yankee-class SSBNs breaking out to get within missile

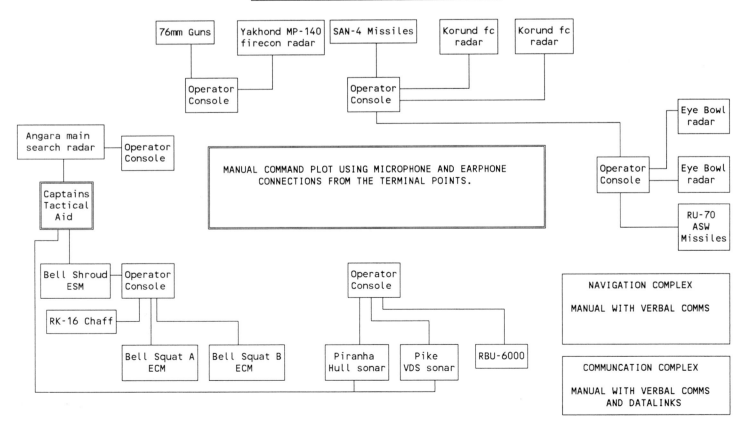

PROJECT 1135 COMMAND SYSTEM
(SIMPLIFIED AND SANITIZED)

The command system of a Krivak-I (Project 1135)–class frigate is typical of pre–Second Captain practice. It is clear that the tactical aid was added well after the ship was completed because it is not connected in any way to the main plot. Unlike Western naval summary plots, this one is horizontal, targets being indicated by markers rather than by grease pencil. This practice is much like that in World War II air-defense filter centers, the shore equivalents of CICs. (Stuart Slade/DMS-Forecast International)

PROJECT 1135P COMMAND SYSTEM - SIMPLIFIED AND SANITIZED

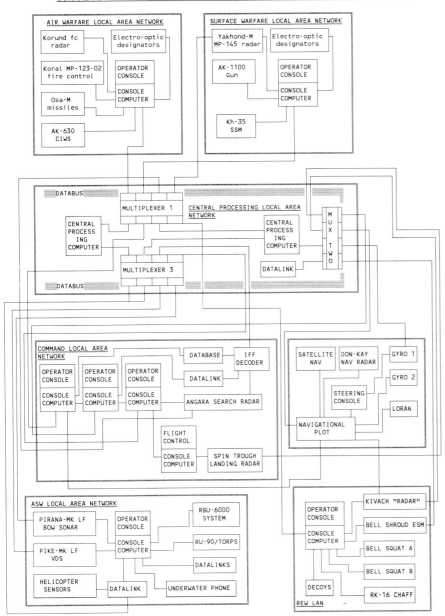

A Krivak-III (Project 1135P) has a fully integrated command system using a Second Captain and a data bus (the single bus has been somewhat distorted to simplify the diagram). This is now a federated CDS using LANs. Note that the Kivach radar is associated with the ECM (radio-electronic warfare, or REW) LAN because it can function as a precision radar direction-finder. The ships were designed as ASW units but taken over as border-patrol craft. This diagram reflects the original design concept, in which the ship's helicopter acted as an ASW sensor, reporting (like a U.S. LAMPS) through a data link into the ASW LAN. This version of the Krivak could dispense with SS-N-14 missiles because SS-N-15s (RU-90s) could be fired from the torpedo tubes. There was also provision for SS-N-25 (Kh-35) antiship missiles, though none have been seen to date. (Stuart Slade/DMS-Forecast International)

range of North America. Ships developed for PSW also conducted strategic ASW in the Mediterranean, where Western SSBNs had to operate in a relatively restricted area. Later, ASW and rocket cruiser (RKR)/antiship groups were formed to protect sanctuaries from which more advanced Soviet SSBNs could fire.

Okean showed that the Western observers were right: turn-around time for information was so long that virtually all the ships would have been sunk. The solution was the "Second Admiral," on board the first true Russian flagships.

Two *Sverdlov*-class cruisers were converted to command ships to test the RKR (*Zhdanov*) and PSW (*Adm.* Senyavin) command systems. They were followed by the *Kirov* (RKR) and *Kiev* (PSW) classes. A parallel program produced submarine brigade flagships (the existing command tenders, beginning with the *Volga*, already performed a kind of flagship function). The converted cruisers were tested in Okean 75 (1975). At least 1 participant understood their

true significance; the player representing the U.S. Navy made every effort to destroy them (including notionally crashing airplanes into them). It became painfully obvious that the loss of a flagship would completely dislocate an operation. Hence the very heavy antiaircraft batteries of the last ships of the *Kirov* class.

Like surface attackers, submarines are cued by the central command (in their case, via submarine tender–flagships). The most striking, and best-publicized, case was the interception of the nuclear carrier *Enterprise* en route to Vietnam in February 1968, by a November-class submarine. Each brigade (3 divisions, 2 submarines each, 1 of which is active in peacetime, the others being retained for mobilization) attacks just 1 target before retiring, so there is no need to signal back the status of the boats (so that the central command does not order attacks by empty submarines). Under some circumstances, particularly PSW, surface ships could control nearby supporting submarines by acoustic signals. In ASW operations, sub-

PROJECT 671RTMK COMMAND SYSTEM (SIMPLIFIED AND SANITIZED)

SECOND CAPTAIN LOCAL AREA NETWORK

| COMMAND CONSOLE 1 | COMMAND CONSOLE 2 | COMMAND CONSOLE 3 | COMMAND CONSOLE 4 | DATALINK |
| CONSOLE COMPUTER | CONSOLE COMPUTER | CONSOLE COMPUTER | CONSOLE COMPUTER | SPECIAL DATALINK |

NAVIGATION AND PLOTTING LOCAL AREA NETWORK

| GYRO-1 | GYRO-2 | DATALINK | OMEGA/LORAN | GLONASS |
| STEERING CONSOLE | | | NAVIGATIONAL PLOT | |

RADIO-ELECTRONIC WARFARE LOCAL AREA NETWORK

- SNOOP TRAY 2 "RADAR" — RADAR SCAN CONVERTER
- DATALINK — OPERATOR CONSOLE
- ESM THREAT LIBRARY
- BRICK PULP ESM — CONSOLE COMPUTER
- PARK LAMP DF

VIKING CENTRAL PROCESSING LOCAL AREA NETWORK

| MAIN COMPUTER 1 | MAIN COMPUTER 2 | MAIN COMPUTER 3 |

MULTIPLEXER 1 — DATABUS — MULTIPLEXER 2 — DATABUS — MULTIPLEXER 3

SENSORS SUITE LOCAL AREA NETWORK

- BARRACUDA LF A/P BOW SONAR
- AKULA FLANK ARRAYS
- CHANEL PASSIVE INTERCEPT
- PASSIVE RANGING SONAR
- ACOUSTIC COUNTERMEASURES
- MULTIPLEXER 4 — DATABUS — MULTIPLEXER 5
- PERISCOPES
- WAKE SENSOR SYSTEM
- PITHON TOWED ARRAY
- FIRE CONTROL SONAR
- UNDER-ICE NAV SONAR
- MINE AVOIDING SONAR
- UNDERWATER TELEPHONE

| OPERATOR CONSOLE 1 | OPERATOR CONSOLE 2 | OPERATOR CONSOLE 3 |
| CONSOLE COMPUTER | CONSOLE COMPUTER | CONSOLE COMPUTER |

WEAPONS CONTROLS LOCAL AREA NETWORK

- 53cm TORPEDO TUBES
- 65cm TORPEDO TUBES — 65CM TORPEDO TUBE CONTROL
- NUCLEAR RELEASE

| TORPEDOES CONTROL | MISSILES CONTROL | ESCAPE & EVASION | MAIN COMPUTER 4 |
| CONSOLE COMPUTER | CONSOLE COMPUTER | CONSOLE COMPUTER | |

The command system of a modernized Victor-III– class submarine (Project 671RTMK) is built around a single data bus (broken up in this diagram to simplify arrangement). The special data link in the "Second Captain" LAN is to authorize the release of nuclear weapons (note the special nuclear-release lock in the weapons-control section). The net computing power of the 4 command consoles in the "Second Captain" network exceeds that of the main computers. The Viking system is modeled on the Norwegian MSI-90U. Note that, as in the Krivak-III, the surface-search radar is included in the ECM system because of its ESM role. Note, too, that there is a special data link associated with ESM, allowing units to pass data so as to triangulate targets. (Stuart Slade/DMS-Forecast International)

marines probably often avoid IFF problems by operating in a scouting line, firing long-range weapons only over a limited forward sector.

No distant commander could efficiently control a submarine brigade against fast high-value targets; Okean 70 proved that each brigade needed its own submarine flagship. As in surface flagships, the key piece of technology was a compact computer, which might be called a "Second Commodore." Units of the Alfa, Echo-II, Victor-I (at least 2 flagships), Victor-II (at least 1), and Victor-III (at least 3) classes were converted. The special communications versions (SSQ) of the Hotel- and Golf-class strategic submarines were probably interim or experimental submarine flagships. Submarines intended to operate closer to the coast, such as Tangos, were probably never converted to flagship configuration. Nuclear submarines, with their global reach, were a very different proposition. It appears that Kilos were built in brigades of 7, each including a flagship.

The external marks of a submarine flagship are a larger Pert Spring satellite-communications antenna, a more elaborate Park Lamp VLF antenna, and a larger UHF communications antenna (Shotgun). Presumably, the flagship receives target and command information via a satellite or long-haul radio. Because each submarine has Pert Spring and Park Lamp, she can also receive instructions directly from home. The flagship probably uses her acoustic communications to bring brigade units to periscope depth for LOS radio contact during the approach to the attack area; once in the area, communication is probably limited to stereotyped acoustic messages.

The Soviets reportedly much favored brigade attacks conducted at maximum range, so as not to risk the attacking submarine. "Browning shots" of pattern-running torpedoes would generally be fired into formations such as convoys. Coordinated bow shots were favored against fast high-value targets such as carriers. Such tactics favor the use of the wake-following torpedoes now in service.

Bell Thumb data link (successor to Bell Crown) on the mainmast of the destroyer *Bezuderzhannyy* in 1993. (Author)

Bell Crown is broadly equivalent to Link 11, connecting "Second Captains," probably mainly for radar data. The antenna consists of an upward-facing radome, a smaller downward-facing radome, and a third radome pointed horizontally outboard. All 3 may be mounted together, or separated vertically and horizontally by short lattice masts (as in a *Slava*). The earliest form was Bell Cap. Tested in 1973–74, this link is on the *Kiev, Moskva, Kirov, Slava,* Kara, Kresta-II, *Udaloy,* and *Sovremennyy* classes. **Bell Thumb** is the successor system. **Bell Strike** is a special link for ESM data. **Bell Hop** connects Bear-Ds with surface units and submarines; reportedly, it is nearly a direct copy of the U.S. postwar AEW link (Bellhop) used with APS-20 radars (Big Bulge is closely related to APS-20). **Bell Spike,** on board *Kirov-* and *Slava*-class cruisers, may be a surface-to-air link controlling land-based fighters (Su-27s) operating over the sea. The antenna is a very sharp spike resembling the end of a toothpick. **Fig Jar** command-fires RBU-6000s (and presumably transmits sonar data). The dedicated antenna, a squat cylindrical radome with a flat top pointing up at the end of a yardarm, was probably superseded in small ASW ships by a link in which Strut Curve is the receiver (Grishas, all of which have Strut Curve, lack Fig Jar). Fig Jar is on board *Moskva,* Kara, Kresta-I/II, Kynda, Mod Kashin, Mirka, Petya, and Poti classes. It may be on board *Kiev, Kirov, Udaloy,* and Krivak classes. (The developed form is Bell Jar.)

Missile video data links are **Fish Bowl** (2 in Nanuchkas, for SS-N-9 [P-50] missiles), **Front Door** (formerly Trap Door in *Kiev*-class carriers, for SS-N-3 and -12: in *Kiev, Slava,* Echo-II, Juliett classes), and **Light Bulb** (2 in a *Sovremennyy* or *Neustrashimyy,* 2 in the surface-effect ship *Sivuch,* 1 in a Tarantul-II or -III, and 2 in some Nanuchkas, to control P-80, P-100, P-27, P-270, and P-50 missiles, respectively; also in Krivaks and the one Osa converted to carry Kh-35 [SS-N-25] missiles). The submarine **Rim Hat** includes an SS-N-22 (P-100) data link (on Akula, Sierra, and Typhoon classes). The **Plinth Net** SS-N-3 missile video link, in effect the prototype for Fish Bowl and Light Bulb, is now nearly extinct (on Kynda and Kresta-I classes). Surface ships generally carry 2 video-data-link antennas, 1 on each side, for 360-deg coverage; Tarantul-IIs/IIIs carry only a single masthead unit. Since the link is almost certainly directional, the

missiles can engage only 1 target or 1 group of targets (shifting between missiles flying close together) at a time. Therefore, it seems unlikely that SS-N-9s or -22s can be maneuvered to approach a target simultaneously from different directions; they are probably limited to stream attacks. Although conceived as a high-capacity missile data link, **Light Bulb** is now reportedly used as a general-purpose high-capacity link analogous to NATO **Link 16 (JTIDS).** That explains its presence aboard some AGIs and on some nonmissile ships. SS-N-12/19 ships carry **Punch Bowl** (EORSAT/RORSAT receiver) to acquire targeting data.

Shot Dome/Shot Rock are small radomes, typically located above the bridge, in all modern combatants (and backfitted in some older destroyers, now discarded). They are directional antennas to alert a ship to turn on her transmitter for bridge-to-bridge communication. The size suggests microwave frequency, which would normally limit the system to LOS and thus make it difficult to intercept.

Some radars (certainly Plank Shave and Strut Curve) function as highly directional data-link receivers.

EORSATs/RORSATs are, respectively, ESM (for radar sidelobe emissions) and side-looking radar ocean-reconnaissance satellites conceived as targeters for Soviet warships, probably specifically for the SS-N-19 missile. The satellites down-link directly to the Punch Bowl antenna on board the missile shooters; satellites can also cross-link information to a command center ashore, or store it for later dump. Both satellites were probably conceived in parallel, but RORSAT appears to have been canceled as part of the defense cuts of the late 1980s. EORSAT became operational in March 1980. Satellites occupy near-circular 276–86-mile orbits (period 93.3 min) inclined at 65 deg. They last 22 months. Location accuracy at the surface may be as good as 1.3 nm. Five or 6 satellites lie in 2 orbital planes (so that a second EORSAT follows the first along the same path over the target); pairs of EORSATs replace the former RORSAT-EORSAT combination. Paired fixes give an estimate of a target's course and speed. Two constellations of ELINT satellites provide data only to a ground station: (i) 6 satellites in 6 orbital planes spaced 60 deg apart, mean altitude 443 miles, inclination 82.5 deg, launched by SL-14; (ii) newer series, larger satellites, inclination 71 deg, altitude 579 miles, normally 4 in orbit (SL-16 booster). Presumably, these satellites cue shooters and the EORSATs on which they rely.

The new **Irida** HF surface-wave radar is similar in concept to the Marconi system described above; it has been under test since about 1990 on the Black Sea and at Nakhodka on the Sea of Japan. Each system covers a 90-deg sector out to 280–300 km; it detects ships and can handle up to 100 air targets. Peak power is 64 kW (average 16 kW, using 4 4-kW transmitters at 7–15 MHz). Accuracy is 3–5 deg and 3–4 km. The transmitting array cannot be more than 50 m from the shoreline, and it is 500 to 1,500 m from the receiver.

Weapon Developers and Manufacturers

Weapons are developed and produced by the scientific research institutes (NII), the experimental design bureaus (OKB; sometimes machine design bureaus, MKB, or special design bureaus, SKB), and the research-production organizations (NPO). Many OKBs, formerly known by the name of the chief or founding designer, have recently been renamed. Each ministry has central NIIs; aircraft and aerodynamic missiles are the responsibility of TsAGI, the Central Aero- and Hydrodynamic Institute. The ballistic-missile equivalent is TsNIIMash at Kaliningrad, a Moscow suburb. Services have their own NIIs assigned to particular areas. The NII produces a preferred basic design solution, versions of which different design bureaus (OKBs) develop (for many years the relationship between the U.S. Naval Research Laboratory and radar-making companies was not too different). That is why so many Soviet military aircraft or missiles of a particular generation look so alike. NPOs, authorized in 1968, are an attempt to bring design bureaus into direct contact with the producing factory.

NPO Altair in Moscow integrates naval surface-to-air missile systems; most of the missiles are developed by the P. D. Grushin (Fakel) MKB in Khimki, near Moscow, which was originally part of the Lavochkin aircraft design OKB. Naval cruise missiles are developed by the V. N. Chelomey OKB (now NPO Mashinostroyenie) in Moscow and by the Berezhniak OKB (now Raduga MKB) in Dubna, near Moscow. Raduga missiles are made in Ukraine. Chelomey develops long-range weapons (SS-N- 3s/9s/12s/19s/22s) and Berezhniak (who split from the MiG OKB in 1957) shorter-range and air-launched weapons (SS-N-2s/7s, P-270s, AS-1s/4s/5s/6s, Kh-41s, SS-N-14s). The 2 bureaus apparently compete in the intermediate-range category (SS-N-9s/22s). They adopted different guidance concepts. Berezhniak missiles are fired at a range and bearing with respect to the launch platforms. Chelomey missiles are fired to geographic coordinates, and hence are better suited to concentration fire from dispersed platforms.

The Lyulev SKB (NPO Novator) at Sverdlovsk developed the later antisubmarine missiles (SS-N-15s and -16s), as well as the Alfa coast-defense missile and the R-72/K-172 (AAM) and the land-based SA-4 and SA-11 air-defense systems. NPO Uran in St. Petersburg is responsible for torpedoes. It was formed in 1976 out of the Gidropribor OKB (in St. Petersburg) and the Dvigatel plant; torpedoes are tested at Feodosiya on the Black Sea and at Kakhadka in the Pacific.

V. P. Makayev OKB (Mach NPO) in Miass (near Chelyabinsk) has developed most of the naval ballistic missiles, the main exceptions probably being SS-N-17s and -20s, which may have been developed by Chelomey.

Zvezda OKB in Kaliningrad develops tactical air-to-surface missiles, although it is now subject to competition from Vympel and Raduga (Kh-41). Zvezda developed the SS-N-25 (Kh-35), which has an air-launched variant.

Vympel (Pennant) MKB in Moscow, formerly OKB-134, consolidated AAM development, formerly under several aircraft OKBs, in the early 1960s. Zvezda was an offshoot of OKB-134. Another offshoot, S. P. Nepobidimy OKB in Kolomna, is responsible for short-range antiaircraft missiles (SA-7s/14s/16s, which have naval equivalents). To confuse matters, there is also a quite distinct TsNPO (Central NPO) Vympel formed in 1992, which is responsible for antiballistic missile work. The Agat Moscow Research Institute develops missile seekers.

NPP Region in Moscow develops and makes aircraft rockets, laser-guided bombs, and the APR-2 torpedo.

NPO Fazotron, in Moscow, is responsible for air-to-air radars, for the Positive-E target-designation radar, and also for recent naval ECM systems (Kursk/Bell Nip and Flat Track).

STRATEGIC WEAPONS

The Soviets developed strategic (i.e., nuclear) naval cruise and ballistic missiles in parallel. Ballistic missiles were developed mainly by Makayev, cruise missiles by Chelomey. Modified versions of the German V-1 and V-2 were tested both in towed submarine barge form and on board submarines. V-2 barges (with which the U.S. Navy experimented unsuccessfully) were built in several experimental series (perhaps 300 were made); no more than about 20 were on hand at any time, and none was successful. Missile exhaust blew the barge apart as the missile fired, throwing it off course.

The experimental submarine installations were Whiskey Single Cylinder (firing SS-N-3s) and a single-tube Zulu (Project 611A) carrying a single Scud (first firing in September 1955). The next step was 2 missiles/submarine (Whiskey Twin Cylinder) and a 2-tube Zulu (Project 611B, carrying SS-N-4s [R-13s]). Ballistic missiles were raised to the top of the sail, fueled, and then fired. Apparently, they had to be kept well clear of the surface of the sea, e.g., to avoid icing. The surface-launched missiles were sufficiently satisfactory to justify the production of parallel series of diesel and nuclear cruise- and ballistic-missile submarines: SS-N-3–firing Whiskey Long Bin (4 missiles) and Echo-I (Project 659: 6 missiles); and SS-N-4– firing Golf (Project 629) and Hotel (Project 658) (3 missiles each, in sail tubes above a necked-down pressure-hull section, so that missiles could be hoisted for surface firing). Parallel diesel and nuclear designs were necessary mainly because the production of nuclear reactors was limited.

The next missiles (SS-N-5s [R-21s] and P-35s/SS-N-12s) were designed to fire submerged; an SS-N-5 was popped out of its tube by gas or air before igniting. Because it did not have to be raised well above the water for firing, it no longer had to be carried in the submarine's sail (existing ballistic-missile submarines rearmed with or redesigned for SS-N-5 did retain their sail tubes). In the new Project 667, the missiles were moved down alongside the necked-down pressure-hull section: 3 could be accommodated on each side. A par-

allel Project 666 would have carried 6 P-35 strategic cruise missiles, also between the outer and pressure hulls, angled up at 45 deg. Parallel diesel submarines presumably would have been similarly armed.

In 1959 Khrushchev ousted the Soviet Navy from the land-attack role in favor of the new land-based Strategic Rocket Forces. The missile-firing submarines now had to attack ships. Salvos of ballistic missiles (in effect, long-range artillery) fired at choke points would intercept ships passing through; cruise missiles would be fitted with seekers. The new SS-N-6 (RSM-25 Zyb) ballistic missile (the tactical-technical requirement for which was issued in 1960) could be fired far more promptly than SS-N-5s (to reach the choke point in time to make use of a warning that, e.g., a carrier group was passing through). The planned ultimate antiship ballistic weapon, SS-NX-13, had a homing (antiradar) maneuverable reentry body. Because it did not appear until about a decade after the new mission had become obsolete, it was never deployed. As an interim step, the existing Echo-I cruise-missile submarine was lengthened to accommodate another pair of launchers and modified to handle a new guidance technique, to become Echo-II (Project 675, see below).

About 1960 Projects 666 and 667 were lengthened to double their missile batteries, to 12 SS-N-5/6s or P-35s (another necked-in pressure-hull section was added abaft the full-diameter section housing the reactors). In 1962 work on the cruise-missile version was stopped because of problems with the P-35 missile. The only available cruise missile, the earlier SS-N-3, could not be fired submerged; it required an elevating tube outside the submarine's hull. That limited a submarine of this size to 8 missiles, and there was no point in building a new type. Instead, a second batch of Echo-IIs was ordered. The ballistic-missile version was redesigned in 1963–64 to carry 16 SS-N-6s rather than 12 SS-N-5s and, moreover, to carry them inside the pressure hull, as in contemporary Western SSBNs. It became the Yankee class (Project 667A). The redesign seems to have been prompted by a compromise of Western submarine-construction or missile-guidance technology.

The new diesel ballistic-missile submarine (Project 652) was dropped (possibly in favor of continued Golf production), probably because it could not be stretched to provide the sort of salvo needed for the new anti–battle group mission. The diesel cruise-missile submarine was redesigned as Juliett (Project 651), carrying 4 SS-N-3s in elevating launchers. The big nuclear cruise-missile submarine almost certainly inspired the current Oscar, with her SS-N-19s (which superseded SS-N-12s). With the fall of Khrushchev, the Soviet Navy was allowed back into the strategic attack role.

Under the Bush-Yeltsin agreement, all naval tactical nuclear weapons (including cruise missiles) are to be withdrawn. That eliminates existing **SS-N-21**s (RKP-55s, designed by Lyulev) at sea. The nonnuclear Kh-65 was developed from the equivalent Raduga **AS-15** (RKV-500, Kh-55A/B; the coincidence with the RKP-55 designation may mean that SS-N-21 was adapted from AS-15). Surely a nonnuclear alternative to the parallel SS-N-21s, equivalent to current Tomahawks, will follow. The Victor-III trials ship for SS-N-21 had a 2-missile pod added to her hull forward of her sail, apparently a prototype for deployment on Victors. Since the submarine probably lacked the appropriate mission computer, these missiles would surely have been loaded with preselected flight plans. That would not have been appropriate for tactical nonnuclear use. Presumably, only submarines designed to carry SS-N-21s (and, therefore, fitted with the appropriate computer) will carry any tactical variant: Akula, probably Sierra, and Yankee-Notch. Raduga's larger **SS-N-24** was canceled about 1990 because of defense cuts; its air-launched equivalent, AS-19, was canceled in 1992. It (and presumably also SS-N-24s) carried 2 warheads, with which it could attack targets as much as 100 km apart (much as a bomblet-carrying Tomahawk can attack targets in sequence). AS-19's designed range was 4,000 km [2,160 nm].

An **SS-N-20**/RSM-52 Mod 2 was probably tested in 1988, and a completely new SLBM (presumably to be SS-N-26) is reported under development. For treaty purposes, SS-N-20 is credited with 10 RVs; **SS-N-23** (RSM-54) is credited with 4, although as many as 10 have been reported in the past. SS-N-8 is RSM-40 Vysota; SS-N-18 is RSM-50 Volna. **SS-N-18** Mods 2 and 3 are obsolete. **SS-N-6** (RSM-25) and **SS-N-17** (RSM-45) are now extinct, all Yankee-class submarines having been dismantled.

The following information on SLBMs was released for the START Treaty in 1991:

	SS-N-6	SS-N-8	SS-N-17	SS-N-18	SS-N-20	SS-N-23
Diameter	1.5 m	1.8 m	1.54 m	1.8 m	2.4 m	1.9 m
Length without warhead	7.1 m	13.0 m	10.6 m	14.1 m	9.5 m	14.8 m
Launch Weight	14.2 t	33.3 t	26.9 t	35.3 t	90 t	40.3 t
First Stage	13.5 t	52.8 t	—	—	—	—
Throw Weight	650 kg	1,100 kg	450 kg	1,650 kg	2,550 kg	2,800 kg

The launch weight of SS-N-20 includes components jettisoned at launch; without them, the missile weighs 84 t.

STRIKE WARFARE

In July 1992 the Antonov OKB announced a maritime-patrol version of the An-72 (Coaler). **An-72P** employs an inertial-navigation system linked to its EO sensors. Its autopilot can be used to calculate ship's course and speed. A data link can send the image back to a control center. The first 3 aircraft were delivered to the Pacific Border Guards, to replace An-24s. This airplane has also reportedly been sold to Iran, in a deal that also may have included Tu-22 Backfire bombers. In theory, the totally passive An-72P can identify targets, cueing the Backfires without exposing them to detection by hostile ESM. The airplane carries SFP-2A flares for night operation. Endurance is 5.3 hr at 160–90 kt at 3,300 ft. The airplane is armed with a 23-mm gun in a starboard under-fuselage fairing, and has eyeball-type windows aft of its flight deck.

Big Bulge is reportedly descended from the U.S. S-band APS-20, widely used after World War II for both airborne early warning and surface search. The Bear-D uses Big Bulge mainly to obtain a picture of the OTH target for missile ships, down-linking the video to them. It has back-to-back antennas, 1 transmitting the linked video while the other transmits and receives radar pulses. The data can also be passed to other aircraft, particularly Hormone-A helicopters, for re-transmission (cross-linking). Such dissemination allows dispersed strike units to attack together to saturate target defenses. The Hormone Big Bulge radar is also used for surface search, e.g., to investigate ESM contacts.

Many air-to-surface missile/aircraft control systems ("complexes": radar, computer, and data links) are designated in a K series (the K designator is *not* the missile designator):

—KS: For the AS-1 (KS-1) missile, with Kobalt-N radar, is obsolete.
—K-10S: For the K-10 (AS-2) missile, with EN radar (probably Puff Ball); in naval service in 1961, superseded by K-26. The airplane was designated Tu-16K-10 (Badger).
—K-11: For the KSR-2M missile (AS-5), with Rubin-1 (probably Short Horn) radar.
—K-16: For the KSR-2P (AS-2) missile; the airplane is Tu-16K-11–16 (1962). Presumably, this is a modified K-11 with a Rubin radar.
—K-20: For the AS-3 (Kh-20) strategic missile (Bear-C); extinct.
—K-22: For the AS-4 (Kh-22: in Tu-22 Blinders and -22M Backfires), replacing K-20 in all Bear-Cs.
—K-26: Multimissile type, for the K-10 (AS-2), Kh-22 (AS-4), and KSR-5 (AS-6) missiles. The airplanes were originally Tu-16K-10–26s (presumably, K-26 is a modified K-10) or Tu-95K-26s (modified Bear carrying an AS-6 missile). Information supplied during CFE negotiations: Tu-16 versions all have a target-detection range of 50–100 km (accuracy 300–400 m, angular accuracy 0.75 [probably deg]); fire-control cycle time is 300–600 sec. The system can fire 2 missiles against 1 target. Versions of Tu-16 vary in the number of sensors (1–3). This system was adapted to Blinder (Tu-22Ks) and Backfire (Tu-22Ms) bombers carrying the AS-4 missile. It has a new radar (Down Beat, with the same range accuracy), presumably a modified Short Horn. The latest Backfire version (Tu-22M2 and -22M3) employs 4 sensors and can detect targets at 150–200 km. It can handle 2 targets simultaneously (which implies that a Backfire carries no more than 2 missiles at a time, even though it has 3 hard points). Angular accuracy is 0.3 (probably deg). Fire-control cycle time is 5–10 min. The earlier Tu-22Ms and the Tu-22K Blinder used 2 sensors and were credited with a target-detection range of 100–150 km (accuracy and fire-control cycle time were the same, suggest-

ing that the radar was a less-powerful version of the same device, and that the computer was the same). Each version handles 1 target at a time.

Klon (**Square Tie** radar) controls SS-N-2A/B/C missiles on board Osa-class missile boats and Charlie-I– class submarines (SS-N-7 is a modified SS-N-2C). The operator designates targets on the CRT, using a *vilka* (fork, i.e., a pair of strobes) and a movable range marker, both controlled by a joystick. Two consecutive detections suffice for autotracking to begin (typically, the radar is turned off once the computer has calculated range and range rate; it is turned on intermittently to check the accuracy of the tracker). The FCS commands the missile to fly on autopilot until it is about 3.5 nm from the predicted target position, when the seeker is turned on (it then has just enough time to receive 8 returned pulses from the target, then lock-on).

Korrell (**Plank Shave** radar) controls SS-N-2D (P-20M system); it can accept data-linked commands. In a Tarantul, a 2-part command console is in a space abaft the bridge. Corrections are cranked into the left-hand panel. The right-hand side carries a Plank Shave CRT in a hood (range scales 1, 5, 25, 50, and 75 km) and a target-indication receiver; the firing panel is below it. Deviations from standard conditions are cranked in, e.g., temperature, wind speed, and direction. The console shows range to target, ship's deviation from attack course (10- or 0.1-deg increments), seeker's range setting (1.0- or 0.01-km intervals), free flight time (10- or 0.1-sec intervals), and correction to attack course (0.1-deg intervals). The targeting method is also set on this console: (i) autonomous, using Plank Shave and a calculated lead angle, (ii) third-party targeting (target's coordinates, speed, and course are manually entered), (iii) without lead angle (used when target's speed and course are unknown or the target is maneuvering violently and, presumably, against a fixed target), and (iv) data link (remote control).

The Plank Shave radar console and the analog (gears plus some electrical components) FCS computer are in a separate space below

Plank Shave radar on board the Tarantul-class missile boat *Hiddensee*. (Author)

decks, near other FCS equipment. Given Plank Shave (Harpoon) data, Korell computes missile's course and flight time, based on target's range and bearing, the desired range from the target at which the missile's guidance system is to be switched on, change of range and bearing as the target steers a presumably straight course, true wind direction and speed, and the average cruise speeds of the missile and the ship. The missile's search-sector setting is a function of range to target, given in a table. The missile's speed depends on temperature (the average varies from 299 m/sec at $-20°C$ to 316 m/sec at $+10°C$). Typically, the missile is set to search within ± 5 deg (± 15 deg when no lead angle is used). Set cruise height is 25 or 50 m [80 or 160 ft]. The seeker turn-on point is set at 5, 10, or 15 cables [0.25, 0.5, or 0.75 nm] from the computed target position.

If Plank Shave or the computer fails, or if the ship is observing radar silence, the missile can be fired on the basis of data manually input from other radars (Bass Tilt or a navigational radar) or the optical viewer (periscope) in the roof of the bridge (in the "viewer" mode the missile is fired without any lead angle). When other radars are used, the ship's course is held manually. Free-flight range is set as the difference between the target's estimated range and the seeker's turn-on range. If the target's range is estimated by eye, free-flight time is set as the shortest possible (3–4 km) so that the seeker is turned on as early as possible.

The Plank Shave console below decks has a rectangular B-scan (20 deg × 20 cables [1 nm], centered on the expected target location) alongside a PPI, to indicate the range gates applied to the target. The radar can sector-scan within an 80-deg sector. The target's relative-speed limits are ± 80 kt; the maximum computed target range is 80 nm (maximum solution range 60 nm). The missile's range is 55 nm (effective limits are 8 and 80 km [5 and 43 nm]).

To line up the missile's gyros, the ship must keep a steady (combat) course when preparing to fire missiles; the computer takes over the helm. The bridge unit can change heading within ± 3 deg. Missiles fly straight paths; they cannot dogleg. Full missile warm-up from cold condition (Readiness Level II) takes 400 sec. Missiles can be held fully warmed up for 30 min, and in a 200-sec mode for 8 hr (the last 60 sec is running up the gyro, altimeter, and rocket-speed indicator).

Air-to-Surface Weapons

"Kh" in the designations below is the English version of the Cyrillic letter "X." In 1993 the Russians began using instead the Polish equivalent, H, so a missile called Kh-29 here is X-29 in Russian and may be marked H-29 at a show.

AS-2 (K-10, K-10S, K-10M [nuclear], RSL-1) and **AS-5** (KS-11, KSR-2M, KSR-2P) are extinct (any surviving Egyptian AS-5s probably are not operational). Both were developed by the MiG bureau.

AS-4 (Kh-22) versions are Kh-22, -22MP, and -22N; -22MP is probably an antiradar version. Designer: Raduga.

AS-6 Kingfish (KSR-5) versions are KSR-5 (1968 version), -5N (improved), and -5P (antiradar). In 1993 loitering antiradar and target versions (KSR-5NM[MV]) of AS-6 were shown at Abu Dhabi. Designer: Raduga.

AS-7 Kerry (Grom, Kh-23/66) was introduced in the mid-1960s. Kh-66, for the MiG-21, was the first Soviet tactical air-to-surface missile. Kh-23, a slightly modified version originally intended for the MiG-23, began a new numbering series. It was carried by naval Forgers (Yak-38s and -38Ms) and presumably by some land-based naval aircraft. It was followed by the improved Kh-23M, which is carried by the newer-generation strike aircraft of the mid-1970s (Su-17 series); presumably, it is tied to their standard avionics, particularly their FCS radar. That may mean that the radar tracks the missile. The missile may use semiactive terminal homing (like the much-larger AS-1s); some AS-7s have dielectric nose cones, which would not be used with any form of command guidance. Kh-23M platforms: Su-17M3s, Su-20s, Su-22s, and Su-22M3 and -22M4 export strike aircraft. Another version, KhA-23, is limited to the Su-17R reconnaissance airplane.

Users: Bulgaria, CIS, India, Iraq, Poland, Romania (as A921).

Designer: Zvezda.

AS-9 Kyle is Kh-28 (range 80 km) and -28E (range 120 km), an ARM carried by Badgers, Backfires, Fencers, and Fitter-Cs and -Ds. Designer: Zvezda.

AS-10 Karen (Kh-25)/**AS-12** Kegler (Kh-25M/Kh-27): Kh-25 (Izdeliye 69) is a command-guided solid-fuel missile evolved from Kh-

23 (AS-7). Kh-25M is a more-versatile second-generation version: Kh-25MD, Kh-25MK (export), Kh-25MP (antiradar, Izdeliye 711), Kh-25MR (radio command, Izdeliye 711), Kh-25ML (laser-guided, Izdeliye 713). Effective range depends on the guidance technique: 8 km for radio command, 10 km for laser guidance, 40 km for antiradar. All are 275 mm [10.8 in] in diameter. Kh-25MR is 3.83 m long (span 0.82 m, weight 320 kg, warhead 140 kg). Kh-25MP is 4.353 m long (warhead 89.6 kg, overall 320 kg); Kh-25ML is 4.255 m long (warhead 89.6 kg, overall 300 kg). An EO (television-guided) version, presumably Kh-25MT, was shown at the 1992 Moscow Air Show (length 4.04 m, weight 300 kg, warhead 90 kg, launch range 2–20 km, altitude 100–10,000 m, maximum flight speed 800 m/sec). There is also a similar IIR version. The antiradar version (Kh-25MP) is 4.355 m long (310 kg, warhead 90 kg); launch range is 2.5– 60 km (altitude 100–15,000 m), and maximum speed is 900 km/sec. There may also be a KhA-25 version. Reportedly, Kh-25MP/AS-12 is a lighter-weight successor to AS-9, for the Su-24 Fencer, Su-25 Frogfoot, and Tu-22M Backfire. It entered service about 1978. The frequency band is preselected. The seeker is described as a "unified anti-radar seeker type A, A' and A." Kh-27 is a modified Kh-25MP (-27PO for Su-17Rs, -27PS for MiG-27s). Designer: Zvezda.

AS-11 Kilter (Kh-58, Izdeliye 112) is a large, solid-fuel, antiradar missile broadly comparable to HARM. It entered service about 1978. Kh-58U (as carried by Su-17M3s) is 38 cm × 4.8 m with span 1.45 m [15 × 189; 57 in], weighing 640 kg [1,141 lb]; warhead is 160 kg [353 lb]. Range is 50 km [27 nm]. AS-11 is carried by Su-17M3s/M4s/Rs, Su-24Ms, and MiG-25BM Foxbat-Fs. Presumably, it can also be carried by the large carrier-based fighters. Reports of a nuclear version have not been confirmed. A version specifically intended to deal with Patriot and similar systems was announced at the 1992 Moscow Air Show. It is 5 m long (650 kg, span 1.17 m), with a minimum launch range of 10 km (maximum 160 km) and a maximum speed of Mach 3.6; the missile carries a B-band passive seeker. No warhead weight was given. An antiship version, Kh-58A (38 cm × 5.0 m, span 1.17 m, 650 kg), was announced at the same time; it carries a 150–200-kg SAP warhead and uses inertial guidance plus a mm-wave active terminal seeker. Maximum flight altitude is 30 km, and maximum flight speed is Mach 4. Range against a cruiser is 60–70 km, against a larger ship ("supership") is 150–180 km. Designer: Zvezda.

The EO-guided **AS-13** Kingbolt (Kh-59, Ovod), carried only by the Su-24M Fencer, was shown at Dubai in 1991. Its seeker is probably related to that of the Kh-29T/AS-14. Dimensions: 42.5 × 585 cm; span 1.35 m [16.7 × 230 in; 53 in]; weight 875 kg [1,929 lb], warhead 250 kg [551 lb]. Versions are Kh-59, -59A (antiship), and the turbojet-powered -59M (Ovod-M, **AS-18**) air- and ship-launched version announced in Moscow in 1992. The TV-guided aircraft version is launched at 100–5,000 m, cruising at 600 or 1,000 m. Launched at 115 km [62.9 nm], it flies at 860–1,000 km/hr [470–547 kt] and has a CEP of 2–3 m. The missile is locked on by using a data link in a pod aboard the aircraft; it is analogous to the U.S. SLAM. Dimensions: 38 × 569 cm; wingspan 130 cm; total weight 920 kg (320-kg penetrating or 280-kg cluster warhead). An air-launched radar-guided (inertial midcourse) version is 510 cm long (850 kg, 315-kg HE warhead). The shipboard-radar version, which may be the weapon planned for the sole Nanuchka-IV, weighs 1,000 kg and is 530 cm long. It cruises at 1,026 km/hr [561 kt] to a maximum range of 200 km [109 nm]. Designer: Zvezda.

The **AS-14** Kedge (Kh-29, 9M721, Izdeliye 64) family of rocket air-to-surface missiles, developed by Vympel, supersedes Zvezda's Kh-23 (AS-7) and Kh-25 (AS-10/12). AS-14 entered service about 1980. It is carried by Fencer-Ds (Su-24s), Fitters (Su-20s/22s), Floggers (MiG-23s/27s), and Frogfoots (Su-25s), and can be used against shipping. There are 4 fixed rear fins, 4 fixed canards, and 4 movable canards controlled by the modular guidance unit. There are 2 basic series, Kh-29 and the improved Kh-29M. There are at least 4 subversions: Kh-29D, Kh-29L/29ML (laser; same seeker as in Kh-25ML), Kh-29MP (passive radar homing, i.e., ARM), and Kh-29T (TV, i.e., EO). Kh-29ML is carried by Su-17Ms, -24Ms, -25s; Kh-29T by MiG-27Ds/Ks/Ms and Su-17M4s, -24Ms, -25s. Kh-25MP is carried only by Su-17M4s. There are also KhA-29M and -29T versions. NATO designations: Kedge-A laser-guided, Kedge-B EO. Kh-29L: 38 cm × 3.875 m, span 1.0 m [15 × 153; 39.4 in], weight 657 kg [1,449 lb], warhead 317 kg [699 lb]. Range is 2–10 km (launch altitude 0.2–5 km). Kh-29T has the same dimensions (overall weight 688 kg, same warhead; wing and fin span also given as 0.97 and 1.1 m; launch altitude 0.2–10 km, range 3–12 or 4–30 km, depending on launch altitude). Kh-29MP: warhead 250 kg, range 12 km. Aerodynamic range is reported as 30 or even 40 km [44,000 yd]; effective range is probably limited by the airborne designator. Iraqi Mirage F1EQ-5s carried 2 underwing and used a French Thomson-CSF ATLIS laser-designator pod. Developed for the 10-km AS-30L, ATLIS could guide AS-14 out to a range of 12–15 km. There may be an alternative ground-designated mode, the airplane dropping it beyond defensive range.

Kh-65 (sometimes R-55) is the nonnuclear air-launched antiship derivative of AS-15 (Kh-55A), carried by Su-24MRs: 51.4 cm × 6.04 m, wingspan 3.1 m, 1,250 kg, range 280 km [153 nm]. There is also a land-attack version that uses a form of TERCOM navigation, plus the Russian equivalent of GPS, carrying a 410-kg cluster or penetrating warhead, with a maximum range up to 500–600 km, altitude 40–110 m, speed Mach 0.48–0.77, CEP 18–26 m. A Kh-65S3 version shown at Abu Dhabi has some stealth shaping. Designer: Raduga.

Raduga's **AS-16** Kickback (Kh-15A) is an antiship version of a short-range strategic (defense-suppression) missile equivalent to the U.S. SRAM. It is launched into a ballistic trajectory (climb before descent), and its mm-wave active radar seeker corrects its aim point. Maximum flight speed is Mach 5, with a solid-fuel rocket motor. Dimensions: 45.5 × 478 cm [17.9 × 188 in], fin circle diameter 92 cm [36.2 in], weight 1,200 kg, warhead 150 kg [2,646/331 lb]. Range depends on the target: up to 60 km for a fast attack boat, up to 100 km for a destroyer, up to 150 km [82 nm] for a cruiser. The missile can be carried underwing or in a rotary launcher (on a Backfire or Blackjack; capacity 12 missiles). Given the original AS-16 mission, there is surely an antiradar version.

Zvezda's **AS-17** (Kh-31) was expected to enter service in 1993. It uses mixed rocket-ramjet propulsion as in the larger Kh-41 (boost rocket in the tail, 4 ramjets wrapped around the body). It is carried by Su-17M4s and Su-24Ms. Dimensions: 375 mm × 4.9 m; span 1.15 m [14.8 × 193 in; 45.3 in]; weight 600 kg [1,323 lb]; warhead 100 kg [221 lb]. The first version, Kh-31P, is an air-to-surface ARM; an air-to-air passive/active version, intended specifically to destroy AWACS and similar aircraft, was announced at the Moscow Air Show in 1992. It is 5.232 m long and weighs 600 kg (warhead 90 kg); launch height is 100–1,500 m, and maximum range is about 200 km. Maximum flight speed is 1,000 m/sec [1,968 kt]. Presumably, the active-homing feature counteracts any attempt by the AWACS to avoid the missile by turning off its own radar. A dedicated antiship active-radar version, Kh-31A, was first seen at Minsk in 1991. It is 5.232 m long and weighs 650 kg, with a 90-kg warhead. It is launched 5–70 km from the target, at an altitude of 50–15,000 m; maximum flight speed is 1,000 m/sec (it hits the target at up to 350 m/sec).

Comparable with the Franco-German ANS, it is the first supersonic antiship missile to arm tactical aircraft.

Raduga's **Kh-41** (Moskit; no NATO designation), a large, new, rocket-ramjet radar-guided antiship missile first shown at Minsk in 1992, looks like a scaled-up AS-17, and is probably the successor to AS-4/6 (designed by the same bureau, Raduga). An Su-24 or -27 can carry 1 underbody; presumably, a Backfire can carry 2 underwing. Dimensions: 76 × 974.5 cm [29.9 × 383.7 in], weight 4,500 kg [9,923 lb]. The SAP warhead weighs 320 kg [706 lb]. Speed is Mach 3.0 at high altitude and Mach 2.1 at low altitude (5–15 m). The launching airplane can acquire the target itself and fire the missile at high altitude (range 250 km, including a 50-km low-altitude run-in), or it can launch at low altitude on the basis of data-linked target information (range 150 km). Launch velocity is 200–470 m/sec [393–925 kt]. At Abu Dhabi in 1993 the Russians were seeking funds to develop a ship-launched version—a new, longer-range missile. See also the Raduga 3M-80 described below.

All bomb designations indicate type by prefix, then weight in kg with suffix for details (AB means *aviatsionnaya bomba*).

Guided bombs (KAB, *korrektiruyemaya aviatsionnaya bomba*, correctable aircraft bombs): KAB-500 and -1500 laser (L) bombs and a 500-kg EO (Kr) bomb (fire-and-forget correlation seeker). At least the 500-kg versions may have rocket tails. The laser seeker resembles that of a Paveway; the EO seeker is the full diameter of the bomb body. KAB-500Kr E/O bomb: 350 × 3,050 mm (tail span 850 mm; 560 kg, including 380-kg warhead; 200 kg of explosive); dropped at 0.5–5.0 km altitude, speed 550–1,100 km/hr [300–600 kt], accuracy 4–7 m. KAB-500L laser bomb: 400 × 3,050 mm (534 kg, including 195 kg of explosive); KAB-1500L-Pr laser bomb: 580 × 4,600 mm (tail span 850 mm folded, 1,300 mm unfolded); weight 1,500 kg, including 1,100-kg warhead. KAB-1500L-Pr is dropped at an altitude of 1–5 km [3,300 to 16,500 ft] at 550–1,100 km/hr [300–600 kt]; accuracy is 7–10 m [23–33 ft]. The bomb penetrates 2 m of reinforced concrete or 10–20 m of soil. A similar KAB-1500L-F carries a blast (rather than SAP) warhead (1,560 kg, including 1,180-kg warhead). There are also KAB-500D and KAB-1500Ya.

General-purpose Bombs (FAB Series):

High Drag: FAB-250, -500, and -1500. FAB-500M-54: 474 kg (warhead 201 kg HE), 450 × 1,500 mm. FAB-1500M-54: 1,550 (675) kg, 630 × 2,765 mm (finspan 792 mm). FAB-3000, -5000, and -9000M-54 were all developed for heavy aircraft such as Badgers. Weights and dimensions were, respectively, 3,067 (1,387) kg/332 × 82 cm (finspan 79.2 cm); 5,247 (2,207.6) kg/332.4 × 106 (133) cm; and 9,407 (4,927) kg/500 × 120 (150.4) cm.

Low-Drag: FAB-100, -250, -500, -750, -1000. Examples: FAB-500M-62, 497 kg, 400 × 2,430 mm; FAB-500 ShN (with pronounced

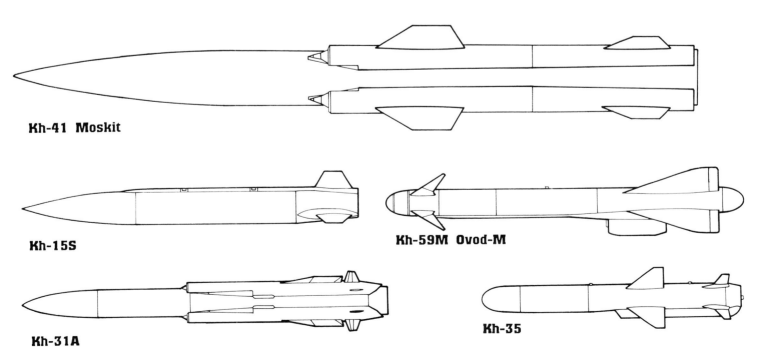

Kh-41 Moskit

Kh-15S

Kh-31A

Kh-59M Ovod-M

Kh-35

The new Russian air-launched antiship missiles. Note how much larger Moskit (Kh-41) is than all of the others. Kh-15S is the aeroballistic missile based on the Soviet equivalent of the U.S. SRAM. Both Ovod-M and Kh-35 (SS-N-25) have shipboard equivalents. (S. Zaloga)

boat-tail), 513 kg (221 kg of explosive), 450 × 2,188 mm; FAB-500TS, 500 kg (108 kg of explosive), 400 × 1,500 mm (delayed action, to dig a 7.6-m crater). F means *fugasnaya*, demolition (HE). A published photograph shows a low-drag bomb being retarded by the Soviet equivalent of the U.S. ballute.

Low-Drag Blast-Fragmentation: OFAB-100, -250. Examples: OFAB-100–120, 120 kg, 273 × 1,060 mm; OFAB-250–270, 266 kg, 320 × 1,420 mm. OFAB means *oskolochno-fugasnaya*, fragmentation/HE.

Demolition (Thin-Case): ODAB-500, -1100. OD means *obyomno-detoniruyushchaya*, volume-detonation. ODAB-500P: 466 (145) kg, 227.8 × 50 cm.

Concrete Penetrators: BetAB-250 and -500. Example: BetAB-500ShP, possibly rocket-boosted, 424 kg, 325 × 2,805 mm, penetrates 550 mm. Bet means *betonoboynaya*, concrete-piercing.

Incendiary: ZAB-100, -250, -350, -500; there is also a ZAP-200 incendiary container weapon. Z means *zashigatelnaya*, incendiary. ZAB-500W: 378 (118) kg, 249 × 40 cm (finspan 57 cm). ZAB-500–400 is entirely unstreamlined, with a flat nose: 410 (160) kg, 149.8 × 45 (57) cm. There are also ZB-250, -360, and -500. ZB-500SzM is streamlined: 317.5 (260) kg, 250.3 × 50 cm. There are also 2.5-kg ZAB bomblets.

Cluster Bombs: RBK-250, -500; there is also an RAB-120 carrying fragmentation bomblets. RBK means *razovaya bombovaya kasseta*, single-use bomb cassette. RBK-250–275 AO-1SCh is 325 × 2,119 mm, 275 kg, carrying 150 AO-1SCh bomblets (each 49 × 156 mm, 1.2 kg), effective over a 4,800-m² area. Alternatively, it may carry 60 A0–2.5RT antipersonnel bomblets (90 × 150 mm, 2.5 kg, each about as effective as a single 81-mm mortar round) or 30 PTAB 2.5 antitank bomblets (68 × 362 mm, 2.8 kg with 0.45-kg warhead). There are also PTAB-1.5, -2, -5, and -5/1 antitank bomblets. RBK-500 AO 2.5RT (500 × 2,500 mm, 504 kg) carries 108 bomblets, effective over a 6,400-m² area. RBK-500 ShOAB-0.5 (450 × 1,500 mm, 334 kg) carries 565 bomblets, effective over a 300 × 400 m area. There are also fragmentation bomblets (RAP-2.5, -3.5, -16), incendiary bomblets (ZAB-2.5, 91 × 135 mm, 2.7 kg with 1.72-kg warhead), and a 14.5-kg self-guided bomblet, SPBE-D. The latest version of RBK-500 can carry 12 BETABs (runway-cratering bomblets) or 108 AO-2.5 RTMs (antipersonnel) or 268 PTAB-1Ms (antitank) or 12 SPBE-Ds. RRAB (no weight given) contains incendiary bomblets. AK-2 is a dispenser for 240 1-kg chemical bomblets (mustard and Lewisite). DPT-150 is a reported cluster-bomb designation (54 PTAB-1.5s, 44 RAP-2.5s, or 34 RAP-3.5s).

KMGU (*koneteyner malogabaritnykh gruzov universalnyi*, "small universal cargo container") is a 500- or 1,000-kg cluster bomb, which can be dropped at 700–1,200 km/hr to open at 30–1,500 m in altitude. KMGU-2: 370 × 46 cm (finspan 46 cm), casing 170 kg (total weight about 525 kg).

Dispensers: PKPE-1 contains 29 70-mm tubes, each containing 2 or 3 submunitions, launched laterally by a small charge; the submunitions are either blast-fragmentation grenades or shaped charges (similar to the RPG-7 warhead). A helicopter or ground-attack airplane typically carries 2, firing to each side. UPAE-1500 (listed in 1991 CFE documents) may be an analogous aircraft dispenser.

Chemical weapons: The Soviets displayed high-drag bombs of World War II vintage and presumably have developed modern low-drag equivalents. VAP-200 is a container bomb; VAP-1000 (BATT) is a dispenser (700 liters of hydrogen cyanide for low-altitude spraying); and KhAB-500 is a unitary bomb filled with 180 kg of phosgene. VAP is probably a general dispenser designation, and newer weapons include an NOV-AB series of bombs containing nonpersistent toxic agents and an SOV-AB series containing persistent toxic agents.

Rockets (S-series):

—S-5: 9 warheads include HEAT, high explosive, fragmentation, and chaff. Typical burnout speed is 620 m/sec [2,034 ft/sec]. S-5KO: 55 × 1,006 mm, 4.5 kg, warhead 0.263 kg, range 1.8 km—can penetrate 170 mm of armor. S-5 was designed to attack both aircraft and surface targets; it corresponds broadly to the U.S. 2.75-in FFAR. Because it was not lethal enough against large bombers, S-5 was superseded by the 220-mm ABRS-220 (102 kg with 30-kg warhead, effective range 1.2–1.6 miles) and by the ROFS-325 submunition rocket (carrying 38 bomblets). Pods: UB-16 and -32 (the number is the number of rockets). UB-32A: 481 × 2,080 mm, 254 kg loaded/109 kg empty.

—S-8: 80-mm rockets. S-8KO: 80 × 1,445 mm, 11.65 kg (war-

head 3.6 kg), range 2.0 km—penetrates 420 mm of armor. There may also be V-8 and V-8M, probably chemical rockets. Pod: UB-8 for 20 rockets. UB-8M1 (sometimes B-8M1) is 410 × 3,550 mm, 400/160 kg. UB-8V20: 521 × 1,720 mm, 342/100 kg.

—S-13: 122-mm rockets. S-13T, 122 × 2,892 mm, 67 kg (warhead 31.8 kg), range 2.5 kg—penetrates 1,000 mm of concrete. S-13OF is a demolition/fragmentation version (68 kg, warhead 32.2 kg, 1,800 fragments). A photograph of S-13T shows no fins at all; the rocket may be spun by its exhaust. Pod: UB-13 for 5 rockets; 410 × 3,558 mm, 510/160 kg.

—S-24: 240-mm rockets. S-24B, 240 × 2,330 mm, 235 kg (warhead 123 kg, 4,000 fragments), range 2.0 km. S-24B has 4 fixed fins, like those of the old U.S. 5-in HVAR.

—S-25: 340-mm rockets. S-25OF is 340 × 3,310 mm (body 260 mm), 480 kg (warhead 190 kg, attacks 1,820-m² area), 600 m/sec, range 3.0 km. S-25: 420/260 × 3,310 mm (370 kg), 540 m/sec. S-25OFM is a fragmentation version: 3,307 mm long, with a bulged warhead (150 kg, total weight 381 kg, 6,500 fragments). Other versions: S-25L (laser-guided, range 7 km), S-25M, S-25MD. Unlike the smaller S-24, which is launched like a conventional ASM, S-25 is carried in a single-shot O-25 pod. It has flip-out fins.

SS-N-2 Styx was adapted to submarine use when the SS-N-9 program was delayed (the NATO designation is **SS-N-7**); a very slightly modified SS-N-2C arms Charlie-I–class submarines (the shorter missile is accommodated by inserting a plug in the tube). The folding-wing version of SS-N-2 was presumably developed specifically for submarine launching because wing folding makes little difference in surface applications. Compared to SS-N-2, SS-N-7 has a plastic nose cap and different tail fins, to improve its hydrodynamics. Both versions of SS-N-2C have nuclear variants (-2C flies far enough so that its launching boat is not harmed, and no air burst can harm a submerged submarine). The FCS is the same Klon that equips surface platforms. The submarine typically gets an ESM fix, take a quick radar range (without scanning), then another range and bearing, inserts them into the Klon, dead-reckons target position ahead, and dives deeper to run in and fire. The submarine's attack sonar cannot support a long-range attack. Alternatively, a nuclear

An Osa-class missile boat shows the 2 main variants of SS-N-2D (P-20M): the forward missile shows the pimple of an IR seeker (the after missile is radar-guided). (Royal Navy)

SS-N-7 can be fired at a target in the first CZ, the warhead yield making up for any inaccuracy in target location. Charlie-I–class submarines cannot be modernized to Charlie-II (SS-N-9) configuration because SS-N-9 requires a different sort of FCS. This weapon is to be replaced by SS-N-25 (Kh-35) in Russian service.

India makes Styx under license.

Users: Algeria (3 Nanuchkas [2C], 9 Osa-IIs [2B], 2 Osa-Is [2A]), Angola (2 Osa-IIs), Bulgaria (3 Osa-IIs [2B], 3 Osa-Is [2A]), Cuba (13 Osa-IIs, 5 Osa-Is), Ethiopia (4 Osa-IIs [2B]), Finland (4 Osa-IIs [2B], as MTO-66), India (5 Kashins [2C], *Delhi* class [SS-N-2D, not SS-N-22 as reported], 3 *Godavari* class [2C], *Trishul*, 12 *Khukri* class [2D], 24 Tarantul class [2D], 3 Nanuchka class [2C], 8 Osa-II class [2B]), Libya (3 Nanuchkas [2C], 4 Type 400s [2C], 12 Osa-IIs), North Korea (1 Soho class [2A], 2 Najin class, 4 Soju class, 8 So Hung class, 16 Osa-Is, 8 Komars), Poland (1 Kashin, 4 Tarantuls [2D], 8 Osa-IIs [2A]), Romania (1 *Muntenia* [2C], 6 Osa-Is), Russia (2 Mod Kashins [2C], 19 Tarantul-IIs [2E], 2 Tarantul-Is [2D], 16 Matkas [2D], 25 or fewer Osa-IIs [2B/C], 28 or fewer Osa-Is [2A]), Somalia (2 Osa-IIs), Syria (8 Osa-IIs [2B], 6 Osa-Is [2A]), Vietnam (8 Osa-IIs), Yugoslavia (2 Kotors [2C], 2 Konis [2C], 1 Type 400 Kobra, 6 *Rade Končar*s [2B], 10 Osa-Is). SS-C-3 (Rubezh-A) coast-defense version: Algeria, Bulgaria, Finland, India, Iraq, Libya, Poland, Romania, Russia, Syria, Yemen, Yugoslavia. The earlier SS-C-2 (AS-1) may survive in Cuba and Egypt.

The following are versions of Styx:

—SS-N-2A (P-15, 4K40, 50-Kh), with an X(I)-band seeker, was introduced in 1958, on board Komar- and then Osa-class missile boats. SS-N-2B (P-20, 1964) had folding wings, for more compact stowage. There may have been an alternative IR seeker. Dimensions (2A): 0.78 × 5.76 m; span 2.4 m. Weight: 2,300 kg.

—SS-N-2C (P-20K), introduced in 1967, has increased range (45 nm) and a radar altimeter allowing the missile to cruise toward its target at 25 or 50 m. This missile probably originated in a 1961 project for a 50–70-km patrol-boat missile. It is considerably longer than SS-N-2A (dimensions: 0.78 × 6.6 m; span 2.4 m; weight 2,400 kg). P-20K was different enough from P-20 that NATO originally assigned it a new designation, SS-N-11. It is on board converted destroyers (such as Mod Kashins) and also on many small missile craft. P-21 is the IR version.

—SS-N-2D (P-20M) is in export Tarantuls and probably in Russian Matkas. P-22 is the IR version. A Tarantul typically carries 3 radar and 1 IR missiles. P-20M can use the P-20 FCS but generally uses Korell/Plank Shave. The Russians estimated that 3 hits would destroy a light cruiser, 1 or 2 hits would destroy a destroyer or frigate. If the missile itself is 95% mechanically reliable, the hit probability depending on the radar target, the Russians estimated that 1 missile boat carrying 4 weapons (typically 3 radar and 1 IR) could destroy 1 missile destroyer or missile frigate; 1 or 2 missile patrol boats, landing ships, or unprotected minelayers; or 2 or 3 unescorted transports. The IR version, which homes on the target's IR plume, has to be launched more than 30 deg from the direction of the sun and is ineffective in visibility less than 100 m (i.e., thick fog and drizzle or snow).

—P-27 (SS-N-2E?) is somewhat longer, with the V-band seeker developed for 3M-80 (it was the interim weapon, arming Russian Tarantul-IIs, pending completion of 3M-80 development). Unlike other Styx platforms, the craft carrying this missile have **Light Bulb** and **Band Stand** radomes like Tarantul-IIIs (they lack the Plank Shave radar of export Tarantul-Is). It probably follows that P-27 shares the guidance package of P-270, including some capability to send its radar picture back to the launch platform (via Light Bulb), which tracks the missile (using the radar in Band Stand) and can apply some degree of course correction. Given the absence of any other onboard radar, the device in Band Stand probably doubles as a surface-search set, to designate targets for fire-and-forget attack. P-27 was probably exported for the first time when 2 Tarantul-IIs (formerly thought to have been Tarantul-Is) were transferred to Bulgaria in June 1990.

—SS-N-7 (P-20L) is a submarine-launched version. Dimensions: 0.78 × 7.0 m; span 2.4 m. Launch weight: 2,400 kg.

3M-80 (P-270) is a Raduga ship-to-ship missile announced at Abu Dhabi in 1993. It, rather than SS-N-22 (P-80/P-100), is carried by Tarantul-III–class missile boats. It is similar in configuration to AS-17 and Kh-41, about halfway between in dimensions: 130 × 938.5 cm (with wings folded), 3,950 kg with a 300-kg warhead, speed

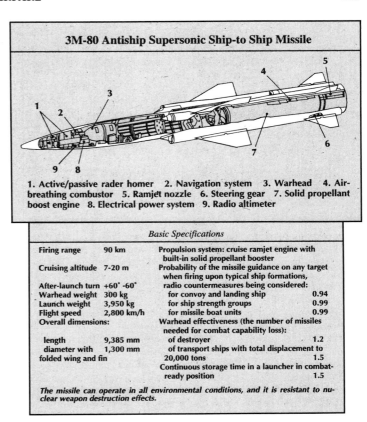

3M-80 Antiship Supersonic Ship-to Ship Missile

1. Active/passive rader homer 2. Navigation system 3. Warhead 4. Air-breathing combustor 5. Ramjet nozzle 6. Steering gear 7. Solid propellant boost engine 8. Electrical power system 9. Radio altimeter

Basic Specifications			
Firing range	90 km	Propulsion system: cruise ramjet engine with built-in solid propellant booster	
Cruising altitude	7–20 m	Probability of the missile guidance on any target when firing upon typical ship formations, radio countermeasures being considered:	
After-launch turn	+60° -60°		
Warhead weight	300 kg	for convoy and landing ship	0.94
Launch weight	3,950 kg	for ship strength groups	0.99
Flight speed	2,800 km/h	for missile boat units	0.99
Overall dimensions:		Warhead effectiveness (the number of missiles needed for combat capability loss):	
length	9,385 mm	of destroyer	1.2
diameter with	1,300 mm	of transport ships with total displacement to 20,000 tons	1.5
folded wing and fin		Continuous storage time in a launcher in combat-ready position	1.5

The missile can operate in all environmental conditions, and it is resistant to nuclear weapon destruction effects.

The 3M-80 rocket-ramjet missile arms Tarantul-class missile boats. This sketch was released at the Abu Dhabi military show in 1993. (Bill Clipson)

2,800 km/hr (1,510 kt), range 90 km (as in SS-N-2C), flight altitude 7–20 m, capable of a 60-deg turn after launch. The characteristics suggest that this was the intended successor to Raduga's Styx. Raduga claims that 1.2 missiles suffice for a mission kill of a destroyer, or 1.5 for a transport. Shelf life is 1.5 yr. Claimed lock-on probability (in the face of ECM) is 0.94 for a convoy or landing ship, or 0.99 for a battle group or small combatant group. The seeker can be switched to an ARM mode. The associated canister is 1.5 × 8.8 m. Iran reportedly bought 8 of these missiles in mid-1992. Design work began in 1983, the missile first flew in 1985, and it entered service in 1987. Like P-80, P-270 has an autopilot that samples wave height so the missile can descend to the lowest safe cruising altitude.

Tarantuls, which fire P-270, have **Light Bulb** missile radar-video-receiver radomes. It would seem to follow that, unlike the export version, the Russian version of the missile provides the launch platform with missile radar video, and can be commanded to a limited extent. Similarly, P-27 ships (Tarantul-IIs) have Light Bulb and a Band Stand radome (they lack the Square Ties of Tarantul-Is). It would seem to follow that, like the longer-range Chelomey missiles described below, these weapons are tracked as they fly out and are commanded in accord with their radar video.

The Chelomey OKB's Shaddock (**SS-N-3/SS-C-1**) was the first Soviet OTH ship-launched anticarrier missile. Although all the platforms (Echo-I–class submarines and Whiskey-class conversions) designed to use the missile solely in its original strategic role have been discarded, the nuclear-armed nonhoming strategic version probably survives. In 1944 V. N. Chelomey was assigned to adapt German cruise missile (V-1) technology, within a main design bureau (OKB) developing offensive missiles, without reference to the service that would fire them (other main bureaus were concerned with nuclear weapons and with defensive missiles). His straight-winged, twin-pulse-jet 16-Kh missile flew late in 1946, but the intermittent pulse-jet explosions either destroyed it or blew it badly off course. A twin ramjet 10-Kh was more successful. Rocket-boosted, it required a long launcher to accelerate it to flying speed. Such launching ramps appeared as early as 1950 around Leningrad (probably to attack targets in Denmark and Germany) and near Vladivostok (to attack Japan). Later offered to China (PRC), 10-Kh became the basis for C-101 (the V-1 ancestry shows in the Chinese missile's rectangular vertical fin).

V-1 flew a straight course from its launcher (the only adjustment was in the duration of the flight, as measured by revolutions of a small propeller driven by the airstream). Chelomey developed a new autopilot that flew the missile to preset geographical coordinates (hard-wired at the factory), so a single launcher could attack multiple targets (albeit not too far from its heading). When the missile reached the set coordinates, its engine cut out (as in a V-1). Presumably, the coordinates were coded. One security advantage of such a system (compared, say, to a system in which the range and bearing were set) was that no battery commander could choose to fire at anything but the assigned target.

10-Kh was slow. The next step, 15-Kh, was to substitute a turbojet with a ventral intake, flanked by a pair of rocket boosters. Missiles still needed a short guide rail, which projected from the missile's container. 15-Kh entered service late in 1948 or early in 1949 and remained in ground service through the late 1960s; it was probably deployed on the Chinese border. By this time there was interest in attacking targets farther afield. A single 15-Kh container was mounted on board some Whiskey-class submarines (about 20 such launchers were made).

By 1949 TsAGI advocated a new generation of swept-wing transonic forms. Chelomey redesigned 15-Kh with a longer fuselage, a tapered nose, and sharply swept (rather than straight) wings. The vertical fin was moved below the fuselage, and the horizontal tail was eliminated. Because it had the same power plant, 20-Kh was not much faster than 15-Kh.

As Project 82R, the postwar battle cruiser (Project 82) was modified to fire the new surface-to-surface cruise missiles. Although Project 82 died on Stalin's death, 82R survived until 1955, with the lead ship in the water, about two-thirds complete. Khrushchev killed big-ship projects (including a carrier) late in 1955, almost certainly to free scarce resources for the rocket-missile military he favored (and also for civilian purposes) by replacing his naval chief, Admiral Kuznetsov, with Admiral Gorshkov. Kuznetsov's demise left only submarines and smaller surface units as possible long-range cruise-missile platforms. The ultimate (in effect, production) Whiskey-class SS-N-3 conversion, Whiskey Long Bin, was probably intended to make up in part for the shore-bombardment firepower lost with Project 82R.

20-Kh was too bulky to go in even so large a ship as Project 82R in worthwhile numbers. Chelomey folded the wings, popping them out as the missile left its launcher. Missiles could, therefore, be stowed side by side in a compact trainable quadruple launcher, reloaded using a monorail connecting the superstructure magazine (with 2 reloads per tube) and the launcher. The folding-wing version was designated P-5 (4K95; it is SS-N-3). It carried a 200-kT warhead. One 15-Kh Whiskey submarine was modified to carry a single launch cylinder. That left excess space; others (Whiskey Twin Cylinder) were completed with paired launch cylinders. The cylindrical launcher was also attractive to the army, which adopted the new weapon as S-35 (the Western designation was SS-C-1). It remained in service as late as the mid-1970s. P-5D had a radar (Doppler) rather than a barometric altimeter, which made it possible to fly higher. It took 35–40 min (far more than Western experts have estimated) to set up the missile, e.g., to run up gyros, during which the launching platform had to run a steady course. A surface ship might well be unable to reach a predesignated launch point. For 82R, then, Chelomey redesigned the autopilot so that the launch ship fed in its own position at the time of launch, the missile navigating from it to the preset target coordinates. This version (with folding wings) was designated P-6.

Over its production run the missile was refined aerodynamically, and the thrust of its turbojet roughly doubled, so that maximum speed increased from about 470 kt [about 540 mph] to better than 600 kt [about 690 mph, close to Mach 1; some reports have the missile barely exceeding Mach 1].

Chelomey's OKB was abolished in February 1953 (for political reasons, according to his Russian biographer). In 1954 Chelomey found a new home in the naval weapons R&D organization (NII-4) by selling the idea of a ship-launched antiship cruise missile using a command-guidance system based on his earlier surface-to-surface work. It was first applied to the existing, well-tested 15-Kh airframe (NATO designation **SS-N-1**, Soviet P-1): a TWS shipboard radar (Sun Visor, in a destroyer director) tracked both the missile and its surface target. 15-Kh missiles and launchers made surplus when SS-N-3 appeared were apparently used (the missiles were modified with folding wings).

An analogous guidance system was applied to the much bigger and faster P-5/6 as P-7 (command guidance was used to keep the missile on track, i.e., to correct for autopilot drift, not to change the assigned target coordinates). The new TWS radar was Scoop Pair. It appeared in a Project 82R drawing, so it must have been conceived before late 1955. Since the missile would fly well beyond the ship's horizon, the radar could only confirm that it was flying to roughly the coordinates that some other system (such as a Bear-D) reported for the target. The next step (P-10) was to accept changes in target coordinates set in the autopilot, e.g., to compensate for navigational error. The P-10 designation was originally assigned to an unsuccessful Beriev competitor to P-5, tested in 1957 on board a Zulu-class submarine, which did not have pop-up wings and which required a separate launch ramp.

The antiship role seems to have lapsed briefly after the 1955 naval purge. The platforms actually adopted for SS-N-3, the Kynda-class (Project 58) cruiser (with the new quadruple launcher but with only 1 reload/tube), the modified Whiskey-class submarine, and the new Echo-I– and Juliett-class submarines, were all conceived purely for land attack (the short-range Styx, conceived about 1954, was the favored antiship missile).

About 1957 Chelomey's OKB began work on a much faster strategic cruise missile, the rocket-ramjet P-35 (**SS-N-12**); a number of contemporary Soviet weapons, such as SA-6, used similar forms of propulsion. Because it paralleled SS-N-5, the new missile could be fired submerged. That was never done because, once it had been adapted for the antiship role, SS-N-12 needed midcourse guidance provided by a surfaced platform.

As in the case of the ballistic weapons described above, after 1959 the cruise missiles had to be adapted to the new antiship role. As an interim measure, the command-movable aim point feature was revived. A P-5 series missile so guided would be ineffective at long range because it was so slow (the target might well move out of the way while the missile flew). SS-N-12, about twice as fast and fitted with a seeker, would be as effective as 4 SS-N-3s. As an interim measure, the existing Kynda design was modified for antiship attack, with a pair of Scoop Pair radars (but only a single guidance package, which could be connected to either radar). The Echo-class submarine was redesigned (see Strategic Weapons, above).

A new light cruiser, to carry 4 SS-N-12s, was designed: Kresta-I (Project 1134). Its attack would so disrupt an enemy formation that other cruisers (1134s armed with 8 shorter-range missiles, Ametysts [P-50s/**SS-N-9s**]) could close in. P-50 would also arm a very fast submarine, Papa (with 10), and 6 (2 triples) would replace the forward twin 3-in mount on a new coastal frigate.

None of this came to pass as planned. It seems to have proven extremely difficult to combine a rounded radome (needed for the sensor of a really satisfactory antiship missile) with the sort of smooth airflow the P-35 ramjet needed. As P-25, SS-N-3 soldiered on with part of the planned SS-N-12 guidance package. Although work on P-35 continued, most effort shifted to a redesigned SS-N-3, which became SS-N-19. The Papa-class submarine proved too expensive and too complex, so a less expensive but slower submarine, Charlie, was designed. P-50 (SS-N-9) was slow to develop, so as an interim measure, SS-N-2 (Styx), was adapted to underwater launch (see above). The surface-ship program was overtaken by a new requirement for ASW (actually, PSW). It appears that an unsuccessful Raduga OKB competitor to P-50, a rocket (P-50 is a turbojet), was adapted to carry an ASW torpedo or nuclear depth bomb as SS-N-14. The P-50 Kresta version and the coastal frigate (Krivak) were redesigned to carry it. The Nanuchka-class missile boat seems to have been conceived to replace P-50 firepower lost when the Krivak was redesigned.

Like their predecessors, P-25, -35 (as adapted to attack ships), and -50 were all designed to fly to a particular preset geographical (rather than ship-centered) point because the supporting surveillance system would locate a target in geographical coordinates. Unlike their predecessors, they have radar seekers, which they turn on (and lock onto the largest radar target) when they arrive. The P-25 radar picture was transmitted back to the launching ship (received by Plinth Net) to become the basis for targeting the next missiles fired. The ship's Scoop Pair tracks a pair of outgoing missiles. In a submarine, 1 element of Front Door/Front Piece served the Scoop Pair role; the other was equivalent to Plinth Net. The single antenna can apparently track only 2 beacons simultaneously. The submarine cannot fire a second salvo until the first has locked on, so the salvo interval is about 15 min. This antiship version had a 20-kT RK-55

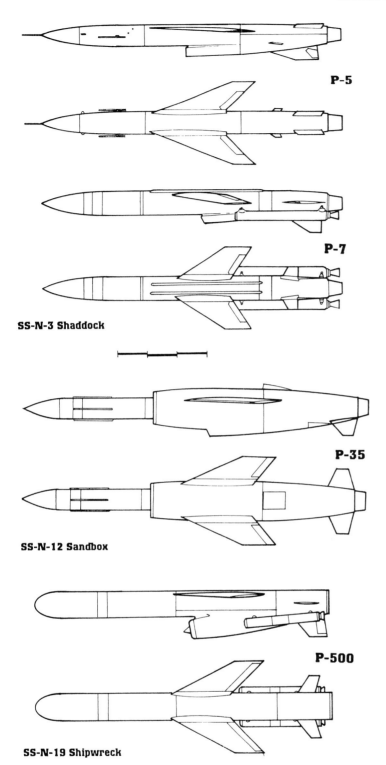

P-5

P-7

SS-N-3 Shaddock

P-35

SS-N-12 Sandbox

P-500

SS-N-19 Shipwreck

Russian long-range ship-launched antiship missiles, all designed by the Chelomey OKB. Early versions of P-35 had the ramjet air intake extending much farther forward. (S. Zaloga)

nuclear warhead (lower yield was acceptable because the missile was more likely to hit a target). The P-50 FCS is a smaller version of that developed for P-25/P-35. The missile sends its radar video back to a **Fish Bowl** or **Light Bulb** antenna. It is tracked by an antenna inside the **Band Stand** radome. Like a longer-range shooter, the missile boat receives its target data from a third party. Submarines firing the missile presumably also generally rely on third-party information, and probably have their own more limited video data link and tracker, usable at periscope depth. P-50 was never exported; Nanuchka-IIs for client states have SS-N-2Cs, and their Band Stands contain Square Tie targeting radars. Submarines firing the missile probably also use the video link because their sonars cannot provide the sort of performance required for long-range targeting. P-50 has not been

exported; Nanuchkas produced for Soviet client states are armed instead with SS-N-2Cs.

Early P-35s had the P-25 guidance package; for a considerable time both missiles were in production, probably with the same guidance package. Most such missiles have nonnuclear warheads. An improved package (in this missile and in later P-25s) can fly a search pattern around the preset coordinates. The shipboard operator can use a missile's radar video to select its target. These missiles also have an ARM version, which presumably takes its target signature from Rum Tub. Most missiles equipped with these more sophisticated guidance packages have nonnuclear warheads. SS-N-12 was later improved with a better engine (for speed and range) and with a much better autopilot that could be programmed for waypoints and other midcourse maneuvers. These weapons are carried only on board *Kiev*-class carriers and *Slava*-class cruisers (the missiles on board modernized Juliett- and Echo-II–class submarines are SS-N-19s). It is not clear whether any SS-N-3s survive (many were lost in the explosion of the Northern Fleet's ammunition dump in 1984). The only remaining platforms are 1 Kresta-I– and perhaps 1 Kynda-class missile cruisers.

With the failure of P-35, Chelomey turned to a redesigned P-5 using a new turbojet to achieve much the same speed, about twice that of P-25: P-500 (**SS-N-19**). The new engine was released to the design bureau in 1964. Compared to SS-N-3, P-500 has a fuller nose, accommodating a much larger radar dish. The P-500 designation presumably reflects its relationship with P-5.

As carried by *Kirov*-class missile cruisers and by *Kuznetsov*-class carriers, P-500 can be tracked and controlled via the ship's main air-search radar. Like its predecessors, SS-N-19 has a video data link back to the firing ship. In 1 version, the missile snakes, to examine each target in its search area in turn, and transmits back data that are assembled on board the ship to form an ISAR radar image for automatic comparison with an image already held on board ship. If they match, the missile is ordered to attack. If not, the missile retains the target as an alternate and goes on to examine the next contact. If it passes out of the target area without finding the appropriate target, it automatically turns 180 deg and attacks the last target seen. The ship's ISAR image is formed by her helicopter's radar or by a supporting Bear. There are also conventional radar and ARM versions (the latter said to be intended specifically to attack Aegis ships), and the standard radar seeker can switch to ARM mode in flight (though in that case it is less sensitive than the dedicated ARM version). Warheads: nuclear (200 or 350 kT), 1,000-kg unitary shaped-charge high explosive, and bomblet (primarily for antiship attack, but also usable against land targets: 750 × 1 kg, a mix of incendiary, AP, HE, which can be varied to meet requirements). The bomblet attack mode implies that the missile can approach at a very low angle.

SS-N-19 is so fast (and probably has so good a search pattern) that it can function without midcourse guidance. An Oscar-class missile submarine can, therefore, fire the missile submerged, on the basis of information provided by a satellite via the Punch Bowl down-link antenna. The Punch Bowl/SS-N-19 combination (rather than the reported SS-N-12) was installed on modernized Echo-II–(Project 675M) and Juliett-class submarines.

Chelomey's **SS-N-22** Sunburn (P-80) is the larger, faster, and lower-flying rocket-powered successor to SS-N-9, on board *Sovremennyy*-class missile destroyers. Equipped with a radar (rather than barometric) altimeter, P-80 samples wave heights to fly at a minimum safe altitude (7– 20 m [23–66 ft]). A folding-fin version, P-100, can be fired from 65-cm torpedo tubes and from the torpedo catapults of the *Neustrashimyy* class (the ship normally carries 8 P-100s, 8 SS-N-16s, and 8 torpedoes). There is probably also a shore version. A vertically launched version is under development; a sketch of a *Sovremennyy* variant shown at Abu Dhabi in 1993 showed 24 such missiles aft. The Chelomey OKB states that the missile will fit a U.S. Mk 41 launcher. A sketch of a submarine's vertical launcher was shown at Moscow in 1992.

Like that of P-500, the P-80/P-100 seeker can operate in ISAR mode; there is also an unbriefed mode in which the missile sends back target video, and the operator on board ship decides whether to attack. Missile video is received via the ship's **Light Bulb** antennas, and the missile itself is tracked by the radar inside the **Band Stand** (which reportedly operates at lower frequency, NATO D- rather than F-band, than that of the radar in the Nanuchka **Band Stand**). The missile can also be used in fire-and-forget mode. There is also an ARM version. There are 3 warheads, a 250-kg shaped

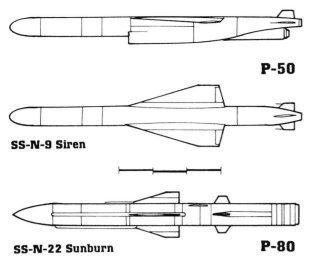

The family of medium-range ship-launched antiship missiles designed by the Chelomey OKB. P-80 and its folding-wing variant, P-22, are not related to the Berezhniak (Raduga) 3M-80 rocket-ramjet, which arms the Tarantul (Project 1241) class. Both missiles have been designated SS-N-22 in the West. As of mid-1993, P-80/P-100 had been shown publicly only in the form of a poster at the 1992 Moscow Air Show, but it seemed likely that the missile itself would be displayed at the 1993 show. (S. Zaloga)

with an underbody air scoop. It and P-80/P-100 were associated with 3 platforms: a modified Nanuchka (carrying 1 missile on each side), an attack submarine, and a shore launcher.

Dimensions are as follows:

—SS-N-3: 0.96 × 9.1 m (length overall, including booster, 10.2 m), span 3.2 m; launch weight 4,700 kg
—SS-N-9: 2.1 × 8.8 m (forebody diameter 0.78, aft body depth abaft jet intake, 0.87 m), span 2.1 m; launch weight 2,952.5 kg
—SS-N-12: 1.6 × 11.7 m, forebody diameter 0.78 m, span 3.2 m; launch weight just over 5,000 kg
—SS-N-19: 0.96 × 10.2 m, span 3.2 m
—SS-N-22: 0.52 × 9.4 m (fin span 1.8 m); the *Sovremennyy* canister is 1.85 × 9.6 m. A Chelomey OKB poster (at Moscow in 1992) gave the range as 130 km [70 nm].

P-numbers were originally assigned in blocks of 5 (beginning with P-5) and then in blocks of 10. Probable missing weapons, with their likely designators, are a large intercontinental-range Ilyushin submarine-launched strategic cruise missile (P-30), a failed rocket-ramjet Styx follow-on (contemporary with P-35: P-40), the failed Raduga competitor to P-50 (P-60, hence the 60-RU designation for the first version of SS-N-14), a failed supersonic Styx follow-on similar in configuration to P-80 (P-70; attempted cures would have been P-170 and then the successful P-270), and a failed Raduga competitor to P-80 (P-90). P-27 was almost certainly inserted into the series very late (P-25 had already been assigned), and its relationship with P-270 seems clear.

SS-NX-25 (Kh-35), Zvezda's turbojet-powered Harpoon-like missile, was shown in Moscow in 1992 in both ship- and air-launched versions (it is suitable for Ka-27 and -28 helicopters), and for coast defense. There is also a submarine version, the Russian equivalent of Sub-Harpoon. The planned ship platform was the KRK "Uran"; drawings of a Tarantul carrying 4 quadruple launchers have been displayed. Kh-35 is now being mounted on board modernized Krivak-class frigates. A triple Kh-35 launcher can replace a single SS-N-2 on board an Osa, and a sextuple launcher can replace the usual triple SS-N-9 launcher on board a Nanuchka. Some boats may have been refitted. Zvezda states that Kh-35 can use the shipboard or aircraft electronics of a Harpoon. It is advertised partly as a "Harpoon"-like target for training and testing. The canister was first seen on board the East German *Sassnitz* ("Bal-Com-10").

The program began in 1983, at which time the East German Zeiss organization was expected to develop an EO seeker. The missile is to enter service in 1994. A Kh-35 sales brochure indicated that 1993 was the "technical project deadline of any carrier [platform] armed [with] this missile." Dimensions: 42 × 440 cm (600 kg, including 145-kg warhead). Fin span (diagonal) is 93 cm. Air-launched IIR and active-radar versions are 375 cm long (480 kg), with a range of 5–130 km, launch altitude 200– 5,000 m, and flight altitude 5–10 m (speed 300 m/sec).

The "Gepard" corvette advertised at the 1993 Abu Dhabi show, armed with SS-N-25, had both **Light Bulbs** and **Band Stand**. In other systems (SS-N-9/22 and probably P-27), Band Stand tracks the outgoing missile, which sends back its radar video via Light Bulbs; the

charge, a bomblet warhead (in a swollen section), and, presumably, a nuclear warhead.

In June 1993 it was announced that the U.S. Navy was negotiating to purchase 1,000 P-80 missiles at a unit price of $600 thousand to serve as supersonic targets. The original supersonic-target requirement had been framed to simulate precisely this missile. The RN is reportedly considering purchasing the same missile to upgrade Type 22 Batch 1 and 2 frigates. RFPs to adapt P-80 to U.S. launchers have been issued. The design was started in 1972, the missile first flew in 1976, and it entered service in 1980. The same basic airframe configuration was used for Kh-58 (AS-11) and for an unsuccessful successor to SS-N-2 (P-27 was the interim replacement, followed by 3M-80).

At Paris in June 1993, Chelomey displayed a drawing of a successor "Anti-Ship Missile 2000" with some antiradar shaping and

Light Bulb missile-targeting down link (for SS-N-22) on board the destroyer *Bezuderzhannyy* in 1993. (Author)

The air-launched version of Kh-35 (SS-N-25), "Harpoonski." (S. Zaloga)

ship corrects the missile's course (e.g., redirects it to another target) based on this combination. The "Gepard" sketch suggests that SS-N-25, quite unlike the U.S. Harpoon, which it outwardly resembles, has such a semi-command mode. Ships converted to fire SS-N-25 (Krivaks and 1 Osa) seem to have Light Bulbs radomes but lack the associated Band Stand. The ship's main search set can presumably provide limited missile tracking on a TWS basis, perhaps in analogy to the dual search/missile-track role of Band Stand in a Tarantul-II/III. On the other hand, drawings of several ships, most of them modified versions of existing types armed with SS-N-25, distributed at Abu Dhabi in 1993 showed no special antennas. Thus it would seem that the missile can also be fired in a U.S.-style fire-and-forget mode.

At Abu Dhabi in 1993 Lyulev announced a new coast-defense missile, Alpha. The 8.5-m, 7,000-kg (200-kg warhead) missile flies 200 km at subsonic speed (220–240 m/sec [about 440–470 kt]), then when 20 km from the expected target position it accelerates to supersonic speed (700 m/sec [about 1,380 kt]), either by shedding its wings or by firing a second stage.

Also at Abu Dhabi, NPO Barrikady of Volgograd announced a mobile 130-mm gun "complex" in 3 8 × 8 vehicles: a gun, a command vehicle, and a generator vehicle. It can handle targets moving at up to 200 kt and at ranges up to 20 km; it can destroy a target (probability 0.8) in 1–2 min and can control 2 guns. The radar auto-tracks 4 targets (acquisition range 35 km). An associated optronic system covers a 135-deg sector. The control vehicle can be up to 1,000 m from the guns. The gun fires at least 10 rnd/min, and the vehicle carries 40 rnd. The associated Krasnopol laser-guided shell can cope with target speeds up to 19 kt. Elevation limits are +50/−5 deg.

At Defendory (October 1992) a truck-mounted version of the **BM 21** rocket launcher was advertised to counter midget submarines and swimmers; range is 500–3,000 m. All 40 rockets can be ripple-fired in 20 sec.

ANTIAIR WARFARE

Where real designations are known, they are given in parentheses; names are mostly NATO nicknames.

Cheese Cake is a surface-search radar, in a flat circular radome, atop the bridge of at least some Matka-class missile boats. It is analogous to the Kivach-3 of a Tarantul.

Cross Dome (Positive-E, 1RL144) is a new radome-enclosed small-ship search/target-acquisition/surface-fire-control radar (in Parchim-II, Pomornik, and the Indian *Khukri*). In a *Neustrashimyy*, it acquires targets for the CADS-N-1 system and controls the ship's helicopter. It has been identified with the search element of the Cross Swords fire-control set (hence the name), but most likely it uses the same transmitter with a different antenna. The -E suffix stands for *esminets*, destroyer. This is probably the Podberezovik ("barber," after its shape) radar described at Abu Dhabi in 1993: peak power 110 kW, maximum elevation 30 deg, data rate 5 sec (12 rpm); detects a 7-m² target at 1,500 m altitude at 300 km [162 nm]. Minimum range is 5 km. Total weight is 13 t (antenna 3.0 t). For target acquisition, the radar scans at a higher speed, probably 60 rpm. In

Peel Cone. (Royal Navy)

the case of the land-based Tunguska (2S6), which has a lower-powered version of this radar with a smaller antenna (Positive-T, for tank, 1RL144M), range in this mode is reduced to 18 km [9.8 nm]. There is also probably an intermediate mode better adapted to low-flier detection; the Indians claim 70–75 nm for the radar on the *Khukri*.

Curl Stone-A is the enclosed surface-search/navigational radar on the *Dergach* surface-effect missile corvette.

Peel Pair is a back-to-back radar mounted only on board Soviet Nanuchkas (not export craft, which use Don-2 or Mius instead).

Plank Shave (Garpun) supersedes Square Tie. There are 3 operating modes: radar, ESM (DF on a jamming strobe), and directional data-link receiver. Radar scan modes: 360 deg, sector scan, and directional. Presumably, the directional mode is used to find the range to a target indicated by an ESM cut. At least in a Tarantul, the data link takes over operation of the ship (including missile firing); it does not provide a tactical picture. The name means Harpoon.

Users: India (*Khukri,* Tarantul classes), Libya (Koni class), Poland (Tarantul class), Russia (Tarantul, Matka classes)

Sky Watch has apparently been entirely unsuccessful. Development funding was reportedly cut about 1990. The superstructure of the second full-deck carrier, the incomplete *Varyag,* is suited to a conventional mechanically scanned radar.

Strut Curve is Fut-B, MR-302; note the connection with Slim Net (Fut-N). Like Plank Shave, Strut Curve can act as a data-link receiver, in this case to accept commands for concerted ASW action (presumably, using the RBU-6000 launcher). Presumably, it supersedes the combination of Slim Net and a dedicated data-link receiver, perhaps Fig Jar.

Users: Algeria (Koni class), Bulgaria (Koni, Poti classes), Cuba (Koni class), Ethiopia (Petya-II class), Libya (Koni class), Romania (*Muntenia,* Tetal, Poti, Cosar,

Peel Pair radar on a Nanuchka. (Royal Navy)

The island of the carrier *Adm. Kuznetsov.* (Royal Navy)

Croitor classes), Russia (Grisha-I/II/III, Petya-II [and modified Petya-I], Mirka-II [most have Slim Net], Poti, *Ivan Susanin*, T-58 picket, Ropucha, Ugra, Lama [or Slim Net] classes), Syria (Petya class), Vietnam (Petya class), Yugoslavia (*Kotor*, Koni classes)

Ball End (Ryf) *Users:* Albania (T-43 class), China (PRC) (T-43 class), Syria (T-43 class)

Big Net (MR-500 Echo) *Users:* India (Kashin class), Poland (Kashin class), Russia (Kashin and Kresta-I classes).

Head Net C (Angora-M, MR-310U) *Users:* India (Kashin class), Poland (Kashin class), Russia (Kresta-I/II, Kara, Kynda, Kashin, Krivak, *Ivan Rogov* [Top Plate in *Migrofan Moskalenko*], *Smol'nyy*, Artika classes). Head Net was reportedly copied from the Dutch Signaal DA-02.

Kivach, normally considered a surface-search radar, is often connected to ESM equipment, for fine ESM cuts (as in a Krivak-III).

Mius (X-band surface-search) *Users:* Algeria (Nanuchka)

Nyada (MR 212: X-band surface-search radar) *Users:* Russia (Gorya, *Aleksandr Brykin*, Vishnaya class AGIs)

Pot Drum (MR 102) *Users:* Angola (Shershen class), Bulgaria (Shershen class), Cambodia (Stenka, Turya classes), Congo (Shershen class), Cuba (Stenka, Turya classes), Egypt (Shershen class), Ethiopia (Turya class), Guinea-Bissau (Bogomol class), North Korea (Shershen class), Romania (Shanghai-II and Epitrop classes), Seychelles (Turya class), Russia (Stenka [or Peel Cone], Turya classes), Vietnam (Shershen, Turya classes), Yugoslavia (Shershen class)

Pot Head (Reya) *Users:* Albania (Shanghai-II class), Cape Verde Islands (Shershen class), China (PRC) (Haijui, Hainan, Shanghai-II [or Skin Head], 25-m classes), Congo (Shanghai-II class), Cuba (SO 1 class), Ethiopia (Mol class), Mozambique (SO-I class), North Korea (Najin, Taechong, Shanghai-II, SO-I [or Don-2], P-6/Sinpo [or Skin Head], Nampo classes), Sierra Leone (Shanghai-II class), Somalia (Mol class), Tanzania (Shanghai-II class), Vietnam (SO-I class), Zaire (Shanghai-II class)

Skin Head (Zarnitsa) *Users:* Albania (Huchuan class), China (PRC) (P-4 and P-6 classes), Guinea-Bissau (Shantou class), North Korea (Najin, Chodo classes), Tanzania (Huchuan class), Vietnam (Shanghai-II class)

Slim Net (Fut-N) *Users:* Bulgaria (Riga class), China (PRC) (Riga class), India (Petya-II and Ugra classes), Indonesia (Don class), North Korea (Najin class), Russia (Riga, Mirka [or Strut Curve] classes)

Snoop Head *Users:* Russia (Alfa- and Oscar-I classes)

Snoop Pair *Users:* Russia (Typhoon-, Sierra-, Akula-, and Oscar-II–class submarines)

Snoop Plate *Users:* Albania (Whiskey class), Algeria (Romeo class), China (PRC) (Wuhan, Ming, Romeo classes), Bulgaria (Romeo class), North Korea (Romeo class), Syria (Romeo class)

Snoop Slab *Users:* Russia (Echo-II– and some Juliett-class submarines)

At least in Victor-III, **Snoop Tray** (MRK-50; export version MRK-50E) is closely associated with ESM; it is presumably used mainly for high-precision DF cuts for targeting. Submarines have a 2-way data link allowing them to share ESM information for cross-bearings.

Users: Algeria (Kilo class), Cuba (Foxtrot class), India (Kilo, Foxtrot classes), Iran (Kilo class), Libya (Foxtrot class), Poland (Kilo, Foxtrot classes), Romania (Kilo class), Russia.

Russian versions:

—Snoop Tray 1: Charlie-, Echo-, some Tango-, Foxtrot-, November-, Victor-I–, Lima-, Hotel-, Bravo-, and some Romeo-class submarines.
—Snoop Tray 2: Delta-I/II/III/IV–, some Echo-II–, Charlie-II–, Victor-II/III–, some Tango-, Kilo-, India-, and Yankee-Notch-–class submarines.

Spin Trough *Users:* Angola (Yevgenya class), Benin (Zhuk class), Bulgaria (Poti, Zhuk, Sonya, Yevgenya, Polnocny, Vydra classes), Cape Verde Islands (Zhuk class), Congo (Zhuk class), Cuba (Sonya, Yevgenya, Polnocny, Zhuk classes), Egypt (Toplivo 2 and Okhtenskiy classes), Ethiopia (Zhuk class), Guinea-Bissau (Poluchat-I class), India (Pauk, Yevgenya classes), Libya (Polnocny class), Mozambique (Zhuk, Yevgenya classes), Nicaragua (Zhuk, Yevgenya classes), Russia (Krivak [or Don-2], Mayak, T-58 picket, Zhuk, Sonya, Zhenya, Yevgenya, Alligator [or Don-2], Polnocny, Vydra, *Smol'nyy* classes), Seychelles (Zhuk class), Somalia (Poluchat-I class), Syria (Natya, Zhuk, Yevgenya, Polnocny classes), Vietnam (Sonya, Yevgenya, Zhuk classes), Yemen (Zhuk, Yevgenya, Polnocny classes).

This is the helicopter-landing radar in a Krivak-III.

Square Tie (Rangout)/Type 331 (PRC designation) *Users:* Algeria (Nanuchka, Osa classes), Angola (Osa class), Bulgaria (Osa class), Cuba (Osa class), Egypt (Osa class), Ethiopia (Osa class), India (Nanuchka, Osa classes), Libya (Nanuchka, Osa classes), North Korea (Soho, Soju, Sohung, Osa, Komar classes), Poland (Osa class), Romania (Osa class), Somalia (Osa class), Syria (Osa classes), Vietnam (Osa class), Yemen (Osa class), Yugoslavia (Osa class)

Top Plate (Fregat) *Users:* Russia (*Kuznetsov, Kirov, Slava,* on 8 Udaloy-class, 5 Sovremennyy-class destroyers, Krivak-IIIs [after the first 2], *SSV-33,* later *Artika* class).

Fregat-MA (probably Half Plate) data given at Abu Dhabi in 1993: S(E)-band planar array with less than 30-dB sidelobes; peak power 30 kW (i.e., pulse-compressed), with a 4-sec data rate; max elevation 55 deg. Detects a 7-m^2 target above 5,000 m at 130 km [70 nm], a 500-m^2 ship at 30 km; min range is 3 km. Total weight 7.5 t (antenna 2.2 t). The associated Poima-E ADT processor carries 20 target tracks (5 t).

Half Plate *Users:* Russia (Half Plate A: *Aleksandr Brykin*; Half Plate B: later Grisha-Vs, superseding Strut Pair)

Top Sail (MR-600 Voshkod) *Users: Moskva, Kiev,* Kresta-II, Kara

Top Pair *Users: Kirov, Slava* classes

Top Steer *Users:* Russia (2 *Kiev*s, 2 *Kirov*s, 2 *Slava*s, first 3 *Sovremennyy*s)

Plate Steer *Users:* Russia (Sovremennyy-class destroyers *Osmotritel'nyy* and *Bezuprechnyy*)

The first postwar generation of Soviet naval radars included separate target-indication sets (which rapidly scanned a narrow beam across their antennas, to give high resolution, while they rotated) and dedicated range-only FCS radars. The first modern FCS radars, Hawk Screech and Owl Screech, embodied a horizontal or diagonal rapidly scanning feed; the radar itself scanned the horizon. These radars operate in TWS mode: the console measures the movement (in range and bearing) of a designated target, transmitting the rates to an FCS computer. The operator monitors rate-aided tracking. In theory, such a radar can track several slow-moving targets simultaneously. The external mark of TWS operation is the cylindrical radar feed, housing a spinner.

The next generation (Drum Tilt, Bass Tilt) added a dedicated tracker, initially in the form of a tilting plate, which the operator kept centered on the target. Like their predecessors, these radars scan the horizon until their operators designate targets for precision tracking (TWS/rate-aided tracking suffices for surface targets). In the next generation, Kite Screech, the scanning and tracking mechanisms are moved into the radar enclosure. Missile-guidance radars use the same TWS technology, although they may have a rough equivalent of monopulse in the form of SWC (scan with compensation).

A CADS-N-1 combined gun-missile mounting. Above each Gatling gun are 4 guide rails for missile tubes, which are loaded vertically from below.

Kolonka, the standard Russian optical backup director, is shown on board the missile destroyer *Bezuderzhannyy*. That it has no computing function whatever is obvious from its use of a simple ring sight. (Author)

Hot Flash, the CADS-N-1 radar array, consists of a pair of vertical orange peels, which can train as well as elevate. One tracks the target, the other the outgoing bullets; like the Western Goalkeeper and Phalanx, CADS-N-1 uses closed-loop spotting for its guns (the missiles are optically guided).

Kolonka is a simple optical director, used to control light automatic guns, such as AK 230s, which lack any on-board controls. Kolonka carries a very simple sight with speed rings; it is not a lead-

Vympel (Bass Tilt) GFCS consoles in the below-decks weapons-control space of the Tarantul-class missile boat *Hiddensee*, showing the television (top) and radar screens. The device at right is the ballistic computer, with separate dials showing the bearings of the 76-mm and 30-mm guns. The guns are fired from the main console, which has bearing repeaters for the 2 30-mm guns (to the right of the radar scope); below them are dials showing how many rounds remain. A switch selects long or short bursts. (Author)

computing sight like the old U.S. Mk 14 used in the Mk 51 and 63 FCSs. The operator has a pair of pistol grips, triggers on both of which must be depressed to fire. Lights on the operator's side of the director show which guns the operator controls, and also whether the operator is in control.

Bass Tilt is 2 different radars:

—MR-105 Turel (controls 1 gun) *Users:* India (*Ranvir* [Kashin class]), Poland (Kashin class), Russia (*Kiev, Kirov, Slava*, Kara, Kresta-II [not in all], Kresta-I [only *Vitse Admiral Drozd*], *Udaloy, Sovremennyy*, Mod Kashin, Krivak-III, Babochka, Pomornik [units 2 and 3], *Aleksandr Brykin, Berezina*, SSV-33 classes)

—MR-123 Vympel (controls 2 guns) *Users:* Guinea-Bissau (Bogomol class), India (*Khukri*, Tarantul, Pauk classes), Poland (Tarantul class), Russia (Parchim-II, Grisha-III/V, Dergach, Tarantul, Nanuchka-III, Svetlak, Pauk, Matka, Muravey classes).

In at least the -123 version (which may also be designated Koral), it has a TV camera and a laser range-finder. Peak X(I)-band power is 250 kW (beam 1.8 deg); scan rate is 15 rpm. Scan rate in elevation (for target acquisition) is 5 Hz (field 3.6 deg). The target tracker is monopulse; claimed accuracy is 1 mrad in angle and 5 m in range. Instrumented range is 45 km (30 km with MTI). Maximum elevation is 85 deg. Total weight is 5.2 t.

Cross Sword *Users:* Russia (*Kuznetsov, Gorshkov, Udaloy* class)

Drum Tilt (Rys, MR-104) *Users:* Algeria (Koni, Osa, Polnocny classes), Angola (Osa, Shershen, Polnocny classes), Bulgaria (Koni, Osa, Shershen, Polnocny classes), Cambodia (Stenka class), Cuba (Koni, Osa, Polnocny classes), Egypt (Osa, Polnocny classes), Ethiopia (Osa, Mol, Polnocny classes), Finland (Osa class), India (Kashin class, *Godavari* class, *Trishul*, Osa, Natya, Polnocny classes), North Korea (Osa, Shershen classes), Libya (Koni, Osa, Natya, Polnocny classes), Poland (Osa, Mod Obluze, Polnocny classes), Romania (*Muntenia*, Tetal, Osa, Epitrop, Cosar classes), Russia (Osa, Stenka, *Gorya*, Natya-I, Yurka classes), Somalia (Osa, Mol classes), Syria (Natya, Osa classes), Vietnam (Shershen, Yurka classes), Yemen (Osa, Polnocny classes), Yugoslavia (*Kotor*, Koni, Osa classes)

Eye Bowl *Users:* Russia (*Kirov, Udaloy*, Krivak classes).

The 2 dishes track a single missile (1 tracks horizontally, the other vertically, using the standard scanning mechanism). Eye Bowl is, in effect, the missile-tracking element of Head Lights.

Front Dome (Orekh) (C-band tracker-illuminator for SA-N-7, 3 per launcher) *Users:* Russia (*Sovremennyy* class and test ship *Provornyy*)

Hawk Screech (Yakor') *Users:* Algeria (Koni class), Bulgaria (Koni class), Cuba (Koni class), Ethiopia (Petya-II class), India (Petya-II class), Libya (Koni class), Romania (*Muntenia*), Russia (Petya, Mirka, Don, Amga [alternative to Muff Cob] classes), Syria (Petya class), Yugoslavia (Koni class).

This fully stabilized radar, conceived in 1949, introduced TWS techniques to Soviet radar technology.

Like Peel Group, **Head Lights** (Grom, 4K65) is a TWS radar; 1 of each pair of dishes is scanned vertically, the other horizontally. Previous suggestions that Head Lights is a monopulse radar are entirely incorrect. The name means Thunder.

Users: Moskva, Kiev, Kara, Kresta-II classes

The mounting of **Kite Screech** (MR-145 Lev; may be Yakhond-M system) carries an autotracking TV camera and a laser range-

Front Door B (formerly Trap Door) erected on a *Kiev*-class carrier. (Royal Navy)

finder; the FCS is digital. The X(I)-band search beam is 1 deg wide (300 kW peak power); the K-band tracker beam is 0.25 deg wide (25 kW). Instrumented range is 75 km, and maximum elevation is 75 deg. Accuracy: 0.5 mrad, 5 m. Weight: 8 t. The system tracks its own shells for correction and can direct 2 guns (e.g., 2 AK-100s on a *Udaloy*) simultaneously.

Users: Russia (*Gorshkov, Kirov, Slava, Udaloy, Sovremennyy,* Krivak-II/III)

Muff Cob (MR-104 Bars) *Users:* Algeria (Nanuchka-II class), Bulgaria (Poti class), Cambodia (Turya class), Cuba (Turya class), Ethiopia (Turya class), India (*Godavari,* Nanuchka classes), Libya (Nanuchka class), Romania (Poti, Cosar classes), Russia (*Moskva,* Kresta-I/II, Grisha-I/II, Poti, T-58 picket, Turya, Ugra, Amga [alternative to Hawk Screech], *Berezina* classes), Vietnam (Turya class), Yemen (Ropucha class)

Owl Screech (Yakhond, MR-114; there may be an MR-140 version)

Users: India (Kashins), Poland (Kashins), Russia (*Kiev,* Karas, Kashins, Krivak-Is, *Ivan Susanin, Smol'nyy* class)

Peel Group (Yatagan) *Users:* India (Kashin class), Poland (Kashin class), Russia (Kynda, Kresta-I, Kashin classes)

Pop Group (Osa-2M, MPZ-301, 4P33) *Users:* Algeria (Nanuchkas, Konis), Bulgaria (Konis), Cuba (Konis), India (Nanuchkas), Libya (Koni class), Russia (*Kiev, Kirov, Slava,* Kara, Krivak, Grisha-V, Nanuchka classes), Yugoslavia (Kotor, Koni classes).

At least in a Krivak, the radar is called Korund (Osa is the full system).

In **Scoop Pair** (Binom), 1 antenna group is used for each quartet of SS-N-3 missiles; it consists of 2 separate stabilized antennas (top and bottom), each provided with a pair of horns and 2 superimposed reflectors, about 4.2 m wide. With dual polarization, each antenna set could handle 2 sets of signals, to control 2 missiles. The system dates from the late 1950s, when the Soviets were using TWS systems to control surface-to-air missiles. Presumably, Scoop Pair is an application of much the same technology.

Users: Russia (Kresta-I, Kynda classes)

Sun Visor (Yakor-2M) *Users:* Bulgaria (Riga class), China (PRC) (Riga class), Indonesia (Don class), Russia (Riga, Don classes)

Top Dome *Users:* Russia (*Kirov, Slava* classes and *Azov* [test ship])

Squeeze Box *Users:* Russia (*Sovremennyy* class and amphibious ships with 140-mm bombardment rockets; uncovered version in *Pomornik*)

Tee Plinth *Users:* Russia (*Moskva, Kiev, Slava,* Kresta-I/II, Kara, Kynda, Mod Kashin classes; *Soobrazitelnyy* was probably the test ship)

One of these EO devices is located approximately above each 30-mm Gatling gun on board a *Sovremennyy*-class destroyer (and also close to each Front Dome SA-N-7 guidance radar, which lacks any EO element). It probably incorporates a television tracker (this one was photographed when the destroyer *Bezuderzhannyy* was anchored in New York), but it may also incorporate a laser dazzler. Its NATO nickname is unknown. (Author)

Watch Box bridge periscope on board the *Bezuderzhannyy*. (A. L. Raven)

Tin Man *Users:* Russia (*Novorossiysk, Gorshkov, Kirov* classes)

There is an AEW version of the Helix (Ka-27) helicopter. A model of a twin-engine AEW airplane with a rotodome (resembling the E-2C) was shown at the Moscow Air Show in August 1992, but this project appears to have died.

Slot Back (RP-29, N-019 Zhuk) is the Doppler look-down/shoot-down multifunction radar of the Su-27 and the MiG-29, possibly in different versions. The original MiG-29 radar used an inverse Cassegrain antenna. At the 1991 Paris Air Show a new Zhuk (Beetle) radar, which had a flat-plate (slotted-waveguide-array) antenna and a digital processor, was shown. It was a 3-channel monopulse system with a high PRF for air-to-air pulse-Doppler operation. It appeared to have a 65–70-deg scan. The Germans credit MiG-29s with essentially this radar but a different antenna. Range is 90–110 km in search mode, with lock-on at about 70 km (somewhat less in look-down). At the 1992 Moscow Air Show it was reported that Zhuk flight tests were nearly complete; the new radar would equip MiG-29M and possibly -29S fighters.

This TWS radar maintains good enough track on 4 targets to engage them with active-radar or IR weapons. This was probably the first Soviet software-controlled radar, suited both to air-to-air combat and to ground attack. Modes: TWS, simultaneous engagement in look-up and look-down modes; real-beam or SAR mapping, terrain-following and -avoidance. Reportedly, Soviet Slot Backs have 5 alternative operating modes, but export radars are limited to 3 (based on observed cockpit configurations). These numbers probably correspond instead to the number of sensors on the airplane; in material released for CFE, the Soviets credited the Su-27 and MiG-29 with 5 sensors: radar, IRST, laser ranger, a helmet sensor (to which missile seekers can be slaved), and ESM. Presumably, the last 2 are not cleared for export.

The following is CFE data on the Su-27 intercept radar (released in May 1991). The airplane can track 10 targets simultaneously, engaging 1 with a data-linked missile. "C2 cycle time," presumably the data-link refresh rate, is 60 sec. Typical detection range is 70 km (but in a table of tactical fighters, the Su-27 radar is credited with a range of 54 km); accuracy is 50 m in range, 0.6 deg in elevation/ bearing, and 10 m/sec in target speed). It appears that the Soviets considered this the best of their interceptor multifunction radars; they rate its quality as 1.00 on a scale on which the MiG-31 radar is 0.5 (similarly the MiG-23P radar). The MiG-29 radar has similar performance. Recent reports suggest that the MiG-29 radar has a very narrow search sector, perhaps only 30 deg wide (1 report suggests

10 deg), which would be appropriate for a ground-controlled intercept system but would be less effective for an aircraft operating from a carrier without any associated AEW system.

The MiG-29 weapons-system computer apparently selects which weapon to fire based on radar input. The system automatically interrogates a target; it can be set either not to fire on a positive IFF reply, or else to disregard the reply. Thus standard practice is to operate with the trigger depressed, relying on IFF to protect friendly aircraft. The trigger and other weapons switches are widely separated and are probably difficult to press in quick succession. An Iraqi pilot apparently failed to set his system to avoid engaging friendly aircraft (or suffered an IFF failure) and, therefore, shot down his wingman early in the Gulf War. Apparently, similar failures occasionally resulted in Russian losses during training. The full weapon system incorporates an IRST and, reportedly, a wide-angle helmet-target designator. A Russian pilot reportedly explained the system as a whole as an attempt to avoid emissions in intercepting a target. Typically, the radar operates in dormant mode. A clear-air target is acquired and tracked by IRST (which incorporates a laser ranger); the radar is used only when it disappears into a cloud. The pilot uses the helmet to cue AA-10 missile seekers (IR and radar).

NPO Fakel (the Grushin OKB, founded in 1953) was responsible for most major surface-to-air missile systems, including SA-N-1, -3, -4, -6, and -9. NPO Altair is responsible for adapting ground-forces weapons for naval service.

SA-N-1 Goa (M1 Volnya-M; V-600 missile) *Users:* India (Kashin class), Poland (Kashin class), Russia (Kresta-I, Kynda, Kashin classes).

The twin launcher (ZIF-101) carries 16 V-600 missiles in twin drums.

The **SA-N-3** Goblet (V-611 missile, Shtorm system) provides a missile capacity per launcher of 22 in Kresta-II (B-187A launcher) and *Moskva* and 36 in Kara (B-192 launcher) and *Kiev* classes.

SA-N-4 Gecko (9M33 missile, 4K33 or Osa-M system ["complex"]) *Users:* Algeria (Koni, Nanuchka classes), Bulgaria (Koni class), Cuba (Koni class), India (*Godavari*, Nanuchka classes), Libya (Koni, Nanuchka classes), Russia (*Kirov*, Kara, Krivak, Grisha, Nanuchka, Sarancha, *Ivan Rogov, Berezina* classes), Yugoslavia (*Kotor*, Koni classes).

The cover of the 20-rnd ZIF-122 launcher (ZIF-122) reportedly leaks.

SA-N-5/8 is fired either from a hand-held tube or from the East German–designed FASTA-4M launcher. Early Kilo-class submarines probably have platforms for missile operators. SA-N-5 Grail is

Strela 2M (9M32 missile). SA-N-8 Gremlin is 9M39 (Igla-M). SA-N-8 uses the same launcher but has greater range. SA-N-10 is a quadruple launcher, reloaded vertically through a single hatch in its base, firing the successor missile, SA-16 Gimlet (9M313 Igla-1). The 2 launcher arms elevate separately, so that each can line up with the reloader. Range is 3 km [1.6 nm]; targets between 32 and 11,500 ft, and at speeds up to 680 m/sec [1,300 kt], can be engaged. SA-N-10 is on board Kilo-class submarines (at least later ones: total 8 missiles) and the AGI **Ural** (SSV-33).

FASTA-4M

Users: Guinea-Bissau (possibly in Bogomols), India (Tarantul, Natya classes), Russia (Pauk, Tarantul, Natya classes), Libya (Natya class), Poland (Tarantul class). Single missiles: Algeria (Kilo class), Cuba (Osa, Turya classes), Egypt (Osa class), India (Kilo class), Poland (Kilo class), Romania (Kilo class), Russia (some Osa class, minecraft, landing ships, auxiliaries), Yemen (Polnocny class)

SA-N-6 Grumble (Fort; Ryf for export) corresponds to the land-based S-300PMU (SA-10), designed specifically to deal with low-flying cruise missiles; the missile is 48N6E. Guidance is by track-via-missile. Missiles are carried in revolver-type 8-rnd vertical launchers, 1 fired every 4–5 sec. They are loaded in their canisters and are considered good for 10 yr before overhaul. The missiles ignite only after they clear the ship's deck. At least on a *Slava*, banks of cannisters are angled slightly outboard so that missiles will not fall back on deck if their motors fail. Each Top Dome can handle 3 targets simultaneously, controlling 6 missiles. Maximum slant range against targets at 2,000 m [6,600 ft] and higher altitudes is 90 km [49 nm]; against low-altitude targets (25 m [80 ft] and less), 25 km [13.7 nm]. Maximum speed at interception is 4,200 km/hr [2,296 kt]. The land-based equivalent must be a somewhat larger missile because its maximum range is 150 km [82 nm] and its speed at intercept is 6,450 km/hr [3,526 kt].

SA-N-7 Gadfly (Uragan; Shtil for export; possibly also Smerch) is the naval version of SA-11. The successor, SA-17, is longer but very similar and uses the same systems; presumably, there is a naval version. Photographs of SA-N-7 on its launcher show the missile in a somewhat awkward position; the launcher may be designed to accommodate the larger SA-17 equivalent. As displayed in Moscow in 1992, this system is available in 24-, 48-, 72-, and 96-rnd versions: 1 launcher per 24 missiles. Different versions can have 2, 4, 6, 8, 10, or 12 firing channels (guidance antennas); presumably, the **Sovremennyy** version has 6 channels for 48 missiles. Like the U.S. SM-2, this missile has a commandable autopilot. Commands are sent up after burnout, to avoid interference from the motor plume. The launcher fires a missile every 12 sec. The missile's magazine has an area of 5.2 m² and a depth of 7.42 m; weight (empty) is 30 t. The

A Fasta-4M quadruple launcher for SA-N-5/8 missiles, on board the Tarantul-class missile boat *Hiddensee*. The launching tubes are placed in the clamps shown; the device is entirely self-contained. (A. D. Baker III)

An SA-N-7 launcher on the destroyer *Bezuderzhannyy* shows protected hatches (probably for loading). Two similar hatches are on the other side of the ship. (Author)

antennas of the 6-channel version weigh a total of 7.1 t; total system weight (without missiles) is 96 t, with a tactical crew of 19. Total electrical load is 320 kW. Missile dimensions: 40 × 555 cm (fin span 86 cm); weight 690 kg (warhead 70 kg). Missiles maneuver at up to 20 G; max speed is Mach 3. The system engages 1 target per guidance radar; maximum range for a crossing target is 18 km for an aircraft, 6 km for an ASM. Altitude limits are 15–15,000 m for aircraft, 10–10,000 m for an ASM. Maximum target speed is 420–830 m/sec for an aircraft, 330–830 m/sec for an ASM (depending on altitude). Ranges (closing target) are 3.5–25 km for aircraft above 1,000 m, 3.5–18 km for aircraft below 1,000 m, and 3.5–12 km for ASMs. Claimed 2-shot kill probability is 0.81–0.96 for aircraft and 0.43–0.86 for ASMs. Maximum FCS-radar elevation angle is 70 deg. The engagement console has a round PPI alongside a rectangular scope, presumably a B-scan. The missile uses a radio proximity fuze.

SA-N-9 (Kinzhal; Klinok export) guides up to 8 missiles against 4 targets in a 60 × 60–deg sector, and it can also control 30-mm guns. Response time is 8–24 sec, and missiles are fired at the rate of 1 every 3 sec (20/min). Targets at 3.5 km in altitude [11,480 ft] are detected at 45 km [49,200 yd]. Maximum range is 12 km [6.6 nm]; minimum is 1.5 m. Altitude limits are 10 m and 6,000 m. Maximum target speed is 700 m/sec (acceleration 300 m/sec^2). Maximum missile speed is 850 m/sec. The single-stage (dual-thrust) missile is 9M330 (length about 2.8 m, 165 kg with 15-kg warhead). Systems can accommodate 24–64 missiles (i.e., 8/rotary launcher). Without ammunition, the system weighs 41 t, and it requires 13 personnel. The system employs 4 types of consoles: a 1-operator console carrying a rectangular CRT and a pair of small alphanumeric screens (as well as a keyboard and trackball), corresponding to a fire channel; a monitoring console; a large-CRT weapons-control console (presumably for target assignment), showing the target-acquisition-radar picture); and a smaller console carrying a CRT and a large alphanumeric screen. The latter (which is set apart from the other consoles) is probably the interface with the ship's "Second Captain."

SA-N-11 (9M311) is the missile component of the CADS-1 (Steelet; also Kortika/Kashtan) system. Launched from a disposable tube, it is a navalized SA-19. The mount carries 8 missiles, plus guns. The missiles are autoreloaded from a 48-rnd below-decks magazine, perhaps in analogy to the standard Soviet bombardment-rocket launcher. 9M311 is a 2-stage rocket with a larger-diameter booster. Effective system range is 500–8,000 m (guns down to 500 m, missiles

The 3M330 (SA-N-9) missile, on display in Moscow in 1992. (S. Zaloga)

from 1,500 to 8,000 m [8,750 yd]; altitude limits are 15 m (0 m with guns) and 4,000 m [about 13,000 ft], and maximum target speed is 500 m/sec. Lethal radius is 5 m with a 9-kg warhead. Maximum missile speed is 900 m/sec (average 600 m/sec). Targets are tracked electro-optically; a brochure claims that the system can engage up to 6/min. Each missile container weighs 57 kg (dimensions 225 × 170 × 2,562 mm). Missile length is about 2.55 m; maximum diameter is about 145 mm. The system consists of a command module and a combat module (i.e., the mounting proper); total weight is 13,500 kg. Swept radius of the turret is 2,760 mm, and maximum height is 2,250 mm. One command module can control up to 6 combat modules (i.e., it can presumably engage up to 36 targets/min). The associated guns in the current naval version are 30-mm Gatlings; they are an interim installation until the twin-barrelled 30-mm/115s (2,500 rpm for each of 2 on the mount, elevating at 30 deg/sec) already used on the analogous land-based Tunguska are available in sufficient numbers. The export version has only the guns and their closed-loop spotting system; 1 such mount replaces the usual pair of 30-mm Gatlings on board a Tarantul (PN-952). Kortika seems to be the name of the overall system, and Kashtan is the export name for the Gatling-gun version.

AA-8 (Aphid, R-60, also Izdeliye 62) is a lightweight, short-range, IR missile, designed as a supplemental fighter weapon and a strike-aircraft self-defense missile. It is small enough to be carried on a twin-rail launcher, APU-60-IIM. There are both IR and semiactive-radar versions. Data below refer to the IR type. AA-8 seems to lack lethality. For example, in October 1988 an AA-8 failed to kill a British Aerospace 125 business jet carrying the president of Botswana, when the missile was fired by an Angolan MiG-21. The missile is smaller than a Sidewinder and cannot be launched head-on. R-60 was accepted for service use about 1975. An improved R-60MK is designed for very short ranges (minimum range is 400 m; K means *kratkoe-deistviye*, short-range). This missile has been widely exported. Dimensions: 13 cm × 2.0 m; span 52 cm [5.1 × 78.7 × 20.5 in]; weight 55 kg [121 lb] with 6-kg warhead. Range 7 km [7,650 yd], max speed Mach 3.0.

AA-10 Alamo (R-27, Izdeliye 470 series) is the current long-range, 2-stage (boost-sustain in long-range version) air-to-air missile, broadly equivalent to Phoenix or AMRAAM. It was developed specifically for the new MiG-29 and Su-27. Work began in the early 1970s, and R-27 entered production in 1982. Guidance is inertial with midcourse command update and semiactive or IR terminal homing. Target altitude can be 20 m–27 km [66–88,600 ft]. R-27EM is a new semiactive version announced in 1992: 26 × 47.8 cm; wingspan 80 cm; fin span 97 cm (350 kg with 39-kg continuous-rod warhead); range 0.5–170 km, speed Mach 4.0. Maximum launch range is for a target closing the launch platform. Semiactive radar versions are R-27R and -27RE; IR versions are -27T and -27TE. An active R-27AE version (maximum range 130 km), to engage small targets (such as cruise missiles) down to very low altitude (3 m), was disclosed in 1992. The E suffix indicates a longer booster and a boost-sustain motor, for greater range (booster diameter 26 vice 23 cm, wingspan 80 vice 77 cm). Literature distributed at the 1992 Moscow Air Show did *not* indicate any midcourse update for the IR versions, but that would surely be needed. R-27R (Alamo A) weighs 253 kg, is 4.0 m long, and has a launch range of 25 km and a maximum range of 80 km. The earlier semiactive R-27RE (Alamo C) weighs 350 kg and is 4.7 m long; maximum range is 130 km (broadside 27 km, tail on 0.5 km). Maximum target acceleration is 8 G. R-27T (Alamo B) weighs 245 kg, is 3.7 m long, and has a broadside launch range of 24 km and a maximum range of 70 km. R-27TE (Alamo D) weighs 348 kg, is 4.5 m long, and has a launch range of 30 km and a maximum range of 120 km. A short-range R-27PS IR version is designed to be retrofitted to MiG-27D and -27K strike fighters.

The R1 version, in production for MiG-29s since 1986, uses a 9B-1101K semiactive seeker. It locks on at altitudes between 20 m and 25 km at vertical separations of up to 10 km (for target airspeeds of up to 3,500 km/hr and acceleration up to 8 G). It locks onto a 3-m^2 target at 25 km. The missile can be launched 1 sec after receiving target designation, and its autopilot is radio-corrected at ranges of up to 25 km (30 sec of flight time). The seeker is 219 × 1,173 mm (33.5 kg).

The alternative monopulse-Doppler, active-radar seeker incorporates a 1-kg programmable computer with up to 32 kbyte of ROM and 32 kbyte of RAM. Maximum launch range against a 5-m^2 target is 70 km; the missile locks on at 20 km. A MiG-29 can provide midcourse guidance at up to 50 km. The radar is ready in 1.5 sec (after

AA-11 (R-73, foreground) with AA-10 (R-27) behind it, at the 1992 Moscow Air Show. (S. Zaloga)

having been warmed up for 2 min). Dimensions: 200 × 600 mm (14.5 kg without radome).

The unusual configuration, with inverse-tapered wings abaft small strake foreplanes, and with short-span tail fins, was adopted to confer good maneuverability at high angles of attack. The difference between long and short range is in the length of the rocket motor, hence its burn time. The longer-burning motor may also be used to provide the missile with greater terminal maneuvering power at constant range. In the radar version, the longer motor is probably intended to take advantage of the higher illuminating power available in an Su-27. Since AA-10 is a new missile, it probably uses an inverse-monopulse seeker, like that of current Sparrows. AA-10 is exported with the MiG-29 fighter (and presumably with the Su-27), so customers include Cuba, China (PRC), India, Iran, and Serbia.

AA-11 Archer (R-73, Izdeliye 72), a short-range, dogfight missile first reported in 1986, replaces AA-8 and is reportedly a generation ahead of AIM-9M. Performance, reportedly as demonstrated during

An R-77 (AA-12) missile shows its unusual honeycomb (lattice) tail fins, at the 1992 Moscow Air Show. (S. Zaloga)

the Gulf War, considerably exceeds Western estimates; AA-11 may justify production of AIM-9R. R-73 in effect bridges the gap between the short-range R-60 (AA-8) and the long-range R-27 (AA-10). The design bureau sometimes calls it RMD (Short-Range Missile). AA-11 uses thrust vectoring for very high maneuverability. Target altitude is 20 m–20,000 m. This missile apparently introduced an off-boresight seeker to Soviet practice; hence the introduction of a helmet sight (to designate its target) in the Su-27 and MiG-29. Targets can be designated 45 deg off axis (60 deg in the modified RMD-2). They can maneuver at up to 12 G. RMD-2 can deal with target altitudes down to 10 m, and can fire at nose-on targets at 40 km. Dimensions: 17 × 290 cm; wingspan 51 cm (105 kg with a 7.4-kg continuous-rod warhead). Speed Mach 2.5. Range 30 km nose on, 0.3 km tail on.

AA-12 (R-77, Izdeliye 170) is the Russian equivalent of AMRAAM, to attack look-up and snap-down targets. It uses the first active-radar seeker in a Russian tactical missile (the big R-33/AA-9 has 1). The most unusual feature is its lattice tail fins, which look like honeycombs perpendicular to the line of flight. Each honeycomb consists of a mesh of narrow wings. Similar fins are on the SS-23 land-based ballistic missile. They should retain attached airflow at angles of attack as high as 50–60 deg. Because individual vanes can be close without interacting, a large effective wing area can be obtained in a small space. At supersonic speed, such a lattice can achieve several times as much lift as a monoplane wing in the same space (3 times at Mach 4). The lattice enjoys practically a constant coefficient of lift at varying angles of attack throughout the speed range, a particularly useful feature when the center of gravity shifts significantly in flight (because of fuel burnout). The lattice wing is also much smaller, hence has smaller hinge moments, and needs smaller actuators. The missile can deal with target maneuvers at up to 12 G. This fire-and-forget missile can be used by a multichannel FCS. Further planned improvements are installation of an IR guidance system and an enlarged motor for maximum range as great as 150 km (vs. AEW aircraft). The model of this missile shown at the 1992 Moscow Air Show carried the dummy designation AAM-AE, but the number above is almost certainly correct. AA-12 was first shown at Minsk in February 1992. As of mid-1992, first deliveries were scheduled for fall 1992. Dimensions: 20 × 360 cm (175 kg); range is approximately 100 km forward aspect, 35 km rear aspect. NPO Vympel displayed a vertically launched version, for ships or ground troops, at Abu Dhabi in February 1993.

Novator showed its new **R-72** missile (export designation AAM-I, prototype designation probably R-172) at Abu Dhabi in February 1993. Like the shorter-range R-77, it combines commandable mid-course inertial guidance with an active terminal seeker. It has conventional tail fins and a large-diameter booster. Development began in 1991. An Su-27 can carry 7, but the intended platform is the Su-35. Dimensions: 0.514 × 6.0 m (750 kg with 75-kg adaptive fragmentation warhead). Maximum launch range is 400 km (216 nm), and the missile can be ordered to turn as much as 180 deg after launch. Target speed can be up to 4,000 km/hr [2,160 kt]; maximum target acceleration is 12.25 G; altitude can be 3–30,000 m. R-72 can engage targets as small as 0.05 m² (air-to-air missiles). It can be launched at 700–2,500 km/hr [380–1,250 kt] and from 50–17,500 m. m. The missile is catapult-launched.

The following are previously unreported shipboard guns:

—**AK-630M1-2** (announced at Abu Dhabi in 1993) is a double (under-and-over) version of AK-630, firing 10,000 rnd/min and carrying 4,000 rnd (shell weight 0.384 kg). Weights: 2.5 t empty, 6.5 t loaded. This is a 30-mm/54 gun with a muzzle velocity of 880 m/sec. Elevation limits are +90/−25 deg (elevation rate 50 deg/sec, traverse rate 70 deg/sec to ±180 deg). 80% of all rounds are within 11 mrad on each firing cycle. These guns are controlled by a Vympel system (MR-123–02).
—**AK-306** (1980) is a lightweight (self-contained) version of AK-630. AK-630 weighs 1,000 kg (without ammunition) but requires an additional 800 kg off-mount; -306 weighs 1,100 kg altogether (less ammunition). It fires 900 rnd/min (compared to 4,500–6,000 for -630) and stows 500 (rather than 1,000) rnd/mount. The gun is AO-18P (rather than AO-18). Control is by optical sight only (-630 uses radar or optical sighting). There may also be a 3-barrel version.
—**BP-30** (1976) is a 30-mm automatic grenade launcher equivalent to the U.S. Mk 19. It is a 1-operator single mount firing a lightweight shell (28 kg) at low velocity (185 m/sec); it fires

400 rnd/min, and the standard mount carries 400 rnd. Maximum range is 1.75 km.
—**UTES-M** (1976), a twin (side-by-side), enclosed, remote, 12.7-mm mount fires 700 rnd/min; elevation limits +85/−12 deg; the mount carries 200 rnd; total weight is 725 kg. Effective range is 2,000 m (altitude 1,500 m).

The larger guns shown at Abu Dhabi were **AK-100** (100-mm/59) and **AK-176M** (76.2-mm/59).

	100-mm	76-mm
Velocity	880 m/sec	850 m/sec
Shell Weight	15.6 kg	5.9 kg
Capacity	60 rnd/min	120 rnd/min
	322 ready-use rnd	152 ready-use rnd
Mount Weight	35 t empty	11.2 t empty
		13.1 t loaded
Train/Elevation Rates	30/20 deg/sec	35/30 deg/sec
Elevation Limits	+85, −10 deg	+85, −15 deg
Horizontal Range	21.5 km	15.5 km

ESM/ECM

Bell Crown, Bell Strike, Bell Thumb, and Fig Jar, often listed as ECM, are all data-link antennas. Many radars (e.g., Plank Shave, Strut Pair) can take precise ESM cuts for targeting, after which a few pulses will be sent for precise ranging. They do not rotate quickly enough to search for signals.

Reportedly, **Amber Light** is a self-protection deception jammer, for use when a submarine has surfaced, at which time it may be immune to attack by conventional ASW torpedoes, but may be attacked by radar-guided missiles (Akula and Sierra classes).

Bald Head is the ESM in Alfa- and Oscar-class submarines, integrated with the Snoop Head search radar. Compared to the later Rim Hat, Bald Head lacks any separate RWR array; presumably, the idea was to use the main ELINT spirals for both warning and ESM. Combining the radar and ESM masts reduces radar signature because the 2 masts tend to create reinforcing echoes.

Bell Bash/Bell Thump/Bell Nip replace Zaliv (Bell Clout/Slam/Tap) in large cruisers; the associated directional noise jammer is the electronically scanned Wine Flask. One Bell Thump or Bell Bash is paired with each Side Globes radome in a *Kiev*, so presumably the same radome can accommodate 2 different ESM arrays. A pair of radomes is assigned to each Wine Glass (2 Wine Glasses to a side of a ship). The approximate dimensions of the 2 ESM radomes are as follows: Bell Bash, 0.6 × 0.7 m; Bell Thump, 0.6 × 0.75 (plus a small radome less than 0.2 m in diameter alongside it). The short-range defense (deception) jammers of the earlier system are eliminated.
Bell Nip (Kursk) is a new-generation Ka/Ku-band short-range self-defense (deception-jammer) system. Each of 2 cones is atop a cylinder carrying 2 rows of spirals; the outputs of vertical pairs of spirals

The carrier *Kuznetsov* has a new, more highly integrated EW system. The large flat-faced housing with 3 flat circular (cavity-backed spiral) antennas is Flat Track. Atop it are a pair of Wine Flask jammers, each atop its ESM array (with monopulse DF antennas). Between the 2 Wine Flasks are 2 Bell Pushes, arranged vertically. The platform above carries the Bell Crown data-link antenna. The 2 large radomes below Flat Track are Wine Glass ESM sets for OTH-T (they replace the earlier Rum Tub). No NATO nickname has been reported for the 2 smaller antennas outboard; they may be K-band deception jammers cued by Flat Track. (Royal Navy)

are combined to overcome multipath (due to reflection off the sea). That is probably particularly important to counter sea-skimming missiles. Each cone contains an omni receiver in its top, feeding a frequency-memory loop that the antenna below it uses to transmit deception signals. In *Slavas*, Rum Tub, which is usually used for OTH-T, cues Side Globes; Bell Nip is mounted between the pair of Rum Tub antennas (there are no Bell Bashes/Thumps).

Users: Kuznetsov, Slava, Kirov (Adm. Nakhimov, Petr Velikiy) classes, Novorossiysk (was in Minsk, now stricken). Bell Nip alone (for short-range self-protection) is in Ropuchas, Turyas, Stenkas, and Svetlaks.

In the *Adm. Kuznetsov*, Bell Nip is superseded by **Bell Push**, a pair of truncated cones. They are presumably equivalent to the omni and transmitter elements of Bell Nip, the DF function having been taken over by the elements under the 2 Wine Flasks (and by Flat Track, which is presumably part of the same system). In the *Kuznetsov*, the combination of Bell Bash/Bell Thump/Bell Nip is replaced by a combination of 2 Flat Tracks and arrays immediately under each Wine Flask jammer. As in Bell Nip (Kursk), there are 2 ports, vertically paired, for each frequency range in each direction. However, this system can achieve finer DF cuts by interferometry (beam preforming). In this sense, Bell Nip and the new system including Flat Track correspond to modern Western system such as UAA-2. The earlier Zaliv and Bell Bash/Bell Thump are amplitude-

The *Adm. Nakhimov* (ex-*Kalinin*) shows the successor system to Zaliv. Wine Glass radomes (passive missile targeting) flank Bell Thump and Bell Bash; the radome in the middle is probably the Bell Crown data link. Bell Bash and Bell Thump have very similar radomes, but the structure under Bell Thump is taller. (Royal Navy)

This detail view of the *Kuznetsov* shows the Wine Glass (formerly Football B) and the probable K-band jammers more clearly (Flat Track is above them). (Royal Navy)

The *Sovremennyy*-class destroyer *Bezuderzhannyy* shows standard destroyer ECM equipment. Two 10-tube chaff launchers are visible atop the bridge (1 only partly visible, to the extreme left). The big radome to the right is Bell Shroud; the associated Bell Squat radome is visible below it. Another, shallower, Bell Squat is mounted on the yardarm. It is probably the noise-jamming element of the system. The big radome to the right is the missile-targeting Wine Glass; the empty platform above Bell Shroud is intended for a second Wine Glass. At the extreme right of the photograph is the Light Bulb targeting down link. (A. L. Raven)

Zaliv is shown on a Russian auxiliary. Almost hidden to the left is Bell Slam; to its right are Bell Tap and Bell Clout; the small radome on the mast is Shot Rock (communications). (Royal Navy)

comparison DF systems like the old British UA-8/9/10. No NATO code name is known for the higher-frequency arrays associated with Flat Track. Both Bell Nip and Flat Track (and the associated higher-frequency arrays) were developed by Fazotron.

Bell Clout/Bell Slam/Bell Tap/Bell Nest (Zaliv) are double-radome combinations consisting of a larger ESM dome (containing a monopulse DF array and, probably, an omni for pulse analysis) above a smaller radome containing a nondirectional deception (i.e., blip repeater) jammer. In an analog system like this one, a blip repeater probably has to be quite close to the receiver. Lack of directionality is acceptable in a self-defense repeater, whose role is to cause weapons or close-in fire-control radars to break lock. Dimensions (diameter × height, upper/lower components) are as follows: Bell Clout, 0.8 × 1.0/0.6 × 0.8; Bell Slam, 0.5 × 0.5/0.4 × 0.4; Bell Tap, 0.4 × 0.3/0.25 × 0.3 m; Bell Nest, 1.2 m total height. The sizes imply that respective frequency ranges are L, S/C (2–8 GHz), C/X (7.5–18 GHz), and K-band. Zaliv first appeared in the Kynda class, with the earlier Watch Dog ESM set triggering Top Hat noise jammers. In later classes its ESM component was used to point and set Side Globes long-range noise jammers. In short-range deception mode, the wide-open receiver in the radome above keys the jammer. Bell Tap first appeared in the Osa (Project 205) class, mounted on the mast below the Square Head IFF antennas. The bigger Bell Slam and Bell Clout came later. The Kashin class had only Bell Slam plus Top Hot (many were fitted to take the jammer, but the jammer was not carried). Kanins had Bell Slam and Bell Tap plus Watch Dog. Most Nanuchkas have only Bell Tap, plus a higher-frequency version, **Bell Nest**. Kyndas have the full Zaliv but no Side Globes. In all other cases (*Moskva*, Kresta, Kara classes) the full Zaliv system is provided to control Side Globes. In the *Kiev* and *Kirov* classes, Zaliv is superseded by the combination of Bell Nip, Bell Bash, and Bell Thump.

Users: Russia (*Moskva*, Kara, Kresta-I/II, Kynda, Kashin [Bell Slam only], Nanuchka*, possibly Gorya* and Alligator-I/II/III/IV*). Starred types carry only Bell Tap. Osas, Tarantuls, Pauks, possibly Natyas, Babochkas, and Muraveys, and export Nanuchkas carry the ESM portion of Bell Tap (in Nanuchkas, the antenna is in the big Band Stand radome). In coastal-patrol, mine, and ASW craft, the system is probably intended to provide cross-bearings for missile shooters. Export Pauks (for Bulgaria, Cuba, and India) may have Bell Tap.

Bell Push supersedes Bell Nip; it consists of 2 truncated-cone elements, from which waveguides extend. It appears without Flat Track in the *Kirov* and *Slava* classes.

Users: Kuznetsov, Kirov (only *Adm. Nakhimov, Petr Velikiy*), *Slava*, Nanuchka, Ropucha II classes

Bell Shroud/Bell Squat (Start) is a small-ship (destroyer/frigate) combination to deal with the new (1960s) threat of Ku-band aircraft radars, e.g., on board A-6s. This combination first appeared on board Kashins modernized as "tattletales," which would have been subject to air attack in the Mediterranean; it is also on board Krivaks, which would face Tornadoes and Buccaneers in the North Sea and the Norwegian Sea. Bell Shroud itself is essentially Watch Dog with 2 additional rows of ports for monopulse detection of higher-frequency signals. The usual outfit is 4 Bell Squats for 2 Bell Shrouds. In analogy to Top Hat, Bell Squat presumably exists in separate noise- and deception-jamming versions. They are not externally distinguishable, but the Bell Squats mounted on top of Bell Shrouds are probably for deception. The 2 Bell Squat radomes, 1 with a dimple on top and 1 flat, differ only because they were cast by 2 different factories using different techniques. Bell Squat contains a rotating antenna on top of a square flat plinth: thus it can deal with only 1 target at a time. Approximate dimensions: Bell Shroud, 1.7 × 1.2 m; Bell Squat, 0.6 × 0.4 m.

Users: Poland (Kashin destroyer), Russia (*Sovremennyy, Udaloy*, Kashin-Mod, Krivak, *Ivan Rogov* classes, *Berezina* [AOR], and *Aleksandr Brykin* [AS])

This is the yardarm Bell Squat on board the *Bezuderzhannyy*. (A. L. Raven)

Brick Pulp: These passive threat-intercept and -warning systems for submarines were delivered from the late 1960s on, beginning with the Victor and Charlie classes. Brick Pulp is a cleaned-up and enlarged Stop Light B, with the same pimple for omni RWR. It is probably an enlarged Bald Head (including lower-frequency elements) plus an omni warner, presumably too tall to accommodate any integrated search radar. This system introduced spiral (vice horn) antennas for its CVRs. Since they have lower gain, the substitution would imply the use of better amplifiers. Brick Group, a formerly reported version, does not exist (its Brick Spit element was a misidentified snorkel intake). Charlie-I/II, Echo-III, Echo-V (Echo modified for special operations), export Kilos (for Algeria, India, Iran, Libya, Poland, and Romania), Victor-I/II/III, Delta-I/II/III/IV, Papa (now discarded).

The **Half Cup** (Spektr-F) laser detector array was first seen in the *Udaloy* class (ships have 4). The associated countermeasure is a series of smoke bombs spaced around a ship's deck, to make laser guidance impossible; they resemble old-fashioned depth charges. A single main-control station supports 2–12 85-kg detectors; claimed effectiveness is 95% probability of detection of a single laser pulse.

Half Hat is a new small-combatant ESM antenna and jammer in a half-cylindrical vertical radome, typically at the end of a yard. It looks like a smaller and lighter version of part of Wine Flask. Approximate dimensions: 1.2 × 0.8 m.

Users: Neustrashimyy, sole Nanuchka-IV, all Tarantul-IIIs, "Dergach" class (Project 1239), Svetlak class. Some units of the following classes have it: Nanuchka-III, Tarantul-I/II, Pauk.

The **Rim Hat** ESM system is integrated with the back-to-back Snoop Pair radar. The 4 visible spirals at the bottom of the dome are for CVRs for radar warning. The big pot, hinged at 1 side (and carrying the paired radar antennas), covers 4 tiers of spirals on a truncated cone, 8 per tier, for instantaneous direction-finding. The 2 Snoop Pair antennas differ: the 1 with the small feed is the conventional radar; the other, with a broad feed, is for data linking (for the P-100 missile) and for fine DF cuts on selected signals (accurate to within a fraction of a degree). The active element can obtain a range on a selected signal. It also functions as a conventional radar. The paired radars nod, e.g., to follow the P-100 missile. Rim Hat/Snoop Pair is associated with the 65-cm-torpedo tube, i.e., with both the big wake-following torpedo and the P-100 (SS-N-22) missile. Installations: Akula, Sierra, and Typhoon classes; probably also on board some Victor-IIIs (Project 671 RTMK version). Reported on Uniform and Yankee Notch classes, but that is unlikely.

Rum Tub is a long-range ESM set designed to target the SS-N-12 and -19 antiship missiles. It probably provides the necessary signatures to the ARM versions of these missiles. Reportedly, it is based on compromised UAA-1 (British) and SLQ-17 (U.S.) technology. It is a mechanically scanned lens system. Rum Tub is a set of 4 radomes, divided into quadrants; each is split horizontally into a wider base and a narrower top, and each segment is further split into segments (5 at the base, 6 at the top), each segment showing 2 square plates, 1 atop the other. The appearance is quite unlike that of earlier Soviet radomes. Rum Tub appeared about 1974; it was initially in-

stalled on board the first 3 *Kiev*-class carriers and the cruiser *Kirov*, the *Slava* class, and then the modernized cruisers *Kerch* and *Petropavlovsk*. Thus it is associated with the SS-N-12 and -19 missiles. Its presence on board the 2 modernized cruisers (which lack long-range weapons of their own) may indicate an intention to use them as pickets (e.g., for target triangulation) to support missile-shooters. Other later Kara-class cruisers show empty platforms adapted to a radome of Rum Tub size. In *Slavas*, Rum Tub provides both OTH-T data and ESM support for Side Globes long-range jammers. Approximate dimensions: 2.1 m wide × 1.8 m high. Wine Glass is the successor system.

Side Globe (Gorzuf) is a series of mechanically steered, long-range directional noise jammers, intended to neutralize aircraft targeting radars in the L–X-bands. Presumably, the burn-through range of the radars would be within the effective range of the ships' SA-N-3 defensive missiles. Delaying engagement would also allow the ship to fire off her antiship missiles, in the "battle of the first salvo." Both concepts failed to take into account the U.S. shift to K-band attack-aircraft radars (in the A-6 and A-7). Hence the appearance of Bell Slam/Bell Clout/Bell Push as a supplemental defense. One radome on each side of a ship works in each of L-, S-, C-, and X-bands (each contains a jammer flanked by a pair of tracking antennas for monopulse DF). The jammers are triggered by Zaliv (Bell Clout/Slam/Tap). The sheer size of the Side Globe radome suggests a very high gain antenna, and reportedly Soviet jammers produce very high effective radiated power (lethal to humans within 40–50 ft). Reportedly, too, the massive tower masts on which Side Globe is mounted conceal substantial cooling systems and also shield personnel from radiation. Side Globe appeared in 1967 (on board the *Moskva*). Approximate dimensions: 1.8 × 2.2 m (length includes coned-in section at base).

User: Russia *Kiev, Moskva, Adm. Ushakov* (ex-*Kirov*), *Slava* class, Kresta-I/II and Kara classes.

Wine Flask is the successor system.

Squid Head is Bald Head plus the directional CVRs (for RWR) used in Rim Hat. In some classes it replaced Stop Light. Presumably, the main ESM system was not suitable for warning. Directional warning would have been necessary for submarines operating in a formation; otherwise, none of them would have been able to use their radars for ranging (the omni warners would have picked up the transmissions and caused the submarines to dive). Hence the directional warners (here and in Stop Light C), presumably associated with group tactics. Installations: Juliett-IIs (replaced Stop Light C), Tangos (Stop Light in early units), Russian Kilos, Echo-IVs. Squid Head may have replaced Stop Light C in the India class (now discarded).

Stop Light (Machta) appears in 3 forms. Stop Light A is a basic ESM set, derived from the surface-ship Watch Dog: it provides a directional display of an incoming signal, with facilities for manual analysis. It does not provide quick threat warning (i.e., automatic threat recognition) for crash-diving. Stop Light B adds a pimple for omnidirectional RWR. Stop Light C is a retrofit, adding a dome in place of the pimple, presumably for directional RWR. It was installed in Yankee-I– (replaced by Brick Pulp) and Juliett-I–class submarines, now discarded, plus the 2 India-class rescue submarines (probably replaced by Squid Head). Stop Light A survives only in Whiskey-class submarines in Albania and China.

Stop Light B Users: Algeria (Romeos), Bulgaria (Romeos), Cuba (Foxtrots), Egypt (2 Romeos), India (Foxtrots), Russia (Echo-IIs, Foxtrots, Julietts), Serbia (*Heroj*), Syria (Romeos)

Top Hat A is a noise jammer, **B** a deception jammer. Top Hat seems to have been conceived as part of the Kashin class's suite, triggered by Watch Dog. These ships later received Bell Tap. Approximate dimensions for Top Hat: 0.4 × 0.36 and 0.58 × 0.54 m. The carriers *Kiev* and *Novorossiysk* are sometimes incorrectly credited with 4 Top Hat A and 4 Top Hat B radomes (they have Bell Thump and Bell Bash).

Users: India (Kashin, Polnocny classes), Libya (Polnocny [Top Hat A only]), Russia (*Moskva* [Top Hat A only], Kynda, Kashin-I classes)

Watch Dog B incorporated an omni antenna feeding a pulse analyzer or IFM (the dimple atop the cylinder). Stop Light A/B was the submarine equivalent. The addition of the omni may have been connected with the use of a jammer or chaff. Reportedly, the Soviets considered the Top Hat/Watch Dog combination equivalent to the

The *Neustrashimyy* shows data-link radomes above and ESM below on her mainmast, with Wine Glass (OTH-T) below the Half Hat radomes. The openings for the torpedo catapults are clearly visible below the mainmast. This photograph was taken in July 1991. (Hans Vanhoefen)

Watch Dog. (Royal Navy)

U.S. WLR-1/3/ULQ-6. Watch Dog was conceived as a warning receiver to protect raiding *Sverdlov*-class cruisers from maritime-patrol aircraft. Based on wartime German submarine RWR technology, Watch Dog was later used to trigger the first Soviet jammer, Top Hat. An improved version (presumably with the earliest Soviet digital processor) may have been installed, unsuccessfully, on the Kynda class. Watch Dog is Bisau.

Watch Dog A Users: Albania (T-43 class), Algeria (Polnocny class), Bulgaria (*Druzki*, Polnocny, T-43, Poti classes), Cuba (Polnocny class), Egypt (Polnocny, T-43 classes), Ethiopia (Polnocny class), Indonesia (T-43 class), Poland (Polnocny B class), Romania (Poti class), Russia (Riga, Polnocny A/B classes), Syria (Polnocny, T-43 classes), Vietnam (Polnocnys), Yemen (Polnocnys)

Watch Dog B Users: Algeria (Koni-II class), Bulgaria (*Smeli*), Romania (*Marasesti*, Tetal, Cosar classes), Cuba (Koni class), Ethiopia (Petya-II class), India (Kashin, Petya-II, Polnocny classes), Libya (Koni and Polnocny classes), Poland (Polnocny-C class), Russia (Kashin-I, Grisha-I/II/III, Mirka-II, Petya-I/II, Parchim-II, Poti, Polnocny-C, Polnocny-B [mine countermeasures], Yurka, Ugra, Pinega, Malina, Lama, Don, Andizhan, Amga classes), Serbia (Koni-I/IVs), Syria (Petya-IIIs), Vietnam (Petya-II/IIIs)

Wine Flask (formerly Modified Football), a long-range electronically steered noise jammer superseding Side Globes, first appeared in the cruiser *Frunze*, completed in 1984, and in the carrier *Novorossiysk*. Each radome covers a stack of 4 cylindrical antennas, covering all 4 bands (L, S, C, X). Each shows 2 rows of antenna ports, presumably to provide vertical beam-steering. The 4 antennas on each side of the ship are paired horizontally (with Bell Nip between them). Approximate dimensions: 0.6 × 1.2 m. Reportedly, Wine Flask and Wine Glass (which appeared in the late 1980s) are derived

in part from Rapids technology compromised about 1980–83. The *Adm. Gorshkov* is unique in lacking Bell Bash and Bell Thump. Instead, a box under each Wine Flask jammer carries an array of small radomes covering monopulse ESM antennas, in what must be a more-integrated system. The entire jamming combination (modified Wine Flasks and Bell Nips) is carried on top of the upper of 2 Flat Tracks.

Users: Kuznetsov, Gorshkov, Novorossiysk, Kirov classes (except *Adm. Ushakov*) and later *Udaloys* (2 radomes at the base of the mainmast, in *Adm. Kharlamov, Adm. Levchenko, Adm. Pantaleyev, Adm. Vinogradov, Simferopol*)

Wine Glass (formerly Football) supersedes Rum Tub as a missile-targeting ESM set. Unlike Rum Tub, Wine Glass is electronically scanned. Presumably, electronic scanning makes for better DF accuracy against fleeting signals. Under the radome are 3 flat phased arrays, each covering a 60-deg arc, probably using much the same techniques as Flat Rack (which covers the high I/J/K-bands). The *Sovremennyy* was completed with 4 Wine Glass radomes, but the more usual complement is 2, 1 on each side of the forward superstructure.

Users: Kuznetsov, Adm. Gorshkov, Kirov class (except *Adm. Ushakov*), *Sovremennyy* class (except *Bezuprechnyy, Osmotritel'nyy, Otchayannyy*), *Udaloy* class (last 5 only; only *Simferopol* has all 4; first 7 have empty platforms), *Neustrashimyy*, Tarantul-III class. *Neustrashimyy* probably has the set because she can fire SS-N-22s (P-80s) from her torpedo catapults. Also reported in "Dergach" (Project 1239) and Svetlak and in some Nanuchka-III, Tarantul-I, and Pauk-I/II classes. If these listings are correct, it is presumably in the ASW craft to provide cross-bearings for missile shooters.

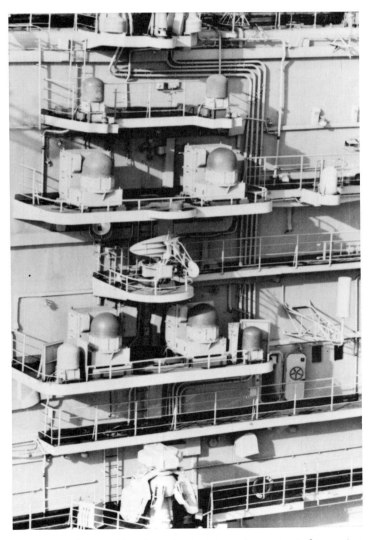

Wine Flask, the current jammer, is shown clearly on board the carrier *Adm. Gorshkov* (ex-*Baku*). The object next to it is the larger of 2 Bell Pushes, which appear to be the innards of Bell Nip (without the conical radomes); note that Bell Push is incorrectly identified in the main text. A second Wine Flask is barely visible to the left of the Bell Push. The pair of radomes (large and very small) at middle left is Bell Thump; a Side Globes radome is visible below it. (Royal Navy)

The carrier *Adm. Gorshkov* shows 4 Wine Glasses for OTH missile targeting, on the 2 big platforms. Above the upper platform is 1 carrying Bell Thump and Bell Bash; a similar pair is outboard of the 2 Wine Glasses on the lower main platform. Above the upper platform is 1 carrying 2 Wine Flask jammers with Bell Push between them. Bell Bash/Bell Thump are the ESM associated with the jammers. This is an intermediate step leading toward the integrated system (ESM below jammer) in the *Kuznetsov*. (Royal Navy)

A Wine Glass missile-targeting radome (for SS-N-22) on board the *Sovremennyy*-class destroyer *Bezuderzhannyy* in 1993. At left is a Bell Squat, probably the deception jammer because it is closest to the Bell Shroud ESM array (not visible here). (Author)

The trainable twin 152-mm **decoy** launcher (RK-2, ZiF-121) loads vertically from below and trains and elevates to fire. It was designed to deploy an active rocket-boosted parachute decoy about 1 m long. Reportedly, the Soviets preferred an active decoy to chaff on the theory that large-scale use of chaff would tend to jam their own radars. This device was not particularly successful; there are also 140-mm chaff (TSP-47, 36.1 kg), IR (TST-47, 37.5 kg), and combined IR/chaff (TSO-47) rounds, each 1.105 m long. This first Soviet decoy launcher was introduced in the Kara class (and then retrofitted to the Kyndas and Krestas), and for some time it was the only one carried. Other installations: *Kiev, Moskva, Berezina.*

The lightweight, 10-tube, 120-mm barrage launcher (RK-10 or KT-216) is used in large numbers, to fire as many as 80 rnd at once. Rounds: SR-50 chaff, SOM-50 IR/laser (i.e., IR and aerosol), SK-50 chaff/IR/laser, each 1.226 m long. It first appeared in the *Udaloy* class in 1989. One Krivak, *Bodryy,* has 10 10-tube chaff launchers in place of the usual 4 16-tube units.

The fixed 82-mm RK-16 16-tube chaff/IR decoy launcher of East German design was originally for light units. Rounds (all 653 mm long): TSP-60 chaff (8.3 kg) and TST-60U IR (8.5 kg). Installations include Mod Kashins, Krivak-I/IIs, Tarantuls, Pauks, Nanuchkas, Matkas.

ASW WEAPONS SYSTEMS

Surface ships can monitor sonobuoys. For example, in a Krivak-III, the monitoring antennas (Long Fold) are at the ends of the foremast yardarms.

Early postwar patrol aircraft, such as the Be-6, essentially duplicated World War II PBY avionics in a new airframe (eventually, simple sonobuoys were carried). The later Be-12 (Mail) carries a dipping sonar but is otherwise much like the earlier aircraft. The first modern maritime-patrol aircraft, May (Il-38), was originally designed for Indonesia, to patrol the archipelago against surface craft (presumably, to cue Badgers armed with antiship missiles). It, therefore, had only a search radar (with on-board terminal), crude ESM, and a manual plotting table. When Sukarno fell, about 30 had been completed. These aircraft were diverted to the Soviet Navy. Some, equipped as intended for Indonesia, were sent abroad (e.g., to Socotra and Cam Ranh Bay) for maritime patrol (surface surveillance). The Soviets preferred to use austerely equipped aircraft abroad to avoid compromising their ASW technology. Others were modified for ASW, to

work with Kara-class cruisers, with radar, sonobuoys, transponders, MAD stingers, and ESM. Each sensor fed its own terminal; there was a manual plot in the "battle area" abaft the cockpit (this system corresponded broadly to that of the U.S. P-3A). A data link from the Kara reported in the battle area. Each Kara could control 4–6 Mays via its "Second Captain."

In a **Bear-F** (Tu-142), the equivalent of the shipboard BIP is the "battle station" abaft the flight deck. Bear-F Mods include changes in sonobuoy signal processors, Mod 1 having virtually none (i.e., using the old BM-series broad-band buoys). At least some aircraft may data-link with Il-38 Mays (the 2 are often seen together, except in the Mediterranean). Although different generations of aircraft are well defined, all Bear-Fs are essentially hand built, so there are 12 or 13 subvariants.

Mod 0 (Tu-142, first flown in 1968) combined the May system with a Bear airframe with a redesigned wing. Only 15 were made, 5 of which were transferred to India. The other 10 were used for R&D, then reconditioned as Mod 3s. Mod 1 (1974) is identifiable by its numerous ram-air intakes and the absence of a chin radome. It has 3 sonobuoy terminals, a belly radar, ESM, and a MAD stinger. Each sensor reports electronically to a plotting table in the "battle area" abaft the cockpit. This area also contains a weapons-release station (in previous aircraft the pilot manually dropped weapons on command).

Work on Mod 2 (Tu-142M) began in 1972; the prototype flew on 4 November 1975, and this version (essentially Mod 3 without its full electronic suite) entered service in 1980. The battle station was approximately doubled in size (the forward fuselage was lengthened by 9 in), and a fully equipped galley and bunk areas were added. ESM was more elaborate than in Mod 1, and there were more data links for operation with surface ships (in addition to Karas) and with submarines (a new feature). There were also transponders and much enhanced airborne track keeping. This version had a very crude airborne "Second Captain" computer. Mod 2 introduced self-defensive weapons (jammers and chaff). This may have been the first version to use Type 75 LOFAR sonobuoys.

All earlier aircraft were converted to the Mod 3 version (1982), which has enlarged weapons bays (27 and 14 m), a new Ladoga MAD (very similar to the U.S. ASQ-81) reporting to 2 stations rather than 1 (this was the first version with the MAD boom on top of the tail fin), and 2 ESM terminals. This version had 3 sonobuoy terminals (perhaps for different types of buoys: broad-band, Julie, and LOFAR) and 1 radar terminal. All reported to a *work area* in the battle station, which was now an airborne command center. There were 12 data links (air–air, air–surface, air–subsurface). This version required its own gas-turbine generator. It had a full "Second Captain"–type tactical computer, which processed ESM data directly. Its output was fed directly to the weapons-control station for weapons release, both for the airplane and for the other platforms it controlled. In a reversal of the earlier arrangement, a single Mod 3 could control several Kresta-IIs. In this version and Mod 4, there is a self-defense "complex" with several terminals (for jammers and chaff). Mods 3 and 4 have full satellite-communications capability.

Mod 3 apparently handles (or handled) several different sonobuoy types. A May 1986 photograph of a Bear-F Mod 3 over the Pacific shows a mix of buoys in the bomb bay, all carried horizontally in racks. The forward bay carries large buoys in 2 vertical racks, probably 9 per rack (i.e., 1 attack per rack). The middle section carries smaller buoys, each about half the length of the large ones. The after section carries torpedoes. The after bay also carries buoys (2 large vertical racks). The larger buoys are probably the earlier broad-band type (BM series); the small ones are likely to be Type 75 LOFAR buoys. This particular airplane dropped 9 large buoys, each retarded by a parachute, in 3 close groups of 3; presumably, each buoy of a group was set to place its hydrophone at a different depth. The group of 3 triplets would form a line barrier. As modernized to carry only Type 75–series buoys, Mod 3 carries 100 rather than the 70 of earlier versions.

The current Mod 4 uses a data bus and has been heavily modified to use the new LIDAR (see below); the big box under its nose carries FLIRs, LLLTV, LIDAR, and a new radar altimeter. This version has a communications room separate from the battle station (but the data links feed directly into the battle station). Mod 4 carries 100 Type 75 Series L (LOFAR-type) sonobuoys. This version reinstates the chin radome and carries a short-range navigational radar (thimble) on its nose. Fairings are revised. The projected maritime-patrol version of the new Albatros (Be-44; NATO nickname Mer-

TUPOLEV TU-95 BEAR FOXTROT MOD.4
(simplified and sanitized)

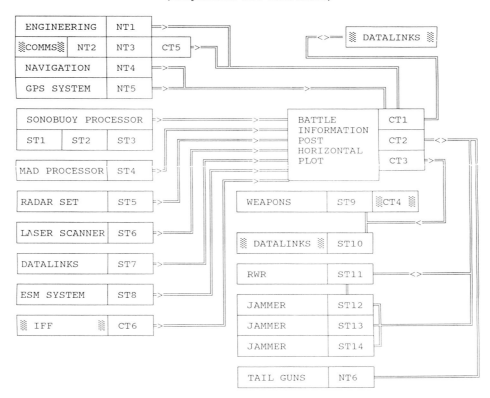

```
NT = Normal terminals usually associated with aircraft functions
ST = Sensor terminals equipped with tracker balls
CT = Command terminals with tracker balls, touchpads and cardkey access
▒  = Command-encrypted system with cardkey access
```

The command system of a Bear-F Mod 4 maritime-patrol aircraft shows an organization similar to that of a ship or, for that matter, to a U.S. P-3C. The laser scanner is the Amethyst LIDAR to detect shallow submarines. (Stuart Slade/DMS-Forecast International)

maid) flying boat will probably have much the same ASW system as Bear-F Mod 4. Mod 4s' maximum weapons load is about 16,000 kg (up to 12 APR-2E torpedoes [which replace short 53-cm torpedoes], 4–8 nuclear depth bombs, as well as conventional bombs for ASW and ASMs, in a rotary launcher).

Like a Bear-F, an **Mi-14** Haze has a weapons system built around an airborne "Second Captain." Each of 4 sensor consoles (fore to aft: MAD, radar, sonobuoys, dipper) preprocesses its data, feeding detection data into the computer (track supervisor, weapons-system overseer). The computer is on the port side forward, with the weapons-control computers (separate units for torpedoes and nuclear depth bombs) aft. Opposite it are the sensor terminals, all in a row, with the dipping-sonar console roughly abeam the sonar winch. Some helicopters may also have an EO-sensor console. As in a ship, the "Second Captain" processes ESM data directly. The "Second Captain" computer allocates targets and transfers them to the weapons-control station. The helicopter carries 44 Type 75 Series S LOFAR buoys in 20 top-loaded drop tubes. Readouts are paper (presumably LOFARgrams) and CRTs. The helicopter data link connects it to a ship or to a shore station (when it operates inshore).

Kalmar, the weapons system of Polish Navy Mi-14PW ASW helicopters, may be an export version of the Soviet system described above. In Polish service, the Mi-14PW replaced an ASW version of the Mi-4, the Mi-4M (the first Mi-14PWs arrived on 15 July 1981). The navigator forward is the system operator, using head-down displays (i.e., using the "Second Captain" track-keeping and tactical computer). The sensors are the APM-60 MAD, streamed at the end of a cable, and the OKA-2 dipping sonar (a 1990 description mentions no sonobuoys). A modified ASW version, Mi-14PW-M, with improved equipment (not specified) was introduced in the mid-1980s. The weapons are bombs, depth charges, and torpedoes, carried on pylons and in special containers. The IFF is Chrom Nikiel. The chin radar is designated 12-M. Bulgaria, Cuba, Libya, North Korea, Poland, Romania, Syria, and Yugoslavia operate the export version of Mi-14.

Ka-25/27 helicopters process their sonobuoys on board. Ka-25 originally carried 12 broad-band buoys without a processor. It now carries 3 Type 75 Series S (LOFAR) buoys. The larger Ka-27 carries 12 Type 75 Series S buoys. Presumably, it was specially designed to accommodate the processor and the LOFAR buoys, which were back-fitted into the smaller Ka-25. On the newest ASW ships (*Neustrashimyy, Udaloy,* and Krivak-IIIs), Ka-27PL data is data-linked to the ship's combat system, as in a LAMPS III.

Sonars

At least in the recent past, standard submarine practice in approaching major surface targets was to use a wide-open ESM receiver as the initial sensor. Ducting practically guaranteed that signals could be received beyond the target's radar horizon. As soon as a good bearing was established, the submarine would switch to her long-range passive sonar. The Russian set, introduced in the Foxtrot class, presumably was similar to the German GHG and was far from wide open. The operator selected a particular bearing and listened. Given an initial bearing, target detection would have been far more likely, and the target could be tracked fairly precisely for the approach. More recent passive bow arrays and towed arrays presumably *are* wide open (i.e., use some form of beam preforming) and, therefore, can more easily be used as primary search sensors.

The **sonar-countermeasure** system first installed in Victor-Is uses an intercept receiver (Chanel) copied from the Anglo-French Type 2019 (PARIS) but using 3 (Victor-Is) or 5 (Victor-IIIs, backfitted to Victor-Is and -IIs, and also in Sierras and Akulas) signal receivers around the sail, linked to a computer; the associated jammer uses 2 transducers aft of the main bow sonar (for deception in range and direction); it also launches small-diameter decoys. "Large evasion devices" (BGTs) are actually nuclear torpedoes (see below). At Abu Dhabi in 1993 Gidropribor displayed a GPD-3 Impostor acoustic decoy (noise or deception [echo-repetition] jammer, presumably a nonnuclear alternative to a BGT). Two can be carried in

The bow sonar of a *Udaloy*, visible just beneath the surface in very clear water. (Royal Navy)

tandem in a torpedo tube, launched either automatically (to counter torpedoes) or manually to counter surface-ship sonar. The 3.9-m decoy weighs 797 kg and can operate to a depth of 250 m [820 ft].

Generations of surface-ship sonars can probably be associated with foreign sources. Moose Jaw (Orion) and Mare Tail are probably versions of the British Type 177 (at different frequencies). The roughly contemporary Bull Nose is probably derived from Type 184. The next generation reportedly derives from French scanning sonars (which themselves derive from U.S. practice, quite different from the British): Horse Jaw, Bull Horn, Horse Tail. The first really big Soviet sonar was the 6-m-diameter cylindrical Rubin, designed about 1960 for the Papa-class submarine.

The *Neustrashimyy* has a new sonar broadly comparable to SQS-53C, with digital reception *and* transmission. A drawing of the export version of an *Udaloy*-class destroyer shows a sonar window in the forefoot and a side panel further aft, presumably analogous to the U.S. SQQ-23 PADLOC (passive location by triangulation).

Artika, the large searchlight sonar in the forefoot of Romeo- and Foxtrot-class submarines, replaces a smaller searchlight, carried farther aft, in the keels of Whiskey-, Zulu-, and Quebec-class submarines. Leningrad is the associated analog torpedo FCS. Unlike contemporary Western systems, it turns torpedoes through 2 gyro angles in sequence. The torpedoes of a spread, therefore, emerge in parallel, and thus can hit despite errors in target range (the single gyro angle applied by standard Western systems causes the torpedoes of a spread to diverge so much beyond the estimated range that the target is unlikely to be hit). Both Artika and its smaller-diameter predecessor, Feniks, were accorded the same NATO nickname, Pike Jaw. Feniks's typical range (active only) is 2.0 nm (4 kyd).

Akula is the Victor-III's flank array, about a third as long as the submarine, probably inspired by the British Type 2007, compromised about 1972–73 (an earlier version corresponded to the British Type 186). There is also an unnamed passive ranger, presumably equivalent to the French DUUX-2.

Barracuda is the bow array in Victor-IIIs (and presumably later units). It consists of a sphere (of about 1,000 elements) operating at 0.5–5 kHz (3.5 kHz active) wrapped in a 27-stave (20 double, 7 single) linear array operating passively at 3.5 kHz, i.e., at the standard U.S. and British active submarine frequency. Presumably, Barracuda was inspired by the U.S. BQQ-2.

Kashin (Project 61) and Petya (Project 159) introduced a new combination of scanning-search/target-indication (Titan, MG 312) and attack sonars (Vychegda, MG 311) to support the new RBU-6000; active range was 5 km (about 5,500 yd). The sonar dome also accommodated a Khosta acoustic communications/IFF device. Titan was apparently the surface-ship equivalent of the contemporary Hercules (NATO Wolf Paw) submarine scanning sonar (active and passive ranges 2.0 nm). The successor sonars in German (and presumably Russian) Parchims were MG 322 and MG 329 (possibly with an MG 16 mine-avoidance set). Konis were limited to MG 322T, presumably incorporating an elevating beam for attack, as in the earlier U.S. SQS-4 series. A recent brochure for an export Grisha shows an MGK 335MS hull sonar, a relatively small unit at the fore

end of a large dome. The searchlight hull sonar of the old 201M class ("SO 1") is MG 11.

Bull Nose (Piranha) operates at 4.5, 5.0, and 5.5 kHz with a 380-Hz bandwidth (CW and FM pulses); pulse widths are 30, 60, and 120 msec. Typically, the same consoles control RBU-6000 and process data from its smaller sonar (which is in a separate dome about 60 ft abaft the main dome). Krivak-IIIs have a solid-state version. Estimated ranges: 3 nm passive, 5 nm active. These figures correspond to SQS-23 performance. Mod Kashins (including the Indian ships) have a different keel (rather than bow) sonar, Platina (Platinum).

Elk Tail is the VDS for the Grisha class and Ka-25 helicopters. Range: 2.5 nm active, 1 nm passive.

Horse Jaw's instrumented ranges are 30/60/120 km [16.2, 32.4, 64.8 nm, i.e., out to the fourth CZ in the Mediterranean]. Reported estimated direct-path range is 8 nm. This sonar is probably broadly equivalent to DUBV 23.

Horse Tail's performance: active 8 nm, passive 4 nm and first CZ.

Reportedly, Mare Tail (Vega) uses stepped-frequency transmission, possibly something like the steps in the old British Type 177. Performance: 4.0 nm active, 2 nm passive. The version in a Krivak is Pike (Pike-MK in Krivak-IIIs). Mare Tail (probably Pike) may be carried by some Mi-14 helicopters.

Moose Jaw (Orion) reaches the first CZ in both active and passive modes (instrumented range 40 km [21.6 nm]).

Rat Tail is the 14–15-kHz dipping sonar of the Ka-27 helicopter. Range 3 nm active, 1 nm passive.

Shark Fin's active range is 2 nm, passive range 4 nm.

Shark Gill (MRK-400): An export version, Shark Gill E, is carried on board Kilo-class submarines. The full LF Shark Gill suite includes an active component (range typically 6 nm); both the standard and the export versions have typical passive ranges of 9 nm (and first CZ). The export Kilo combat system (MVU-110EM) autotracks 2 targets and allows manual tracking of 3 more; it can engage 2 targets with straight-running or wire-guided torpedoes. Presumably, there are 3 analog commutators (beam-formers): 2 trackers and 1 continuous scanner, the latter feeding 3 rate-aided (semi-manual) trackers.

Foal/Stork Tail dipping sonar of an Mi-14 (Haze) helicopter. (Royal Navy)

Dipping sonar of a Ka-27 Helix helicopter. (Royal Navy)

This is much the same as in the U.S. BQQ-1 (the spherical component of BQQ-2), the sonar that probably inspired Barracuda, except that in the U.S. case the scanner fed a single bearing-time recorder. In a Kilo, the associated mine-detection sonar (possibly Mouse Roar) is MG-519; the sound-velocity meter is MG-553, and the cavitation detector is MG-512.

Shark Tail (Pithon) is the SSN towed array; range is 15 nm direct path and first and second CZs. It is 8 cm × 80 m long, with 50 hydrophones, operating at 20– 200 Hz; it is streamed on a 756-m cable (diameter 37.5 mm). In a Victor-III, it has full DEMON processing.

Shark Teeth: Late Foxtrots have the passive-only Shark Teeth E (effective range 7 nm and first CZ). The full Shark Teeth suite includes an active pinger (range 6 nm).

Users: Delta-I/II/III, Yankee, Charlie-I/II, modernized Echo-II, Victor-I/II, and Tango classes.

The pinger may be the Kerch described below (Rubin would probably have been too large).
Squid Arm, an Alfa-class sonar suite (including the Mouse Roar HF sonar), was introduced in 1970. Reportedly, this MF sonar is also used on board export Kilo-class submarines, so the Squid Arm sonar may be Shark Gill. The main cylindrical element may be the 4-m–diameter Kerch, which can steer the beam both vertically and horizontally. Active range is 5 nm, passive range 5 nm (and first CZ).
Steer Hide's performance: active and passive ranges 5 nm.
Trout Jaw is an MF passive sonar. Typical range is 4.0 nm.
MG 69 and 79 are minehunting sonars in the Natya and Sonya classes. MG 7 is a 300-kHz mine-avoidance sonar that a Krivak-III can lower from a forward davit.
Bear-F Mod 4s carry an **ASW LIDAR**, Amethyst, using a blue-green laser. It scans from side to side (out to a 45-deg angle) as the airplane moves forward, covering a 100-m-wide swath. The pilot must maintain constant altitude (100 m) and ground speed (100 m/ sec [about 200 kt]); Amethyst must be shut down whenever the airplane turns. Each line in the display (representing 1 scan) deviates up and down to indicate range (in effect, depth). Lines are spaced 1 m apart (in scale). Very high projections or deep troughs extend over

adjacent lines, creating a shadow effect. The back-and-forth scan forms a green line on a standard Russian 525-line screen, measuring 20 × 25 cm, with a frame rate of 100 Hz (corresponding to the rate of forward motion; each screen corresponds to a 500-m-long swath). Because the screen is relatively short, the image is compressed vertically. It is somewhat distorted toward the sides because the beam slants so steeply there. The system is calibrated to 50 m in depth but is said to be ineffective below 100 ft [about 30 m]. Apparently, some operators learn to interpret it within about 15 min, but others never do. That is reminiscent of sonar recognition, which also involves inherent talents. The series of images is automatically recorded on a standard 3-hr videotape.

The drastic limits on aircraft motion suggest that the system is mechanically range-gated, perhaps by a disk rotating in front of the receiver. Much must depend on the sensitivity of the receiver, so it probably burns out if it is *not* protected. Hence the injunction against turns (which drastically change the angles and ranges to the sea surface). Aircraft speed is tightly limited (within about 1%) because the system must process only 1 pulse at a time, inserting that range into the horizontal scan. If the airplane moves too quickly, part of 1 line is inserted into the next (presumably the equivalent of the second-time- around problem in radar).

The current standard **sonobuoy** is Type 75, a LOFAR buoy.
R-500, which is probably BM-1, is made under license in Romania. It exists in both air-dropped and anchored form. The anchored long-life version is 340 mm × 1.55 m (maximum width 430 mm, length including anchor 2 m); total weight less anchor is 98 kg (including 57-kg battery). A small boat typically drops a line of 18 buoys. Each has a single radio channel and transmits for up to 4 sec at a time. It has a maximum rated detection range of 10 cables (0.5 nm). The buoy transmits only when it detects sound, which is indicated at 1 of 7 intensity steps. The anchored version can be used in depths of up to 70 m [230 ft], and it lasts 7–20 days. This is an analog buoy: the audio signal modulates the radio signal. The receiver is R-550E (for helicopters) or R-550N (for patrol boats). The receiver automatically listens for each buoy's channel (48.9–53.8 MHz) and automatically DFs that transmission within better than 30 deg, using 4 dipole antennas. The buoy transmission is indicated within 7 sec. Display definition is 1 deg (digital) or 30 deg (CRT: signaling area 350 deg at 9 deg).

Raduga's **SS-N-14** Silex (Metell), derived from an unsuccessful alternative to Chelomey's SS-N-9, is broadly equivalent to Malafon or Ikara. It is a command-guided, powered missile carrying a homing torpedo or nuclear depth bomb. The original nuclear-depth-bomb version was 60-RU; the original torpedo version was 70-RU. Carrying a new torpedo (presumably the short 53-cm type), it became 80-RU; the dual-purpose (ASW and antiship) version shown at Abu Dhabi in 1993 was 85-RU. Launchers: KT-100 on Karas and Kresta-IIs, KT-106 on Krivaks (all paired 4-missile fixed launchers), also on the *Udaloy* and *Kirov* classes (reloadable twin launcher). In Krivak-IIIs, the *Frunze*, and modified *Udaloy*s, it is superseded by torpedo-tube-launched SS-N-15 (90-RU). Against targets in direct-path range, detected and tracked by hull sonars, the missile is commanded to drop its torpedo immediately above the submarine's position. Krivaks are limited to this mode. Against a more distant target (e.g., detected by an airplane cooperating with the ship, or in the CZ), the attacking ship sends a helicopter to the submarine's estimated position. The helicopter uses sonobuoys and a dipping sonar to localize the submarine, hovering almost directly over it. The missile is fired directly at the hovering helicopter, which orders the torpedo dropped at the appropriate moment (presumably via a link back to the launching ship). Without the helicopter, attack range must be limited roughly to the horizon, about 10 nm. The missile typically flies at 400 m; maximum range is 50 km (speed Mach 0.95). Dimensions (85-RU): 57.4 × 720 cm (full depth, including underslung weapon, is 135 cm); weight is 4,000 kg.

Kresta-II– and Kara-class cruisers control their SS-N-14s via their Head Lights surface-to-air guidance radars; presumably, the ASW missile shares the command guidance system of the SA-N-3. Krivaks and *Kirov*s are limited to Eye Bowl guidance radars. They track the SS-N-14 (given classical Soviet TWS techniques, it takes 2 antennas to track in elevation and bearing). In the case of a *Kirov*, the helicopter is probably tracked by the Top Dome missile-control radar. Krivaks do not work with aircraft, so no associated air tracker is needed. Ships equipped with Eye Bowl have trainable SS-N-14 launchers, so it would be easier for them to gather the missile into the tracking beam. At least the 85-RU version is dual-purpose, with an antiship seeker and an explosive charge in the airframe forward of the torpedo. A shore-based version was developed specifically to deal with U.S. submarines operating close inshore. It seems not to have been deployed but was advertised at Abu Dhabi in 1993.

The Lyulev OKB developed **SS-N-15** (90-RU) and **-16** (100-RU). SS-N-15 Starfish (90-RU), the Soviet copy of the U.S. SUBROC, was originally armed with only a nuclear warhead and was probably intended as the primary weapon of Victor-II–class submarines. Maximum range is 25 nm. There is now a torpedo-carrying (UMGT) version. In addition to submarines, it arms the missile cruisers *Frunze* and *Kalinin* (it is fired from 533-mm torpedo tubes). In these ships it is fired like a torpedo, dives into the water, stabilizes itself, and then ignites. In effect it replaces SS-N-14. It was apparently chosen to arm the Krivak-III and modified *Udaloy*, although the appropriate torpedo tubes may not have been fitted. At Abu Dhabi in 1993, Novator offered an export version carrying a 742-kg APSET-95 electric torpedo: 533 mm × 8.166 m, 2,445 kg. The Russian version carries the much lighter APR-2 torpedo, and thus probably enjoys a greater range.

SS-N-16 Stallion (Veder/Vodopod, 100-RU), the dual-capable successor to SS-N-15, was apparently conceived in the mid-1970s in parallel with SS-N-22 (P-80/P-100). Because all Soviet homing torpedoes of that era were substantially larger and heavier than the U.S. lightweight torpedo that SUBROC could carry, SS-N-16 had to be much larger than a 21-in tube; presumably, it was the first Soviet 65-cm weapon. Larger size bought about twice the range of the earlier weapon. The range and, to a lesser extent, the course of the Mach-2.5 SS-N-16 can be corrected in flight using the data link developed to correct the course of the SS-N-22 antiship missile. SS-N-16 seems to have been conceived from the first in alternative surface-ship (Veder) and submarine (Vodopod) missiles, both carrying the same torpedo (Orlan) to 100–120 km [54–65 nm]. The current payload is the short 53-cm torpedo. Thus far the only definite surface-ship application is the *Neustrashimyy*, which has 6 large torpedo catapults (similar to those in French ships) rather than the usual 53-cm tubes (she carries 16 reloads). According to a recent Russian book, this weapon is fired from the SUW-N-1 launcher of the *Moskva* class.

As revealed in the Mike submarine's sinking, **torpedo** loadouts are quite limited, probably no more than 2 reloads per tube (with the tubes themselves sometimes unloaded in peacetime). Thus Mike carried a total of 12 torpedoes (2 of them nuclear, probably the BGTs described below) and 7 "special devices," probably decoys. A Victor-III–class submarine assigned to ASUW carries 2 salvos of 65-cm torpedoes and 1 of SS-N-16 ASW missiles (3 conventional, 1 nuclear). The extra torpedoes allow for some shots at ASW surface ships on the way out to the patrol area, and probably also for some self-defense against submarines on the way home. The SS-N-16s are to help break through a submarine barrier on the way home. Akula,

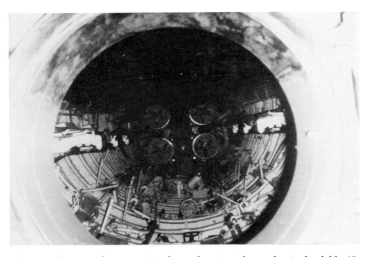

The torpedo room of a Victor-III–class submarine shows the 4 reloadable 65-cm tubes. Two more 53-cm tubes, which are not reloadable, are outside the pressure hull. They fire straight-running nuclear torpedoes intended to force a hostile submarine, firing a wire-guided torpedo, to break away. Reload trays are faintly visible in the shadows below the lower tubes and alongside the upper ones. (Royal Navy)

designed as a cruise-missile carrier (PLARK), has 4 reloadable 21-in tubes (for 12 SS-N-21s), plus a pair of 65-cm tubes (for 3 torpedo-carrying SS-N-16s and 1 nuclear-armed -16). Both classes also carry a pair of 53-cm straight-running nuclear torpedoes (BGTs, large [*bolshoi*] "escape/evasion devices") in nonreloadable tubes. They would be fired down the noise strobe of an approaching wire-guided torpedo, in hopes of forcing the launching submarine to evade. The outfit of 2/submarine is probably standard.

The submarine and surface-ship torpedo data that follow come mainly from a Russian source, ca. 1991, and may include all weapons then operational. Older torpedoes probably survived because analog FCSs could not be adapted to newer ones. Some data come from brochures distributed at the 1993 Abu Dhabi show. DT, APSET-95, USET-95, and TEST-96 were all associated with Gidropribor, so the numbers probably indicate planned dates of introduction. Gidropribor also mentioned USET-93, SET-92K, and DST-92 (possibly an alternative designation for DT), but details are lacking.

The first 65-cm torpedoes were **65–73** (500-kg warhead) and **65–76** (nuclear); both run at 14-m depth [46 ft] and achieve a range of 50 km at 50 kt. There is probably also a newer 65-cm torpedo carrying a 900- or 1,000-kg warhead. A **DT** long-range thermal torpedo described in 1993 is 65 × 1,100 cm [433 in], 4,500 kg with a 450-kg [992-lb] warhead with proximity and contact fuzes. It can be fired either as a wake-follower or as a straight-runner; in each case the torpedo can turn successively through 2 angles. The gas-turbine power plant uses a steam-gas (presumably Walter) mixture. The NATO designation for the big torpedo is 65–80 (reportedly 9.1 m long, with 900-kg or 50-kT warhead). A 65-cm ASW torpedo has also been reported.

The first modern Soviet unguided, submarine antiship torpedo was probably **53–57** (NATO designation 53–56): 45 kt/18,000 m, run depth 14 m, warhead 300 kg, straight-running only. **53–61** was an improved version with 2 settings (15 km at 55 kt or 22 km at 35 kt, running at 15 m, in a straight, pattern, or circular run. 53–61M of 1963 added a passive homer. **53–65** replaced 53–61: 12 km at 65 kt or 22 km at 45 kt. It was a passive homer. It was upgraded in 1969 to 53–65M, with an improved passive homer. 53–65K is a 53–61 upgraded to –65 standards and usable by surface ships (19 km at 45 kt). The export version is 53–65KE. The current standard torpedo has the NATO designation **53–83**; it has an engine and warhead based on those of the U.S. Mk 48. As an example of standard surface-ship loadouts, a Kashin (Project 61) normally carried a mix of 53–57 and SET-53 (ASW) torpedoes.

53–56V (submarines) and **–56VA** (torpedo boats) are standard air-steam–powered export torpedoes, replacing 53–39. Both have pattern-running modes based on the wartime German FAT (53–56VA is preset by the torpedo FCS of Shershen-class or later torpedo boats). The exploder is an inertia-pendulum with 4 deg of freedom, so it can work at any impact angle.

	53–56VA	53–56V
Dimensions	533 × 7,490 mm [21 × 295 in]	
Weight	1,750 kg [3,859 lb]	1,900 kg [4,188 lb]
Speed/Range	51 kt/4,000 m	41 kt/8,000 m
	39 kt/8,000 m	
Warhead	310 kg	400 kg

The mechanical FCS on Romeos and Foxtrots is designed to work with 53–56 and probably cannot easily be adapted to alternatives. These torpedoes are spindle-set.

NATO designations 53–65 (wake-follower), 53–68N (20-kT nuclear), and 53–70VA (560-kg conventional) have been published.

BGT is the straight-running 53-cm nuclear evasion weapon (15 km at 55 kt). The first 53-cm electric antiship torpedoes were **SAET-60** (1961, 42 kt/13,000 m) and **SAET-M** (1969, 35 kt/15,000 m), both with 300-kg warheads. -M may be -60M, an upgraded version, possibly with more than gyro guidance. **SAET-80** appeared in 1980 (submarines only, 48 kt/18,000 m, maximum depth 100 m, warhead 80 kg).

The following are electric 53-cm ASW torpedoes:

—**SET-53** (1959, so probably actually SET-53–59): 8 km at 23 kt, effective to 200 m, 100-kg warhead, active/passive guidance, a pirated U.K. Mk 20; fired by submarines and surface ships
—**SET-53M** (1964, upgraded): 14 km at 29 kt, 200-m depth, 100-kg warhead—small because of bulky electronics

—**SET-65** (submarines only; the first serious Soviet ASW torpedo, probably actually SET-53–65): 15 km at 40 kt, 460-m depth, 250-kg warhead, active/passive guidance
—**SET-65Ch** (1972; a conversion of 53–65): 15 km at 45 kt, 460-m depth, 250-kg warhead, active/passive
—**SET-72** (ships and submarines, dual-purpose, 1972): 41 kt/8,000 m, depth 950 m, warhead 80 kg, i.e., probably atomic
—An export SET-65E was described at Dubai in 1993: 53.3 × 780 cm [307.1 in], 1,700 kg with 205-kg warhead

The published NATO designations of other electric torpedoes are

—straight-running ET-80–66N: 53 cm × 7.7 m, 10 km at 35 kt or 40 km at 20 kt, 20-kT nuclear
—ET-80A (80–67): 53 cm × 7.8 m, wire-guided and active/passive acoustic, 15 km at 35 kt, 270 kg, on surface ships and submarines (probably including Grisha V)

TEST-68 (1968) was probably the first submarine-launched wire-guided ASW torpedo (29 kt/24,000 m, depth 250 m, warhead 200 kg). The successor **TEST-71** (1971) was faster and could dive deeper (35 kt/25,000 m, 400 m). **TEST-E** (1977, probably TEST-53–77E) was a surface-ship equivalent (1977: 40 kt/20,000 m, 400 m, warhead 200 kg; it may have a nuclear version). All of these torpedoes have active/passive seekers. TEST-71ME was described at Abu Dhabi in 1993: 53.3 × 793.5 cm [312.4 in], 1,820 kg with 205-kg warhead (practice version 1,445 kg). It is electrically powered. An electrically powered **TEST-96** described at Abu Dhabi in 1993 could be fired by surface ships or submarines (it follows surface-ship wakes in its terminal phase, or homes actively or passively against submarines): 53.3 × 800 cm [315 in], 1,800 kg with 250-kg warhead.

AT-24 (1973: NATO 53–72) is a short 21-in [53 cm × 4.6 m] missile-payload torpedo: 40 kt/38,000 m (the range figure is probably a misprint in the Russian original), 400-m [1,300-ft] maximum depth, 100-kg warhead. It arms SS-N-14s and probably -16s. **UMGT-1** (1981), a modified MGT, is the SS-N-15 nonnuclear payload: 41 kt/8,000 m, maximum depth 500 m, warhead 60 kg. NATO lists E45–75A (45 cm × 3.9 m, 8 km at 38 kt) as the SS-N-16 and SUW-N-1 warhead.

AT-1 was the lightweight, passive, air-dropped, ASW homing torpedo introduced in the 1960s, in aircraft such as the Il-38 May (2 AT-1s, 144 RGB-1 and 10 RGB-2 buoys) and the Ka-25 Hormone (1 AT-1). It was also carried by Tu-142 Bear-Fs, Ka-27 Helixes, and Mi-14 Hazes. Target depth could be 20–500 m (the initial search setting was 20–200 m); THE torpedo's speed was 27 kt. Acquisition range was 500–1,000 m, and running range was 5,000–10,000 m [about 5,500–11,000 yd].

The replacement **APR-2E** was introduced in the 1980s and is carried by ASW airplanes (such as Bear-Fs) and helicopters (such as

Ka-27s and Mi-14s). It probably arms the conventional version of SS-N-15. It was shown (in poster form) at the 1992 Moscow Air Show. APR means *aviatsiya protivo raketny* (airborne ASW rocket), but in this case rocket probably merely means solid-fuel. The "E" probably means export version. APR-2E has a smaller diameter than previous homing torpedoes. Dimensions: 35 × 370 cm [14 × 146 in], weight 575 kg [1,267.3 lb], maximum speed 115 km/hr [62.9 kt]. The warhead is described as equivalent to 100 kg [220 lb] of TNT. Homing is by a correlation-phase system with maximum range of 1,500 m [1,640 yd], pattern 90 × 45 deg, maximum resolution (signal/noise) 0.4, bearing accuracy up to 2 deg. Endurance is 1–2 min (listed as combat-mission fulfillment time). Kill probability (with a designation error of 300–500 m) is 70–85%. Maximum depth is 600 m [1,968 ft], and maximum target speed is 80 km/hr [44 kt].

The standard unguided air-dropped depth bomb is **PLAB-250–120** (there was or is also a nuclear depth bomb): total weight 123 kg, 150 × 24 cm (28 cm across the tail fins). Sink rate is 16.2 m/sec. The claimed effectiveness increases with depth, to 1.2–1.5 times near-surface effect at 200 m, and 4–8 times at 600 m.

45–54VT (1,075 kg) and **45–56NT** (1,035 kg) were the standard antiship torpedoes carried in pairs by Il-28 naval bombers in the 1950s, and probably still used by China (PRC) on its H-5 (Il-28 copy) bombers. The 45-cm missile-payload torpedo has probably been superseded by UMGT-1, above.

The escape/evasion torpedoes (BGTs) are the functional successors to the 40-cm **MGT** (1961), a submarine-launched antiship (antiescort) torpedo, probably equivalent to the U.S. Mk 37 in concept: it was to be fired aft as the submarine tried to escape (6 km at 25 kt, run at 10 m, warhead 50 [also given as 80] kg; pattern or S run; probably SET-40–62). MGT was presumably designed for the Echo-, Hotel-, Juliett-, and November-class submarines. These were *not*, as often stated, ASW torpedoes; they loitered to find an approaching escort, and their run-depth limit protected the firing submarine. The 40-cm surface-launched ASW torpedoes, **SET-40** (NATO E40–63, 1962, 40 cm × 4.5 m, 7.5 km at 29 kt, 200-m run depth, 50-kg charge, active/passive homing) and **SET-U** or **USET** (1968, 400-m depth, 30-kg charge), are quite separate. They may have superseded an unsuccessful 345-mm weapon. **USET-80** (1980) is a submarine-launched dual-purpose torpedo (48 kt/18,000 m [also given as 15 km at 40 kt], depth 1,000 m, 80-kg warhead). **USET-95** (40 × 470 cm, 650 kg, 80-kg HE), announced at Abu Dhabi, can be launched by both surface ships and submarines; it follows surface-ship wakes and homes actively and passively on submarines. A 40-cm **APSET-96** torpedo described at Abu Dhabi is suitable for airplane or helicopter launch, with a drag parachute (40 × 384.5 cm, 650–720 kg with 60-kg warhead, active-passive homing in both planes, with proximity and contact fuzes). NATO lists E40–75 (40 cm × 4.5 m, 12 km at 30 kt) as the current standard shipboard lightweight ASW weapon.

A full ASW rocket system (RPS) consists of the RBU (launcher) plus the RGB (rocket), the UDB (depth fuze), and the PUSB (firing control device).

RBU-12000 was introduced in 1989, presumably to replace RBU-6000; it has 10 larger-diameter barrels. The reported Soviet designation is RPK-5, Udav; there is also a 6-barrel RBU-10000, Leevyen (Heavy Rain). Range: 216–10,000 m. In the *Kuznetsov, Adm. Gorshkov, Kalinin, Andropov.*

RBU-6000's range is 5,700–6,000 m. Kresta-IIs and Karas have 144 RGB-60 rnd (6 salvos per launcher), Kashins have 192 rnd (8 salvos per launcher). The bomb can be fitted with the guidance system of the S3V depth bomb described below. This weapon can be used for shore bombardment.

Users: Algeria (Koni class), Bulgaria (Koni class), Cuba (Koni class), India (Kashin class), Libya (Koni class), Poland (Kashin class, *Kaszub*), Russia (*Kiev, Kirov, Slava,* Kresta, Kara, *Udaloy,* Kashin, *Neustrashimyy,* Krivak, Parchim, Grisha, Petya-II classes), Yugoslavia (*Kotor,* Koni classes)

RBU-2500 (Katyusha) fires the RGB-25 rnd; the system as a whole is Smerch. Bomblet dimensions are 312 × 1,340 mm (85.0 kg, including 26 kg of explosives). Lethal radius is 5 m. Sinking speed is 11 m/sec (depth settings 10–320 m). Flight time is 3–25 sec. The loadout in a Riga-class frigate was 128 rnd (4 salvos/launcher).

Users: India (Petya class), Romania (Tetal, Poti classes), Russia (Petya-III class), Syria (Petya class), Vietnam (Petya class)

RBU-1200 (Uragan system) fires RGB-12 (50 rnd: 252 × 1,228 mm; weight 71.5 kg, including 32 kg of explosives). Lethal radius is

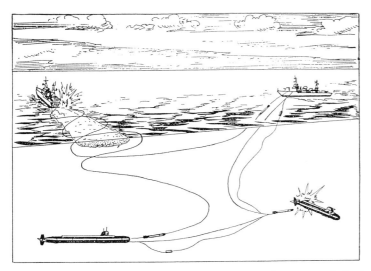

Gidropribor's drawing shows the wire-guided TEST-96 electric torpedo fired by submarines and surface ships against a submarine and (as a wake-follower, at left) against a surface ship. Note that a wire dispenser is fired with the torpedo. (Gidropribor)

RBU-12000 on board the *Adm. Gorshkov* (ex-*Baku*). (Royal Navy)

6 m. Sinking speed is 6.85 m/sec (depth settings are 10–330 m). Flight time is 3–16.3 sec. At the maximum range, 1,450 m, bombs are spread over a 70 × 150–m area.

Users: Bangladesh (Jianghu class), Bulgaria (Riga class; also has MBU-600 Hedgehog), China (Jianghu, Jiangdong, Jiangnan, Haijui, Hainan, Shanghai classes), Cuba (SO 1 class), Egypt (Jianghu class), Finland (*Turunmaa* class), North Korea (Soho, Najin, Hainan, SO 1 classes), Pakistan (Hainan class), Romania (*Democratia* and Shanghai classes), Russia (Mayak class), Thailand (Jianghu class), Vietnam (SO 1 class)

RBU-1000: 60 RGB-14 rnd (5 salvos/launcher) in a Kara or Kresta-II, 48 rnd (4 salvos/launcher) in a Kashin. This is a dedicated antitorpedo weapon.

SUW-N-1 (Viyuga): The rocket is 82-R; the launcher (in a *Moskva*) is RPK-1 (18 rnd). According to a recent unofficial Russian book, 16 SS-N-16s can be carried instead.

Users: Kiev class (except *Adm. Gorshkov*) and *Moskva* class (being discarded). *Kiev* class launchers may fire SS-N-14s.

The **S3V** guided depth bomb, advertised at the 1992 Moscow Air Show, is designed to attack targets down to a depth of 600 m [1,968 ft]. It is guided by an active pinger in the nose, actuating tail fins; the bomb can glide at an angle as great as 60 deg to the vertical. Diving speed is 16.2 m/sec [53.1 ft/sec]. Dimensions are 211 × 1,300 mm and weight is 94 kg (warhead 19 kg). Compared to a conventional PLAB bomb, kill probability is 1.2–1.5 times higher in shallow (less than 200 m) water and 4–8 times higher in deeper water, down to 600 m.

MINE WARFARE

Cluster Bay is RVM; **Cluster Gulf** is the UEP mine.

At Abu Dhabi in 1993 Gidroprobor (see Torpedoes, above) announced a variety of mines: KPM, MSHM, SMDM, and the MDM series. **KPM**, made by the V. V. Kuibyshev Machine-Building Works in Petropavlovsk (Kazakhstan), is an anti–landing craft, horned, moored mine (water depth 5–20 m, case depth 0.5–2.0 m) laid at 4–6 kt by small craft with a draft of about 2 m (70 × 140 cm, 745 kg including 48 kg of TNT equivalent). Weight and dimensions include the anchor.

MSHM is a moored rising mine firing a maneuvering underwater rocket probably based on S3V (hence a development of RVM, whose rocket rose only vertically). It can be laid by surface ships (at 4–15 kt), submarines (at 4–8 kt), and aircraft (at up to 600 kt) in water 60–300 m deep (i.e., for the continental shelf). Dimensions: 53.3 × 400 cm, 820 kg including 250 kg of HE. The designation **PMK-1** has been reported for an unguided rising rocket mine for use in depths of 200–400 m.

SMDM is a self-propelled bottom mine (submarine-launched, at up to 20 kt) equivalent to the U.S. Mk 67, converted from a 53-cm (length 790 cm, weight 1,980 kg, including 480 kg of HE) or a 65-cm (1,100 cm, 5,500 kg, 800 kg of HE) torpedo, to be laid in depths of 4–100 or 8–150 m, respectively. Version 1 adds a 53.3-cm mine module to a torpedo, containing a warhead and an acoustic-magnetic trigger. Version 2 adds a similar module to the warhead of a 53- or 65-cm torpedo.

MDMs are all bottom mines. MDM-1 (laid by ships at 4–15 kt and by submarines at 4–8 kt in, respectively, 12–120 and 20–120 m of water) has both acoustic and magnetic (induction) channels. Dimensions: 53.3 × 286.0 cm (960 kg, including 120 kg of HE). The surface-laid MDM-2 (79 × 230 cm, 1,413 kg including 950 kg of HE) has a 3-channel acoustic exploder (initial detector feeding a difference detector and a guard channel to avoid sweeps; the outputs of the 2 channels are compared to decide whether to explode); it is laid in 12–35 m of water against surface ships or 12–125 m of water against submarines. MDM-3, -4, and -5 are aircraft- and ship-laid antiship and antisubmarine bottom mines (MDM-5 can also be laid by surface-effect craft). Laying speeds: up to 540 kt from aircraft, up to 100 kt by surface-effect craft, 4–15 kt from ships. All use combination acoustic/magnetic/hydrodynamic (pressure) exploders. MDM-3's warhead is 300 kg of TNT equivalent. The aircraft version is 45 × 158 cm (525 kg) to be laid in 15–35 m of water. The surface-ship version is 80 × 152.5 cm (in packing) (635 kg with bogie car), for laying in 8–35 m of water. MDM-4 (950 kg of TNT equivalent) is 65 × 278.5 cm (1,370 kg), to be laid in 15–50 m of water (to 250 m against submarines). The corresponding surface version is 69 × 230 cm (1,420 kg); minimum laying depth is 12 m. MDM-5 (1,350 kg TNT equivalent) is 63 × 305.5 cm (1,500 kg), to be laid in 15–60/ 300 m water. The surface version is 63 × 240 cm (1,470 kg); minimum laying depth is 8 m.

UDM is a universal influence mine to counter surface ships and submarines, laid by surface ships and aircraft (and possibly also by submarines). Total weight is about 1,000 kg (charge weight 650 kg). In its magnetic version, the mine releases a sensor that floats closer to the surface (an acoustic sensor is in the main body; presumably, it releases the magnetic sensor when it detects a likely target). The magnetic sensor is brought closer to low-signature targets such as mine-countermeasures craft and surface-effect landing craft. The Iraqis used this mine during the Gulf War. It may be the mine otherwise described as sectionalized.

The MCM system in the Gorya class (Project 1260) was apparently inspired by Western rising mines, particularly Captor. Twenty units (to be built over 5 yr) were planned, but the program was deferred (more likely abandoned) as too expensive. The lead ship cost 41 million rubles, of which only 5 million went into the hull. She was intended to carry 2 CTICH submersibles ("self-propelled remote-controlled seeker-destructor" in Russian), each carrying 2 100-kg demolition charges (20 such charges would have been embarked). Presumably, the submersibles would have been launched by cranes extending out through the 2 sliding doors in the deckhouse. The planned outfit also included 2 special deep-water sweeps, Anaconda and Cobra, each employing a pair of old SET-40 torpedoes towing a sweep wire between them (the ship has special 40-cm torpedo tubes). Anaconda would have cut through mine cables; Cobra would have used cable-cutting charges.

Gidroprobor's helicopter sweep was described at Abu Dhabi in 1993. The 5 × 3 × 3 m, 3-ton hydrofoil can be towed at up to 21.6 kt, producing a maximum sweep current of 1,000 amperes. On-board generator fuel suffices for 4 hr. The active magnetic loop is 180 m long, and the electrode is 40 m long.

ADDENDUM

SURVEILLANCE/COMMAND/CONTROL

The Chilean CDS is **SP-100**, developed by SISDEF (Compania de Ingenieria de Sistemas de Defensa, Ltd.), a joint venture of Ferranti and the ASMAR shipyard; it replaces ADAWS I on the Chilean "County" class, beginning with *Alm. Condell*, and it will be installed on the four *Leander*s (which currently have no integrated CDS). SP-100 is a fully distributed system using multifunction tactical consoles (CONTACs), each of which has 80486DX-66 and TMS34020 processors; software is written in ADA. The consoles have color displays, touch-sensitive screens, trackballs, and keyboards. It seems likely that SP-100 is derived from Ferranti's earlier **System 500**, which was also fully distributed.

The new Indian Type 16 frigates are to have a Bharat Electronics Ltd CDS, the first developed by India, using 3 workstations (with Barco 19-in displays) linked by an FMC Unicom LAN. This system, reportedly based on the Italian **INS-10**, may also be installed on board Type 15 (*Delhi* class) destroyers and, in more compact form, aboard Indian-built Tarantul fast attack boats.

Elbit displayed a new federated (workstations plus central computer) CDS, the **Naval Action Information System** (NAIS), at the 1993 Paris Air Show. Each tactical console has 2 19-in raster scan displays. The system can interact with up to 6 data link nets simultaneously and may also be used to command other ships and aircraft. Presumably NAIS is an export version of the *Eilat* CDS.

Ferranti's **ADAWS 2000** has been adopted for HMS *Ocean*, the new British helicopter carrier (LPH).

The first fully operational **SSCS**-equipped British Type 23 frigate will be HMS *Westminster*, now (fall 1993) working up. SSCS is now a color system (red for hostile, blue for friendly, green for neutral, white for unknown targets) using the experimental graphics tested in the DRA RRASL system (e.g., airplane silhouettes pointing in the direction of flight). The new graphics are described by a new NATO standard (STANAG).

At RNBAEE 1993, Dowty announced a new small-ship CDS, IMPACT (integrated modular powerful adaptable C2 system technique). Presumably it builds on SMCS/SSCS experience. IMPACT uses the UNIX operating system and would run on commercial workstations. The software is built around a track management data base with access to a "geographic and encyclopedic database" from which predictions can be made. Existing CDS systems generally use a track data base, but only the large ones (such as ACDS Block 1) connect the real-time track data with background data (e.g., intelligence files) for tactical advice. Dowty appears to be arguing that modern workstations are now so powerful that such performance can be extended to fast attack craft. The company offers to assemble customized systems from existing commercial hardware *and software*.

Upgraded Indonesian **Boeing 737** maritime patrol aircraft carry a 5-console Boeing **DPDS** (Data Processing and Display System), derived from the abortive P-3C UPDATE IV, integrating onboard sensors (the **SLAMMR** and **APS-504(V)5** radars and a Texas Instruments **AAS-36**) and the aircraft navigation system. The pilot (the aircraft commander) has 2 repeater screens. Video can be transferred to the

Consoles of the Royal Navy's new SSCS command system, for the Type 23 frigate. (BAeSEMA; Cliff Bolton photograph)

Indonesian Air Force headquarters via a data link and a system of HF relay stations. The new system processes SLAMMR radar data in real time; formerly the film it produced had to be processed after landing.

STRATEGIC WARFARE

The U.S. Navy is reportedly interested in a torpedo-tube ballistic missile for conventional or nuclear strike, possibly to fit the 30-in tube in the new *Seawolf*. Experience with Tomahawk has inspired interest in conventional deterrence, possibly using a Trident variant carrying bomblets.

STRIKE WARFARE

Recent tests reportedly show that **Exocet Block II** can evade closed-loop spotting point defense guns such as Phalanx and Goalkeeper. By sensing the spotting radar pulses, the missile can estimate where the outgoing salvo is headed. The gun system corrects its aim on the basis of an estimated miss distance, just as the old surface fire-control systems corrected their aim against moving ships. In the past, small agile ships could often avoid destruction by steering deliberately towards the splash of the last salvo, in the knowledge that the next salvo would be corrected to hit where they would have been, had they not steered. Apparently the missile guidance or ESM system now has sufficient computing power for it to make similar use of spotting radar, dancing clear of the bursts. It is not clear whether the CIWS radar designer cannot negate such countermeasures by providing a series of deceptive pseudospotting signals.

Reportedly the Exocet tests convinced the French navy that close-in gun systems were futile. The British reached similar conclusions based on the expectation that future antiship missiles would be hypersonic. The French also reportedly became convinced that stealth measures applied to Exocet could so reduce its infrared signature that heat-seeking point defense missiles like Sadral would soon be outmoded. Hence, reportedly, the French decision to form a joint venture with Short Brothers and their current interest in the laser-guided Starstreak.

Harpoon has now been sold to Taiwan for *Knox*- and *Perry*-class frigates, in the latter case for firing from Mk 13 launchers (these ships will still carry canisters for the locally built Hsiung Feng II missile).

AAW

The Chinese Type 88C (Dardo with twin 37-mm guns) has been sold to Thailand for the Type 25T frigates *Naresuan* and *Taksin*.

Barak has reportedly been bought by Colombia for installation on board *Padilla* class frigates; South Africa is reportedly to receive it on board three "Minister" class fast attack craft. At the Paris Air Show, IAI reported that the system had already been delivered to 2 of 3 export customers, probably Chile and Singapore. Series production began in 1992.

Signaal's X-band **APAR** is now a joint project between Canada, Germany, and the Netherlands, for the midlife upgrade of the Canadian "City" class, the planned German F124 class, and the planned Dutch AAW frigate (LCF frigate). Other elements of the consortium now include DASA of Germany (front-end processor) and Northern Telecom of Canada (to manufacture the Tx/Rx modules, using MMIC technology). A single-face rotating Engineering Development Model will be built. Characteristics: vertical coverage 70 deg; instrumented range 75 km for horizon search, 150 km air search and track, 32 km surface search; capacity over 200 tracks. APAR will guide Sea Sparrow, Evolved Sea Sparrow, and SM-2 missiles.

Ericsson of Sweden is no longer involved in the 3-D version of the C(G)-band (5 cm) **Sea Giraffe**; this is now wholly a Marconi product, designated **S1812**. The long-range mode, previously described, is limited to 5 beams, covering 25 deg in elevation. A new maximum cover mode uses all 8 beams, for continuous cover to 57 deg; scans at 15 RPM, instrumented range 66 km. The former short-range mode is now called a target indication mode. A new splash-spotting mode (15 RPM scan rate, 33 km instrumented range; a 10-m^2 splash is

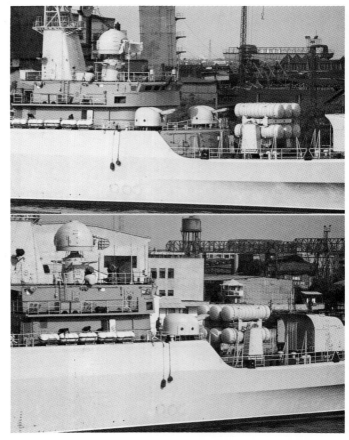

Dardo-type twin 37-mm gun mounts on board a Chinese Jangwei-class frigate (pennant number 539), 1992. Their fire control radar (a dish) is just visible above the Wok Won (modified Soviet-designed Wasp Head) 100-mm director. The fat tubes are for the CY-1 ASW rocket, similar in concept to ASROC. (*Ships of the World*)

The Chinese version of Dardo is shown on board a Jangwei-class (pennant number 539) frigate, 1992: the Rice Lamp director is on a short lattice mast above the helicopter hangar. The large radar to the right is Pea Sticks. (*Ships of the World*)

detected at 33 km with a P_d of 0.8). The weight of the phased-array antenna has increased to 250 kg (below-decks weight is 670 kg). The antenna consists of a stack of 6 elements, each of which is a stack of 3 boards. Presumably the boards are the radiating elements, replacing the slotted waveguides of earlier planar array radars. The spine of the antenna contains a stack of phase shifters and an elevation power divider.

Much the same antenna technology seems to have been incorporated in a new 3-D Marconi S(E/F)-band (2.8–3.1 GHz) naval radar revealed at the RNBAEE show in September 1993, **S1834**. It probably couples the transmitter/receiver and signal processor of the the 2-D **S1830** with a new 12-beam planar array consisting of 44 stacked boards (2.438 × 2.28 m, gain 33 dB, beam 3.1 × 3.1 deg [for lower-elevation beams]). Total height, including the pedestal, is 3.47 m (the antenna is tipped back at a slight angle). The antenna scans at 10 or

MW-08 on board a Portuguese MEKO 200 frigate. The elements of the ARGO-Systems ESM system are also visible (masthead omnis and direction-finding spirals at the base of the radar platform), as are the antennas of the Telegon HF/DF system (surrounding the pole mast). (Signaal)

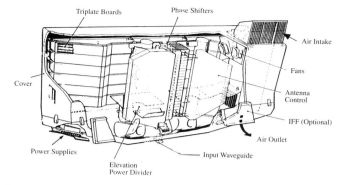

The antenna for Marconi's S1812 small-ship 3-D radar, front and back. Note the elaborate cooling arrangements. (Marconi Radar Systems)

IRSCAN (right) with Goalkeeper aboard the Dutch M-class frigate *Willem van der Zaan*. (Signaal)

20 rpm (selectable). Both radars automatically detect and track up to 300 targets; both automatically detect and plot jamming strobes; both have ECCM features including pulse-to-pulse and burst-to-burst (for MTI) frequency agility, PRF stagger and PRF discrimination (to avoid jammers with the wrong PRF), and fixed and moving notched filters. Each has 4 controllable sectors and can function in an RF-silent waiting mode. Each uses a coherent transmitter (explicitly TWT in the case of S1834) with solid-state amplifiers and signal processors. S1834 transmitter data: peak power 170 kW (2 kW mean); pulse width 6–18 microsec (compressed to 0.4 microsec); PRF 600–1,500. Instrumented range is 100 nm (187 km), and maximum height for accurate height finding is 80,000 ft. S1834 has a long-range mode using 5 beams (up to about 6 deg) out to maximum instru-

The antenna of Marconi's new S1834 3-D radar for frigates. (Marconi)

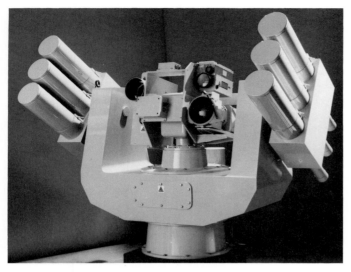

The Shorts-Radamec SR-2000 close-in system, announced at RNBAEE 1993. In the center are the laser range finder and TV camera on one side, and the thermal imager on the other. The flat plate in the middle covers the 2 missile guidance lasers. (Radamec)

mented range, and a high-level 12-beam mode (up to 60 deg) with an instrumented range of about 60 nm.

Corrected data on **ST1803** released at RNBAEE 1993: the long pulse is now 1.33 rather than 1.0 microsec, and instrumented non-MTI range is 48 km. Elevation limits are −28/+83 deg.

At RNBAEE 1993, Radamec announced a new low-cost System 1000 for EO surveillance, in both land/coastal (1000L) and naval (1000N) versions. In the naval version, a 2-axis stabilized director carries a daylight TV camera and a thermal imager, both of which produce standard TV images for both display and tracking. The below-decks console contains a television screen and a touch screen for control, plus a joystick. System 1000 is credited with the ability to detect a fishing vessel at about 10 km. The system can detect and track surface and air targets and can be tied into a radar or tactical display system to receive or transmit target indication (cueing) data.

At RNBAEE 1993 (September 1993), Shorts and Radamec announced a new short-range defensive system, **SR-2000**, which carries 6 Starburst missiles on a standard Royal Navy Radamec pedestal carrying a Type 2400 electro-optical sensor. It can acquire targets at 12 km and intercept them at 4.5 km (about 2.5 nm), a range consistent with the need to destroy a hypersonic missile (such as an SS-N-22) far enough out to protect the ship from the fragments. There is no deck penetration (the system is controlled from a below-decks console), above-decks weight is 750 kg (plus a 180-kg cabinet and a 100-kg control console), and the cost is less than £2.5 million (described as less than a third as much as Goalkeeper). SR-2000 would be cued by the ship's CDS or by a separate radar.

Reportedly the Royal Navy plans to adopt a very short-range system (VSRAAD) including a microwave search radar cueing up to 4 SR-2000s (carrying **Starstreak** rather than Starburst missiles) to replace Goalkeeper and Phalanx. The first installation will be in the new helicopter carrier HMS *Ocean*. Reportedly the Royal Navy is no longer interested in gun-missile systems for close-in defense. Apparently the French navy has made a similar decision. The Starstreak version of SR-2000 will be offered to selected NATO navies, presumably including that of France.

SPQ-9 is being upgraded with a new larger (taller) antenna (i.e., for a narrower vertical beam width, to deal more effectively with sea skimmers), a new receiver, a new signal processor, and an APG-68 transmitter.

ELECTRONIC WARFARE

More data on the latest French submarine ESM system, **ARUR-13** (DR-3000U), is now available. It is fitted in the *Rubis* class and is offered for export on board Agosta 90B– and Scorpène-class boats. The system has separate ESM and ELINT modules and can handle 1 million pulses/sec in the C–J-bands. Elevation coverage is −10 to

+45 deg. Sensitivity is −68 dBm; dynamic range is 60 dB. The associated library contains 4000 radar signatures for 192 platforms.

The DR-2000U systems in German Type 206 submarines originally had no automatic radar identification unit, so the Thorn-EMI SARIE 2 was bought (SARIE 1 compares emitters with ones listed on a paper tape; SARIE 2 uses magnetic tape). Up to 6 possible identifications can be displayed, along with the received parameters. SARIE 2 has about 4 times the library capacity of SARIE 1; up to 1,000 comparisons are made in less than 350 msec. SARIE was heavily used by the Royal Navy, in the UA-8/9/10/13/15 series. The output of the stand-alone SARIE is manually input into the submarine's ISUS CDS.

Reportedly the Royal Navy plans to select *Siren* as its stand-off jammer because it (and not the rival *Carmen*) can produce CW jamming signals, which are regarded as an essential feature. Apparently the ISAR imaging guidance system of the Russian P-80 missile (SS-N-22) can defeat pulse, but not CW, jammers.

A contract to upgrade **Type 670** has reportedly been canceled; the jammer is to be withdrawn as an economy measure.

Sky Guardian/Mentor are now being modified with 68020-series 32-bit processors. Mentor A* now includes a digital IFM (previously available only in Mentor B); Mentor B+ includes a wider frequency-measuring capability, better DF accuracy, and a more elaborate display. UAG, based on Mentor and now being tested in the British AOR *Fort Victoria*, uses 7 68020s in its console and one in the display in the ESM space; it tracks up to 200 emitters and reportedly has up to 3000 warner (library?) channels.

Shield III is a new GEC-Marconi Combat System chaff/IR decoy system using a 68040 processor in place of the Z-80 of Shield II, an Ethernet LAN, and a new touch-screen (plasma) control system. The first order, reported in July, was for 12 systems for a new class of 45-m fast attack craft for Singapore (the *Victory* class have Shield II). Design options: 2 cross 6-barrel for fast attack craft, 2 cross 9-barrel for corvettes, and 4 straight 6-barrel for frigates. Current munitions are P6 (sequentially deployed IR) and P8 (time-fuzed chaff), but the system has growth potential for an active offboard jammer, and integration with a torpedo defense system was studied in 1992–93.

The next version of **ALR-67**, (V)3, is to begin flight tests in the spring of 1994. **ECP-510** production was approved in March 1993, so all existing ALR-67s should be updated by late 1994. The upgrade was reportedly adopted because the original ALR-67, which had been designed before the Soviets fielded pulse-Doppler aircraft radars, was deficient when tested against them in 1988.

The 95 existing **ALQ-165**s will probably be installed on board F-14s. A license has been approved for export. Loral, Raytheon, and Lockheed Sanders have all proposed alternatives. For the F/A-18, Loral will offer a modified **ALQ-178**, which it is producing for Turkish F-16s. It may be tested against the Raytheon **ALQ-187**, derived from the DIAS jammer developed for Greek F-4s and A-7s. Raytheon may also offer a jammer based on its pod and decoy programs.

ARGOSystems **AR-900** is the core of 3 new programs: APECS III, CLOAC (Compact Lightweight Omnidirectional Advanced Electronic Countermeasures System), and an MPA system.

ASW

New data on the Australian **Kariwara** and **Narama** towed arrays is now available. Kariwara acoustic sections can be made in lengths from 70 to 2000 m; standard diameter is 40 mm. The array can be used as a bottom sensor or it can be towed. Towing speed is 4 to 15 kt. Narama offers a listening speed of up to 20 kt (30 kt survival speed) for a 50 mm × 2000 m array. Surveillance speed would be 2–5 kt, tactical speed 10–15 kt. Thomson Pacific claims performance equivalent to much larger diameter conventional arrays.

Finnyard of Finland has announced a new **Sonac Passive Towed Array (PTA)**, which is now in service with the Finnish navy, towed by *Rauma*-class fast attack craft. It is specially designed to work in shallow water, using an active depressor to maintain depth (down to about 50 m). Operational towing speed is 3 to 12 kt. The 78-m array (including VIMS) is towed on a 600-m cable (2 twisted wire pairs and 2 optical fibers around a Kevlar core) streamed from the depressor, which is on a 100-m steel armored cable (3 twisted wire pairs and 2 optical fibers). Both the towed body and the depressor

A Chinese Jangwei-class frigate (pennant number 539) shows the sextuple CY-1 launcher forward. She has a centerline anchor, indicating the presence of a large bow sonar dome. The ships shows no other ASW weapons but does carry a helicopter in a hangar aft. The foremast carries, top to bottom, an Eye Shield target-acquisition radar and a Rice Lamp AA fire-control radar (for her 37-mm guns, in Dardo-style mounts). Atop the bridge is a Wok Won FCS with Sun Visor radar for her 100-mm guns (in the enclosed mount). Aft is the low-frequency Pea Sticks long-range air-search radar. Empty racks amidships are probably for C-801 missiles in box launchers. (*Ships of the World*)

Bow arrays for the BSY-2 sonar of the *Seawolf* class: the big sphere is the passive element. Note the conformal array surrounding the spheres. (U.S. Navy)

The new Australian submarine HMAS *Collins*, rolled out of its assembly shed on 28 August 1993, displays elements of her French sonar system: the intercept transducer projecting above the bow, the flank array, and the 3 ranging arrays along her casing (superstructure). (Australian Submarine Corp. via Rockwell International)

carry pingers for depth control. A single winch drum (total weight 1,200 kg) handles the hydrophones and both tow cables. Frequency coverage is 20–800 Hz, and the system uses an adaptive beamformer. The signal is digitized at the hydrophones and transmitted back to the ship on a fiber-optic cable. The parameters of the array electronics (amplification, own ship noise cancellation) are controlled from the ship. Finnyards claims that its effective towing ship noise canceller makes a short tow cable possible, so that PTA can maneuver easily to operate in shallow and narrow waters. The main displays are: broadband surveillance (waterfall, up to 30 min of history); narrowband surveillance (spectral estimates of signals from various directions, up to 10 min of history); combined wide- and narrowband (up to 10 min of history); target spectral analysis; navigation with tracked target data (geosit display); sound-ray path analysis; and depressor movement history. The system also provides audio (from a selected direction) and transient alarm with audio replay. Optional extensions include interfaces with a ship's radar and her CDS, the ability to exchange information with a sister system on another ship, a target classification and identification system, a BT,

and a display video printer. The PTA prototype was delivered to the Finnish navy in 1991, and the first production system was delivered in the summer of 1993.

Finnyards also offers a hybrid small-boat dipping sonar (HDS) for active and passive surveillance in shallow water. The 60-kg dipping body is 25 cm × 2.7 m. In the water, it extends three 2-m receiving legs, hydrophones on which are used to form 36 beams. The ODT transmit beam is 15 deg wide in the vertical. It can be tilted slightly up or down. In active mode, HDS produces both CW and spread-spectrum pulses and can provide Doppler spectrum analysis. The display can be circular or rectangular, with a separate target-tracking window with zoom. In passive mode, HDS provides wideband surveillance over 360 deg, and it can do narrowband analysis on 8 beams. It can detect transients, and it can display jammers. Transmitting and receiving electronics are in the dipper; digitized data goes up the cable to the onboard computer. A BT on the dipping body provides data from which the optimum dipping depth can be estimated.

Atlas Elektronik (formerly KAE) has announced an **ASA 92** active towed array system, operating at 1 or 2 kHz. The active body (approx 2.3 × 0.8 × 0.9 m) is towed on a 400-m cable; the array is towed on a 250-m (35-mm diameter) cable towed by the active body. The hydrophone section is 24 m long (diameter 70 mm), with 20-m VIMs at both ends. The system can be combined with a torpedo warner. Towing depth is 30 m or more (maximum depth is probably about 300 or 350 m).

The new Korean Type 209 submarines are armed with **SUT Mod 2** torpedoes. The indigenous heavy torpedo program is in trouble and may be abandoned.

ATAS: Reported sold to Taiwan (for the *La Fayette* class) and to Pakistan for Type 21–class frigates.

NLCAW: The USN withdrew 3 June 1993, leaving only Norway and Germany; the program, now in the feasibility phase, must now choose between a mini-torpedo and a guided-depth bomb. Both partners are now seeking further participants; Denmark and Sweden are interested. Current competitors: STN (Systemtechnik Nord) vs. NFT/Diehl/Whitehead. Since STN was in partnership with Lockheed on the anti-mine torpedo, the Lockheed mini-torpedo has probably survived.

The sonar processor for the British **Merlin** helicopter has been designated **AQS-950**. The projected British maritime patrol aircraft processor, which is to incorporate the French Sadang 2000, is **AQS-951**. The U.S. **ALFS** sonar is now designated **AQS-22** (presumably the failed Bendix alternative was AQS-21).

The U.S. **ADAR** sonobuoy, intended as the receiver for the current Improved E2R program, or as a passive detector of fast submarines, generally resembles Barra in configuration, with 5 × 125-in arms unfolding umbrella-style from a 4-ft central mast, and a total of 40 omnidirectional hydrophones, each with its own pre-amplifier; deployed diameter is 20 ft.

In May 1993, the last British **Mk 46** torpedo was handed over to Alliant Techsystems; the weapon is no longer in British service.

MINE WARFARE

As of the summer of 1993, the naval component of the U.S. Special Operations Command was calling for proposals for devices to be the basis for a new family of shallow-water MCM systems (special forces are responsible for clearing surf zone mines ahead of amphibious forces). Sidescan sonar processing is to be improved to include "true zoom," a feature that selects frequency, repetition-rate, and beamwidth to match screen resolution to acoustic resolution (1-ft² object at 100 yd at 6 kt). Sonars are also to be linked to GPS so that detected objects can be designated and their positions stored. Tests in 1992 showed that sidescan sonars could detect mines in water only 6 ft deep. A multibeam sidescan sonar (for a faster search rate than a conventional single-beam sonar) is to be suited to installation under a 24-ft rigid inflatable boat (nominal range 100 yd in water depth 6–21 ft, usable in Sea State 3). The request also includes a new swimmer (hand-held) sonar (resolution less than 3 in at 20 yd, field of view approx 45 × 10 deg) and a new mine destruction charge (less than 5 lbs, effective 16 in from the mine).

The reported sale of AQS-17 to Indonesia apparently was not consummated.

A standard U.S. Mk 105 mine clearance sled used by HM-12; at Norfolk, 7 July 1992. (Jürg Kürsener)

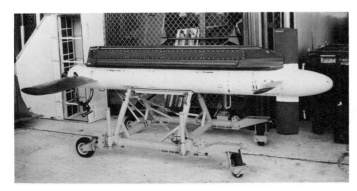

AQS-14 helicopter mine detection sonar used by HM-12; at Norfolk, 7 July 1992. (Jürg Kürsener)

RUSSIAN SYSTEMS

In a recent article, Admiral Felix Gromov, the Russian Naval C-in-C, stated that in future the Russian navy would be equipped with a conventional land attack missile as well as with antiship and anti-submarine missiles. The Rubin submarine design bureau is currently offering an "Amur" export submarine design that may incorporate an external cruise-missile launching pod similar to the SS-N-21 pod designed for the "Victor" class. One natural conclusion would be that an SS-N-21 land attack version, analogous to Tomahawk, is being developed. No such missile was displayed at the 1993 Moscow Air Show, however.

British official sources indicate that several missile tubes, probably including those for SS-N-9 and -22, have housed several quite different weapons without any external indication. Chelomey displayed a rocket-powered submarine-launched missile, probably the original Ametyst/P-50/SS-N-9, and a model of its turbojet-powered successor (described in a poster as the first suited to both submarine and surface launch, hence clearly also a missile designated SS-N-9 in the West).

The **Chelomey** (Mashinostroyenie) design bureau announced 3 new antiship missiles at the 1993 Moscow Air Show: **Alpha, Bastion,** and **Yakhont. Alpha** appears to be the "Missile 2000" a photograph of which appeared at the 1993 Paris Air Show. It is described as effective against both land and sea targets, suitable for firing by aircraft, from a 3-missile ground-mobile truck launcher, from ships, and from submarines. It can be supplied in a launching tube (similar to that shown for Yakhont, below), but it can also be fired from a vertical launcher (an 8-round Western-type cellular launcher is illustrated in the Chelomey brochure) or from a 4-tube submarine vertical launcher. Two missiles are shown under the wing of an attack airplane. A drawing of the fire control system console shows 2 side-by-side CRTs with a third above. It is tempting to associate each CRT with the tellback of 1 missile attacking 1 target, in which case

The Korell (P-20M) FCS computer on board the *Hiddensee,* showing its computing gears. (Author)

The Chelomey bureau's 1993 poster advertising Alpha, a missile it described at the Paris Air Show as the weapon of the year 2000. (S. Zaloga)

This solid-fuel rocket-powered missile was described by the Chelomey bureau, which developed it, as the first submerged-launched antiship missile in the world. It is probably the original Ametyst/P-50 (SS-N-9). It is possible that the missile carried by Nanuchkas is a turbojet version carrying the same guidance package. SS-N-7 (P-20L) now appears to have been a modified P-20 airframe carrying a guidance package that Berezhniak developed for a competing missile. (S. Zaloga)

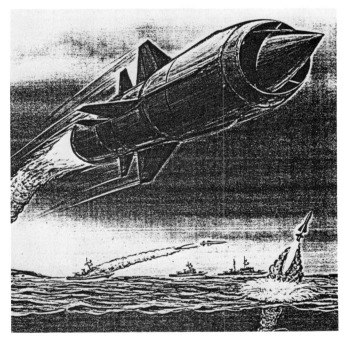

Yakhont, as sketched by the Chelomey bureau. This missile is almost certainly a ramjet version of P-80, designated P-80K or P-80U. Terminal attack speed is probably Mach 3.5. The canister in which the folded-up version of the missile lies is probably 65 cm in diameter. (Mashinostroyenie)

The Yakhont canister alongside an SS-N-3 missile at the 1993 Moscow Air Show. (S. Zaloga)

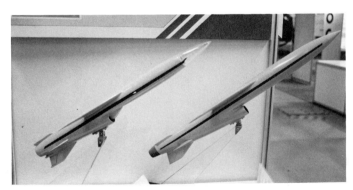

Chelomey OKB models of 2 versions of SS-N-3; that on the left is the guided version for submarines and surface ships. The nose is transparent to display the radar antenna; the missile on the right is autopilot-guided. (S. Zaloga)

a single system can handle 2 targets simultaneously (the third CRT is presumably for target assignment). Chelomey provided no data on this weapon.

Yakhont is a new ramjet missile, designed for firing from ships (including large missile boats), submarines, and ground mobile launchers. An illustration of a submarine launching showed the missile rising from a tube abaft the submarine's sail, rather than from a torpedo tube. A poor-quality photograph of a surface-ship launching appears to show the frigate *Neustrashimyy*. Stated maximum range is 300 km (164 nm); speed is Mach 2–2.5. The missile can fly at minimum height along its entire path, or it can fly a lo-hi-lo path (14 km initial phase, to avoid giving away the location of the launcher). Yakhont is currently in production, probably for later units of the *Sovremennyy* class. The new **Bastion** coast defense missile, which is not yet in service, is apparently a variant of Yakhont. It is carried on a 3-missile transporter truck; up to 24 can be salvoed

together under the control of a single command system. No dimensions were offered.

Reportedly the Chelomey design bureau has offered the P-80 missile system to a Western navy at a price of $600,000 per missile, plus $1 million for the shipboard ISAR targeting terminal, plus additional payment for adaptation of the ship's radar as a data link receiver for the missile. Reportedly, too, the bureau has decided not to release information on P-80/P-100 because it thinks sales to Western navies, which may not like publicity, are imminent.

A data sheet on the land-based SA-17 missile (successor to SA-11, equivalent to the naval SA-N-7) was distributed at Moscow in 1993: the missile is 0.4 × 5.5 m (710–720 kg, warhead 50–70 kg), with a maximum speed of 1,200 m/sec. Presumably there is a naval version.

Raduga and TsAGI are engaged in a program of ramjet missile development. A series of models of advanced types of ramjet were

Novator's Alpha coast-defense missile, at the 1993 Moscow Air Show. The hump forward indicates the warhead section, which separates for its high-speed terminal run. (S. Zaloga)

A Kh-15S aeroballistic antiship missile, at the 1993 Moscow Air Show. (S. Zaloga)

Wind-tunnel models of next-generation ramjet-powered missiles, displayed by Raduga at the 1993 Moscow Air Show. (S. Zaloga)

Novator's 400-km air-to-air missile, R-72, shown at the 1993 Moscow Air Show. The dark line indicates the sensor of a proximity fuze. (S. Zaloga)

displayed at the Moscow Air Show; presumably they indicate likely directions of development. A sketch of the current type, with separate ramjet inlets around the missile body, was dated 1973–78. It is effective between Mach 1.0 and Mach 3.5. The next stage (1980–85) shows a large conical splitter in a single under-body intake, effective between Mach 2 and Mach 4.5. The 1985–1990 version has a flatter divided intake, effective between Mach 2 and Mach 6. The 2000 version has a further divided intake, and presumably the flat underbody shape forward of the intake provides some compression. It is considered effective between Mach 4 and Mach 8. The wind-tunnel shapes are interesting because to the extent that they represent "TsAGI solutions," they are the shape of future Russian tactical missiles.

Vympel displayed a new 175-kg rocket-ramjet version of its honeycomb-finned **R-77**, which it calls **PBB-AE**. Rocket-ramjet propulsion was adopted to provide low-to-medium level performance equivalent to the high-altitude performance of the original R-77, including a range of 80 to 100 km. There is also a surface-to-air version, **PBB-AE-ZPK**, which is vertically launched, with a gas-dynamic unit to tip the missile into the appropriate direction. It has a larger booster. Neither the original R-77 nor the new version has yet attracted any Russian orders, but Vympel is making some R-77s on speculation.

The proposed "Amur" type submarine is credited with the capability to carry "high-speed underwater missiles" as well as torpedoes and torpedo tube–launched antiship missiles. This may refer to SS-N-15/16, or perhaps to some type of underwater rocket (in the past, short-range underwater rockets have been studied, at least in the United States).

An antitorpedo version of the RBU-12000, **UDAV-1N**, was announced at the 1993 Moscow Air Show. Effective range is 100–3000 m, and the system fires within 15 sec of target detection. Claimed hitting probability of a single salvo (10 rounds) is 0.9 against a straight-runner and 0.76 against a homer. The launcher is auto-

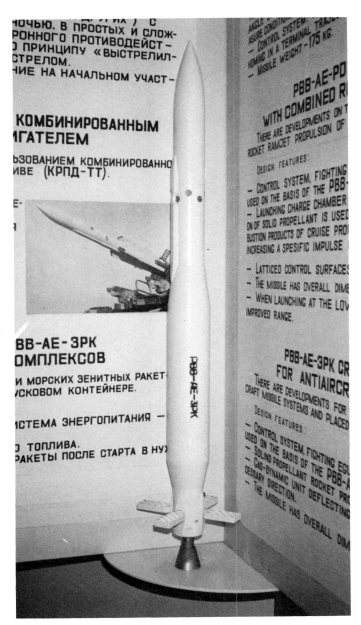

A model of the rocket-ramjet version of R-77, at the 1993 Moscow Air Show. (S. Zaloga)

A Kh-58E (AS-11) missile at the Moscow Air Show, 1993. (S. Zaloga)

The Ovod-M (Kh-59M, AS-18) electro-optically guided cruise missile, at the 1993 Moscow Air Show. (S. Zaloga)

The Kh-65SE antiship air-launched cruise missile, at the 1993 Moscow Air Show. (S. Zaloga)

SAN-11, the missile of the CADS-N-1 gun-missile system, on a poster at the Moscow Air Show. (S. Zaloga)

A Peel Pair radar on board a Nanuchka III, 1989. The large vertical cylinder is the Stump Spar radio antenna. Note the difference between the two antennas of the pair.

mated and fires both decoys and depth charges; it is also used (as has long been known) against submarines and swimmers (which the Russians call "diversion forces").

Details of Russian minehunting sonars have now emerged. The sector-scan (over a 90-deg sector) search sonar (probably MG 89) operates at 12–50 kHz, with range settings of 300 and 1,000 m. Angular accuracy is 0.5 deg (1 deg near the beam edge). The associated shorter-range sonar, presumably intended as a classifier but de-

Top Plate in a *Udaloy*. Note the back-to-back IFF interrogators atop the 2 planar arrays.

Top Steer aboard the *Sovremennyy*-class destroyer *Otlichnyy*. Note the waveguide cross-connecting the 2 antennas, and the narrower waveguide (presumably for IFF) leading into the feed of the 2D element of the radar.

Plate Steer on board the *Admiral Gorshkov* (ex-*Baku*). Compared to the cylindrical reflector in Top Steer, the flat planar array in Plate Steer should have far lower sidelobes, which should improve its performance and also better protect it from jamming.

Cross Sword (SA-N-9) director in a *Udaloy*. The flat array consists of phase-shifters, which focus and steer the beam produced by the external feed. Front Dome (Orekh, for SA-N-7) has a similar configuration, although all of it is covered by a radome.

scribed as a counter to underwater weapons and swimmers, operates over a 45-deg sector (which can be enlarged to 90 deg) with range settings of 100 and 500 m. Accuracy at these ranges is, respectively, 0.5 deg/1 m and 1.5 deg/3 m. Scanning is electronic.

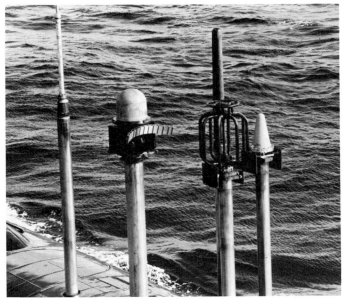

Masts of an Oscar-class missile submarine: left to right, they are HF communications, Snoop Head/Bald Head (radar/ESM), Shot Gun (VHF/UHF communications), Park Lamp (VLF/LF receiver), and Pert Spring (satellite navigation).

Snoop Pair (atop Rim Hat), on a Typhoon-class strategic submarine. Note the differences between the feeds of the 2 antennas.

The Bass Tilt radar on board the Tarantul-class fast attack boat *Hiddensee*. In search mode, the flat plate antenna directs the 3-deg beam. After each scan, it tips up by 3.6 deg; the maximum elevation can be set at 18–36 deg. Once a target has been designated, the monopulse cluster alongside the tilting plate locks on for precision tracking. In a later version, the tilting plate may elevate continuously, so that the radar scans helically. Maximum target speed is 700 m/sec. An associated MTI can eliminate static targets. Antenna gain is about 30 dB; peak power is 200 kW. Pulse width is about 0.5 microsec (PRF is 1,800 or 3,600).

Antennas on board a Typhoon-class strategic submarine: left to right, they are Pert Spring, HF communications, Park Lamp, Shot Gun, and Snoop Pair/Rim Hat.

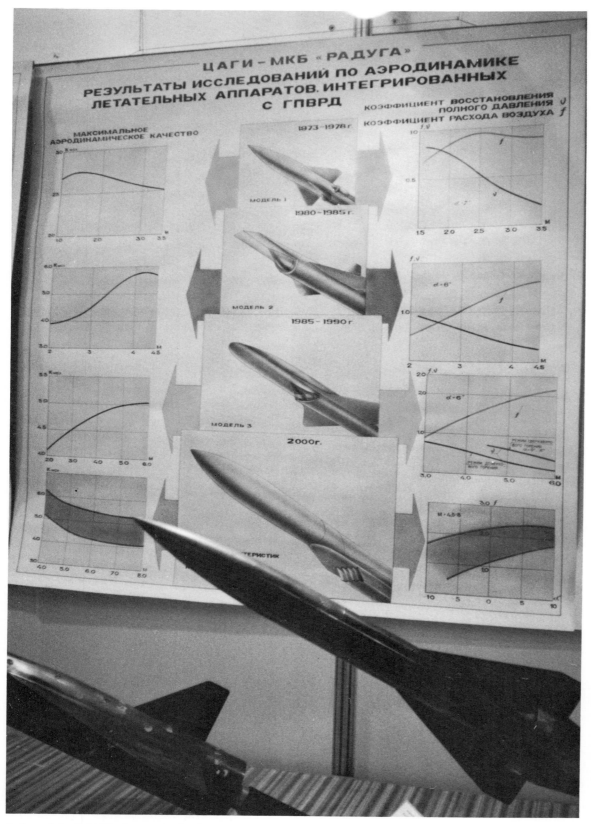

A chart of the TsAGI-Raduga ramjet development program, displayed at the
1993 Moscow Air Show, with a wind-tunnel model of the earliest series (as
typified by Kh-31/AS-17 and by 3M80) in the foreground. (S. Zaloga)

CADS-N-1 mount on board the cruiser *Kalinin*.

PK-16 decoy launcher with 3 rockets in place, on board a *Udaloy*.

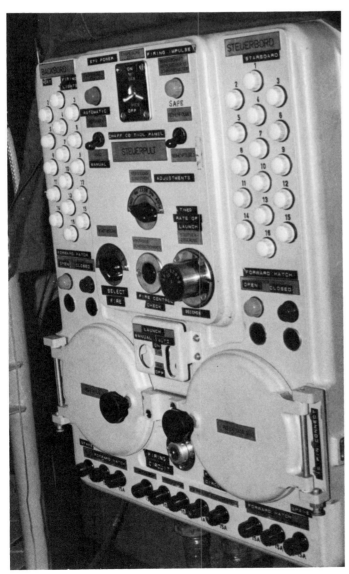

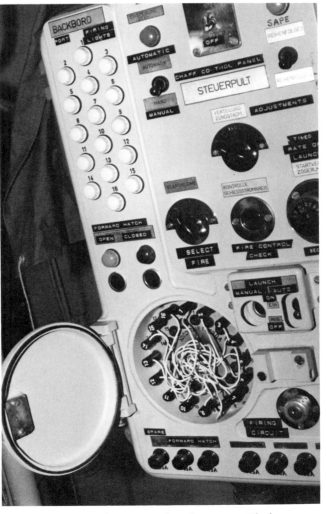

PK-16 control board on the ex–East German Tarantul-class attack boat *Hiddensee*, showing the plugboard for arranging launch sequence. The boat carried chaff tuned to 1–2, 2–4, 4–8, and 8–12 GHz. The Russians also developed special antilaser aerosol rounds. (Author)

A model of the 85-RU (SS-N-14) missile, at the 1993 Moscow Air Show. (S. Zaloga)

An APR-2E aerial torpedo, with a KAB-500 Kr guided bomb alongside. (S. Zaloga)

Two rarely photographed North Korean warships show a variety of Russian-supplied weaponry. These ships are a "Najin"-class frigate (pennant number 531) and a "Sariwon"-class corvette (pennant number 671), the latter based on an old Russian minesweeper design. The frigate has 100-mm guns (as in the old "Riga" class) fore and aft, with twin standard 57-mm guns superfiring over them. Each of the 3 small shields protects a twin (over-and-under) 25-mm gun. Note also the twin 30-mm guns with their Drum Tilt FC radar. The 2 fixed SS-N-2 Styx launchers came from a Komar-class missile boat. Radar antennas visible forward, top to bottom, are unidentified (probably not, as reported, Skin Head), Pot Drum, Square Tie (for SS-N-2 targeting), and Slim Net (air search). Forward, the "Sariwon" carries a tank turret, as in many Russian river gunboats. The 4 mounts around the funnel are probably twin 25-mm; the 2 aft are twin 57s. The radars are Don-2 and Pot Drum. Both photographs were taken by a Japanese P-3C while the ships were operating in the Sea of Japan supporting a North Korean missile test on 29 May 1993. (*Ships of the World*)

INDEX

Page numbers in bold indicate pages in this volume. All other page numbers refer to the 1991/92 edition.

INDEX

INDEX

INDEX

INDEX

INDEX

INDEX

INDEX

ABOUT THE AUTHOR

Norman Friedman is recognized worldwide as a leading naval writer and defense analyst who specializes in technical and strategic issues. His work shows both an understanding of current technology and profound appreciation of history and its application to the present. As a consultant to various U.S. governmental agencies and defense contractors, he has examined the technology of national mobilization, Soviet responses to U.S. naval innovation, the utility of ballistic-missile defense, and strategic conflict with the Soviet Union, among other subjects.

Praised for his ability to explain complex technology to the layman, Friedman has written many successful books on naval ships and weapons that combine technical analyses with an examination of the historical, political, and economic influences on design and development.

His popular illustrated design histories published by the Naval Institute Press include *U.S. Destroyers*, *U.S. Aircraft Carriers*, *U.S. Cruisers*, *U.S. Battleships*, and *U.S. Small Combatants*. Among his others books are *U.S. Naval Weapons*, *Naval Radar*, *The Postwar Naval Revolution*, and *Submarine Design and Development*.

Friedman writes articles on a wide range of defense subjects that appear regularly in journals throughout the world. He also contributes a monthly column on world naval developments for the Naval Institute's *Proceedings* magazine.